SOLOMON ZEITLIN'S
Studies in the Early History of Judaism

SOLOMON ZEITLIN'S
Studies in the Early History of Judaism

*Selected with an introduction
by the author*

VOLUME II

KTAV PUBLISHING HOUSE, INC.
NEW YORK

© COPYRIGHT 1974
SOLOMON ZEITLIN

Library of Congress Cataloging in Publication Data

Zeitlin, Solomon, 1892-
  Solomon Zeitlin's Studies in the early history of Judaism.

  Includes bibliographical references.
  1. Judaism--History--Ancient period--Addresses, essays, lectures. 2. Jews. Liturgy and ritual--Addresses, essays, lectures. 3. Bible. O. T.--Addresses, essays, lectures.
BM173.Z442   296'.09'01   72-5816
ISBN 0-87068-209-1

MANUFACTURED IN THE UNITED STATES OF AMERICA

TABLE OF CONTENTS

FOREWORD	VII
INTRODUCTION	XI
An Historical Study of the Canonization of the Hebrew Scriptures	1
Some Reflections on the Text of the Pentateuch	43
Were there Three Torah-Scrolls in the Azarah?	54
The Apocrypha	58
Jewish Apocryphal Literature	88
The Book of Jubilees Its Character and Its Significance	116
The Book of "Jubilees" and the Pentateuch	147
The Legend of the Ten Martyrs and its Apocalyptic Origins	165
The Assumption of Moses and the Revolt of Bar Kokba	181
The Pharisees: A Historical Study	226
The Sadducees and the Pharisees—A Chapter in the Development of the Halakhah	259
The Pharisees and the Gospels	292
The Origin of the Pharisees Reaffirmed	344
The Essenes and Messianic Expectations	357
The Origin of the Idea of the Messiah	394
Proselytes and Proselytism During the Second Commonwealth and the Early Tannaitic Period	407
The Offspring of Intermarriage	418
The Jews: Race, Nation, or Religion	425
Who is a Jew? A Halachic-Historical Study	470
The Names Hebrew, Jew and Israel: A Historic Study	500
Jewish Rights in Palestine	515
Jewish Rights in Palestine, Arnold J. Toynbee—Jewish Rights in Eretz Israel (Palestine)., Solomon Zeitlin—Correspondence	531
The Ecumenical Council Vatican II and the Jews.	582

FOREWORD

It was my intention to have the essay "The Canonization of the Hebrew Scriptures and the Pharisees" in volume I, but due to technical difficulties it appears in this volume.

The term canon is a Greek word, *kanon,* and comes from the word *kane,* which means "reed." It was suggested that the Greek word *kanon* is derived from the Hebrew word קנה . Paul used the word *kanon* in the meaning rule. In his Epistle to the Galatians (6, 16) he said, "And as many as walked according to the rule *kanoni,* peace [be] on them." The word *kanon* in the early Church literature denotes rule or instruction, "Rule of Truth," "Rule of Faith" *regula fidei.* Between the years 140-200 C.E. the New Testament was formed under the name canon. It consisted of the Hebrew Bible and the New Testament, while other writings which were circulated among the early Christians were considered Apocryphal, i.e., spurious, false.

The Hebrew Bible was canonized in three stages. In the year 444 B.C.E. under the leadership of Ezra and Nehemiah, the Five Books of Moses became holy, maintaining that they contained the words of God spoken to Moses. The Five Books of Moses became known as the Torah —the constitution of the Judean people. Shortly after the Restoration there were other books circulated which claimed that they contained the words of God transmitted to Moses by an angel, such as the book of Jubilees, which was originally called the Torah of Moses. They were rejected.

Approximately two centuries after the canonization of the Pentateuch, the Torah, other books were assembled and canonized under the name *Neviim.* They were held to have been composed by prophets who spoke in the name of God; Joshua, Judges, Samuel, Kings, Isaiah, Jeremiah, Ezekiel, twelve small prophesies included in one book named The Twelve, Hagai, Zecharaiah, and Malachi. They were divided into two parts, נביאים ראשונים Former Prophets and נביאים אחרונים Later Prophets. The prophetic books which were composed before the Restoration were called Former Prophets while the books which were composed after the Restoration, such as Hagai, Zecharaia, and Malachi, were called Later Prophets נביאים אחרונים With the canonization of the books of the prophets the Hebrew canon was completed. The sages maintained that after the death of the last three prophets "prophesy ceased in Israel".

FOREWORD

There were more books that were held in high esteem but not included in the canon. Psalms were chanted in the Temple and some books of wisdom were not included in the canon. In the year 65 C.E., a third section was added to the Hebrew canon, consisting of Psalms, Proverbs, Job, Daniel, Ezra-Nehemiah, Chronicles, Lamentations, and Ruth. The Song of Songs was included in the canon after a long discussion between the schools of Shammai and Hillel while the book of Kohelet was rejected. This section was called *Ketubim* and it was held that these books were "inspired"—Holy Scriptures. At the time of the destruction of the Second Temple the Hebrew canon contained three sections and consisted of twenty-two books. Each section has a different sanctity. The *Torah* is considered the most sanctified book followed by the *Neviim* and the *Ketubim*.

At the Conclave at Jabneh ca. 100 C.E., the canonization of the book of Kohelet was brought up again and after a debate the view that the book should be a part of the canon prevailed, and thus Kohelet was canonized. At that time the Hebrew canon consisted of twenty-three books. It seems that neither at the Conclave of 65 C.E. nor at the Conclave of Jabneh was the canonization of the book of Esther ever brought up. The book of Esther was canonized at the Conclave of Ousha ca. 140 C.E. In my Introduction to the book of Judith, I endeavored to show that the book of Judith was written to mitigate the ambivalence of many Jews toward the book of Esther for not alluding to prayers and Divine Revelation. The sages were reluctant to include the book of Esther in the Hebrew canon. It was accepted due to public pressure. The book was very popular among the people.

In this volume I have included four essays on the Pharisees. One essay deals mainly with the halakic controversies between the Sadducees and the Pharisees. This essay was originally written in Hebrew and translated by Rabbi Mordekai Shapiro. The halakic contentions between the Morning-Bathers and the Pharisees is discussed in the essay "The Origin of the Pharisees Reaffirmed." Disputations between Jesus or his disciples with the Pharisees are related in the essay "The Pharisees and the Gospels." Having all of the halakic controversies between the Pharisees and their opponents in one volume (incidentally, for the first time), it will help the reader to have a full comprehension of the Pharisees and for what they stood, and he will be able to form an authentic idea of the Pharisees and their philosophy of Judaism. I also believe that the reader will recognize where I deviate from other historians with regard to the origin and the philosophy of the Pharisees.

In this volume is also included the essay "The Origin of the Idea of

FOREWORD

Messiah," in which I demonstrate that the historians actually echoed the view of the theologians and thus vitiated the history of the Jews during the Second Commonwealth.

Volume I contained twenty-two essays dealing with the development of the calendar, the semi-festivals, and Josephus as a man and his role during the war against the Romans. The volume also contains the essays "The Origin of the Synagogue," "The First Canonization of the Hebrew Liturgy" wherein I maintain that the synagogue as a house of worship came into existence when prayers were standardized, and that was after the destruction of the Second Commonwealth. It was at that time the synagogue as a permanent institution, as a house of worship, came into being.

The two volumes contain forty-five essays, the fruit of more than a half century of intensive research of the sources: the Tannaitic literature, Apocryphal literature, the writings of Josephus, and the vast Hellenistic literature which not only has a bearing on the history of that period but also supplies additional material for the history of the Second Jewish Commonwealth.

It is well known that sources are sometimes very ambiguous and complicated—sometimes contradictory. In examining the sources, I applied both methods, the external and the internal. By external evidence I mean the verification of the text by an examination of various readings found in different manuscripts. By internal evidence I mean the scrutiny and analysis of the text. I particularly emphasized the importance of the usage of terms. To give an example, one of my contentions is that the synagogue was not originally a house of worship because the Hebrew term is *Bet Ha-K'nesset* and not *Bet Ha-Tefillah*. The word *Bet Ha-Tefillah* is found in the Bible while the term *Bet-Ha-K'nesset* is a later term, never occurring in the Bible. Again, the term "sanhedrin" never occurs in the Tannaitic literature before the destruction of the Temple; it is always referred to as *Bet Din*. In studying the tenet of Messiah, I was struck by the fact that in the Bible *Meshiaḥ* is used as an adjective but not as a proper name. The idea of Messiah as a redeemer not only does not occur in the writings of Josephus but also not in the Apocryphal literature. If the Jews believed in a supernatural Messiah we would expect the term Messiah to occur in the books of the Maccabees and in the book of Judith. Again, the Mishneh says one who does not believe in resurrection and that the Torah is from Heaven will not share a portion in the future world; however, the belief in Messiah is not mentioned. Normative Judaism believed that God would redeem the Jews from their enemies.

The monographs and essays which are embodied in these volumes formed the basis of the *Rise and Fall of the Judaean State*.

FOREWORD

The readers of these two volumes and the *Rise and Fall of the Judaean State* will undoubtedly note my fundamental deviation from all those who wrote on the history of the Jews during the Hellenistic and Roman periods.

The essay "Who is a Jew?" was first published in *JQR* April, 1959, and was reprinted by B. Litvin *Jewish Identity,* 1965., ed. by Dr. Sidney B. Hoenig.

These essays harbor a certain amount of unavoidable repetitiousness. This is due to the nature of the subjects and the time of publication of the essays. I hope the reader will be patient.

SOLOMON ZEITLIN
Dropsie University
August, 1973

INTRODUCTION

This volume contains twenty three essays that have appeared in various periodicals and magazines during a period of over forty years and in which I deal mainly with the canonization of the Hebrew Scriptures and with Jewish apocryphal literature. Also included are essays on Second Commonwealth sects—the Pharisees, the Sadducees, and the Essenes; the origin of the idea of the Messiah; proselytism during the Second Commonwealth; and the question of who is a Jew.

The Hebrew canon consists of three parts: the Torah—Pentateuch; Neviim—Prophets; Ketubim—Writings, Holy Scriptures. The Pentateuch was canonized in the year 444 B.C.E.; the Prophetic Books were canonized in the early Hellenistic period; the Ketubim were canonized in the year 65 C.E., shortly before the destruction of the Temple. At the time of the fall of the Judaean state, the Hebrew canon consisted of twenty-two books; the Torah, five books; the Prophets, eight books, and the nine books of the Ketubim—Daniel, Ezra-Nehemiah, Chronicles, Psalms, Proverbs, Job, Lamentations, Song of Songs and Ruth. The Book of Kohelet was canonized in Jabneh, approximately in the year 100 C.E., while the Book of Esther was canonized still later, at the Conclave at Ousha, about the year 140 C.E.

The Book of Esther was popular, it was read on the days of Purim. After the destruction of the Temple, and particularly after the catastrophe of Bar Kokhba, the Book of Esther became even more popular because Jews felt that the story of the book was a consolation. Haman strove to annihilate the Jews. He did not succeed, and he himself was destroyed and he was hanged on the gallows. It happened to those who schemed to destroy the Jews and it could happen again. The fortunes could again be reversed. Undoubtedly, there was a popular outcry to include the Book of

INTRODUCTION

Esther in the Holy Scriptures. The sages were at first reluctant to include the Book of Esther in the Hebrew canon, but finally yielded. We may postulate that the canonicty of the Book of Esther was forced on the rabbis by public pressure.

When the Book of Esther was accepted in the Hebrew canon the sages endeavored to find in it passages which showed that the book was an inspired one, i.e., the author of the book had been inspired by the Holy Spirit and thus the Book of Esther could be considered a part of the Holy Scriptures, but not all the sages agreed about the inclusion of the Book of Esther in the canon. Samuel an Amora of the third century said that the Book of Esther does not defile the hands, i.e., the Book of Esther is not a Holy Book and thus not a part of the Hebrew Bible. When he was reminded that he, himself had said once, that the Book of Esther was "inspired", he retorted that it was "inspired" for reading on the days of Purim but it was not "inspired" for the inclusion in the Hebrew Bible.

I

The history of the canonization of the Hebrew Scriptures has been dealt with by many scholars, mostly Christians, from whom we have an extensive literature. Scholars who have dealt with the subject base their theories mainly on the writings of the Church Fathers, by-passing the tannaitic literature; and those who have utilized this literature, misconstrued it.

In the essay "An Historical Study of the Canonization of the Hebrew Scriptures," I deal primarily with the third section of the Hebrew canon, the Ketubim. While the study is based mainly on the words of the Tannaim, who were responsible for its canonization, the writings of the Church Fathers have not been ignored. In presenting my argument for the canonization of the Hebrew Scriptures in the year 65 C.E. and the exclusion of Kohelet and Esther from the Hebrew canon at that time, I differ considerably from those who have hitherto dealt with the subject. In this essay the reader will find the underlying reasons for not including the Book of Jubilees, Ben Sira, Tobit, Susanna, and Judith in the Hebrew canon. In the Talmud the expression, "the Holy Scriptures defile the hands" occurs quite frequently. Here I explain why the sages decreed that the Holy Scriptures defile the hands.

II

In the books of the Torah there are dotted letters. In "Some Reflections on the Text of the Pentateuch," I try to show that the dots were placed on the letters to indicate that they were inserted in the text through error. I also maintain that many words crept into the Pentateuch by error, and that the correct text is to be found in the rabbinic literature. In other words, we have no Masoretic text.

III

The Talmud relates that there were three Torah scrolls in the Azara. In "Were There Three Torah Scrolls in the Azara?" I point out that this statement is a legend. Shortly after the destruction of the Second Temple, the sages introduced the five final letters as well as the *matres lectionis* into the Bible. In order to give authority to these innovations, they maintained that three Torahs were found in the Temple, and that two of them had the final letters and the *matres lectionis*.

The term apocrypha means hidden, secret, something mysterious. The early Church Fathers applied the term apocrypha to those books which they considered false, spurious, heretical. The Tannaim applied the term "outside books" to all those not included in the Hebrew canon. Some they considered heretical. Books outside of the canon did not defile the hands. The term defiling of the hands therefore became a criterion for those books which were considered part of the Hebrew canon and therefore holy.

IV

In "The Apocrypha," I deal with the story of the martyrdom of the mother and her seven sons. In the Second Book of Maccabees the story is placed in the time of Antiochus Epiphanes and, the book relates, that they were put to death because they disobeyed the laws of the king and refused to eat forbidden food. In the Talmud, the story is placed in the Roman period and the reason given for the death penalty is that they refused to worship idols. In the Fourth Book of Maccabees, which is an apocalyptic book, these martyrs were called saints. Neither book ever claimed they were of the family of the Maccabees. The Church accepted the story and called the mother and the seven sons, Maccabees and saints. The Fourth Book of Maccabees had a great influence on the Church. According to its author, the children died to atone for the sins of the people, and the idea of atonement became the focal point in Christianity. Dying to atone for the sins of others never became a tenet of normative Judaism.

In this essay I advance the theory that the Fourth (Second) Ezra was

INTRODUCTION

composed in Cyrene during the reign of Trajan. The author of the book propagated the idea that God will send the Messiah, who will be called *Vir,* Man. The Apocalypse of (Second) Baruch was written in the land of Judaea before the revolt of Bar Kokhba. The author of this book propagated the idea of the coming of the Messiah who would establish a Jewish state and restore the Temple. The Greek text of these books no longer extant, had a great influence on the Jews and helped the fanatics to instigate the revolts against the Romans. The revolts in Cyrene and in Egypt against the Romans brought added suffering and catastrophe to the Jewish people.

The apocryphal books as well as those that were written by the apocalyptists emanated from the genius of the Jewish people; they were the product of that twilight period between the closing of the Hebrew canon and the dawn of Christianity. These books were banned, however, because some of them contradicted the established halakha, while others were in opposition to the views of the Pharisees. The new sect of Judeo-Christians considered that some of the books of the apocalyptists were "inspired." The sages were apprehensive that the sect would maintain that these books had a place in the Hebrew canon. They therefore decreed that those who read them would be excluded from sharing a portion in the future world.

Most of these books were written in Hebrew and Aramaic. However, they have been preserved only in the Greek language. In the majority of cases, the Greek translation is full of misreadings and misrenderings, due to the fact that many of the translators were not sufficiently acquainted with the original languages. These writings were transmitted by the Church; thus we find in many passages the thought and the dogma of the Church.

V

In "Jewish Apocryphal Literature" I show that when the Hebrew canon became well-established, the ban against the "outside books" automatically disappeared. The Book of Ben Sira is quoted in the Talmud. The Book of Judith was read in some synagogues on Hanukkah, while the Book of Baruch was read in the synagogues on the Ninth of Ab.

VI

The general opinion is that the Book of Jubilees was composed during the second century B.C.E. Scholars are divided as to its authorship. Some maintain that the author was a Pharisee, others that he was a Sadducee, still others, that the author of the book was an Essene. Those who are of

INTRODUCTION

the opinion that the author could not have been a Sadducee or a Pharisee base their argument on the author's placing the Festival of Weeks in the middle of the third month, i.e., Sivan. The Pharisees maintained that the Festival of Weeks always fell on the fiftieth day after the Omer was brought to the Temple. The Sadducees, on the other hand, maintained that the Festival of Weeks must always fall on a Sunday; consequently, the author could not have been a Pharisee or a Sadducee.

The Book of Jubilees was written originally in Hebrew and was later translated into Greek. Neither the original Hebrew nor the Greek are extant. What we do have is an Ethiopic rendition and some Latin sections which were translated from the Greek. In my essay I try to demonstrate that the Greek translator misunderstood the Hebrew. The Greek translator read the Hebrew word in Jubilees the same as in the Pentateuch, *shabuot*, (sing. *shabua*), and therefore rendered it "Weeks", following the Septuagint which rendered the word *shabuot* correctly as the Festival of Weeks. However, in reality the word in the Book of Jubilees was meant to be read *shebuoth* (sing. *shebua*) and had the connotation of oaths which God made with Noah and Abraham. In commemoration of these oaths, according to the author, it was ordained that the Jews celebrate the Festival of Oaths in the middle of the third month.

With regard to the date of the composition of the book, I maintain that it was written at the period when the solar calendar was changed to lunar-solar, a change which the author of Jubilees strongly opposed. The title of the book originally was The Laws of Moses; the title Jubilees came to us from the Church Fathers.

VII

In the essay "The Book of Jubilees and the Pentateuch," I try to substantiate the theory that the so-called Book of Jubilees was not composed by a Sadducee, a Pharisee, or an Essene, but that it was written in opposition to the Pentateuch. According to the author, the laws were given to Moses through the medium of the Angel of Presence, and many of the laws recorded in the Ten Commandments were actually enacted long before the time of Moses.

VIII

The midrashim tell of ten sages who were put to death by the Romans. Their names vary in the different midrashim, and scholars have labored to identify them. In "The Legend of the Ten Martyrs and its Apocalyptic Origins," I advance the theory that the midrash about the ten martyrs is, in essence, not history but a legend. This does not mean that the Romans did not torture and slay many sages, they did; but the story of the ten martyrs is based on the apocalyptic ideas of ransom. According to the author of the Book of Jubilees, the Day of Atonement was instituted as a day of fast and affliction to redeem the sin of the ten sons of Jacob who sold their brother Joseph into slavery, which occurred on the tenth day of the seventh month, Tishri. The story of the ten martyrs, as recorded in the midrash, also reflects the idea of redeeming the sin of Jacob's sons. The idea of ransom, to say the least, is not in accordance with normative Judaism. The Book of Jubilees had a great influence on the apopcalyptists, the forerunners of the Christians. The tenet of dying in order to atone for the sins of others became the cornerstone of Christianity. A liturgical poem about the ten martyr sages, that undoubtedly had its origin in the Book of Jubilee, is recited in the synagogues on the Day of Atonement.

IX

It is generally believed that the Assumption of Moses was composed before the destruction of the Second Temple. As to the authorship of the book, scholars are divided: Some maintain that the author was a Sadducee, others that he was a Zealot, while still others argue that the author was a Pharisaic Quietist. In "The Assumption of Moses and the Revolt of Bar Kokhba" I contend that the book could not have been written before the Bar Kokhba period, since the author designated the years according to the era of *anno mundi*. He gave the date of Moses' death as "two thousand five hundred after the creation of the world." The manner of designating the year by *anno mundi* was not used by the Jews before the destruction of the Second Temple. It came into vogue shortly after the revolt of Bar Kokhba. The fact that the author designated the years according to the era of *anno mundi* mitigates against the theories that this book was composed before the year 70 C.E.

In this essay I endeavor to establish that the so-called book of the Assumption of Moses was written in the year 140 C.E. and that it is an important document for the history of the revolt of Bar Kokhba. The author was among those who opposed the revolt against the Romans. He considered the revolt a secular movement and referred to the leaders of the Bar Kokhba period as "devourers of the goods of the poor," and "deceitful and impious men." The author did not believe in a Messiah. He held that God would rule the world, and predicted that God would reveal himself in the year 4250 *anno mundi,* i.e., 490 C.E. The book and its prediction are referred to in the Talmud.

INTRODUCTION

X

The term Pharisee is defined in the *Oxford Universal Dictionary:* "One of the ancient Jewish sects distinguished by their strict observance of the traditional and written laws, and by their pretentions to superior sanctity. 2) A person of this disposition. 3) A self-righteous; formalist; hypocrite." The *American College Dictionary,* defines the term Pharisee: "One of an ancient Jewish sect which believed in the validity of the oral law and in the free interpretation of the written law by seeking to discover the inner meaning. 2) A pharisaic, self-righteous or hypocritical person." Pharisaism is defined as: "The doctrine and the practice of the Pharisees. 2) Rigid observance of external forms of religion without genuine piety; hypocrisy."

This hostile attitude toward the Pharisees and Pharisaism is due to the influence of the Gospels, particularly the Gospel according to Matthew, where the Pharisees are referred to as hypocrites. Similarly, the Church Fathers always assumed a hostile attitude when writing about them. Since the period of the Reformation many theologians, Protestants and Catholics, have assumed a more liberal attitude toward the Pharisees, but the general view of the New Testament still prevails. Very few among the liberal Protestants consider the Pharisees as sincere people devoted to their religion.

The literature on the Pharisees is extensive, but confusing. Their origin is placed in the second century B.C.E., at the time of Jonathan the Hasmonean. The word Pharisee has been interpreted by some to mean separatist, because Pharisees separated themselves from the *am ha-aretz,* by others, to mean interpreter, one who interpreted the Torah, while still others maintain that because the Pharisees were very scrupulous and observed the laws of purity, the word itself, Pharisee, connotes separatist, to separate oneself from unclean things and from the heathens.

In "The Pharisees: A Historical Study," I propound the idea that the term *Perushim*, Pharisees, was actually a nickname, a term of reproach and contempt espoused by their opponents, the Sadducees, who considered them heretics: they were named *Perushim* because they separated themselves from God and the Torah.

The origin of the two groups, the Sadducees and the so-called Pharisees, goes back to the time of the Restoration shortly after the canonization of the Pentateuch. The early Sadducees were the followers of Joshua, the high priest of the family of Zadok who stood for the establishment of a new community—a theocracy—and believed in the law as given in the Pentateuch denying the validity of the Oral Law. Many Judaeans supported

INTRODUCTION

Zerubbabel, a scion of the royal Davidic family, and believed that the new community should be ruled by secular leaders. They maintained that both the Written and the Oral Law were of divine origin and that the laws as given in the Pentateuch could be interpreted in accordance with the needs of the people and the demands of the times. They also held that Yahweh is a universal God, not an ethnic God and, thus, favored proselytism. The high priests who were descendants of the family of Zadok considered these views heretical. They nicknamed those who held these views, *Perushim*, because they separated themselves from the people, the Judaeans, and from God, while the priests named themselves *Zedokim*, Sadducees, descendants of the high priest of Zadok.

The sages never called themselves *Perushim*. This alone militates against the theories that the term Perushim has the connotation of separatists from the *am ha'aretz, i.e.* that they were scrupulous in observing the laws of purity and thus separated from the unclean and the heathen, or that they were called so because they interpreted the Torah. In the tannaitic literature, the expression is never "the Perushim said" but "the sages said." The word *Perushim* occurs only in the dialogues between the Zedokim, the Sadducees and the *Perushim,* the Pharisees.

XI

It is a generally held view of the Pharisees that they were very rigid in their interpretation of the Halakha, the law, although there is no record in the tannaitic literature of laws that were enacted by the Pharisees. We do have dialogues between the Sadducees and the Pharisees in regard to the application of the law. All of the dialogues that took place between these groups are collated in, "The Sadducees and the Pharisees—A Chapter in the Development of the Halakha." I believe that this is the first time that the disputations between the Sadducees and the Pharisees have been collected in one essay. In placing them together we can have a better understanding of the origin and historical background of the disputations.

The controversies between the Sadducees and the Pharisees reflect their different attitudes towards religion, law, and the social and economic problems of the people. The center of these disputations is Pentateuchal law and its application in life. The Sadducees demanded the rigid observance of the Pentateuchal law. The Pharisees strove to amend the Pentateuchal law in order to bring religion into consonance with the requirements and demands of ever changing life. The Pharisees were the true leaders of the people: They endeavored to make religion the concern of the entire people by

INTRODUCTION

working to eradicate superstition; they contended that in order to meet the vicissitudes of life, the Pentateuchal laws must be interpreted and amended. This essay presents an ample number of examples of these attitudes.

The Sadducees sought to monopolize the Temple service by devising means of excluding the masses. According to Pentateuchal law, sacrifices were to be brought to the Temple every morning and afternoon. The Sadducees maintained that these daily sacrifices should be considered a matter of private concern. Any individual who wished to provide lambs for the daily sacrifices could do so directly or could donate to the Temple treasury the money required for purchasing them. Obviously, the wealthy Sadducees were the only ones who could afford this luxury. The Pharisees, on the other hand, maintained that the daily sacrifices should not be considered the responsibility of the individual, but should be provided by the entire community. The Pharisees instituted a law that animals for the daily sacrifices were to be purchased out of those funds in the Temple treasury to which each Jew contributed his equitable portion. Thus the Jews as a whole could participate in the Temple service. The enactment of laws by the Pharisees concerning priests and ritual purity provide other examples of their liberalism and their desire to eradicate class distinction.

There is a controversy recorded about the offering of incense in the Holy of Holies on the Day of Atonement. The Sadducees maintained that the high priest should put the incense upon the fiery coals in the censer while he was yet outside the Holy of Holies. In this way the smoke arising from the incense would obstruct his vision when he went beyond the curtain and entered the Holy of Holies. The Sadducees following the words of the Pentateuch literally, believed that God was somehow especially present in the Holy of Holies. They were apprehensive that the high priest would die on entering the Holy of Holies if he saw God. The Pharisees on the other hand contended that the high priests should enter the Holy of Holies with open eyes. God was invisible and could not be seen with human eyes, thus there was no fear that the high priest would see God and die. They maintained that God is everywhere and is not confined to the Holy of Holies. To eradicate the notion that God has form and could be seen by a human being, the Pharisees maintained that the high priests should not prepare the smoking incense outside of the curtain. He was to carry the censer with the fiery coals and the incense separately. Only when he was inside the curtain and within the Holy of Hollies was he to put the incense upon the coals in the censer, make it smoke, and offer it. With this law the Pharisees sought to eradicate superstition and raise religion to a higher level. They were not

INTRODUCTION

always successful, for superstition is very tenacious as its continued prevalence indicates.

According to the Pentateuchal law, if water is poured upon seed, the seed becomes susceptible to ritual uncleanliness. The law makes no distinction between seed attached to the soil and seed detached from it. If this had been rigidly upheld, it would have brought havoc to the economic life of the people. It would have made it impossible for those who were scrupulous in observing the laws of ritual purity to use grain imported from Egypt, since the Egyptians irrigated their fields and under this law their seed was thus susceptible to ritual uncleanliness. But grain from Egypt was often a necessity because of frequent poor harvests and famine in the land of Judaea. The Pharisees interpreted the word "seed" in the Pentateuch to mean only seed detached from the soil, holding that only a detached seed upon which water was poured was susceptible to ritual uncleanliness. With this interpretation the Pharisees made it possible for the people of Judaea to import grain from the rich granary of Egypt. The Pharisees' intention was to ease the law so that it should not be a burden on the people. Their credo was that halakha was given for man, and not man for halakha.

From time immemorial, man has been troubled with the problem of why the virtuous suffer and the wicked prosper. The Pharisees offered a solution to this vexing problem by teaching a belief in life after death. They maintained that reward was in store for the virtuous and punishment for the wicked in the future life. The Pharisees affirmed that all men, as the children of God, were under His Providence. Yet, although they believed that every action depended on fate and God, they also believed in freedom of the will— that man could act virtuously if he so desired. Accepting freedom of will, they still believed that not only did fate play a part in man's actions, they virtually identified fate with the Providence of God. They also taught that the soul is immortal. Their conception of afterlife was limited to immortality of the soul, not to a resurrection of the body. The Sadducees denied both resurrection and Providence, since neither is explicitly mentioned in the Pentateuch.

XII

The essay "The Pharisees and the Gospels" enumerates the disputes between Jesus, or, rather, his disciples, and the Pharisees. The word "Pharisees" has become a synonym for "hypocrites," due to the Gospels, particularly Matthew, that identified the Pharisees with hypocrisy. In Matthew

INTRODUCTION

23.13 the expression "Pharisees, hypocrites" is used in Jesus' name. Before presenting the historical background of these disputations, a short analytical study of the Sermon on the Mount is in order.

The Sermon on the Mount is a conglomeration of the sayings of Jesus, which, it must be stressed, were recorded at least two generations after his death. His followers were of differing traditions and, thus, we find confusion and contradiction in the sayings of Jesus as recorded in the Sermon on the Mount and in other passages of the Synoptic Gospels. The Sermon on the Mount, must be placed in its proper historical perspective. Several terms supposedly used by Jesus were not in vogue during his lifetime, but came into usage after the destruction of the Second Temple. The words "Gehenna" and "synagogue"—synagogue as a house of prayer—were first used in the Judaean literature after the destruction of the Second Temple. Similarly, "You cannot serve God and mammon," could not have been authored by Jesus, since the word "mammon" was not used by Judaeans during his lifetime. "Mammon" is Hebrew *mammon,* meaning money, wealth. During the Second Commonwealth, i.e., during the lifetime of Jesus, the word used for money was *kesef,* and the word *nekhasim* had the connotation of property, wealth. *Mammon* as money, wealth, came into vogue two generations after the death of Jesus.

There are other anachronisms in the episodes given in the Gospels. To cite several examples: Matthew (17.24–26) relates that when Jesus came to Capernaum, "they that received the two drachmas, (half-shekel) came to Peter, and said, Doth not your teacher pay (two drachmas)?" He saith, Yes. And when he was come into the house, Jesus prevented him, saying, What thinkest thou, Simon? of whom do the kings of the earth take custom or tribute? of their own children or of strangers? Jesus said unto him, Then are the children free." Jesus could not, have said this. The two drachmas— half-shekel— had to be paid by the Judaeans, the "children," and were collected by the emissaries of the *Bet Din,* the court. No stranger could give half a shekel to the Temple. This episode, if it ever took place, could have happened only after the destruction of the Temple. Josephus writes that when the Romans conquered Judaea, Emperor Vespasian imposed a special tax of two drachmas on the Jews to be paid annually to Jupiter Capitolinus, the amount formerly contributed by the Jews to the Temple. A special office was established under the name *Procurator,* to collect this tax called *fiscus Judaicus,* which was levied upon those who professed the Jewish faith regardless of where they lived, whether in Judaea or in other parts of the Roman Empire. It was a religious tax, not an ethnic tax, and was also collected from proselytes who accepted Judaism.

INTRODUCTION

To set this episode in its proper perspective: it must have occurred *after* the destruction of the Second Temple. When the Roman collectors came to get the half-shekel, Jesus maintained that as taxes were collected from strangers, not from "children" he was not obliged to pay. Jesus considered God to be the only ruler and himself the son of God. In order not to give offense, however, Jesus said to Peter (Matthew 7:27), . . . "go thou to the sea, and cast a hook, and take up the fish that first cometh up; and when thou hast opened his mouth, thou shalt find a piece of silver; (shekel); that take, and give unto them for me and thee." Although Jesus maintained that he was not obliged to pay the half-shekel, he paid it in order not to offend the Roman authorities.

Jesus' disposition to compromise in order not to antagonize the Roman authorities is manifested in another, more famous, instance (Matthew 22: 17–21). When asked, "Is it lawful to give tribute unto Caesar or not?" Jesus perceived that the questioners were trying to place him in a difficult position. "[Jesus] said, Show me the tribute coin. And they brought unto him a dinar. And he said unto them, Whose is this image and inscription? They said to him, Caesar's. Then said he unto them, Render therefore unto Caesar the things which are Caesar's; and unto God the things which are God's."

The following statement by Matthew cannot have been made by Jesus; it is anachronistic: "Woe unto you, scribes and Pharisees, hypocrites! for ye compass sea and land to make one proselyte." The term proselyte, *ger,* one who embraced Judaism, came into usage either a few years before the destruction or after the destruction of the Second Temple. During the time of Jesus a convert to Judaism was called *mumar, metaboles,* changer, a person who changed his religion, his mode of life, and accepted Judaism. Neither was the term rabbi in usage during the Second Commonwealth; it came into vogue after the destruction of the Second Temple.

In the Sermon on the Mount (Matthew 5:27–30) Jesus said, "You have heard that it was said, by them of old time, You shall not commit adultery: but I say to you, that whosoever looks at a woman lustfully has already committed adultery with her in his heart. And if your right eye causes you to sin, pluck it out, and cast it from you; it is better that you lose one of your members than that your whole body be thrown into Gehenna." The admonition ascribed to Jesus, "One who looks at a woman lustfully has already committed adultery with her in his heart," is not new. Philo and the author of II Maccabees relate that maidens were kept indoors so as not to be seen in public. According to the author of the Twelfth Testament, looking at a woman lustfully was considered a moral sin. According to the

INTRODUCTION

sayings of Jesus, to remove this moral sin a person had to pluck out his eye. This is contrary to the nature of mankind; it is not realistic. No man who has looked lustfully at a woman would maim himself by plucking out his eye, but would continue to live in moral sin. The sages recognized the weakness of human nature and made it possible for a man committing a moral sin to live a righteous life. They introduced the principle of *tshuba,* returning to God, repentance. When a man repented, his moral sin was forgiven; God being merciful accepted his repentance.

Many sayings in the Sermon on the Mount are not realistic—they are contrary to human nature—particularly the saying "Love your enemy." This is generally considered the apogee of the Sermon on the Mount, but it is a utopian statement. Is it conceivable that a man who was wronged should be enjoined not to hate the person who may have, even unintentionally, committed a crime against him? A person may forgive and tolerate one who has injured him or a member of his family; but how can one expect a person to love an enemy who has harmed him or someone close to him? This is humanly impossible. Hillel's Golden Rule that a person should not injure another since he himself does not want to be injured, is more realistic. People can be educated in accordance with his principle.

With regard to the disputations regarding halakha, we note the same views: Jesus sought the ethical side while the Pharisees, who were the leaders of the people, had to apply the law to maintain order. Some of these disputations between Jesus, or the disciples of Jesus, and the Pharisees could not have taken place during the lifetime of Jesus. We refer to the disputation about washing the hands before meals, about which, according to the Gospels of Mark and Matthew, Jesus became so infuriated that he violently attacked the Pharisees by calling them hypocrites. The Gospels record: (Mark 7:1-6) "Then came together unto him the Pharisees and certain of the scribes which came from Jerusalem. And when they saw some of his disciples eat bread with defiled, that is to say, with unwashed hands, they found fault. For the Pharisees, and all the Judaeans, except they washed their hands oft, eat not, holding the tradition of the elders. . . . He answered and said unto them, Well hath Isaiah prophesied of your hypocrites" . . . In "The Pharisees and the Gospels," I show that the institution of washing the hands before meals came into vogue after the destruction of the Second Temple.

In the same essay I have also tried to demonstrate the difference between the Synoptic Gospels and the Gospel according to John. In the former we note the great animosity toward the Pharisees, while in the latter the animosity is directed against the Jewish people.

INTRODUCTION

In sum, the phrase "Pharisees, hypocrites," could not have come from Jesus. It is possible that some of the disciples, in the heat of the argument with the Pharisees, used diatribes against them. The followers of Jesus were originally members of the Apocalyptist Pharisees. They might have accused their teachers or their fellows of not stretching the halakha as they would have liked to. We have to remember that the followers of Jesus were Jews, and the Pharisees considered them heretics for breaking the laws

XIII

One theologian, in his books and monographs during the last few decades, has followed the general view that the Pharisees came into being during the second century B.C.E., at the time of the Hasmoneans. In a recent article, "The Origin of the Pharisees Reconsidered," he wrote, "The Pharisees existed as a distinct group as early as the fourth century B.C.E." This is a complete reversal of his previous theory and brings him much closer to my view that they came into being at the latter part of the fifth century B.C.E. However, in the eassy "The Origin of the Pharisees Reaffirmed," I wrote, while I am glad to obtain converts to my views, I must reject Dr. Finkelstein's theory. His premise is unacceptable. He bases his theory on the *Tosefta Yadaim* where a controversy between the Morning-Bathers and the Pharisees is recorded. The Morning-Bathers came into being either shortly before or soon after the destruction of the Temple, when the Pharisees declared that washing the hands was sufficient to render a person pure in the case of minor impurities such as nocturnal pollution. Furthermore, Dr. Finkelstein has not presented the historical background for the rise of the Pharisees. Parties which mold the life of a people are not the result of a whim of a person; they do not spring from a vacuum. We do not not know of any great events in the beginning of the fourth century B.C.E. which could have caused a split among the Judaeans and given rise to the Pharisees. In this essay I reaffirm that the Pharisees came into being after the canonization of the Pentateuch, when the conservatives, the Sadducees, upheld the written laws, the Pentateuchal laws, but denied the validity of the unwritten laws.

The opinion that the Pharisees originated during the Hasmonean period as well as the view that they came on the historical arena at the 4th century must be disregarded. No causation was given for the rise. A group which existed for centuries and had such profound influence over the people must have had causes for its emergence. We must conclude that the

INTRODUCTION

Pharisees arose during the time of the Restoration when the Pentateuch was canonized, then the question arose over the validity and the binding of the oral law. The Sadducees maintained that these laws were not binding while another group held the opposite views.

This clash of ideologies brought about the emergence of the group known as the Pharisees who maintained that the oral laws are as binding as the written laws.

In order to have a full understanding of the Pharisees and the development of their ideological views, one must deal with the history of the Judaeans during the Second Commonwealth. The emergence of parties and their influence on the people are a result of political, social, and religious forces and thus are interwoven with the history of the people. As the history of the people must be studied step by step, so must the history of the parties also. The error committed by those who wrote about the Pharisees was that they did not subject themselves to the discipline that an historian should undergo. They did not take into consideration the development of the ideologies of the Pharisees step by step nor their interconnection with the history of the Judaeans. One cannot write on the Pharisees without taking into consideration the historical development of the Judaeans. The history of a people may have a zigzag course and deviate, but the main characteristics always remain. This is also true of parties. The Sadducers and the Pharisees adapted themselves to ever-changing historical forces, but their main characteristics remained.

XIV

Josephus, enumerating the sects that existed during the Second Commonwealth, also describes one he calls the Essenes. Philo calls them Essaioi. The Pharisees and the Sadducees are mentioned in the tannaitic literature, thus we know their Hebrew names, *Perushim* and *Zedokim;* but the Essenes are never mentioned in tannaitic literature. Incidentally, the Essenes are never mentioned in the New Testament either. The Essenes were a Judaean sect, thus they must have had a Hebrew name. What was it? And when did this group arise on the historical arena? The answer to these two queries is given in the eassy "The Essenes and Messianic Expectations."

The Hebrew name of the Essenes was *hasidim* and this appelation is used in the two books of Maccabees. Josephus named them Essenes, which has the connotation of oracle and prophecy. In enumerating the vestments of the high priest Josephus rendered the word *Hoshen, essen,* and

INTRODUCTION

adds that this word signifies *logion,* oracle. In describing the Essenes, Josephus said that the members of the group wore linen cloth on their loins. It was believed that the *ḥoshen* or essen was the means of giving the power of prophecy to the person who wore it. The Essenes who wore the loin cloth were credited by Josephus with the power of prophesying. Thus Josephus called this group Essenes. Similarly, Josephus called the followers of Judah the Galilean, the founder of the fourth Philosophy, *sicarii* because they wore a dagger called *sica* under their garment.

The *hasidim,* the pious people, arose at the time of Antiochus Epiphanes. They joined the army of Judah Makkabee. However, when freedom was won by the Hasmoneans, the *hasidim* opposed the establishment of a free Jewish state: they were interested in the freedom of religion, but not in the establishment of an independent state. They were particularly opposed to the family of the Hasmoneans, because they were not descendants of Zadok. *The hasidim* opposed the election of Simon as high priest. They believed that he had no right to enter the Holy of Holies and thus they considered the Temple profaned.

The idea of the two messiahs, one a scion of the Davidic family, and another a descendant of the family of Ephraim, is discussed at length in this essay. The expectation of the coming of the Messiah almost became a tenet among the Jews. Christian as well as Jewish theologians have interpreted certain biblical and apocryphal passages as referring to the messiah, Christian theologians to their messiah and the Jewish to theirs. To cite a few examples: The verse in Genesis 49.10, "The sceptre shall not depart from Judah, nor the ruler's staff between his feet, as long as men come to Shiloh; and unto him shall the opinions of the people be." Origen interpreted this passage as referring to "Christ of God," Jesus. The Targum according to Jonathan, interpreted it as referring to the Jewish mashiaḥ. This view was shared by Jewish historians. There is no idea of messiah to be found in the Bible or in the apocryphal literature. The word mashiah is used in the Bible as an adjective, not as a noun. The term messiah as a noun appears only in the late apocalyptic literature. The prophets speak of a millennium—a period of happiness when there will be no more wars between nations and people will live in peace with one another.

XV

In "The Origin of the Idea of Messiah," I endeavor to show that during the Second Commonwealth the Jews did not expect a messiah—a supernatural person—who would save them from their enemies. They believed that God himself would rescue them from the yoke of the pagans. The

INTRODUCTION

historians of the Second Commonwealth vitiate their work with their idea of messianic expectations. They interpret certain biblical passages as referring to a messiah. These historians who are deluded with the idea of messianic expectation during the Second Commonwealth are not only deceiving their readers, they are distorting Jewish history of that period. Messianic expectations arose only after the destruction of the Second Temple. During the Second Commonwealth the Apocalyptists expected a messiah, but the Judaeans, in general, including the Pharisees, the Sadducees, and the Essenses, had no ideas about the coming of a messiah. In neither the works of Philo nor of Josephus is there any mention of a messiah, neither is there any inkling of messianic expectation to be found in the apocryphal literature.

Besides the afore-mentioned groups the Sadducees, the Pharisees and Essenes, undoubtedly, there were many that denied Revelation and the belief that the Five Books of Moses were given by God on Mount Sinai. Many did not believe in a future world. We may assume that there were some Gnostics. However, they were individuals; they were not organized groups with a definite ideology and philosophy. From the time of Herod to the destruction of the Temple Pharisaism was the normative way of life of the Judaeans.

XVI

The term for a convert to the Jewish faith in the rabbinic literature is *ger, a* proselyte. However, in the Pentateuch, *ger* means "sojourner," one who came to live in a particular country or city for a while. In the Pentateuch, the children of Israel are called *gerim,* those who came originally from Canaan and sojourned in Egypt. The concept of conversion does not occur in the Pentateuch. Yahweh was an ethnic god, the god of the descendants of Abraham, Isaac, and Jacob who took them out of Egypt, the land of slavery. Hence, those who were not descendants of Abraham, Isaac, and Jacob could not worship Yahweh. After the Restoration, Yahweh was no longer held to be an ethnic god, the god of the Judaeans alone. He was recognized to be the God of the entire universe. Hence, anyone could accept Him. Thus conversion not only became possible, but desirable. The term used for a convert to the Judaean faith was *munar,* "a changer."

The historical development of proselytism is presented in the essay "Proselytes and Proselytism During the Second Commonwealth and the Early Tannaitic Period." Originally, a *ger,* a proselyte, did not have to undergo specific rites. He had to follow the two main Pentateuchal tenets:

INTRODUCTION

to love Yahweh with all his heart and to love his fellow man as himself. However, circumcision was a mandatory rite by which he showed that he joined the people of Judaea and distinguished himself from the heathens. The rite of baptism of proselytes was instituted after the destruction of the Temple.

The sages regarded proselytes very highly and extolled those who gave up their religion and accepted the God of Israel, commending them even more than those who were born Jews. They compared the proselytes to Abraham, who had been brought up in idol worship and had recognized the universality of God. It is true that the Talmud records one hostile opinion about proselytes, but this is the only such statement. The generally favorable attitude is quite evident from the halakha. According to the Palestinian Talmud *Kidushin,* even one who embraces Judaism for personal motives, as for love, is considered a bona fide proselyte. According to the halakha, the rites of conversion must be witnessed by three men, who constitute a *Bet Din*. However, even if it is performed under the supervision of one man, the conversion is still valid. The sages were particularly lenient with the conversion of women. According to the Book of Ezekiel, a priest may marry from the children of the house of Israel. According to R. Jose, a priest may marry a daughter of a proselyte. R Simon was of the opinion that a priest may even marry a girl who embraced Judaism when she was not yet three years and a day old. According to the Pentateuch, Moabites and Ammonites were never to be allowed to enter the community of Yahweh. Nevertheless, Ruth, who was a Moabite, said to her mother in-law Naomi, "Thy people are my people, thy God is my God." Although she was a Moabite she became a member of the Jewish people. According to the Book of Ruth, which became a part of the Hebrew canon, King David, the pride and glory of the Jewish people, was a descendant of Ruth, a proselyte.

A *ger* was one who accepted Judaism without qualification. The term *ger,* a sojourner, was still used for a foreigner, a heathen, who lived in the land of Judaea. However, the word *toshab* was added. He was designated a *ger toshab* and had to observe the Noachite laws, i.e., *jus gentium*.

XVII

The question of whether the Jews constituted a nation, a race, or a religious group was debated in the period of the Jewish Emancipation. This problem was taken up also by the Jews themselves. Some of them argued that the Jews were a nation while others were of the opinion that they formed only a religious group.

INTRODUCTION

These questions were partially answered with the establishment of the State of Israel. The establishment of the State of Israel came almost two thousand years after the destruction of the State of Judaea by the Romans in 70 C.E.

Israel is a sovereign state—a nation like all other nations of the world. Israel is an equal member in the United Nations. Anyone who lives in the State of Israel is an Israeli. In Israel there are Jews and Arabs—most of them Muslims, some of them are Christians. All are members of the State of Israel.

During the Second Commonwealth, most of the Jews lived outside of Judaea. In my essay "The Jews—Race, Nation or Religion," I analyze the relationship of the Jews of the Diaspora and the Judaeans. Although the term "race" is a comparatively new term, it has not yet been established etymologically whether its origin may be Slavonic or even Semitic from the word ראש —head (cf. *We Europeans,* by Julian S. Huxley and A. C. Haddon, London, 1935, p. 18). However, the conception of race was known in the period of the Second Commonwealth and was used in the sense of the descendants of a particular person or of a clan. In the Bible the word זרע, בני has a connotation of race which the Greeks defined by the term *genos*. In the Talmudic literature, race is sometime defined by the word גזע .

In the same manner, the term *nation*, although a modern term, can very well be applied to the time of the Second Commonwealth. A unity of a certain group occupying a definite territory and closely associated with each other by common history, governed by same laws, was considered a *polis* . . . a city—or in a wider sense an *ethnos*—a nation.

The meaning of *ethnos* and *genos* may be best demonstrated by the manner in which they were used by the Greek writers. Aristotle, in *Politics,* VII, 6, says "the nations *ethne* inhabiting the cold places and those of Europe are full of spirit but somewhat deficient in intelligence and skill . . . the peoples of Asia on the other hand are intelligent and skillfull in temperament . . . the Greek race *Hellenon genos* participates in both characters, just as he occupies a middle position geographically . . . the same diversity also exists among the *Greek nations* compared with one another." When Aristotle speaks of the Greek in general he uses the term *genos;* when he discusses the different states of Greece he uses the term *ethnos*. In the biblical literature the word *gentile* גוי is used to designate *ethnos,* nation (*ethnos*) ומי כעמך כישראל גוי אחד בארץ "who is like thy people Israel, a nation one in the earth"; (II Sam. 7, 23). "and I will make them one nation in the land . . . and there shall be no more two nations" (Ezek. 37.22). The word *goy* was used in the Talmud when referring to Gentiles;

INTRODUCTION

in the New Testament as well as in the writings of the Early Church Fathers, the terms *ethnos* was always applied to non-Jews, Gentiles.

During the Second Commonwealth as well as in modern times a great segment of the Jews lived in the Diaspora. In Egypt alone there were a million Jews, and as many Jews lived in the Mediterranean islands and in Babylonia. They were not known as "Jews." Their nomenclature was "Israelite" or "Hebrew." However, the bond between the Judaeans and their coreligionists in the Diaspora was great. They were united not only by their religion but also by culture and history. There was also an ethnic element which united them. Judaism was the genius of one people. Also, the belief that they descended from common ancestors, Abraham, Isaac, and Jacob, forged the union between all Jews.

In this essay I endeavor to show that the Judaeans during the Second Commonwealth constituted a nation. The Jews of the Diaspora: Egypt, Asia Minor, and Babylonia were not under the political leadership of the Judaeans. They were citizens of their own respective countries and were called Hebrews or Israelites. What really united them with their brethren in Judaea was their religion. The Jews who lived in the Diaspora used to go from time to time particularly during the holidays to Jerusalem, the Holy City, to worship. The Jews hoped for the time when all the adherents of their religion would be gathered together in Judaea.

In this essay I confine myself not only to the halakot of the Tannaim but also I take into consideration the entire literature of that period; the Apocrypha, Josephus, Philo, the New Testament, the Greco-Roman writers, as well as the writings of the early Church Fathers.

XVIII

According to the tannaitic law, the offspring of a union between a Jew and a non-Jewish mother, are not considered as Jews. On the other hand, the offspring of a union between a non-Jew and a Jewess, are considered full-fledged Jews. What was the underlying reason for this law? Many hypotheses have been offered in explanation.

In the essay "The Offspring of Inter-Marriage," I have proposed the theory that this law was enacted shortly after the Restoration to frustrate the schemes of Sanballat, the governor of Samaria, who schemed to build a temple on Mount Gerizim, the sacred mountain of the Samaritans and make it supreme over the Temple of Jerusalem In order to accomplish this, he gave his daughter in marriage to Manasseh the grandson of the High Priest Eliashib. The offspring of this union, if he were male, would be a *kohen,* a priest of the Zadokite family. Thus the temple of Mount Gerizim would not only become competitive with the Temple in Jerusalem but

INTRODUCTION

would overshadow it, since the priests on Mount Gerizim would be descendants of the High Priest, the family of Zadok. The spiritual leaders in Jerusalem fully grasped the designs of Sanballat and saw a danger not only to the Temple in Jerusalem, but also to the entire Judaean community. To avoid this peril, they enacted a law that the offspring of a mixed marriage where the mother is not a Jewess is not a Jew. Sanballat's daughter was not Jewish; she was a Horonite. Hence, according to the enacted law, the grandchildren of Sanballet were not only not priests, but were not Jewish.

XIX

Who is a Jew has become a vexing problem in modern days, particularly after the establishment of the State of Israel, when that state enacted the "Law of Return" granting all Jews the right to migrate to Israel and claim automatic citizenship. In the essay "Who is a Jew?—A Halachic-Historical Study," I set forth the various views of the Jews held by the non-Jewish world (as a religious community, as an ethnic group, and as a nation), and how the halakha defines a Jew.

The question first arose after the French Revolution. The liberals in the National Assembly of France argued that the Jews were a religioue community, like Catholics and Protestants, and thus were entitled to all the rights of citizenship, like Catholics and Protestants. The reactionaries, on the other hand, maintained that the Jews constituted an ethnic group, a nationality, and therefore could not enjoy French citizenship but should be protected by French law as aliens. The reactionaries' views about the Jews was a continuation of Church policy, throughout the ages, Christians had regarded Jews as an ethnic group and the Church had maintained that the Jewish religion was all ethnic and not a universal religion. The Jews themselves did not raise the question of who they were. Jews the world over, regardless of where they lived, considered themselves bound together by religion, by culture, by history, and, also, by ancestry, as they believed that they were the children of Abraham, Isaac, and Jacob. They were a kindred people, whose history went back thousands of years. The Jews did not adopt their religion as other people adopted Christianity. They created it. Jews and their religion entered the historical arena simultaneously.

According to the halakha, a person born of parents who were Jews is a Jew. (The law stating that non-Jewish mothers bore non-Jewish offspring as was mentioned before, was enacted shortly after the Restoration. It was a nationalist-political move.) According to the halakha, if a Jew

INTRODUCTION

converts to another religion, he is still a Jew. He may be a wicked person, but he is still a son of God. If a Jew accepts another religion while married to a Jewess, the marriage remains valid, and if she wants to remarry, she has to obtain a *get*—a writ of divorce. Even if a non-Jew converts to Judaism, reverts to his old religion and later marries a Jewess, the marriage is valid; and if his wife wants to divorce him, she has to obtain a *get* from him. It is clear that not only is a Jew born of Jewish parents still considered a Jew even if he accepts another religion, but, according to the halakha, even a proselyte turning back to his old religion is considered a Jew. If a Jewess marries a non-Jew their offspring is a Jew. Even further, if this offspring is female and she marries a non-Jew, her offspring according to halakha, is a Jew. If a Jew dies without any issue, and leaves a brother who adopted another religion, the wife must get a levirate divorce from her apostate brother-in-law.

With regard to conversion to Judaism, the halakha is very lenient. The male proselyte has to go through the rites of circumcision and baptism. A female has to go through the rite of baptism. The ceremony must take place in the presence of three males; however, if the woman is baptized in the presence of one person, it is considered a bona fide conversion. If a proselyte changes his mind and readopts his old religion or accepts another religion and then wants to return to Judaism, he need not go through any ceremony, because according to the halakha he never left the Jewish faith.

XX

Throughout their long history, the Jews have had different nomenclatures—Hebrew, Jewish, and Israel. These different names have different meanings. In the essay "The Names Hebrew, Jew, and Israel" I elucidate the changes of names throughout the history of the Jewish people.

The term Children of Israel occurs in the Pentateuch. The term Hebrew occurs in the Pentateuch and in the Prophetic books only in connection with slaves or with foreigners. During the time of the First Temple, the people who lived in the north were called Israelites, while those who lived in the south were called Judaeans—Jews. During the Second Conmmonwealth, those who lived in Judaea were called Judaeans—Jews, while some of their brethren who lived in the Diaspora called themselves Hebrews, and others called themselves Israelites. When he was in Judaea, Paul proclaimed himself to be a Judaean—a Jew; when he was in the Diaspora he called himself a Hebrew or an Israelite, since the people who lived there used these terms. The Jews who lived in the Diaspora were closely

INTRODUCTION

bound to Jerusalem and the Temple. Adopted from the term Judaeans, the term Judaism, in the sense of religion, was coined by them. Since then the term Jew has become identified with Judaism.

XXI

Antagonists of a Jewish state in the Land of Israel maintain that the Jews have no historic or legal rights in Palestine. In the essay "Jewish Rights in Palestine" I advance numerous arguments for the legal as well as other rights of the Jews to Palestine since the Jews never relinquished their claim to the land. The Jews are the only people who, from the earliest time to our own day, are identified religiously, historically, and legally with Palestine—which they have always called *Eretz Israel,* the Land of Israel.

XXII

Professor Arnold J. Toynbee is one of the greatest antagonists of Jewish rights in Palestine having propagated his opposition to the establishment of the Israeli state in articles and lectures. I invited him to write a scholarly article for the *Jewish Quarterly Review* in which he would present his arguments against the rights of the Jews in Palestine. I wrote that I would reply in the same number. He consented.

In the July 1961 issue of the J.Q.R. his article, "Jewish Rights in Palestine" appeared. In the same issue I replied with the article "Jewish Rights in *Eretz Israel* (Palestine)." After reading my reply, Professor Toynbee sent me a letter and asked me to publish it. His letter was published in the 1962 issue with my reply. The dialogue as well as the correspondence appeared in a separate essay and these also are included in this volume. I shall not make any comments, but leave it to the reader to be the judge.

XXIII

For over eighteen centuries the Jews have been accused of the Crucifixion of Jesus. This accusation was propagated at the beginning of the second century and has continued to our own day. To this day Jews are occasionally called Christ killers, deicides. The accusation is theological not historical: early Church leaders placed the onus of the Crucifixion upon the leaders of the Jews, in order to substantiate the truth of Christianity. It was Church theology to emphasize that the Jews are

INTRODUCTION

deicides and thus accursed, destined to suffer and live in degradation as eternal witness to the "truth" of Christianity. Historically, the Jews were not responsible for the Crucifixion; Jesus was crucified as the king of the Judaeans, as a rebel against the Romans. The Judaeans of that time were a vanquished people, under the yoke of Rome. The high priest who was the ecclesiastical leader in the Temple was an appointee of the Romans, charged by them with the civil management of the people, responsible to the Roman authorities for the tranquility of Judaea. The Jewish religious leaders had no part in the Crucifixion of Jesus. A serious historian must differentiate between theology and history.

It has been generally assumed that this libelous accusation against the Jews has been the great cause for anti-Semitism. That the Jews crucified Jesus was taught in the schools and preached from the pulpit throughout the ages, and has helped perpetuate an animosity toward the Jews, which has in turn brought great sorrow and dire suffering upon an innocent people. Undoubtedly the seed of this teaching was also instrumental in aiding the Nazi slaughter of six million innocent Jews, particularly in Poland and Lithuania where the Church held sway over the masses. It began with the destruction and burning of the synagogues in Germany. The Christian world must *atone* for their guilt toward the Jewish people for using the Crucifixion of Jesus as a pretext for persecuting them throughout the ages.

Many Christians recognize the danger of anti-Semitism and honestly try to eliminate this cancer gnawing the vitals of civilization. One American Christian theologian, an associate editor of *Christianity Today,* presents a remedy for the elimination of anti-Semitism. In the issue of March 13, 1964, he wrote: "The Jewish people would help eliminate anti-Semitism if they would admit, as honesty could do without violating the terms of the Jewish faith, that they did destroy a man. There is little, if indeed anything, in such an admission in current Jewish concern about anti-Semitism. Let Jews, if they must, regard Christ as only a man but let them admit that honesty and integrity demand the destruction of a man by their ancient leader's insistence that he be put to death."

No one can admit that he has committed a crime in which he had no part. The Jewish people, even under their duress of anti-Semitism, could not and would not admit that their religious leaders had any part in the crucifixion of Jesus.

Many Christian leaders recognized the danger of anti-Semitism and acknowledged the injustice done to the Jews. Pope Pius XI, in one of his encyclicals, said that in spirit we are all Semites. This attitude and spirit were followed by the great humanitarian and saintly Pope John XXIII.

INTRODUCTION

In the dark days of the holocaust when millions of Jews were destroyed in the gas chambers, he interceded whenever he could and saved the lives of many. The present pope, Paul VI, summoned an Ecumenical Council Vatican II. In 1964, in my essay "Ecumenical Council Vatican II and the Jews," I present some of the declarations drafted toward non-Christian religions and also the relationship of the Jews to the Ecumenical Council. Some declarations read as follows: "May they never present the Jewish people as the rejected, cursed, or guilty of deicide. All that happened to Christ in His Passion cannot be attributed to the whole people then alive, much less to that of today." . . . "Everyone should be careful, therefore, not to expose the Jewish people as a rejected nation, be it in Catechetical tuition, in preaching God's Word or in worldly conversation, nor should anything else be said or done which may alienate the minds of men from the Jews. Equally, all should be on their guard not to impute to the Jews of our time that which was perpetrated in the Passion of Christ." Let us hope that this declaration approved at the Ecumenical Council Vatican II, November 20, 1964, will be fully adhered to by the Church leaders.

In my essay, I express concern and apprehension with regard to the dialogues between Jews and Christians which became popular in the 1960's. I expressed the view that dialogues between Jews and Christians with regard to religion is contrary to the history of true Judaism. Jews and Christians are members of one human society, having a common interest in the welfare of their country. They are members of one fellowship. They are separated only by their religions. The Jews do not wish to convert the Christians to Judaism nor do they wish to be converted to Christianity. The events of the last few years have demonstrated how sound were my apprehensions.

AN HISTORICAL STUDY
OF THE
CANONIZATION OF THE HEBREW SCRIPTURES

Reprinted from *Proceedings of the American Academy of Jewish Research,* Vol. 3, 1933.

PREFACE

The literature dealing with the canonization of the Hebrew Scriptures is quite extensive. The scholars who have dealt with the subject based their theories on the testimony of the church fathers, whereas the testimony of the Tannaim was either entirely ignored or misconstrued. It is true that the church fathers, particularly Origen, were very much interested in the Sacred Scriptures of the Old Testament, and Melito, the Bishop of Sardis, even journeyed purposely to Palestine to ascertain first hand, which of the books were canonized, and which were not. However, these were outsiders and their testimony must be taken with a grain of salt. Their information was most likely gathered from the Hellenized Jews. The Tannaim, and they only, are responsible for the canonization of the Hebrew Scriptures and therefore their words are absolute.

In this essay I endeavored to give a historical study of the canonization of the Hebrew Scriptures, based on the words of the Tannaim. Yet, I did not ignore the passages of the church fathers, and the Hellenized Jews.

In the discussion of the numerous passages of the Tannaitic literature, I have offered a few new interpretations, differing greatly from those which have been accepted previously (particularly in Chapter 3). At first sight, the reader may, under the influence of the commentaries, and of the modern literature, be reluctant to accept them. I trust that a careful study of this essay will convince the scholar of the soundness of my interpretations and views.

In this treatise, the first chapter deals with the canonization of the Prophetic books. In the second chapter, I gave the history of the canonization of the Hebrew Scriptures. The third chapter is devoted to the subject "The Holy Scriptures Defiles The Hands," which I believe presents for the first time the underlying motives of the Tannaim in declaring that a book of the Scriptures defiles the hands. The last chapter is concerned with the question why such books as Jubilees, Ben Sira, Tobit, Susanna and Judith were not included in the Canon.

The place of the composition of the books Tobit, Susanna, Judith, according to the general consensus of opinion of scholars, is Palestine. Therefore, I have omitted the discussion of this particular subject. However, in my forthcoming book, The History of The Jews During the Second Commonwealth, this matter will be dealt with.

The full bibliography of the literature on the *extra canonical* books has not been included in this essay, since all this literature can be readily found in Charles, *The Apocrypha and Pseudepigrapha of the Old Testament*, Vol. 1, and E. Schürer, *Geschichte des Judischen Volkes im Zeitalter Jesu Christi*, Vol. III, the more recent literature can be obtained in the various encyclopedias.

I wish to extend my gratitude to my friend, Professor Alexander Marx, for his kindness in reading through the proofs of this essay while I was abroad.

October, 1932.

AN HISTORICAL STUDY OF THE CANONIZATION OF THE HEBREW SCRIPTURES

I

The Canonization of the Prophetic Books

Though the word "canon" or a word similar to it, is never used in rabbinic literature with reference to the Bible, the principle of canonization, however, is quite applicable. The term "canon" is used mainly with reference to books which are considered divine, therefore authoritative; whereas the books which are not canonized are not only of no authority and hence not binding, but are not allowed to be read.

The Hebrew Bible is divided into three sections: תורה Laws, נביאים Prophets, כתובים Hagiographa,—Scriptures. The first section, the Pentateuch, according to the opinion of most scholars, was already canonized at the time of Ezra.[1] The second section, the Prophets, likewise, was canonized in the early Hellenistic period. Ben Sira, in enumerating the number of the Prophets, mentions the twelve minor prophets as contained in one book.[2] The author of the second book of Maccabees also tells us that Nehemiah "collected the books about the Kings, the prophets, and the books of David . . . so did Judas collect all the writings."[3] That the second section of the Bible, namely the Prophets, was canonized in the pre-Maccabean period, can be shown from a

---

[1] See H. E. Ryle, *The Canon of the Old Testament*, London, 1892; Buhl, *Kanon u. Text des Alten Testamentes*, Leipzig, 1891; Comp. also Wood's article on the Old Testament in Hasting's Dictionary of the Bible. Also J. Fürst, Der Canon des Alten Testament, Leipzig, 1868; G. Wildeboer, The Origin of the Canon of the Old Testament, London, 1895.

[2] Ben Sira XLIX, 10. Comp. Ryle, *Ibid*.

[3] II Maccabees 1, 13, 15.

1

passage in the early Tannaitic Literature, where it is stated that Shammai (Shemaiah) in his endeavor to introduce a new law, cited for his support a verse from the book of Samuel.[4] This means of deriving a new law could not have been followed unless the book of Samuel had already been canonized, for those books which were not canonized were not authoritative, and no new laws could have their validity based on such non-authoritative works.

Some scholars are of the opinion that the Prophets might have been canonized much before the destruction of the Temple. Nevertheless, there was not an unanimous agreement on some of the Prophetic books. The Book of Ezekiel was in danger of being removed from the Canon.[5] These scholars base their assumption on the Talmudic passage: had it not been for Hananiah ben Hezekiah, the book of Ezekiel would have been withdrawn, נגנז, because its words conflicted with the words of the Torah.[6] From the Sifre we learn some of the points of disagreement between the Prophet and the Pentateuch. The Prophet Ezekiel states, "That the meal offering shall be an ephah, for a bullock, and a ephah for a ram, and for a lamb."[7] According to the Pentateuch, however, the meal offering for a bullock was to be three tenth deals; for a ram, two tenths deals, and one tenth deal for a lamb.[8] Hananiah ben Hezekiah succeeded in reconciling this seeming contradiction by stating that Ezekiel wished to teach that any measure, whether large or small is called ephah.[9] Another discrepancy between Ezekiel and the Pentateuch is given in the Tractate *Menaḥot*. Ezekiel states "in the first day of the first

---

[4] שמאי [שמעיה] אומר משום חני הנביא שולחיו חייב שנאמר אותו הרגת בחרב בני עמון Kid. 43a, See S. Zeitlin, The Semikah Controversy between the Zugoth, *J.Q.R.N.S. VII.*

[5] Bertholet, *Das Buch Hesekiel*; Ryle, Ibid.; Graetz, *Geschichte*, III; Derenbourg, *Essai* p. 296.

[6] ברם זכור אותו האיש לטוב [אלעזר בן] וחנינה בן חזקיה שמו שאלמלא הוא נגנז ספר יחזקאל שהיו דבריו סותרין דברי תורה Shab. 13b.

[7] Ezek. XLVI, 11.

[8] Num. XXVIII.

[9] רבי אלעזר בן חנינה בן חזקיה אומר איפה לפר ואיפה לאיל ואיפה לכבש וכי מידת אילים וכבשים אחת היא אלא מלמד שאיפה גדולה ואיפה קטנה קרויה איפה Comp. Men. 45a. איפה לפר . . . אמר ר' שמעון וכי מידת פרים ואלים אחת היא אלא שאם היו להם פרים מרובין ולא היו נסכים יבאו פר אחד ונסכיו . . .

month thou shalt take a young bullock, without blemish, and cleanse therewith the sanctuary."[10] From the Pentateuch, however, we learn, that on the new moon a bullock was to be offered as a burnt offering,[11] which is obviously in contradiction with Ezekiel's passage where the bullock was not a burnt offering but a sin offering. Rabbi Judah being perplexed with these conflicting passages said that only Elijah would be able to interpret this passage of Ezekiel. Rabbi Jose's opinion was that there is no discrepancy between the Torah and Ezekiel, and the passage in Ezekiel has no bearing upon the new month sacrifice. He refers to the sin offering of the dedication of the second Temple, which was celebrated on the new moon of the first month (Nisan).[12]

The prevailing opinion among the modern scholars is that the early teachers of the Talmud were not only opposed to the last chapters of Ezekiel because of the evident halakic conflict with the Torah, but also for his theosophical speculations related in the first chapter, namely his description of the Chariot (Markaba).[13] Here again Hananiah ben Hezekiah was the man who was responsible for having Ezekiel retained in the canonical books. It once happened, we are told in the Talmud, that a lad was reading in his teacher's house (school) in the Book of Ezekiel, and so absorbed himself in the *Hasmal*, that a fire came out from the *Hasmal* and consumed him. Therefore, the Rabbis sought to withdraw, לגנוז, the book of Ezekiel. But Hananiah ben Hezekiah said to them, "If he (the lad) was wise, are then all wise?"[14] Consequently, through the efforts of Hananiah ben Hezekiah the book was not excluded from the canon. Professor Torrey goes a little farther and maintains that the objection of the Jewish Teachers to the book of Ezekiel was not because of its conflict with the

---

[10] Ezek. XLV, 18. בראשון באחד תיקח פר בן בקר וחטאת את המקדש.
[11] Num. XXVIII, 11.
[12] ר' יהודה אומר פרשה זו אליהו עתיד לדורשה אמר לו ר' יוסי מילואים הקריבו בימי עזרא כדרך שהקריבו בימי משה, וכל נבלה וטרפה מן העוף . . . . . לא יאכלו הכהנים כהנים הוא . . . Men. 45a הא ישראל אכלי . . . אליהו עתיד לדורשה
[13] Ryle, The Canon, p. 193.
[14] ת"ר מעשה בתינוק אחד שהיה קורא בבית רבו בספר יחזקאל והיה מבין בחשמל ויצאה אש מחשמל ושרפתו ובקשו לגנוז ספר יחזקאל אמר להם חנינה בן חזקיה אם זה חכם הכל חכמים Hag. 13a.

words of the Torah. "The real cause of the controversy" according to Torrey, "was hidden and that out of necessity under a mere pretext." The entire story as given in Shabbat is "good humor camouflaged, nothing else." He is of the opinion that the real cause for the objection to the Book of Ezekiel lies in the fact that the book is not the product of the prophet Ezekiel, but was compiled much later. The entire book is pseudo-Ezekiel.[15]

The theory that the book of Ezekiel was in danger of being excluded from the canonical books, is based entirely on the talmudic passage where it is stated בקשו לגנוז. The word גנז has different meanings. It may mean "to store away" some very precious thing,[16] or it may mean "to store away from the possibility of destruction." This latter definition of the word גנז is frequently found in the Talmud.[17]

Many scholars have rendered the Hebrew word גנז wrongly by interpreting it as "hidden": בקשו לגנוז ספר יחזקאל they wanted to remove the Book of Ezekiel from the Canon, that is, to declare it an Apocryphal book. The word גנז never occurs in the Talmudic literature in that sense. It occurs only in the sense of storing something away because of its great value; or it refers to a book which is not fit for public reading any more, and which should not, however, willfully be destroyed. This is indicated by a story related in the tractate *Shabbat*. Once R. Gamaliel was standing on the hill of the Temple, and a translation of the Book of Job was brought before him. He said to one of the masons: "store it away under the rubble," (so acc. to Tal. Jer. ibid.). R. Jose, the son of Juda, says that a trough of mud was put upon the book. But Rabbi did not accept this testimony of R. Jose, giving two objections for not accepting the validity

---

[15] C. Torrey, *Pseudo-Ezekiel and the Original Prophecy*; Comp. also Budde, Zum Eingang des Buches Ezechiel, *Journal of Biblical Literature*; 1931, 20ff., S. Spiegel, Ezekiel or Pseudo-Ezekiel, *The Harvard Theological Review*, Oct. 1931.

[16] Pes. 119a; גנוזה לצדיקים לעתיד לבא B. B. 11a; אבותי גנזו למטה ואני ננזתי למעלה Yom. 52b. Comp. II Maccabees, II, "Jeremiah found a cavernous chamber, in which he placed the tabernacle, and the ark, and the altar of incense; and he made fast the door." ובאוצרות בית המלך גנז ספר רפואה Pes. 56a. II Kings, XVIII, 15, the Targum has ובגנזי בית מלכא; see ibid., XX, 17.

[17] תשמישי קדושה נגנזין Meg. 26b and passim.

CANONIZATION OF THE HEBREW SCRIPTURES

of the story. First, there was no mud on the Temple Mount; secondly, the book could not be destroyed willfully.[18] From here we can see that the word גנז must be interpreted in the sense of preserving as opposed to destruction. Again, in the Talmud it is stated that the Holy Scriptures, when translated into one of the foreign languages, although they were not supposed to be read on the Sabbath; nevertheless, in case of a fire, such books were to be saved, regardless of the Sabbath.[19] Books in such a class were to be stored away from destruction. On the other hand, the heretical books, which had the name of the Deity written in them did not have to be saved, and were to be burned immediately even though the divine name was in them. But Rabbi Jose of Galilee says "on week days, one may examine the portion where the name of the Deity appears, and this part is to be stored away from destruction, while the rest should be burned."[20] Here again, we see the word גנז is in opposition to שרף used to denote destruction by burning. The same thought is expressed frequently in the Talmud. A Scroll which is in a state of decay גונזין should be buried by the side of a scholar.[21] Another Rabbi said that the wrappings of the scrolls which were in a state of decay should be used as shrouds.[22] Here again we see the word גנז is applied to those sacred books which could not be used any more for public reading because they were in a state of decay. Such books had to be buried, but not destroyed. Similarly a scroll in which the name of the Deity was written in gold must be stored away.[23] Such a scroll may not be used in the synagogue, as the law states

---

[18] מעשה באבא חלפתא שהלך אצל רבן גמליאל ברבי לטבריא ומצאו שהיה יושב על שלחנו של (יוחנן הנזוף) ובידו ספר איוב תרגום וקרא בו אמר לו זכור אני ברבן גמליאל אבי אביך שהיה עומד ע״ג מעלה בהר הבית והביאו לפניו ספר איוב תרגום ואמר לבנאי וגנזו תחת הנדבך] ר׳ יוסי בר׳ יהודה אומר, ערובה של טיט כפו, עליו אמר ר׳ שתי תשובות יש בדבר ... וכי מותר לאבדן ביד Shab. 115a.

[19] היו כתובים תרגום וכל לשון מצילין אותן מפני הדליקה... אין מצילין ואפילו הכי Ibid. מצילין אותן וגונזן אותן. Comp. Tosefta, Ibid. XIII. גניזה בעו.

[20] ספרי מינין אין מצילין אותן אלא נשרפין הן במקומן הן ואזכרותיהם Tosefta, Ibid. ר׳ יוסי הגלילי אומ׳ בחול קורא את האזכרות וגונז ושורף את השאר.

[21] ספר תורה שבלה גונזין אותו אצל תלמיד חכם Meg. 26b.

[22] מטפחות ספרים שבלו עושין אותן תכריכין למת מצוה וזו היא גניזתן Ibid.

[23] מעשה בתורתו של אלכסנדרוס שהיו כל אזכרותיה כתובות בזהב ובא Trac. Sef. I, 9. מעשה לפני חכמים וגנזו.

that letters of the Deity must not be written in gold.[24] Since the name of God, however, is found in the scroll, it should not be destroyed, and must be stored away.

The word גנז is found in tannaitic literature in reference to sacred objects which for one reason or another became unfit for use. Such objects had to be stored away in a particular place and could not be destroyed. A Mishna tells us that the stones of the altar which were defiled, were stored away in the Temple area by the Hasmoneans.[25] According to the first book of the Maccabees, the stones were stored away in the Mountain of the House until a prophet should come to decide concerning them.[26] The altar which was profaned by the Syrians could not be used further. On the other hand, the stones could not be destroyed. Similarly the knives which were used in the Temple, when they became unfit for further use, were not thrown away, but were stored away in a particular place in the Temple.[27] In the same manner, if a book of the Bible which was found by the rabbis not fit to be used in the synagogue for some reason or other, because it contradicted other canonical books of the Bible,[28] or if it contradicted itself[29], or if there were found in it some heretical ideas,[30] such a book had to be stored away and could not be used further in the synagogue, but that did not mean that the book was excluded from the canon. If we should say that the word גנז is to be interpreted as meaning exclusion of the book from the canon and to make it as ספרים חצונים, that would be the same as saying that they are profane and should be destroyed, as ספרים חצונים were not allowed to be used even privately[31] and had to be destroyed.

The very passage from which the scholars want to deduce that the Book of Ezekiel was to be classified among the apocryphal

[24] Ibid.
[25] Mid. I, 6. בה גנזו בני חשמונאי את אבני המזבח ששקצום מלכי יון.
[26] I Mac. IV, 46.
[27] Mid. IV, 7. Zeb. 88. ששם גונזים את הסכינים, סכין מטרפת . . . וננוזה.
[28] Shab. 13b. נגנז ספר יחזקאל שדבריו סותרין דברי תורה.
[29] Shab. 30b. בקשו חכמים לגנוז ספר קהלת מפני שדבריו חותרין זה את זה.
[30] Mid. R. Q. I בקשו חכמים לגנוז ספר קהלת מפני שמצאו בו דברים מטין לצד מינות.
[31] San. X, 1.

books, is based entirely on a faulty reading. The story relates that a youth who was reading in his teacher's house (school) in the book of Ezekiel, and absorbed in the Hasmal, when a fire came out from Hasmal, and consumed him. Therefore they sought to withdraw the book of Ezekiel. Hananiah ben Hezekiah said to them, "If he (the lad) was wise, are then all wise?"[32] In En Jacob the reading is יהושע בן גמליאל instead of חנינה בן חזקיה. Rabinowitz in his Variae Lectiones, דקדוקי ספרים, substitutes שמעון בן גמליאל Simon ben Gamaliel, for he says that there is no rabbi by the name of Joshua ben Gamaliel.

I believe, however, that the original reading was יהושע בן גמלא Joshua ben Gamala. We recall, that this man, according to the Talmud, was responsible for instituting the public schools in Palestine and in some way made the study of Hebrew letters compulsory.[33] When the Rabbis sought to remove the book of Ezekiel from being studied in the schools, Joshua ben Gamala opposed them, and argued that the study of the book of Ezekiel in the public schools is not dangerous. "If he (the lad) was wise, are then all wise?"

Since the name of Joshua ben Gamala rarely occurs in the Talmud, and was quite unknown to the scribes of the Talmud, some scribe changed the name to Joshua ben Gamaliel. While other scribes, being unfamiliar with the name of Joshua ben Gamala, and knowing that the book of Ezekiel was quite frequently connected in the Talmud with the name of Hananiah ben Hezekiah, consequently changed the name in this passage from Joshua ben Gamala to Hananiah ben Hezekiah. Undoubtedly the original text had Joshua ben Gamala, and not Hananiah ben Hezekiah, for if the text had Hananiah ben Hezekiah, no scribe would have amended it to read יהושע בן גמליאל Joshua ben Gamaliel (or יהושע בן גמלא Joshua ben Gamala), as Joshua ben Gamala was hardly known to the scribes of the Talmud and there was no man by the name of יהושע בן גמליאל.

The word גנז in relation to Ezekiel should be interpreted as stored away from public reading; that is, it should not be studied

---

[32] Hag. 13a.
[33] B. B. 21a. יהושע בן גמלא שמו שאלמלא הוא נשתכחה תורה מישראל .... תיקן שהיו מושיבין מלמדי תינוקות.

11

and interpreted in the academies of learning. The story which is recorded in Talmud Chagiga illustrates this idea quite clearly. When the lad tried to interpret the matter of the Hasmal the rabbis decided to store away this book from further study in the schools. In the tractate Shabbat we are told that the rabbis were of the opinion that the Book of Ezekiel should not be studied in the academies, "for its words conflict with the words of the Pentateuch."

The entire tannaitic literature gives us no inkling whatsoever that the Book of Ezekiel was threatened with being withdrawn from the canon and declared an apocryphal book, in which case it would be forbidden to be read. Of all the portions of the Bible, which, according to the Mishna and *Tosefta* of *Megillah*, were not allowed to be read,[34] the book of Ezekiel is not even mentioned. From this we may conclude that the rabbis did not oppose the reading of Ezekiel. We do find, however, a statement that the first chapter of Ezekiel, the *Markaba*, was read publicly,[35] which shows clearly that the rabbis had no objection at all to the first chapter of Ezekiel. What they maintained was that this chapter should be interpreted and discussed only by men who were both mature and scholarly.[36] Some rabbis were of the opinion that the first chapter of Ezekiel should not be read as *Haftarah*. Rabbi Judah, however, maintained that the first chapter can be used even as an *Haftarah*.[37] It is out of the question to assume that the rabbis at this late date dared to declare the Book of Ezekiel apocryphal, for the Prophets were already canonized, and the rabbis did not possess the authority of withdrawing any book from the Canon. Ben Sira had Ezekiel already in his list of the Prophets, and the order of the Prophets as given by Ben Sira is almost identical with the record in the Talmud.[38]

---

[34] See Mishna, Meg. IV, 10; Tosefta, Ibid. IV.
[35] Tosefta, Ibid. והמרכבה קורין אותה לרבים.
[36] Hag. II, 1, אין דורשין .... במרכבה ביחיד.
[37] M. Meg. IV, 10. אין מפטירין במרכבה ור' יהודה מתיר.
[38] Ben Sira, XLVIII–XLIX; Isaiah, Jeremiah, Ezekiel and the Twelve Prophets. According to the Talmud the order was Jeremiah, Ezekiel, Isaiah and the Twelve Prophets. However, in our Masoretic Bibles is in the same order as that which Ben Sira gives.

II

THE CANONIZATION OF THE SCRIPTURES

The third part of the Bible is the Scriptures—Hagiographa. This section of the Bible is likewise authoritative. The *Tannaim* in expounding the Law many a time quote the *Ketubim* in support, which meant that the words of the Scriptures were authoritative, and upon their passages, new laws were based. The question now arises, was this group, called the *Ketubim*, canonized at the same time with the group called Prophets, or was this group canonized at a later period, and if so, when?

Ben Sira in giving the list of the Prophets does not mention by name any of the books of the Scriptures.[39] We may assume from this that although the books of the Scriptures may already have been written, they were not yet canonized. Josephus in his book "Against Apion" stated that the Jews had twenty-two books. Of these, five are the books of Moses, thirteen are the prophetic ones, and the remaining four books contained the Hymns to God and the precepts.[40] So in the time of Josephus the Bible was already canonized and contained twenty-two books, divided into three parts, the Pentateuch, the Prophets, and a third part comprising four books of Hymns and precepts. A *Baraita* in the Talmud, however, gives the canon as consisting of twenty-four books, the prophetic books being eight in number, and the Scriptures consisting of eleven.[41]

The question is, which of the books that the Talmud had in the third group, the Hagiographa, did Josephus place in the second group, the Prophets. This cannot be ascertained, and many speculations have been offered by students of the Bible. Many scholars are of the opinion that Josephus probably had in his Canon, among the Prophets, the Books of Daniel, Ezra, Nehemiah, Chronicles, and Job, while in the third group, the Hagiographa, he had the remaining four books: Song of Songs, Psalms, Ecclesiastes,

---

[39] Although Ben Sira may have quoted some phrases or passages from the books which are known to us as Kethubim, he does not refer to them by name. Comp. S. Schechter, The Wisdom of Ben Sira, Cambridge, 1899.
[40] *Against Apion*, I, 8.
[41] B. B. 14b.

and the Proverbs. The Book of Ruth was added to Judges and Lamentations to Jeremiah.[42]

The fact remains that Josephus had in his Canon, twenty-two books, instead of twenty-four. Did he append two books of the Scriptures to the Prophets, namely, Ruth to Judges, and Lamentations to Jeremiah, as many scholars maintain? On the other hand, should we assume that the Hebrew Canon at the time of Josephus consisted of only twenty-two books, while two more books were added at a later period, which made the Hebrew Canon consist of twenty-four books, and this final canonization of the Bible is recorded in the Baraita? The latter hypothesis is, I believe, the correct one, namely that the Jewish Bible at the time of the destruction of the Temple consisted of twenty-two books and the Books of Ecclesiastes and Esther were added later.[43]

From tannaitic literature we learn that there were varying opinions in reference to the Book of Ecclesiastes in relation to the defilement of the hands. Rabbi Judah said that "the Book of *Kohelet* defiles not the hands, and with respect to Song of Songs, there was a difference of opinion." Rabbi Jose said "Song of Songs defiles the hands, and with respect to Kohelet there is a dispute."[44] From all the passages we learn that the rabbis differed as to the Book of Ecclesiastes. According to everyone, the Song of Songs defiles the hands. From this we may safely conclude that the

---

[42] Comp. Ryle, *The Canon*, p. 165; W. Robertson Smith, *The Old Testament*, London, 1892, p. 164. Comp., also, Thackeray, Josephus, The Man and the Historian, 1929, p. 79.

[43] Josephus had in his Canon the Five Books of Moses, Thirteen Prophets, 1. Joshua, 2. Judges, 3. Samuel, 4. Kings, 5. Isaiah, 6. Jeremiah, 7. Ezekiel, 8. The Twelve Minor Prophets, 9. Ezra and Nehemiah, 10. Job, 11. Daniel, 12. Chronicles, 13. Psalms. In the third group, the Scriptures, he placed: 1. Proverbs, 2. Song of Songs, 3. Ruth, 4. Lamentations. αἱ δὲ λοιπαὶ τέσσαρες ὕμνους εἰς τὸν θεὸν καὶ τοῖς ἀνθρώποις ὑποθήκας τοῦ βίου περιέχουσιν. With ὕμνους εἰς τὸν θεὸν he refered to the Song of Songs, and with ὑποθήκας he refers to Proverbs, in which advice is given for the conduct of human life.

[44] M. Yad. III, 5. ר' יהודה (מאיר) אומר שיר השירים מטמא את הידים וקהלת מחלוקת
ר' יוסי אומר קהלת אינו מטמא את הידים ושיר השירים מחלוקת אמר ר' עקיבא חס ושלום לא
נחלק אדם מישראל על שיר השירים שלא תטמא את הידים שאין כל העולם כדאי כיום שניתן
בו שיר השירים לישראל שכל הכתובים קדש ושיר השירים קדש קדשים ואם נחלקו לא נחלקו
אלא על קהלת אמר ר' יוחנן בן יהושע בן חמיו של ר' עקיבא כדברי בן עזאי כך נחלקו וכך
גמרו. Comp. reading in Meg. 7a; see additional note.

Song of Songs was canonized before the time of Akiba. The only difference of opinion among the early Tannaim was concentrated on the Book of Ecclesiastes. Some were of the opinion that the Book of Ecclesiastes does not defile the hands, therefore was not included in the Canon, while others maintain that there was a dispute among the early rabbis in reference to this Book, but there is no positive statement found to the effect that the Book of Ecclesiastes defiles the hands. In other words, there is no statement found in the controversy between the Tannaim that the Book of Ecclesiastes defiles the hands, which means that *Kohelet* was not included in the Canon at the time of the destruction of the Temple.

The difference of opinion between Rabbi Judah and Rabbi Jose can be summarized as follows: Rabbi Jose states that the Book of 'Song of Songs' was unanimously accepted in the Canon and hence defiled the hands, while the Book of Ecclesiastes was rejected, but after a dispute between the Schools of Shammai and Hillel, the Shammaites being against and the Hillelites for. The Shammaites won because they had a majority in the Assembly when the eighteen measures were adopted. Rabbi Judah, on the other hand, was of the opinion that 'Ecclesiastes' was unanimously rejected, while 'Song of Songs' was accepted only after a discussion.

In the famous gathering of the Shammaites and Hillelites which took place in the house of Hananiah ben Hezekiah, a few years before the destruction of the Temple, the question arose as to which of the books of the Scriptures should be canonized and should defile the hands and which should not; the status of the Book of *Kohelet* was descussed, the Hillelites maintaining that Ecclesiastes should be included in the Canon and hence defile the hands, while the Shammaites were against the defilement of the hands. At this gathering the Shammaites were victorious and all the amendmends of the Hillelites were rejected and therefore Koheleth was not included in the Canon. Thus Rabbi Simon says that the Book of Kohelet is [ר' שמעון אומר קהלת] מקולי בית שמאי ומחומרי בית הלל[45] i.e. Kohelet, according to the Shammaites, does not defile the hands, as this Book is not sacred. From this we may further infer that

---

[45] Ibid.

the canonization of the third group, Hagiographa, did not take place before the year sixty-five, and only in that gathering Kethubim was added to the Bible.

The Book of Esther was likewise added to the Canon much later. According to the Talmud the Book of Esther also does not defile the hands,[46] which means that the Book was not canonized. That the Book of Esther was not included among the Scriptures which were canonized in the year sixty-five can be proved from the fact that in Megillat Taanit, where all the semi-holidays are recorded, the Festival of Purim is among them.[47] Had the Book of Esther been canonized, the holiday of Purim would not have been placed in the Megillat Taanit. The author of this chronicle in giving the list of the semi-holidays, states that fasting is prohibited on the holidays and on the days before them. If the Book of Esther was already canonized in the year sixty-five, it would have been unnecessary for the author of the Megillat Taanit to state that on the day of Purim fasting is prohibited. He does not mention the day of the New Moon when fasting is likewise prohibited, because the feast of the New Moon is mentioned in the Bible. Furthermore, when the Tannaim wanted to prove that the day of Purim is a day of rejoicing and that no Jew is allowed to fast on that day, they inferred this from the Megillat Taanit.[48] It would not have become necessary for the Tannaim to infer this law from the Megillat Taanit if they had had the Book of Esther in the Bible. The rabbis of the later period, however, when they wanted to prove that the day of Purim is a festival and that no Jew is allowed to work on this day, they inferred this law from the Book of Esther itself,[49] which goes to show that at the time of the early Tannaim, although the day of Purim was observed, the Book of Esther was not yet canonized. The Book of Esther was canonized at a much later period, some time after the Hadrianic period. Public opinion was primarily responsible for the canonization of

---

[46] Meg. 7a. אסתר אינה מטמא את הידים.

[47] בארבעת עשר ובחמשה עשר ביה יומי פוריא. Comp. S. Zeitlin Meg. Taanit, pp. 65–68.

[48] Yer. Meg. 70–71. Comp., also, B. T. 18b. Meg. 5b.

[49] Meg. 5b.

this Book. The rabbis were never anxious to have this book among the Hebrew Scriptures, but the Festival of Purim was celebrated for many centuries before the destruction of the Temple; already at the time of the Maccabees Purim was a holiday. The author of the second book of the Maccabees called it the Festival of Mordecai.[50] The Book of Esther was recited annually on Purim, but nevertheless it was not considered "inspired" and so was not included in the Scriptures.[51] The rabbis, however, after the Hadrianic period could not keep this Book out of the Canon any longer, due to the importance which was laid on the reading of the Megillah on the Festival of Purim, and thus they were compelled to include it in the Bible. The canonicity of Esther was due, therefore, to pressure of public opinion, and did not originate at the academies. This idea is borne out in the Talmud, where it is related that Esther sent to the scholars and said: "Inscribe my Book for posterity".[52] The scholars were at first reluctant to accept it, but finally yielded, and we may say that the canonicity of the Book of Esther was forced on the rabbis. Therefore as late as the third century, it was recorded in the name of Samuel that Esther does not defile the hands—that is, Esther does not belong to the Canon. "The Book of Esther was inspired that it

---

[50] II Maccabees, XV, 36. The author of I Maccabees in recording that Nicanor was slain on the 13th of Adar, does not mention that it was a day before Purim. From this many scholars deduce that the Festival of Purim was not observed in Palestine during the Second Commonwealth and was brought over from the Diaspora at a much later period. This theory is erroneous. Elsewhere I have shown that the year 152 A.S., 161 B.C.E. was a leap year, that is, the Jews had two months of Adar. Nicanor was killed on the 13th of Adar and therefore the author of I Maccabees who wrote this book shortly after the Hasmonean victory, knew quite well that Nicanor was killed on the first Adar, which was not a day before Purim. On the other hand, the author of II Maccabees, who drew his material from the books of Jason of Cyrene and compiled his work in the Diaspora at a much later period, not knowing that the year when Nicanor was killed had two Adars and having before him only the material of Jason, where it was recorded that Nicanor was beheaded on the 13th of Adar though that it was an ordinary year and added the words "the day before Mordecai," and that is the reason why we have the day of Mordecai mentioned in the second book, while it is entirely passed over in the first book. Comp. S. Zeitlin, Meg. Tannit, P. 118.

[51] Meg. 7a. אסתר ברוח הקודש . . . נאמרה לקרות ולא נאמרה לכתוב.
[52] Ibid. שלחה להם אסתר לחכמים קבעוני לדורות.

should be read on Purim, but it was not inspired to be written down." According to Eusebius, Melito, Bishop of Sardis, in the third quarter of the Second Century journeyed to Palestine to learn the exact number of the books of the Hebrew Canon. In his list Lamentations and Esther were not yet included, as Lamentations was probably added to Jeremiah, while Esther was probably not yet included in the Canon.[53]

The Hebrew Canon consisted of three parts, Torah, תורה Prophets, נביאים, and Hagiography, כתובים. Each of these had not only different degrees of sanctity,[54] but they were also canonized at different periods, the Torah at the time of Ezra, the Prophets some time in the Hellenistic period before the Maccabeans; they consisted of eight books, Joshua, Judges, Samuel, Kings, Isaiah, Jeremiah, Ezekiel, and the twelve Minor Prophets, and the Hagiographa were canonized in the year sixty-five, five years before the Temple was destroyed, and comprised the following nine books: Psalms, Proverbs, Job, Daniel, Ezra-Nehemiah, Chronicles, Ruth, Lamentations and the Song of Songs. The book of *Kohelet* was added some time in the beginning of the Second Century in the Academy of Jabneh.[55] Esther was added later in the Academy of Oushah. Although the Kethubim were compiled before the Roman period, and were known to the people, and the Psalms were chanted by the Levites in the Temple, and some of them may even have been translated into Greek nevertheless, the canonization of Kethubim came at a much later period, namely, in the year Sixty-five. The author of the Prologue to Ecclesiasticus refers to the books of the third group as other books—thus he says: "My grandfather, Jesus,

[53] Eus., *The Church History*, IV, 26; Ibid. VI, 25. The Church Fathers had different books and in different order in the Hebrew Canon. Their testimony must, however, be taken with a grain of salt, as they were outsiders and most likely they followed the order of the Septuagint. For more about the Hebrew canon, according to the Church Fathers, comp. Ryle, *The Canon*. (According to IV Ezra, 14, there were twenty-four books in the Bible, while another reading has ninety-four.)

[54] Tos. Meg. IV, 20.

[55] Yad. III, 5. אר״ש ב״ע מקובל אני מפי ע״ב זקנים ביום שהושיבו את ראב״ע בישיבה, תורה נבוכי הזמן שער י״א Comp. also, Krochmal ששיר השירים וקהלת מטמאים את הידים. Graetz, Kohelet, 1871.

seeing he had much given himself to the reading of the Law and to the Prophets and the other books of the Fathers."[56] In the year 132 B.C.E. when the grandson of [Joshua ben Sirach wrote his Prologue to "The Wisdom of Sirach," the Hebrew Canon was not yet tripartite, as Kethubim was not yet canonized.

III

"The Holy Scriptures Defiles the Hands"

In the preceding pages we pointed out that books which were canonized defiled the hands. The question now arises why a book of the Scriptures defiled the hands. What is the underlying reason for such laws? The whole subject of the "Defilement of the Hands" presents many difficulties. The Sadducees indeed questioned the law, as to the reason why the Holy Scriptures should defile the hands.[57] The answer which was given by Jochanan ben Zakai to the Sadducees[58] does not throw much light on the origin of this Halakah. There is another problem which has to be solved. Why should the hands be defiled, and not the whole body? From what we know about the Laws of defilement in the Pentateuch, we learn that if any part of the body—a hand or leg touched any unclean thing, the person is considered defiled, and must go through all the laws of Purification.

The laws of Levitical cleanliness are the most complicated in the Talmud. Therefore, to understand the expression that the Holy Scriptures defile the hands, we believe it would not be out of place to give a short survey of the Laws of Impurity, and their development. According to the Biblical Laws, if a person touched a dead body, he is unclean for seven days, and for that period of time he must leave the camp. At the end of the seven days, he

---

[56] ὁ πάππος μου Ἰησοῦς ἐπὶ πλεῖον ἑαυτὸν δοὺς εἴς τε τὴν τοῦ νόμου καὶ τῶν προφητῶν καὶ τῶν ἄλλων πατρίων βιβλίων ἀνάγνωσιν. In the same Prologue the author refers again to the third group as 'others,' "The Prophets and the others who followed after them." "The Prophecies and the rest of the books."

[57] Yad. IV, 6. אומרים צדוקים קובלין אנו עליכם פרושים שאתם אומרים כתבי הקודש מטמאים את הידים.

[58] Ibid. לפי חבתן היא מטמאוֽן.

must bring a sacrifice.⁵⁹ Any person who comes in contact with this man must leave the camp for one day, and he can only return to the camp after sunset, and after he has taken the prescribed bath. Likewise, the man who experienced pollution had to undergo the same grades of purification.⁶⁰ They are all called in the tannaitic literature ראשון לטומאה, which is the first degree of uncleanliness. A ראשון לטומאה can transmit its impurity, and any object which comes in contact with this "first degree" becomes a "second," but the "second" can not transmit any further. However, if the "second" comes in contact with Terumah, the Terumah becomes a "third" and it is unfit to eat, and must be burned.⁶¹ Terumah which is unclean in the "third degree" can not transmit its impurity to others. If it comes, however, in contact with an object which is "sacred" the latter is defiled.⁶²

The Tannaim who strove to bring religion into agreement with life, amended to the Laws of "impurity." They interpreted the word מחנה to mean Camp of God, or Camp of the Levites.⁶³ By this amendment the laws of temporary banishment for the "first degree" could only apply to the Sanctuary proper, and to the "Azarah" (the camp of the Levites) but the unclean person is not banished from the City.

The person who was unclean in the "first degree" had still to wait until the evening, and mere bathing of the body in water would not be sufficient to render the person pure. This was a great hardship for the Jews during the Second Commonwealth, as it hampered them in their daily life. So the Tannaim further amended the Laws of Impurity. They explained that the biblical law, which says that a man who is unclean must wait until sunset, refers only to the priests in the case of eating Terumah.⁶⁴ Otherwise mere washing of the body suffices to make a person pure, and it was not necessary for him to wait until sunset.

---

⁵⁹ Num. XIX, 11.
⁶⁰ Ibid. XIX, Deut. XXIII.
⁶¹ M. P., XI, 4. Hag. 24.
⁶² Ibid., Pes. 18b.
⁶³ Ibid., 68a. See S. Zeitlin, Les Dix-huit Mesures. R.E.J., Vol. 68.
⁶⁴ Sifra Shemine. משתחשך ולתרומה יום מבעוד לחולין טהור . . . הערב עד יטמא. See Idem, Takkanot Ezra, J. Q. R., N. S. VIII.

Even the prerequisite of washing the body to render the person clean, the early Tannaim considered a hardship, and they modified the law by instituting the *washing of the hands* as a sufficient substitute to render the person pure. This Takkana the Talmud ascribed to Solomon, who instituted "washing the hands."[65] On the other hand, according to the Talmud, Shammai and Hillel decreed the "defilement of the hands." The Talmudist[66] as well as the modern scholar[67] interchanged the Takkana of Solomon of washing the hands with G'zerah of Shammai and Hillel, "The defilement of the hands," and so complicated the entire subject of "washing the hands" and "The defilement of the hands."

I have shown elsewhere that the washing of the hands, and the defilement of the hands had nothing to do with each other. The former is a Takkana, an amendment of the early law, while the latter is a decree.[68]

The G'zerah of the defilement of the hands, according to the Talmud, was decreed by Shammai and Hillel. This decree was aimed particularly against the Priests. A Mishna in Hagigah tells us that after every holiday, all the vessels of the Azarah were dipped in water. The Priests said to the worshippers "Be careful

---

[65] Shab. 14b. Idem. The Halaka in the Gospels and its Relation to the Jewish Law in the Time of Jesus, H. U. C. A. Vol. 1. בשעה שתיקן שלמה עירובין ונטילת ידים.

[66] Shab. 14b. בשעה שתיקן שלמה גזר .... ואכתי שלמה שלמה גזר.

[67] Comp. הגרון in II–V. איש שלום

[68] According to Shab. 14b. Solomon instituted the Takkanah of washing the hands בשעה שתיקן שלמה עירובין ונטילת ידים. while Shammai and Hillel decreed defilement of the hands שמאי והלל גזרו טומאה על הידים. Dr. Klausner in the second edition of his book מפני הדברים הברורים ש.שמאי והלל גזרו' על נטילת ידים says on p. 492 ישו הנוצרי (שבת י"ד ע"ב) .... בטלה דעתו של ש' ציטילין שנטילת ידים היא מי"ח דבר שנתקנו רק בימי החורבן. If Dr. Klausner would be careful in the subject matter which he treats, he would find out that there is no mention made anywhere in the Talmud that שמאי והלל גזרו על נטילת ידים Shammai and Hillel decreed washing of the hands. What they really decreed was defilement of the hands שמאי—שמאי והלל גזרו טומאה על הידים Yer. Sh. 3d, טהרת ידים. והלל גזרו על טהרת ידים. Any student of the Talmud is aware of the difference between נטילת ידים and נזרו טומאה על הידים. Furthermore, error follows error. He wrongly ascribes to me that I said that washing of the hands is one of the eighteen measures which were adopted shortly before the destruction. What I really said was the defilement of the hands is one of the eighteen measures which were adopted before the destruction.

not to touch the vessels that can not be readily dipped, such as golden altar, or the candelabra."[69] The reason for dipping all the vessels in water after every holiday was due to the fear that the Israelites who came for the holidays to worship, might have handled the vessels in the Azarah. Therefore the priests insisted that the vessels should be purified. However, such vessels which were handled only by the Priests did not need purification. The Pharisees who strongly opposed any distinction between Priests and Israelites, insisted that even vessels touched by the Priests required purification. This is undoubtedly the decree of defilement of the hands which the Talmud ascribed to Shammai and Hillel; namely vessels touched by Priests in the Temple are defiled, just as when they were touched by the Israelites.[70]

Some Tannaim objected to the decree that any vessel of the Temple touched by the hands requires purification. This disapproval is well borne out by Rabbi Akiba's statement in which he declares: "We can prove our point that there is no defilement of the hands in the sanctuary,"[71] as Rabbi Akiba was likewise opposed to the decree that the hands defile the vessels in the Temple.

In the previous pages we believe we have shown the underlying reasons of the Takkana of washing the hands, as well as the decree of the defilement of the hands. We shall now endeavor to show the meaning of the statement that the Holy Scriptures defiled the hands. The decree of the defilement of the hands was aimed chiefly against the priests, just as were most of the other eighteen decrees which the schools of Shammai and Hillel adopted in the year sixty-five.[72] The purpose of these decrees was to make it impossible for the priests to eat the Terumah. One of these measures was Sefer,[73] The Book, i. e., that if Sefer "The Book" came in contact with Terumah, the Terumah became defiled and could not be eaten by the priests, but had to be burned. This decree was directed against the Priests and the Sadducees. The

---

[69] Hag. III, 7–8. ואומרין להם הזהרו שלא תגעו בשלחן [ובמנורה].
[70] S. Zeitlin, The Halakah in the Gospels, H. U. C. A., Vol. 1.
[71] Pes. 19a. אמר ר' עקיבא זכינו שאין טומאת ידים במקדש.
[72] S. Zeitlin, Les Dix huit Mesures, R. E. J., 68.
[73] הספר ... אלו פוסלין את התרומה ..... שמונה עשר דבר גזרו.

Sadducees accepted only the laws of the Pentateuch and rejected the Oral Law. The Pharisees who stressed the Oral Law very much and were anxious that the Oral Law should be studied in the Academies in preference to the Written Law,[74] declared that "The Book," the Pentateuch, or any other Books which are canonized, i. e. Holy Scriptures, if they touch Terumah, the latter is rendered unfit for use. With this decree they made it impossible for the Priests to read the Pentateuch, and to eat Terumah, as the latter would be unfit for use. According to the Talmud "The Book" does not defile but only renders the Terumah unfit.[75] Thus the Book was put in the "second degree" of defilement which only makes Terumah unfit, and not ordinary food. With the decree that "The Book" makes Terumah unfit, the Pharisees did not gain their entire end, as the Priests could avoid contact of the "Sefer" with Terumah. So they decreed that "The Book" which is only of the "second degree" of defilement, makes the hands which touch the book not impure in the "third degree" but in the "second degree."[76] Therefore the hands which touch "The Book", as well as the "Sefer" itself make the Terumah unfit for eating. With this they accomplished their end, i. e., that the Priests could not read "The Book" and if they read it, the hands that touched it were declared in the "second degree," and hence they could not touch Terumah until evening, as washing the body was not sufficient to render them pure in connection with Terumah.[77]

So the book which is considered sacred in order that it should not be used was declared by the early Tannaim as defiling the hands. In consequence of this decree any sacred thing which cannot be used defiles the hands. For example, any part of the pascal lamb which was left over until after midnight defiled the hands, and so נותר portions of sacrifices left over beyond the

---

[74] Yer. Shab. 15c. שהמשנה קודמת למקרא ... העוסק במקרא מידה שאינה מידה.
[75] Shab. 13b. פוסלין את התרומה.
[76] Yad. III, 2. כל הפוסל את התרומה מטמא את הידים להיות שניות .... כתבי הקדש שניים מטמאים את הידים.
[77] Comp. also B. K. 114b. מעשה באדם אחד שהיה מסיח לפי תומו תרומה משחשך שאמר זכורני כשאני תינוק ומורכבני על כתיפו של אבא והוציאני מבית הספר והפשיטני את כתנתי והטבילוני לאכל בתרומה לערב.

legal time, defiled the hands, פסח אחר חצות and נותר are holy, but cannot be used by anyone and therefore defile the hands.[77a]

Only the "Book," the Torah, which was in the Azarah[78] (otherwise called ספר עזרא[79]) did not defile the hands, the reason most likely for this being that it should not defile the High Priest when he read the Torah on the Day of Atonement.[80] However, if this "Torah" was taken out from the Azarah, then it did defile the hands just as all the "Books" did. On the other hand, if somebody brought into the Azarah any of the Prophetic books, or any part of the Pentateuch or other books, they did defile the hands,[81] as only the Sefer of the Azarah was excluded from the decree of defilement of the hands.

When the "Scriptures" were canonized, they were considered holy and were placed with the first two sections, namely, the Pentateuch and the Prophets. As "The Book," i. e., The Pentateuch and the Prophets, which according to the decree of the "eighteen measures," defiles the hands, so the "Holy Scriptures" also, as a part of the Hebrew Canon, defile the hands. Scriptures which were written before the Maccabean period and were popular among the Jews much before the destruction of the Temple, like

[77a] M. Pes. X, 9. הפסח אחר חצות מטמא הידים הפגול והנותר מטמא את הידים.

[78] Kelim 15, 6. כל הספרים מטמאין את הידים חוץ מספר העזרה.

[79] Tos. Ibid. B. M., V. 8. The Pentateuch which was kept in the Azarah was sometimes called the book of Ezra, as the belief apparently was that Ezra, who was a scribe, עזרא הסופר not only canonized the Five Books of Moses, but wrote the copy of the Pentateuch which was in the Azarah. Comp. also M. K., 111, 4, Jer. Tan. 68a.

[80] Yom. VII, 1. חזן הכנסת נוטל ספר תורה . . . . וכהן הגדול עומד ומקבל וקורא. Anything which was in use in the Temple did not defile other objects. Ordinary liquids are susceptible to Levitical uncleanliness, but wine and oil which are used in connection with the sacrifices are not susceptible to Levitical uncleanliness. M. Kelim, 15, 6. ונבלי בני לוי טהורין, כל המשקין טמאין ומשקה בית מטבחייא טהורין.

[81] Tosefta, Kelim, B. M. 15, 8; ספר עזרא שיצא לחוץ מטמא את הידים ולא ספר עזרא בלבד אלא אפילו נביאים וחומשים וספר אחר שנכנס לשם מטמא את הידים. The expression ספר אחר used in this Tos. refers most probably to the Kethubim. It is interesting to note that the translator of Ben Sira used the identical expression ἄλλων πατρίων βιβλίων in connection with the Kethubim. This particular Tosefta was compiled apparently before the Kethubim were canonized and therefore he used the expression ספר אחר in referring to the books which later became known as Kethubim. Comp. Jer. Meg. 70d בספר אילו הכתובים.

Ben Sira, etc. do not defile the hands, since they were not included in the Canon.[82] Hence any book that defiles the hands is canonized. The book which does not defile the hands is not sacred, and is not included in the Canon. The Tannaim opposed the reading of the Kethubim on Saturday, and they declared that the "Holy Scriptures" should not be read on Saturday before Minhah.[83] This law, that the "Scriptures" should not be read on Saturday, was followed even in the later periods. A story is told that once when Purim fell on Saturday, the Megillah was read after Minhah.[84] From another story we learn, when the eve of the fast of the Ninth of Ab fell on Saturday, the Book of Lamentations was likewise read after Minhah,[85] as neither the Book of Esther which the Jews read annually on the Feast of Purim, nor the Book of Lamentations, which was read annually on the fast day of Ab, could be read at the proper time, when these days fell on Saturday.

IV

The Reason for the Exclusion of Jubilees, Ben Sira, etc. from the Hebrew Canon

In the previous pages we tried to show that the "Scriptures" were added to the Hebrew Canon in as late a period as the year sixty-five. We are now confronted with the following problem: Why were books like the Jubilees, Ben Sira, Tobit, Susanna, Judith, written in the Pharisaic spirit before the Maccabean period, not included in the Canon? In order to understand why these books were not included in the Canon, we shall take each book up separately and show the reasons why the Tannaim declared these as extra canonical.

---

[82] Tos. Yad. II, 13. ספרי בן סירא וכל ספרים שנכתבו מכאן ואילך אינן מטמאין את הידים.

[83] Tos. Shab. XIII, 1; Yer. Ibid. 15c.

[84] Yer. Meg. 74b.

[85] Yer. Shab. 15c. דלמא רבי ור' חייא רבא .... פושטין במגילת קינות ערב תשעה באב שחל להיות בשבת מן המנחה ולמעלה ... למדנו שלשה דברים ... אין קורין בכתבי הקודש אלא מן המנחה ולמעלה.

Jubilees.[86] The Book of Jubilees, or the Little Genesis, as it is sometimes called, contains the history from the Creation to the Exodus, dividing it into Jubilee periods of forty-nine years each. This Book was written, according to some scholars, between the year 135 and 105 B.C.E., that is before the rupture between John Hyrcanus and the Pharisees. This date of the compilation of the Book of Jubilees is not supported by the contents of the Book. From internal evidence we will be able to show that this Book was written at a much earlier period. First, the Laws of Sabbath are very strict and primitive and not at all according to the Pharisees of the period of John Hyrcanus. Again, the Book is divided into cycles of forty-nine years, called Jubilees. We are at a loss to understand why an author should write a book, call the book Jubilees and stress so much the observance of the Jubilees, when for many centuries Jubilees were no longer in existence among the Jews. Furthermore, the author complains against the leaders of the Jews for changing the calendar from a solar to a lunar-solar one, and thus disturbing the seasons, and making the year ten days shorter. The author bitterly complains that with this change the Jubilee years will be destroyed and profane days will become holidays. This, we believe, is sufficient evidence that the Book of Jubilees was written at a very early period when the Jews changed the solar calendar to a lunar-solar one, and many of the Jews opposed this innovation. The author expresses his opposition in the book: "And command thou the children of Israel that they observe the years according to this reckoning—three hundred and sixty-four days, and (these) will constitute a complete year, and they will not disturb its time from its days and from its feasts; for everything will fall out in them according to their testimony, and they will not leave out any day nor disturb any feasts . . . And all the children of Israel will forget, and will not find the path of the years, and will forget the new moons, and seasons, and sabbaths, and they will go wrong as to all the order of the years. For I know and from henceforth will I declare it unto thee, and it is not of my own

---

[86] On the literature, and text, editions, of the Book of Jubilees, consult Schürer, Gesch. Vol. III; Charles, *The Apocrypha and Pseudepigrapha of the Old Testament*, Vol. II, p. 1–10.

devising; for the book (lies) written before me, and on the heavenly tablets the division of days is ordained, lest they forget the feasts of the covenant and walk according to the feasts of the Gentiles after their error and after their ignorance. For there will be those who will assuredly make observations of the new moon—how (it) disturbs the seasons and comes in from year to year ten days too soon. For this reason the years will come upon them when they will disturb (the order), and make an abominable (day) the day of testimony, and an unclean day a feast day, and they will confound all the days, the holy with the unclean, and the unclean day with the holy; for they will go wrong as to the months and sabbaths and feasts and jubilees. For this reason I command and testify to thee that thou mayst testify to them; for after thy death thy children will disturb (them), so that they will not make the year three hundred and sixty-four days only, and for this reason they will go wrong as to the new moons and seasons and sabbaths and festivals, and they will eat all kinds of blood with all kinds of flesh."[87]

The above quotation shows quite clearly that the Book of Jubilees was written when the question of the change in the calendar was still an issue among the Jewish people.[88] Otherwise, we couldn't account for the author arguing so forcibly against the change in the calendar, if this question had already been settled centuries before. To say that the Book of Jubilees was written in the second century before the Common Era is as utterly out of the question as to presume that anyone should

---

[87] Jubilees, VI, 32–38.

[88] See S. Zeitlin, *Some Stages of the Jewish Calendar*, 1929; Idem. Notes relatives au calendrier juif, *R. E. J.*, Vol. 89, 1930. In these essays I have shown that the Jubilee Year consisted of forty-nine days, which were added after seven cycles of seven years. These days were called the Jubilee Year. They began with the Sunday after the Day of Atonement up to the day before the Festival of Succoth. As to the question whether the Jews observed the Jubilee Year or whether it was economically possible for the Jews to keep the laws connected with the Jubilee Year, that is another matter; but one thing, I believe, is sure and that is, that the Jews had the Jubilee Year, as well as the Sabbatical Years at one time before the change of the calendar from the solar system to solar-lunar system occurred. It is most likely that the Jews did not observe the laws of the Jubilee Year, as they did not observe at the time of the first Temple many laws which we have in the Pentateuch.

write a book now in refutation of Sabbatai Zevi as the true Messiah. The issue of Sabbatai Zevi is dead for centuries and no man would raise this question again.

How can it be possible for an author so forcibly to argue against a calendar which for many centuries had already been discarded? The Book of Jubilees, in my opinion, is one of the earliest books of Jewish literature. The idea of the author was to give the history of the Creation and the laws in a Midrashic form, and it was written at a time when the change in the Jewish calendar occurred. The author being a very conservative Jew, opposed this change very bitterly, since with this change the Jubilee year disappeared from the Jewish calendar. We may classify this book as apocryphal to the Pentateuch. When the Pentateuch was canonized this book (and many like it) was excluded. And hence there could be no question about the canonization of this book in the year sixty-five, when the "Scriptures" were canonized.

There is no inkling found in the entire tannaitic literature to the effect that there was a controversy between the Pharisees and Sadducees on the question of the calendar. The controversy between the Pharisees and the Sadducees in relation to the Festival of Pentecost has no bearing whatsoever on the calendar. The Sadducees maintained that the Festival of Pentecost should be on a Sunday, since the Bible has ממחרת השבת, the morrow after the Saturday, regardless of the day of the month, while the Pharisees, on the other hand, maintained that the Pentecost should always fall on the fiftieth day after the first day of Passover, regardless of what day of the week it was. The phrase ממחרת השבת was interpreted as referring to the morrow of the first day of Passover.[89] The notion of the scholars that the Pharisees were against having Pentecost on Sunday is untenable, as this view is not borne out by the sources. The Pharisees maintained that the day of the Omer should always be on the sixteenth of Nisan, regardless of the day of the week and so Pentecost should always be on the fiftieth day after the Omer was sacrificed, i. e. the sixteenth of Nisan, again regardless of the day of the week.[90]

[89] Men. 65a.
[90] The reader will find a more detailed discussion of the controversy between the Pharisees and Sadducees on the question of Pentacost in an article by the

CANONIZATION OF THE HEBREW SCRIPTURES

Ben Sira.[91] The reason why the rabbis did not include Ben Sira among the Scriptures is given in *Tosefta Yadayim*, where it is stated ספרי בן סירא וכל ספרים שנכתבו מכאן ואילך אינן מטמאין את הידים Ben Sira and all the books which were written from that time on do not defile the hands. The reason why the books which were written מכאן ואילך do not defile the hands is due to the fact that the rabbis were of the opinion that prophecy ceased from Israel after Daniel in the Persian period.[92] Therefore all the books written after that time cannot be considered a part of the Holy Scriptures. The Book of Ben Sira was written in the Hellenistic period and that was the reason for its exclusion from the cannon.

Ben Sira gives a description of a high priest Simon. With whom is this Simon to be identified? Some scholars are of the opinion that the high priest mentioned in the book refers to the Simon who flourished from 300 to 270 B.C.E.,[93] while others are of the opinion that it refers to Simon who was high priest of the Jews in 219–179.[94] The translator of the Book of Ben Sira, in his Prologue, calls the author of the original version his ὁ πάππος. If we should take the term ὁ πάππος in its usual sense of grandfather, then we would say that the Simon who is mentioned in Ben Sira refers to Simon II, and the original version of Ben Sira was written between 185–75 B.C.E. On the other hand, if we should assume that the word ὁ πάππος means ancestor, then Ben Sira could have lived many generations before the translator, and the Simon mentioned in the book may refer to Simon I, and the composition of the original book of Ben Sira may therefore be assigned to the first half of the third century B.C.E. Elsewhere we have pointed out that the Simon referred to by Ben Sira is the second one.[95] We may further substantiate this theory by a

---

writer, entitled, "The Date of the Crucifixion According to the Fourth Gospel" in the *Journal of Biblical Literature* 1932, pp. 266–77.

[91] On the text, editions, and Bibliography, consult Charles, *Apocrypha*, Vol. I, pp. 268–315.

[92] Seder Olam Rabba, XXX.

[93] Graetz, Gesch. III.

[94] Derenbourg, Essai; III, Krochmal מורה נבוכי הזמן שערי'.

[95] נר מערבי 1924.

passage from Ben Sira. In chapter 50:24 we read as follows: "May His mercy be established with Simeon,

And may He raise up for him the covenant of Phinehas; May one never be cut off from him;

And as to his seed, (may it be) as the days of heaven." This can be applied only to the time from 180–175 B.C.E., when the sons of Joseph (who was a grandson of Simon I and a priest also), Simon and Menelaus, tried to usurp the office of high priest from Onias the son of Simon II.[96] Ben Sira, as a pious Jew and much devoted to Simon II, prays to God that the priesthood should not cease from Simon's lineage and that the covenant of Phinehas should never be broken with Simon's children.

Tobit.[97] The story of this Book is as follows: Tobit, a pious Jew, of the tribe of Naphtali, with his wife Anna and his son Tobias, was taken into captivity by the Assyrians to Nineveh. Even in captivity Tobit was very scrupulous with regard to the Jewish laws and customs. He took particular pains in burying the bodies of his countrymen who had been put to death by the Assyrians and were not allowed by the Government to be buried. Once on the Feast of Pentecost Tobit sent out his son to bring some poor Jew to partake of the holiday meal with him. Tobias returned saying that there was a Jew lying in the street strangled. Tobit rose at once from his table without finishing his meal, hid the man, and at night buried him, for which the king ordered that he be put to death. Instead of being rewarded for his praiseworthy deeds, he was visited with a great affliction, and upon returning from burying the dead, he lay down to sleep in his courtyard. Then a sparrow's dung fell upon his eyes, and in consequence he became blind. Helpless and reduced to poverty, his wife, Anna, reproached him for the misery which they had to endure. One day under such provocation Tobit prayed to God that he should die. At the same time there lived in Ecbatana in Media, a pious

---

[96] That Simon, Menelaus and Lysimachus were priests and that they were the sons of Joseph of Tobias, the writer will endeavor to show in a separate essay.

[97] On the texts, editions, and literature see Schürer, *Gesch.* III; Charles, *Apocrypha*, Vol. I, pp. 174–201. See also the article by Marshall in Hasting's Dictionary of the Bible.

CANONIZATION OF THE HEBREW SCRIPTURES

Jewess, called Sarah, the daughter of Raguel, who had been married seven times, and all her husbands had died on the bridal night by the evil spirit Asmodeus. Sarah was reproached by her maid for having slain them. She likewise prayed for death. The prayers of both were heard and the angel Raphael was sent to deliver both from their affliction. The aged Tobit recalled in the midst of his distress that he had once left ten talents of silver with Gabael of Rages in Media, and he sent his son, Tobias, for the money. When Tobias sought a guide, the angel Raphael offered his services, pretending to be a man by the name of Azarias, and these two set out on their journey to Media with a favorite dog. On the way, while Tobias was bathing in the River Tigris, a great fish leaped up out of the water and he caught it. Upon the advise of Raphael, he cut out its heart, liver and gall, to be used as a medicament later on. Passing through Ecbatana they stopped at Raguel's house, and Tobias asked for Sarah in marriage. Raguel consented, and he wrote an instrument of cohabitation, even that he gave her to him to wife according to the decree of the Law of Moses. In the evening, as the newly married couple entered the bridal chamber, Tobit acting under the instructions of Raphael, burned the heart and the liver of the fish and this odor caused Asmodeus to disappear. The wedding was celebrated for fourteen days. Thus, during the fourteen days, Raphael took the opportunity to go to Rages to take the money from Gabael. After the marriage festivities were over, Tobit returned to Nineveh to his parents, accompanied by Raphael, and took half of his father-in-law's wealth with him. Tobias, upon meeting his father, applied the gall of the fish to his father's eyes, and his sight was instantly restored. Tobit wished to reward the faithful Azarias, whereupon the latter disclosed his identity, and returned to heaven. Full of gratitude to God, Tobit chanted a song of thanksgiving to God. He continued to live in health and prosperity for many more years.

From the contents of the Book we can safely say that the Book was written by a very pious Jew, who stressed the observance of the Jewish Law and particularly those relating to burying the dead. He also wants to show that God may test a man, as he tested Abraham and Job. He may even give power to Asmodeus to test the man, as he tested Job, but in the end He will reward the righteous man.

As to the time of the composition of this Book, various dates have been advanced by scholars. Schürer is of the opinion that the Book was written in the course of the last two centuries before Christ. Ewald fixes it around 350 B.C.E.[98] On the other hand, Graetz[99] ascribes it to the period of Bar Kokba, and Kohut goes a little further and believes that the Book was written some time in the year 226 of the Common Era.[100] The chief reason for which Graetz places the composition of this Book at such a late date is that the principal object of the Book is to stress the duty for every pious Jew to bury the dead, even at the risk of his own life, as God would in the end reward him for it, and such a time in Jewish history, according to Graetz, was in the period of Hadrian, when those of the slain in Bettar were not allowed to be buried. We believe, however, that Graetz's theory is quite untenable, as his chief argument for giving such a late period of the Book of Tobit, is that Hadrian did not allow those Jews slain in battle to be buried. This custom of not allowing enemies to be buried prevailed among all the nations. Josephus tells us that during the civil war in Jerusalem, when the Zealots slew their enemies, they left them without burial, and any relative who buried his kin was punishable by death.[101] And so the Psalmist complains that "the bodies of thy servants have they given to be meat unto the fowls of the heaven, the flesh of thy saints unto the beasts of the earth. Their blood have they shed like water round about Jerusalem; and there was none to bury them."[102]

We believe that Schürer is quite right in saying that the Book was written in the course of the two centuries before C. E. To be more exact, we would say that the Book was written during

[98] *History of Israel*, Vol. V, 209.

[99] *Monatschrift f. Gud. Jud.*, 1879.

[100] Geiger's, Z. vol. X. 49.

[101] B. J. IV, 6, 3; "They left the dead putrefying in the sun. For burying a relative, as for desertion, the penalty was death."

[102] Psalms LXXIX, 2–3. נתנו את נבלת עבדיך מאכל לעוף השמים בשר חסידך לחיתו ארץ שפכו דמם כמים סביבות ירושלים ואין קובר.

CANONIZATION OF THE HEBREW SCRIPTURES

the revolt against the Syrians when many pious Jews were slain and their bodies were left unburied.

Furthermore from internal evidence, namely the Halakah recorded in this Book, we may conclude that it was written in an early period. The author relates that when Raguel gave his daughter in marriage to Tobias, he wrote an instrument of cohabitation,[103] which means he wrote a document (shtar) in giving away his daughter. This is the old Halakah, which says that a woman may be acquired as a wife by "shtar."[104] This law, however, was later amended. Instead of the "shtar" which had to be written by the father of the bride, a Ketubah was introduced, which was to be written by the groom. The Talmud ascribes this amendment to Simon ben Shetach.[105] In the Book of Tobit, we are told, however, that Raguel, the father, wrote the "shtar," and not Tobias, the husband. This indicates clearly that the Book was written before the time of Simon. It must, therefore, have been written either before the Maccabean period, or at the very latest in the early Maccabean period.

Now, if we are correct in assuming that the book was written in such an early period, why was it not included among the Kethubim when the latter were canonized in the year sixty-five? This difficulty is easily removed if we recall that "Tobit" still had the old Halakah which was already modified at the time of the canonization of the Kethubim. If there was a disagreement between a Prophetic book and the Pentatuech, the rabbis tried to reconcile it, but they would never canonize a book which was in direct contradiction with their Halakah. That is sufficient reason for not including the Book of Tobit among the Kethubim.

Susanna.[106] The contents of the book of Susanna is as follows: In the early period of the captivity in Babylon, there lived a woman named Susanna, beautiful, virtuous, and pious, a daughter

---

[103] VII, 11–13.

[104] Kid. I, 1. האשה נקנית בשלשה דרכים בכסף בשטר ובביאה.

[105] Shab. 14b. שמעון בן שטח תיקן כתובה לאשה. Comp. Yer. Ket. 32c; Tos. Ibid. XII, 1. A more detailed discussion of the origin of the Ketubah, will be found in an article by the writer, entitled, "The Origin of the Ketubah," which will appear shortly in the *J.Q.R.*

[106] On the texts, editions, and literature, comp. Charles, Vol. I, pp. 638–646.

of a priest. She was married to a man by the name of Joakim, who was rich and very much respected in the community. There were two elders in Babylon who were also judges. One evening they saw Susanna walking in her husband's garden, and their passion for her was aroused, and they tried to coerce her to lie with them, saying to her, "if you will not consent to our lust, we shall say that we saw you sin with a young man." But Susanna repulsed them with scorn and said that she would rather die than sin against God. The two judges to protect themselves accused Susanna, and summoned her to appear before the assembly. The two elders appeared as witnesses, telling the people that they saw Susanna lying in the park with a young man, who managed to escape before he could be arrested. Susanna protested her innocence, but the people of the assembly had to take the evidence of the two witnesses and condemned Susanna to death. As they were leaving the assembly house to lead her to be executed, a young man, by the name of Daniel, reproached the community, by saying that, without any examination or knowledge of the truth, they had condemned a daughter of Israel, and he undertook to prove the innocence of Susanna. He cross-examined the two elders separately, and put the same question to each, and asked them under what kind of tree did the adultery occur. Each gave the name of a different tree. The people being convinced of the innocence of Susanna and the malevolence of the two judges, put the two elders to death.

The author may not have had any motive in writing this story, but he certainly reflects his theological point of view; a man should rather prefer death to sinning against God, and he who trusts in the Lord, will be rewarded by him in the end. On the other hand, hypocrisy, as practiced by the judges, will meet with a just penalty.

As to the date of the composition of Susanna, we shall endeavor to establish this from the contents. The author of this book, in giving the story of Susanna, would certainly present the institutions and laws as they existed in his time. We are told in the book that Susanna was summoned before the assembly of the people. Apparently the institution of the Sanhedrin was not yet in existence at that time, otherwise the author would certainly have mentioned the fact that Susanna was summoned to appear before the Sanhedrin. This proves that the story was written before the existence of the Sanhedrin, which means that it was written before the time of Simon II. Furthermore, Daniel in cross-examining the witnesses, asked the name of the tree under which the act of adultery was committed. In giving different trees, (which according to the Tannaim was called הכחשה) Susanna was not only acquitted, but the witnesses were put to death. This is the biblical law: "Then shall ye do unto him, as he had thought to have done unto his brother."[107]

The early Tannaim maintained that false witnesses can be put to death only in the case of an alibi, that is, if other witnesses come to testify that the said witnesses were together with them in a different place at the time that the supposed crime took place. If, however, their testimony does not agree, as in the case of the trial of Susanna, the defendent cannot be convicted, and the witnesses are free from punishment.[108] This law was already in existence at the time of Simon ben Shetach.[109] The author of the book tells us that when Daniel found that the two witnesses were not in agreement about the tree, they were put to death. This clearly shows that the book was written before the time of Simon ben Shetach.

The reason why the book "Susanna" was not included among the Scriptures can be readily understood, for the Halakah recorded in "Susanna" is early Halakah and did not agree with the Halakah which existed in the year sixty-five. This was sufficient reason for excluding this book from the Scriptures, just as the book of Tobit was excluded.

Judith.[110] The following is a brief account of the Book of Judith: Nebuchadnezzar, after conquering Media, sent a large force, under the leadership of his general Holofernes to take vengeance on Judea because the Jews had not come to his aid. Holofernes laid waste the various countries, demolished their temples, and their

---

[107] Deut. XIX, 19.
[108] M. Mak. I; Comp. M. San. V, 11.
[109] Comp. Mak. 5b; Tos. San. VI, 6.
[110] On the texts, editions, and literature see Charles, pp. 242–247; Schürer, *Gesch.* III.

35

gods, and demanded that Nebudhadnezzar alone should be worshipped as God. The Jews who had but lately returned from the Exile, resolved to resist Nebuchadnezzar with all their might and to defend their country and their religion. Joakim, the high priest in Jerusalem, sent instructions to Bethulia to stop the passes leading to the Capital. Holofernes called a council of officers to decide how to proceed with the campaign against the Jews. One officer, called Achior, an Ammonite, warned Holofernes that God in Heaven protects the Jews and no one can do them any harm unless they sin. This speech displeased Holofernes, and Achior was delivered to the enemy in Bethulia. Holofernes then laid siege to Bethulia. After this had lasted for forty-seven days, the water supply of the city gave out, and the inhabitants of the city suffering very severely, demanded that their leaders surrender the city to the enemy. When the distress in the city had reached a climax, a wealthy, beautiful and very pious widow, by the name of Judith, resolved to save her people by a great act of daring. Prepared by praying and strict observance of the Jewish law, she made her way to the camp of the enemy, taking a single maid servant with her and a bag of "pure" food. Holofernes was captivated by her beauty, and he invited her to his camp. On the evening of the fourth day, Judith was invited to participate at a banquet, which was given in her honor. After the guests had departed, she was left alone with Holofernes. When the general was lying intoxicated upon his bed, Judith decided that this was the most opportune moment for carrying out her design. She took his sword and cut off his head. Then she and her maid servant managed to leave the camp without being observed and made their way to Bethulia, taking the head of Holofernes with them. When the enemy discovered that their general had been betrayed by the Jewess, they fled in all directions, hotly pursued by the Jews, who killed a great number of them. Achior, seeing the wonders of God, had himself circumcized and became converted to Judaism. The Jews celebrated this great victory with sacrifices to God and with great rejoicing.

The author believed that Israel's troubles were due to their sins, and if the Jews would follow God's commandments and observe the laws, he would deliver them from all their enemies who threatened their religion and their country. Judith, because she was devoted to God, and because she strictly observed the dietary laws, was able with God's help, to conquer Holofernes.

The original language of this book is commonly accepted to have been Hebrew. Schürer rightly points out that Judith was written in the Hellenistic period when the Jewish religion, as well as their country, were threatened by the Syrians.[111]

Graetz's opinion that the book of Judith was written at the time of Trajan,[112] is not even to be considered, as Clement of Rome, who died before Trajan, already in his Epistle to the Corinthians, gives an account of the Book of Judith. He says: "The blessed Judith, when her city was besieged, asked the elders to suffer her to go out into the camp of the strangers. So she gave herself up to danger, and went forth for love of her country and her people in their siege, and the Lord delivered over Holofernes by the hand of a woman. Not less did Esther also, who was perfect in faith, deliver herself to danger, that she might rescue the nation of Israel from the destruction that awaited it; for with fasting and humiliation she besought the all-seeing Master of the Ages."[113] Furthermore, the author of the Book of Judith relates that when Achior was converted to Judaism, he was circumcised. If the book had been written after the destruction of the Temple, as Graetz assumes, then why does the author fail to mention that Achior was baptized, for baptism was already a necessary requirement for proselytes.[114] We must, therefore, assume that the book

---

[111] Schürer, Ibid.
[112] *Gesch.* III.
[113] LV.
[114] The institution of baptism for proselytes came into existence in the year sixty-five, when the Gentiles were declared in a state of זב. Büchler, in an article in the *J.Q.R.*, 1926, entitled, *"The Levitical Impurity of the Gentile in Palestine before the Year Seventy,"* does not accept the date of the year sixty-five as a terminus *a quo* for this institution. He claims that in the year 17-18 the Gentiles were already considered unclean. His argument is based on a statement found in the Talmud: Yom. 47a ערבי עם דברים סיפר אחת פעם קמחית בן ישמעאל ר' על עליו אמרו תחתיו ושמש אחיו ישבב ונכנס בנדיו על מפיו צינורא וניתזה בשוק אחד .Tos. Yom. IV, 20 שיצא צינורא וניתזה ערבי המלך עם לדבר. According to Büchler the high priest concerned here was Simon (Ishmael), the son of Kamethis, who was appointed by Gratus in the year 17-18, and so at that time the Gentiles were already considered in a state

was written before the destruction of the Temple, when baptism was not yet a requisite for conversion to Judaism.

In order to understand why Judith was not included in the Scriptures it is only necessary to recall that the Book of Esther which is quite similar to it, was not included in the Canon until a very late period, for the rabbis had been opposed to the inclusion of the Book of Esther in the Canon. Only through pressure of public opinion was this book finally included, as the Book of Esther had been read for centuries on the festival of Purim. It may be true that the Book of Judith was connected with the festival of Hannukah[115] and may have been read during the days of Hannukah, but the festival of Hannukah itself was not very popular among the Jews during the Second Commonwealth, when the Hasmonean dynasty was overthrown by Herod. Moreover a statement is found in tannaitic literature that a fast was declared on Hannukah.[116] The festival of Purim, however, was always very popular with the Jews. The Book of Jubilees, Ben Sira, Tobit, Susanna, Judith, and other similar books, such as, First Maccabees, the Wisdom of Solomon, or books of an Apoca-

of Levitical impurity. However, after critical examination of all the passages in the tannaitic literature, relating to this episode, we believe that Dr. Büchler's theory is not acceptable. The story recorded in the Palestinian Talmud reads as follows: שיצא לדבר עם המלך ערב יום הכפורים וניחזה צינורא של ריק מפיו על בנדיו וטימאהו ונכנס יהודה אחיו ושימש תחתיו. This version is found several times in the Palestinian Talmud, and it is undoubtedly the correct one. It is hardly conceivable that the high priest would go out from the Temple on the Day of Atonement to take a promenade with an Arab—or to talk over matters with him. The text in the Babylonian Talmud is corrupt. In place of ערב it has ערבי. Dr. Büchler furthermore quotes the following passage from the Talmud to prove his point: כי אתא רב דימי אמר בית דין של חשמונאי גזרו ישראל הבא על הנכריה חייב משום נש׳נא Ab. Zarah, 36b. But Rav Dima was an Amora who lived in the fourth century and hence his statement cannot overthrow my thesis, as we have shown from many passages of tannaitic literature that Gentiles were not subject to Levitical impurity and do not transmit it. הבהמה והגוים אין Tos. Oh. I, 4, הגוי והבהמה הנוגעים במת כלים הנוגעים בהן טהורין. Tos. Zab. II, 1, הגוים והגר התושב אינן מטמאין בזיבה Tos Neg. VII, 10, מקבלים טומאה There is no reference found anywhere in the Tannaitic literature or in the Hellenistic literature before the destruction of the Temple that baptism was a requisite for conversion to Judaism. See also Craetz, III, n. 19.

[115] See Zunz, *Gottesdienstliche Vortrage*, p. 131.
[116] Yer. Tan. 70d. מעשה שגזרו תענית בחנוכה בלוד.

lyptic nature, which were written in the Hebrew language, or in the Greek language, were considered ספרים חצונים and these books were prohibited from being read, and anyone who read these, according to the rabbis, would not share a portion in the world to come, while such books which have no connection whatsoever with Judaism,[117] as the books of Hamerum (Homer), were not prohibited from being read.

The early Jewish literature may be divided into two sections כתבי הקודש the Holy Scriptures, and the Extra-Canonical Books ספרים חצונים. The term ספרים גנוזים which occurs in modern Hebrew literature, and is used quite frequently by modern scholars, is an erroneous one, as no such term is found in the Talmud, and there were no books of that name.[118]

The Jewish tradition connects the canonization of the Hebrew Scriptures with the Great Synagogue. This Essay, I believe, sopports this tradition. Many scholars have denied the existence of the Great Synagogue. They considered it a rabbinical fiction.[119] I believe, that of the scholars who dealt with the historical question of the Great Synagogue, some did not penetrate into the history of that period, while others did not fully comprehend the sources in the original language. Had they made a thorough investigation of the tannaitic literature, they would not have come to such a hasty conclusion. The institution of the Great Synagogue was not a myth and the rabbis did not invent it. It was a reality and it had great influence in helping to shape the history of the Jews during the Second Commonwealth.

[117] M. San. X, 1. ואלו שאין להם חלק לעולם הבא ... ר' עקיבא אומר אף הקורא בספרים החצונים; Yer. ibid. 28a הקורא ... כגון סיפרי בן סירא וספרי בן לענה, אבל ספרי המירם בהן כקורא באיגרת.

[118] Comp. Charles, *Apocrypha* V. I, p. VII,

[119] Kuenen, Over de mannen der groote Synagogue 1876; Robertson Smith, The Old Testament, p. 169; "It has been proved in the clearest manner that the origin of the legend of the Great Synagogue lies in the account given in Neh. viii.–x ... and everything that is told about it, except what we read in Nehemiah, is pure fable of the later Jews." Compare also H. E. Ryle: The Canon of the Old Testament, Excursus A. Kohler, H. U. C. A., Vol. I, p. 388, "Without going into detail, it can be positively asserted that the organization is a fictitious product of the Rabbinical schools."

The Great Synagogue was not a permanent institution which existed at the time of Ezra only and lasted up to the time of Simon the Just but it was something like a constitutional assembly which gathered from time to time when the need for such assemblies arose. One such assembly met at the time of Ezra upon the return from the Exile. Another one met at the time of Simon the Priest II (The Just); while another such assembly met in the year 141 B. C. E. when the High Priesthood was given to the family of the Hasmonaim.[120] Still another Great Synagogue assembled in the year 65 C. E., after the great victory which the Jews had over the Roman general Cestius, when a new government was established and a constitution was drafted, and in that period the Hebrew Scriptures, that is, the last part, the Kethubim, were canonized.[121]

---

[120] See S. Zeitlin, The Origin of the Synagogue, Proceedings of the American Academy for Jewish Research, 1930–31. Comp. George F. Moore, Judaism, III, p. 10.

[121] Idem. Megillah Taanit, p. 108.

ADDITIONAL NOTE

כל כתבי הקדש מטמאין את הידים שיר השירים וקהלת מטמאין את הידים ר' יהודה (מאיר) אומר קהלת אינו מטמא את הידים ומחלוקת בשיר השירים ר' יוסי אומר שיר השירים מטמא את הידים ומחלוקת בקהלת ר' שמעון אומר קהלת מקולי בית שמאי ומחומרי בית הלל (so according to Meg. 7a) אמר ר' שמעון בן עזאי מקובל אני מפי ע"ב זקן ביום שהושיבו את ר'אב"ע בישיבה ששיר השירים וקהלת מטמאים את הידים אר"ע חס ושלום לא נחלק אדם מישראל על שיר השירים שלא חטמא את הידים שאין כל העולם כלו כדאי כיום שניתן בו שיר השירים לישראל שכל הכתובים קדש ושיר השירים קדש קדשים ואם נחלקו לא נחלקו אלא על קהלת א"ר יוחנן בן יהושע בן חמיו של ר"ע כדברי בן עזאי כן נחלקו וכך נמרו. M. Yad. III, 5.

"All Holy Scriptures defile the hands. The 'Song of Songs' and 'Ecclesiastes' defile the hands. Rabbi Judah said,—'Ecclesiastes' does not defile the hands but as to the 'Song of Songs,' there was a difference of opinion. Rabbi Jose said 'Song of Songs' defiles the hands but in the matter of Ecclesiastes there was a controversy." (So according to the reading in Meg. 7a which undoubtedly is the correct one). Rabbi Simon, (a Hillelite) said "Kohelet is מקולי בית שמאי and מחומרי בית הלל." (According to the school of Shammai, Kohelet does not defile the hands. This corresponds to the statement of Rabbi Jose, a Hillelite, that 'Kohelet' was rejected, but only after a dispute between the schools of Shammai and Hillel).

Rabbi Simon ben Azzai said, "I have a tradition received from the 72 elders that on the day when R. Eleazar ben Azariah was made president, it was determined that the 'Song of Songs' and 'Kohelet' defile the hands." Rabbi Akiba denied that there had ever been a controversy with respect to the book of Song of Songs. If ever there had been a controversy, he said, it was only in the matter of the book of 'Ecclesiastes.' From this statement of Rabbi Akiba we may deduce that the Song of Songs was accepted into the Canon before the destruction of the Temple. This agrees with the opinion of Rabbi Jose that שיר השירים מטמא את הידים. Rabbi Johanan the son of Joshua, the son of Rabbi Akiba's father-in-law concurs in Ben Azzai's statement that the Court of Jabneh decreed that 'Kohelet' as well as 'Song of Songs' defile the hands. This means that the Book of Kohelet was added to the Hebrew Scriptures then.

It has been shown in Chap. III that anything which is sacred but cannot be used is מטמא את הידים defiles the hands. With this view in mind, we can understand the underlying reason for the decree that בשר תאוה מטמא את הידים. The Tosefta of Ma'aser Sheni 1, 8 read as follows: לוקחין חיה ועוף לבשר תאוה (אבל לא לזבחי שלמים) משנוזר שיהא בשר תאוה מטמא את הידים אמרו אין לוקחין חיה לבשר תאוה אבל לוקחין העוף לבשר תאוה. One may buy with the money which was redeemed *Ma'aser Sheni* any חיה ועוף לבשר תאוה. Since the decree that בשר תאוה מטמא את הידים i. e. flesh of the animal which was bought with the money with which the *Ma'aser Sheni* was redeemed, defiles the hands, one may not purchase any beast. The reason for this is quite clear since בשר תאוה is still sacred but yet cannot be used for secular purposes, one may not purchase with this money any beast which is not fit for the altar הלוקח בהמה לזבחי היה לבשר תאוה אין לוקחין (Comp. M. Ma'aser Sheni 1, 3 שלמים או חיה לבשר תאוה יצא העור לחולין. This Mishna most likely dates back to the period before the decree בשר תאוה defiles rhe hands.) One may however buy a fowl for בשר תאוה since a fowl is permitted as a sacrifice אבל לוקחין העוף לבשר תאוה. Comp. Jer. ibid. Chap. 1, 52d, particularly the statement בראשונה היו אומרין לוקחין בהמה לבשר תאוה והיו מבריחין אותו מעל גבי המזבח חזרו לומר לא יקחו אפילו חיה אפילו עופות. Comp. also ibid. 1, 15, הלוקח בהמה לזבחי שלמים בשוגג יחזרו דמיה למקומה במזיד תעלה ותאכל במקום, בזמן הזה תמות. אמר ר' יהודה במה דברים אמורים בזמן שמתכוין ולקחה בתחילה לשום שלמים אבל במתכוין להוציא מעות של מעשר לחולין בין בשוגג בין במזיד בשר תאוה יחזרו דמים למקומן. More on the question of redemtion of Ma'aser Sheni or בשר תאוה will be discussed ar length in my forthcoming book on the development of the Halakah.

SOME REFLECTIONS ON THE TEXT OF THE PENTATEUCH

WHEN A SCRIBE in ancient times made an error in copying a text he placed dots above the erroneous letter or word. According to the Sifre there are ten places in the Pentateuch where dots were placed above words and letters.[1] It is stated in a Midrash that Ezra said "If Elijah comes and says to me, 'Why didst thou write [these words]?' I shall say to him, 'That is why I dotted these passages.' And if he says to me, 'Thou hast written well,' I shall remove the dots."[2] It is evident from the statement ascribed to Ezra that the sages were in doubt as to whether these ten places over which dots were placed belonged to the original text of the Pentateuch or came into the text by error. Following are the ten places:

1—Genesis 16.5, ישפט יהוה ביני וביניך "Adonai judge between me and thee." The Masora has a dot on the *yod* of the word ביניך. It is evident from the Sifre, however that the dots were placed on the letter *caf* indicating that the correct word should have been ובינה "between me and her," i.e., between me and Hagar.[3]

2—Gen. 18.9, ויאמרו אליו איה שרה "And they said to him 'where is Sarah?'" Dots were placed above אליו "to him." It is clear from the text that the three men spoke to Abraham. Therefore אליו "to him" is superfluous and the dots were placed above it to indicate that it was written by error.[4]

---

[1] An excellent essay on the dotted words in the Pentateuch was written by the late Prof. Ludwig Blau, *Masoretische Untersuchungen*, Strassburg, 1891, and I have followed him in the first part of my article.

[2] כך אמר עזרא אם יבא אליהו ויאמר לי מפני מה כתבת כך אומר אני לו כבר נקדתי עליהן ואם אומר לי יפה כתבת אעבור נקודה מעליהן.

[3] שלא אמרה לו אלא על הגר בלבד.

[4] תני משום רבי יוסי למה נקוד על איו שבאליו לימדה תורה דרך ארץ שישאל אדם באכסניא שלו.

Reprinted from the *Jewish Quarterly Review*, New Series, Vol. 51, 1961.

The text originally had ויאמרו איה שרה אשתך "They said, 'Where is Sarah, thy wife?'"

3—Gen. 19.33. In the account of the relation of Lot's daughters with him, it is said in respect to the older daughter: ולא ידע בשכבה ובקומה "And he knew not when she lay down nor when she arose." The Masora has a dot above the letter *waw* of the word ובקומה. We may safely conclude that dots were above the entire word ובקומה "when she arose" to indicate that the word did not belong in the text. Lot did not know when she lay down but he was aware when she arose.[5]

4—Gen. 33.4. In the account of the meeting between Esau and Jacob it is stated וירץ עשו לקראתו ויחבקהו ויפול על צוארו וישקהו "And Esau ran to meet him (Jacob) and embraced him and fell on his neck and kissed him." Dots are placed above the word וישקהו "and he kissed him," indicating that it is superfluous,[6] since it is stated in the same sentence that he embraced him.

5—Gen. 37. וילכו אחיו לרעות את צאן אביהם בשכם "And his brethren went to pasture their father's flock in Shechem." There are dots above the particle את which indicate that it is superfluous. We may assume from the statement in the Sifre that dots were originally placed above the words את צאן אביהם בשכם "their father's flock." [7] Accordingly the original text read: וילכו אחיו לרעות בשכם "And his brethren went to pasture in Shechem."

6—Numbers 3.39 כל פקודי הלוים אשר פקד משה ואהרן "All that were numbered of the Levites, whom Moses and Aaron numbered." Dots were placed above the name Aaron, indicating that it should be omitted. It is evident from the text that the Levites were numbered by Moses only [8] and that therefore the name Aaron should be omitted.

[5] ולא ידע בשכבה ובקומה נקוד על בקומה (בשכבה) לומר בשכבה לא ידע ובקומה ידע.
[6] שלא נשקו בכל לבו.
[7] שלא הלכו אלא לרעות את עצמם.
[8] שלא היה אהרן מן המנין.

7—Numbers 9.10. בדרך רחקה "In a journey far off." A dot was placed above the letter *heh* in the word רחקה. The word דרך in Hebrew is masculine and the *heh* in the word indicates the feminine form, the phrase בדרך רחקה is ungrammatical and hence the dot above the *heh* indicates that it should be omitted. It is probable that dots were above the entire word רחקה "far off." According to this a person on a journey even not far from the temple could sacrifice the pascal lamb on the 14th day of the second month.[9]

8—Numbers 21.30. ונירם אבד חשבון עד דיבן ונשים עד נפך אשר עד מידבא. The J.P.S. translation rendered this verse, "We have shot at them—Heshbon is perished—even unto Dibon, and we have laid waste unto Nophah, which reached unto Medeba." According to the tractate Seforim a dot was placed above the letter *resh* in the word אשר.[10] The entire verse is obscure. The Septuagint renderd this verse καὶ τὸ σπέρμα αὐτῶν ἀπολεῖται Ἐσεβὼν ἕως Δαιβὼν καὶ αἱ γυναῖκες ἔτι προσεξέκαυσαν πῦρ ἐπὶ Μωάβ "And their seed shall perish (from) Esebon to Daebon and their women have yet farther kindled a fire against Moab." Neither does the rendering of the Septuagint make sense of this verse. Rashi interprets the phrase סר ניר, מדיבור ניר לשון מלכות השימונום עד נפח. He follows the rendering according to the Targum Onkelos. Neither the Targum Onkelos nor Rashi's explanation is satisfactory.

9—Numbers 29.15. ועשרון עשרון לכבש, "And a tenth a tenth for every lamb." Upon the first עשרון "tent" dots were placed so to indicate only one tenth was necessary for every lamb.[11]

10—Deut. 29.28. הנסתרות ליהוה אלהינו והנגלות לנו ולבנינו

[9] אפילו בדרך קרובה
אף על פי שאין שם אלא נקודה אחת מלמעלן אתה דורש
את הנקודה ומסלק את הכתב

[10] ריש נקוד

[11] Cf. Sifre כיוצא בו עשרון עשרון נקוד על עשרון שלא היה אלא עשרון אחד בלבד
See men. 87 אמר רבי יוסי למה נקוד ו שבאמצע עשרון של עשרון של יום טוב הראשון של חג

עד עולם "The secret things belong unto the Lord, our God, but the things that are revealed belong unto us and our children forever." According to Aboth R. Nathan dots were placed above the words לנו ולבנינו.[12] In connection with this passage it is stated in the Sifre that dots were placed but it does not indicate where.[13] L. Blau is correct in assuming that dots were originally placed above the words ליהוה אלהינו "unto the Lord, our God."[14] The original text was הנסתרות והנגלות לנו ולבנינו עד עולם "The secrets and the revealed things belong unto us and our children forever." A scribe later added the words "the Lord our God" to indicate that secret things belong to God while only revealed things belong to men. Since the original text did not have the words "the Lord our God," dots were placed above them by another scribe to show that they were not an integral part of the text. Later editors would not permit the name of God to be dotted and they removed the dots and placed them above the words.

Regarding these ten passages it was stated that Ezra said if Elijah would ask him why he wrote these words he would answer that he placed dots above them to indicate that they were inserted in the text through error. We have through internal evidence endeavored to show that the dotted words were not in the original text of the Pentateuch but were inserted later.

There are other words in the Pentateuch which we dare say came into the text through error. The Text in Deut. 6.20 has מה העדת והחקים והמשפטים אשר צוה יהוה אלהינו אתכם Both the Palestinian Talmud and the Sifre (erroneously called Mekilta) have אתנו "us"[15] instead of אתכם "you" as it is in the Pentateuch. The Septuagint also reads "us". We may safely assume that the original text in the Pentateuch had אתנו "us".

[12] נקוד על לנו ולבניו ועל ע שבעד
[13] כיוצא בו הנסתרות לײ אלהינו והנגלות לנו ולבנינו עד עולם נקוד
אמר להם עשיתם הגלוים אף אני אודיע לכם את הנסתרות
[14] Blau, *op. cit.* [15] Yer. Pes. 10, אשר צוה יי אלהינו אותנו.

Deut. 28.66 the text has ופחדת לילה ויומם "And thou shall fear night and day." The Targum according to Jonathan has ותהון דחלין יומם ולילי. The day precedes the night. The reading in the Septuagint is the same. The original reading of the Pentateuch undoubtedly was in accordance with the reading of the Targum of Jonathan "day and night." The word *day* precedes night throughout the Pentateuch.

Exodus 34.25 ולא ילין לבקר זבח חג הפסח "Neither shall the sacrifice of the feast of the passover be left unto the morning." The Targum of Jonathan has ולא יבתון לצפרא בר ממדבחא תרבי נכסת פסחא "the slaughtering of the passover (pascal lamb)." There can be no doubt that its text is the correct reading. The term חג "feast" was placed only before המצות unleavened bread, חג המצות the Feast of Unleavened Bread. The word חג "feast" was never placed before to pascal lamb. Therefore the reading in the Pentateuch חג הפסח is incorrect.[16]

It can be shown that different readings existed in the Pentateuch from rabbinic literature (The Targumim are also to be considered rabbinic literature).

Exodus 28.40. The text reads as follows ופתחת עליו פתוחי חתם קדש ליהוה "And thou shalt make a plate of pure gold, and engrave upon it, like the engraving of a signet: Holy to YHWH." It is evident from this verse that the words "Holy to YHWH" were inscribed on the plate worn by the high priest. Josephus stated in his book, *Jewish War* that the high priest wore a crown of gold whereon the sacred letters four vowels, i.e., the tetragrammaton YHWH were embossed.[17] He does not state that the word "holy" was inscribed there. He states also in his book *Antiquities* that the high priest had to wear a plate of gold "bearing graven in sacred characters the name of God."[18] Here he likewise said that the name of God, i.e., the tetragrammaton, was engraved on the plate.

It is stated in the Talmud that the words "Holy to YHWH"

---

[16] Cf. Ex. 23.18, ולא ילין חלב חגי עד בקר' see also Yer. Pes. 5.
[17] 5.6, 6 (231-32).
[18] 3.7, 6 (178).

were engraved in two lines on the plate. The tetragrammaton was above the first line while קדש ל "Holy to" was engraved on the second line.[19] It is stated that Rabbi Eleazer, the son of Jose, said that when he was in Rome אני ראיתיו "I saw it" and the words Holy to YHWH were engraved on the line.[20] I dare say that we have to accept the version of Josephus. He was a priest, claiming to be a member of the high priestly family. He served in the Temple and undoubtedly carefully observed the vestments of the high priest, particularly the gold plate which was worn so ostentatiously. He could not have made a mistake in omitting the word *holy* if it had been engraved on the golden plate.

The statement in the Talmud that the words "Holy to YHWH" were engraved in two separate lines on the golden plate was made by rabbis who lived long after the destruction of the Second Temple. They did not witness the services of the high priest. The statement of Rabbi Eleazar is ambiguous. He did not say that he saw the plate in Rome but said, "I saw it." Possible his statement referred to other vessels which were taken from the Temple by the Romans on which "Holy to YHWH" was written. Later the rabbis regarded his statement as a reference to the golden plate worn by the high priest. I venture to say that the original text of the Pentateuch did not have the letter *lamed* perfixed to the tetragrammaton. ועשית ציץ זהב טהור ופתחת עליו פתוחי חתם קדש יהוה. This passage should be rendered as follows, "And thou shalt make a plate of pure gold and engrave upon it the engravings of a holy signet: YHWH. The letter *lamed* which is prefixed to the tetragrammaton was inserted in our text of the Pentateuch on the basis of the satement in the Talmud.

Gen. 13.16. The text has אם יוכל איש למנת את עפר הארץ גם זרעך ימנה "If a man can number the dust of the earth then

---

[19] Shab. 63, ציץ כמו טס של זהב וכתוב עליו בב שיטין יו״י ד ה״א למעלה וקודש למד למטה

[20] Ibid. אמר רבי אלעזר ברבי יוסי אני ראיתיו בעיר רומי וכתוב קדש לה בשיטה אחת. See also Suk. 5; Yer. Yoma 4.1; *JQR*, Jan. 1961, p. 215.

shall thy seed also be numbered." The Targum Onkelos has
"As a כמא די לא אפשר לגבר לממני ית עפרא דארעא אף בנך לא יתמנון
man cannot number the dust of the earth they seed also shall
not be numbered." Thus there were two readings and it is
difficult as to which is correct.

Gen. 26.32. The Text has ויאמרו לו מצאנו מים "We have
found water." The Septuagint has οὐχ εὕρμεν ὕδω "We
have not found water." The Midrash in commenting on this
passage said "We do not know if they did or did not find
water." [21] Apparently the author of this Midrash had two
readings of the Pentateuch. One was לא with an *alef*, indicating that the servants of Isaac did not find water, while
another reading was לו with a *waw* indicating that they told
Isaac that they found water.

Gen. 4.8. The text reads ויאמר קין אל הבל אחיו ויהי בהיותם בשדה
"And Cain spoke to Abel his brother. And when they
were in the field." The Targum Jonathan has איתא ונפוק
תרוינן לברא לברא והוה כד נפקו תרויהן לברא "Let us go out into
the field." This version is also found in the Septuagint. The
problem confronting us is whether this version given in the
Targum and the Septuagint was in the Pentateuchal text and
our text is incorrect, or whether this version is just an explanation to elucidate the text. This problem must remain
unsolved for lack of evidence.

Numbers 10.35-36. Dots were placed above and beneath
to indicate that these verses do not belong to this section of
the Pentateuch.[22]

The Pentateuchal text had no matres lectionis nor punctu-
ations in ancient times. Punctuation was introduced in the
Middle Ages to facilitate the reading of the text. Many
of the punctuation marks however were wrongly placed and
thus distorted the meanings of the passages. I shall cite only

---

[21] ויבאו עבדי יצחק ויאמרו אין אנו יודעים אם מצאו או לא מצאו.

[22] Sifre, ויהי בנסוע הארון נקוד עליו מלמעלה ומלמטה מפני שלא היה
זה מקומו
cf. also Shab. 115, סימניות מלמעלה ולמטה שאין זה מקומה.

one example of many. We have in Lev. 27.2-3 איש כי יפלא נדר בערכך נפשת ליהוה והיה ערכך הזכר מבן עשרים שנה. The J.P.S. renders this passage, "When a man shall clearly utter a vow of persons unto the Lord, according to thy valuation, then thy valuation shall be for a male from twenty years old." This rendering makes no sense and is due to the faulty punctuation of the word בְּעֶרְכְּךָ. The correct punctuation should be בְּעֶרְכְּךָ. This reading is supported by the Targum of Onkelos, which has גבר ארי יפריש נדר בפורסן נפשתא קדם יי ויהי פורסניה דדכרא מבר עשרין ועד בר שתין שנין
The rendering of this passage should be, "When a man shall clearly utter [argue] a vow unto the Lord in the valuation of persons, then the valuation shall be for a male from twenty years old." [23]

Some passages in the Pentateuch are ambiguous and presented difficulties for the rabbis and commentators. The text in Deut. 33.8-9 reads ללוי אמר ..... האמר לאביו ולאמו לא ראיתיו ואת אחיו לא הכיר ואת בניו לא ידע
Does it convey that Moses spoke to Levi or that he spoke to God of Levi? If Moses spoke to Levi then verse 10 has to be rendered in the second person, "Who says to his father and mother I have not seen thee." However if Moses spoke to God of Levi verse 10 has to be rendered in the third person. "His father and mother he did not see." There are other ambigous passages in the Pentateuch which posed difficulties for the commentators who presented differented interpretations of the text.[24]

The Pentateuch is the most sacred book to the Jews and was copied with great care and reverence. Nevertheless errors crept in. The prophetic books were not regarded as holy as the Pentateuch and Scriptures still less. In these books a greater numbers of errors crept in.

There have been many translations of the Bible. The earliest

---

[23] Cf. also Abraham ibn Ezra *ad loc.* וכ״ף בערכך על דעת כל המדקדקים נוסף והטעם בערך
[24] See *JQR*, Jan. 1958, pp. 269-70.

was the Septuagint and it has been translated in all languages since. It has been well said that a translator must know the language from which he translates the language in to which he translates and also be well versed in the contents of the text. Many renderings in the Septuagint are not in accordance with the so-called Masoretic text. This may be explained by the fact that there were variant readings in the biblical text at the time of the compilation of the Septuagint, and that the translators made use of a text which is no longer extant. Many renderings however do accord with the biblical texts as cited in rabbinical literature, but not found in the so-called Masoretic text. On the other hand it is evident from the rendering of many biblical passages as given in the Septuagint that the translators did not understand the Hebrew text and thus mistranslated and distorted many biblical passages.

We have also a Latin translation of the Bible known by the name Vulgate. There were two translations of the Pentateuch into Aramaic; one is the Targum Onkelos and the other is the Targum of Jonathan. The former is more literal while the latter is more homiletic and also halakic. The Targum Onkelos is not only a literal translation but also conveys the spirit of the biblical passages.

The Bible has been translated into all the modern languages since the Reformation. There is an English translation by the Jewish Publication Society of America. Numerous errors crept into this translation because the translators followed the Septuagint variants rather than the rabbinic translations and interpretations. Apparently they overlooked the fact that the Bible was written by the Jews, for the Jews and preserved by the Jews in the language in which it was written.

The Jewish Publication Society of America is now contemplating a new translation of the Bible for which the Society is to be congratulated. There is real need for a good translation into English. But the editors should *not* follow the methods employed by the editors of the Revised Standard Edition wherein the fidelity to the text was sacrificed for style.

Josephus, in his book *Against Apion*, blamed the Greek historians for sacrificing accuracy of facts for style.[25]

The Society has made a draft version of the book of Genesis. Many renderings of the text are questionable and I trust that they will be eliminated in the final version. Here are few given in the spirit of constructive criticism.

Chapter 4.1 "And the man had intercourse with his wife Eve." Aside from indelicacy of language, it is incorrect to translate the word האדם "the man," the proper rendering is Adam. One must go by the meaning of the passage and not by grammatical form. There are many so-called grammatical inaccuracies in the Bible. Both the Targum Onkelos and the Septuagint have Adam and not "the man."[26]

Chapter 14.3 the text has ים המלח. It is translated "the Dead Sea." The note states, "Heb. Salt Sea." It should be reversed. The text should have "Salt Sea" as in the Hebrew text while the note should be "Now known as the Dead Sea." Diodorus, Strabo, Josephus and Pliny the Elder named this sea, the Sea (lake) of Asphalt. As far as I know the historian Justin was the first to use the term "Dead Sea" for this lake—*mortuum mare dicitur*.[27] The name Dead Sea has recently become more familiar because of the discovery of Hebrew scrolls. One must not sacrifice faithfulness to the Pentateuch text for popularity.

Chapter 49.10 the text has עד כי יבא שילה. It is rendered "So that tribute shall come to him." There is a note by the editors, "Shiloh, understood as *shai loh* 'tribute to him,' following the Midrash." It is true that the Midrash interpreted these words to mean "a gift to him" but these words were rendered homiletically by the rabbis to combat the contention of the early Church fathers that this passage is a prophecy of the coming of Jesus. The rabbis interpreted this passage

---

[25] 5. (23-27).
[26] Cf. also Deut. 4.32, למן היום אשר ברא אלהים אדם על הארץ The JPS has "since the day that God created man upon the earth". It is incorrect to translate the word אדם "man", the proper renderin is Adam. Cf. also Targum Onkelos,די ברא יי אדם על ארעא.
[27] *Justini Historiarum*, 36.

homiletically as referring to the Jewish Messiah, "a gift to him" to the Messiah. One must be on guard and steeped in rabbinic literature to enable one to distinguish between the factual and homiletical interpretations of the biblical passages by the rabbis.

Variants of the biblical texts found in Hebrew manuscripts and the Septuagint were collated. It is time to collate the various readings found in the rabbinic literature. They are essential for the proper understanding of the Bible. However they are to be placed on the margin of the text. The biblical text must not be altered, it is sacred. The vocalizations of the words in the Bible are faulty in many places, not only in the prophetic books and the Ketubim but even in the Pentateuch. These faulty vocalizations are the cause of wrong renderings of the text and should be changed accordingly. They are not sacred. It seems that those who vocalized the text misunderstood many passages in the Bible.

A dispatch was recently received from Israel which states that the Hebrew University was contemplating the publication of the Bible which would include a collation of all the variants found in rabbinic literature. It was also stated that the variants in the book of Isaiah, supposedly found in a cave near the Dead Sea, would also be included. One wonders if the readings of this scroll, written by a semi-literate person lacking knowledge of Hebrew, will be included. Following are some of the faulty readings:

למטלים ובשקלו דבר ים אשו [28] מת [29] פלטיש אכס זוהז [30]

In collating variants of the biblical text and the talmudic texts one has to distinguish between a genuine reading, which must be taken into consideration, and a reading by an ignorant scribe, which must be totally ignored. The scroll of Isaiah does have some good readings. Many of its variants are on a par with the readings in rabbinic literature. Most of the variants however are worthless and have no value for a proper text of Isaiah. *(To be continued)*

[28] For אשור   [29] For חמת
[30] For זאת. See *JQR*, July, 1950, *ibid.* Oct., 1960, pp. 164-65.

WERE THERE THREE TORAH-SCROLLS IN THE AZARAH?

IN THE PALESTINIAN TALMUD a statement is found that there were three *Seforim* (Torahs) in the Azarah. In one was written מעון אלהי קדם (Deut. 33. 27); in the other two the reading was מעונה instead of מעון. The majority rule was followed; the reading of the one was disregarded the reading of the two was accepted. In one Torah, the reading was וישלח את זעטוטי בני ישראל (Exodus 24. 5) and in the other two the reading was נערי בני ישראל instead of זעטוטי בני ישראל. The reading of the two was adopted while the reading of the one was disregarded. Again the reading in one Torah was היא with a *yod* while the reading in the other two was הוא with a *waw*. The reading of the one was disregarded and the reading of the two was accepted.[1] This statement with some minor variants is found in the Sifre,[2] Aboth d'Rabbi Nathan[3] and Soferim.[4]

The scholars who dealt with this statement accepted it as historical fact that there were three Torahs in the Temple Court and that these had different readings. The Sages, in fixing the text of the Torah, followed the majority rule, accepting the reading of the two books as against the reading of the one. The scholars were in doubt only as to the period

[1] שלשה ספרים מצאו בעזרה ספר מעוני וספר זעטוטי וספר היא באחד מצאו כתוב מעון אלהי קדם ובשנים כתוב מעונה אלהי קדם וקיימו שניים ובטלו אחד באחד מצאו כתוב וישלח את זעטוטי בני ישראל ובשנים כתוב וישלח את נערי בני ישראל וקיימו שנים ובטלו אחד באחד מצאו כתוב אחד עשר הוא ובשניים מצאו כתוב אחת עשרה ההיא (cf. Soferim 6.4) וקיימו שנים ובטלו אחד. Yer. Tan. 4. 2.
[2] Deut.
[3] 46. (ed. Schechter) cf. also ibid. 34.
[4] 6. 4.

when the Sages fixed the reading of the three Torahs which were in the Azarah.

We are confronted with grave complexities with regard to the historicity of the entire statement. We know from tannaitic sources that there was one *Sefer*, Torah, in the Azarah.[5] It is unthinkable that there were three Torahs in the Temple which differed in their readings. On the Day of Atonement, the high priest read portions from the Torah which had been handed to him by his subordinates.[6] It is unbelievable that there were three Torahs with different readings. If there had been three Torahs, how could the overseer have known which was the Torah with the correct text to be handed to the high priest? And, if it was known that a Torah had a defective text, the question confronting us is: How could a Torah with a defective text have been kept in the Temple?

It is stated that in the two Torahs the reading was נערי בני ישראל while in the one instead of נערי was זעטוטי. In some of the texts quoting the statement זאטוטי בני ישראל was written with an *aleph* while in other texts it has an *ayin*. A story is given in the Talmud that when the seventy men translated the Pentateuch for Ptolemy they changed the reading of זאטוטי[7] to וישלח את זאטוטי בני ישראל to וישלח את נערי בני ישראל. If זאטוטי was written with an *aleph*[8] it is an Aramaic, having the connotation small, little. If זעטוטי was written with an *ayin*[9] it is a Greek word ζητητικος meaning research, researches for wisdom. If the translators changed the word נערי they would not have substituted for it the word זאטוטי, which is Aramaic, and has the same connotation as the Hebrew word נערי. Thus we must assume that if they changed the word נערי it was to זעטוטי, researches for wisdom. If we take the state-

---

[5] M. Kelim, 15, 6, Tos. *ibid.* B.M. 15. 8, [ספר עזרה] עזרא (ספר). M.M.K. 3. 4.
[6] M. Yoma 7. 1. חזן הכנסת נוטל ספר תורה ונותנו לראש הכנסת וראש הכנסת נותנו לסגן והסגן נותנו לכהן גדול וכהן גדול עומד ומקבל וקורא.
[7] Meg. 9. וישלח את זאטוטי בני ישראל ... ואל זאטוטי בני ישראל לא שלח ידו
[8] Meg. *ibid.*, Sof. 6. 4.
[9] Yer. Tan. 4. 2.

ment in the Talmud as a historical fact that there were or were found three Torahs and that one Torah contained the word זעטוטי instead of נערי, it would mean that a Torah with a Greek word inserted was kept in the Azarah. Such would be impossible even to contemplate.

I venture to say that the statement about the three Torahs in the Azarah has no historical basis although it is found in the Palestinian Talmud and recorded in other rabbinic literature. It is an *Aggadic* statement. Any story or legend, however, must have some historical basis. What is the historical background for the statement about the three Torahs in the Azarah?

During the Second Commonwealth the biblical books did not have the *matres lectionis*. The letters *aleph, he, waw* and *yod* were not used as vowels to define how to pronounce words. They were consonants. Nor were the five final letters of *kaph, mem, nun, pe* and *ṣade* employed in the Holy Scriptures. During the second century CE the *matres lectionis* were introduced in the Bible. A little later the five final letters were introduced into the Holy Scriptures. Some scrolls of the Bible had the *matres lectionis* while others still contained the archaic writing without the *matres lectionis*. The Sages who wanted to establish the text of the Bible with the *matres lectionis* quoted the story that three Torahs were or were found in the Azarah. In one the text had מען and in the other two the text had a *he* appended as a vowel. They disregarded the writing without the *he* and accepted the writing with a *he*. They thereby affirmed that *matres lectionis* should be used in the Bible and cited the authority of the decision made during the Second Commonwealth.

Again during the second through the third centuries in some of the scrolls of the Torah the text had זאטוטי in place of נערי. If we accept this assumption we have to assume that this Aramaic word crept into the Torah. If, however, we accept the reading זעטוטי then we have to assume that the Greek word ζητητιχος was Hebraized to זעטוטי and also crept into the

Torah. In establishing the text the Sages sought to eliminate the Aramaic word or the Hebraized Greek word. They substantiated this on the basis of the legend of three Torahs found in the Azarah, saying that in one the text had זאטוטי, זעטוטי while in the other two the text had נערי. The text of the one had been disregarded, considered unfit.

The word הא without a vowel had the connotation of either she or he. When the *matres lectionis* was introduced in the Bible, in many instances the word הא was written היא with a *yod*, she. In other cases it was written הוא with a *waw*, he. The Sages in establishing the correct text of the Bible brought in the story of the three Torahs found in the Azarah as authority for their text.

The *aggadah*, the story of the Torahs found in the Azarah, is not a historical fact. The Temple did not contain Torahs with different readings. The *aggadah* of the three Torahs was brought in the third century in order to give authority to the introduction into the Bible of the *matres lectionis* and the establishment of the biblical text.

THE APOCRYPHA

The term Apocryphal books refers to the scriptures outside of the canon. The word apocrypha is of Greek derivation, having the meaning "hidden" and refers to books which were not allowed to be read and hence were hidden.[1] The rabbis however, speak of such writings as "outside books", ספרים חצונים i. e. books outside of the canon. Rabbi Akiba said, "Anyone who reads outside books will not share a portion in the future world."[2]

These books were written by Jews and with few exceptions in the Hebrew or the Aramaic tongue. They were preserved however by the Church and not by the Synagogue. In like manner through the Church the writings of Josephus and Philo have come down. Many books and treatises on the Apocrypha were written by Christian scholars all over the world. The best edition on the Apocrypha is by R. H. Charles, *The Apocrypha and Pseudepigrapha*.[3] Notable contributions on the Apocrypha were also issued in this country, to mention one, Goodspeed's *The Story of the Apocrypha*.[4]

Because of the fact that these books came to us through the Church, many interpolations are found in them inserted for theological purposes. Besides, the translations were made by men not well acquainted with the Semitic

---

[1] ἀπόκρυφα.
[2] San. X, 1.
[3] *The Apocrypha and Pseudepigrapha of the Old Testament in English With Introductions and Critical and Explanatory Notes To The Several Books*, Oxford, 1913.
[4] *The Story of the Apocrypha*, Chicago, 1939.

Reprinted from the *Jewish Quarterly Review*, New Series, Vol. 37, 1947.

language nor with the historical background of this literature. Hence, the translations of the Apocrypha are filled with errors.

A book on the Apocrypha was recently published by the noted scholar and Semitist, Charles C. Torrey.[5]

He divides his book into two parts. Part one is a general introduction in which he gives a full account of the Apocryphal books from the time of their composition to modern days. He deals particularly with the controversies in the Church centering around these books. In this introduction, he defines the term apocryphal, and is correct in pointing out that the theory which connects the word apocrypha with the Hebrew word *ganaz* is erroneous. I have pointed out elsewhere that the word *ganaz* has the connotation "store away" referring to something of great value, something very precious which should not be destroyed.[6] However, ספרים חצונים "outside books" may be destroyed, since they were profane and were not allowed to be used, even privately; those who used them were denied a share in the future world. Dr. Torrey suggests that the reason "outside books" came to be termed apocrypha "hidden" is probably to be found in the oft quoted passages in the Apocalypse of Ezra, Chapters XII and XIV. He quotes Chapter XIV, VI where Ezra wrote that the Most High said, "I brought forth (Moses) up to Mt. Sinai ... and told him many wondrous things ... and commanded him saying, these words shalt thou publish openly and these shalt thou hide."

Professor Torrey's hypothesis is striking and he is most likely correct in his assumption. The term apocrypha used

---

[5] *The Apocryphal Literature, A Brief Introduction*, New Haven Yale University Press, 1945.

[6] See S. Zeitlin, *An Historical Study of the Canonization of the Hebrew Scriptures*, 1933, pp. 4–8.

by the Church did originate in the Book of Ezra. The Jews never applied the word apocrypha to extra-canonical books. They divided the books into two categories: those which were canonized and were called Holy Scriptures and those which were outside of the canon and were termed ספרים חצונים "outside books." The Jews were not only prohibited from reading them; it was optional to destroy them.[7] In this introduction Dr. Torrey gives an historical survey of the controversies in the Church in regard to Apocryphal books in the pre-Reformation period, as well as later. He presents considerable information with which the general student of the Bible is not acquainted. This introduction has a great value for those interested in the attitude of the Church toward the Apocryphal books.

I AND II MACCABEES

The second part of the work deals with the Apocryphal books proper and to each of these Dr. Torrey furnishes an introduction. This literature may be divided into two branches, historic and apocalyptic. In this review I shall treat of only a few of the historic and of the so-called Apocalyptic books. Of the historic books, I and II Maccabees hold the most prominent positions. Dr. Torrey first gives a synopsis of I Maccabees. He holds that the author was an eye-witness of the early uprising of the Hasmonean and that he was a staunch adherent of this family, who, he believed, was divinely appointed to save Israel.[8] Dr. Torrey places the rededication of the Temple in the year 164 B. C. E. and the death of Antiochus Epiphanes in the year 163 B. C. E.[9] In his opinion the Jews regained their independence in the year 141 B. C. E.

[7] San. X, 1; Yer. *ibid.* X, 1.
[8] P. 72.   [9] P. 70.

The Second Maccabees, as is well known, is an epitome of a larger book written by Jason Cyrene. Dr. Torrey holds that the sources "at the disposal of Jason of Cyrene must have been mainly oral."[10] The Epitomist wrote this book in Alexandria. The date that Torrey assigns to this book is shortly after 124 B. C. E.

It is surprising that Dr. Torrey did not mention that there are not only chronological divergencies but also chronographical discrepancies between these two books. According to I Maccabees Lysias' second expedition against the Jews occurred in the year 150 A. S.,[11] but according to II Maccabees it occurred in the year 149 A. S.[12] A difference between these two books exists also as to the date of the death of Antiochus Epiphanes (the fourth). According to I Maccabees he died after the rededication of the Temple,[13] but according to II Maccabees his death took place before the rededication.[14] Concerning these discrepancies, particularly as to the date of the rededication of the Temple, scholars of note have been divided.[15] Some are of the opinion that the First book is more historic, while others hold that the Second book is more historic. Dr. Torrey is silent on this problem.

In describing the events of the I Maccabees, he says that the purification of the Temple and the rededication of the

---

[10] P. 76.

[11] 6, 18–21, "So they came together, and besieged them in the hundred and fiftieth year, and he made mounts for shot against them, and other engines."

[12] 13, 1–26. "In the hundred forty-ninth year, it was told Judas that Antiochus Eupator was coming with great power into Judaea."

[13] 4, 36–61; 6, 1–16.   [14] 9, 1–28; 10, 1–5.

[15] Compare Niese, *Geschichte*, III, pp. 174; 230-1; Die beiden Makkabaerbücher, *Hermes*, XXV, 1900, pp. 502–5; Bevan, *The House of Seleucus*, II, p. 172. Comp. also Clinton, *Fasti Hellenici*, III, p. 84; Unger, Die Seleukidenära der Makkabaerbücher, *Sitzungsberichte der Philos.-Philol.-Hist. Cl. der k. b. Akademie der Wiss. zu München*, 1895; Schürer, *Geschichte*, I.

new altar occured in the year 164 B. C. E., while the death of *Antiochus Epiphanes* and the accession of his son Antiochus V occurred in the year 163 B. C. E.[16] It is well known that the author of the I Maccabees dates the years according to the Seleucidean Era. According to the I Maccabees Antiochus Epiphanes died in the year 149 and his son Antiochus V and Lysias besieged the Temple Mount in the following year,[17] which would be according to Torrey's reckoning 162 B. C. E. The author of I Maccabees says that the Jews were at a great disadvantage in the siege, having nothing to eat because it was the sabbatical year.[18] Now the sabbatical year extended from the autumn of 164 B. C. E. to the autumn of 163 B. C. E.[19] How can Dr. Torrey reconcile his statement? As a matter of fact the rededication of the Temple actually took place in the autumn of the year 165 B. C. E., while the siege of the Temple Mount by Antiochus V occurred in the year 150 A. S., i. e. 164–3 B. C. E. Thus, the siege took place during the sabbatical year.[20]

Dr. Torrey is right in assuming that the author of I Maccabees was a witness of the Hasmonean struggle from

[16] "The thrilling narrative of the first victories gained by the Jews under the leadership of Judas Maccabeus is followed by the account of the purification of the temple and dedication of the new altar, in the year 164. The course of the subsequent history while Judas was in command runs as follows. Campaigns against the surrounding nations (chap. 5). Death of Antiochus Epiphanes in Persia, and accession of Antiochus V Eupator, year 163. Further wars with the Syrians." P. 70.

[17] 6, 16–20. "So king Antiochus died there in the hundred forty and ninth year." καὶ τεσσαρακοστοῦ καὶ ἑκατοστοῦ. So they came together, and besieged them in the hundred and fiftieth year. καὶ συνήχθησαν ἅμα καὶ περιεκάθισαν ἐπ' αὐτοὺς ἔτους πεντηκοστοῦ καὶ ἑκατοστοῦ.

[18] 6, 49, "But with them that were in Bethsura he made peace ... because they had no provisions there to endure the siege, it being a sabbatical year (sabbath to the land) σάββατον ἦν τῇ γε.

[19] See S. Zeitlin, *Megillat Taanit*, Ch. III.

[20] *Idem., Ibid.* pp. 33–44.

its beginning. This book was based mainly on oral tradition. We cannot, however, agree that II Maccabees, which was based on the works of Jason of Cyrene must have been founded mainly on oral tradition. We must bear in mind that the epitomists not only abridged the works of Jason, but also added new material. The story of the martyrdom of Eleazar and the seven brothers unquestionably does not come to us from Jason, but from the additions of the epitomists. Likewise, the proemium, as well as the passages dealing with the festival of Hanukkah, was not written by Jason, but by the epitomists. In many instances, the epitomists detached a number of passages and sometimes disturbed the sequence of events.[21] In Chapter 1 of the II Maccabees we have a letter from the Jews of Judea to the Jews of Egypt. There are in Chapter XI letters addressed to the Jews by King Antiochus and by the Romans. Many scholars doubt the authenticity of these letters.[22] However, Dr. Torrey gives little more than a page to these important letters.

The Book of Judith

Dr. Torrey is of the opinion that the Book of Judith has no historical background, but is edifying fiction. He advances a very striking and original hypothesis, that Bethulia is a pseudonym for the city of Shechem, while Betomasthen is really a pseudonym for Samaria.[23] This book according to him, was written shortly after 120 B. C. E. He passes over many important and difficult problems in the book, such as the use of the words "Hebrews" and the "Children of Israel" throughout and not the word "Jews." When

---

[21] *Idem.* Hanukkah, *JQR.* XXIX, 1938, pp. 19–32.
[22] See Niese, Op. Cit.
[23] Pp. 88–92.

Judith came to the camp of her Holofernes and was asked who she was, she replied that she was a daughter of the Hebrews.[24] In the Book of Esther with which the story of Judith is almost identical we are told that after the Jews won a victory over the enemies "many of the people of the land" became Jews, the author using the term "Judaized."[25] However, in the Book of Judith, the author relates that when the Jews won the victory over Holofernes army Achior, the Ammonite circumcized himself; and[26] the author did not use the expression "Judaized" but "he joined the people of Israel."[27]

The term "Jews" is used in most of the other apocryphal writings. In the II Maccabees we find the word "Jews" many times alongside the term "Hebrews." We must bear in mind that II Maccabees was based on a work written outside of Palestine and in Greek. In the Testament of the Twelve Patriarchs, the term "Hebrews" appears just twice.[28] Thus, we are confronted with the problem as to why the author of Judith always used the term "Hebrews" and "Israel" and not "Jews," particularly since Dr. Torrey assumes that the book was written so late and in Palestine. It seems more likely that the book was written in the Diaspora. Judith was written to offset the Book of Esther. It is well known that in this biblical book the name of God or Jerusalem is not mentioned. The author of Judith on the other hand, glorifies the service of the Temple, the priesthood and the seat of Jerusalem. The author also stressed the desirability of proselytism. In Deuteronomy

[24] θυγάτηρ εἰμὶ τῶν Ἑβραίων. (10.12)
[25] מתיהדים.
[26] 14, 10, "And when Achior had seen all that the God of Israel had done, he believed in God greatly, and circumcised the flesh of his foreskin, and was joined unto the house of Israel unto this day."
[27] καὶ προσετέθη πὸς τὸν οἶκον Ἰσραήλ.
[28] *The Testament of Joseph* 12, 2; 13, 3.

it is stated that an Ammonite shall not enter the community of God, "even the tenth generation they should not enter into the community of God forever."[29] The author of the Book of Judith relates that Achior, the Ammonite circumcized himself and joined the House of Israel.

Dr. Torrey says that "the post-Maccabean time" of the book "is indicated by 3.6 and 6.2, where the allusion to Antiochus Epiphanes and his efforts to establish a state religion with himself as the Deity, seems plain." In Chapter 6:2, we have the following: "And who art thou Achior and the hirelings of Ephraim, that thou hast prophesied among us as today and hast said, that we should not make war with the people of Israel because their God will defend them? And who is God but Nabuchodonosor?" This passage does not necessarily refer to Antiochus; compare II Kings 18: "Hath any of the Gods of the nations ever delivered this land out of the hand of the king of Assyria? Where are the Gods of Hamath, and of Arpad? Where are the Gods of Sepharvaim, of Hena, and Ivvah? Have they delivered Samaria out of my hand? Who are they among all the Gods of the countries that have delivered their country out of my hand, that God shall deliver Jerusalem out of my hand?"

THE BOOK OF JUBILEES

On the authorship of the Book of Jubilees wide differences of opinion exist and various hypotheses have been set forth. Some say that the author was a Pharisee, while others hold that he was a Sadducee.[30] A divergence of opinion also exists with regard to the date of its composition.

[29] Deut. 23, 4.
[30] See S. Zeitlin, *The Book of Jubilees, Its Character and Its Significance*, Philadelphia, 1939, and the literature there quoted.

The prevailing opinion is that the book was written during the reign of John Hyrcanus, about the end of the second century B. C. E. Elsewhere I advanced the theory that the book was composed some time in the fifth century B. C. E.[31] Dr. W. F. Albright, in *From the Stone Age to Christianity*, accepted this theory in part and placed the composition in the early third century B. C. E. and possibly even in the late fourth century B. C. E.[32]

Dr. Torrey believes that the Book of Jubilees was composed during the second half of the last century B. C. E.[33] and later than the Book of Enoch. He states that the angelology and the demonology had been more fully developed in the former book than in the Book of Enoch.[34] However, an examination of the angelology in the two books, makes it quite clear that the Book of Enoch was a later composition. It is true that in both books, angels play an important part, but we should bear in mind that angels figured in the Bible, especially in the Pentateuch. In the Book of Jubilees, as in the bibilical books of the pre-exilic period, they are not as yet designated by proper names. However, in Enoch, the angels are so designated, e. g. Gabriel, Michael, Uriel, Raphael, etc. This proves unquestionably that the Book of Jubilees was written at the

---

[31] *Ibid.* pp. 8–16.

[32] "S. Zeitlin hàs now (1939) published a strong argument for a still earlier date and has even suggested that it might belong to the early post-exilic age. While this date is demonstrably much too high, he shows that the book is older than the time of the disputes between the Pharisees and Sadducees, which began about the middle of the second century B. C., and that it even opposes many pentateuchal laws and traditions." P. 266.

[33] "The second half of the last century B. C. may be conjectured as the period within whose limits the composition of Jubilees is to be placed. There appears no good ground for a more definite dating." P. 128.

[34] "The development of angelology and demonology has progressed farther than in Enoch." P. 127.

time when in Jewish theology names had not yet been assigned to the angels, while Enoch was written at a later period when names had already been assigned to them. Similarly, demons in Jubilees are not mentioned by name anymore than they are in the Bible. However, in the Book of Enoch, they are so mentioned, and this shows a later development.

Dr. Torrey assumes that Jubilees is of a late date because the names of *Beliar* and *Mastema* are found there. He admits that the word *Beliar* is derived from Belial,[35] a word found in the Bible. As a matter of fact, Beliar is a corruption of Belial and thus we find in the Book of Jubilees the expression "the sons of Beliar"[36] just as we find in the Bible "the sons of Belial."[37] Why Dr. Torrey says that the noun *Mastema* (enmity) in Hos. 9.7, 8 was interpolated later than the Septuagint version[38] when the verb וישטם[39] and also וישטמהו[40] are already mentioned in the Pentateuch is not clear. The fact that the Septuagint (Hos. 9.8) has μανία (madness) is no proof that the word *Mastema* is of a later period. There are many places in the Septuagint where the Greek translater has misread the Hebrew text. According to Dr. Torrey the word *Mastema* in verse 8, is a later interpolation and is not "represented in either Syriac or Targum."[41] This is not exact. The phrase ורבה משטמה is rendered in the Targum ותקופו חטאך which shows that the Targum already had the word *Mastema* in the text. In Zech. (3.1, 2) the word *satan* is rendered in the Targum חטאה.[42]

---

[35] "Beliar is derived from the "Belial" of the Hebrew scriptures, the phonetic variation having merely the purpose of gaining a proper name." (note 111).
[36] 15, 33.
[37] I Sam. 2.12.   ובני עלי בני בליעל.   [38] P. 127.
[39] Gen. 27.41.   [40] Ibid., 49.23.
[41] P. 127, note 111.
[42] וחטאה קאים על ימיניה לאסטאה ליה.

Dr. Torrey further says: "From the passage 4.17–21 especially it is certain that the author of the work was well acquainted with the Book of Enoch."[43] The passage to which he refers is as follows: "And he was the first among men that are born on earth who learnt writing and knowledge and wisdom who wrote down the signs of heaven according to the order of their months in a book, that men might know the seasons of the years according to the order of their separate months." The fact is, however, that the relation was reverse. The author of Enoch based his book on this particular passage in Jubilees where Enoch is described as the first person to learn the signs of heaven, the order of months, and the seasons of the year. That the Book of Jubilees antedated the Book of Enoch is clear. Furthermore, the months in the Book of Jubilees are still designated by numerals instead of names.[44]

It is surprising that Dr. Torrey bases his theory of the lateness of the Book of Jubilees on such flimsy grounds, while ignoring the reasons which sustain the theory of an earler composition. Thus, this book does not betray any trace of the controversies between the Pharisees and the Sadducees. It was written in opposition to the Pentateuch. I shall give only a few examples to sustain this view. According to the Pentateuch, the Festival of the First Fruit is also called *Shabuot*, the Festival of Weeks and is so called because it is to be celebrated seven weeks after the offering of the Omer. Seven times seven days are to be counted from the day of the offering of the *Omer*, and the fiftieth day is the day of the Festival.[45] It was therefore called *Pentecost* by the Hellenistic Jews.[46] In the Book of

[43] P. 127.
[44] Comp. *JQR.*, 1945, pp. 188–9.
[45] Lev. 23.15–16; Num. 28.26.
[46] II Mac. 12.32.

Jubilees, *Shabuot* which is also referred to as the Festival of the First Fruit is not connected at all with the *Omer*, but is traced to the covenant which God made with Noah and confirmed with Abraham.[47] Elsewhere I pointed out that even the name *Shabuot* in the Book of Jubilees has not the connotation of "weeks" but means "Oaths," referring to the oaths of the covenants which God made with Noah and Abraham.[48]

Furthermore, according to the Pentateuch, the year of release is the seventh year,[49] but according tc Jubilees it is the fifth.[50] According to this book, "God appointed the sun to be a great sign on the earth for days and for sabbaths and for months and for feasts and for years and for sabbaths of years and for jubilees and for all seasons of the year,"[51] while the Pentateuch assigns both the sun and the moon as signs of the seasons of the year.[52] The calendar system in the Book of Jubilees is purely Solar. Dr. Torrey says, "The whole history of the world is divided into 'jubilee' periods, cycles of 7 x 7 years." To this he adds in parentheses ("See Lev. 25.12").[53] The jubilee period in the Book of Jubilees consisted of forty nine years, whereas according to the Pentateuch, it consisted of fifty years: "And ye shall hallow the fiftieth year ... it shall be a jubilee unto you.[54] So again the Book of Jubilees is in opposition to the Pentateuch.

The name of this book, Jubilees, came to us through the Church. The original Hebrew title is not known. It may have been called "The Laws of Moses," as the Pentateuch

---

[47] 6.21.
[48] *The Book of Jubilees*, pp. 6–8.
[49] Lev. 25.4.
[50] 7.37.
[51] 2.8.
[52] Gen. 1.14.
[53] P. 127.
[54] Lev. 25.10–11.

is referred to in the Book of Prophets[55] and Hagiographa.[56] The Book of Jubilees had a profound influence on Judaism and particularly, on Christianity. It is regrettable that scholars have not yet fully utilized this book for the history of the development of Judaism and Christianity.

THE FOURTH MACCABEES

The Fourth Maccabees primarily deals with the Jewish martyrs, supposedly of the Maccabean period. It gives an account of the martyrdom of the priest Eleazar and of the seven brothers, a story based on the Second Maccabees. Dr. Torrey properly points out that the Fourth Maccabees does not emphasize belief in resurrection of the dead as does the Second Maccabees "but rather the doctrine that all souls, whether righteous or wicked, exist forever after death."[57] "The good will be in eternal happiness," he says, "with the fathers of Israel and with God; the wicked will be in torment, burning in everlasting fire."[58]

These books rather represent different points of view of Judaism at that period. The story of the martyrdom of Eleazar and the seven brothers recorded in the Second book of Maccabees came from the Epitomist and not from Jason of Cyrene. The Epitomist emphasized two fundamentals of Judaism. First, he insisted, the misfortunes which fell upon the Jews were not to destroy them, but rather to chastise them, for although God punished the Jews, he never would forsake them.[59] Secondly, the author stressed the idea of resurrection. This is clear from the words of one of the brothers who said, as he was put to death by Anti-

---

[55] II Kings 14.6.
[56] Neh. 8.8.
[57] P. 104.
[58] Ibid.
[59] 6.12, ἀλλὰ πρὸς παιδείαν τοῦ γένους ἡμῶν εἶναι.

ochus, "The King of the World shall raise us up who have died for His laws unto everlasting life."[60] Only those who follow the laws of God will be resurrected as brought out in the words of another brother to the King Antiochus: "Thou shalt have no resurrection to life."[61]

The author of the Fourth book of Maccabees still emphasized both resurrection and the observance of the laws as in the case of Eleazar, who refused to eat the flesh of the pig, because it was prohibited.[62] However, the main thought of the author of the Fourth Maccabees was to stress, not the idea of resurrection, but that of *atonement*. It is true that he says that the seven brothers died for their piety to God; but the point was that they died to ransom the iniquities of the Jews. The seven brothers were tortured and died to atone for the sins of the people and through their blood "Providence delivered Israel."[63] This idea of dying in order to atone for the sins of others, never became a part of Judaism, but it became a cornerstone of Christianity. The idea of atoning for the sins of someone else, was first brought forth in the Book of Jubilees. We are told there that on the tenth day of the seventh month, the sons of Jacob sold their brother Joseph into slavery. For this reason, said the author of the Book of Jubilees, "It is

---

[60] 7.9, ὁ δὲ τοῦ κόσμου βασιλεὺς ἀποθανόντας ἡμᾶς ὑπὲρ τῶν αὐτοῦ νομων εἰς αἰώνιον ἀναβίωσιν ζωῆς ἡμᾶς ἀναστήσει.
[61] Ibid. 14, σοὶ μὲν γαρ ἀνάστασις εἰς ζωὴν οὐκ ἔσται.
[62] 5.14–35.
[63] ὥσπερ ἀντίψυχον γεγονότας τῆς τοῦ ἔθνους ἁμαρτίας καὶ διὰ τοῦ αἵματος τῶν εὐσεβῶν ἐκείνων καὶ τοῦ ἱλαστηρίου τοῦ θανάτου αὐτῶν ἡ θεία πρόνοια τόν 'Ισραὴλ προκακωθέντα διέσωσε. They having as it were become a ransom for our nation's sin; and through the blood of these pious men and the propitiation of their death the divine Providence delivered Israel that before was evil entreated. 17, 22. Comp. also 6, 29. ἵλεως γενοῦ τῷ ἔθνει σου ... καθάρσιον αὐτῶν ποίησον τὸ ἐμὸν αἷμα καὶ ἀντίψυχον αὐτῶν λάβε τὴν ἐμὴν φυχήν. Make my blood their purification and take my soul to ransom their souls. Comp. also J. Klausner, מישו עד פאולוס.

ordained that the children of Israel should afflict themselves on the tenth day of the seventh month... that they should make atonement for themselves... once a year for their sins; for they had grieved the affections of their father regarding Joseph, his son."[64] The author held that the sin of the ten sons of Jacob, who sold Joseph into slavery, had not been atoned, and that hence the Jews had to afflict themselves annually on the day on which Joseph was sold in order to attain atonement for this sin which their forefathers committed.[65] The author of the Fourth Maccabees even went further. He held that those who died for piety to God did not do so only for their own sins, but more so for the sins committed by the children of Israel. With their blood the martyrs redeemed the iniquities committed by the children of Israel.[66] It is no wonder that this book became very popular with the early Christians and was held in great esteem by the Church. Even the name of this book, the Fourth Maccabees, came from the Church for originally it had another title. The Church held that the seven brothers and Eleazar, who became martyrs, were Maccabees. It even regarded them as Christian Saints.[67] Neither in the Second nor in the Fourth book is there any indication that these martyrs were Maccabees. The story is not history, but legend, and became very popular among the Jews. It is recorded in the Talmud,[68] but there the martyrdom is described as taking place during the Roman period.

According to the talmudic version seven sons refused to worship foreign gods, and each one quoted verses from the

[64] Ch. 34, 10–20. Ed. Charles.
[65] Comp. S. Zeitlin, The Legend of The Ten Martyrs, *JQR*, 1945.
[66] Comp. 6, 28–9.
[67] Comp. Townshend, Introduction The Fourth Book of Maccabees, Ed. Charles.
[68] Git. 57a.

Pentateuch against worshipping such gods.[69] Neither the idea of resurrection nor of atonement is mentioned in the Talmud in connection with the martyrdom of the seven sons. The story is also recounted in the Midrash of Lamentations.[70] Here again, they are described as being tortured because they did not want to worship idols.[71] (The name of Eleazar is not mentioned either in the Talmud or the Midrash). The story of the martyrdom of Eleazar and the seven sons is fully related in Josippon.[72] The author apparently made use of the Second Book of Maccabees.

In the Fourth Book of Maccabees, the seven brothers were called saints,[73] but they were not so called in the Talmud. These two types of literature, the Apocalyptic and the Normative-Pharisaic, represent different points of view of martyrdom. According to the Apocalyptists, who were the forerunners of the Christians, those who died for their religion shed their blood to ransom the people.[74] They were saints.[75] However, according to the Pharisees, who were the founders of rabbinic Judaism, Jews were under command to die for the sanctification of God.[76] A

---

[69] זו אשה ושבעה בניה, אתיהו קמא לקימה דקיסר אמרו ליה פלח לע"ז אמר להו כתוב בתורה אנכי ד' אלהיך אפקיה וקטליה, ואתיהו לאידך לקימה דקיסר אמרו ליה פלח לע"ז אמר להו כתוב בתורה לא יהיה לך אלהים אחרים אפקיה וקטליה ....

[70] 1.51.

[71] מעשה במרים בת נחתום שנשבית היא וז' בניה ... א"ל השתחוה לצלם, א"ל ח"ו איני משתחוה לצלם א"ל למה א"ל מפני שכך כתוב בתורתנו אנכי ד' אלהיך ... הוציא השביעי ... אמר בני השתחוה לצלם ... ולא עוד אלא שנשבענו לאלהינו שאין אנו ממרין אותו באל אחר.

[72] ... סרוח, אז נתפשו שבעה אחים עם אמם ושלחום למלך ובדיל בשר חזיר מתועב שוספו באכזריות חמה, וכשר בשרם התז. ויובא האחד לפני המלך ויאמר מה לך להרבות דברים אתנו או ללמדנו כבר למדנו מאבותינו והנה אנחנו נכונים לקבל עול ד' ועול תורתו .... Ed. Günzbourg. Comp. II Mac. Ch. 7.

[73] ἱεροὶ μείρακες; ἱερὸν γὰρ εὐσεβείας ...

[74] Comp. Epistle to the Romans, 3.25, ὃν προέθετο ὁ θεὸς ἱλαστήριον διὰ τῆς πίστεως ἐ τῷ αὐτοῦ αἵματι. Comp. also I Cor. 15.22; John 1.29; Irenaeus, Contra Haereses.

[75] Tertullian, Ad Martyras, 1; Scorpiace, 9.

[76] ישראל מצווין על קידוש השם. (Yer. San. 21b.)

Jew is supposed to die rather than transgress the precepts of God.[77] He is only fulfilling his duty as a Jew, he is merely a pious man, a righteous man,[78] but not a saint. The Talmud relates that Rabbi Akiba[79] as well as Rabbi Judah ben Baba,[80] and Rabbi Haninah ben Teradyon[81] were put to death by the Romans. These men were not considered saints; they died for the sanctification of God, fulfilling their duty under their religion. Judaism does not recognize martyrdom as a ransom for the people. The Jewish martyrs died because they refused to disobey the laws of God.

The ideas of the Fourth Book of Maccabees and the Book of Jubilees exerted an influence upon some Jewish factions, and these ideas subsequently found their way in the Talmud, particularly in the Midrash. They represent only individual points of view, but not rabbinic Judaism. I have elsewhere shown that the story of the Ten Martyrs, who were supposed to die to redeem the sin of their forefathers, is only a legend and was influenced by the teachings of the Apocalyptic literature.[82] During the Middle Ages, however, the term "saint" was applied to the Jews who died for their religion, but this is a later development and may be due even to the influence of the Church.

The Second Book of Maccabees simply relates that the mother of the seven sons died,[83] while the Fourth Book of the Maccabees says that when she was about to be put to death, she cast herself into the fire so that no man could touch her body.[84] In the Talmud it is recorded that she committed suicide by throwing herself off the roof of a

---

[77] יהרג ואל יעבור.
[78] צדיק, חסיד.
[79] Ber. 61b.   [80] San. 14a.
[81] Ab. Zarah 18b.
[82] *JQR* 1945. Pp. 1–11.
[83] 7.41.   [84] 17.1.

building.⁸⁵ According to the Midrash, she lost her reason and then threw herself from the roof.⁸⁶ The author of Josippon, who followed the Second Book of Maccabees, sometimes interpolates some of his own views and relates that after the death of her youngest son, she prayed to God that He should take her to her sons. On finishing her prayer, she died and fell upon the bodies of her children.⁸⁷

There was another purpose which the author of the Fourth Book of Maccabees had in mind, and that was in making an apology for observing some of the Jewish precepts. When King Antiochus offered swine's flesh to Eleazar, who refused to eat of it, even under the threat of torture and death, Eleazar delivered an apologetic discourse for refusing to eat unclean food. "For believing our law to be given by God, we know also that the Creator of the world, as a Lawgiver, feels for us according to our nature. He has commanded us to eat the things that will be convenient for our souls and has forbidden us to eat meats that would be to the contrary."⁸⁸ The author who lived in Egypt thus apologized to the Hellenistic world for abstaining from certain foods. The Jews had to obey the command of God, because these were given to them for their own benefit.

---

⁸⁵ Git. 57b אף היא עלתה לגג ונפלה ומתה, יצתה ב"ק ואמרה אם הבנים שמחה.
⁸⁶ לאחר ימים נשתטית אותו האשה ונפלה מן הגג ומתה לקיים מה שנאמר אומללה יולדת השבעה.
⁸⁷ ... ויאמר ותפרוש כפיה השמימה ותפרוש. על פניהם עמדה והאשה השביעי גם ומת. ויהי כדברה שלמה נפשה ותצא רוחה, ותפל על בניה ותלך עמהם. According to the Talmud, the mother committed suicide. The rabbis considered suicide a crime against God, and, therefore, according to them whoever committed suicide would not share a portion in the Future World. However, the rabbis were most lenient to those who committed suicide in order to escape the torture of their persecutors. Eusebius extolled these victims as martyrs. (*Ecc. Hist.* VIII) However, Augustine condemned such practice, unless instituted by special revelation. (*De Cevitate Dei*, 1.16–25.)
⁸⁸ 5.25–26.

The author also introduced the idea of *faith*,[89] with a distinctly religious significance. It is well known that Christianity is based on *faith*, while Judaism is a *nomocracy*, the rule of the law. Although the author stressed the observance of the law, he added another doctrine, that of *faith*. Of the mother of the martyrs, he says that she "willingly surrendered death through faith in God."[90] In another passage, he has her speak the following words, "And ye, also having the same faith unto God."[91] Again he says of her that she gave "an example of nobleness of faith."[92]

Dr. Torrey says: "It is quite plain, however, that the Fourth Maccabees represents no particular school; nor does its author appear as an advocate of any 'system' made up from Greek and Jewish elements; his philosophy is merely a part of his general culture."[93] We must disagree with Dr. Torrey that the author represents no particular school. We also cannot accept the assumption of the scholars that he was an orthodox Jew.[94] Palestinian Jewry dominated by the rabbis, emphatically rejected the idea of atonement, the doctrine that a persons by his death can redeem the sins committed by others and they also rejected the view of faith as a religious doctrine. The Jews of the Diaspora, particularly of Egypt, on one hand were influenced by the teachings of the Apocalyptists of the *Pharisaic* sect, and on the other hand, by the Hellenistic philosophy. The Fourth Maccabees represent a synthesis of the views of these two schools. The author was not an

---

[89] πίστεως, *fides*.
[90] 15.21, ἁπάσας ἡ γενναία μήτηρ ἐξέλυσε δια τὴρ πρὸς θεὸν πίστιν.
[91] 16.22, καὶ ὑμεῖς οὖν τὴν οὑτὴν πίστιν πρὸς τὸν θεόν.
[92] 17.2, καὶ δείξασα τὴν τῆς πίστεως.
[93] P. 104.
[94] Comp. Introduction to the Fourth Book of Maccabees, Ed. Charles.

orthodox Jew; he did not represent the theology of the rabbis.

As we mentioned before, the title Fourth Maccabees originated in the Church. The actual title was *On the Supreme Power of Reason*.[95] According to the author, the passions were implanted in man by God, but were to be controlled by reason. Reason the author says, "is not extirpator of the passions, but their antagonist.[96] He illustrates this idea by showing that the passions were controlled by reason by all the Jewish patriarchs, Jacob, Joseph, Moses, David.

The book was composed some time in the first decades of the first century C. E. or even a few years previously.[97] The author was a senior contemporary of Philo. The Fourth Maccabees was written before Philo composed his works. One may say that the influence of the book manifests itself in Philo's works. In any event it had an extensive influence on the ideas of Christianity and also on some tendencies of Judaism, particularly mysticism.

Fourth Maccabees vividly portrays the family life of the Jews of the time.[98] It also describes the methods of education in vogue in Egypt. The author states that the father taught his children the Pentateuch and the Prophets, (which had already been canonized) and recited the stories of the Patriarchs particularly the tale of Isaac, who

[95] περὶ αὐτοκράτορος λογισμοῦ.
[96] 3.5. οὐ γὰρ ἐκριζωτὴς τῶν παθῶν ὁ λογισμός ἐστιν, ἀλλ' ἀνταγωνιστής.
[97] In the Fourth Book of Maccabees, the term "Jews" is never found, only the term "Hebrew." In the Second Book of Maccabees, it is said that the mother spoke to her youngest son in the "vernacular language." πατρίῳ φωνῇ. But, in the Fourth Book, it is said that she spoke to him in the "Hebrew tongue." Ἑβραΐδι φωνῇ. The term "Jew" does not appear in the Fourth Book of Maccabees, but, when the author speaks about the Jewish religion, he calls it *Judaism*, Ἰουδϊσμον.
[98] 18.6–9.

had been offered as a burnt-offering and the account of Joseph in prison. He also informs us that the Psalms of David were chanted by the father before his children.[99]

The Fourth (Second) Ezra And Apocalypse (Second) Baruch

The Fourth Ezra and the Second Baruch are the two latest books of Apocryphal literature. They were both composed in the first part of the second century C. E. after the destruction of the Second Temple. Scholars differ as to which book preceded the other. Schürer and Wellhausen were of the opinion that the Second Baruch was the earlier, while Renan, Dillmann, and Gunkel[100] are of the opposite opinion. Dr. Torrey places the Fourth Ezra first, holding that Baruch was a later composition.

Torrey gives a summary of the Fourth Ezra. He correctly points out that the present Fourth Ezra is the work of different authors. He is of the opinion that "the approximate date of the Apocalypse was originally provided by the Eagle Vision,"[101] and places the date in the time of the Emperor Domitian, i. e. at the end of the first century C. E. The reference to the death of the Eagle, where it is said that he "shall die upon his bed and yet with pain," is according to Dr. Torrey to Nero's suicide.[102] Box is of the opinion, however, that the words may refer to Trajan's death.[103] Thus, he would put the Vision of the Eagle towards the end of the second decade of the second century C. E.

[99] *Ibid.* 10-19. ὃς ἐδίδασκεν ... τὸν νομον καὶ τοὺς προφήτας ... τῶν ὑμνογράφον ἐμελῴδει ὑμῖν Δαυϊδ λέγοντα.
[100] Comp. Introduction to Fourth Ezra, ed. Charles.
[101] P. 119.
[102] P. 121.
[103] *Ezra-Apocalypse, General Introduction.*

It seems to me that Dr. Torrey and the other scholars have missed the entire purpose of the author or authors of the book. We learn from Josephus that after the temple was burned in the year 70 C. E., the members of the Fourth Philosophy, the Sicarii (the nationalists) and the Apocalyptists fled to Egypt and to the cities around Cyrene where they began to agitate against the rule of the Romans and for the establishment of the Kingdom of God.[104] The Jewish leaders of Alexandria, who feared for their own welfare, delivered many of them over to the Romans.[105] Josephus further tells us that the Sicarii and the Apocalyptists who succeeded in escaping to these countries, nevertheless continued to spread their revolutionary ideas that only God was the Lord and that they appealed to the Jews to revolt against their oppressors. A man named Jonathan of Cyrene assembled around him many Jews of the poorer class and led them forth into the desert promising them a display of signs and the appearance of supernatural power.[106] The Book of Fourth Ezra is one of the remnants of the propaganda of these Jewish fanatics.

It is well known that the Sicarii and the Apocalyptists were responsible in a great measure for the war against the Romans and the catastrophes which befell the Jews in the year 70 C. E. The Sicarii resorted to terror to promulgate their ideas, and the Apocalyptists propounded the view that God would send a Messiah, who would save the Jews from pagan oppressors and establish the Kingdom of

---

[104] B. J. VII, 10, 1, τοῖς γὰρ ἐκ τῆς στάσεως τῶν σικαρίων ἐκεῖ διαφυγεῖν δυνηθεῖσιν οὐκ ἀπέχρη τὸ σῴζεσθαι πόλιν δὲ καινοτέροις ἐνεχείρουν πράγμασιά καὶ πολλοὺς τῶν ὑποδεξαμένων ἔπειθον τῆς ἐλευθερίας ἀντιποιεῖσθαι καὶ Ῥωμαίους μὲν μηδὲν κρείττους αὐτῶν ὑπολαμβάνειν θεόν δὲ μόνον ἡγεῖσθαι δεσπότην.
[105] Ibid.
[106] Ibid. II, 1.

God.[107] Disregarding the great calamity which befell the Jews, the Sicarii and the Apocalyptists did not abandon their ideas; these found expression in the so-called Fourth Ezra. Ezra, supposedly the author of this book, sought to solve the problem as to why the Jews were suffering and to determine when the end of their suffering would come. "And why" asked the author "have they who have denied Thy promises been allowed to tread under foot those that have believed Thy covenants? If thou did so much hate Thy people, they ought to have been punished with Thine own hands."[108] "And now, oh Lord, behold these nations which are reputed as nothing, lord over us and crush us, for we Thy people whom Thou hast called Thy first born, Thy beloved, are given up unto their hands. If the world has indeed been created for our sakes, why do we not enter into the possession of our world? How long shall this endure?[109] The answer is given by the Vision of the Eagle, that Rome shall be destroyed, that the Jewish oppressors shall suffer and that the Messiah "shall reprove them for their ungodliness, rebuke them for their unrighteousness

---

[107] *Ibid.* 11, 13, 3-4. "Besides these there arose another body of villains, with purer hands but more impious intentions, who no less than the assassins ruined the peace of the city. Deceivers and impostors, under the pretense of divine inspiration fostering revolutionary changes, they persuaded the multitude to act like madmen, and led them out into the desert under the belief that God would there give them tokens of deliverance." . . . πλάνοι γὰρ ἄνθρωποι καὶ ἀπατεῶνες προσχήματι θειασμοῦ νεωτερισμοὺς καὶ μεταβολὰς πραγματευόμενοι δαιμονᾶν τὸ πλῆθος ἔπειθον καὶ προῆγον εἰς τὴν ἐρημίαν ὡς ἐκεῖ τοῦ θεοῦ δείξοντος αὐτοῖς σημεῖα ἐλευθερίας.

[108] 5.29-30. *et conculcaverunt eum qui contradicebant sponsionibus tuis quique tuis testamentis non credebant. et si odiens odisti populum tuum, tuis manibus debet castigari.*

[109] 6.57-9. *et nunc, Domine, ecce istae gentes, quae in nihilum deputatae sunt, coeperunt dominari nostri et devorare nos. nos autem populus tuus, quem vocasti primogenitum, unigenitum, aemulatorem carissimum, traditi sumus in manibus eorum: et si propter nos creatum est saeculum, quare non haereditatem possidemus cum saeculo? usquequo haec?*

reproach them to their faces with their treacheries. For at the first he shall set them alive for judgment; and when he had rebuked them, he shall destroy them."[110]

In the Vision of the Man from the Sea, the author states that it was revealed to him, that the Man, *Vir*,[111] whom the Most High called His son and had kept for many ages would appear. "He shall stand upon the Summit of Mount Sion ... My son shall reprove the nations that are come for their ungodliness ... shall reproach them to their face with their evil thoughts and with the tortures with which they are destined to be tortured — which are compared unto a flame; and then shall he destroy them without hard labor (by the Law) ... He shall destroy the multitude of the nations (*gentes*) that are gathered together, He shall defend the people that remain. And then shall he show them very many wonders."[111a]

It is significant that the author does not mention that the Messiah, the Man, will establish a Jewish state, rebuild the Temple and reinstate the sacrifices. The theology of this book is based on pure theocracy — God himself will rule the world. True, he speaks about rebuilding the city of Sion, but this is not an earthly sign, but heavenly.[112] Thus, it would seem that the author or authors of the Fourth Ezra were of the Apocalyptic school, which indeed,

---

[110] 13.29–38.

[111] *Et tunc revelabitur filius meus, quem vidisti ut virum ascendentem.* (32)

[111a] *Ibid.* 37–38. *ipse autem filius meus arguet quae advenerunt gentes impietates eorum, has quae tempestati adpropiaverunt, et improperabit coram eis mala cogitamenta eorum et cruciamenta quibus incipient cruciari, quae assimilatae sunt flammae, et perdet eos sine labore per legem quae igni assimilata est.* Comp. Box, *op. cit. ad. loc.*

[112] Comp. ch. 8.52. Box rightly said that the author refers to a Heavenly Jerusalem and a Heavenly Zion. Compare his "Additional Note On the Heavenly City," p. 198.

was not interested in the establishment of a Jewish state, but in the lordship of God over the universe.

The book was not composed in Palestine, but in the Diaspora, — in Egypt or most likely in Cyrene during the reign of Trajan. The Vision of the Eagle, which refers to one of the Roman Emperors and says that he "shall die upon his bed, and yet with pain," refers to the Emperor Nerva. The Roman historian, Dio, says that the Domitian would have slain Nerva, too, along with his other victims, but one of his astrologers told him that Nerva would die within a few days.[113] This saved Nerva from the sword of Domitian. When Nerva became Emperor he was held by the Romans in contempt because of his old age.[114] The soldiers under the command of Casperius Aelieenus revolted against him in the second year of his reign.[115]

Thus, in establishing the theology, the date and the place of the composition of this book, we may shed light upon a very important, but most obscure period in Jewish history. According to the Roman historian, Dio, a revolt of great magnitude under the leadership of a certain Andreas, broke out in the region of Cyrene. The revolt spread to different cities, Alexandria and to other localities in the region of

---

[113] *Epitome* of Book 67.
[114] *Ibid.* 68.
[115] *Ibid.* Dio also relates that Calpurnius Crassus had formed a plot with some others against Nerva. Many plots were formed against the emperor, who was held in contempt because of his age. Nerva, thus, was forced to surrender some of his friends, Petronius and Parthenius, to his great sorrow. See E. Cary, *Dio's Roman History*. The Loeb Classical Library.
According to Box, this passage "one of them shall die upon his bed and yet with pain. But as for the two who remain the sword shall devour them" refers to the death of Trajan and Lusius Quietus, who were executed by Hadrian. It seems to me that the one who shall die upon his bed refers to Nerva and the two who shall be destroyed by the sword are Petronius and Parthenius.

Cyrene, with great rapidity.[116] The Jews gave vent to their anger not on men alone, but avenged themselves on the gods as well, by destroying their images as well as the temples. According to the same historian, 220,000 persons were killed.[117]

The Christian historian Eusebius, also tells us of the great revolt and of the plundering of the land of Cyrene by the Jews. He says that they were under the leadership of a certain Lucuas.[118] From the descriptions of the two historians, it is clear that the revolt was in Cyrene and in Egypt and not in Palestine. It was not instigated against the Romans for the purpose of establishing a Jewish state in Palestine, but against the pagans in general, the Greeks and the Romans.[119] According to Eusebius, the Jews were incited by some terrible and infectious spirit and the entire hatred was concentrated against their fellow citizens, the Greeks.[120] Thus, the revolt was a Messianic movement, not to establish a political state, but to establish the Kingdom of God.

According to Dio, the leader of this revolt was a certain Andreas. According to Eusebius, his name was Lucuas. Some scholars believe that the leader had two different names. In truth, neither Andreas nor Lucuas was his proper name. In Fourth Ezra, it is related that the *Man, Vir*, whom the Most High had kept for many years would

---

[116] *Epitome* 68. Καὶ ἐν τούτῳ οἱ κατὰ Κυρήνην Ἰουδαῖοι Ἀνδρέαν τινὰ προστησάμενοι σφῶν τούς τε Ῥωμαίους καὶ τοὺς Ἕλληνας ἔφθειρον.

[117] *Ibid.*

[118] *Ecc. Hist.* IV, ἡγουμένου αὐτῶν Λουκούα.

[119] From an inscription from Cyrene, we learn of the devastation of a temple of Apollo. See V. Tcherikover, *The Jews In Egypt In The Hellenistic-Roman Age In The Light Of The Papyri.* Ch. 6.

[120] *Ecc. Hist.* IV, ἔν τε γὰρ Ἀλεξανδρείᾳ καὶ τῇ λοιπῇ Αἰγύπτῳ καὶ προσέτι κατὰ Κυρήνην ὥσπερ ὑπὸ πνεύματος δεινοῦ τινος καὶ στασιώδους ἀναρριπισθέντες ὥρμηντο πρὸς τοὺς συνοίκους Ἕλληνας στασιάζειν.

appear and destroy all the nations which had oppressed his people.[121] He is called *Vir*. The original Greek would have been ἀνδρεῖος, Andreas. Thus, according to the author, the Messiah was called man, ἀνδρεῖος. When the revolt broke out, the pagans considered the head of the revolt one called Andreas, "man" and it is thus recorded by the pagan historian, Dio. The Christian historian, Eusebius, however, states that the revolt was led by a certain Lucuas. Lucuas, in Greek literature, has the meaning not only of wolf, but also of "destroyer" and "devourer," an opprobious epithet signifying crulety. The Talmud also relates that the pagans called the altar Lucuas because it devoured the animals which were brought as sacrifices to God.[122] Either the pagans nicknamed the leader of the Jews, Lucuas, for his cruelties or, later the Christians who called Jesus "Man" or "Son of Man" called the leader of this revolt, not *man*, but used the term, Lucuas, destroyer.

This revolt which brought great misfortune upon the Jewish people was fomented by the teachings of the Jewish fanatics, the Apocalyptists. These were the forerunners of Judeo-Christians, who still insisted upon observing the laws.

Dr. Torrey correctly assumes that the Apocalypse of Baruch is a later compilation than the Fourth Ezra. The Book of Baruch was composed during the time of Hadrian, while as we stated before, the Fourth Ezra was composed in the time of Trajan. We cannot however, agree with

---

[121] Comp. ch. 13. *Et dixi ego: Dominator Domine, hoc mihi ostende, propter quod vidi virum ascendentem de corde maris. et dixit mihi: sicut non potest hoc vel scrutinare, vel scire quis, quid sit in profundo maris, sic non poterit quisque super terram videre filium meum, vel eos qui cum eo sunt, nisi in tempore diei.* Comp. also ch. 12.

[122] Suc. 56b. תנו רבנן מעשה במרים בת בילגה שהמירה את דתה... כשנכנסו יוונים להיכל היתה מבעטת בסנדלה על גבי מזבח ואמרה לוקס, לוקס עד מתי אתה מכלה ממונם של ישראל. See also Tosefta *ibid*. Yer. *ibid*.

Dr. Torrey when he says that "the Apocalypse of Baruch does, in fact, look like an enlarged and (in intention) improved edition of the 'Second Esdra's' Apocalypse."[123]

These two books present different philosophic views of the Messiah and two different attitudes toward the Jewish people. According to the Fourth Ezra, the Messiah will herald the Kingdom of God,[124] while, according to Baruch, the Messiah will establish a Jewish state in Palestine.[125] Herein lies the main difference between these two books. According to Fourth Ezra, the Jews are the chosen people. With the arriving of the Messiah, idol worship will be destroyed. The Kingdom of God will be proclaimed and all the people will join the Israelites.[126] According to the Book of Baruch however, the Messiah will only establish a Jewish state and the nations who oppressed the Jews will be destroyed, but the nations who did not oppress them, will be spared.[127] According to Baruch, the Temple will be restored and the sacrifices will be reestablished,[128] while the Fourth Book of Ezra does not mention the restoration of the Temple. The Fourth Ezra was composed before the revolt of the Jews against the pagans in Cyrene and in Egypt. The Book of Baruch was written in Palestine

---

[123] P. 124.

[124] Comp. ch. 6.25–28; 7.33–34.

[125] 44; 68.5-6. "And, at that time, after a little interval, Zion will again be builded and its offerings will again be restored, and the priests will return to their ministry, and also the Gentiles will come to glorify it." *et illo tempore post modicum iterum aedificabitur Sion, et constituentur iterum oblationes eius, et sacerdotes revertentur ad ministerium suum, et iterum venient gentes ut glorificent eam; veruntamen non plene sicut in initio: sed erit post haec, erit ruina gentium multarum. hae sunt aquae lucidae, quas vidisti.*

[126] Comp. 9.7–8.

[127] 72.4–6. *omnis populus qui non noscit israel, neque conculcavit semen Iacob, ipse est qui vivet; et hoc, quia subiicientur ex omnibus gentibus populo tuo. omnes illi autem qui dominati sunt vobis, aut noverunt vos, isti omnes in gladium tradentur.*

[128] See above note 125.

before the revolt of Bar-Kokba, and these two revolts of the Jews which brought much suffering and catastrophe were influenced by these two types of propaganda literature.

It is of great significance that in the Apocalypse of Baruch the name of God is not mentioned, but the terms *Dominus*, Κύριος, Lord, *Dominator.Domine* (Oh Lord, my Lord),[129] and Almighty, *Altissimum*, are employed.[130] The name *Fortis* δύναμις "Power" also appears as the name of God.[131] The term, "Power" as the name for God appears in only these two books of the entire Judeo-Hellenistic literature. The term, "Power," in this sense, is also mentioned in the Synoptic Gospels.[132] In the tannaitic literature, the term גבורה "Power"[133] is one of the attributes of God.

There are very important differences concerning sin and evil in these two books.[134] However, due to the lack of space, I shall not discuss them now. Nor shall I deal with the important books, Enoch, the Testament of the Twelve Patriarchs, the Psalms of Solomon and the Assumption of Moses.[135]

In this article, I have demonstrated on the one hand the importance of the Apocryphal literature for an understanding of Judaism and early Christianity. On the other hand, I have pointed out the lack of understanding

---

[129] δεσποτα κυριε.

[130] In the Fourth Ezra, the name of God is only mentioned in chapter VII.

[131] 46, 54, and passim.

[132] Ὁ δὲ Ἰησοῦς εἶπεν Ἐγώ εἰμι καὶ ὄψεσθε τὸν υἱὸν τοῦ ἀνθρώπου Καθήμενον ἐκ δεξιῶν τῆς δυνάμεως. (Mark 14.62; Mat. 26.64; Luke 22.69.)

[133] אנכי ולא יהיה לך מפי הגבורה שמענו.

[134] There are two excellent translations and commentaries on these two books, by Box, *The Ezra-Apocalypse* and Oesterley, *II Esdras*. An article on Baruch, which has great merit, was published in the Jewish Encyclopedia by L. Ginzberg.

[135] I shall deal at length in the near future with these two books as well as with the rest of the Apocryphal books.

among the students of the Apocryphal literature. Even Professor Torrey, a most renowned Semitic scholar, a man of great erudition and originality of thought, has not fully penetrated the veil of mystery behind the Apocryphal literature. He points out many mistakes in the translation of the Apocryphal books. He calls them the "traditional nonsense."[136] He blames them on the translators, who were not well versed in the Semitic language in which these books were written. However, there are many more mistakes in the translations than Dr. Torrey has mentioned, and they are not only due to the fact that the translators were not well versed in the Semitic languages, but rather due to the fact that the translators did not fully comprehend the historical background of the Apocryphal writings.

There is indeed a crying need for a proper translation and a scholarly introduction to these Jewish books which had been thrown aside in time of emergency by the Jews, but which should now be reclaimed by them.

---

[136] P. VI.

JEWISH APOCRYPHAL LITERATURE

The word ἀπόκρυφα apocrypha means "hidden, secret, something mysterious." It is found a number of times in the LXX.[1] It occurs once in Maccabees I, 1.23;[2] and also several times in Ben Sirah,[3] having the meaning "secret". It is found in the Gospels, e.g., according to Mark 4.22; Luke 8.17, and in Colossians 2.3, where the meaning is "hidden."

The early Church Fathers applied the word apocrypha to those books which they considered false, spurious, and heretical. Tertullian says, "But why need we care since these philosophers have also made their attacks upon those writings which are condemned by us under the title of apocryphal, certain as we are that nothing ought to be received which does not agree with the true system of prophecy."[4] In a similar vein St. Augustine says... "We reject.... the apocryphal books which are so called, not because of any mysterious regard paid to them but because they are mysterious in their origin, and, in the absence of clear evidence, have only some obscure presumption to rest upon."[5] This was their attitude to some books called apocryphal.

---

[1] Deut. 27.15; Is. 4.6; Ps. 17.12; 27.5.
[2] ἀποκρύφους
[3] 14.21; 23.19; 39.3.
[4] *De Anima*, 2, *Quid autem si philosophi etiam illa incursaverunt quae penes nos apocryphorum confessione damnantur certos nihil recipiendum quod non conspiret germanae et ipso iam aevo pronatae propheticae paraturae.*
[5] See *Contra Fastum Manichaean*, 11,2. ...*Apocryphi non quod habendi sunt in aliqua auctoritate secreta sed quia nulla testificationis luce declarati de nescio quo secreto nescio quorum presumtione prolati*

Reprinted from the *Jewish Quarterly Review*, New Series, Vol. 40, 1950.

It seems that Origen employed the term apocrypha also in the sense of spurious and in general for books which are not in the Hebrew Canon and for works considered unreliable by the authorities. In his letter to Africanus he maintains that the story of Susanna is not spurious and, although not found in the Hebrew Book of Daniel, it is used in every Church of Christ.[6] He further says that the story that the Prophet Isaiah was sawn asunder is found in an apocryphal work and is sustained by tradition.[7]

The books now commonly known as apocrypha, however, were greatly esteemed and considered to be of divine inspiration. Clement of Rome called Judith "the blessed".[8] The Apostolic Fathers and the later Church Fathers cited the now commonly known apocryphal books with the introductory words "it was written"[9] just as they did the "Holy Scriptures." Clement of Alexandria frequently refers to the book of Tobit as one in which "it was written."[10] Barnabas, in quoting a passage from Enoch, states that it is one in which "the Scripture says"[11] and as for the Fourth Ezra he calls the author, a prophet.[12]

Athanasius (fourth century) divided the various books into three categories: 1—Books that were canonized and

---

sunt. Comp. also *De Civ. Dei*, 15,23. *Omittamus igitur earum scripturarum fabulas quae apocryphae nuncupantur eo quod earum occulta origo non claruit partibus a quibus usque ad nos auctoritas veracium scripturarum certissima et notissima successione pervenit. In his autem apocryphis etsi invenitur aliqua veritas tamen propter multa falsa nulla est canonica auctoritas.*

[6] ἐωσάνναν γραφῇ ... ὡς λανθάνοντὸς με τοῦ μέρους ... ἐν πάσῃ ἐκκλησίᾳ χριστοῦ παρα δὲ ἑβραίοις μὴ κειμένων.

[7] σαφὲς δ'ὅτι αἱ παραδόσεις λέγουσι πεπρῖσθαι 'Ησαΐαν τον προφήτην καὶ ἐν τινι ἀποκρύφῳ.

[8] 'Ιουδὶθ ἡ μακαρία, 1.55.

[9] γραφή.

[10] Storm. 2.23.

[11] 4. περὶ οὗ γέγραπται; 16, λέγει γὰρ ἡ γραφή.

[12] 12.

considered holy; 2—Books that do not belong to the canon but should be read in the churches for their high ideals or for instruction; 3—Apocrypha—spurious books for which authority was claimed because of their religious and historical contents and titles.[13] Rufinus (fourth century) similarly divided the books into three categories—canonical, ecclesiastical and apocryphal.[14] The books commonly known as apocryphal were included in the ecclesiastical section. Since the term ecclesiastical was applied to these books they were so named by Rufinus.

Cyril of Jerusalem (315 – 386) maintained that there are only twenty-two books in the Hebrew canon and rejected the rest as apocryphal.[15] His junior contemporary Jerome also enumerates only twenty-two books in the Hebrew canon and adds, *Quidquid extra hos est inter apocrypha ponendum*.[16] Thus Jerome used the word apocrypha in a wider meaning. The books which Rufinus classified as ecclesiastical Jerome termed apocryphal. Jerome actually was the first to name these books apocrypha. He was more exact than Cyril of Jerusalem. At the Council of Hippo (393) and again at the Council of Carthage (397) the books which Jerome held were apocrypha were canonized. Since Augustine was present at the Council of Carthage, it is undoubtedly due to his great influence that these books were canonized. The authority that Augustine wielded in this very important matter is remarkable. In the Codex Amiatinus (about 541) of Jerome's own Vulgate the apocryphal books are included together with the Hebrew canon against the opinion of Jerome himself.

Jerome's definition of Apocrypha was not lost, however.

[13] Βιβλία κανονιζόμενα, Ἀναγιγνωσκόμενα, Ἀπόκρυφα,
[14] *Canonici . . . . . . ecclesiastici . . . . caeteras vero scripturas apocryphas nominarunt quas in ecclesiis legi voluerunt.*
[15] *Catech.* 4.33.
[16] *Prologus Galeatus.*

The reformers of Germany and England in the sixteenth century adopted his definition and his opinion. In Luther's complete edition of the German Bible, 1534, Judith, Wisdom, Tobias, Sirah, and I Maccabees, additions to Esther and Daniel and the Prayer of Manasseh were classified under the title of Apocrypha, i.e., books which are not holy but useful and to be read. In the English Bible of 1539 these books were also collected under the title of Apocrypha.

In the Council of Trent, the Old Testament canon was reaffirmed as adopted in Carthage. In April 1546 it was declared, "If any one does not receive these entire books, with all their parts, as they are accustomed to be read in the Catholic Church and are found in the ancient edition of the Latin Vulgate, as sacred and canonical, let him be anathema."[17]

Thus there was a division between the churches. According to the Protestant Bible the following books are considered apocryphal and in the King James Bible of 1611 the following order is given: 1 — First Esdras; 2 — Second Esdras; 3 — Tobit; 4 — Judith; 5 — Additions to the Book of Esther; 6 — The Wisdom of Solomon; 7 — Ecclesiasticus; 8 — Baruch, the Epistle of Jeremiah; 9 — The Additions to Daniel; The Song of the Three Holy Children; Susanna; Bel and the Dragon; 10 — The Prayer of Manasseh; 11 — I Maccabees; 12 — II Maccabees.

In the Vulgate and its official English translation (Douay) these apocryphal books are incorporated in the Old Testament and are regarded as holy and of divine inspiration. Tobit is placed after Nehemiah and is followed by Judith and Esther with Additions. The Book of Wisdom (Solomon) is placed after Song of Songs and is followed by Eccle-

---

[17] *Si quis autem libros ipsos integros cum omnibus suis partibus prout in ecclesia catholica egi consuererunt et in veteri vulgata Latina editione habentur pro sacris et canonicis non susceperit . . . anathema esto.*

siasticus. Baruch and the Epistle of Jeremiah came after Lamentations. The story of Susanna and Bel and the Dragon are appended to the book of Daniel. Maccabees I and II are placed at the end of the Old Testament canon.

The division between the Catholics and the Protestants on the place of the apocryphal books in the Holy Scriptures, may be easily explained. The Catholic Church became acquainted with the Holy Scriptures through the LXX, the Greek translation of the Hebrew text, which was considered holy and divinely inspired, for Justin Martyr said the translation itself was made through divine power.[18] The apocryphal books which were translated into Greek were incorporated together with other books of the Holy Scriptures and thus the Catholics accepted the entire *Septuagint* as one holy unit. We also must bear in mind that the early Church Fathers, as was remarked before, quoted from these books as from the Holy Scriptures.

The leaders of the Reformation in Germany and in England, who were very much influenced by Hebrew studies, followed the Hebrew canon. They rejected those books which were not included in it. They supported Jerome who rejected these books, calling them apocrypha. The name was adopted by the reformers and is in vogue in our own time.

Thus, according to the Catholic Church, there are two branches of this literature — the Old Testament, which includes the commonly known apocrypha literature, and the pseudepigrapha. According to the Protestant Churches this literature is divided into three sections (following Rufinus): The Hebrew Canon, the apocrypha, in the sense used by Jerome, and the pseudepigrapha.

To understand the place of the apocrypha in the syna-

---

[18] *Justin's Hortatory Address to the Greeks*, 13. Comp. also St. Augustine *De Civ. Dei*, 18, 43.

gogue, or rather the value of these books for the history of Judaism, I shall make a few observations regarding the history of the Hebrew Canon.

The Hebrew Bible is divided into three sections תורה Laws, נביאים Prophets, כתובים Hagiographa — Scriptures, The first section, the Pentateuch, was canonized at the time of Ezra. The second section, the Prophets, was canonized in the early Hellenistic period. Ben Sirah, in enumerating the number of the Prophets, mentioned the twelve minor Prophets as being contained in one book,[19] which would indicate that the prophetic books were canonized. From Ben Sirah we may infer that the Hagiographa was not yet canonized. In giving the list of the Prophets he does not mention any of the books of the Scriptures by name. Some of them had already been composed and Ben Sirah made use of them but they were not yet canonized. Josephus, in his book *Against Apion*,[20] states that the Jews have twenty-two books. To this he adds that five are the Books of Moses, i.e., Pentateuch, thirteen books he classified as prophetic, while the remaining four, he says, contain hymns to God and precepts for the conduct of human life.[21] According to a Baraita the Hebrew Canon consists of twenty-four books: the Five Books of Moses and Eight Prophetic Books and Eleven Books of the Scriptures.[22] There is not only a discrepancy in the number of books of the Hebrew Canon but also in the number of Prophetic Books. I shall presently explain the reason for this. But one thing is certain that at the time Josephus wrote his book *Against Apion* 93–94 C. E. there had already been three sections of the Hebrew Canon.

[19] 49.10.
[20] 1.8.
[21] ὕμνους εἰς τὸν θεὸν καὶ τοῖς ἀνθρώποις ὑποθήκας τοῦ βίου περιέχουσιν.
[22] B. B. 14b.

In my essay *An Historical Study of the Canonization of the Hebrew Scriptures* I maintained that the third section of the Hebrew Scriptures was canonized a few years before the destruction of the Temple, namely, in the year 65 C. E. The books canonized at that time were the Psalms, Proverbs, Job, Daniel, Ezra, Nehemiah, Ruth and Lamentations.[23] There were differences of opinion with regard to the Song of Songs and Ecclesiastes. After a controversy between the Shammaites and the Hillelites the Song of Songs was finally canonized, while Ecclesiastes was rejected.[24] The Hebrew canon of that time consisted of twenty-two books, which is in accordance with the statement made by Josephus. The question of the canonization of Ecclesiastes was brought up again at the Academy of Jamnia. According to some Shammaites the question of the canonicity of the Song of Songs was also brought up at this conclave.[25] This, however, was denied by Rabbi Akiba, who stated that the question of canonicity was only with regard to Ecclesiastes,[26] and at this assembly the Hillelites gained the majority and Ecclesiastes became a holy book, part of the Hebrew Canon.[26a] At a later time at the Assembly of Usha the Book of Esther was added to the Hebrew Canon,[27] thus making the final number of the Hebrew Canon twenty-four books.

These twenty-four books were considered inspired and holy. The rabbinic term for them was 'they defile the

---

[23] Pp. 9–12.
[24] *Ibid.*
[25] Comp. Mishna Yad. 3.5; Tal. Meg. 7a, ר׳ יהודה (מאיר) אומר שיר השירים מטמא את הידים וקהלת מחלוקת ר׳ יוסי אומר קהלת אינו מטמא את הידים ושיר השירים מחלוקת. ר׳ שמעון אומר קהלת מקולי ב״ש ומחומרי בית הלל.
[26] אמר ר׳ עקיבא חס ושלום לא נחלק אדם מישראל על שיר השירים שלא תטמא את הידים שאין כל העולם כדאי כיום שניתן בו שיר השירים לישראל שכל הכתובים קדש ושיר השירים קדש קדשים ואם נחלקו לא נחלקו אלא על קהלת.
[26a] אמר ר׳ שמעון בן עזאי מקובל אני מפי ע״ב זקן ביום שהשיבו את ר׳ אב״ע בישיבה ששיר השירים וקהלת מטמאים את הידים.
[27] See S. Zeitlin, *op. cit.*, p. 12.

hands,'[27a] while those books which were excluded from the Canon were called ספרים חצונים, 'outside books.' The theory that the word *ganaz*, mentioned in the Talmud, refers to the books which were rejected, and thus had to be hidden, is erroneous. On the contrary, the word *ganaz* in the Talmud applies to books or any other precious things which must be stored away either because of their sacredness and great value and which must not be used because of their state of decay or for some other reason.[28] This term is also applied to precious objects, to be stored away because of the possibility of their destruction.[28a]

It was pointed out that at the Assembly held in 65 C. E. the word *ganaz* was used in connection with the Book of Ezekiel,[29] meaning that they wanted to remove this book from the Canon, hide it, i.e., to declare it an apocryphal book. Those who maintain this theory are in error. First — at no assembly was it ever debated what books should be excluded from the Canon but the question was what books should be included. Second — no assembly had the authority to remove the Book of Ezekiel from the Canon. It had been canonized and considered holy for centuries. Third — as we have pointed out — the word *ganaz* never had the connotation of the meaning declaring a book apocryphal.

The phrase בקשו לגנוז is to be interpreted to mean that the sages wanted to store away the Book of Ezekiel from the public reading and not to be interpreted in the academies since some expressions were contradictory to some

---

[27a] כתבי הקדש מטמאים את הידים.
[28] Comp. B. B. 11a, אבותי גנזו למטה ואני גנזתי למעלה; Pes. 119a, משנגנז תשמישי קדושה נגנזין; Meg. 26, הארון גנזו עמו צנצנת המן and passim.
[28a] Meg. 26b, ספר תורה שבלה גונזין אותו אצל ת"ח מטפחת ספרים שבלו עושין אותן תכריכין למת מצוה וזו היא גניזתן.
[29] Shab. 13b, ברם זכור אותו האיש לטוב [אלעזר בן חנינה בן] חזקיה שמו שאלמלא הוא נגנז ספר יחזקאל.

pentateuchal passages.[30] The meaning of the sentence בקשו לגנוז ספר יחזקאל, to withdraw from study and public reading is corroborated by a passage in the Talmud Hagiga. A story is related that a lad in his school was reading (studying) the Book of Ezekiel and was absorbed in the *Hasmal* when a fire came forth from the Hasmal and consumed him. Therefore they (the sages) sought to withdraw the Book of Ezekiel.[31] Hananiah ben Hezekiah [Joshua ben Gamala][32] said to them, "If he (the lad) was wise, are then all wise?"[33] So Joshua ben Gamala, who was responsible for the institution of the public schools in Judaea,[34] saved the book from being withdrawn from the elementary schools. Similarly the sages with their interpretation of the contradictory passages in Ezekiel saved it from being withdrawn from the academies.

At the conclave held in the year 65 C. E. and at the conclave of Jamnia at the end of the first century there were many controversies as to which books were of divine inspiration and hence to be included in the Canon and which were written by wise men and thus to be excluded. We know that there were great disputes over the Book of Ecclesiastes at both conclaves. (According to some sources the inclusion of the Song of Songs in the Canon was strongly disputed.) There must have been opposition to other books of which we have no historical records. On the other hand there must have been many in favor of the inclusion of a number of the books in the Canon which are now commonly called apocrypha, particularly those books which bore such

[30] וכל נבלה וטרפה שהיו דבריו סותרין דברי תורה; comp. also Men. 45a, מן העוף... לא יאכלו הכהנים הוא... הא ישראל אכלי.

[31] ת"ש מעשה בתינוק אחד שהיה קורא בבית רבו בספר יחזקאל והיה מבין בחשמל ויצאה אש מחשמל ושרפתו ובקשו לגנוז ספר יחזקאל.

[32] אמר להם חנינה בן חזקיה, the original reading was יהושע בן גמלא, see S. Zeitlin, *op. cit.*, p. 7.

[33] אם זה חכם הכל חכמים.

[34] See B. B. 21a.

titles as Enoch, Ezra, Wisdom of Solomon, Baruch, etc. The author of the Epistle of Barnabas, who lived in the time of Rabbi Akiba called the Book of the Fourth Ezra a prophetic book, and refers to Enoch as a part of the Holy Scriptures.[35] In the year 65 C. E. the Apocalyptists were still an influential sect among the Jews, and the Judaeo-Christians were still a part of the Jewish people, and they considered the Book of Enoch and similar ones as prophetic books. Thus the rabbis had to be on their guard to define clearly which were Holy Scriptures and which were not. The books which were canonized were called כתבי הקודש Holy Writ, and those books which had religious pretensions but were excluded were called 'outside books'. Since some of the 'outside books' were considered inspired and prophetic by the Judaeo-Christians and the Apocalyptists, the rabbis banned these books and decreed that those who read them would be excluded from sharing a portion in the future world. Only those books which had religious pretensions were under this ban but secular books which had no pretensions to inspiration were not banned. The books of Homer were not banned[36] but a book like Ben Sirah was under the ban[37] because it was a book of wisdom similar to the Book of Proverbs. The Book of Ben Sirah was excluded on the principle that it was written after prophecy had ceased in Israel. Haggai, Zecharia and Malachi were the last prophets.[38]

In due time, when Hebrew Canon had been well estab-

---

[35] See above p. 224.
[36] Comp. M. Yad. 4,5. אומרים צדוקים קובלין אנו עליכם פרושים שאתם; Yer. אומרים כתבי הקדש מטמאין את הידים ספרי הומירס אינן מטמאין את הידים San. 28a, אבל ספרי המירוס... הקורא בהן כקורא באגרת.
[37] אלו שאין להם חלק לעולם הבא... ר' עקיבא אומר אף הקורא בספרים החיצונים כגון ספרי בן סירא.
[38] Tos. Yad. 2. ספרי בן סירא וכל ספרים שנכתבו מכאן ואילך אינן מטמאין את הידים. The phrase מכאן ואילך has the meaning from the time when prophecy ceased in Israel.

lished and there was no longer any fear of introducing other books into the Canon, the ban automatically disappeared and therefore we find that the rabbis in the Talmud and the Midrash quote passages from Ben Sirah.[39] In quoting Ben Sirah they used the term כתיב 'it is written'[40] just as when they quoted the Holy Scriptures. A Babylonian Amora of the fourth century, named R. Joseph, declared that one was not allowed to read the Book of Ben Sirah.[41] Undoubtedly he based his prohibition on the words of Rabbi Akiba. When his pupil Abbaye asked the reason for this he could not give an explanation.[42] Finally, however, he declared that the better passages in the Book of Ben Sirah may be read and interpreted like the verse of the Holy Scriptures.[43] Not only was Ben Sirah read and interpreted but, according to the testimony of the Apostolic Constitution, the Book of Baruch together with the Lamentations was also read in the Synagogues on the Fast Day of Ab.[44]

The reason that the books nominally known as the Apocrypha, called by the Talmud 'outside books' were excluded from the Canon was that they revealed the time of their composition, like the Book of Ben Sirah and the Book of the Hasmonean (I Maccabees). They were written after prophecy had ceased in Israel, and therefore could not be inspired.

Some books were not included because they were written in a foreign language, Greek, and outside Judaea, like II Maccabees, so-called III Maccabees, so-called IV Maccabees, and the Letter of Aristeas and similar books.

[39] Hag. 13a; Yeb. 63b; Nida 16b.
[40] כדכתוב בספר בן סירא; כתוב בספר בן סירא.
[41] Tan. 100b. רב יוסף אמר בספר בן סירא נמי אסור למקרי.
[42] א'ל אביי מאי טעמא אליטי משום דכתיב... באורייתא נמי כתיב...
[43] אמר רב יוסף מילי מעליותא דאית בה דרשינן.
[44] Καὶ γὰρ καὶ νῦν δεκάτῃ τοῦ μηνὸς γορπιαίου συναθροιζόμενοι τοὺς θρήνους Ἱερεμίου· ἀναγινώσκουσιν ... καὶ τὸν Βαροὺχ.

Other books were excluded because they were the products of dissenters and in opposition to normative Judaism. They were written by the Apocalyptists and were considered inspired by the early Christians.

Some books while written in the spirit of normative Judaism were excluded from the Canon because of passages that were in contradiction to the established halaka. We refer to the books like Tobit, Susanna and Judith. From the contents of the Book of Tobit we see that it was written by a very pious Jew who stressed the observance of the Jewish Law. The author's thesis was that God may test a man as He had tested Abraham and Job, that God may even give the power to Asmodeus (Satan) to test the man as he tested Job, but that finally He will reward the righteous man. The book relates a story similar to that in the Book of Job but it was not canonized. We may postulate that there was a controversy as to the canonization of the Book of Job. Apparently it was accepted because of Job's popularity;[45] in fact, he was considered a prophet who lived during the time of Moses. This belief was held by some of the rabbis of the Talmud[46] as well as by Origen.[47]

The author of the Book of Tobit relates that when Raguel gave his daughter in marriage to Tobias he wrote an instrument of cohabitation, i. e., a writ כתובה[48] in giving away his daughter. This is the old halaka which says that a woman may be acquired as a wife by a writ.[49] This law, however, was later amended. Instead of the writ which had to be written by the father of the bride a *ketuba* was intro-

---

[45] Comp. B. B. 14b–16a. משה כתב ספרו ופרשת בלעם ואיוב. See also *Contra Celsum*, 6.43, ἐν τῷ ἀρχαιοτέρῳ καὶ Μωυσέως αὐτοῦ Ἰωβ.
[46] See B. B. *ibid*.
[47] *Op. cit.*
[48] συγγραφὴν βιβλίου συνοικήσεως, 7. 14.
[49] Kid. I.1. האשה נקנת בשלשה דברים . . . בכסף בשטר ובביאה.

duced which was to be written by the groom.[50] The Talmud ascribed this amendment to Simon ben Shetach.[51] Thus in the year 65 C. E., during the time of the conclave, the halaka was that the groom was supposed to write a *ketuba*, while according to the Book of Tobit the father wrote the writ. Thus it contradicted the halaka. If there were contradictions in the prophetic books the sages tried to reconcile them but they could not canonize a book which was in contradiction to the halaka. That is why a book like Tobit was classified as an 'outside book.'

Similarly the Book of Susanna was written by a pious Jew in accordance with normative Judaism. The doctrine of the book is that a man should rather prefer death to sinning against God, and that he finally will be rewarded if he trusts in God. On the other hand sinners and hypocrites will meet with just punishment. The author, in giving the story of Susanna, relates that when she was accused of adultery by the two elders, Daniel, in cross-examining them, asked them the name of the tree under which the act of adultery was committed. As they each named a different tree Susanna was not only acquitted but the elders were put to death. This is the biblical law: "Then shall ye do unto him as he had thought to have done unto his brother."[52] According to the halaka which was promulgated by the Pharisees, if the witnesses do not agree and contradict one other, as in the case of the trial of Susanna, the defendant cannot be convicted but the witnesses cannot be punished.[53] Only if an *alibi* was shown by two other persons that those witnesses who testified against the defendant were with them at a distant place at the time that

---

[50] S. Zeitlin, "The Origin of the Ketuba," *JQR*, 1933, pp. 1–7.
[51] Shab. 14b; Ket. 82b; Tos. Ket. 12,1.
[52] Deut. 19.19.
[53] See Mishna San. 5.1, בזמן שמכחישין זא״ז עדותן בטילה.

the crime was supposedly committed, the testifying witnesses were called זוממים *false* and were put to death. Hence the story of the trial, as given in the Book of Susanna, is in contradiction to the adopted halaka and that was a good reason for its exclusion from the Canon.[54]

Origen gives the reason why the story of Susanna is not included in the Hebrew Canon though it is found in the Greek version appended to the Book of Daniel and used in the Churches.[55] He says it is due to the fact that the Jews purposely removed from their books passages containing scandals against elders, rulers, and judges.[56] In a like manner the story that Isaiah was sawn asunder is not found in the Hebrew books.[57] It is strange that Origen, who had Jewish teachers and was learned in Hebrew did not understand the Jewish spirit. The Jews never hid any scandals con-

---

[54] Some scholars believe that the Book of Susanna was composed in Babylonia, basing this on the fact that the plot of the story was laid in Babylonia. This is erroneous. That this book was written in Judaea is substantiated by internal evidence. Since the youth (Daniel) addresses one of the men who accused Susanna, "O, seed of Sidon (Canaan) and not of Judah" it is apparent that the book was written in Palestine and not in Babylonia, since he contrasts Sidon (Canaan) with Judah. Had this book been written in Babylonia he would not have made a comparison with Phoenicia but would have named a wicked city like Ninevah or Babylon. Furthermore the first six verses of the Book of Susanna, where Babylonia is mentioned, are not found in the earliest translation of the Septuagint but are given only in Theodotion's version. It is probable that the first six verses were prefixed to the book because of the ill feeling of the Palestinian Jews toward the Babylonian Jews, thus making Babylonia the locale of the story and demonstrating the corruption of the rulers of Babylonian Jewry. The ill feeling of the Palestinian Jews toward their brethren in Babylonia, which existed shortly after the destruction of the Second Temple, is demonstrated in the Talmud. Comp. Men. 100a, תניא נמי הכי ר' יוסי אומר לא בבליים הם אלא אלכסנדריים הם ומתוך ששונאים את בבליים קורין אותן על שם בבליים. The Theodotian version is based on the later revised story of the Book of Susanna.

[55] *Ad Africanum*, 2.
[56] Ibid. 9.
[57] Ibid.

nected with their leaders but openly reproached them. That King Manasseh killed the prophet Isaiah is mentioned in the Talmud.[58] It is most probable that the sages drew from the apocryphal book for the story of the martyrdom of Isaiah.

The story in the book of Judith is very similar to that in the book of Esther. In both books a woman saved the Jewish people from annihilation by their enemies. Some believe that the Book of Judith is even superior and that Judith was a greater heroine than Esther. The question is why such a book was not included in the Hebrew Canon. To answer this we must remember that the Book of Esther was not included in the Canon until a very late period, as the sages had been opposed to its inclusion in the Canon. Only through pressure of public opinion was this book finally included, as the Book of Esther had been read for centuries on the festival of Purim.[59] Thus the people put pressure upon the rabbis to include the Book of Esther in the Hebrew Canon and it finally became a part of the Canon at the conclave of Usha after the year 140 C. E. There was no such public pressure on the rabbis for the inclusion of the Book of Judith in the Canon.

There is another reason why the Book of Judith was not included in the Canon. The author relates that after Judith brought the head of Holofernes into the city, Achior, an Ammonite, was circumcised "and was joined unto the house of Israel."[60] According to the Pentateuch an Ammonite can never join the community of God. [61] During the Second Commonwealth this law was amended to refer only to the

---

[58] Comp. San. 103b. משנת ר' אלעזר בן יעקב קב ;שהרג ישעיה; Yeb. 49b, ונקי וכתוב בה מנשה הרג את ישעיה.

[59] Meg. 7a, אסתר ברוח הקודש נאמרה ... נאמרה לקרות ולא נאמרה לכתוב.

[60] 14.10, καὶ προσετέθη πρὸς τὸν οἶκον Ἰσραήλ.

[61] Deut. 22.4.

male line and not to the female line;[62] an Ammonite woman could accept Judaism and be received into the Jewish community. Some of the sages maintained that even a male Ammonite may become a Jew and be a member of the Jewish community[63] but this view was opposed by some of the rabbis.[64] It is related that Achior was circumcised but not baptized.[65] In the early halaka baptism was not required; however, after the year 65 C. E. baptism became a *sine qua non* for anyone accepting Judaism.[66] This was sufficient reason for not including the Book of Judith in the Hebrew Canon as it was not in agreement with the accepted halaka.

In the course of time, however, Judith the heroine became connected with the Hasmoneans. Rabbi Samuel, the grandson of Rashi, said that as the miracle connected with Purim was brought about through Esther, so the miracle with respect to Hanukkah came about through Judith.[67] There is even a likelihood that in some parts of the Diaspora the Jews read the Book of Judith in the synagogues during the days of Hanukka.

Origen, in his epistle to Africanus, wrote that the books of Tobit and Judith were not even found in the Hebrew Apocrypha.[68] As was previously stated he used the term Apocrypha in the sense of spurious and false. Indeed in his time the Jews had no Index, not only against books like Tobit, Judith and Ben Sirah but even not against the so-

---

[62] Comp. Yeb. 76b, עמוני ולא עמונית.
[63] Comp. Yad. 4. Tos. *ibid.* 2.17. בו ביום בא יהודה גר עמוני... מה אני לבא בקהל... א"ל ר' יהושע מותר אתה... כבר עלה סנחריב מלך אשור ובלבל את כל האומות... והתירוהו לבא בקהל.
[64] *Ibid.* עמוני ומואבי אסורים ואיסורין; Yer. Yeb. 8, א"ל ר' גמליאל אסור אתה איסור עולם.
[65] 14.10, καὶ περιετέμετο τὴν σάρκα τῆς ἀκροβυστίας αὐτοῦ.
[66] See S. Zeitlin, "L'origine de L'institution du Baptême pour les proselytes", *REJ*, 1934.
[67] Comp. Tosefot Meg. 4a שאף הן היו באותו הנס פירש רשב"ם שעיקר הנס היה על ידן, בפורים ע"י אסתר בחנכה ע"י יהודית.
[68] *Ad Africanus*, 12.

called ספרים חצונים 'outside books.' The Hebrew Canon was established and there was no fear of the inclusion of other books. Christianity became a separate definite religion and there was no threat to Judaism from Judaeo-Christians. (Incidentally at that time the Judaeo-Christians had already been disseminated by their fellows, the pagan Christians.) The ban against books such as Tobit, Judith, Ben Sirah and orher 'outside books' was automatically annulled. Hence Origen is quite right when he says that the books of Tobit and Judith are not found in the Hebrew Apocrypha; they were not considered spurious. It is true that the synagogues never recognized these 'outside books' as holy but the Jews read them as ecclesiastical writings.

The apocalyptical books were not canonized because they were not in the spirit of normative Judaism. The Pharisees fought the Apocalyptists and considered some of them false prophets.[69] Normative Judaism maintained that prophecies ceased in Israel at the time of the Persian period and that there have been no prophets since then. In general the entire philosophy of the books was antagonistic to normative Judaism. The precepts of the Torah were not their main principles. The Apocalyptists laid more stress on ethics and faith.

The only apocalyptical book which became a part of the Hebrew Cannon is the Book of Daniel. The last six chapters of this book, which deals with apocalyptic revelations, were added to the original book of Daniel, the author of which was supposed to live in the Persian period when prophecy was not yet closed. The visions of Daniel were interpreted as prophesying the events of Alexander the Macedonian, the Seleucids, the Ptolemies, and particularly the profanation of the altar by Antiochus Epiphanes

[69] Comp. S. Zeitlin, "The Assumption of Moses and the Revolt of Bar Kokba," *JQR*, 1947.

and the rededication of the Temple by the Hasmoneans.[70] Daniel's prophecies were fulfilled and hence the rabbis in 65 C. E. had no apprehension of including the Book of Daniel in the Canon. For them it was history but they did not want to include any book which dealt with revelations of things to come.

Josephus in his book *Antiquities*, written at the close of the first century C. E. interprets some of Daniel's visions referring to the Romans as foretelling the capture of Jerusalem and the destruction of the Temple by them.[71] The book of Daniel became the most speculative book in the history of Judaism and Christianity. The rabbis of the Middle Ages assumed that many of Daniel's revelations allude to the date of the coming of the Messiah,[72] while Christianity from the early days of Hippolitus[73] and Julius Africanus[74] interpreted some of the apocalyptical passages as alluding to Jesus and to the days of the anti-Christ.

Some books, like the Fourth Ezra and the Apocalypse (second) of Baruch, were not canonized, not only because they were apocalyptic books but because they were composed after the close of the Canon. The Fourth Ezra was composed in the Diaspora in the first quarter of the Second Century during the revolt against Trajan,[75] while the Apocalypse of Baruch was composed during the time of Hadrian.[76] The Assumption of Moses was composed at an even later period. Fortunately the date of its composition can be deduced from the book itself, and that is 140 C. E.[77]

---

[70] Comp. also *Seder Olam*, 30. והצפור השעיר מלך יון... ועמד מלך גבור הוא אלכסנדרוס מקדן שמלך י"ב שנה.

[71] 10.11, 7 (276).

[72] Comp. The Commentaries of Saadia Gaon and Rashi *ad loc.*

[73] See his Commentary on Daniel.

[74] The extant writings.

[75] S. Zeitlin, "The Apocrypha," *JQR*, 1947.

[76] *Idem, ibid.*

[77] *Idem.*, *JQR*, pp. 34–37.

The Book of Jubilees is not of the apocalyptic school. It is a book of laws and gives the history of the Hebrews from the Creation to the time of the Exodus. It was composed in the pre-Hellenistic period and was rejected when the Pentateuch was canonized. In my essay on the Book of Jubilees[78] I demonstrated that this book was written by men of a school which opposed the Pentateuch on the ground that the Pentateuch was not revealed by God. They maintained that the book commonly known as the Book of Jubilees was revealed by God. Most likely the original name of the Book of Jubilees was תורת משה the Laws of Moses. Therefore there could no longer be any question of its canonization in the conclave of 65 C. E. or at the meeting in Jamnia since it had already been rejected.

The apocryphal literature may be divided into two sections. First — those books written in the spirit of normative Judaism but which were for some reason not canonized, either because it was known that they were composed after prophecy had ceased in Israel or that some of the passages contained therein contradicted the established halaka. Second — books that were composed by the apocalyptists, which were in opposition to normative Judaism. Normative Judaism regarded the Apocalyptists as destructive. Both sections were classified by the Tannaiam as 'outside books' and the ban applied to the reading of this entire literature. However, in due time, as was before remarked, not only was the ban annulled but the books which belonged to the first section, like Ben Sirah, were cited in the Talmud and the Midrash in the same terms as applied to the Holy Scriptures.

I Maccabees, which we have good reason to believe had the original title ספר בית חשמונאים, The Book of the House of

---

[78] *The Book of Jubilees, Its Character and its Significance*, Philadelphia, 1939.

the Hasmoneans, was used by the sages throughout the ages. The term Hasmoneans, which is frequently mentioned in talmudic and midrashic literature, became known from this title.[79] As noted before, the Book of Judith was read in the synagogues and the heroine became associated with Hanukkah. Some midrashic literature of the Middle Ages betrays the influence of the Book of Judith. This type of literature became a part of Jewish ecclesiastical books and the apocalyptic literature was venerated. The Book of Enoch is often mentioned in the Zohar and midrashic literature. There is a Midrash Noah which is a product of apocalyptic literature.[80] Some of the testimony of the Twelve Patriarchs was re-translated into Hebrew and became a part of midrashic literature, like the Hebrew Testament of Naphtali[81] and also מדרש ויסעו. These stories became so popular among the Jews that they were incorporated in the well known booklet ספר הישר.

The influence of the apocalyptic literature on Judaism is notable. The entire conception of angelology— the power and the activity of the angels, is traceable to the book of Enoch.

---

[79] I Maccabees is a compilation of two parts of different books. Chapters 1–13 were written by a contemporary early in the reign of John Hyrcanus and re-edited after the destruction of the Temple. Chapters 14–16 are part of another book. These two portions were combined into one book during the first decade after the destruction of the Temple. The original title of the book was ספר בית חשמונאים the *Book of the Hasmoneans*. The title Maccabees originated with the Church Fathers. The word Maccabees is never mentioned in the Talmud but Hasmoneans. Comp. the author's *Introduction to I Maccabees*, ed. Dropsie College, 1950, pp. 48–9.

The author of *Halakot Gedolot* said that the elders of the School of Shammai and Hillel wrote (edited) *Megillat Bet Hasmonai*, זקני בית שמאי ובית הלל כתבו מגלת בית חשמונאי the author adds ועד עכשיו לא עלה לדורות which means that this book was not canonized. The term לדורות sometimes has the meaning of canonization. Comp. Meg. 7a שלחה להם אסתר לחכמים קבעוני לדורות.

[80] See A. Jellinek, *Bet ha-Midrash*, vol. 3.

[81] R. H. Charles, *The Greek Versions of the Testaments of the Twelve Patriarchs*, Oxford, 1908.

The idea of the two Messiahs, the son of Joseph and the son of David, mentioned in the Talmud,[82] is actually derived fron the Book of the Fourth Ezra.[83] The legend of the Ten Martyrs and the reading of the Midrash describing the martyrdom of the Ten Scholars on the Day of Atonement is due to the influence of the Book of Jubilees and the Testimony of the Twelve Patriarchs.[84] The theology based on the future world—גן עדן, Paradise, גיהנום, Hades, as portrayed in the apocalyptic literature, left a great mark on Judaism.

The belief that the Messiah will reveal himself in the year 4231 A.M. (471 C.E.), which is stated in a Baraita in the Talmud of Abodah Zarah,[85] is based on the apocalyptic book The Assumption of Moses. From the Talmud it is evident that not only the book was used but the date of the Messiah is based on this apocalyptic book.[86]

Furthermore the whole conception of the Messiah as supernatural was not in the spirit of normative Judaism during the Second Commonwealth. The Jews believed in a Redeemer who would be sent to them by God, similar to David. The idea of a supernatural Messiah arose through the influence of apocalyptic literature.

The history of Jewish mysticism, including Cabbala and Hasidism, is a part of the chain of development of apocalyptical literature showing the antagonism of the apocalyptists toward normative Judaism and Rabbinism.

In short, the books originally called ספרים חצונים 'outside

---

[82] Suk. 52a.

[83] Comp. C. C. Torrey, "The Messiah son of Ephraim", *JBL*, 1947, pp. 253–77.

[84] S. Zeitlin, "The Legend of the Ten Martyrs and its Apocalyptic Origins", *JQR*, 1945.

[85] 9a, במתניתא תנא (אחר) ארבעת אלפים ומאתים ושלשים ואחת שנה לבריאת עולם אם יאמר לך אדם קח לך שדה שוה אלף דינרים בדינר אחד אל תקח.

[86] S. Zeitlin, *JQR*, 1947, p. 36.

books' became venerated, ecclesiastical books. Therefore we shall apply the term apocrypha in the sense of ecclesiastical books to this literature; it is Jewish Apocrypha Literature, as differentiated from the canonized books called Holy Scriptures.

To say that the apocalyptic literature influenced Christianity would not convey the full purport of this literature. Apocalypticism was the forerunner of Christianity. Without knowledge of this literature it would be impossible to have a full comprehension of primitive Christianity. The idea of Messiah, Christ, is actually based on the apocalyptic literature. Original sin, atonement, ransom, martyrdom and even the conception of non-resistance, as is found in the Sermon on the Mount, have their origin in this literature. It would not be an exaggeration to say that the apocalyptists had more influence on Christianity than the Hebrew Bible. It is true that the Church Fathers, in proving the truth of Christianity, always referred to the Hebrew Bible. This is not because the apocalyptic literature was not considered the main source of Christianity, but because in order to combat the Jews they had to prove that Jesus was the true Messiah from those books which were sacred to the Jews.

Since the apocryphal books which were originally rejected by the Jews and were venerated by the Christians the Church preserved them, and it is due to the Church that this product of Jewish genius has been preserved for posterity.

These apocalyptic books have come to us in Greek translations. The original Aramaic and Hebrew writings were lost. Many passages of the Bible were wrongly rendered into Greek as the translators misconstrued many words, particularly when these words had synonyms. This is well known to every student of the Bible. However, these mistranslations have been noted since we have had the original Hebrew with which to make comparisons. Unfortunately, however, the original text of the Apocrypha is lost and we have nothing with which to compare it. To give a few examples: In the Book of Jubilees the reading is, "For this reason it is ordained and written in the heavenly tablets that they should celebrate the Feast of Weeks in this month once a year to renew the covenant every year."[87] In this book the Festival of Weeks is placed in the middle of the third month, i. e., in the middle of the month of Sivan. According to the Pharisees the Festival of Weeks, Pentecost, is celebrated on the fiftieth day after the first day of Passover. Scholars therefore advanced a theory that the Book of Jubilees is a Sadduceean work.[88] In reality however the original text had the word שבועות the Festival of Oaths, the festival in commemoration of the oaths which God made with Noah and Abraham. The Greek translator mistranslated the word שבועות oaths to שבועות weeks. The original reading is borne out by the text itself.[89] The mistranslation of the Greek misled modern scholars who misconstrued the Book of Jubilees in its entirety.

Two other examples of mistranslation of Hebrew words by the Greek translator may be cited from the book — The Assumption of Moses. In Chapter Eleven the Latin has (what is a translation of the Greek version) *dominum verbi* of which Charles remarked, "I cannot suggest the origin of this phrase."[90] The original Hebrew text undoubtedly had דבר "leader,"[91] which the translator misread and translated

[87] 6.17.
[88] R. Leszynsky, *Die Sadducaer*, 1912, pp. 179–236; G. H. Box, *Introduction to the Book of Jubilees*.
[89] S. Zeitlin, *The Book of Jubilees*, pp. 6–7.
[90] *Ad loc.*
[91] Comp. San. 8a א״ל משה ליהושע אתה והזקנים שבדור... אמר לו הקב״ה טול מקל והך על קדקדם דבר אחד לדור ואין שני דברין לדור.

"word." In Chapter Four the Latin is *devenient*. Modern scholars have found it very difficult to explain this word.⁹² However it is simple. The Hebrew had ירדו "They shall rule." The Greek translator read it ירדו and translated "They will descend."

I shall quote two other examples in which the Greek misunderstood the Hebrew. In I Maccabees the Greek reading is δύο καὶ τριάκοντα "thirty-two men were on the elephant."⁹³ Scholars have observed that even for an Indian elephant thirty-two men would be too many and have suggested an emendation.⁹⁴ However the Hebrew text had שני שלשים "two officers," which the Greek translator misread שני ושלשים thirty-two.

In Chapter 9.15 the Greek has ‘Αζώτου ὄρους "Mount of Azotus," which does not make sense. The city of Ashdod was in the plain. Abel amends the text to read ‘Αζωρου ορους⁹⁵ which is also incorrect as no such place as "Mount of Azorus" is known. Oesterley says, "The text is clearly corrupt,"⁹⁶ and he is right. The Hebrew text had אשדת הפסגה "the slope of the mountain" while the Greek translator misunderstood the word אשדות to mean "the city Ashdod." These are but a few examples of which there are many hundreds of misreadings by the Greek translator.

Only with a great deal of painstaking research and knowledge of Semitics and particularly of the spirit of Judaism of that period can these errors be discerned. Merely to detect the errors is not sufficient to establish the original text. Since these books were used in the Church many interpolations were included and some of them are of con-

---

⁹² *Devenient* cannot refer to a going up to Jerusalem .... which is an easy corruption of ירבו (Charles).
⁹³ 6.37.
⁹⁴ Rahlfs emended the text to read four τεσσαρες.
⁹⁵ *RB*, pp. 1924, pp. 385–7; comp. also C. Torrey, *JBL*, 1934, p. 34.
⁹⁶ P. 97.

siderable proportions. On the other hand many scholars assume that where the word Christ is found it must have been interpolated by the Christians.[97] However this is not always the case as the word Messiah, Christ, was used by the Apocalyptists. The so-called Christological passages, which some scholars believe to have been added by the Christians, actually came from the hands of the Apocalyptists.

We can fully understand why the Christian scholars have contributed so much to our knowledge of apocryphal literature while Jewish scholars neglected it. It is true that some Jewish scholars wrote historical treatises on different books of the Apocrypha but there is not a scientific edition of the apocryphal literature among Jews.[98] The Jews neglected the genius of their own people. While it is true that the Christian scholars in their studies of apocryphal literature contributed greatly to the cause of scholarship, they did not penetrate deeply into the spirit of Judaism of that period. Goethe has well said that to understand the poetry of the poet one must go to his land.

It is fortunate that Dropsie College has undertaken to edit the Jewish apocrypha, which in a time of emergency had been considered 'outside books' but later became a part of the great Jewish literature and made a deep impression on the development of Judaism.

The author of II Maccabees relates that Judah Maccabee collected the "books about the Kings and the Prophets and the Books of David." This undoubtedly refers to those books which Ezra did not canonize and which were considered 'outside books'. Judah preserved them for posterity and later they became the Holy Scriptures. Dropsie College

---

[97] Comp. Charles, *op. cit.* V.2. pp. 291–2.
[98] A. Kahana in his editing הספרים החצונים was the first attempt of a scientific edition of the Jewish Apocryphal Literature.

in collecting and editing the Jewish Apocryphal Literature is following the example of Judah Maccabee. It seeks to disclose to the modern world the great literature, the fruit of the Jewish genius, which fed and sustained modern religious thought.

APPENDIX

Jewish Apocryphal Literature is to be divided into the following sections: Halakic books dealing with the law; Historic books; Legends and stories based on historical plots; Books of Wisdom; Prayers and Hymns; Midrash; Apocalyptical books dealing with prophecies and visions.

A. Halakic

1. The Book of Jubilees or The Laws of Moses

B. History

2. First Ezra
3. First Maccabees or The Book of the Hasmoneans
4. Second Maccabees or Maccabees

C. Legends and Stories

5. Judith
6. Tobit
7. Third Maccabees or On Providence
8. Fourth Maccabees or The Supreme Power of Reason
9. The Additions to Daniel
10. Susanna
11. The Story of the Three Guardsmen
12. Bel and the Dragon

13. The Rest of the Book of Esther
14. Baruch
15. The Epistle of Jeremiah
16. The Letter of Aristeas

D. Books of Wisdom

17. The Wisdom of Sirah
18. The Wisdom of Solomon

E. Prayers and Hymns

19. Prayers of Azariah and the Hymn of the Three Men
20. Prayers of Manasses
21. Psalms of Solomon

F. Midrash

22. The Books of Adam and Eve
23. The Lives of the Prophets
24. The Testament of Job
25. The Martyrdom Isaiah
26. Pseudo Philo

G. Apocalyptical Books

27. Enoch
28. The Testament of the Twelve Patriarchs
29. II Enoch or The Book of the Secrets of Enoch
30. II Baruch or The Apocalypse of Baruch the son of Neriah
31. IV (II) Ezra or The Apocalypse of Ezra
32. III Baruch or The Apocalypse of Baruch
33. The Assumption of Moses

H. Miscellaneous

In this category are books of which only fragments are extant in the writings of the Church Fathers, also books which are not primarily Jewish. Following are some of the titles of books which may be included in the Jewish Apocryphal Literature:

34. Ezekiel the Tragic Poet
35. Philo the Poet
36. The Sibyllian Oracles
37. Demetrius
38. Eupolemus
39. Artapanus
40. Aristeas[99]

---

[99] To his Second Volume of *Apocrypha and Pseudepigrapha* Charles appended *Pirke Aboth, Sayings of the Fathers* and *Fragments of the Zadokite Work*. In his Introduction he explains the reason for the inclusion of the former as being the chief work on ethics in the Talmud. This may be true but certainly it is not an apocryphal book. It is no more apocryphal than the other tractates of the Mishna.

As to the *Fragments of the Zadokite Work*, Charles, in accepting Schechter's point of view (with reservations), that the work is of the pre-Christian period, included it in the Second Volume. However this work was written by a Karaite between the 9th and 11th centuries C. E. In order to combat rabbinism the author represented the book as having been written during the time of the Temple and tells of the opposition expressed against the Pharisees. But as forgerers cannot escape detection since they employ the words and terms of their time not known at the time when the books were supposedly written, the author of the *Fragments of the Zadokite Work* fell into the same trap. The inclusion of this work in apocryphal literature was a disservice to students who, believing it to be a work of the pre-Christian period, depended on Charles.

An excellent and important book on the apocrypha by Robert N. Pfeiffer entitled *History of the New Testament Times with an Introduction to the Apocrypha*, has recently been published by Harper and Brothers.

THE BOOK OF JUBILEES
ITS CHARACTER AND ITS SIGNIFICANCE

THE Book of Jubilees,[1] or, as it is sometimes called, the Little Genesis,[1a] relates the history of the Hebrews from the Creation to the Revelation of the Law by God to Moses through the medium of the Angel of the Presence. The author divides this period into Jubilees, each forty-nine years long. The date of the Revelation is given as "forty-nine Jubilees . . . and one week and two years,"[2] in the first year of the Exodus, i. e., 2410 A. M. It is well known that the original language of this book was Semitic, either Hebrew or Aramaic.[3] The book was early translated into Greek, and the Greek was further translated into Ethiopic. Only the latter version in its entirety and fragments of the Greek have survived, while the original was lost.[4]

I

AUTHORSHIP

There exists wide difference of opinion as to the authorship of this book and the date of its composition, and various hypotheses have been put forth. Some maintain that the

---

[1] οἱ Ἰωβηλαῖοι.
[1a] ἡ λεπτὴ Γένεσις.
[2] 50.4.
[3] Jerome, Ep. LXXVIII; comp. Jubilees, ed. Charles, Introduction; Hermann Rönsch, *Das Buch der Jubiläen*, Leipzig, 1874.
[4] Charles, *The Ethiopic Version of the Hebrew Book of Jubilees, edited from Four Manuscripts*, Oxford, 1895; comp. idem, *The Book of Jubilees*, Introduction, pp. 2-4, (*The Apocrypha and Pseudepigrapha*, Vol. II);

Reprinted from the *Jewish Quarterly Review*, New Series, Vol. 30, 1939.

author was a Sadducee,[5] others take him to have been a Pharisee,[6] while still others make him a member of another sect.[7] The scholars who believe the book to be of Sadducean origin base their theory upon some of the laws recorded in it, which prove to them that the book could not have been written by a Pharisee. The author upholds the *lex talionis* — an eye for an eye — which the Pharisees opposed. The Pharisees held that a man whose eye was put out should be compensated by money. The same scholars maintain further that the book could not have been written by a Pharisee, since the author in describing the Festival of Tabernacles does not mention the ceremony of pouring water on the altar, to which the Pharisees attached great importance. The Sadducees vigorously opposed this ceremony, and the author's silence on the subject proves to them his adherence to the Sadducean sect. The purely solar calendar of the Book of Jubilees precludes the possibility of Pharisaic authorship, since the Pharisees employed a solar-lunar calendar. According to the Pharisees the Festival of Weeks should be on the fiftieth day after the first day of Passover while the Book of Jubilees gives the middle of the third month, i. e., the fifteenth of Sivan, as the date of the festival.[7a]

The scholars who believe the author to have been a Pharisee also base their assumption upon some of the contents of the book. The author was a believer in immortality and in the existence of angels, both of which doctrines were de-

---

see Dillmann, *Das Buch der Jubiläen*, (Ewald's *Jahrbucher d. bibl. Wissensch.*, 1850–1); idem, *Pseudenpigraphen des A. T.* in Herzog's *R. E.*, XII. There is also extant an old Latin version. Comp. Schürer, *Geschichte*, III, p. 274 and the literature there quoted.

[5] Rudolf Leszynsky, *Die Sadduzaer*, Berlin, 1912, pp. 179–236; comp. also Box, Introduction to *The Book of Jubilees*.

[6] Charles, Introduction to *The Book of Jubilees*, p. 1 (*The Apocrypha and Pseudepigrapha*, Vol. II).

[7] See Box, op. cit.

[7a] Ibid.

nied by the Sadducees. The author believed in a Messiah of Davidic descent, while the Sadducees did not. Some of the laws recorded in the book are in agreement with tannaitic Halakah. The calendrical system employed in the Book of Jubilees cannot be Sadducean, since according to the Sadducees the Festival of Weeks should fall on the fiftieth day after the morrow of the Sabbath, while according to the Book of Jubilees it occurs on the fifteenth of Sivan.[8]

Some who sought to reconcile the divergent views of the scholars, ascribed the same motive to the author of the book, and stated that he was a sectarian who sought to bring about a compromise between the Pharisees and the Sadducees. Some maintain that the author of the book was a Hasid,[9] since the laws recorded in the book are very rigid, in the spirit of the Hasidim. Others take him to have been an Essene,[10] while still others call him a Jewish Christian.[11]

It is strange that both the scholars, who maintained that the book was of Sadducean origin because some of its laws contradict the Pharisaic law, or was of Pharisaic origin because some of the laws are in opposition to the Sadducean principles, failed to notice that some of the laws of the Book of Jubilees are also at variance with the laws of the Pentateuch. According to the Pentateuch, the Jubilee year is the fiftieth year,[12] whereas in our book it is the forty-ninth.[13] In the Pentateuch, the year of release is the seventh year,[14]

---

[8] See Charles, op. cit.
[9] See Box, op. cit., p. xxix.
[10] Jellinek, *Über der Buch der Jubiläen*, 1855.
[11] Singer, *Das Buch der Jubiläen oder die Leptogenesis*, 1898. According to Frankel, *Monatsschrift*, 1856, the author was a Jewish Hellenist. Comp. Dillmann in *ZDMG*, 1857. Beer, *Das Buch der Jubiläen*, Leipzig, 1856, ascribed the authorship of the book to a Samaritan; see Schürer, *Geschichte*, III, 274.
[12] Lev. 25.11.
[13] Passim.
[14] Lev. 25.4.

while in our book it is the fifth.[15] According to the Book of Jubilees, "God appointed the sun to be a great sign on the earth for days and for sabbaths and for months and for feasts and for years and for sabbaths of years and for jubilees and for all seasons of the years,"[16] while according to the Pentateuch both the sun and the moon serve as signs for the seasons and the years.[17]

The account of the origin of the festivals given in the Book of Jubilees differs entirely from that set forth in the Pentateuch.[18] According to Leviticus, the Festival of Tabernacles was instituted in commemoration of the tabernacles in which the Israelites dwelt during their wanderings in the desert after the Exodus.[19] The Book of Jubilees tells that the festival was instituted by Abraham in commemoration of his deliverance from his enemies and of God's promise that the children of his son, Isaac, "should be unto the Lord a people for (His) possession above all nations and that it should become a kingdom of priests and a holy nation."[20]

According to the Book of Jubilees, there were four Days of Remembrance in the year, namely, the first days of the first month, of the fourth month, of the seventh month, and of the tenth month.[21] According to the Pentateuch, there is only one Day of Remembrance, the first day of the seventh month.[22] According to the Pentateuch the Fast of Atonement is on the tenth day of the seventh month[23] and

---

[15] 7.37.
[16] 2.8.
[17] Gen. 1.14. According to the Book of Jubilees (7.30), the blood of killed animals should be covered if it is beast, cattle or fowl. According to Lev. 17.13, only the blood of beast or fowl should be covered.
[18] Except Passover when the same reason for the celebration of this festival is given.
[19] Lev. 23.43.
[20] 16.18–31.
[21] 6.23–28.
[22] Lev. 23.24.
[23] Ibid. 27–32.

no reason is given for the origin of this fast day. However, the Book of Jubilees tells us that on the tenth day of the seventh month Joseph was sold into slavery by his brethren. "For this reason it is ordained for the children of Israel that they should afflict themselves on the tenth day of the seventh month — on the day that the news which made him weep for Joseph came to Jacob his father — that they should make atonement for themselves thereon with a young goat on the tenth day of the seventh month, once a year for their sins; for they had grieved the affection of their father regarding Joseph his son. And this day hath been ordained that they should grieve thereon for their sins, and for all their transgressions and for all their errors, so that they might cleanse themselves on that day once a year."[24]

Pentecost, besides being called the Festival of First Fruits, is also referred to in the Pentateuch by the name of *Shabuot*, the Festival of Weeks.[25] It is called *Shabuot*, because it is to be celebrated seven weeks after the offering of the Omer. Seven times seven days are to be counted from the day of the offering of the Omer, and the fiftieth day is the day of the festival.[26] It was, therefore, called Pentecost by the Hellenistic Jews, while in the Pentateuch it is called *Shabuot*, the Festival of Weeks. In the Book of Jubilees, *Shabuot*, which is here also referred to as the Festival of First Fruits,[27] is in no way connected with the Omer, and nothing is said of the counting of either weeks or days. Jubilees traces the origin of *Shabuot* to the covenant that God made with Noah, never again to destroy the human race by flood, while Noah swore both for himself and his seed never to eat blood. The festival was confirmed by Abraham, when God made

---

[24] 34.18–19.
[25] Num. 28.26; Ex. 34.22.
[26] Lev. 23.15–16.
[27] 6.21, "For it is the חג השבועות and the feast of first-fruits: this feast is twofold and of a double nature."

the covenant with him which took place in the middle of the third month, i. e., on the fifteenth of Sivan.

I venture to say that even the name Shabuot in the Book of Jubilees has not the connotation of "weeks," but means "oaths," referring to the oaths of the covenants which God made with Noah and Abraham. It was stated before that this book was originally written in Hebrew, and, therefore, we may safely assume that the name of the festival was חג השבועות. The Greek translator, who had before him the Septuagint translation of the Pentateuch, where חג השבועות was correctly translated as the Festival of Weeks, ἑορτὴν ἑβδομάδων,[28] translated also Festival of Weeks, ἑορτὴν ἑβδομάδων, which is not the meaning here at all.[29] That the word שבועות in Jubilees is derived from the word שבועה oath, and not from שבוע week, is quite evident from the context. "And Noah and his sons swore that they would not eat any blood that was in any flesh, and he made a covenant before the Lord God for ever throughout all the generations of the earth in this month. On this account He spake to thee that thou shouldst make a covenant with the children of Israel in this month upon the mountain with an oath, and that thou shouldst sprinkle blood upon them because of all the words of the covenant, which the Lord made with them for ever. And this testimony is written concerning you that you should observe it continually, so that you should not eat on any day any blood of beasts or birds or cattle during all the days of the earth, and the man who eats the blood of beast or of cattle or of birds during all the days of the earth, he and his seed shall be rooted out of the land . . . He set His bow in the cloud for a sign of the eternal covenant that there should not

---

[28] Deut. 16.10; Ex. 34.22.
[29] It is well known that homonymous words are sometimes mistranslated in the Septuagint, e. g., comp. II Kings 6.5.

again be a flood on the earth to destroy it all the days of the earth. *For this reason it is ordained and written on the heavenly tablets, that they should celebrate the feast of Sh'buot[30] in this month once a year, to renew the covenant every year* ... And do thou command the children of Israel to observe this festival in all their generations for a commandment unto them: one day in the year in this month they shall celebrate the festival. For it is the feast of *Sh'buot* and the feast of first fruits: this feast is twofold and of a double nature: according to what is written and engraven concerning it, celebrate it." This quotation proves to my mind beyond all doubt that the Festival of *Shabuot* was instituted according to Jubilees, in commemoration of the covenants, and has nothing to do with the Omer, while in the Pentateuch the Festival of Shabuot is to be celebrated seven weeks after the offering of the Omer.[31] According to the Book of Jubilees, Shabuot was chronologically the first festival, and was already observed by Noah and Abraham. The Festival of Tabernacles was observed by Abraham, while Passover was instituted in commemoration of the Exodus, and was chronologically the last in the cycle of festivals. According to the Pentateuch, however, Passover was the first festival. Shabuot, being agricultural, was to be celebrated after the Jews settled in Palestine,[32] while the Festival of Tabernacles was instituted, according to the Pentateuch, in commemoration of the deliverance of the Jews from Egypt and their sojourn forty years in the desert.[33]

[30] In the English edition of Jubilees, we have the "Feast of Weeks." However, it is well known that this translation is based on the Ethiopic, which was translated from the Greek, while the Greek translator, as we pointed out, mistook the words שבועות to mean "Feast of Weeks."
[31] Lev. 23.9–17.
[32] Ibid. 40–43.
[33] According to the Book of Jubilees the Sabbath was instituted in commemoration of Creation. The same reason is given in the First Decalogue. However, in the Second Decalogue the Sabbath is associ-

Furthermore, the Ten Commandments, which according to the Pentateuch were revealed to the entire congregation of Israel on Mount Sinai, in the third month after the Exodus, are not mentioned at all in the Book of Jubilees. Some of the precepts included in the Ten Commandments had, according to the Book of Jubilees, already been given long before the Exodus, i. e., the Sabbath, which had been ordained on the seventh day of Creation, and the law of homicide, which had been given at the time of the murder of Abel by Cain.[34] While the precept of the commandment "Honor thy father and thy mother" was already set forth by Noah, so also was the precept "Love thy neighbor as thyself."[35] The first two commandments had already been given at the time of Abraham.[36]

According to the Pentateuch, after the Revelation, God summoned Moses to the mountain to receive the tablets of the Law. Moses remained on the mountain forty days and forty nights. The author of the Book of Jubilees begins his account with God's summons to Moses to come up to the mountain to receive the tablets of the Law, containing all the precepts, ordained since the days of Creation and practiced by the Patriarchs.

II

The Date of Composition

The same wide divergence of opinion that exists with regard to the author of the book exists also with regard to the date of its composition. It is placed anywhere between the

---

ated with the Exodus. It seems to me that the reason of the Exodus is not given for the origin of the Sabbath, but for the principle that the servants shall rest on that day. ויום השביעי שבת ... לא תעשה כל מלאכה אתה ובנך ובתך ועבדך ואמתך ... למען ינוח עבדך ואמתך כמוך וזכרת כי עבד היית בארץ מצרים ... על כן צוך ... לעשות את יום השבת.

[34] 4.32.
[35] 7.20.
[36] 20.8.

early Maccabean and the early Christian period, between 160 B. C. E. and 50 C. E.[37] The prevailing opinion is that the book was written some time during the reign of Simon the Maccabean, or his son, John Hyrcanus.[38] The dating of the book follows necessarily from the assumption that it must have been written either by a Pharisee, a Sadducee, or some other sectarian. Thus, the dating of the book is placed between the Maccabean and the early Christian periods.

However, the calendar employed in the Book of Jubilees bears witness to the early composition of the book. The calendar used by the author was a solar calendar of 364 days. During the Maccabean period it was already universally known that the solar year contained $365\frac{1}{4}$ days. The author's primitive conception of the calendar points conclusively to an early date.

Some students who maintain that the book was written during the time of the Maccabeans base their theory on the expression found in Jubilees 32.1, that Levi, son of Jacob, was ordained priest "of the Most High God." This title was assumed by the Maccabean priest; hence, according to them the book was written during the Maccabean period.[39] This argument is not persuasive since we know that the title "priest of the Most High God" is already found in the Pentateuch, and therefore could be used by the author of the Book of Jubilees. Some scholars argue that the omission of any mention by the author of Jubilees of the ceremony of the libation of water during the Festival of Tabernacles proves that the book was written before the rift between John Hyrcanus I and the Pharisees, circa 110/9 B. C. E.[40]

---

[37] See Box, op. cit., p. xxii.
[38] Charles, op. cit., p. 1; Box, op. cit., p. xxx.
[39] Charles, op. cit., p. 6.
[40] Idem, op. cit. Comp. also Klausner, p. 173, ב, היסטוריה הישראלית.

This argument is without foundation, as we have already pointed out in the previous pages that the author of the book was neither a Pharisee nor a Sadducee, and we shall show in the course of this paper that the book was written in a very early period, in the pre-Hellenistic time. Therefore, the silence of the author on the ceremony of the libation of water during the Festival of Tabernacles may be readily understood. Neither is the ceremony mentioned in the Pentateuch.

Some scholars maintain that chapter 23, which is essentially eschatological, refers to the Maccabean period, when the Jews were severely persecuted by Antiochus.[41] This chapter reads in part as follows: "For calamity followeth on calamity, and wound on wound, and tribulation on tribulation, and evil tidings on evil tidings, and illness on illness, and all evil judgments such as these, one with another, illness and overthrow, and snow and frost and ice, and fever, and chills, and torpor, and famine, and death, and sword, and captivity, and all kinds of calamities and pains. And all these will come on an evil generation, which transgresseth on the earth: their works are uncleanness and fornication, and pollution and abominations ... And He will wake up against them the sinners of the Gentiles, who have neither mercy nor compassion, and who will respect the person of none, neither old nor young, nor any one, for they are more wicked and strong to do evil than all the children of men. And they will use violence against Israel and transgression against Jacob, And much blood will be shed upon the earth. And there will be none to gather and none to bury." However, passages parallel to this chapter are found in the Pentateuch. Deuteronomy 28 reads, in part, as follows: "The Lord will cause thee to be smitten

[41] Charles, op. cit.; Box, op. cit.

before thine enemies; thou shalt go out one way against them, and shalt flee seven ways before them; and thou shalt be a horror unto all the kingdoms of the earth. And the carcasses shall be food unto all fowls of the air, and unto the beasts of the earth, and there shall be none to frighten them away . . . Thou shalt beget sons and daughters, but they shall not be thine; for they shall go into captivity . . . The stranger that is in the midst of thee shall mount up above thee higher and higher; and thou shalt come down lower and lower."[42] From this parallel we may, therefore, assume with assurance that Jubilees 23 has no bearing upon the Maccabean period.

Scholars who maintain that the Book of Jubilees was written during the lifetime of John Hyrcanus I adduce support for their theory from the statement in 38.14 that the sons of Edom were subject to the sons of Jacob, "until this day," meaning to the days of the author.[43] This would indicate that the book was written in the days of John Hyrcanus, who conquered and subjugated the Edomites. This is not conclusive enough proof for dating the composition of the book so late, during the lifetime of John Hyrcanus, when other internal evidence points to an earlier date. The expression "until this day" is very common in the Bible,[44] and does not necessarily refer to the time of the composition of the particular book. Furthermore, we may assume that the expression "until this day" is a gloss. This Book of Jubilees was written in Hebrew and was in some ways popular with certain groups among the Jews. When John Hyrcanus conquered the Edomites, the words "until this day" may have been added to the text.

[42] Comp. also Lev. 26.14–26; Isa. 65.20; Ezek. 20.16-39.
[43] Comp. Klausner, op. cit.
[44] Deut. 2.22; 3.14, עד היום הזה. See also Judg. 1.21, 26; 6.24; I Sam. 30.25.

Charles[45] is of the opinion that the author of Jubilees was well acquainted with the book of I Enoch. He bases his theory on the passage in Jubilees 4.17-18, which reads as follows: "And he [Enoch] was the first among men that are born on earth who learnt writing and knowledge and wisdom and who wrote down the signs of heaven according to the order of their months in a book, that men might know the seasons of the years according to the order of their separate months. And he was the first to write a testimony, and he testified to the sons of men among the generations of the earth, and recounted the weeks of the jubilees, and made known to them the days of the years, and set in order the months and recounted the Sabbaths of the years as we made (them), known to him." According to Charles, the statement in Jubilees, that Enoch was the first man to learn the wisdom of the signs of heaven and the order of the months and the seasons of the years, reveals an acquaintance on the part of the author with I Enoch, which deals with the calendar. The fact is, however, that the relation was reversed. The author of I Enoch based his book on this particular verse in Jubilees, where Enoch is described as the first man to learn the wisdom of the signs of heaven, the order of the months, and the seasons of the years. That the Book of Jubilees antedated I Enoch is quite evident. In both books angels play an important part. While in Jubilees, as in the biblical books of the pre-exilic period, they are not yet designated by proper names,[46] in I Enoch every angel bears a proper name, e. g., Gabriel, Michael, Uriel, etc. This proves that the Book of Jubilees was written at a time when Jewish theology had not yet assigned names to the angels, while I Enoch was written at a later period.

[45] Op. cit.
[46] They were called the *angels of presence* and the *angels of sanctification*. Comp. Isa. 63.9, ומלאך פניו, "The angel of His presence." See also Ex. 32.11. Comp. Isa. 6.10; Ezek. 11.

The designation of the months by numerals rather than by names shows that the Book of Jubilees could not have been written in a late period, when the months were already known by definite names, such as Nisan, Sivan, Tishri, etc. If the book had been written during the Maccabean period or later, the author could not have failed to refer to the months on which the main festivals occur by their names, viz. Nisan, Sivan, Tishri.

That the Book of Jubilees could not have been written as late as the Hellenistic period can further be demonstrated from the fact that the author connects the festival of שבועות with the covenants that God made with Noah and Abraham, contradicting thereby the Pentateuch. Such a novel idea could not have been introduced in the Hellenistic period, when not merely the festival was firmly established, but also its name, derived from the meaning ascribed to it by the Pentateuch. Josephus called the festival Pentecost, i. e., the fiftieth day after Passover,[47] as did Philo.[48] Even the Second Book of Maccabees, which was written about 125 B. C. E.,[49] calls the festival Pentecost and Feast of Weeks.[50]

Finally, the calendar employed in the Book of Jubilees shows that the book could not have been written during the Maccabean period. The author still used the primitive solar calendar which contained 364 days, while as we have already previously pointed out during the Hellenistic period it was universally known that the duration of the solar year was 365¼ days.

[47] *Ant.* 3, 10, 6, "On the fiftieth day, which the Hebrews call *Asartha*.
[48] "The festival ... its name of pentecost from the number of fifty," (πεντηκοστὸς) *de Specialibus Legibus*, 11, 179.
[49] II Macc. 12.31, 32 — ἑβδομάδων, πεντηκοστὴν.
[50] About the date of composition of the Second Book of Maccabees, see S. Zeitlin, "Hanukkah," *JQR*, XXIX, 25, 32.

Furthermore, the author protests vigorously against the change from the solar to a solar-lunar calendar, thereby disturbing the seasons and making the year shorter by ten days. As a result of this change, he complains, the Jubilee years will disappear and the profane days will be declared holy. This proves that the Book of Jubilees was written at the time when the calendar was changed from solar to solar-lunar time, and some Jews opposed this innovation. The author expresses his opposition to the change in the following words: "And command thou the children of Israel that they observe the years according to this reckoning — three hundred and sixty-four days, and (these) will constitute a complete year, and they will not disturb its time from its days and from its feasts; for everything will fall out in them according to their testimony, and they will not leave out any day nor disturb any feasts ... And all the children of Israel will forget, and will not find the path of the years, and will forget the new moons, and seasons, and sabbaths, and they will go wrong as to all the order of the years. For I know and from henceforth will I declare it unto thee, and it is not of my own devising; for the book (lieth) written before me, and on the heavenly tablets the division of days is ordained, lest they forget the feasts of the covenant and walk according to the feasts of the Gentiles after their error and after their ignorance. For there will be those who will assuredly make observations of the new moon — how (it) disturbs the seasons and comes in from year to year ten days too soon. For this reason the years will come upon them when they will disturb (the order), and make an abominable (day) the day of testimony, and an unclean day a feast day, and they will confound all the days, the holy with the unclean, and the unclean day with the holy; for they will go wrong as to the months and sabbaths and feasts and jubilees. For this reason I command and testify to thee that thou mayst testify to them; for after thy death thy children will disturb (them), so that they will not make the year three hundred and sixty-four days only, and for this reason they will go wrong as to the new moons and seasons and sabbaths and festivals, and they will eat all kinds of blood with all kinds of flesh."[51]

This quotation shows clearly that the book was written when the change of calendar was recent and still an issue among the Jews. How can we otherwise account for the author's forceful arguments against the change of calendar, if we should assume that the book was written during the Maccabean period. The calendar had already been changed centuries earlier and had long ago become a dead issue. To say that the Book of Jubilees could have been written in the first or even in the second century B. C. E. betrays a lack of comprehension of the history of that period. The lunar-solar calendar was definitely and firmly established, and writing a book at that period in support of the solar calendar is in the same category as writing a book today to prove, centuries after the issue of Sabbatai Zevi had been settled, that Sabbatai Zevi was not the true Messiah.[52]

There was never, as some maintain, any controversy between the Pharisees and Sadducees as to the calendar. There is no reference whatsoever, in all of tannaitic literature, to such a controversy. The Pharisees and Sadducees differed only in regard to the Festival of Pentecost. The Pharisees maintained that Pentecost is to be celebrated on

---

[51] 6.32–38.

[52] See S. Zeitlin, *An Historical Study of the Canonization of the Hebrew Scriptures*, 1931, pp. 22, 24. On the calendar employed in the Bible and in the early days of the Second Jewish Commonwealth, see idem, "Notes relatives au calendrier juif," *REJ*, 1930.

the fiftieth day after the offering of the Omer on the sixteenth of Nisan, regardless of the day of the week. They rendered the words ממחרת השבת to mean the morrow of the first day of the festival. The Sadducees maintained that Pentecost should be celebrated on the fiftieth day after ממחרת השבת, the morrow of the Sabbath, and it was therefore always to fall on a Sunday. The Mishna, Rosh Hashanah, which tells us that on one occasion the Boethusians (Sadducees) hired two men to bear false testimony with regard to the birth of the new moon and mislead the Rabbis in the fixation of the new month,[53] bears on the same controversy. The witnesses tried to mislead the Rabbis into fixing the first day of Nisan on a Saturday so that the fiftieth day after the Omer would fall on a Sunday, in accordance with the Sadducean view, and yet at the same time be acceptable to the Pharisees. That this story refers to a controversy between the Pharisees and Sadducees with regard to Pentecost and not the calendar is borne out by the Tosefta and the Palestinian Talmud.[54]

III

THE ORIGINAL LANGUAGE OF THE BOOK

We have already pointed out that the general opinion among scholars is that the Book of Jubilees was written in a Semitic language, most likely Hebrew. This is quite evident from the many Hebraisms found throughout the book.[55] It is well known that the Book of Jubilees differs

---

[53] R. H. 2.1, משקלקלו הביתוסים התקנו. Comp. ibid. 22b, פעם אחת בקשו ביתוסין להטעות את החכמים שכרו ביתוסין שני עדים ובא להטעות החכמים לפי שאין ביתוסין מודין שתהא עצרת (אלא) אחר השבת.

[54] Tos. R. H. 1.15. Yer. ibid. 57a, ומה קלקול הוה תמן שהיו אומרים עצרת לאחר השבת.

[55] See H. Rönsch, op. cit.; Littmann, op. cit. Charles, op. cit., p. 4, § 6.

in many readings from the masoretic text of the Pentateuch, but agrees with the Septuagint or other translations or versions of the Pentateuch. This is explained by many scholars by the fact that the translator of Jubilees made use of the Septuagint.[56] Dr. Büchler, in a very interesting article,[57] disputes the generally accepted opinion and maintains that the author of the Book of Jubilees, not the translator, used the Septuagint. According to Dr. Büchler, therefore, Jubilees was originally written in Greek and hence was not composed in Palestine. Dr. Büchler presents what appears to be on the surface a very strong case. However, after a careful examination of all his arguments, we must say that they are not persuasive and cannot disprove the view that the original language of the book was Hebrew. The proofs he adduces in support of his arguments are not conclusive. The mere mention of demons in the book proves to Dr. Büchler that it was written outside of Palestine, under Persian influence, as were, according to him, the books of Tobit, Enoch, and the Testaments, in which demons play an important part. However, in these three books the demonology is already fully developed. In Enoch, the demons are designated by name,[58] which is a late development. The angels are designated by names in all three books. In the Book of Jubilees, on the other hand, only the words *Satan* and *Mastema* are found, in the same manner as in the biblical books of the preexilic and exilic periods.[59] The angel who figures in the Book of Jubilees is called the Angel of the Presence, and and not by a proper name, as is common in Enoch and the other books. Dr. Büchler aims to prove that the author of

---

[56] See Charles, op. cit.; Box, op. cit.
[57] "Studies in the Book of Jubilees," *REJ*, 1926, pp. 253–74.
[58] Enoch 54.6; 69.4–8.
[59] Comp. Deut. 32.17, וזבחו לשדים. Zech. 3, והשטן עומד על ימנו לשטנו. I Chron. 21.1, ויעמוד שטן על ישראל.

Jubilees made use of the Septuagint, from the following passage: "the son of Mâsêq, the son of my handmaid, is the Dammasek Eliezer."[60] This passage agrees with the reading of the Septuagint but differs from the reading of the Pentateuch; the reading is ובן משק ביתי הוא דמשק אליעזר.[61] However, the agreement of the Septuagint reading with that of Jubilees is not sufficient proof that the author of Jubilees used the Septuagint. It is quite possible that two readings existed in the Pentateuch, one of which was accepted by the Septuagint and the author of Jubilees, and the other was incorporated in the masoretic text. This can be demonstrated from a passage in Gen. 26.32, where we read ויאמרו לו מצאנו מים, "we have found water." The Septuagint reads here καὶ εἶπαν οὐχ εὕρομεν ὕδωρ, "we have not found water." The reading of Jubilees agrees with the Septuagint. This does not imply that the author of Jubilees relied upon the Septuagint, but rather upon a different reading whose existence can be proven from another source. In the Midrash we read ויבאו עבדי יצחק ויאמרו. אין אנו יודעים אם מצאו או לא מצאו.[62] From this we can readily see that the Midrash had two readings and could not determine whether the servants of Isaac found water or did not find water. On the other hand, the Book of Jubilees sometimes agrees with the masoretic text of the Pentateuch where it differs with the Septuagint. In the blessing of Isaac to Jacob, we read in the masoretic text "the sons of your mother," a reading shared by the Book of Jubilees, while the Septuagint reads "the sons of your father." Another instance is Gen. 3.17, ארורה האדמה בעבורך, "cursed is the ground for thy sake," and similarly in Jubilees, while the Septuagint reads "cursed is the ground for thy work."

[60] 14.2.
[61] Gen. 15.2.
[62] Midrash Rab. to Gen. 64.

Sometimes the reading of Jubilees disagrees with both the masoretic text and the Septuagint. אם יוכל איש למנות את עפר הארץ גם זרעך ימנה, "if a man can number the dust of the earth, then shall thy seed also be numbered."[63] The Septuagint reads in the same way. The text in Jubilees, on the other hand, reads "though a man may number the dust of the earth, yet thy seed shall not be numbered." It is interesting to note that the Targum according to Onkelos, which seldom deviated from the masoretic text, also reads "thy seed shall not be numbered," אף בנך לא יתמנון. The Targum either had another reading, which agreed with that of Jubilees, or was influenced by the book. If the latter be the case, the Book of Jubilees was certainly not written in Greek, for no book, not written in the Hebrew language, could have any influence on the Targum.

According to Charles, the account given in Jubilees 12.25-6: "And the Lord God said: Open his mouth and his ears, that he may hear and speak with his mouth, with the language which hath been revealed; for it had ceased from the mouths of all the children of men from the day of the overthrow (of Babel). And I opened his mouth, and his ears and lips, and I began to speak with him in Hebrew in the tongue of the creation" proves that the book was written in Hebrew, since a work which claims to be from the hand of Moses could have been written only in Hebrew, the sacred tongue in which God created the universe. Büchler counters this with the retort that "as the author himself did not avail himself of the opportunity of stating explicitly that his book was written in Hebrew, the argument proves nothing."[64] Dr. Büchler's criticism is not convincing. Do any of the prophets ever mention that they are writing in Hebrew or is there any indication in the books of the Pen-

[63] Gen. 13.16.
[64] Büchler, ibid., p. 267.

tateuch that they were written in Hebrew? If the Book of Genesis were lost and only its Greek translation survived, Büchler might be tempted to say, on the basis of similar reasoning, that it was written in Greek. The author of Jubilees certainly did not expect his book to be lost, but rather was certain that it would be accepted as the word of God to Moses.

Dr. Büchler argues further that the Book of Jubilees could have been written only in Greek, since the author had certain ideas and facts to propound. He could achieve his purpose only by writing his book in Greek. He not only had peculiar ideas about the origin of the festivals, but he also contradicted many of the statements about the laws of the Pentateuch. Had he written in Hebrew he could not have advanced his purpose, for his readers, who were well versed in the Pentateuch, would have rejected his writings. Only by writing in Greek for Hellenistic Jews, who had only a superficial acquaintance with the Pentateuch in its Greek translation, could he hope that his ideas would be accepted.[65]

Dr. Büchler follows the general opinion that the Book of Jubilees was written by a sectarian at a late period when the authority of the Pentateuch was already firmly established, and the author desired to add to the familiar account some aggadic material. He differed also with some of the pentateuchal laws. However, as we already pointed out, Jubilees is entirely against the Pentateuch. The author not only differs in his account of the origin of the festivals,

---

[65] Pp. 273–74, "Written in Greek for readers who were only superficially acquainted with the Pentateuch from a Greek translation or a Greek remodelled presentation, it impressed its doctrines upon such without exciting contradiction, and inculcated into such minds novel details and forms of religious practices, known to them only partly from life, by means of invented stories, the method, character and trend of which were familiar to them from Jewish-Hellenistic writers."

but of their nature as well. He differs throughout with the biblical account of the revelation by stressing the fact that the Patriarchs already observed many of the commandments and precepts. He opposes strenuously the institution of a new calendar. The character of the Book of Jubilees clearly shows that this book was intended to take the place of the Pentateuch. The Pentateuch derives its authority from its being the word of God to Moses. Jubilees, therefore, also pretended to be the word of God, given to Moses. Such a book could not have been written in any language but Hebrew. Dr. Büchler is quite right that such a book, written in Hebrew, would provoke controversy and irritate the instructed reader.. This book not only irritated the reader, but also called forth great opposition and was justly suppressed. That this book was written in Hebrew is quite evident not only from the many Hebraisms[66] it contains, but also from the marked influence it had on rabbinic literature. Although the book was outside of the Canon and its reading was banned, since it was written in Hebrew it circulated among the Jews, and that part of it which did not directly contradict the Pentateuch exercised an influence upon later literature. Similar is the case of Ben Sirach, which was extra-canonical.[67] Its reading was banned, yet the book is quoted in the Talmud.[68]

IV

IMMORTALITY AND MESSIANIC HOPE

The doctrine of immortality as expressed in the Book of Jubilees is pointed to by Charles as proof of the Pharisaic authorship of the book.[69] The passage in question reads as

---
[66] Comp. Rönsch, op. cit. Charles, op. cit., p. 4.
[67] Sanh. 100b.
[68] Ibid., passim.
[69] Charles, op. cit.

follows: "And their bones will rest in the earth, And their spirits will have much joy, And they will know that it is the Lord who executeth judgment, And showeth mercy to hundreds and thousands and to all that love Him."[70] Box already pointed out that this passage would rather indicate a Sadducean[71] origin, since it does not speak of the resurrection of the body, a doctrine denied by the Sadducees. The idea of immortality as expressed in Jubilees is very vague, which reveals, to my mind, that the book was composed in pre-Hellenistic times, when the concept of immortality was not yet crystallized. In the Second Book of Maccabees, written about 125 B. C. E., the concept of immortality was already well defined.[72]

Those who ascribe this book to a Pharisee adduce support from Isaac's blessing of Judah "And to Judah he said: 'May the Lord give thee strength and power, To tread down all that hate thee; A prince shalt thou be, thou and one of thy sons, over the sons of Jacob; May thy name and the name of thy sons go forth and traverse every land and region. Then will the Gentiles fear before thy face, And all the nations will quake. In thee shall be the help of Jacob, And in thee be found the salvation of Israel.'"[73] This passage they maintain refers to a Messiah, of the family of David, which is in accordance with the Pharisaic doctrine, while the Sadducees anticipated a Messiah from the priestly family. Box, however, is of the opinion that this passage does not

---

[70] 23.31.

[71] Box, op. cit.

[72] 7.9, "but the King of the world shall raise us up, who have died for his laws, unto everlasting life." 12.44, "for if he had not hoped that they that were slain should have risen again, it had been superfluous and vain to pray for the dead. And also in that he perceived that there was great favour laid up for those that died godly." Comp. also Isa. 26.19, יחיו מתיך נבלתי יקומן הקיצו ורננו שכני עפר. Comp. Daniel 12.2, ורבים מישני אדמת עפר יקיצו.

[73] 31.18–20.

refer to the Messiah, but that it may be an allusion to the historical David.[74] Leszynsky suggests that the author in this particular passage may have in mind Judas Maccabeus.[75] This passage, however, has nothing to do with the idea of the Messiah, and its parallel may be found in Gen. 49.8-10, where the identical thoughts are expressed. "Judah, thee shall thy brethren praise; Thy hand shall be on the neck of thine enemies; Thy father's sons shall bow down before thee. Judah is a lion's whelp ... The sceptre shall not depart from Judah, Nor the ruler's staff from between his feet, As long as men come to Shiloh; And unto him shall the obedience of the peoples be."

The scholars who maintain that the author of Jubilees was a Sadducee derive support for their theory from 32.1, wherein it is stated that "Levi dreamed that they had ordained and made him the priest of the Most High God, him and his sons for ever;" since it was expected in certain quarters among the Sadducees that the Messiah would spring from the priestly ruling house.[76] This passage, however, has no reference to the Sadducean doctrine on the messianic expectation. A parallel passage is found in the Pentateuch: "and it shall be unto him, and to his seed after him, the covenant of an everlasting priesthood."[77] The difference between the pentateuchal passage and that of Jubilees lies in this. In the Pentateuch Phineas received the priesthood as an eternal heritage for himself and his seed forever, while according to Jubilees it was granted to Levi. In the blessing of Moses, Levi is designated not as a priest solely, but also as a leader of his people.[78]

[74] Box, op. cit.
[75] Leszynsky, *Die Sadduzäer*, pp. 225–26.
[76] Box, op. cit.
[77] Num. 25.13; comp. Ben Sirach 23–24.
[78] Deut. 33.8–11.

Dr. Büchler discerned Hellenistic influences in the Book of Jubilees.[79] In the account of the Exodus we are told that the Israelites despoiled the Egyptians in return for the servitude which the Egyptians had imposed upon them.[80] The thought — that the Israelites carried off the spoils of the Egyptians as a just recompense for their long servitude — is also expressed by Philo.[81] The passage in Jubilees, however, does not indicate any Hellenistic influence at all. Philo, wishing to defend the Jews against the charges of their enemies that they robbed the Egyptians upon leaving the country, made use of this account in the Book of Jubilees.

I believe, moreover, that the words "in return for the bondage in which they had forced them to serve," were added by the Greek translator. This is very evident from the context. We are told that the prince of the *Mastema* was bound, in order "that he might not accuse (before God) the children of Israel on the day when they asked the Egyptians for vessels ... in order to despoil the Egyptians in return for the bondage in which they had forced them to serve." If the Israelites despoiled the Egyptians in return for the bondage in which they were held by them, what grounds would the prince of the *Mastema* have for accusing the Israelites? They merely took the reward for their labor. We may, therefore, safely assume that the original Hebrew text did not contain the expression "in return for the bondage in which they had forced them to serve."

---

[79] "Traces des Idées et des Coutumes Hellénistiques, dans le livre des Jubilés," *REJ*, 1930, pp. 321–48.

[80] 48.18.

[81] *De Vita Mosis*, 1.141, "they took out with them much spoil ... And they did this not in avarice, or, as their accusers might say, in covetousness of what belonged to others. No, indeed. In the first place, they were but receiving a bare wage for all their time of service."

The Greek translator added these words for apologetic reasons.[82]

This method of translation was not uncommon. We are told that when the seventy men translated the Pentateuch into Greek (Septuagint), they introduced a number of changes.[83] Some of these changes are still found in the Septuagint, i. e., where the Hebrew reads ויכל אלהים ביום השביעי מלאכתו, the Septuagint has καὶ συνετέλεσεν ὁ θεὸς ἐν τῇ ἡμέρᾳ τῇ ἕκτῃ.

Dr. Büchler seems to find Hellenistic thoughts in the Book of Jubilees because he followed the prevalent view in ascribing the book to the late Hellenistic period.

V

The Calendar

The calendar employed in the Book of Jubilees is a very simple one. It has a solar year of 364 days divided into twelve months of thirty days each. Since twelve times thirty is 360, an additional day was added at the end of every third month, i. e., to the third, sixth, ninth, and twelfth months, so that each season of three months consisted of ninety-one days, thirteen weeks. The entire year consisted of fifty-two weeks.[84] The reason for adding one day at the end of each third month was the fact that ninety-one, being divisible by seven, makes all the festivals fall on the same day of the week on which they occurred when first instituted. Passover would always fall on Sunday, Sh'buot[85] on Thursday, the Days of Remembrance

---

[82] Philo made use of the Greek translation of the book.
[83] Sef.,1.8.
[84] 6.22, 31.
[85] When I refer to שבועות as mentioned in the Book of Jubilees, I transliterate it *Sh'buot*, while the name שבעות as given in the Bible I transliterate *Shabuot*.

on Sundays, the Day of Atonement on Tuesday, Tabernacles on Sunday. According to such a calendar, the festivals would always be on the same day of the week every year, "for ever and ever." For this reason the author objected strenuously to the change to a lunar-solar calendar, "for it would render the unclean days holy and the holy days profane."

As simple as this calendar is, students of the book succeeded in complicating it, for the reason that they failed to understand the purpose of the book and labored under a wrong hypothesis in ascribing it to a Pharisee or Sadducee. According to Jubilees, Sh'buot falls in the middle of the third month, i. e., the fifteenth of Sivan. According to the Pentateuch, the festival of Shabuot is to be celebrated on the fiftieth day after the offering of the Omer, which was brought on "the morrow of the Sabbath." Epstein[86] maintains that the author of Jubilees so devised his calendar that the fiftieth day of the Omer would coincide with the fifteenth of Sivan. But the calendar of Jubilees, with Nisan and Iyar each having thirty days, would not make the fiftieth day of the Omer fall on the fifteenth of Sivan. If the morrow of the Sabbath is taken as the morrow of the first day of Passover, the fiftieth day of the Omer will fall on the fifth of Sivan; if it is taken to mean the morrow of the last day of Passover, the fiftieth day of the Omer will be the twelfth of Sivan, contradicting the statement of Jubilees that Shabuot is to occur in the middle, i. e., on the fifteenth, of the third month. Therefore, Epstein advances the theory that the author employed two calendars side by side, one civil and the other ecclesiastical. The civil year had twelve months: eight months of thirty days and four months of thirty-one days; while the ecclesiastical year consisted of thirteen months of twenty-eight days

[86] "Le Livre des Jubilés," REJ, 1890–1891.

each. Box already pointed out that it is difficult to believe that the author of Jubilees employed two calendars, side by side, and proposed a solution of his own, namely, the addition of a week at the end of every third month, so that the year contained eight months of twenty-eight days and four months of thirty-five days. According to this calendar, the fiftieth day after the last day of Passover would fall on the fifteenth of Sivan — the last seven days of Nisan, twenty-eight days of Iyar, and fifteen days of Sivan, making a total of fifty days. Box himself noticed a difficulty in his own solution, namely that the middle day of the third month, which contains thirty-five days, would not be the fifteenth of the month.[87] Box, therefore, says that the term "middle" is used loosely. Box's hypothesis is as untenable as Epstein's. There is no evidence whatsoever in the Book of Jubilees for the use of two calendars or of a calendar in which two months of twenty-eight days were followed by a third of thirty-five days. Furthermore, there is sufficient evidence in the book to discount the theory of a calendar such as Box suggests. In the account of the Deluge we are told, "and the water prevailed on the face of the earth five months, one hundred and fifty days."[88] Now, if the author of Jubilees employed a calendar in which every two months of twenty-eight days were followed by a third of thirty-five days, five months would amount to 154 days, since the flood began in the second month and ended in the seventh.[89]

[87] Box, op. cit.
[88] 5.27.
[89] On the surface it appears that the statement "five months — one hundred and fifty days" contradicts also our assumption of a calendar in which two months of thirty days were followed by a third of thirty-one days, for these same five months would contain 152 days. However, a close study of the text removes this apparent contradiction. There are five chronological months, but only 150 full mathematical days. We are told that the flood began on the seventeenth

Both Epstein and Box encounter difficulty in understanding the calendar of Jubilees because they follow the accepted opinion that the Festival of Shabuot mentioned in Jubilees was to be celebrated on the fiftieth day after the offering of the Omer, as recorded in the Pentateuch. We have already pointed out that there is not the slightest reference to the Omer in the Book of Jubilees, nor is Shabuot in any way connected with Passover or with the counting of weeks or days. The word שבועות itself, as we have already demonstrated, has not the connotation of "weeks" but of "oaths."

VI

Character and Purpose of the Book

In the foregoing paragraphs we have maintained that the Book of Jubilees was written in Hebrew and in the early period of the Second Commonwealth. We have shown that it was not written by a Pharisee or a Sadducee or any other sectarian and was not composed in the Maccabean period or later. We demonstrated that its laws are in many cases at variance with those of the Pentateuch. We are now confronted with the problem of the author's purpose in writing this book.

It is well known that Genesis and the first eleven chapters of Exodus, which tell the history up to the time of the Exodus from Egypt, contain very few precepts. The pro-

---

day of the second month *in the evening*. The seventeenth day, therefore, is not counted. The flood ceased five months later, i. e., on the sixteenth of the seventh month. Again, the sixteenth of the month is not counted. We therefore have only 150 full days, but the space of time covered is a period of five chronological months, from the seventeenth of the second month to the sixteenth of the seventh month.

It seems that the author, when he wants to stress the completeness of a period of time, uses the proper word to specify the fact, as in the account of Adam's sojourn in the Garden of Eden, where seven complete years are specified, 3.17.

hibition against eating blood and the law of homicide are connected with the story of Noah,[90] and the law against the eating of the sinew of the thigh-vein is in some way connected with Jacob,[91] and circumcision with Abraham.[92] Even the precept of the Sabbath is not given at Creation. No doubt many Jews were puzzled why the precepts were not revealed to the Patriarchs. A reflection of this in rabbinic literature may be seen in the question of R. Isaac, as to why the Torah began with the account of Creation and not with the commandment of the paschal lamb,[93] the first precept given to the Hebrew people. Very likely many Jews wondered how it was possible that the Patriarchs did not observe the laws of God, and why, therefore, the children of Israel were chosen as God's favorite people. The Rabbis had these problems in mind when they said that the Torah was in existence before the creation of the world,[94] that Abraham observed all the laws,[95] that the Patriarchs instituted the prayers.

The author of Jubilees had intended to write, in opposition to the Pentateuch, an account of the Hebrews that would solve all these problems. The book tells that when God summoned Moses to Him on the sixteenth day of the third month after the Exodus from Egypt, He gave him the tablets on which were inscribed all the laws from Creation to the Exodus. These laws were observed by the Patriarchs and by the children of Israel, but were rejected by the rest of mankind. For this reason God had chosen them of all the peoples of the earth to be His people, and redeemed them from the land of Egypt. The author

---

[90] Gen. 9.   [91] Ibid. 32.
[92] Ibid. 17.
[93] See Midrash, Tanhuma to Gen., ed. Buber; comp. Rashi, Gen. 2.
[94] Midr. Rab. to Gen.
[95] Mishna Ḳid. 4, שקיים אברהם אבינו כל התורה כולה. Comp. also Yoma 28a.

connected the festivals with the patriarchs, the Festival of Tabernacles with Abraham, the Festival of Sh'buot שבועות with Noah and Abraham. According to the Bible, the Festival of Shabuot שבעות, Festival of Weeks, is purely an agricultural one. The author of the Book of Jubilees connected this Festival with the covenant which God made with Noah and Abraham.

It is possible that similar books were written by the same author or by one of his group, continuing the account to cover the rest of the laws, but were lost. Judging from the one extant work, we need not be sorry for the loss. The book is permeated by a chauvinistic spirit and, if it had been accepted in the Canon, it would have served to isolate the Jews from the rest of humanity.[96] Its laws are primitive in their severity, and could be observed only by a primitive people. The Jews were far too advanced in thought to accept such a book. We must, however, be thankful to the Church for preserving this one book, which throws interesting light on the life and thought of the Jews during the early part of the Second Commonwealth.

The titles of the book "Jubilees" and "Little Genesis," came to us through the Church. The former title is based upon the reckoning of time according to the Jubilee years which is employed in this book, while the latter title was given to it to distinguish it from the first book of the Pentateuch, Genesis. The original Hebrew title of the book is not known to us. From the beginning of the book we may readily assume that the author wished his work to be designated as תורת משה "The Law of Moses", or חוקי משה,[97]

---

[96] Comp., e. g., chap. 30.

[97] "This is the history of the division of the days of the law and of the testimony ... as the Lord spake to Moses on Mount Sinai when he went up to receive the tablets of the law and of the commandment, according to the voice of God as He said unto him: 'Go up to the top of the Mount.'"

as the Pentateuch is referred to in the books of the Prophets[98] and Hagiographa.[99] The Book of Jubilees in its Hebrew original[100] exercised a great influence upon rabbinic and apocalyptic literature, and in its Greek version influenced extensively Hellenistic Jewish writing and early Christian thought.

To summarize: I believe this essay demonstrates that the Book of Jubilees was written by a man, or a school of men, who opposed many of the pentateuchal laws and traditions. The author took care to give reasons for most of the precepts, which are not given in the Pentateuch. To the festivals, he ascribes origins and causes different from those given in the Pentateuch. The book was written during the pre-Hellenistic period when it could be hoped that opposition to the Pentateuch would not be wholly futile.

I consider the Book of Jubilees to be one of the most important documents of the history of the Jewish religion. This book dates from an obscure period of Jewish history, the early part of the Second Commonwealth, of which there are but meager literary remains. The Book of Jubilees sheds new light on the canonization of the Pentateuch, and affords a new perspective for the early history of the Second Jewish Commonwealth.

---

[98] II Kings 14.6.
[99] Nehem. 8.8.
[100] The Hebrew was still extant in the days of Saadia Gaon; see Epstein, *REJ*, 1890; see also Klausner, 171, ב, היסטוריה ישראלית. Comp. also S. Schechter, *Documents of Jewish Sectaries*, I, 16.

THE BOOK OF "JUBILEES" AND THE PENTATEUCH

THE title Jubilees was not the original one of the book, but came to us from the Church Fathers; the reason for this nomenclature is due to the fact that the author in relating the history of the Hebrews from the Creation to the Revelation divided the book into jubilees, each one consisting of forty-nine years, the date of the Revelation being given as the forty-ninth jubilee ... one week [of years] and two years, i. e., in the year 2410 A. M. Some called this book the Little Genesis because the author gave the history of the Hebrews from Adam to Moses; however, as we pointed out elsewhere,[1] the book most likely had another title. From the first paragraph of the book we may readily assume that the book was designated תורת משה, the Law of Moses, or חוקי משה, in the same manner as the Pentateuch is referred to in the books of the Prophets[2] and in the Hagiographa.[3]

All the writers who dealt with this book assigned it to the second century BCE, specifically to the time of John Hyrcanus.[4] Some ascribed the book to Sadducean origin,[5] others to Pharisean origin,[6] and some ascribed it to Essene origin.[7] The reason given for the Sadducean origin of the

---

[1] *The Book of Jubilees*, Philadelphia, 1939.
[2] I Kings 2.3; II Kings 14.6.
[3] Neh. 8.8.
[4] Charles, *The Apocrypha* ... V.II, "The Book of Jubilees was written in Hebrew by a Pharisee between the year of the accession of Hyrcanus to high-priesthood in 135 and his breach with the Pharisees some years before his death in 105 B. C."
[5] R. Leszynsky, *Die Sadduzäer*, Berlin, 1912.
[6] See above n. 4.
[7] Jellinek, *Über das Buch der Jubiläen*, 1855.

218

Reprinted from the *Jewish Quarterly Review*, New Series, Vol. 48, 1957.

book is that according to the author, the Festival of Weeks, Pentecost, was to be celebrated in the middle of the third month,[8] on Sunday, which would correspond to the Sadducean point of view. The writers who advanced this theory did not comprehend the book. The Festival of Weeks, or as it was called, Pentecost, depends on the offering of the *Omer* which was to be offered on the "morrow after the Sabbath."[9] The Israelites had to count seven weeks, i. e., forty-nine days after the "sheaf of the wave" offering, and the fiftieth day was to be a festival.[10] This festival sometimes is called the Festival of Weeks and sometimes the Festival of Pentecost, because it is on the fiftieth day after the sacrifice of the *Omer*; so from the Pentateuch it is clear that the time of the Festival of Weeks depends on that of the sacrifice of the *Omer*. During the Second Jewish Commonwealth this festival was the concluding feast of the Festival of Unleavened Bread, Passover. The Festival of Weeks was called by Josephus as well by the sages of the Second Jewish Commonwealth the festival of *Atzereth*[11] which means the concluding feast.

In the book of Jubilees there is no mention about the *Omer*, or about seven weeks. There is no connection between this festival and the *Omer*, and this is contrary to the Pentateuch. The writers who had a pre-conceived notion that the Jewish apocryphal books must be either of Saducean or Pharisean origin failed to grasp the spirit of the books and hence were led astray. The author of the so-called book of Jubilees was in opposition to the Pentateuch; he did not connect the so-called Festival of Weeks with the *Omer*, or with the Festival of Unleavened Bread,

---

[8] Comp. Box, Introduction to the *Book of Jubilees*, p. xviii.
[9] Lev. 23.10–11.
[10] *Ibid.* 23.15–21; Deut. 16.9–10.
[11] Ḥag. 2.4, *passim*.

and hence it could not be either Sadducean or Pharisean; as a matter of fact, as I have pointed out, this festival was not called the *Festival of Weeks* by the author of Jubilees but the Festival of Oaths. This festival was inaugurated according to him in commemoration of the covenants which God made with Noah[12] and Abraham.[13] The Greek translator of the book who found the word שבעות in the text thought it had the connotation of weeks, following the Septuagint translation of the Pentateuch where the phrase חג שבעות was correctly translated the Festival of Weeks; in our book, however, the words חג השבעות[14] have the connotation the Festival of Oaths.

During the Second Jewish Commonwealth the phrase חג השבעות, "Festival of Weeks" was never used for this festival.[15] It was called עצרת *Azereth* in the tannaitic literature, and it was called Pentecost in the book of Tobit,[16] in the Second book of Maccabees,[17] and in the Acts.[18] Josephus in his book *Antiquities* said, "When the seventh week following this sacrifice [i. e., the *Omer*] has elapsed these are the forty-nine days of the weeks on the fiftieth day which the Hebrews called *Asartha*, the word denoting fiftieth."[19] The word *Asartha* does not denote fiftieth. Josephus who heard that this festival was called by the Jews in Judaea *Azereth*, or *Azartha* in the Aramaic form, and heard or noted that the Jews in the hellenistic diaspora, called it Pentecost, the fiftieth, erroneously assumed that the word *Azartha* denotes fiftieth.

[12] Jub. 6.15–6.
[13] *Ibid.* 14.20; 15.1.
[14] Comp. S. Zeitlin, *op. cit.*
[15] Comp. II Macc. 12.31, Dropsie College ed.   [16] 2.1.
[17] 12.31.
[18] 2.1.
[19] τῇ πεντηκοστῇ ἥν Ἑβαῖοι ἀσαρθὰ καλοῦσι σημαίνει δὲ τοῦτο π ͺτηκοστήν Ant. 3.252, see also *ibid.* 13.252; Philo, *de Specialibus Legibus*, 11.179.

The author, or the authors of the book of Jubilees not only differed with the Pentateuch in reference to the Festival of Weeks but also in reference to the Festival of Tabernacles. This festival according to the Pentateuch was instituted in commemoration of the tabernacles in which the Israelites following the Exodus dwelt during their journey through the desert.[20] The author of this book assigned the origin of the festival to Abraham who instituted it in commemoration of his deliverence from his enemies.[21] The author stated that it was ordained in the heavenly tables that the Israelites should celebrate the Feast of Tabernacles for seven days. He further stated that Abraham "took branches of palm trees and fruit of goodly trees, and every day going round the altar with the branches seven times.[22] This is entirely in contradiction to what is written in the Pentateuch about this festival.

Those who ascribe the book to a Sadducean origin assume this because the ceremony of pouring the water on the altar during the Festival of Tabernacles is not mentioned by the author in describing this festival, the ceremony being a Pharisaic custom rejected by the Sadducees. These writers have not fully comprehended this book. The author gave another connotation for the festival of Tabernacles in opposition to the Pentateuch. It is also to be noted that according to the Pentateuch the order of the festivals as they were instituted was first Passover, or the Festival of Unleavened Bread which was instituted in commemoration of the Exodus; the Festival of Weeks, on the fiftieth day after the offering the *Omer*; and the Festival of Tabernacles which was instituted later in commemoration of the journey through the desert where the Israelites dwelt in

[20] Lev. 23.43.
[21] 16.21.
[22] *Ibid.* 30–1.

booths. The order in the book of Jubilees is first the Festival of *Shabuot* and was instituted by Noah and Abraham; the Festival of Tabernacles instituted by Abraham; and finally the Festival of Passover which was instituted in commemoration of the Exodus.

Those who maintain that the book of Jubilees was written in the Hasmonean period say that many of the passages therein are appropriate to that period. The author of the book of Jubilees lays great emphasis on the Sabbath and says that those who do not observe it, ought to be punished by death. Again, the author of the book of Jubilees warned against being seen naked like the Gentiles. This emphasis in the book of Jubilees, they concluded reflects the time of the Hasmoneans as it is described in the books of the Maccabees. Following such logic we could conclude that many portions of the Pentateuch were written in the time of the Hasmoneans. The observance of the Sabbath was stressed in the Pentateuch. We are told that while the Israelites were wandering in the desert, a man who gathered sticks on the Sabbath Day was put to death.[23] The Pentateuch as well as the other books of the Bible lays great stress against the worship of idols. This does not mean that these books were written in the time of the Hasmoneans. The author of the Pentateuch as well as the author of Nehemiah strongly opposed intermarriage. We are told in Genesis that when Noah became intoxicated he lay down naked and that his son Ham on passing by and seeing his father's nakedness, did not cover him. For this he was cursed by his father Noah.[24] Thus, we can readily see that the Pentateuch abhorred nakedness. Again, following the logic of the authors who maintain that the book of Jubilees was written during the hellenistic persecutions because the author opposed nakedness, we could

---

[23] Num. 15.32–35.   [24] Gen. 9.25.

conclude that this passage in the Pentateuch also was written in that period. All the laws and the prohibitions in reference to circumcision, idolatry, intermarriage, and association with the Gentiles are found in the Bible. Only in the book of Jubilees do we find that great stress was laid on the segregation of the Jews from the other nations. In this the author is more chauvinistic even than the author of the book of Nehemiah. Fortunately, the book of Jubilees was never accepted by the Jews.

The phrase "until this day" in 38.14 where it is written that "the sons of Edom have not got quit of the yoke of servitude which the twelve sons of Jacob had imposed on them until this day" proves that the Book of Jubilees was composed during the time of John Hyrcanus when he conquered the Edomites.[25] The phrase "until this day" is found in two other places in this book.[26] If we assume that this phrase indicates the time of composition, we shall have to say that the book was composed in three different periods. The phrase "until this day" in the Bible occurs quite frequently. In Josh. 10.27 we are told that Joshua buried the kings whom he had slain and laid great stones on the mouth of the cave "until this very day."[27] Again, in the same book it says (14.14) "Therefore Hebron became the inheritance of Caleb the son of Jephunneh the Kenizzite until this day." In accordance with this contention we must assume that the Book of Joshua was composed at two different times since the phrase "until this day" refers to different times. To show the absurdity of such a contention we shall quote a few examples. The phrase "until this day" occurs several times in the book of Chronicles. In I Chron. 4.43 it is stated "And they [the sons of Simon] smote the remnants of the Amalekites that escaped and dwelt there until this day." In II Chron. 10.19 it is stated "So Israel

---

[25] Comp. J. Klausner, 205 ,היסטוריה של הבית השני, ג.
[26] 10.33; 45, 12.   [27] עד עצם היום הזה.

rebelled against the house of David until this day." Again, in chapter 21.10 we have "So Edom revolted from under the hand of Judah until this day." Following this faulty contention we must say that this book was composed in different periods since the phrase "until this day" refers to different periods. The phrase "until this day" appears frequently throughout the Bible.[27a] The author of the book of Jubilees who claimed that the book had been revealed by God also used the same phrases and expressions as appeared in the Bible.

In my essay the *Book of Jubilees* I said that the author of the book strenuously opposed a change of the calendar from a solar to a solar-lunar one, and that this indicates that the book was written either at the time of the change or soon after. This book, I said, could not have been written as is generally assumed in the Hasmonean period because the question of the calendar was then no longer an issue. This to my mind, I pointed out, clearly indicates that the book was written in a very early period when the calendar was either in the process of changing or soon afterwards.[28] To this contention it was retorted that my argument is not very convincing since there were many calendars among the Jews.[29] This theory that there were many systems of calendars employed by the Jews during the Second Commonwealth and that even during the Hasmonean period there was not yet a fixed calendar has no validity whatsoever. We have no evidence for such a theory; moreover, some of the theories were based on a misrendering of the biblical text.

It was pointed out that Antiochus Epiphanes sought to revise the Jewish calendar and that Daniel refers to this event, when he stated that the Little Horn should "think

---

[27a] Comp. also Judith 14.10.
[28] S. Zeitlin, *op. cit.*, pp. 8–16.
[29] Comp. H. H. Rowley, *The Relevance of Apocalyptic*, pp. 86–88.

to change times and the law."[30] The text has זמנין; the word
זמנין has the connotation in this passage not of time, seasons,
but of festival. The word זמנים has both the connotation of
time and festival.[31] The word זמנים in the prayers which
came to us from a very early period and that followed the
biblical style has the meaning of festivals. In the *Kidush*
as well as the prayers we have "Blessed be thou O Lord
who sanctifies (the Sabbath) Israel, and the festivals.[32]
Both the words מועדים[33] and זמנים in tannaitic literature
have the connotation of appointed time, seasons and festivals. Daniel was composed during the Second Commonwealth. In fact, King Demetrius I in his letter to the Jews
in which he relieved the Jews from the decrees of Antiochus
wrote that "the Jews may observe and rest on their Sabbath and festivals."[34] We may add that Rashi in his
commentary on Daniel as well as Saadia Gaon in his
interpretation of this passage fully understood that the
word זמנין has the connotation of festivals.[35]

Those who followed the theory that the Jews had a different system of calendars and that there was a gradual
change in the calendar used during the post-exilic age sup-

[30] ויסבר להשניה זמנין ודת.
[31] שמיני.... שהוא זמן בפני עצמו; ג' זמנים בבבל; מועדים לשמחה חגים וזמנים לששון.
[32] חג המצות...זמן חרותנו. מקדש (השבת) ישראל והזמנים. The phrases חג המצות זמן מתן תורתנו, חג הסכות זמן שמחתנו were rendered by all translators "the season of our freedom ... the season of our gladness." In
the prayer book published by the Rabbinical Assembly of America the
word זמן was rendered "season." It is with great satisfaction that we
note that Dr. P. Birnbaum in his translation of the *Sidur* rendered the
word זמן festival. In this Dr. Birnbaum showed that he not only fully
understood the meaning of the phrases חג המצות זמן חרותנו חג השבעות
זמן מתן תורתנו... but that he grasped the spirit of the early Hebrew
literature. My attention has been called to the fact that M. Klein in
his edition of the Sidur correctly rendered the word זמן festival and not
season as has been rendered by so many.
[33] למועד אשוב; עשה מועדים לתורה. [34] I Macc. 10.34.
[35] זמנין ודת ... להעבירם על כל מועדיהם ודתיהם (רש״י), לבטל מישראל ... המועדים והתורה, (סעדיה).

ported themselves on Ezek. 40.1, בעשרים וחמש שנה לגלותנו
בראש השנה בעשור לחדש. They maintain that in the postexilic period the Jews had their *Rosh Hashana* at the beginning of the year on the 10th day of the month, i. e., of Tishri. This theory is based on a faulty understanding of these biblical words. The phrase בראש השנה does not refer at all to the 10th of Tishri as the new year. Ezekiel refers to a new year of an era, that is to say, בעשרים וחמש שנה לגלותנו בראש השנה בעשור לחדש "in the twenty-fifth year of our captivity, in the beginning of the year, on the tenth day of the month." The prophet refers to the tenth of *Ab* not *Tishri*, which began a new year of the era from the period of the destruction of the Temple which was burned in the fifth month (*Ab*) on the tenth day thereof. This was understood by the Tannaim.[36] Symmachus also fully understood this passage.[37]

The Jews, like other nations reckoned their chronology according to different eras; from the Exodus,[38] from the construction of the Temple,[39] and also from the destruction of the Temple. In like manner, in America we say, in the year so and so of independence. This does not imply that the Fourth of July is a civil new year. The Fourth of July is the new year of the era of independence, whereas the first of January is the civil new year. The calendar was used by the Jews in the same way during the Second Commonwealth, the new year always began the first day of

[36] לא זכו למנות לבנינו התחילו למנות לחרבנו בעשרים וחמש שנה לגלותנו בראש השנה בעשר לחדש, Yer. R. H. 1.

[37] Ἐν τῷ πεμπτῷ μηνί, ad loc. Let us hope that the editors of the new translation of the Hebrew Bible will take cognizance of the rabbinic interpretations of the scriptures. It is true that knowledge of the Septuagint and other oriental languages is very important for a proper understanding of some verses in the Bible, but the rabbinic interpretations and the rabbinic versions are more essential. The Hebrew Bible was written by the Jews, was studied by the Jews and was preserved by the Jews.

[38] ויהי בשמנים שנה וארבע מאות שנה לצאת בני ישראל מארץ מצרים.

[39] ויהי מקצה עשרים שנה אשר בנה שלמה.

Tishri; however, they employed different eras in their chronology. In the beginning they reckoned their chronology from the destruction of the Temple which was on the tenth of Ab. Later, before the time of the Hasmoneans, they counted their era from the date of the establishment of the Seleucid dynasty.[40] Still later they counted their eras from the ascendency of the kings.[41]

The biblical calendar was a solar one.[42] In the early part of the Second Jewish Commonwealth the calendar was changed to a lunar-solar-one. The author of the book of Jubilees voiced indignation against the changing of the calendar from a solar to a lunar-solar one, maintaining that by changing the calendar the people would forget and transgress the days of the new moons, the Sabbath and the festivals. His indignation against the changing of the calendar to a lunar-solar proves without any doubt that his book was composed at the time of or about the time of the changing of the calendar.

There are other unimpeachable proofs that this book was composed either at the time of the canonization of the Pentateuch or near that of the canonization, when the Pentateuch was not yet well established among the Jews. As has been mentioned previously, the author gave different reasons for the establishment of the main festivals, Passover, Shabuot and the Festival of Tabernacles. He also changed the order of the festivals from that recorded in the Pentateuch. He opposed many of the laws of the Pentateuch. According to the Pentateuch a certain number of animals had to be sacrificed during the festivals.[43] He gave a different number.[44] According to the Pentateuch the seventh year is the year of release.[45] According to the

---

[40] Comp. I Macc. *passim*.   [41] *Ibid*. 13.42.
[42] Regarding the verses ... יום שני ... יום אחד בקר ויהי ערב ויהי.
Comp. S. Zeitlin, *Religious and Secular Leadership*, p. 79.
[43] Comp. Num. 29.12–34.
[44] 16.22–24.   [45] Lev. 25.4.

author, the fifth is the year of release.[46] No Jew in the Hasmonean period would write a book opposing the laws of the Pentateuch. Of course there were Jews who did not believe in the divine origin of the Pentateuch but these Jews would not write a book and claim that it came from God.

It has been said that during the time of Antiochus Epiphanes many Jews rejected many of the Pentateuchal laws and substituted a hellenistic cult.[47] Again, these Jews would not write such a book as Jubilees and claim that it was written by God on heavenly tables. It has been stated that the Pharisees abrogated many of the laws of the Pentateuch, like the law of *lex talionis*, but this was not true. The Pharisees never abrogated the Pentateuchal laws. They interpreted them. They maintained that "an eye for an eye" was never meant to be taken literally. The idea of the lawgiver was that the injured person should be compensated. In the same manner they interpreted all the laws, maintaining that it was the meaning of the lawgiver. There is a great difference between *abrogation* of the laws and *interpretation* of the laws. The author of the book of Jubilees opposed the laws of the Pentateuch. Such a book could not have been written in the latter part of the Second Jewish Commonwealth. The only scholar who fully comprehended the historical background of the composition of the book, as was brought out in my essay, the *Book of Jubilees*, was Prof. W. F. Albright.[48]

What was the purpose of the author or authors in writing this book? When writing a book, an author must have a message which he desires to deliver. What was the intent of the author of this book? I have previously endeavored to show that this book was written in opposition to the Pentateuch There are references in the historical books

[46] 7.37.   [47] Rowley, *op. cit.*, p. 86.
[48] *From the Stone Age to Christianity*, p. 266.

of the Bible to the "Laws of Moses." But the Pentateuch never became the constitution of the Israelites during the time of the first Temple. The entire Pentateuch is based on the following two statements, "I am your God," and "Thou shalt have no other Gods." These are the quintessence of the entire Pentateuch, and even so today, for the Jewish people. However, we know from the book of Judges that the Israelites worshipped foreign gods; even Solomon did so.[49] The prophet Jeremiah in his castigation of the Judaeans said, "For according to the number of thy cities are thy gods, O Judah; and according to the number of the streets of Jerusalem have ye set up altars to the shameful thing, even altars unto Baal."[50] Even after the burning of the Temple by the Babylonians when the remnants of the Judaeans fled to Egypt, they said to the prophet Jeremiah, "But we will certainly perform every word that is gone forth out of our mouths, to offer unto the queen of heaven, and to pour out drink-offerings unto her, as we have done, we and our fathers, our kings and our princes, in the cities of Judah, and in the streets of Jerusalem."[51] In the northern kingdom the worship of foreign gods was even more prevalent than in the southern kingdom. All the kings, from the first king Jeroboam to Hoshea the son of Elah worshipped idols. There was only a small group of prophets and their followers who consistently castigated the Judaeans and the Israelites for worshipping foreign gods. These prophets were persecuted for preaching monotheism, the establishment, the worship of the God Israel, and many had to leave their homeland, and some of the prophets were looked upon as fools and madmen.[52]

After the Restoration, the Pentateuch was canonized and became the constitution of the new state and there was no longer idol worship in Judaea. Monotheism, the univer-

[49] I Kings 11.5–6.   [50] Jer. 11.13.   [51] *Ibid.* 44.16–19.
[52] Hos. 9.7.

sality of God, was well established and the people were ready to sacrifice their lives for the unity of God. They were ready to sacrifice their lives at a critical time, and did not forsake the Torah even under torture. When the Pentateuch was canonized we do not know. Tradition has ascribed the canonization to Ezra. We must assume that there was some opposition to it. To say that the books were canonized without opposition is contrary to everything we know from our history. When the entire Bible was canonized in the year 65 CE we know there was opposition to at least two books, the Song of Songs and Ecclesiastes; the latter was canonized in the year 90 CE against strong opposition,[53] and the Book of Esther was canonized in the year 140 CE again against a great opposition.[54] There must have been some people who believed other books should be canonized and opposed some of those which were included. But of this we have no record. Therefore we have a right to assume that the canonization of the Pentateuch also was not without opposition. We believe that the book of Jubilees was written in opposition to the Pentateuch.

The doctrines of the author of the so-called book of Jubilees in regard to the giving of the laws to the Israelites differ from those in the Pentateuch. According to the latter, God gave the Ten Commandments to Moses on Mount Sinai while the people remained in the valley, and Moses gave the rest of the Torah at the command of God gradually to the people. The Mishne Torah, the book of Deuteronomy, gives a slightly different version, of the rest of the books. There were no laws given to the people before the

---

[53] Comp. S. Zeitlin, *An Historical Study of the Hebrew Scriptures*, pp. 9–15.
[54] *Ibid.*

first year of the Exodus. According to the so-called book of Jubilees the entire Torah was written on heavenly tables. Many of the precepts were observed by the patriarchs, Abraham, Isaac and Jacob, and even by Noah. Some of the precepts which are included in the Ten Commandments had already been observed at the time of the patriarchs.[55] According to the book of Jubilees, in the first year after the Exodus on the sixteenth day of the third month God told Moses to come up to Mount Sinai and said He would give him two tables of the law. Moses was on the mount forty days and forty nights and God said to the Angel of Presence that he should write for Moses the entire Torah from the beginning of the Creation until the Sanctuary would be built.[56] Thus the entire Torah was received by Moses through a mediator, the Angel of Presence. There is no separation of the Ten Commandments from the rest of the precepts. All the laws were written at the time of the Creation and some of them were observed by the patriarchs, and they were given to Moses on Mount Sinai by the Angel of Presence. Thus the entire philosophy of the book of Jubilees is at variance with that of the books of Deuteronomy, Exodus and the other books of the Pentateuch.

We may surmise from the books of Ezra and Nehemiah that a schism arose after the Restoration between those who were of Judaean origin and those who were of Israelite origin, i. e., between the southerners and the northerners. The Judaeans wanted to have the Temple rebuilt in Jerusalem, where it had stood before the burning, while the people of the north, who were called Samaritans, wanted the new temple to be built on Mount Gerizim, and their contention was well supported by the Pentateuch. Jerusalem, Zion, is never mentioned in the Pentateuch, while

[55] *Idem, The Book of Jubilees.*   [56] I.4–27.

Mount Gerizim is mentioned in connection with the blessing of the people;[57] hence this gives support to the contention of the Samaritans that the Temple should be built on Mount Gerizim. According to the so-called book of Jubilees, God already had commanded in the heavenly tables that the Sanctuary should be built on Mount Zion in Jerusalem.[58] This was God's will. Actually, the Judaeans had no support for their contention that the Temple should be rebuilt in Jerusalem, except the fact that it had stood there before the burning. We find no reference in the Pentateuch to Jerusalem and therefore it could be said that there was no God's will that the Temple should be built in Jerusalem. We therefore must assume that the historical books of the Bible, Joshua, Judges, Samuel and Kings were canonized simultaneously with the Pentateuch. We find in Kings that God has chosen Jerusalem where the Sanctuary should be built.[59]

The Pentateuch prohibited intermarriage with the "seven people" and with the Ammonites and Moabites, also with the Edomites and Egyptians. We learn from the book of Nehemiah that Nehemiah opposed intermarriage with foreign people. The book of Jubilees stressed the prohibition against intermarriage with *any* foreign people, which is not in accord with the Pentateuch. The Pharisees who stressed the universality of god and held that Judaism is a universal religion and is not confined to one race or people did *not* prohibit intermarriage, provided Judaism gained converts.[60]

The Pentateuchal prohibition against intermarriage with the Ammonites was interpreted to refer only to the males

---

[57] Deut. 27.12, comp. also *ibid.* 4–8.
[58] 1.28, 29; 8.19; 18.13.
[59] Comp. II Kings 21.7.
[60] S. Zeitlin, *Judaism as a Religion.*

and not the females;[61] later the male Ammonite also was welcomed in the Jewish community.[62] The heroine of the book of Ruth which was written during the Second Commonwealth was Ruth, a Moabitess, who accepted Judaism. One of her descendents was King David. The purpose of this book was to emphasize that even a Moabitess could enter the Jewish community. One of the heroes of the book of Judith which was written in the Hellenistic period was Achior, an Ammonite, who was friendly to the Jews and after the defeat of Holofernes' army "joined unto the house of Israel unto this day."[63] The author of the book purposely brought an Ammonite into his story in order to show that Ammonite proselytes were welcomed. This attitude of the Pharisees toward the proselytes was in opposition to the philosophy of the book of Jubilees and also to the Pentateuch. In regard to the latter, the passages were interpreted in accordance with the Pharisaic conception of Proselytism.

The calendar employed in the Book of Jubilees was a solar one. The day began with the dawn.[64] The year consisted of 364 days divided into 12 months of 30 days each. Since 12 times 30 are 360, an additional day was added at the end of every third month, i. e., to the third, sixth, ninth and twelfth month, so that each season of three months consisted of 91 days, thirteen weeks. The entire year consisted of 52 weeks. The reason for adding one day at the end of each third month was due to the fact that 91 was divisible by 7, so that all the festivals would fall on the same day of the week on which they occurred when they were first instituted. Passover would always fall on Sunday; Shabuot would fall on Thursday; the days of Remem-

---

[61] Yeb. 8.3. עמוני ולא עמונית מואבי ולא מואבית.
[62] Yad. 4. כבר בא סנחריב מלך אשור ובלבל את כל האומות.   [63] 14.10.
[64] See S. Zeitlin, *The Zadokite Fragments*, pp. 14–17.

brance would fall on Sundays; the Day of Atonement on Tuesday; the Festival of Tabernacles would fall on Sundays. Each jubilee consisted of forty-nine years. In this the author of the book is in contradiction with the Pentateuch where the fiftieth year is the jubilee year.

We may say with certainty that this book was written by a man or a school of men who wanted to substitute it for the Pentateuch. Therefore, it is very evident that this book could have been written only in a period when it could be hoped that the opposition to the Pentateuch and to its inclusion in the canon would have an effect.[65]

It is possible that more books were written by the same group continuing the account of the Israelites until the time of the building of the Temple. Judging from the laws found in this book we need not be sorry for the loss of such books. The laws are primitive in their severity and could be observed only by a primitive people. The leaders of the Jews rightly rejected such a chauvinistic work. This book, however, is very important for a proper understanding of the early period of the Restoration. It throws new light on the period of the canonization of the Pentateuch. For the

[65] In the pseudo-scholarly literature which has grown around the Dead Sea Scrolls like mushrooms we find it maintained that the book of Jubilees is an Essene work and that it greatly influenced those who wrote the Hebrew Scrolls which supposedly were discovered by Bedouin in a cave near the Dead Sea. This hypothesis is not borne out by either the book of Jubilees or the Hebrew Scrolls. This contention is as spurious as all the other contentions of those who maintain the antiquity of the scrolls. The Essenes followed the Pentateuch strictly. The book of Jubilees contradicts many laws of the Pentateuch. In the Hebrew Scrolls there are many references to a messiah. In the book of Jubilees there is no reference whatsoever to a messiah. The calendar in the book of Jubilees was a solar one and the day began with the dawn, while in the Zadokite Fragments (Damascus Documents) the lunar calendar was used, where the day began with the sunset.

An article was published in connection with the solution of the enigma of the Scrolls. This article is full of distortions and half-baked hypoth-

preservation of this book in toto we must be thankful to the Church.

The book, although rejected and suppressed by the spiritual leaders of the Jews, could not be eradicated. Ideas, unlike men, can never be totally destroyed. It has exercised an influence on Judaism, upon rabbinic and apocalyptic literature, particularly through its midrashic contents. This book was used by the Jews despite the prohibition against it. Similarly the book of Ben Sirach although banned and placed among ספרים חצונים nevertheless was used by the sages of the Talmud. The Hebrew text of the book of Jubilees, or its Aramaic form, was still extant in the time of Saadia Gaon.

I shall give a full analysis of the book of Jubilees and its influence on Judaism and early Christianity in the Introduction to the Book of Jubilees which will appear in the series of the Jewish Apocryphal Literature published by Dropsie College.

---

eses, suggesting that Menahem, the son of Judah the Galilean, tried to introduce a new calendar. This assumption belongs to the realm of fiction; it has no validity whatsoever. Judah the Galilean and his son Menahem who were the leaders of the sect called the Fourth Philosophy according to Josephus were in full agreement with the Pharisees except that they rejected the lordship of man.

The author even confused the sect of the Fourth Philosophy with the Zealots. Judah the Galilean was not the founder of the Zealots as was maintained by the author; he was the founder of the Fourth Philosophy. The Zealots were organized long after his death and their leader was Eleazar the son of Simon.

THE LEGEND OF THE TEN MARTYRS AND ITS APOCALYPTIC ORIGINS

THE *Midrash Eleh Ezkerah*[1] tells of ten martyrs who were put to death by the Romans. Their names were as follows: Ishmael, (the High Priest) Simon son of Gamaliel, Akiba, Haninah ben Teradyon, Eliezar ben Shammua, Yeshebab Hasofer, Ḥaninah ben Hakinai, Judah ben Baba, Huzpit and Judah ben Doma.[1a] In the *Midrash of Lamentations* other names are substituted for some of these and in the *Midrash Psalms* there is again a difference of names among the Ten Martyrs.[2] This story of Ten Martyrs, ten scholars being put to death by the Romans, was accepted by all historians. As the sources differ with respect to the identity of the Ten Martyrs, so students differ as to who they actually were.[3]

[1] *Bet ha-Midrash*, Adolph Jellinek, p. 64, מדרש אלה אזכרה.
[1a] ר' ישמעאל ור' שמעון ב"ג ר' עקיבא ור' חנינא בן תרדיון ר' אליעזר בן שמוע ור' ישיבב הסופר ר' חנינא בן חכינאי ור' יודא בן בבא ר' חוצפית המתורגמן ור' יודא בן דמא.

[2]
M. Lam.	M. Psalms
ר' ישמעאל ורבן גמליאל ור' ישבב ור' יהודה בן בבא ור' חוצפית המתורגמן ור' יהודה הנחתום ור' חנניה(א) בן תרדיון ור' עקיבא ובן עזאי ור' טרפון. ואית דמפקין ר' טרפון ומעיילין ר' אלעזר חרסנא.	ר' שמעון בן גמליאל ור' ישמעאל בן אלישע ר' ישבב הסופר ור' חוצפית התורגמן ר' יוסי ור' יהודה בן בבא ור' יהודה הנחתום ור' שמעון בן עזאי ור' חנינא בן תרדיון ור' עקיבא.

[3] Comp. Zunz, *Die Synagogale Poesie des Mittelalters*, 1920, pp. 139–40; Hamburger, *Real-Encyclopädie Supplementband*, pp. 98–100. See also L. Finkelstein, "The Ten Martyrs," *Essays and Studies in Memory of Linda R. Miller.* Dr. Finkelstein places even Julianus and Pappus among the Ten Martyrs. Comp. also S. Krauss, עשרה הרוגי מלכות, השלח, כרך מ"ד.

Reprinted from the *Jewish Quarterly Review*, New Series, Vol. 36, 1945.

Though students recognized that the rabbis named in the Midrashim were not contemporaries, nevertheless they did not question the historicity of the Ten Martyrs. The Talmud, however, never mentions the Ten Martyrs. It relates that Rabbi Akiba was tortured and put to death by the Romans,[4] as were Judah ben Baba[5] and Haninah ben Teradyon.[6] A Tosefta relates that Samuel ha-Koten foretold that Simon and Ishmael would be put to the sword.[7] This ancient source does not say who Simon and Ishamel were. The Midrashim, however, identify Simon with Simon the Prince, son of Gamaliel, who lived before the destruction of the Temple,[8] and identify Ishmael with Ishmael ben Elisha, the High Priest,[9] which also would indicate that he lived before the destruction of the Temple. However, Ishmael ben Elisha lived after the destruction of the Temple.[10] In connection with Huzpit, one of the supposed Ten Martyrs, the Talmud says that his tongue was found lying in the dung.[11] The Palestinian Talmud relates that the tongue of Judah ben Hanaḥtum, another one of the supposed Ten Martyrs, was carried by a dog in its mouth.[12] The Talmudim do not say that either Ḥuzpit or Judah was put to death by the Roman government, although there is a possibility that such was the

---

[4] Ber. 61b.
[5] Sanh. 14a.
[6] Ab. Zarah 18a. See also Semahot 8, ed. Higger.
[7] Tosefto Sotah 13, אף הוא אמר בשעת מיתתו שמעון וישמעאל לחרבא וחברוהי לקטלא; see also Yer. ibid. 9; Semahot 8. Comp. also Mekilta Mish. 18.
[8] Comp. ibid.
[9] Ibid. Comp. also Ab. R. N. 38; M. Eleh Ezkeroh.
[10] Comp. Shab. 12b. אני ישמעאל בן אלישע ... כשיבנה בית המקדש אביא. Comp. אמר ר' ישמעאל בן אלישע מיום שחרב בית המקדש; B. B. 51b, הטאת שמינה also Ber. 7a.
[11] Hulin 142, לישנא דר' חוצפית המתורגמן הוא דהוה מוטלת באשפה. See also Kid. 39b.
[12] Yer. Hag. 2,1, ויש אומר ע״י שראה לשונו של ר' יהודה הנחתום נתון בפי הכלב. Comp. also Mishna Sotah 9,16 שמת בן עזאי פסקו השקדנים.

case. The only hint of this from the Talmud is that they met a violent death. It could have been inflicted by bandits or the Roman government. In any case the Talmud does not connect them with the Ten Martyrs.

As we said before, modern scholars have accepted the story about the Ten Martyrs as historical. However, there are many objections to such acceptance. First, the term Ten Martyrs is never mentioned in the Talmud. If there were Ten Martyrs then we would have to explain why not only the tannaitic literature but even the amoraic literature never used the term. Furthermore, the Talmud describes in detail the torturing of Rabbi Akiba, Rabbi Haninah ben Teradyon and Rabbi Judah ben Baba, but does not associate them with the Ten Martyrs. Again, as was pointed out by other scholars, Simon son of Gamaliel lived before the destruction of the Temple. Thus, he could not be connected with the Tannaim of the later period.[13] Still more, the Tosefta which says that Simon and Ishmael would be killed, does not identify them with Simon son of Gamaliel and Ishmael the High Priest.[13a] Thus, the Talmud speaks only about three sages who were put to death by the Romans; it had been foretold that two sages would be put to death. One talmudic source says

---

[13] See Graetz, דברי ימי ישראל ח' ב'.

[13a] Samuel ha-Koten lived in the time of Rabban Gamaliel II; hence he could not have prophesied the death of Rabban Simon who died long before Samuel. Rabban Simon, the son of Gamaliel I, most likely was assassinated by the *Sicarii* during the civil war in Jerusalem before the destruction of the Temple. Nor could Samuel ha-Koten have prophesied that Simon, the son of Gamaliel II, would meet a violent death. Simon lived after the time of the persecutions and his death was due to natural causes. The Simon, referred to by Samuel ha-Koten, was not Simon the Prince nor was Ishmael, Ishmael, the high priest. Simon and Ishmael, who Samuel ha-Koten foretold would be put to the sword, most likely were among the leaders of the Bar Kokba revolt. It is possible that this Simon may refer to Bar Kokba himself, whose proper name was Simon.

that Ḥuzpit met a violent death, while the other source says that Judah Hanaḥtum met a violent death. There is no reference in the Talmud to the other sages who were supposed to be among the Ten Martyrs. It is indeed strange that if there were really Ten Martyrs why the Talmud is silent about them. Why did not the Tannaim, who lived in the Roman period, speak of the Ten Martyrs? To say that the Tannaim feared the Romans or sought to appease them and therefore were silent about the Ten Martyrs, as some believe, is a hypothesis which cannot be entertained. It is clear that the Tannaim had no fear of the Romans; neither did the Tannaim seek to appease them since they set forth in detail the tortures of the three rabbis.

The story about the Ten Martyrs is undoubtedly a legend. There were no Ten Martyrs. I do not mean to say that there were no martyrs,[14] that the Romans did not kill Jews because they observed the precepts of the Torah and were loyal to Judaism. Thousands of Jews and their leaders were tortured and killed by the Romans. The story of the Ten Martyrs as a group, however, is a legend. Since the story as such is a legend, the scholars who seek to indentify the Ten Martyrs *labor in vain*.

It has been said that ritual comes first and legend follows. Thus, we may say that a legend must have either historical background or some idea behind it. Undoubtedly there was some idea behind the legend of the Ten Martyrs. The problem that now confronts us is what this idea was which led to the legend of the Ten Martyrs.

I believe the Book of Jubilees will give us the first clue to the idea which gave rise to this legend. According to

[14] ושמעתי שהיו אומרים הרוגי מלכות אין אדם Comp. Pes. 50a, הרוגי מלכות. יכול לעמוד במחיצתן מאן נינהו אלימא ר' עקיבא וחביריו משום הרוגי מלכות ותו לא אלא הרוגי לוד.

the Pentateuch the tenth day of the seventh month (Tishri) is a day of atonement. The Pentateuch says: "Ye shall afflict yourselves ... for it is a day of atonement to make atonement for you before God, your God."[15] It does not give either a historical or a theological reason why this tenth of the seventh month was instituted as a Day of Atonement.

According to the Book of Jubilees, on the tenth day of the seventh month the sons of Jacob "dealt treacherously with him, (Joseph) and formed a plot against him to slay him, but, changing their minds, they sold him to Ishmaelite merchants ... And the sons of Jacob slaughtered a kid and dipped the coat of Joseph in the blood and sent it to Jacob their father." The Book of Jubilees proceeds: "For this reason it is ordained that the children of Israel should afflict themselves on the tenth day of the seventh month — on that day that the news which made him weep for Joseph came to Jacob his father — that they should make atonement for themselves thereon with a young goat on the tenth day of the seventh month, once a year for their sins; for they had grieved the affection of their father regarding Joseph his son. And this day has been ordained that they should grieve thereon for their sins and for all their transgressions and for all their errors so that they might cleanse themselves on that day once a year."[16]

The Book of Jubilees, as I had occasion to show elsewhere,[17] is one of the oldest books in Jewish literature. It was written in the pre-Hellenistic period, in opposition to the Pentateuch. The author of this book, or the school

[15] Lev. 23.26–8; Num. 29.7–11.
[16] 34.10–20. *The Apocrypha and Pseudepigrapha of the Old Testament*, Vol. 11, ed. R. H. Charles.
[17] *The Book of Jubilees Its Character and Its Significance*, Philadelphia, 1939.

of men who wrote it, held that the sin of the ten sons of Jacob, who sold Joseph into slavery, had not been atoned, and that hence the Jews must afflict themselves annually on the day on which Joseph was sold, in order to attain atonement for this sin which their forefathers committed. Such an idea certainly could not be sanctioned by the Pharisees, who held that every person was responsible for his own sins, and that children should not suffer for the sins of their fathers.

We do not know what the Prophet Amos meant when he said, "For three transgressions of Israel, yea, for four, I will not reverse it; because they sold the righteous for silver and the needy one for a pair of shoes."[18] However, some of the Midrashim held that these words of the Prophet Amos refer to the sale of Joseph by his brethren into slavery. According to *Pirke Rabbi Eliezer*, the words of the prophet referred to the sale of Joseph to the Ishmaelites for twenty pieces of silver by his brethren, each of whom took two pieces and purchased sandals.[19] The *pseudo-Johnathan* to Genesis also says that the brothers of Joseph bought sandals for the money they received in selling Joseph to the Ishmaelites.[20] Likewise, the author of the *Testament of the Twelve Patriarchs* tells us that Zebulun said that he and the other brothers of Joseph bought sandals for themselves and their wives and their children with the twenty pieces of silver.[21] In the *Testament of Gad* it is related that the brethren[22] sold Joseph for thirty

---

[18] Amos 2.6.

[19] אמר להם ראובן אל תשפכו דם השליכו אותו אל הבור הזה אשר במדבר וימות שם ... ומכרו אותו לישמעאלים בעשרים כסף כל אחד ואחד נטל שני כספים לקנות מנעלים ברגליהם שנאמר על מכרם בכסף צדיק ואביון בעבור נעלים (פרקי ר' אליעזר, ל"ח). Comp. *Midrash Tanḥuma* Gen. ad loc., עמדו מכרוהו בעשרים כסף לכל אחד מהם שני כסף לקנות מנעלים לרגליהם.

[20] וחביני ית יוסף לערבאין בעשרים מעין דכסף וזבנו מנהון סנדלין (Gen. 37.28).
[21] *The Testament of Zebulun* 3, 2.
[22] 2.3.

pieces of gold;[23] ten of these pieces were taken by Simon and Gad while the other twenty were shown (given to their brethren.) It is of interest to note that according to the Gospel of Matthew, Judas Iscariot took thirty pieces of silver for betraying Jesus.[24]

Thus we find in the extra-canonical books the idea that the sin of Joseph's brethren for selling him into slavery was not forgiven, and hence the Jews must make atonement and be redeemed from this sin. We do not learn in the extra-canonical writings how the children of Israel could be redeemed from this sin. In the Apocalyptic literature another sin is mentioned which needs redemption. We refer to the Original Sin, i. e., the sin which Adam committed on Friday, the very day he was created. On that day Adam transgressed the word of God.[25] According to the author of II Baruch, death was decreed because Adam sinned: "Because when Adam sinned," said the author of II Baruch, "and death was decreed against those who should be born."[26] The Original Sin will be redeemed, according to the Apocalyptic literature, by a blameless one who "shall be delivered up for the lawless men, and the sinless one shall die for ungodly men."[27] This view that a righteous man, a sinless one, shall die for the sins of the

---

[23] Comp. also the Septuagint Gen. ad loc. εἴκοσι χρυσῶν.
[24] 26.15,
[25] See Ab. R. N. 1. בו ביום נוצר ... בו ביום הכניסו לגן עדן ... בו ביום סרח בו ביום נטרד.
[26] *Quia quando peccavit Adam et decreta fuit mors contra eos qui gignerentur.* 23.4. Comp. also 1 Cor. 15.22, ὥσπερ γὰρ ἐν τῷ Ἀδὰμ πάντες ἀποθνῄσκουσιν, οὕτως καὶ ἐν τῷ Χριστῷ πάντες ζωοποιηθήσονται; Irenaeus *Contra Haereses* V, 23, *Manifestum est itaque, quoniam in illa die mortem sustinuit Dominus, obediens Patri, in qua mortuus est Adam inobediens Deo. in qua autem mortuus est, in ipsa et manducavit... Quia in ipsa mortui sunt, in qua et manducaverunt, hoc est, Parasceve quae dicitur coena pura, id est sexta feria, quam et Dominus ostendit passus in ea.* Comp. also Ben Sirah, 25.24.
[27] *The Testament of Benjamin* 3.8.

ungodly men, for the sin which was committed generations before, was held by the Apocalyptic sect and became the cornerstone of Christianity.[28] Jesus was crucified on Friday, on the day when the Original Sin was committed, to redeem mankind from it.[29]

The theological conception of the redemption of the Original Sin, that a sinless man, a righteous man, can redeem with his blood a sin committed in antiquity, was in vogue among the Jewish Apocalyptists, but was strongly opposed by the rabbis. This idea of redemption by a blameless man for a sin committed by ancestors had an influence on many Jews long after the destruction of the Temple. Thus, we may understand how the legend arose that ten great men in Israel who were sinless and great scholars, were put to death in order to redeem the sin of the ten sons of Jacob who sold their brother Joseph, into slavery. It is of significance that in the liturgy of the Day of Atonement the story of the Ten Martyrs and of their death for the sin of the ten brothers of Joseph is recited. As we remarked before, the author of the Book of Jubilees stated that the Day of Atonement was instituted to atone the sins of the children of Israel because their forefathers sold Joseph into slavery.

Since the Tannaim strongly opposed the idea that a sinless man should atone a sin committed by somebody else we can readily understand why they did not record the story of the Ten Martyrs. Not only is the story of the Ten Martyrs and their connection with Joseph not recorded in the Talmud but the term *Ten Martyrs is never found.*

[28] Comp. also *The Testament of Joseph* 19, 11, The lamb of God who taketh away the sin of the world; The Gospel according to John 1.29, "Ἴδε ὁ ἀμνὸς τοῦ θεοῦ ὁ αἴρων τὴν ἁμαρτίαν τοῦ Κόσμου.

[29] See S. Zeitlin, Origine de la Divergence entre les Evangiles synoptiques et l'Evangile non synoptique quand à la date de la crucifixion de Jésus, *REJ*, 1926.

The Talmud never speaks of ten scholars who were put to death by the Romans. Only in the *Midrash of Lamentations* is it stated that scholars were put to death, but the *number ten is not used* although there were ten. Only in the Apocryphal Midrash *Eleh Ezkerah*, is the story given of the Ten Martyrs and their connection with Joseph. These ten righteous men were to redeem the sin of the ten brothers of Joseph who sold him into slavery. The story in this Apocryphal Midrash relates that Rabbi Ishmael, upon the request of his colleagues, ascended heaven and asked whether they would be put to death. The angel Gabriel told him that the ten Jewish scholars would be put to death. Then Rabbi Ishmael asked him the reason for this. The reason, replied Gabriel, was that the ten sons of Jacob sold their brother Joseph, into slavery.[30]

In the liturgy of the Day of Atonement we have a poem entitled *Eleh Ezkerah*, in which the story of the Ten Martyrs in narrated in beautiful language. In this liturgy the martyrdom of the ten scholars is connected with the selling of Joseph, based on the *Midrash Eleh Ezkerah*. In this liturgical poem a dialogue between the Roman governor and the Jewish scholars is given. The Roman governor says to the scholars:[31] "Where are your ancestors who sold their brother, handing him over to the Ishmaelites;

[30] ... כיון שהגיע לפסוק וגונב איש ומכרו ... מיד צוה למלאות פלטירו מנעלים ושלח לקרוא לעשרה חכמי ישראל ... אמר להם ומי שגנב איש מאחיו של בני ישראל והתעמר בו ומכרו מה דינו? אמרו לו התורה אמרה מות יומת. ענה ואמר להם א"כ אתם חייבים מיתה, אמרו לו אמור למה. אמר להם על מכירת יוסף שמכרוהו אחיו. ואם הם היו בחיים הייתי דן אותם ועתה שאינם חיים אתם תשאו עון אבותיכם ... אמר לו גבריאל ישמעאל בני חי נפשך שכך שמעתי מאחורי הפרגוד שעשרה חכמי ישראל נמסרו להריגה ביד מלכות הרשעה. אמר לו ר' ישמעאל למה. אמר לו על מכירת יוסף שמכרוהו אחיו.

[31] אלה אזכרה ונפשי עלי אשפכה ... לעשרה הרוגי מלכות ... גבה לב בליעל עובד אלילים וצוה למלאות פלטירו נעלים וקרא לעשרה חכמים גדולים ... גם איה אבותיכם אשר אחיהם מכרוהו לאורחת ישמעאלים סחרוהו, ובעד נעלים נתנוהו, ואתם קבלו דין שמים עליכם כי מימי אבותיכם לא נמצא ככם ואם היו בחיים היית דנם לפניכם, ואתם תשאו עון אבותיכם

for a pair of shoes they gave him away; accept you then the judgment of God, since from the days of your fathers there have been none equal to you; had they been living I would have pronounced sentence against them in your stead, but now you shall bear the sins of your ancestors."[31a]

This liturgical poem, as well as the *Midrash Eleh Ezkerah*, has nothing of the spirit of rabbinic Judaism. It represents, rather, the teachings and the spirit of the Apocalyptic Pharisaic sect, the forerunner of the Christians.[31b]

Among the elegaic poems of *Tishah B'ab* there is one about the Ten Martyrs.[32] However, its author makes no reference to the iniquity of the selling of Joseph by his brothers. Saadiah Gaon also has a poem on the Ten Martyrs in his Siddur in the liturgy for the Day of Atonement.[33] He also does not connect the story of the Ten Martyrs with the selling of Joseph.

It is surprising that none of the students of Jewish history ever questioned the historicity of the story of the Ten Martyrs. They have differed as to what scholars were among the Ten Martyrs and as to whether the martyrdom took place in one period or in different periods. They did not realize that the story was only a legend and did not even breathe the spirit of rabbinic Judaism. It is interesting to note that Gedaliah ibn Yachya, the author of *Shalshelet ha-Kabbalah*, questioned the authenticity of the story. Although he was not a historian and his book *Shalshelet ha-Kabbalah* was far from being a historical book, nevertheless he sensed that something was wrong with the story. He was puzzled first by the fact that all the ten scholars were not contemporaries. Secondly, he marveled that de-

---

[31a] L. Finkelstein, *op. cit.*, p. 31.

[31b] Comp. also Israel Levi "Éléments Chrétiens dans le Pirké Rabbi Eliezer," *REJ*, v. 18, pp. 83–9.

[32] ארזי הלבנון אדירי התורה... הנם קדושי הורני מלכות עשרה.

[33] .זכור תבוסת צאן טבחה לכפירים שואנים

scendants should be punished for the sins of their forefathers. He pointed out that the prophets had often proclaimed that children should not die for the sins of their fathers, and he asked why scholars, righteous men, should be punished, and not sinners. Gedaliah ibn Yachya therefore came to the conclusion that there were no Ten Martyrs. Only those whose names were recorded in the Talmud died in martyrdom, and they died either for their own sins or because of the sins of their generation, but not for sins committed before their time. The authors of the poems which are found in our liturgy, he said, invented the story to strike fear into the hearts of the people on such days as the Day of Atonement and the Fast of the ninth of Ab.[34]

To summarize, I have sought to show that the extra-canonical Book of Jubilees, which was written in the pre-Hellenistic period in opposition to the Pentateuch, exercised a great influence upon certain groups of Jews, particularly upon the Apocalytic Pharisaic sect. This group was the forerunner of the Christians. Thus, the ideas of the Book of Jubilees penetrated deeply into Christianity and also left traces on Jewish thought, and passed into the synagogue. The story thus was woven into the Historical books. The legend of the Ten Martyrs is a direct result of the teachings of the Apocalyptic literature, particularly of the ideas found in the Book of Jubilees.

[34] וראוי שתדע כי כל ימי הייתי תוהה על אשר נשאלתי בהפיוט הנאמרים ביום צו"כ וביום ט' באב... ונראה בהם מיתת עשרה הרוגי מלכות עבור חטא מכירת יוסף... כי בא לי על הדבר הזה קושיות הרבה... אפילו שנקיים שחטאו איך יקבלו בניהם אחריהם עונש הלא הנביאים מצווחים ואומרים ובנים לא יומתו על אבות... אפילו שנניח שיוכלו למות הבנים על חטא האבות איך היה העונש לאלה החכמים ולא לחוטאים ממש... והואיל והיו עשרה שבטים יחד בעת עשות החטא, איך לא היו יחד בעת העונש, וזה כי אלו החכמים לא נמצאו יחד בדור... אומר אני כי שקר נחלו אבותינו להאמין שהאבות יאכלו בוסר ושיני בנים תקהנה ולא הרנו כל החכמים ההם זולתי קצת הכתובים בגמרא... וגם הם לא מתו כי אם בעונם או בעון דור אז ולא בעון זולתם, והפייטנים בדאו זה העניין מלבם להביא מורך בלב ההמון בימים ההם שהם ימי עניו ותשובה.

APPENDIX

THE BOOK OF JUBILEES

In my work on the Book of Jubilees I showed that this book was not written in the period between 160 B. C. E. and 50 C. E. by a Pharisee or Sadducee, as was the consensus of opinion among scholars. In my opinion the book was composed in the pre-Hellenistic period and was written in opposition to the Pentateuch. One of the many arguments I gave in substantiation of my opinion was that the names of the angels are not given in the book although they are prevalent in the later Apocryphal books. Neither are the names of the months given, but they are mentioned by numbers as in the Bible of the pre-Exilic period.[35] The laws given in the book are not Sadducean or Pharisean but are in opposition to the Pentateuchal laws.

Dr. H. H. Rowley, in his recent book *The Relevance of the Apocalyptic*, does not accept my conclusions. He states that the system of indicating the months by number was employed in the majority of the Apocryphal and Pseudepigraphical writings.[36] The only other book in the entire Apocryphal and Pseudepigraphical writings besides the Book of Jubilees, where months are mentioned mostly by numbers is the first Book of Ezra.[36a] The Book of Ezra is likewise one of the earliest books, and was also composed either in the pre-Hellenistic period or not later than the end of the fourth century B. C. E.[37] However,

---

[35] Pp. 8–13.
[36] P. 82.
[36a] Twelve months are designated by numbers, while two months are mentioned by definite names.
[37] See the introduction of Charles ad loc. Even in the Book of Ezra two months are recorded by names, like Nisan (5.6) and Adar (7.5); while in the Book of Jubilees all the months are designated by numerals.

in the other books of the Pseudepigraphical literature some months are recorded by names while others are designated by numbers.

In the book of Maccabees I and II some months are indicated by numbers. However, most of the months are mentioned by name, while in the Book of Jubilees all the months are indicated by numbers. I asserted that the Book of Jubilees could not have been written by either a Sadducee or a Pharisee since the laws of the Book of Jubilees are in direct opposition to the laws of the Pentateuch. Dr. Rowley does not believe that this is conclusive proof since, in his opinion, the Pharisees felt themselves at liberty to reject the *lex talionis* and thus oppose an important Pentateuchal law.[38] There is a difference between rejecting a law and amending a law by legal fiction. The Pharisees never opposed the Pentateuchal laws, but amended them. The Pharisees did not reject the *lex talionis*, but amended it. A lawyer knows the exact difference between rejecting and amending a law, but a theologian ought also to take cognizance of the existing difference.

Dr. Louis Finkelstein, in his essay, "Pre-Maccabean Documents in The Passover Haggadah," [39] adds an appendix on the date of the Book of Jubilees. In his essay Dr. Finkelstein retracts his previous opinion that the Book of Jubilees was written at the time of the Sadducees and Pharisees. Now he places the date 175 B. C. E. as the *terminus a quo* for this book. In arguing for this date Dr. Finkelstein quotes from the books of Macabees I and II, that the charge against Jason was, "his establishment of a gymnasium where the youth of Jerusalem disported themselves naked after the manner of the Greeks."[40] There-

[38] P. 82.
[39] *The Harvard Theological Review*, Vol. XXXVI, 1943.
[40] P. 20.

fore, according to Dr. Finkelstein, the command of Noah to his sons to cover the shame of their flesh would indicate that the Book of Jubilees was written in order to denounce the practice of Jason and his associates. According to such an argument one might say that 175 B. C. E. was the *terminus a quo* for Gen. 9.23–27.[41]

Dr. Finkelstein further defends the date for the Book of Jubilees which he places at the time of the struggle between the Seleucids and Ptolemies for Palestine. To support his theory he quotes chapter 46 of the Book of Jubilees: "And he (Joseph) made them swear regarding his bones, for he knew that the Egyptians would not again bring forth and bury him in the land of Canaan, for Makamaron, king of Canaan, while dwelling in the land of Assyria, fought in the valley with the king of Egypt and slew him there, and pursued after the Egyptians to the gates of 'Ermon. But he was not able to enter, for another, a new king, had become king of Egypt, and he was stronger than he, and he returned to the land of Canaan, and the gates of Egypt were closed, and none went out and none came into Egypt." By such logic one might say that the passage in Ex. 1.9–10 was composed at the time of the struggle between the Seleucids and the Ptolemies for the possession of Egypt. Again, from history we know that the Egyptians had many wars first with the Canaanites, and then with the Assyrians.[42]

Dr. Finkelstein, to support his point of view that the Book of Jubilees was written at the time of the conflict between the Seleucids and the Ptolemies, instances the fact that the author was hostile to Egypt, and notes the verse from the Book of Jubilees: "The people of Egypt

---

[41] וירא חם אבי כנען את ערות אביו . . . ויקח שם ויפת את השמלה . . . ויכסו את ערות אביהם . . . ויאמר ארור כנען עבד עבדים יהיה לאחיו.

[42] See Charles, ch. 46 note to verses 6–9.

abominated the children of Israel." Is this really proof that the Book of Jubilees was composed in that period? Have we not a similar passage in Gen. 43.32: "Because the Egyptians may not eat bread with the Hebrews; for this is an abomination unto the Egyptians." In Genesis we find that the Hebrews were an abomination to the Egyptians, while in the Book of Jubilees which was written to oppose the Pentateuch we read the reverse, that the Egyptians were an abomination to the Hebrews.

The arguments which Dr. Finkelstein has brought in support of the late date of the composition of the Book of Jubilees are far from convincing. From the logic of the arguments of Dr. Finkelstein one could say that some portions of the Pentateuch were also written in the Hellenistic period. The Book of Jubilees was written in a very early period in opposition to the Pentateuch. Therefore we have many parallels with the Pentateuch and many laws in direct opposition to it.

That the Book of Jubilees could not have been written in the Hellenistic period is clear from the fact that all the months are designated by numerals rather than by names.[43] The author connected the festival of *Shabuot* with the covenants that God made with Noah and Abraham, thereby contradicting the Pentateuch. The word שבועות has

---

[43] In the Testament of Naphtali 1.2 (the Testament of the Twelve Patriarchs) the month was specified by number. "When his sons were gathered in the seventh month, on the first day of the month" he told them he was dying. That this month was specified by number is due to the fact that this passage had its origin in the Book of Jubilees, XXVIII, 19. "On the fifth of the seventh month." I believe that the reading in the Testament of Naphtali should have been on the fifth of the month instead of the first day, or the reading in the Book of Jubilees perhaps was the first day instead of the fifth. In I Enoch (60.1; 72) the months were given by numbers, the seventh month, the first month. That is also explainable because these chapters deal with the heavenly luminaries, the calendar, and were based on the Book of Jubilees.

not the connotation of "weeks" but of "oaths." In Mac. II, which was written about 125 B. C. E., the festival of *Shabuot* was already known by the name Pentecost and the Feast of Weeks. Again the calendar employed in the Book of Jubilees and the festival of *Shabuot*, in commemoration of the covenants that God made with Noah and Abraham, shows without doubt that the book could not have been written in the Hellenistic period. The author of the book still used the primitive solar calendar, which contained three hundred and sixty-four days, while during the Hellenistic period it was universally known that the duration of the solar year was 365¼ days.

One of the reviewers of my booklet *The Book of Jubilees* said that if my thesis is correct, "all our intertestamental studies need considerable revision."[44] As a matter of fact the reviewer is right in this assumption. All the theories on the Book of Jubilees and the Pseudopigrapha must be reconsidered and revised.

[44] *Anglican Theological Review* 1940; *Journal of Religion* July, 1940.

THE ASSUMPTION OF MOSES AND THE REVOLT OF BAR KOKBA

Studies in the Apocalyptic Literature

THE little volume which we possess today under the name of the *Assumption of Moses* is actually a composite work consisting of two books, *The Testament of Moses* and a treatise known to the Church Fathers as *The Assumption of Moses*. In his *De Principiis*, Origen mentioned an apocryphal book entitled *The Assumption of Moses*,[1] and, in the *Acts of the Second Nicene Council*, 787 C. E.,[2] a reference is found to a book of the same name.[2a] In a list of apocryphal works, however, mention is made of the *Testament of Moses*.[3]

Now, it chanced that nearly ninety years ago a renowned Italian scholar, Ceriani, discovered in the Ambrosian Library of Milan a palimpsest manuscript of the sixth century which bore no title, but which Ceriani identified

---

[1] *Et primo quidem in Genesi serpens Evam seduxisse describitur: de quo in Adscensione Mosis, cujus libelli meminit in epistola sua apostolus Judas, Michael archangelus cum diabolo disputans de corpore Mosis, ait a diabolo inspiratum serpentem causam exstitisse praevaricationis Adae et Evae.* Lib. III, 2, pp. 303–4. Origenis, *Opera Omnia*, ed. C. H. E. Lommatzsch, t. XXX, Berlini, 1847.

[2] *Acta Synodi Nicaenae* II.

[2a] See below note 4.

[3] See A. Hilgenfeld, *Messias Judaeorum, Libris Eorum Paulo Ante Et Paulo Post Christum Natum Conscriptis Illustratus.* Lipsiae, 1869; pp. 461–2; G. Volkmar, *Mose Prophetie, Und Himmelfahrt.* Leipzig, 1867; pp. 7–9.

Reprinted from the *Jewish Quarterly Review*, New Series, Vol. 38, 1947.

with the passage quoted in the *Acts of the Second Nicene Council*.[4] Since that passage was quoted in the name of the *Assumption of Moses*, Ceriani named the work he discovered *The Assumption of Moses*. Schürer[5] and Charles,[6] however, have pointed out that this *Assumption of Moses* is actually *The Testament of Moses*, while only a small portion of it is *The Assumption of Moses*.

The manuscript which was discovered by Ceriani is defective and badly preserved. Its Latin rendering is imperfect and, at times, ungrammatical.[7] It has no division of chapters and verses, and often many of the letters are undecipherable. The palimpsest itself comes from the sixth century. Undoubtedly, this Latin version was rendered from the Greek, and hence, it may be assumed that it was made not later than the end of the fifth century or the beginning of the sixth. The original language of this book was without doubt Hebrew,[8] but both the Hebrew and the Greek text have been lost.

---

[4] The passage in the Acts of the *Second Nicene Council* reads as follows: Μέλλων ὁ προφήτης Μωυσῆς ἐξιέναι τοῦ βίου ὡς γέγραπται ἐν βίβλῳ ᾿Αναλήψεως Μωυσέως προσκαλεσάμενος ᾿Ιησοῦν υἱὸν Ναυὴ καὶ διαλεγόμενός πρὸς αὐτὸν ἔφη. Καὶ προεθεάσατό με ὁ θεὸς πρὸ καταβολῆς κοσμου εἶναί με τῆς διαθήκης αὐτοῦ μεσίτην. Ceriani identified this with the follwing words found in the manuscript: *Itaque excogitavit et invenit me, qui ab initio orbis terrarum praeparatus sum, ut sim arbiter testamenti illius.* Thus, he came to the conclusion that the manuscript is the *Assumption of Moses* mentioned by the Church Fathers.

[5] *Geschichte*, vol. III.

[6] *Apocrypha and Pseudepigrapha*, vol. II.

[7] Eg. *tunc* for *nunc*, *tib* for *tribus*, *scenae testimonium* for *scenom testimonii*, *cum Moyses* for *tum Moyses*, *occidit* for *occidet*, *docentes* for *dicentes*, *et leges* for *leges et*, *in domum* for *in dominum*. The Greek, as well, of which the Latin is a translation, must have contained some serious mistakes. Comp. note 132.

[8] See Charles, *op. cit.* Comp. idem. *The Assumption of Moses, Translated From The Latin Sixth Century Ms., The Unemended Text Of Which Is Published Herewith, Together With The Text In Its Restored And Critically Emended Form*, London, 1897, pp. XXXVIII–L.

Ceriani published *The Assumption of Moses* in the *Monumenta sacra et profana* in 1861. Five years later Hilgenfeld edited the text;[9] then Volkmar followed and provided a German translation and a commentary.[10] In 1868, Schmidt and Merx again edited this Latin version,[11] and three years later Fritzsche included it in his *Libri Apocryphi Vet Testamenti Graece*, publishing the text of Ceriani on one page and the emended text on the opposite.

The Assumption of Moses which we now have, begins with the statement that in the year two thousand five hundred from the creation of the world[12] Moses summoned Joshua to tell him that he (Moses) was about to pass away, and he gave Joshua instructions how to administer the people. We are also informed that Moses told Joshua to preserve the books which he delivered to him, to set them in order, and to "anoint them with oil of cedar and put them away in earthen vessels in the place which He made from the beginning of the creation of the world." The author then deals briefly with the period from the death of Moses down to his own time. He shows familiarity with the history of the Jewish people — their exile by the Babylonians, their restoration to the land of their fathers, and their tribulations under Antiochus Epiphanes. Next, he tells about the Hasmoneans who usurped the high priesthood and the kingdom. He is aware that Herod ruled for thirty-four years and calls him an "insolent king."[13] Towards the end, the author relates the rest of the history of the Jews, revealing his conviction that the salvation of

---

[9] *Op. cit.*
[10] *Op. cit.*, pp. 137–152.
[11] "Die Assumptio Moses, mit Einleitung und erklärenden Anmerkungen herausgegeben" (*Archiv für wissenschaftliche Erforschung des Alten Testaments*, I. ii 1868).
[12] *Qui est bis millesimus et quingentesimus annus a creatura orbis terrae.*
[13] *Rex petulans.*

Israel would come through the establishment of a theocratic state.

The general opinion is that this book was compiled shortly after the death of Herod, that is, in the first two decades of the first century C. E.[14] As to the authorship of the book, scholars are divided, some maintaining that the author was a Pharisaic Quietist,[15] others that he was a Zealot.[16] Before determining the authorship and the date of the book, however, we must clarify a few important obscurities.

Taxo

In chapter 9, we read: "Then (in that day there) will (be) arise a man of the tribe of Levi, whose name will be Taxo, who, having seven sons, will speak to them."[17]

A considerable literature has been written about the identity of Taxo. Scholars believe that in the identification of Taxo lies the real significance of the book. Hilgenfeld,[18] for example, assumed that the name Taxo means Messiah. He arrived at this conclusion through *gematria*, the letters $T\xi\gamma$ equal 363, and those of המשיח likewise equal 363. Volkmar assumed that the word $T\acute{a}\xi\omega$ was corrupted from $Ta\xi\iota o$, and believed again through *gematria* that it meant Rabbi Akiba, for $Ta\xi\iota o$ equals 431 and רבון עקבא equals 431.[19] Colani holds the opinion that Taxo meant Rabbi Jehuda ben Baba, who was put to death at the time of the Hadrianic persecutions; Colani also arrived at his opinion

---

[14] See below p. 10.

[15] Charles, *op. cit.*

[16] W. J. Deane, *Pseudepigrapha: An Account Of Certain Apocryphal Sacred Writings Of The Jews And Early Christians*, Edinburgh, 1891, pp. 105–6.

[17] *Tunc illo (die erit) [dicente] homo de tribu Levi, cujus nomen erit Taxo, qui habens VII filios dicet ad eos rogans.*

[18] *Op. cit.*, pp. 466–7.

[19] *Op. cit.*, p. 60. However, the name of Akiba has a *yod* in it, עקיבא.

through *gematria*.[20] Hausrath thinks that by the substitutive method of *at bash* שלה was transformed into תכמו, the Greek translator erroneously taking the מ as ס.[21] Shiloh stands here for Messiah. Wieseler thinks that Taxo refers back to תחש, "the badger-like one."[22] This designation he suggests is derived from the fact that the pious dwelt in caves in the earth.[23] Rosenthal points out that שילה is numerically equal to משה and says it has reference to a second Moses who was to rise again.[24] Lattey agrees with Hausrath that Taxo is Shiloh, and that Taxo thus stands for the Messiah.[25] Burkitt[26] and Charles identify Taxo with Eleazar of *II Maccabees*.[27] Holscher agrees with Burkitt that Taxo refers to Eleazar, but says he is another Eleazar of the time of Bar Kokba.[28] Torrey[29] states that Taxo is Mattathis, "the father of the Maccabees and all the Hasmonean dynasty." He writes, "In the numerical value of the letters used, 'Taxo' corresponds exactly to 'the Hasmonean,' in Aramaic, but not in Hebrew.'[30]

These theories cannot be seriously entertained. Some of them are ingenious, but they do not answer the question who is Taxo, who had seven sons and who exhorted them, as we are informed, to observe the law and to die rather than transgress the commands of God. He could not be

[20] *Revue de Theologie*, 1868, pp. 90–4.
[21] *Neutestamentl Zeitgesch.* IV, p. 77.
[22] *Jahr. f. d. Th.* 1868, p. 629. Comp. also Deane, *op. cit.*, p. 119.
[23] Deane is of the opinion that Taxo "is probably the Low-Latin word meaning 'a badger,' equivalent to the Hebrew תחש *tachash*."
[24] *Vier Apokryphische Bücher*, Leipzig, 1885, p. 31.
[25] *Catholic Biblical Quarterly*, 1942. Comp. H. H. Rowley, *The Relevance Of Apocalyptic*, pp. 128–30.
[26] *Jewish And Christian Apocalypses*, The Schweich Lectures 1913, London, 1914, pp. 37–39.
[27] Charles, *op. cit.*, p. 30.
[28] *Zeitschrift für die neutestamentliche Wissenschaft*, 1916, 117–8.
[29] *The Apocryphal Literature*, New Haven, 1945, pp. 114–16.
[30] P. 116.

Mattathis, as Dr. Torrey believes, because Mattathis encouraged his sons to resist and fight the Greeks,[31] while Taxo was opposed to combatting the enemy.[32] Dr. Torrey is of the opinion that the seven sons represent "the seven Hasmonean rulers, from Judas to Antigonus."[33] But, as a matter of fact, there were ·ten rulers from Judas to Antigonus.[34] These are not the only objections that can be raised against Dr. Torrey's theories, as well as those of other scholars. Is it not anomalous that the author of *The Assumption of Moses* should make use of *gematria* for the names Messiah, Hasmonean, Mattathis, Shiloh. Certainly, he would not use the method of *gematria* to arrive at the word Messiah, for none of the apocryphal writers ever adopted this method of *gematria*. Furthermore, the use of *gematria*, I believe, was not known to the Jews during the Second Commonwealth. None of the scholars has suggested any reason why the author should substitute the name of Taxo for that of Messiah or Hasmonean.

I venture to say that the word Taxo is the Greek word Τοξον latinized by the author. *Toxon* means a bow, in the Hebrew *keshet*.

The word *keshet* occupied a conspicuous place in the early Jewish theology. Rabbi Joshua ben Levi said that when a Jew sees the *keshet* in the sky he must fall to the

[31] See I Mac. 2.64–66 . . . ἰσχύσατε καὶ ανδρίζεσθε ἐν τῷ νόμῳ . . . οὗτος ὑμῖν ἔσται ἄρχων στρατιᾶς καὶ πολεμήσει πόλεμον λαῶν.

[32] Ch. 9. In making use of chapter divisions, I follow the edition of Fritzsche. The manuscript itself, as I have said, has no chapter divisions.

[33] *Op. cit.*, p. 116. Comp. also *idem. Jour. Bib. Lit.*, 1943. Comp. also W. Bousset, *Die Religion des Judentums im Späthellenistischen Zeitalter*, 1926, p. 232; J. Lagrange, *Le Judaism, Avant Jesus Christ*, 1931, pp. 237–242.

[34] Judas, Jonathan, Simon, John Hyrkanus I, Aristobulus I, Alexander Jannaeus, Alexandra, John Hyrkanus II, Aristobulus II, Antigonus.

ground.³⁵ According to the Talmud, the *keshet* was created on the sixth day (Friday) at twilight.³⁶ From the Book of Genesis, we learn that when God made a covenant with Noah that "neither shall there any more be a flood to destroy the earth" the *keshet* (bow) was to be the token of the covenant between God and Noah.³⁷ In the Book of Ezekiel, it is related that when Ezekiel saw the chariot, he declared: "As the appearance of the *bow* that is in the cloud in the day of rain, so was the appearance of the brightness around about, this was the appearance of the likeness of the glory of God."³⁸ The author of the Book of Revelation wrote that he saw "a white horse: and he that sat on him had a *bow*; and a crown was given unto him: and he went forth conquering and to conquer."³⁹ The Zohar connects the *keshet* with the coming of the Messiah. It affirms that when the *keshet* appears in very bright colors and the world is lit up by it, then the coming of the Messiah will be near.⁴⁰ Thus, we see that the *keshet* occupied an important position in the early Jewish theology.

³⁵ א"ר אלכסנדרי אמר ר' יהושע בן לוי הרואה את הקשת בענן צריך שיפול על פניו שנאמר כמראה הקשת אשר יהיה בענן . . . הוא מראה דמות כבוד ד' ואראה ואפל על פני. Ber. 59a.
³⁶ עשרה דברים נבראו בערב שבת בין השמשות ואלו הן . . . והקשת. Abot 5.
³⁷ את קשתי נתתי בענן והיתה לאות ברית ביני ובין הארץ . . . והיתה הקשת בענן וראיתיה לזכר ברית עולם בין אלהים ובין כל נפש חיה. Gen. 9.12–16.
³⁸ Ezek. 1.28.
³⁹ καὶ ἰδοὺ ἵππος λευκός καὶ ὁ καθήμενος ἐπ' αὐτὸν ἔχων τόξον καὶ ἐδόθη αὐτῷ στέφανος καὶ ἐξῆλθεν νικῶν καὶ ἵνα νικήσῃ. Rev. 6.2. See also Sirah, 43.11, ἴδε τόξον καὶ εὐλόγησον τὸν ποιήσαντα αὐτό; 50. 7, ὡς ἥλιος ἐκλάμπων ἐπὶ ναὸν ὑψίστου καὶ ὡς τόξον φωτίζον ἐν νεφέλαις δόξης.
⁴⁰ וכד יפקון ישראל מן גלותא זמינא האי קשת לאתקשטא בגוונוי ככלה דא דמתקשטא לבעלה אמר ליה ההוא יודאי כך אמר לי אבא כד הוה מסתלק מעלמא לא תצפי לרגלי דמשיחא עד דיתחזי האי קשת בעלמא מתקשטא בגוונוי נהירין ויתנהיר לעלמא וכדין צפי לי למשיח (פ' נח); כמראה הקשת זה חי עלמין וזה את קשתי נתתי בענן דא מלכות נתתי מן יומא דאתברי עלמא . . . (בראשית); את קשתי נתתי בענן תנינן דההוא קשת אשלחת לבושי ויהיב למשה ובההוא לבושא סליק משה לטורא ומינה חמא מה דחמא ואתהני מכלא עד ההוא אתר (פ' משפטים); קום אנת ר' יוסי הגלילי ואימא דהא מלין שפירין קאמרת בחבורא קדמאה דקשת לא אתייא אלא לאגנא על עלמא למלכא דבכל זמנא דבריה

The author of the *Assumption of Moses* when he wrote או
(τοξου) יקום (יהיה) איש (אדם) משבט לוי ושמו יהיה קשת "*Tunc illo
(die erit) [dicente] homo de tribu Levi, cujus nomen erit Taxo*,"
"then will arise a man of the tribe of Levi whose name will
be Taxo" may have had in mind the prophecy of Zech. 6.12.
כה אמר ד' צבאות לאמר הנה איש צמח שמו ומתחתיו יצמח ובנה את היכל
ד'.[40a] The Church Fathers maintained that this passage
referred to Jesus. The Septuagint translates the word צמח
by Ἀνατολή branch or offshoot. Justin Martyr maintained
that this passage of Zechariah referred to Jesus.[41] He also
rendered the word צמח by Ἀνατολή, but in the sense of
East. The Vulgate renders this passage: *Haec ait Dominus
exercitum, dicens: ECCE VIR ORIENS NOMEN EIUS:
et subter eum orietur, et aedificabit templum Domino. Et ipse
extruet templum Domino.* The word צמח is generally translated in the Vulgate by *germen*.[42] In this passage, however,
the Vulgate renders it *ORIENS, East*. Thus, the Vulgate
definitely follows Justin Martyr in that it gives the translation of Zechariah as "a man whose name is East," meaning, of course, Jesus. The rabbis, likewise, interpret the
word צמח as referring to the Messiah.[43]

The words of Zech. 6.12 present a certain ambiguity.
Does this prophecy refer to Joshua, the priest of the tribe

חב ומלכא חזי למטרוניתא סליק רוגזא דבריה... אלא ודאי ההוא קשת דאתגלייא
בגולתא לא איהו אלא מטטרון דאתקרי שד"י ואיהו עבדו זקן ביתו דשליט בכל דילה
(רעיא מהימנא, פ' פנחס). According to the Zohar, *keshet* is Mattatron,
who is the chief of the angels and is even called שדי, the Almighty.

[40a] He only substituted the word קשת for צמח.

[41] Καὶ Πάλιν Ἀνατολη ὄνομα αὐτοῦ Ζαχαρίας φησὶ. *Dialogue with
Trypho*, 121.

[42] E. g. Jer. 23.5; 33.15; Ezek. 16.7.

[43] Mid. R. Lam. 1, אמר צמח שמו ר' יהושע בן לוי... מה שמו של מלך המשיח
שנאמר הנה איש צמח שמו ומתחתיו יצמח ר' יודן בש"ר איבו אמר מנחם שמו שנא' כי רחק
ממני מנחם. א"ר חניא ולא פלינא חושבנא דדין כחושבנא דדין הוא מנחם הוא צמח
See also Targum Jonathan *ad loc*. הא גברא משיחא שמיה עתיד דיתגלי ויתרבי
ויש פותרים אותו במלך המשיח אבל כל. Comp. also Rashi *ad loc*. ויבני ית היכלא
הענין הזה מדבר בבית שני.

of Levi, or to Zerubbabel of the tribe of Judah? The rabbinic tradition holds that it refers to Zerubbabel.[44] From the text itself, however, we may infer that it refers to Joshua of the tribe of Levi.

A study of the *Assumption of Moses* reveals the fact that the author did not believe in a Messiah but held that God would reveal Himself in this world. The man named Taxo, *keshet*, would herald the coming of God in His full majesty.[45]

Assuming that the word Taxo actually is a latinized Greek word τοξον the fact that in this Latin text we have a Greek word does not present any difficulty. This is not the only place where the author did not translate the Greek but rather transliterated it. Examples of this are: *chedrio*[46] (cedar) κεδρόω; *heremus*[47] (wilderness) ἐρῆμος; and *acrobistia*[48] (uncircumcised) ἀκροβυστία. As to the word Taxo instead of *toxon*, as we should expect if this word is a transliteration of the Greek, we must bear in mind that the Latin translation in general is faulty. There are many other errors both in textual structure as well as in grammar.[48a]

Date of Composition

The same wide divergence of opinion that exists with regard to the word Taxo also exists as to the date of composition and the authorship of *The Assumption of Moses*. Ewald,[49] Wieseler[50] and Dillmann[51] are of the opinion that

[44] See Rashi *ibid.* צמח שמו הוא זרובבל.
[45] Comp. ch. 10.
[46] Ch. 1, 17.
[47] Ch. 3, 11.
[48] Ch. 8, 3.
[48a] See note 7.
[49] *Gesch. des Volkes Israel*, vol. 6.
[50] *Op. cit.*
[51] See the literature given in Herzong's *Real-Encyc.* 3rd ed., XVI, pp. 242–44.

this book was compiled during the first decades C. E. Torrey also accepts this date.[52] Hilgenfeld holds that the book was composed about the year 44–45 C. E.[53] Charles is firm in his belief that it was composed between 7 and 30 C. E.[54] On the other hand, Schmidt and Merx insist that the composition of the book took place sometime between 54 and 64 C. E.[55] Volkmar argues for a still later date, sometime between 137–138 C. E.[56] General opinion among scholars is, however, that *The Assumption of Moses* was compiled *before* the destruction of the Second Temple. This date is out of question and need not even be considered.

The author gives the date of Moses' death as two thousand five hundred years after the creation of the world and thus helps us inadvertantly to establish the date when he lived and wrote it. Now, during the Second Commonwealth, this manner of designating an era by *Anno Mundi*, was not used by the Jews. In the Bible, different eras are given, for example, the era of the Exodus,[57] the era of the destruction of the Temple of Solomon,[58] the era of the different kings.[59] In the Second Commonwealth we also find different eras by which the Jews reckoned their chronology: the era of the Seleucides,[60] the era of the establishment of the Jewish state in the time of Simon the Hasmonean,[61] the

[52] *Op. cit.* p. 116.
[53] *Op. cit.* p. LXXIV.
[54] *Op. cit.*
[55] *Op. cit.*
[56] *Op. cit.* pp. 57–72.
[57] E. g. I Kings 6.1 ויהי בשמונים שנה וארבע מאות שנה לצאת בני ישראל ממצרים.
[58] Ezek. 1.1; 8.1; 20.1; 24.1. See also Yer. R. H. 1.
[59] The dates of the Persian kings are given in the books of the Bible of the post-exilic period, בשנת שתים לדריוש, בשנת שלש לכרש.
[60] This chronology was used in the books of the Maccabees and by Josephus in his book *Antiquities*.
[61] השנה הראשונה לגאולת ישראל.

era of the different kings,⁶² but nowhere is the era of the creation used.⁶³ Only after the destruction of the Second Temple did this manner of designating the era come into vogue.⁶²ᵃ

Thus, we may say with certainty that this book, *The Assumption of Moses*, could have been composed only *after* the destruction of the Second Temple.

Those who are of the opinion that the book was composed in the first two decades of the first century C. E. maintain that the author referred to Herod when he said "He will beget children who, succeeding him, will rule for shorter periods." The statement about the rule of his children for shorter periods is true only regarding Archelaus, who ruled for nine years. It may possibly apply to Herod's grandson, who ruled for four years. But it does not apply to his other children, Philip and Herod Antipas, who reigned longer than their father Herod who ruled for thirty-four years.⁶⁴ The scholars therefore concluded that the book could have been written only after the removal of Archelaus in 6 C. E. and before Philip and Herod Antipas died. This would fix the date of the composition of this book before 30 C. E. However, this is not sufficient proof to assign the book to this early date. The author of our book, in his statement

---

⁶² So Josephus, in his book *The Jewish Wars*, gives the dates of the Roman emperors.

⁶²ᵃ See also IV Ezra 14.48.

⁶³ Josephus, in his book *Antiquities* 1, 3, 3, gives the date of the flood as 2262 after the birth of Adam, the first man. χρόνος δὲ οὗτος ἀπὸ 'Αδάμου τοῦ πρώτου γεγονότος ... In book 8, 3, 1, Josephus says: "From the birth of Adam the first man to the time when Solomon built the Temple there elapsed altogether 3102 years. ἀπὸ δὲ τοῦ πρώτου γεννηθέντος 'Αδάμου ἕως οὗ τὸν ναὸν ᾠκοδόμησε Σολομών .... Josephus never used the term ἀπὸ τῆς κτίσεως τοῦ κόσμου (לבריאת העולם) "after the creation of the world," since there was no such era known to the Jews at the time of the Second Commonwealth.

⁶⁴ From the year 38 to 4 B. C. E.

"Children who, succeeding him, will reign for shorter periods," may refer to those who were kings of Judaea, but Philip and Herod Antipas never ruled over Judaea.

Authorship

On the authorship of the book, wide differences of opinion also exist. Scholars are divided in regard to the sect to which the author belonged. Some hold that he was a Pharisee,[65] while others believe him a Sadducee.[66] Still others are of the opinion that he was an Essene.[66a] On the other hand, some consider him a Zealot,[67] while others maintain that he belonged to the Pharisaic Quietist group.[68] All these scholars who differ as to the authorship of this book base their theories on Chapter VII, which contains, in their opinion, the crux of the argument in the determination of the authorship as well as the date of the book.

As stated above, the condition of the text of this book is unsatisfactory. The Latin translation is full of errors of transcription and, in some places, the text itself is very hard to decipher. Chapter VII is more than defective; it is mutilated. The text of this chapter as it was found reads as follows:[69]

ex quo facto finien	. . . . . . ae . . . . pos . .
tur tempors momen	. . . . initiis tribus ad
to . . . . etur cursus	exitus viiii propter
a . . . . horae iiii ue	initium tres sep
niant coguntur secun	timae secunda tria

---

[65] Dillmann, *op. cit.* Comp. also Schürer, *op. cit.*
[66] See Volkmar, *op. cit.* pp. 105–6.
[66a] Schmidt-Merx, *op. cit.*
[67] See Deane, *op. cit.*
[68] Charles, *op. cit.*
[69] The text here is from the original manuscript published by Fritzsche.

in tertia duae h..ra..
tae et regnarunt
de his homines pes
tilentiosi et impii
docentes se esse
iustos et hi susci
tabunt iram animo
rum suorum qui
erunt homines do
losi sibi placentes
ficti in omnibus suis
et omni hora diei
amantes convivia
deuoratores gulae
s...n...ca....
.....nus diis....
....omnis....
....
....u....o....
rae.....elen
tes.....rum bo
norum comesto
res dicentes se haec
facere propter mi
sericordiam qu...
se et extermina

tores quaeru...
fallaces celantes se
ne possent cognos
ci impii in scelere
pleni et iniquitate
ab oriente usque ad
occidentem dicen
tes habebimus dis
cubitiones et luxu
riam edentes et
bibentes
Et putauimus nos
tamquam principes
erimus et manus
eorum et mentes
inmunda tractantes
et os eorum loque
tur ingentia et su
per dicent noli....
tange ni inquines
me loco in quo...s...
...is d........
su.....us.....
in........
re....raui....

This text was emended and edited by Schmidt and Merx[70] and later re-edited critically by Fritzsche.[71] The English translation by Charles based mainly on these two editions is as follows: "And when this is done the times will be ended, in a moment the (second) course will be (ended),

[70] *Op. cit.*
[71] *Op. cit.*

the four hours will come. They will be forced ....
And, in the time of these, pestilent[72] and impious men will rule, saying that they are just. And these will conceal the wrath of their minds, being treacherous men, self-pleasers, dissemblers in all their own affairs and lovers of banquets at every hour of the day, gluttons, gourmands ....
Devourers of the goods of the poor saying that they do so on the ground of their justice, but (in reality) to destroy them, complainers, deceitful, concealing themselves lest they should be recognised, impious, filled with lawlessness and iniquity from sunrise to sunset: Saying: "We shall have feastings and luxury, eating and drinking, yea we shall drink our fill, we shall be as princes." And though their hands and their minds touch unclean things, yet their mouth will speak great things, and they will say furthermore: "Do not touch me lest thou shouldst pollute me in the place where I stand" ....

Who were the "pestilent and impious men" to whom the author refers? And whom did he have in mind when he said "lovers of banquets at every hour of the day, gluttons, gourmands ...."? Hilgenfeld thinks that they were the Herodian princes.[73] Ewald,[74] Dillmann[75] and Schürer[76] believe them to be Pharisees of the first decades after Herod's death. This passage refers to the Pharisees and to the Sadducees, according to Wieseler.[77] Rosenthal's view is that some verses allude to the Sadducees and others to the Pharisees.[78] Geiger concludes that the passage refers only to the Sadducees.[79] Other scholars say that the

[72] *Pestilentiosi et impii.*
[73] *Op. cit.*
[74] *Op. cit.*
[75] *Op. cit.*
[76] *Op. cit.*
[77] *Op. cit.*
[78] *Op. cit.* pp. 19–22.
[79] See *Jüdische Zeitschrift*, 1868.

author had the Roman procurators in mind,[80] while Volkmar, on the other hand, says that he was thinking of the Sadducees of the time of Nerva and Trajan.[81]

These opinions are untenable. The Pharisees were not inclined towards gluttony nor were they addicted to wine. They were never charged with these vices, even by their bitterest opponents. Furthermore, the book could not have been written by a Saducee. Neither can we accept the theory that this passage is applicable to the Sadducees of the time of Nerva and Trajan, because, after the destruction of the Temple, the Sadducees as a sect ceased to exist. The assumption that one or two verses of this chapter refer to the Pharisees while another verse or two point to the Sadducees is not valid. Neither can we accept the theory that this chapter refers to the Herodian princes or to the Roman procurators. I previously showed that the author's use of the manner of designating an era of the Creation proves unquestionably that this book could not have been written *before* the destruction of the Temple. After the destruction there were no Herodian princes. For the same reason, also, we must reject the opinion that this book was written by a Zealot, because the Zealots, as a party, came into existence in the year 66 C. E., under the leadership of Eleazar, the son of Simon. (Incidentally, we must correct the erroneous assumption of the scholars that the Zealots came into existence at the time of Herod under the leadership of Judas of Galilee... Josephus, in his book *The Jewish Wars*, used the term Zealots forty-eight times. In all but one passage, he refers to the party which was led by Eleazar, the son of Simon.)[82] Since we have refuted the theories of

[80] Beldensperger *Das Selbstbewusstsein Jesu*, 1888, p. 31.
[81] *Op. cit.*
[82] The assertion that the Zealots as a party arose at the time of Quirinius is historically wrong. Josephus applies the term Zealots only to a particular party led by Eleazar, the son of Simon — a party equally

the scholars in reference to Chapter VII, the question now arises as to whom the author indeed had in mind.

To answer this question we must give a short survey of the different parties that existed in Judaea before the destruction of the Temple and of those that survived this catastrophe. It is well known that during the Second Commonwealth three different parties existed among the Jews, the Sadducees, the Pharisees and the Essenes. The Sadducees, besides denying predestination, the Divine influence on man's acts and the authority of the Oral Law, were interested in the Jewish state as a national state, and from time to time they were imperialists. They also denied that God made a covenant with David, thus rejecting the leadership of the Davidic family over the Jews. The ideas of the Pharisees ran diametrically opposite to those of the Sadducees. They believed in Divine Providence, in reward and punishment in the future world and stressed the importance of the Oral Law. They were humble. They held that God made a covenant with David and that the kingdom should belong to his children.[82a] The Pharisees exerted great influence over the masses. The Essenes were successors to the early *Hasidim*. They were highly individualistic in their attitude toward Jewish life. They were strict in their observance of the laws of the Bible, and since they could not observe these laws in the cities where the Pharisees had modified the *Halakot*, they formed communities of their own outside of the cities, where they found it possible to practise their own customs and live their own way of life.

---

opposed to the provisional government, to John of Gischala, and to Simon, son of Giora. The Fourth Philosophy originated at the time of Quirinius under the leadership of Judas of Galilee, while the party of Zealots came into existence in the year 66 and was organized by Eleazar ben Simon. See S. Zeitlin, *JQR*, 1943, pp. 351–2.

[82a] See S. Zeitlin, *Who Crucified Jesus?* Ch. VI.

Besides these three branches of Judaism, there were two others, the Fourth Philosophy and the Apocalyptists. Both of these parties were actually offshoots of the Pharisees.[83] Both believed that God was the only ruler and that there should be no lordship of man over man. Both had a strong attachment to liberty. They preferred to die rather than to accept man as a ruler. Their methods of achieving the freedom of the people, however, were different. The Fourth Philosophy believed in the use of force. They held that terror must oppose terror. Their successors were the *Sicarii*, who were so called because of their use of the *sica*, or dagger.[84] The Apocalyptists were opposed to the use of force or terror. They believed in the revelation of God. They looked forward to the time when God would either reveal Himself and save His people, the Jews, from their foreign yoke, or when He would send a Messiah, a supernatural person, who would save the Jews.

With the fall of the state of Judaea and the destruction of the Temple, the Sadducees disappeared as a group. There was no reason for their existence; there was no longer a Jewish state. The Essenes likewise disappeared as a group; it was no longer possible for them to live under the Romans. The Pharisees, who really were never a group in the strict sense of the word (even the name Pharisees was coined by the Sadducees),[84a] continued to exist after the catastrophe. They were the founders of what has come to be known as Normative Judaism. They adjusted themselves to the new conditions. The *Sicarii* and the Apocalyptists, disregarding the calamities which befell the Jews, clung tenaciously to their views. They continued to preach that God had not forsaken the Jews, that the

---

[83] Comp. *The Jewish Wars*, 2, 8, 2; *Ant.* 18, 1, 6.
[84] *The Jewish Wars*, 2, 17, 6.
[84a] S. Zeitlin, הצדוקים והפרושים.

destruction of the state and the burning of the Temple had only been a test of their piety. God had made them suffer but He would never forsake them. He would reveal Himself or would send a Messiah to save the Jews and punish all their oppressors.

THE SICARII AND THE REVOLT OF BAR KOKBA

The *Sicarii* became more of a secular than a religious group. They were the forerunners or perhaps the very leaders of the Bar Kokba revolt. On the other hand, the Apocalyptists were a purely religious group. Many of them, after the destruction of the Temple, particularly those who believed in a Messiah, joined the Christians. They were the Judeo-Christians. Other members of the Apocalyptists, under the weight of the great catastrophe of the burning of the Temple and the destruction of the Holy City of Jerusalem, became more religious-nationalistic. They believed that God could not have forsaken His chosen people and that He would punish the pagans. They looked forward to a day not remote when God would reveal Himself to His people. This group (the Apocalyptists), whom Josephus called wicked, deceivers and impostors, who, under the pretense of divine inspiration, fostered revolutions,[85] were not the cause of the Bar Kokba revolt. This revolt was of a national-secular character.

---

[85] *The Jewish Wars* II, 13, 3–4. "Besides these there arose another body of villains, with purer hands but more impious intentions, who no less than the assassins ruined the peace of the city. Deceivers and impostors, under the pretense of divine inspiration fostering revolutionary changes, they persuaded the multitude to act like madmen, and led them out into the desert under the belief that God would there give them tokens of deliverance." ... πλάνοι γὰρ ἄνθρωποι καὶ ἀπατεῶνες προσχήματι θειασμοῦ νεωτερισμοὺς καὶ μεταβολὰς πραγματευόμενοι δαιμονᾶν το πλῆθος ἔπειθον καὶ πρῆγον εἰς τὴν ἐρημίαν ὡς ἐκεῖ τοῦ θεοῦ δείξοντος αὐτοῖς σημεῖα ἐλευθερίας.

It was fomented by the ideas of the *Sicarii*. The Palestinian Talmud relates that Bar Kokba himself before battle used to address God as follows: "We do not need Your assistance, but do not help our foe."[86] Also, there is a similar story in the Midrash about two brothers, apparently among the leaders of the revolt, who once went out to fight the Romans. An elderly man met them at the gates of the village and wished them Divine assistance. To this they answered that they did not need His assistance, but hoped that He would not help their foe.[87] This clearly indicates that the Bar Kokba revolt was not a religious but a national-secular revolt to restore the Jewish national state.

It is probable that the Apocalyptists, who believed in the establishment of the Kingdom of God, suffered during this revolt because they did not believe in a Messiah and were not even interested in establishing a Jewish state. Justin Martyr related that during the revolt, Bar Kokba persecuted the Christians, and forced them to deny Jesus.[88] If this was so, it is quite understandable why the Judeo-Christians were persecuted. At that time, they were still a part of the Jewish people. They believed that Jesus was the promised Messiah. They were opposed to a Jewish state. It was to their interest that the revolt of Bar Kokba should fail. They even informed the Roman authorities about the activities of the Jews preparing for the revolt.

[86] וכדדהוה נפק לקרבא הוה אמר ריבונה דעלמא לא תסעוד ולא תכסוף (Yer. Tan. 4).
[87] Midrash Lam. 2, שני אחין היו בכפר חרובא ולא הוה שבקין רומאי עבר תמן דלא הווה קטלי יתיה דנפקין פגע בהון חד סבא א״ל בריא בסעדיכון מן אליון דהא רומאי אתון מן דנפקין פגע בהון חד סבא א״ל בריא בסעדיכון מן אליון נכסוף ולא נסעוד לא ליה אמרו. See also Yer. Tan. 4.
[88] Καὶ γὰρ ἐν τῷ νῦν γεγενημένῳ Ἰουδαϊκῷ πολέμῳ Βαρχωχέβας ὁ τῆς Ἰουδαίων ἀποστάσεως ἀρχηγέτης Χριστιανοὺς μόνους εἰς τιμωρίας δεινάς εἰ μὴ ἀρνοῖντο Ἰησοῦν τὸν Χριστὸν καὶ βλασφημοῖεν ἐκέλευεν ἀπάγεσθαι. *The First Apology*, 31.

For them Jesus was a High Priest and a descendant of the House of David. The leaders of the revolt, on the other hand, regarded them as enemies of the Jewish people, as obstructionists of the revolt and informers to the Romans.

There was a strong division in regard to the revolt even among the leaders of the Jewish people. Many of the rabbis looked upon this revolt as a suicidal act of the Jewish people. Rabban Johanan ben Zaccai had been greatly opposed to the revolt in the time of Nero and Vespasian and had only been saved from death at the hands of the leaders of the revolt by his disciples, who carried him out of the city of Jerusalem in a coffin.[89] In the revolt of Bar Kokba, Rabbi Eleazar of Modin was among those opposed to it. It is said that Bar Kokba heard that Rabbi Eleazar was willing to deliver the city to the Romans, and therefore killed him.[90]

According to the Talmud, the leaders of the revolt during the time of Nero-Vespasian were called בריוני, rebels.[91] Josephus called them λῃσταί, *lestai*, robbers, bandits.[92] According to the Gospel of Mark Jesus was crucified between two *lestai* (robbers).[93] The men who were crucified with Jesus were undoubtedly members of the *Sicarii* who were called *lestai* (robbers). Probably, the

---

[89] See Git. 56a ו*ר'* אחד מצד אליעזר *'*ר בו נכנס ... נפשיך דנח וליטרי ... . See also Midrash Lam. 1, אחד מצד יהושע. לוה ווי בין ... נמלט רבן יוחנן בטיח ובן ברנליה יהושע ור*'* ברישה ר*'*א טען דמית בדמות אפקוני אמר ... . זכאי בן קומי מהלך.

[90] *Ibid*, 2, מדינתא לאשלמא בעי אלעזר ר*'* חביבך כוויבא לבר ואמרין אזלין ... . See וקטליה ברנליה בעיטא חד לי יהב כוויבא לבו רונזה נתמלא ... . אדריאנוס עם also Yer. Tan. 4.

[91] Git. 56a, שבקינהו לא בהדייהו שלמא ונעבוד ניפוק רבנן להו אמרו בריינו הנהו.

[92] *The Jewish Wars* 2. 13, 3 .... ἕτερον εἶδος λῃστῶν ἐν Ἱεροσολύμοις ἐπεφύετο οἱ κολούμενοι σικάριοι.

[93] Καὶ σὺν αὐτῶ σταυροῦσιν δύο λῃστάς. Mark 15.27. See also Mat. 27.38. The rendering in the King James version is "thieves," but is incorrect. The word "thief" in the Gospels is rendered in Greek by the word κλέπτης.

leaders in the revolt of Bar Kokba were also designated by their opponents *lestai*, bandits. A story is told in the Midrash that the son of Rabbi Haninah ben Tradyon joined the לסטים, *lestai* and later disclosed their secrets. For this they killed him.[94] Most likely, the son of Rabbi Haninah ben Tradyon did not join ordinary robbers but the revolutionary group who organized the revolt against the Romans and who were called *lestai* (robbers) by their opponents.

It is true that one of the greatest spiritual leaders of that time, Rabbi Akiba, believed that Bar Kokba was the King Messiah.[95] However, most of his colleagues did not agree with him. One of Akiba's colleagues said to him, "grass will grow through thy jaws and the son of David will not yet have appeared,"[95a] which means that when you will be dead and buried the Messiah will not yet have come. The phenomenon of Rabbi Akiba, one of the greatest teachers of the Jewish religion, joining a secular-national movement is not without parallel in history. There are many cases of men who join movements which are in opposition to the ideology of their social class. Even some of Akiba's devoted disciples did not share his point of view and were not in favor of the revolt against the Romans. Rabbi Judah even tried to justify the enemy. Rabbi Jose

---

[94] Mid. Lam. 3, מעשה בבנו של חניה בן תרדיון שנתחבר ללסטים וגלה את רזן. Comp. also Sem. 12, מעשה בבנו של ר' חניה והרגהו ומלאו פיו עפר וצרורות בן תרדיון שיצא לתרבות רעה ותפסוהו לסטים והרגהו. That the son of R. Haninah ben Teradyon was a learned person and was consulted by rabbis on matters of law is evident from the following Tosefta, תנור מאימתי מקבל טומאה . . . מאימתי טהרתו, אמר ר' חלפתא איש כפר חנניא שאלתי את שמעון בן חנניא ששאל את בנו של ר' חנניא בן תרדיון ואמר משיסיענו ממקומו ובתו אומרת משיפשטו את חלקו כשנאמרו דברי לפני ר' יהודה בן בבא אמר יפה אמרה בתו מבנו (כלים, ב'ק, ד'). This Tosefta confirms my hypothesis that he did not join ordinary robbers but rather *lestai*, "terrorists," followers of Bar Kokba.

[95] Ibid. 2, ר' עקיבא כד חמי ליה להדין (בר כוכבא) בר כוזיבא אמר היינו מלכא משיחא.

[95a] Ibid. א'ל ר' יוחנן בן תורתא יעלו עשבים בלחייך ועדיין בן דוד לא בא.

refused to express an opinion in reference to the Romans Only Rabbi Simon was very militant against them.[96]

Rabbi Joshua, who in his youth witnessed the catastrophe[97] which befell Judaea at the time of Vespasian and lived to see the preparation for the revolt against Hadrian, opposed it. A Midrash relates that when the Jews assembled to take counsel about starting the revolt, Rabbi Joshua told them the well-known fable about the lion and the crane. A lion was choking because a bone was sticking in his throat. He offered a reward to anyone who would remove the bone. A crane responded to the offer, and, probing the lion's throat with her long bill, removed the bone. When the crane demanded her reward, the lion said to her: "You are very well rewarded by coming out of the lion's throat alive."[98] Rabbi Joshua, in relating this fable, indicated that the Jews were fortunate in that they were left alive while among the lions (Romans). It is probable that Rabbi Joshua had in mind the betrayal of the Jews by the Roman government. When Hadrian became emperor after the death of Trajan in the year 117 C. E., while the rightful successor to the throne, Quietus, was still alive and the revolt of the Jews in Northern Africa was still fresh in the emperor's mind,[99] he prom-

[96] Shab. 33b, ר׳ יוסי . . . ר׳ יהודה ואמר כמה נאים מעשיהן של אומה זו פתח ר׳ שתק נענה ר׳ שמעון בן יחאי ואמר כל מה שתקנו לא תקנו אלא לצרך עצמ׳ . . . נשרים ליטול מהם מכס, הלך יהודה בן גרים וסיפר דבריהם ונשמעו למלכות, אמרו יהודה, שעילה יתעלה יוסי ששתק יגלה לצפורי שמעון שגינה יהרג.

[97] We know from the Talmud that Rabbi Joshua attended to duties in the Temple. See Ar. 11b, מעשה בר׳ יהושע בן חנניא שהלך לסייע בהגפת דלתות.

[98] Gen. Rab. 64, והוון קהליא מצמתין בהדה בקעתא דבית רמון, כיון דאתון כתביא שרון בכיין בעיין למטרד על מלכותא . . . אמרין יעול ר׳ יהושע בן חנניה . . . עאל ודרש ארי טרף טרף ועמד עצם בגרונו אמר כל דאתי מפיק ליה אנא יהיב ליה אנגריה, אתא הדין קורא מיצראה דמוקריה ארוך יהיב מוקריה ואפקי׳ א׳ל הב לי אנגרי, א׳ל זיל תהא מלגלג ואומר דעלית לפומא דאריה בשלום ונפקת בשלום, כך דיינו שנכנסנו לאומה זו בשלום ויצאנו בשלום.

[99] See S. Zeitlin, The Apocrypha, *JQR*, 1947.

ised the Jews of Judaea that he would permit them to rebuild their Temple.[100] In 122, when Hadrian was already

[100] Gen. Rab. 64, בימי ר' יהושע בן חנניה גזרה מלכות הרשעה שיבנה ביהמ"ק הושיבו פפוס ולוליאנוס טרפזיון מעכו עד אנטוכיא והיו מספקין לעולי גולה כסף וזהב כל צרכם אזלין אילין כותאי ואמרין ידוע להוא למלכא דהדין קרויתא מרדתא תתבנא ... ואמר להון מה נעבוד וגזירות. אמרין ליה שלח ואמר להון או ישנון יתה מאתריה אין יוספון ... ומן גרמיהון אנון חזרין בהון. Lulianus and Pappas were undoubtedly among the leaders of the revolt of Bar Kokba. With many others, they both were killed in Lydda and were called הרוגי לוד. The rabbis were divided in their opinion about the "slain of Lydda," particularly about Lulianus and Pappas. Some rabbis believed that they were ordinary הרוגי מלכות, "slain by the government," while others believed them "slain for the sake of the Jews and the cause of Judaism." In the Talmud Tan. 18b, the following account is given about Lulianus and Pappas. אמרו כשבקש טוריינוס להרוג את לוליינוס ופפוס אחיו בלודקיא אמר להם אם מעמו של חנניה מישאל ועזריה אתם ובא אלהיכם ויציל אתכם מידי כדרך שהציל את חנניה מישאל ועזריה מיד נבוכדנצר, אמרו לו חנניה מישאל ועזריה צדיקים גמורין היו וראוין היו ליעשות להם נס ונבוכדנצר מלך הגון היה וראוי ליעשות נס על ידו (ואותו רשע הדיוט) ואתה מלך רשע ואינו ראוי ליעשות נס על ידך, ואנו נתחייבנו כליה למקום ואם אין אתה הורגנו הרבה הורגים יש למקום הרבה דובים ... אלא לא מסרנו הקדוש ברוך הוא בידך אלא שעתיד ליפרע דמינו מידך. "Said he to them: 'If ye be of the people of Hananiah, Mishael, and Azariah, your God will come and save you from my hands as he saved Hananiah, Mishael, and Azariah from the hands of Nebuchadnezzar.' They replied: 'Hananiah, Mishael, and Azariah were righteous and pious men and Nebuchadnezzar a noble monarch who was worthy that a miracle should be wrought through him, whilst thou art a wicked king and not fit that a miracle be performed through thee. We deserve death, and if thou wilt not slay us, God hath many other agencies through which to kill us, many bears ... but if thou killest us the Lord will demand our blood of thy hand.' The story concludes that he killed them nevertheless. From this story, it is apparent that Lulianus and Pappas were not considered righteous men like Hananiah, Mishael, Azariah. This story is also given in the tractate Sem. 8. However, there is a gloss אבל כשנמות תדע שאנו מבני בניהם של חנניה מישאל ועזריה. "They said to the king: 'If we shall be killed, then you should know that we are of the children of Hananiah, Mishael and Azariah." Apparently, the author of this gloss considered Lulianus and Pappas righteous men. (Comp. also the Scholia to *Megillat Taanit*.) In the Sifra on Lev. 26.19 ושברתי את גאון עוזכם "and I shall break the power of your pride," the Rabbis said: אילו הגיאים שהם גאונם של ישראל כגון פפוס בן יהודה ולוליינוס אלכסנדרי וחבריו "that is, the haughty who are the pride of Israel like Pappas ben Judah and Lulianus the Alexandrian and their fellows." From this *Sifra*, it is apparent that the rabbis looked upon these two men with an element of contempt. Comp. also Ber. 61b,

secure upon his throne, since Quietus had been executed,[101] he so modified the permission to rebuild that it was tantamount to revoking it. When the Jews found that they had been betrayed by the Romans, they prepared to revolt. Rabbi Joshua, in relating the fable, implied that they should not fight the Romans. However, his advice was not heeded. Rabbi Joshua, who was one of the few sages who experienced the war against Vespasian, also witnessed the beginning of the revolt of Bar Kokba. Rabban Gamaliel, as well as Rabbi Eleazar[102] and most of the disciples of Rabban Johanan ben Zaccai, had died before that revolt had begun. There was no real leadership now. No other Nasi, president, had been chosen in Rabban Gamaliel's place. Some believed that his son, Simon, was not appointed in his father's place because of his youth. In my

אשריך ר' עקיבא שנתפסת על דברי תורה אוי לו לפפוס (בן יהודה) שנתפס על דברים בטלים.
In the *Midrash Koheleth* Rab. 9.8, the following story is related: ר' אחא הוה מתחמיד למחמי אפוי דר' אלכסנדרי אחחמי לי בחלמיה, הראהו תרין מילין, הרוגי לוד אין לפנים ממחיצתם (ברוך שהעביר חרפתן של לוליאנוס ופפוס), ואשרי מי שבא לכאן ותלמודו בידו "Rabbi Alexandri appeared to Rabbi Aha in his dream and showed him two things (I disagree with my friend Dr. Lieberman who insisted that the original reading had "three things"): no compartment beyond that of the slain of Lydda (blessed be He who removed the revilement of Lulianus and Pappas) and happy is he who came here equipped with learning." Rabbi Aha saw in his dream that the "slain of Lydda" were in the future world considered righteous people and thus he proclaimed his thanks to God that the revilement against Lulianus and Pappas was removed. The word חרפה is not to be translated "shame" but "revilement, abuse." Comp. שומעים את חרפתם. Some scribe who erroneously thought that ברוך שהעביר חרפתן של לוליאנוס ופפוס is a part of R. Aha's dream changed תרין "two" to תלת "three."
This Midrash is based on the Talmud Pes. 50 ושמעתי שהיו אומרים ... (1) אשרי מי שבא לכאן ותלמודו בידו, (2) ושמעתי שהיו אומרים הרוגי מלכות אין אדם יכול לעמוד במחיצתן ומאן נינהו אלימא רבי עקיבא וחבריו משום הרוגי מלכות ותו לא אלא הרוגי לוד. For other interpretations of the "slain of Lydda," see S. Lieberman, I. Sonne, *JQR* 1945, pp. 163–69; 1946, pp. 243–46; 1947, pp. 317–23.

[101] Quietus was killed either late in the summer or early in the autumn of 118 C. E.
[102] See B. M. 59b; Sanh. 68a.

opinion, he was not appointed because there was great opposition to religious leadership.[103] Whatever the reason for not choosing him in his father's place, the fact is that the Jews had no Nasi, and no central religious authority existed. There was, indeed, a spiritual vacuum. Rabbi Joshua[104] expressed himself about this period as follows: "Insolence will increase and honor dwindle, the nobility will pervert (justice), the wine will be abundant but wine will be dear."[105] He meant to say that although there would be a good harvest of grapes, the price of wine would rise because of a great demand for it since many people would be addicted to drunkenness.[106] Another younger contemporary, by the name of Phineas ben Jair (the Hasid), said: "Men of arm and men of speech grew powerful."[107] By this he meant to imply that demagogues and men of violence (unscrupulous) would rule the Jews.[107a]

According to the Talmud, two rabbis of great prominence whose parents suffered under the Roman government, were appointed by the Roman government to stamp out robbers and thieves. One was Rabbi Eleazar, the son of Rabbi Simon who, to save his life, had to hide in a cave for many years. The second was Rabbi Ishmael, the son of Rabbi Jose who, in fear of death, fled the country.

---

[103] We may assume from the Talmud R. H. that Rabbi Simon had already attained intellectual maturity before the revolt of Bar Kokba. אמר ר' שמעון בן גמליאל לא היו נוהגין כן ביבנא. Comp. also Yer. *ibid.* 4.

[104] The name of Rabbi Eliezer appears in our printed editions of the Talmud. However, in the Munich manuscript, as well as in עין יעקב, the name of Rabbi Joshua is given. Comp. also משנה ed. H. Lowe.

[105] Sota 9, 16. בעקבות משיחא חוצפא יסגא ויוקר יאמיר הגפן תתן פרייה והיין ביוקר.

[106] See also Targum to Eccl. 7.4, ולב שטיא בחדות בית ליצנותהון אכלין ושתין ומתפנקין ולא יתבין על לבהון סינוף אחיהון.

[107] *Ibid.* רבי פנחס בן יאיר אומר משחרב בית המקדש ... ונברו בעלי זרוע ובעלי לשון.

[107a] Comp. M. Sota 3, הוא היה אומר (ר' יהושע) חסיד שוטה ורשע ערום ואשה פרושה ומכות פרושים הרי אלו מבלי עולם.

The Talmud conceals the story about these two appointees under a veil of legend. When Rabbi Eleazar was reproached for undertaking this work for the government, he replied that he was only "removing the thorns from the vineyard."[108] When Rabbi Ishmael, according to the Talmud, was reproached by Elijah, he said that he had to accept the appointment because it was the decree of the government.[109]

Why did two rabbis of such prominence become informers to help the Roman government eradicate robbers and thieves? Perhaps these so-called "robbers" were the remnants of the rebels who had been active in the revolt of Bar Kokba. It is also possible that some wicked men who had selfish motives took advantage of the revolutionary movement and made use of it for their own designs and attempted to give to their murderous acts the sanction of the party with which they asserted they were affiliated. This was during the time of the revolt against the Romans in the years 65–70.[110] As a matter of fact, whenever revo-

---

[108] B. M. 83b, אתיוה לרבי אלעזר ברבי שמעון וקא תפיס גנבי ואזיל שלח לו . . .
ר' יהושע בן קרחא חומץ בן יין עד מתי אתה מוסר עמו של אלהינו להרינה שלח ליה
קוצים אני מכלה מן הכרם שלח ליה יבא בעל הכרם ויכלה את קוציו.
[109] Ibid. 84a, ואף ר' ישמעאל ברבי יוסי מטא כי האי מעשה לידיה פגע ביה אליהו
אמר עד מתי אתה מוסר עמו של אלהינו להרינה אמר ליה מאי אעבוד הרמנא דמלכא
הוא אמר ליה אבוך ערק לאסיא את ערק ללודקיא.

[110] Comp. S. Zeitlin, *Studies in the Beginnings of Christianity*, 1923. "As a matter of course, whenever revolution is agitated in any nation, some wicked people who have selfish motives will take advantage of the movement and make use of it for their own designs and attempt to give to their act the sanction of the party with which they claim to be affiliated. Thus, it was during the early period of the revolutionary agitation in Judaea, when some bands of robbers, adopting the methods of the Sicarii, killed well-to-do persons, taking their lands and cattle under the pretext that these persons were pro-Romans. Some of the Procurators even extended protection to these robbers and not only had an understanding with them but were often guided by political motives. Their purpose was to bring about a reaction among the Jews against the revolutionists. Their plan was to confuse the rank and file of the people who could not readily distinguish between plain robbers and real revolutionaries whose motives were pure."

lution is agitated in any country, criminals often take advantage of it for their own benefit by adopting the methods of the revolutionists. We thus can understand why these two prominent rabbis, the sons of two great patriots, took upon themselves the task of helping the Romans wipe out this type of criminal who committed crimes while pretending to be acting for the love of the Jews. In any event, we can see from this story the chaotic state of the Jews after the revolt of Bar Kokba.

The Assumption of Moses and the Revolt of Bar Kokba

From the facts given in our short survey of the life of the Jews after the destruction of the Second Temple and bearing in mind that *The Assumption of Moses* was written since that destruction, we may assume that Chapter VII refers to the period prior to the revolt of Bar Kokba. The "pestilent"[111] and "impious men," who, the author says, "will rule," refers to the leaders of the Bar Kokba period. He also calls them "deceitful" and "devourers of the goods of the poor."[112] He was strongly opposed to the revolt. He did not believe in a Messiah. He held that God would rule the world. He even gave the exact time for the revelation of God in this world, which would be 250 "times"

---

[111] *Homines pestilentiosi*. The Greek undoubtedly read λοιμοί while the original Hebrew had פרצים. The passage in Dan. 11.14 בני פריצי עמך is rendered by the Septuagint thus υἱοὶ τῶν λοιμῶν τοῦ λαοῦ. We learn from I Maccabees (15.16–21) that during the time of Simon the Hasmonean the Romans granted the Jewish state the right to extradite and to punish according to the Jewish law any "pestilent" fellows λοιμοί, (Vulgate) *pestilentes*. The word λοιμὸν has a political connotation. The Book of Acts (24) relates that the high priest accused Paul before the Roman governor Felix, calling him λοιμὸν a troublemaker and a mover of sedition among all the Jews throughout the world. See also Taeubler, *JQR*, 1946, pp. 23–6.

[112] (*Paupe*)*rum bonorum comestores*.

after the death of Moses.[113] Since "time" meant a period of seven years, a sabbatical year,[114] 250 times "seven years" equals 1750 years. Since, according to the author, Moses' death occurred in the year 2500 after the Creation, [and 1750 years had passed since his death, therefore] the advent of God would be in the year 4250 A. M., that is, 490 C. E.

In Chapter VIII, the author speaks of "a vengeance" and "wrath" that will visit the Jews as had never afflicted them before. He says that God will stir up against them a king of the kings who will crucify those practicing circumcision. They will be compelled to wear idols in public. They will also be forced to blaspheme their God.[115] The scholars who are of the opinion that this book was written in the first two decades of the first century C. E. regard what is said in this and the following chapters as a forecast of what will happen to the Jews before the advent of God's kingdom. However, Schürer and Charles[116] do not think that these chapters present a forecast but are rather accounts of the tribulations which had already befallen the Jews. They believe that these referred to the persecutions of Antiochus IV. Charles was perplexed by the fact that Chapter VIII appears after the chapter giving an account of the Hasmoneans and Herod. He, therefore, assumed that this chapter was transposed and believed that it belonged after Chapter V.[116a] This theory is unacceptable. There may be dislocations in this difficult book, but, as we pointed out before, it could not have been written before the destruction of the Second Temple. Furthermore, in

---

[113] *Erunt enim a morte — receptione — m(ea) usque ad adventum illius tempora CCL quae fient.*

[114] See Charles, *op. cit.* Volkmar, *op. cit.*

[115] *Et cogentur palam baiulare idola eorum inquinata, quomodo sunt pariter continentibus ea.*

[116] *Op. cit.*

[116a] *Op. cit.*

Chapter IX the author speaks of a man whose name is Taxo, and this chapter is certainly connected with Chapter VIII. Taxo, as we have shown, could not have been Eleazar of the Maccabean period, as Charles assumes. Chapter VIII undoubtedly refers to the Hadrianic persecutions and is not a forecast of future events but is a narration of past events. It is well known that Hadrian suppressed the revolt of Bar Kokba with inhuman cruelty. He not only changed the name of Jerusalem to Aelia Capitolina[117] but strove to destroy the Jewish religion. The edict against circumcision was enforced.[118] The decree against the study of the Torah was likewise enforced.[119] Whoever was found observing the Jewish religion was first tortured and then put to death. Chapter VIII is really an account of the persecutions and tribulations of the Jews after the revolt of Bar Kokba.[120]

We have suggested that Taxo is a latinized Greek word, which means *keshet*, bow. Some have held that the reference to Taxo's seven sons indicates that he was a real person and not an ideal figure.[121] It is probable that the author had Rabbi Joshua in mind when he spoke of Taxo. We must bear in mind that this book is a testament of Moses to Joshua. The verse of Zech. 6.12, which says "behold the man whose name is Zemaḥ (Branch)," referred to Joshua, the high priest. Therefore, we may assume that the word *keshet*, bow, was suggested by the words of Zech. 6.12, and that the author had in mind Rabbi Joshua, who was

[117] See Dio, *Roman History*, 69; Eusebius, *The Church History*, 4.
[118] Yer. Yeb. 8.
[119] Tan. 18a, (כוכבא) הרבה משוכין היו בימי בן כוחבא.
[120] The question may arise, why there was no mention of the destruction of the city and of the burning of the Temple, if the *Assumption of Moses* was compiled after the time of Bar Kokba. We must bear in mind that the text is defective and incomplete. Many passages are missing.
[121] H. H. Rowley, *The Relevance of Apocalyptic*.

opposed to the revolt. Note that Rabbi Joshua was of the tribe of Levi.[122] We must also remember that this verse of Zechariah, which is said to refer to Jesus, is not mentioned by the authors of the New Testament nor by the Apostolic Fathers, although they assumed that numerous passages from the Bible indicated that Jesus was the true Messiah. The first person to associate this verse with Jesus was Justin Martyr who lived in the time of Bar Kokba and hence was a contemporary of our author.[123] We must bear in mind the struggle among the Jewish Apocalyptists in regard to a Messiah. Our author was emphatically opposed to the idea of a Messiah; he believed in the kingdom of God ushered in by God Himself without the instrumentality of a Messiah.

As to the seven sons of Taxo, it is well known that the rabbis called their disciples "sons." We do not know how many disciples Rabbi Joshua had. The author may have had in mind a particular group of seven rabbis as disciples, "sons of Rabbi Joshua." A Midrash tells us that after the revolt was crushed seven rabbis assembled in the city of Usha: Rabbi Judah, Rabbi Meir, Rabbi Jose, Rabbi Nehmiah, Rabbi Simon ben Yochia, Rabbi Eleazar ben Jose, and Rabbi Eleazar ben Jacob.[124]

There is also a possibility that the seven sons were not real persons but were suggested by the prophecy of Zechariah: "For behold the stone that I have laid before Joshua;

---

[122] Comp. Ma'as. Sh. 5, 4; Yer. *ibid*.

[123] Justin Martyr used this verse in a dialogue with Trypho, the Jew. Whether he actually had a debate with a Jew named Trypho is questionable. But it is certain that Justin Martyr wanted to prove to the Jews that Jesus was the true Messiah by quoting a passage from Zechariah.

[124] Mid. R. Song of Songs, 2, בשלפי השמד נחכנסו רבוחינו לאושא ואלו הן ר' יהודה ור' נחמיה ור' מאיר ור' יוסי ור שמעון בן יוחאי ור' אליעור בנו של ר' יוסי הגלילי ור' אליעזר בן יעקב. In the Bab. Talmud Ber. 63b, the text has Jabneh instead of Usha. However, the text of the Midrash is correct, since these rabbis were of the post-Bar Kokba period.

upon one stone shall be seven eyes ... and I will remove the iniquity of the land in one day."[125] The prophecy of Zechariah also speaks of a candlestick of gold with seven lamps.[126] It is well known that the number seven was very popular among the Jews, and there was a great deal of messianic speculation about it.[127]

The Kingdom of God

The author tells us that Taxo said to his seven sons: "Let us fast three (days) and on the fourth day let us go into a cave which is in the field;" and that he added: "and let us rather die than to transgress the commands of the Lord of lords, the God of our fathers. For if we do this and die, our blood will be avenged before the Lord." In the passage following, he describes the kingdom of God. He says that when the Heavenly One will arise from His royal throne, His wrath will burn on account of His sons and the earth will tremble, the high mountains will be made low, and the hills will be shaken and fall. He will appear in order to punish the Gentiles and He will destroy all their idols. Israel will then be happy.[128]

The text is very obscure. There is nothing, however, in it to indicate that the death of Taxo and his seven sons will effect the establishment of the kingdom of God. Furthermore, Taxo said to his seven sons: "Let us fast for the space of three (days)."[129] On the fourth day, they were to

---

[125] 3.9, כי הנה האבן אשר נתתי לפני יהושע על אבן אחת שבעה עינים.

[126] 4.2, מנורת זהב ... ושבעה נרתיה עליה.

[127] Comp. also the Book of Revelation where the number seven is of great significance.

[128] *Quia exurget Summus, Deus aeternus solus, Et palam veniet ut vindicet gentes, Et perdet omnia idola eorum. Tunc felix eris tu Istrahel.*

[129] *Jejunemus triduo, et quarto die intremus in speluncam quae est in agro est, et moriamur potius, quam praetereamus mandata Domini Domimorum, Dei parentum nostrorum. Hoc enim si faciemus et moriemur, sanguis noster vindicabitur coram Domino.*

enter a cave and perish there rather than to transgress the laws of God. "If we do this and die," Taxo said, "our blood will be avenged." It is true that the number three frequently occurs in the Bible. But why did Taxo tell his sons to fast three days and then to enter a cave to perish there, after which God would avenge their blood?

First, we must take into consideration the original Hebrew of the text and the manner in which the book was written. The original Hebrew had צמו or even תענו, which may have the connotation not of *fasting* but of *suffering* and of *affliction*. Neither does the word *triduo* refer to three days. The author of this book frequently avails himself of the use of cryptograms. It was noted before that when the author said "250 times" he actually meant 250 cycles of seven years.¹³⁰ Scholars have already noted that when the author said in Chapter I, "They shall be ruled by chiefs and kings for eighteen years," he actually referred to the fifteen judges¹³¹ and three kings, Saul, David, and Solomon. And when he said "during nineteen years, the ten tribes will be apostates," he actually referred to the nineteen kings of Israel.¹³² When the author said in

---

¹³⁰ See Hilgenfeld, *op. cit.* p. 462; Charles, *op. cit.*

¹³¹ Othniel the son of Kenaz, Ehud the son of Gera, Shomgar the son of Anoth, Deborah, Gibeon, Abimelech, Tola the son of Puah, Jair the Gileadite, Jephthah, Ibzan, Elon the Zebulunith, Abdon the son of Hillel, Samson, Eli (the priest), Samuel.

¹³² Jeroboam, Nadab, Boasha, Elah, Zimri, Omri, Ahab, Ahaziah, Jehoram, Jehu, Jehoahoz, Jehoash, Jeroboam, Zechariah, Shallum, Menahem, Pekahiah, Pekah, Hoshea.

Further, when the author says "seven will entrench the walls" *Et VII circumvallabunt muros* Charles took this to mean that seven kings will bolster the strength and advance the prosperity of Judah. The seven kings, according to Charles, were Rehoboam, Abigah, Asa, Jehoshaphat, Jehoram, Ahaziah, and Athaliah. The Midrash interprets the verse of Jer. 15.9 אומללה יולדת השבעה "she that had borne seven languisheth" as referring to seven wicked kings of Judah, Jehoram, Joash, Ahaz, Manasseh, Amon, Jehoiakim and Zedekiah. אלו שבעה מלכי יהודה רשעים יהורם יהואש אחז מנשה אמון יהויקים צדקיה (מדרש תנחומא, ילקוט

Chapter II, "And they will offer sacrifices throughout twenty years," he really meant twenty rulers of Judah, from Rehoboam to Zedekiah, including Athaliah.

Thus, we clearly see that the author of *The Assumption of Moses* resorted to the use of cryptograms. Instead of rulers, kings, he used the word "years." I venture to say that, when he said "three (days)," he actually had in mind 300 years. We must also bear in mind that the original reading was שלשה ימים. The word ימים sometimes had the connotation of "a year."[132a] We may even assume that the author used *gematria*, since the *Assumption of Moses* was compiled seventy years after the destruction of the Temple. The word ימים equals 100. Hence, שלשה ימים actually meant 300 years.

Taxo's statement to his seven sons that they should fast for three (days) meant that they should suffer for 300 years and that in the fourth hundred year they should go into the cave since the kingdom of God would come. By the words "let us go into the cave," the author had in mind the prophecy of Isaiah that, before the advent

שמעוני). Is this Midrash in contradiction to the *Assumption of Moses*? I believe not. On the contrary, they corroborate each other. The original Hebrew text had חמה *fury, anger*, but the Greek translator took the word חמה to mean *walls*. It is well known that homograph words which have the same spelling but differ in meaning are often mistranslated. Hence, the passage in the Midrash is most likely based on the *Assumption of Moses*.

It is worthwhile to note another mistranslation of the Hebrew. Joshua calls Moses "the lord of the word" *dominum verbi*. Charles remarks "I cannot suggest the origin of this phrase." There is no question in my mind that the Hebrew text had דבר leader. The translator took this to mean דבר word. Comp. Sanh. 8a אָמַל משה ליהושע אתה והזקנים שבדור... אמר לו הקב"ה טול מקל והך על קדקדם דבר אחד לדור ואין שני דברין לדור. Moses was called אדון הדברין the master of the leaders, or דבר רבה like ספרא רבה (Sota 13b).

[132a] Comp. Gen. 24.55, תשב הנערה אתנו ימים, the Targum of Jonathan renders the word ימים as "a year" תיסב ריבא עמנו יומי שתא חדא. Comp. also Lev. 25.29.

of God, the people would go into the caves: "And they shall go into the holes of the rocks and into the caves of the earth for the fear of the Lord and for the glory of His majesty, when He ariseth to shake terribly the earth."[133] The author of the Book of Revelation also says that before the coming of God the people would hide in caves: "And the kings of the earth and the great men and the rich men and the chief captains and the mighty men and every bond man and every free man hide themselves in the caves and in the rocks of the mountains."[134]

THE YEAR OF THE ADVENT OF GOD AND THE YEAR OF THE COMPILATION OF THE BOOK

The author of *The Assumption of Moses* awaited the establishment of the kingdom of God in the fourth century after the compilation of the book. Hence, we can actually fix the date of the writing of this book. We previously pointed out that the advent of God would be in the year 4250 A. M., i. e. 490 C. E.[135] According to the Talmud, the son of David will arrive in the eighty-fifth Jubilee.[136] A Jubilee consists of fifty years. Eighty-five times fifty are 4250 years = 490 C. E. Thus, the Messianic Age given in the Talmud corresponds exactly to the date in *The Assumption of Moses*. Another passage in the Talmud says that the Messiah will come in the year 4291 A. M.[137] I had occasion to point out that the actual reading was 4231,

---

[133] 2.17–9, ונשגב ד' לבדו ביום ההוא, והאלילים כליל יחלף, ובאו במערות צרים ובמחלת עפר מפני פחד ד' ומהדר גאונו בקומו לערץ הארץ.

[134] 6, 15, Καὶ οἱ βασιλεῖς τῆς γῆς καὶ οἱ μεγιστᾶνες καὶ οἱ χιλίαρχοι καὶ οἱ πλούσιοι καὶ οἱ ἰσχυροὶ καὶ πᾶς δοῦλος καὶ ἐλεύθερος ἔκρυψαν ἑαυτοὺς εἰς τὰ σπήλαια καὶ εἰς τὰς πέτρας τῶν ὀρέων.

[135] See above p. 28.

[136] Sanh. 97b, אמר ליה אליהו לרב יהודה אחוה דרב סלא חסידא אין העולם פחות משמונים וחמשה יובלות וביובל האחרון בא אמר ליה בתחלתו או בסופו... אמר ליה עד הכא לא תיסתכי ליה מכאן ואילך איסתכי ליה.

[137] *Ibid.* ד' אלפים ומאתים ותשעים ואחד שנה לבריאתו של עולם.

that is, in the year 471 C. E.[138] Why is 4231 designated as the year of the Messianic age? It is because eighty-four Jubilees are 4200 years; and thirty-one years constitute a majority of the years and decades of the eighty-fifth Jubilee.[139] I believe therefore we may say with certainty that the book, *The Assumption of Moses*, was composed in the year 140 C. E. Three hundred years of tribulations, which the author says the Jews will suffer, would give us 440 C. E. i. e. 4200 A. M., or eighty-four Jubilees. When Taxo told his sons to go into caves on the "fourth" (hundred) because of the beginning of the age of the advent of God, he really meant the eighty-fifth Jubilee, which the Talmud also assigned as the Jubilee of the Messianic Age. The advent of God was expected in the thirty-first year of this Jubilee, i. e. 4231 A. M., or 471 C. E. Thus, 140 C. E., when *The Assumption of Moses* was composed, plus 331 gives us 471, i. e. 4231 A. M., which is the beginning of the Messianic Age.

In a Baraita quoted in the Talmud of Abodah Zarah, it is stated: "If in the year 4231 A. M. (471 C. E.) a man offers you a field worth a thousand denarii for one denarius do not buy it."[140] The reason for this was that the Jews

---

[138] *JQR*, 1946, 166. After I emended the text, I noticed that Rabbi Elijah of Wilno had also emended the text to read שלשים ואחד instead of תשעים ואחד. See ותשעים נמחק ונ"ב שלשים, הנהות הגר"א.

[139] See also Tosefot Ab. Zarah 9b כשיעבור רוב יובל האחרון. In the book of Revelation, it is said that the second millenium "is six hundred threescore and six," because six hundred is a majority of a thousand and three score is a majority of a century and six is a majority of ten. Incidentally, the year 1666 was considered to be the year of the Second Coming and this belief led to the spreading of the movement of Sabatai Zevi, who proclaimed that in the year 1666 he would reveal himself in the Holy Land as the Messiah.

[140] *Ibid.*, אמר ר' חנינא אחר ארבע מאות לחורבן הבית אם יאמר לך אדם קח שדה שוה אלף דינרים בדינר אחד לא תקח, במתניתא תנא (אחר) ארבעת אלפים ומאתים ושלשים ואחד שנה לבריאת עולם אם יאמר לך אדם קח לך שדה שוה אלף דינרים בדינר אחד אל תקח.

either expected the advent of the Messiah or the advent of the Kingdom of God. I have often wondered what was the source of the Talmud for this Messianic Age, 4231 A. M. (471 C. E.). Now we may say with assurance that the source was the book, *The Asssumption of Moses*. As a matter of fact, the rabbis of the Talmud knew about this book. This is evident from a story related in the Tractate Sanhedrin that Rab Hanan sent a message to Rab Joseph, in which he said: "I met a man and he had a scroll written in Assyrian script and in the sacred tongue and he said that he enlisted in the Roman army and among the treasures of Rome he found a scroll, in which it was written that after 4231 A. M. (471 C. E.) the Messianic Age will arrive."[141] This scroll, which was found among the treasures of the Roman Empire, was undoubtedly *The Assumption of Moses*.[141a] We may conclude that not only did the Talmud make use of *The Assumption of Moses*, but that this book was composed in the year 140 C. E., since the date of the Messianic Age given in the Talmud corresponds exactly to the date specified in *The Assumption of Moses*.

Taxo said to his sons: "Let us die rather than transgress the commands of the Lord of lords, the God of our

---

[141] מגילה 97b, שלח ליה רב חנן בר חליפא לרב יוסף מצאתי אדם אחד ובידו מגילה אחת כתובה אשורית ולשון קדש אמרתי לו זו מנין לך אמר לי לחיילות של רומי נשכרתי ובין גנזי רומי מצאתיה וכתוב בה לאחר ד' אלפים ומאתים (ותשעים) ושלשים ואחד שנה לבריאתו של עולם יותם מהן מלחמת תנינים מהן מלחמת גוג ומגוג והשאר ימות המשיח.

[141a] Isaac Abravanel assumed that this Megilah was written by Joseph ben Gorion. והמגלה ההיא דעתי שיוסף בן גריון כתבה והניחה שמה (ברומי) כשאר ספריו וכבר יורה על זה מה שכתב בסוף מאמר הה' מהספר שכתב אל היהודים ובספר שכתבתי אל הרומאים ספרתי על הפלאות אשר עשה מדינת רומי... גם כתבתי אליהם את כל העתידות אחרי מותי עד החרב ותשומם כאשר קבלתי מפי חכמי ישראל קרובים לנביאים וגם מפי חכמי הגוים הנאמנים בחכמתם (מעיני הישועה, על דניאל).
It is indeed strange that a man of such great knowledge was unaware that Josippon was not written by Josephus but was composed sometime at the end of the *fourth* century C. E. This is particularly surprising since Josephus had already been translated into Latin and was read by the scholarly world in the early sixteenth century.

fathers." Scholars improperly interpret this passage to mean that he told them to die in the cave and that God would avenge their blood.[142] But this passage is not connected with the previous passages when Taxo said to his sons: "Let us fast (suffer) for three (centuries) and on the fourth let us go into a cave." When Taxo said to his sons that they should die rather than transgress the commands of the Lord he emphasized that the Jews should not engage in open war against their oppressors but if they were compelled to transgress the precepts of God they should rather die than transgress. He concluded with the following words: "If we do this and die, our blood will be avenged when God will reveal Himself in His full majesty."

The idea that the Jews should not defy their oppressors, the Gentiles, by open warfare is also expressed in a story in the Midrash. The Midrash on Genesis relates that two disciples of Rabbi Joshua changed their clothes during the time of the persecutions (so that they should not be recognized as Jews and be killed). They encountered a Roman captain who said to them: "If you are the sons of the Torah, then you have to give your life for it, and if you are not, then why are you being slaughtered for it?" They answered him: "We are the sons of the Torah and we are ready to be slaughtered for the sake of the Torah but it is not the custom for human beings to commit suicide."[143]

[142] See Charles, *op. cit.*

[143] M. R. 82, שני תלמידים משל ר' יהושע שינו עטיפתן בשעת השמד פגע בהם סרדיוט אחד אמר להם אם אתם בניה של תורה תנו נפשכם עליה, ואם אין אתם בניה למה אתם נהרגים עליה אמרו לו בניה אנו ועליה אנו נהרגים אלא שאין דרכו של אדם לאבד את עצמו לדעת. See also Ab. Zarah 18a, ח"ר כשחלה ר' יוסי בן קיסמא הלך ר' חנינא בן תרדיון לבקרו אמר לו חנינא אחי אי אתה יודע שאומה זו מן השמים המליכוה שהחריבה את ביתו ושרפה את היכלו והרגה את חסידיו ואיבדה את טוביו ועדיין היא קיימת ואני שמעתי עליך שאתה יושב ועוסק בתורה ומקהיל קהלות ברבים וספר תורה מונחת לך בחיקך אמר לו מן השמים ירחמו אמר לו אני אומר לך דברים של טעם ואתה אומר לי מן השמים ירחמו, "When Rabbi Jose ben Kisma was ill, Rabbi Hanina ben Teradion went to visit him. He said to him: 'Brother Hanina, knowest thou not that Heaven (God) has ordained this na-

The Fourth Ezra, the Apocalypse (Second) Baruch and The Assumption of Moses

The Assumption of Moses is the last of the three books of Apocrypha literature which we possess written in the second century C. E. The other two are the Fourth Ezra and the Apocalypse of Baruch. These three books present different philosophic views on Judaism and on the Messianic Age. The authors differ in their attitude toward the Jewish people. According to the Fourth Ezra, a Man — Vir — whom the Most High kept in reserve for centuries, would appear and destroy all the nations that had oppressed His chosen people.[144] *Vir* (the Messiah) would herald the kingdom of God. All the nations would join the Israelites.[145]

tion (Rome) to reign? For though she laid waste His House, burned His Temple, slew His pious and brought His best to destruction, still she is well established. Yet I have heard about thee that thou sittest and occupiest thyself with the Torah and gatherest assemblies and keepest a book of the Law in thy bosom.' He replied: 'Heaven (God) will show mercy.' " To this, Rabbi Jose replied: "I am talking sense to thee and thou sayest Heaven will show mercy."

This story clearly indicates that many of the sages opposed open defiance of the Roman government. Many of the rabbis looked with disapproval upon the revolt of Bar Kokba. The rabbis of the later generations considered this revolt as forcing the coming of the Messiah ahead of time, and hence taught that the Jews committed a transgression. See Mid. Rab. Song of Songs, ארבעה שבועות השביען כנגד ד' דורות שדחקו את הקץ ונכשלו... ואחד בימי כוחבא. See also Targum on Song of Songs, השבעתי יאמר מלכא משיחא משביע אנא עליכון עמי בית ישראל מה דין אתון מתגרין בעמי ארעא למפק מן גלותא ומה דין אתון מרדין בחילוחיה דנוג ומגוג אתעכיבו פון זעיר עד די שיצון עממיא די עלו לאגחא קרבא לירושלים ובתר כן ידכר לכון מרי עלמא רחמי צדקיא ויהא רעוא מן קדמוהי למפרקכון. This Midrash conveyed the following idea: The King Messiah pleaded with the Jews not to revolt against the Roman authorities and not to fight their armies, but to wait until God would redeem them.

[144] *Et tunc revelabitur filius meus, quem vidisti ut virum ascendentem ... ipse autem filius meus arguet quae advenerunt gentes impietates eorum, has quae tempestati adpropiaverunt, et improperabit coram eis mala cogitamenta eorum et cruciamenta quibus incipient cruciari, quae assimilatae sunt flammae, et perdet eos sine labore per legem quae igni assimilata est.* 13.29–38.

[145] See S. Zeitlin, *JQR*, 1947.

There is no mention in the Fourth Ezra of the rebuilding of Jerusalem, Zion and the Temple. The author pictures the Messianic Age as the time of the establishment of the Kingdom of God. On the other hand, the author of Baruch viewed the Messianic Age as the time when the Messiah would establish a Jewish state in Judaea.[146] The author of Baruch states that the kingdom which destroyed Zion would itself be overthrown and subjugated by another which, in turn, would be overthrown, when a third kingdom would arise which also would be destroyed, and then a fourth kingdom would take its place, which would be more terrible than all that had preceded it. And when the time for the fourth kingdom to be destroyed would come, the Messiah would then be revealed.[147] The people of Israel would again find happiness, Jerusalem would be rebuilt, sacrifices would be resumed, the priests would return to their duties.[148] The nations which had not persecuted the children of Israel would be spared by the Messiah, but all those who ruled over the people of Israel would be destroyed by the sword.[149]

---

[146] *Et illo tempore post modicum iterum aedificabitur Sion, et constituentur iterum oblationes eius, et sacerdotes revertentur ad ministerium suum, et iterum venient gentes ut glorificent eam; veruntamen non plene sicut in initio: sed erit post haec, erit ruina gentium multarum. hae sunt aquae lucidae, quas vidisti.* 44; 68.5–6.

[147] *Ecce dies veniunt, et corrumpetur regnum istud quod olim corrupit Sion, et subiicietur illi quod venturum est post ipsum. iterum autem et illud post tempus corrumpetur, et surget aliud tertium, et dominabitur etiam illud tempore suo et corrumpetur. et post ista surget regnum quartum, cuius potestas erit dura et mala magis quam illa quae fuerunt ante ipsum . . . et erit, cum appropinquaverit tempus finis eius ut cadat, tunc revelabitur principatus Messiae mei,* 39, 3–7.

These four kingdoms are undoubtedly Babylon, Persia, Greece and Rome, the last of which the author calls the most terrible.

[148] See note 146.

[149] *Omnis populus qui non noscit Israel, neque conculcavit semen Iacob, ipse est qui vivet; et hoc, quia subiicientur ex omnibus gentibus populo tuo. omnes illi autem qui dominati sunt vobis, aut noverunt vos, isti omnes in gladium tradentur."* 72, 4–6.

The author of *The Assumption of Moses* believed that God would reveal Himself to His people and that His kingdom would be established the world over. Like the author of the Fourth Ezra, he did not approve of the restoration of Zion as a national state and of the rebuilding of the Temple. However, his ideas differ from those of the author of the Fourth Ezra. According to the latter, *Vir* (Messiah) will conquer the enemies of Israel with the sword.[150] According to the author of *The Assumption of Moses*, God will reveal Himself by His own majesty.[151]

The Fourth Ezra was composed in the first decade of the second century before the revolt of the Jews against the pagans in Cyrene and in Egypt.[152] The Book of Baruch was written in Palestine shortly before the revolt of Bar Kokba.[153] The author of *The Assumption of Moses*, who witnessed the suffering of the Jews and the catastrophe which brought about these two revolts, strongly opposed open warfare by the Jews against the Romans. He blamed the "pestilent" (troublemakers) Jews who were responsible for the calamities that befell the Jews as a consequence of the revolt of Bar Kokba. He disapproved of nationalist Jews who believed that Bar Kokba was a Messiah. He was also set against the Judeo-Christians who believed that Jesus was the Messiah.

These three Apocalyptic books are very important for a proper understanding of Jewish history and a true evaluation of Jewish life from the time of the revolt against Trajan to that against Hadrian by Bar Kokba. There are few sources for the history of this revolt. The Roman

---

[150] See note 144.
[151] *Quia exurget Summus, Deus aeternus solus, Et palam veniet ut vindicet gentes, Et perdet omnia idola eorum.* 10, 7.
[152] See S. Zeitlin, *JQR* 1947, p. 246.
[153] *Idem., ibid.*

historian Dio[154] and the Church historian Eusebius[155] gave only fragmentary data about them. References to these revolts in the Talmud and the Midrash are not only fragmentary but are covered with a veil of mystery and legend. Thus, these three books form a great contribution to the comprehension of Judaism and Jewish life in that period. The Fourth Ezra and the Apocalypse of Baruch respectively helped to foment these two revolts. On the other hand, the author of *The Assumption of Moses* regarded the teachings of the authors of these two books as responsible for the acts of the "pestilent" men and the great sufferings of the Jews after the suppression of the Bar Kokba revolt.

The Assumption of Moses was written in Hebrew. The author could not hope to have any influence on the Jews unless the book was written in the sacred tongue. It could not come from Moses in any other tongue than Hebrew. It is true that some Aramaic words are found in this book, but Aramaic words also appear in the Bible, even in the Pentateuch, but the entire language of *The Assumption of Moses* is in the sacred tongue.

Of course, this book is not a testament of Moses to his disciple Joshua. We cannot assume, however, that the author (and for that matter, all the authors of Apocryphal literature) was a deceiver, and really intended to tell the Jews that he had a book written by Moses. On the contrary, we know that all these authors were pious, sincere and humble Jews. There is a possibility that the authors of these books believed that by signing the names of Moses, Enoch, Ezra, Baruch, etc. the books would have a great influence upon the Jews.

There is another possibility that the author of *The Assumption of Moses* believed that if Moses lived in those

[154] *Op. cit.*
[155] *Op. cit.*

troublesome times his message to the Jews would have been the same as his own. Thus, the author concealed his identity in his devotion to his ideas and ideals. Since the author was an Apocalyptist, he may even have had a vision in which he saw Moses who gave him his testament to put into writing.

The Assumption of Moses had a great influence on Jewish thought. As we have seen before, even the date of the Messianic Age, 4231 A. M.–471 C. E. was actually based on this book. This book, however, had no influence on the Church. The ideas in it are diametrically opposed to the ideas of the Church. The author did not believe in a Messiah. One of the purposes of his writing was to oppose the view that Jesus was the Messiah. He does not mention either resurrection, or reward and punishment in a Future World.

Origen says that verse 9 of the Epistle of Jude, "yet Michael the archangel, when contending with the devil, he disputed about the body of Moses, durst not bring against him a railing accusation, but said, the Lord rebuke thee,"[156] is based on *The Assumption of Moses*. This is not historically correct. The archangel Michael is not mentioned in *The Assumption of Moses*. The story of the struggle between the archangel Michael and Satan over the burial of Moses is based on an old Midrash.[157] The fact that Origen mentioned *The Assumption of Moses* in connection with the Epistle of Jude rescued this book from total oblivion. Bishop Evodius, in his Epistle to Augus-

---

[156] See note 1.

[157] Comp. Sifre Deut., אמר לו הקב״ה למלאך המות לך והבא לי נשמתו של משה הלך ועמד לפניו אמר לו משה במקום שאני יושב אין לך רשות לעמוד ואתה אומר לי כך היה סמאל. Comp. also Mid. R. Deut. 11, תן לי נשמתך נער בו ויצא בנזיפה הרשע מצפה נשמתו של משה ואומר יהיה מיכאל בוכה ואני ממלא פי שחוק ... באותה שעה אמר הקב״ה לנבריאל גבריאל צא והבא נשמתו של משה ... אמר למיכאל צא והבא נשמתו של משה.

tine, also says: "In the Apocrypha and in the Mysteries of Moses, a writing which is wholly devoid of authority, it is indeed said that at the time when he (Moses) ascended to the mount to die... there was one body which was committed to the earth, and another which was joined to the angel who accompanied him."[158] This story is likewise based on a Midrash.[159]

The Assumption of Moses is the last literary composition we have of Apocryphal literature. The earliest book is Jubilees, composed in the fifth century B. C. E.[160] Thus, the period of Apocryphal writing extended over half a millenium. This literature represents the *dissenting ideas* in Judaism during the Second Commonwealth. The leaders of Normative Judaism considered these writings pernicious and dangerous. Therefore, the rabbis who called these books "outside books"[161] prohibited the Jews from reading them. They pronounced that "anyone who reads outside books will not have a portion in the future world."[162]

---

[158] *Quamquam et in apocryphis et in secretis ipsius Moysi, quae scriptura caret auctoritate, tunc, cum ascenderet in montem, ut moreretur, ui corporis efficitur, ut aliud esset, quod terrae mandaretur, aliud, quod angelo comitanti sociaretur. sed non satis urguet me apocryphorum proferre sententiam illis superioribus rebus definitis. Epistularum* 158.

[159] Comp. Mid. R. Deut. 11, באותה שעה עמד משה וקידש את עצמו כשרפים וירד הקב"ה משמי שמים העליונים ליטול נשמתו של משה ונ' מלאכי השרת עמו מיכאל וגבריאל וזנואל... א'ל הקב"ה נשמה צאי אל תאחרי ואני מעלה אותך לשמי שמים העליונים ואני מושיבך תחת כסא כבודי אצל כרובים ושרפים. The story about the burial of Moses as given by Clement of Alexandria *The Stromata*, 6, 15, is also based on a Midrash. Comp. also Sota 13b–14a, מלמד שהיה משה מוטל בכנפי שכינה... היכן משה קבור עמדו למעלה נדמה להם למטה, למטה נדמו להם למעלה נחלקו לשתי כיתות אותן שעמדו למעלה נדמה להן למטה, למטה נדמו למעלה. See also Targum of Jerusalem, Deut. 34.6. Some scholars are of the opinion that the phrase "mediator" ἐν χειρὶ μεσίτου, in the Epistle of the Galatians, shows evidence that the author of this epistle was acquainted with the *Assumption of Moses* where Moses is called "mediator" *ut sim arbiter testamenti illius* (1, 14). However, Philo had already called Moses a mediator μεσίτης. *The Life of Moses* III, 19.

[160] See S. Zeitlin, *The Book of Jubilees*, 1939.

[161] ספרים חצונים. [162] כל הקורא בהן אין לו חלק לעולם הבא.

After the catstrophe of Bar Kokba, Normative Judaism became well established. When the rabbis assembled in the town Usha they laid the foundation for the codification of the *Halaka*. The Apocalyptists who, before the revolt of Bar Kokba, still speculated about mysticism, were no longer a power to be reckoned with. Christianity ceased to be a Jewish heretical sect. It became a different religion. It was no longer dominated by Judeo-Christians.

While Normative Judaism then prevailed and there was no longer a struggle between Normative Judaism and the mysticism of the Apocalyptists, nevertheless, the rabbis did not succeed in entirely eradicating the Apocalyptic ideas. During the Middle Ages, we again note the fruits of the Apocalyptists in a new mystic literature upon which the rabbis were again compelled to launch an attack.

In times of crisis, the ideas of the Apocalyptists usually take hold of great masses of the Jewish people. As in the days of the Second Commonwealth, the Apocalyptists, whom Josephus called "deceivers," brought about much suffering of the Jews.[163] Thus, in the Middle Ages, the Cabbalists, the successors of the Apocalyptists, brought great misfortune upon the Jewish people. I refer to Sabbatai Zevi and his followers.

The history of the Second Jewish Commonwealth was written mostly by the students of the New Testament, since they were interested in the origin of Christianity. These writers gave preference to one set of sources: Josephus, the New Testament and the Hellenistic literature. The tannaitic literature, particularly the Halaka, was entirely ignored. It is well known that the legal structure of a nation is the foundation of its existence and that the laws are based on the social, economic and religious life of

[163] See note 85.

the people. The Apocryphal literature was improperly used by the historians because of the numerous errors in the Greek translations and to the improper dating of these books. The Jews had almost entirely ignored this literature. To understand Judaism and the Jewish people, however, we must not only make a study of the literature of Normative Judaism but also of the literature of the *dissenters*. This literature presents a phase of thought among the Jewish people and it had an important influence upon the development of Judaism throughout the ages.[164] Nevertheless, in order to make use of the Apocryphal literature, we must first establish a proper text. There is indeed a crying need for editing anew this great literature which has been so greatly instrumental in shaping western civilization.

---

[164] It is surprising that Dr. G. Scholem, in his book *The Major Trends of Mysticism*, did not take cognizance of the influence of the apocalyptic literature on the Cabbala.

THE PHARISEES
A Historical Study

THERE IS AN EXTENSIVE literature on the Pharisees. This is due to the fact that Jesus, according to the Synoptic Gospels, had disputations with them. In Acts it is stated that Paul said he was a Pharisee.[1] The Church Fathers, in their references to the Pharisees, always assumed a hostile attitude towards them. Christian theologians, Protestants and later Catholics after the Reformation, in their studies on the life of Jesus and the origin of Christianity dealt with the Pharisees. Hence to this day we have a vast literature on the Pharisees written by Christian theologians. There are also studies on the Pharisees written by Jewish theologians.

The general view is that the Pharisees, *Perushim*, were so called because they separated themselves from the *Ame ha'aretz*[2] to avoid not only the uncleanliness of the pagans but also that of their own people who did not scrupulously observe the laws of purity. It has been held that the *Perushim* and the *Haberim* were identical.[3] Although this view is generally entertained by the Christian as well as the Jewish theologians it is historically untrue and should be disregarded. No reference is made in the entire tannaitic literature of antagonism between the *Perushim* and the *Ame ha'aretz*. There are many references to the antagonism between the *Haberim* and the *Ame ha'aretz* and these were only in regard to the laws of purity and impurity, and the laws affecting agriculture,[4] like the laws of tithe. There is no mention

---

[1] Acts 23.6.
[2] Cf. W. O. E. Oesterley, *A History of Israel*, 1932, p. 317; G. F. Moore, *Judaism*, pp. 56-62; E. Schurer, *Geschichte*, v. 2,
[3] J. Klausner, היסטוריה של הבית השני 3, p. 118-122.
[4] Cf. Mishne Demoi, 2.2-3.

Reprinted from the *Jewish Quarterly Review*, New Series, Vol. 52, 1961.

whatsoever of antagonism between these two groups with regard to other precepts and laws. The reason for this is that in the early tannaitic literature the term *Ame ha'aretz* has the connotation of farmers.[5] The urban dwellers, who were scrupulous in their observance of the laws of purity and also in connection with the laws of agriculture, organized themselves as a group known as *Haberim*. They suspected the *Ame ha'aretz*, the farmers, of not observing the laws of purity and impurity,[6] and also the laws in relation to agriculture.[7] They suspected the *Ame ha'aretz* of not giving the necessary tithe to the Levites.[8] Hence they did not associate with the *Ame ha'aretz* nor did they partake of meals with them.[9] To repeat—there is no reference in the entire tannaitic literature of disputations between the Pharisees and the *Ame ha'aretz*. This literature records disputations between the Sadducees and the Pharisees.

It has also been held that the Pharisees separated themselves from the Essenes.[10] This view likewise is untenable since there is no reference in the entire tannaitic literature to any discussion between the Essenes and the Pharisees. If the Pharisees separated from the Essenes, *Hasidim*, we would find record of controversies between them. There is no mention in the tannaitic literature of any dialogues between the Essenes, *Hasidim*, and the Pharisees, while we do find dialogues between the Sadducees and the Pharisees.[11]

It has also been suggested that the term *Perushim* has the connotation of interpreters, interpreters of the Pentateuch.[12] There is no foundation for this view. The Term *Perushim* in

---

[5] See S. Zeitlin, "The Am Haarez" *JQR*, 1932, pp. 45-61.
[6] M. Toh. 7.5; 8.1; Tos. ibid. 8.2,3,4; 9. 11.
[7] M. Demoi, 2. 3; 6. 9; Tos. 2. 2,15,17.20, 21, 22.
[8] Cf. Tos. Sotah 13.10; Yer. ibid. 9.11. מקצתן מעשרין ומקצתן אין מעשרין.
[9] Cf. M. Demoi, 2.3. ואינו מתארח אצל עם הארץ.
[10] J. Klausner, ibid. 3. p. 118; Moore, *op. cit.*. pp. 60-62.
[11] See Mishne Yad. 4.6,7. S. Zeitlin, הצדוקים והפרושים.
[12] Cf. Moore, *op. cit.*

the sense of party, group or a philosophy is not found in the entire tannaitic literature. If indeed the name *Perushim* was adopted by a certain group because they interpreted the words of the Pentateuch, or because they were scrupulous in observance of the laws of purity and separated themselves from those who did not observe these laws, their name would appear in the tannaitic literature, since it was produced by them. We frequently find the expression, "The sages said" [13] of "The sayings of the Soferim," [14] but we never find "The Pharisees said" or "The sayings of the Pharisees". There are no halakot given in the name of the Pharisees.

The foregoing discussion leads us to the conclusion that the term Pharisees, *Perushim*, was not the name adopted by a group of people who followed a certain philosophy. Pharisees, *Perushim*, was a nickname applied to them by their adversaries. Who were their adversaries? The answer is the Zadokites, Sadducees.

The question now confronting us is—when did the conflict between the Sadducees and the Pharisees come about? In other words we must ascertain when the Pharisaism came into being as a philosophy in opposition to the ideas and ideologies of the Sadducees. The general view is that the Pharisees came into being early in the Hasmonean period. [15] There are difficulties in the acceptance of this view. First— What ideological forces brought about the genesis of the Pharisees? The Hasmonean were not of the Zadokite family. Furthermore how could the Sadducees nickname those who opposed them *Perushim*, Pharisees, separatists? From whom did they separate? At that time the Pharisees were in the ascendancy in influence and power while the Sadducees were in decline. Moreover the main contention between these two groups was the question of the validity of oral law.

Speaking historically we cannot assume that the question

---

[13] ·חכמים אומרים·

[14] ·אין דנין דברי תורה מדברי סופרים·

[15] Schurer, *op. cit.* Moore, ibid., Klausner, *op. cit.*

of the validity of the oral law arose in the early Hasmonean period. The Judean community had been in existence for centuries. The Pentateuch was canonized after the return of the Judaeans from Babylonia centuries before the Hasmonean period. What then brought up the question of the validity of oral law at such a late period after the canonization of the Pentateuch? We believe that it came at the time that the Pentateuch was canonized. The Pentateuch does not contain all laws. At the time of the canonization of the Pentateuch the Judaeans had many laws not included in it.[16]

In the writings of the prophets as well as in the Hagiographa there are references to customs and laws that are not found in the Pentateuch. In the book of Jeremiah it is stated that when the prophet bought a field from Hanamel he wrote a deed in the presence of witnesses who affixed their signatures.[17] There is no mention in the Pentateuch of the requirement of a deed and witnesses in the transfer of real property. In the book of Ruth it is said that Boaz told his kinsman that he would have to marry Ruth when he purchased the field from Naomi, "in order to restore the name of the dead to his inheritance." It is further stated that this was the custom, "In former times in Israel concerning redeeming and exchanging, to confirm a transaction, the one drew off his sandal and gave it to the other, and this was the manner of attesting in Israel." [18] This custom of transferring immovable property by the symbolic act of drawing off the shoe is not mentioned in the Pentateuch. From the book of II Kings we learn that if a man did not pay his debts, his creditor had the right to take him into servitude. If he died and left the debt unpaid the creditor could enslave his children. It is said in this book that a woman cried to the prophet Elisha, "Your servant, my husband, is dead and you know that your servant feared Yahweh, but the creditors come to take my

[16] Cf. S. Zeitlin, "The Halaka," *JQR*, 1948,
[17] Jer. 32. 9-10.
[18] Ruth, 4.7.

children to be slaves." [19] This law is not mentioned in the Pentateuch. It is stated in the book of Haggai that God told the prophet to examine the priests on the laws of sanctity and impurity. "Ask now the priests Torah (law) saying 'If one bare hallowed pledge in the skirt of his garment, and with his skirt do touch bread or butter, or wine, or oil, or any food, shall it become holy? and the priests answered and said No.' Then said Haggai, 'If one that is unclean by a dead body touch any of these, shall it be unclean?' And the priests answered and said, 'He shall be unclean' ". [20] These two laws about which Haggai questioned the priests are not found in the Pentateuch, but apparently the prophet thought that they should be familiar with the laws of sanctification and defilement.

It is evident from the book of Genesis that among the early Hebrews a man had to purchase his wife from her father. Jacob paid Laban in manual labor for the privilege of marrying his daughters. [21] David paid King Saul two hundred foreskins of the Philistines for the right to marry his daughter Michal. [22] The Pentateuch makes no mention of a writ in connection with marriage. However such a document is recorded in the Elephantine papyri. [23] We learn from the book of Tobit that when Raguel gave his daughter Sarah to Tobit he called her mother "and wrote an instrument of cohabitation."[24]

Hence it is evident that at the time of the Restoration and the canonization of the Pentateuch there were in vogue many laws and customs which were not found in the Pentateuch. The unwritten laws were as old and perhaps older than some of those embodied in the Pentateuch. The sages of the Talmud recognized this when they said that, "In the days of mourning for Moses thousands of Halakot were forgotten." [25]

---

[19] II Kings, 4. 1.   [20] Hag. 2. 11-13.
[21] Gen. 29. 15-28.
[22] I Sam. 25-27.
[23] Cowley, *Aramaic Papyri of the Fifth Century B.C.*
[24] Tobit 7. 11-14.
[25] Tem. 16. שלשת אלפים הלכות נשתכחו בימי אבלו של משה.

It was at the time of the canonization of the Pentateuch that there arose a difference of views, ideology, in regard to the *Halakot*. One group maintained that only the laws recorded in the Pentateuch are binding and had to be followed, while the customs which had come in vogue among the people, *i.e.* oral law, are not binding. The other group maintained that the customs, oral law, are as binding as the laws given in the Pentateuch. Those two diverse ideologies could only arise when the Pentateuch was canonized and the question of binding of the unwritten law confronted the people.

The validity of the unwritten law has been considered by all peoples. Sophocles made Antigone justify the burying of Polynices, against the order of King Creon, on the basis of "the immutable unwritten laws of god. They were not born today nor yesterday; they die not and none knoweth whence they sprang." [26] Aristotle said that customs are more sovereign than the written laws. [27] Cicero has well remarked that law had its origin ages before any written law existed or any state had been established. [28] Philo, who lived centuries after the Restoration and in a Greek environment, wrote in his book *The Special Laws* "For customs are unwritten laws, the decisions approved by man of old, not inscribed on monuments or leaves of paper, which the moth destroys, but on the souls of those who are partners in the same society." [29]

Taking into consideration that the law givers of all the peoples revered the unwritten law it can hardly be assumed that there was a group among the Judaeans who entirely

[26] ὥστ' ἄγραπτα κἀσιραλῆ θεῶν νόμμα δύνασθαι θνητὸν ὄνθ ὑπερδραμεῖν...

[27] ἔτι κυριώτεροι καὶ περὶ κυριωτέρων τῶν κατὰ γράμματα νόμων οἱ κατὰ τὰ ἔθη εἰσιν. *Politics*, 3. 1287b.

[28] ...*quae saeclis omnibus ante nata est quam scripta lex ulla aut quam omnino civitas constituta. Laws*, 1. 6,

[29] ἔθη γὰρ ἄγραφοι νόμοι δόγματα παλαιῶν ἀνδρῶν οὐ στήλαις ἐγκεχαραγμένα καὶ χαρτιδίοις ὑπὸ σητῶν ἀναλισκομένοις ἀλλὰ ψυχαῖς τῶν μετειληφότων τῆς αὐτῆς πολιτείας. 4. 28.

ignored the value of the unwritten law. No state, large or small, can function only on written laws and ignore the unwritten law. All peoples had unwritten laws.

Josephus, in his account of the rift between John Hyrcanus I and the Pharisees, wrote, "The Pharisees passed on to the people certain regulations handed down by the traditions of the fathers and they were not written in the Laws of Moses, for which reason they are rejected by the Sadducaean group, who hold that only those laws should be considered valid which were written down, and that those which came down by tradition of the fathers need not be observed." [30] Josephus, in *Antiquities*, describing the different sects which existed in Judaea, wrote that "They (Sadducees) do not regard the observation of anything besides what the law enjoins them. They consider it a virtue to have frequent disputations with the teachers of learning." [31]

From Josephus it is evident that the Sadducees rejected the "traditions of the fathers", *i.e.* the unwritten law. Likewise from the tannaitic literature we learn that the Sadducees rejected the unwritten law. Thus we seem to contradict our observation that all peoples have unwritten laws besides the written laws and that no state could exist without unwritten laws. Our observation is supported by the prophetic books and by the Scriptures from which we have the right to deduce that the Judaeans when they returned from Babylonia followed customs which were observed by the people, *i.e.* unwritten laws. What then was the conflict regarding the observance of unwritten laws to which Josephus referred and is substantiated by the tannaitic literature?

[30] νῦν δὲ δηλῶσαι βούλομαι ὅτι νόμιμά τινα παρέδοσαν τῷ δήμῳ οἱ Φαρισαῖοι ἐκ πατέρων διαδοχῆς ἅπερ οὐκ ἀναγέγραπται ἐν τοῖς Μωυσέος νομοις καί διὰ τοῦτο ταῦτα τὸ τῶν Σαδδουκαίων γένος ἐκβάλλει λέγον ἐκεῖνα δεῖν ἡγεῖσθαι νόμιμα τὰ γεγραμμένα τὰ δ' ἐκ παραδόσεως τῶν πατέρων μὴ τηρεῖν, *Ant.* 13. 10,6 (297).

[31] .... φυλακῇ δὲ οὐδαμῶς τινων μεταποίησις αὐτοῖς ἢ τῶν νόμων πρὸς γὰρ τοὺς διδασκάλους σοφίας ἥν μετίασεν ἀμφιλογεῖν ἀρετὴν ἀριθμοῦσιν. 18. 1,4(16)

The difference between these two groups was that one group, while accepting the unwritten law considered that no person could be punished for non-observance of it, that it was not on a par with the written law. Another group maintained that many of the unwritten laws should be on a par with the written laws and should be made statutory laws, thus that new laws could be deduced from them, just as new laws were deduced from the written laws, the Torah. Any one who transgressed the unwritten law would than be as liable to punishment as if he had transgressed the written laws.[32] This was indeed an evasion of the accepted view.

Aristotle, who held that customs are more sovereign than the written laws, wrote, "The written laws involve compulsion, the unwritten do not."[33] In other words he held that a person cannot be punished if he transgressed the unwritten laws. These were valuable for society but were not binding. Philo said, as was noted before, that the unwritten laws are the decisions approved by men of old and that they are inscribed on the souls of those who are partners in the same citizenship. He wrote, "Praise cannot be duly given to one who obeys the written laws, since he acts under the admonition of restraint and the fear of punishment. But he who faithfully observes the unwritten deserves commendation, since the virtue which he displays is freely willed."[34] Thus Philo held that one who transgresses an unwritten law cannot be punished. In other words the unwritten laws are not binding. Most likely Philo copied Aristotle's view as he usually echoed the Greek philosophers.

The clash of the different views on the binding of the oral law on man could not have arisen during the Hasmonean period when the Judaean community had been in existence

[32] Cf. M. Sanh. 10.4. חומר דברי סופרים מדברי תורה.
[33] ... Τὰ μὲν οὖν γεγραμένα εξ ἀνάγκες τὰ δ' αγραφα οὔ ἄλλον δὲ τρόπον εἰ παρὰ τὰ γεγραμμενα ... *Rhetoric* 1.14.
[34] ὁ μὲν γὰρ τοῖς ἀναγραφεῖσι νόμοις πειθαρχῶν οὐκ ἄν δεόντως ἐπαινοῖτο νουθετούμενος ἀνάγκῃ καὶ φόβῳ κολάσεως ὁ δὲ τοῖς ἀγράφοις ἐμμένων ἐκούσιον ἐπιδεικνύμενος τὴν ἀρετήν ἐγκωμίων ἄξιος, *Special Laws* 4.28.

for many centuries. It could come only after the Pentateuch was canonized. Then the question arose—have the laws which were in vogue among the people but were not embodied in the Pentateuch the validity as the Pentateuchal laws and are they as binding? One group, the conservative, headed by the high priests of the family of Zadok, held that the unwritten laws are not on a par with the Pentateuchal laws. Another group, particularly the natives of Judaea and not those who had returned from Babylonia, held that the unwritten laws were on a par with the Pentateuchal laws. Later the followers of this group held that the unwritten laws were more important than the laws of the Pentateuch and even favored them above the Torah. [35] According to the prophetic books of Haggai and Zechariah two men headed the return of the exiles to Judaea. One was Joshua, of the family of Zaddok, the grandson of the High Priest Seraiah, who had been killed by the Babylonians, the other was Zerubbabel, of the Davidic family, grandson of King Jehoiachin. From these books we also know that there was a clash between the two men, rather a clash was between the two factions headed by them. Those who maintained that the new community should be organized on a religious basis were the followers of Joshua, while those who believed that the Judaean community should be organized under civil authority were the followers of Zerubbabel, who was a scion of the family of David. Thus the clash was between the followers of the priestly family, the Zadokites, and those who were followers of the Davidic family. Apparently Zerubbabel and his followers contemplated the use of force against their opponents. The prophet Zechariah said to him, "This is the word of Yahweh unto Zerubbabel, saying: 'Not by might nor by power, but by My spirit' said Yahweh"[36] Zechariah tried to affect a reconciliation between Zerubbabel and Joshua. When the Judaeans remaining in Babylonia sent gold and silver

[35] חביבים מדברי תורה. Yer. Sanh. 10.4.
[36] 4.6.

to Jerusalem, Zechariah stated in the name of Yahweh that crowns were to be made for both men. He further declared, "the counsel of peace shall be between them both." [37] The prophecy was not fulfilled. Peace was not established between the two leaders nor harmony between their ideologies.

The followers of Joshua were victorious. [38] The defeat of Zerubbabel and his disappearance did not, however, eradicate the view that the new community should be headed by a secular leader, by a scion of the family of David, rather than by a high priest of the family of Zadok. This view had many adherents, particularly among those who were not among the former exiles but had remained in Judaea. After the Restoration a profound change took place in Judaean religion which revolutionized the history not only of the Judaeans but the entire western world. From the prophetic books we learn that King Solomon built a House for Yahweh. [39] It was termed the House of Yahweh throughout the Bible. When the Babylonians conquered Judaea they burned the House of Yahweh. [40] We also know from the books of Ezra and Nehemia that the people who returned from Babylonia built a House for Yahweh. [41] However, in the tannaitic literature as well as in the apocryphal books and in the writings of Josephus the term House of Yahweh does not appear. The term given is Sanctuary, [42] the Sacred House, sometimes simply the House [43] but never House of Yahweh. This is not a matter of change in terms but a change in the entire idea of God among the Judaeans. Originally Yahweh was an ethnic God of the people, descendants of Abraham,

---

[37] 6. 13.

[38] The forces which brought about the victory of Joshua over Zerubbabel will be dealt with in my forthcoming book *The Rise and the Fall of the Judaean State*: Published by The Jewish Publication Society of America.

[39] Cf. I kings 6.1.

[40] II Kings 25. 9; Jer. 52. 13.

[41] Cf. Ezra 3.8; Neh. 10.36.

[42] בית המקדש.

[43] הבית.

Isaac and Jacob with whom Yahweh made a covenant to be their God and their children to be His epople. When Yahweh took the children of Abraham, Isaac and Jacob out of bondage in Egypt he thus became the God of their descendants.[44] The Judaeans who were the descendants of Abraham, Isaac and Jacob became the chosen people of Yahweh. Foreign people could not join the Judaeans, no converts could become part of the Judaean community or accept its religion. There is no reference to proselytism in the Pentateuch. The word *ger*, there, has the connotation of sojourner in the Pentateuch, one who lived in a foreign country. The Pentateuch refers to the children of Israel as *gerim* who lived in the land of Egypt.[45] There were, however, those who opposed these ideas, maintaining that Yahweh is not only the God of the Judaeans but the God of all peoples. The prophet Amos said, "O children of Israel? saith Yahweh, have not I brought up Israel out of the land of Egypt and the Philistines from Caphtor and Aram from Kir?"[46] What the prophet Amos said was that Yahweh takes care of other peoples besides Israel.

In the prophecies which have come down to us under the name of Isaiah there is a challenge against the building of a House for Yahweh. It is said, "Thus saith Yahweh heaven is my throne and the earth is my footstool. What is the house which you would build for Me and what is the place which will be My rest?"[47] These words were uttered not as a prophecy but as a challenge to those who returned from Babylonia and began to build a house and called it the House of Yahweh. The prophet protested against the building of a House for Yahweh, He is everywhere.

It is understandable that the views held that the oral law is on a par with the Pentateuchal laws, that the leadership of the new community should be vested not in the hands of

---

[44] Cf. Lev. 26. 13, 45; Deut. 4.20, 6.20; 29,24; Judg. 2. 12; 6.8-9. S. Zeitlin, "Judaism as a Religion," *JQR*, 1943, pp. 331-332.
[45] Cf. Ex. 23.8; Lev. 19.34, 25.6.
[46] 9.7.
[47] Is. 66.1.

the high priest but that a scion of the family of David should rule, and that Yahweh is not only the God of the Judaeans but the God of all the peoples was considered heretical in the eyes of the high priestly family, the *Zadukim*, Sadducees. Those who held these heretical views were nicknamed *Perushim*, Pharisees, separatists, separated from the Judaean people, from God. The word *Perushim* was a nickname created by *Zadukim* as a term of reproach and contempt.[48] Those who separated from the uncleanliness of the people of the land, the pagans, were signified by the term נבדלים separatists.[49] Those Judaeans who did not conform with the norm laid down by the high priestly family, the *Zedukim*, were called פרושים separatists, who had separated from the people of Judaea.

If, as we maintain, the *Perushim*, Pharisees, came into being shortly after the time of the Restoration and the name given them was one of opprobrium, why does not their name found in the book of Ezra? The name Pharisee first occurs in *Antiquities*—where Josephus relates the history of Jonathan the Hasmonean.[50] This is readily explained. The book of Ezra is tendentious (showing its genuineness) giving all the credit to those who returned from exile and ignoring those Judaeans who remained in the land after Babylonia had conquered the country. As was noted before, not only the poorest class remained but many members of the military class as well as many of the royal family.[51] The prophets Haggai, Zechariah and Malachi were Judaeans, they were not of those who returned from exile. The encouragement and prophetic words to the returned exiles came from the prophet Isaiah, a Judaean.[52]

At that time the arch enemies of the Judaeans were the Samaritans. Their name is ignored in the books of Ezra and

[48] Cf. S. Zeitlin, הצדוקים והפרושים.
[49] Cf. Ezra 7.21; 9.1.
[50] 13. 5, 9(171-173; *Jewish War*, 2.8,
[51] Cf. II Kings 25.22-25; Jer. 40.6-14; 41.1.
[52] Is. chs. 48-52.

Nehemiah. In the book of Ezra it is said that when the people who had returned from exile began to build the House for Yahweh the adversaries of Judah and Benjamin heard that the children of the exiles were building a Temple to Yahweh and offered to join them. [53] The author does not indentify the adversaries. We learn from Josephus that they were the Samaritans. [54] Sanballat was the leader of the Samaritans, who strove to prevent the building of the House for Yahweh. His name does not occur in the book of Ezra. Nehemiah does mention a man named Sanballat but does not identify him as the head of the Samaritan group. The books of Ezra and Nehemiah ignore mention of those who were their enemies. They even ignored mention of those Judaeans who had remained in the country. They passed in silence all those opposed to their views. They ignored mention of those who did not follow the doctrines laid down by the leaders who had returned from exile and by the high priestly families, the *Zadukim*. That is the reason there is no reference to the heretics *Perushim*, Pharisees in the books of Ezra and Nehemiah.

The leadership, religious as well as secular, of the new Judaean community was held by the high priest of the *Zadokite* family. [55] The Pharisees had no voice in managing the new community. After the triumph of the Hasmoneans, who were victorious over the Syrian oppressors, they also succeeded in the removal of the high priest of the *Zadokite* family from leadership. The Pharisees who supported the Hasmoneans were now in the ascendant. Josephus, in relating the history of Jonathan, the Hasmonean, made reference to the three sects which now dominated the Judaean community.

Though during the long period from the time of Ezra to

[53] Ezra 4.1. וישמעו צרי יהודה.
[54] *Ant.* 11. 4, 3 (84).
[55] Ibid. 4,9(111), For the high priests were at the head of affairs until the descendants of the Hasmonaean family came to rule as kings. Οἱ γὰρ ἀρχιερεῖς προεστήκεσαν τῶν πραγμάτων ἄχρις οὐ τοὺς Ἀσαμωναίου συνέβη βασιλεύειν ἐκγόνους.

the Hasmonean the Pharisees did not dominate the life of the Judaeans, nevertheless their influence in shaping the Judaean religion was of great significance. As was noted before in the biblical books the Sanctuary was called the House of Yahweh but there voices against such nomenclature since Yahweh is the God of the universe, He is everywhere, no house can be built to him. Ben Sirach, who wrote Ecclesiastes, circa 200 BCE, in writing about the Babylonians who captured Jerusalem, said that they burned the Sanctuary. [56] He did not say that they burned the House of Yahweh as is stated in the biblical books. In speaking of about Zerubbabel and Joshua, he refered to them as those "who in their time builded the house and set up a holy temple to the Lord." [57] He does not call it the House of Yahweh as it is called in the biblical books. Again, in his glorification of the High Priest Simon, son of Onias, he wrote, "who in his life repaired the house again, and in his days fortified the temple." [58] The author of the first Book of Maccabees, in describing the desolation and profanation of the Temple by the forces of Antiochus Epiphanes, did not call it the House of Yahweh but Sanctuary. Similarly, in his account of the victory over the Syrians, he also called it the Temple, not House of Yahweh. [59] This change of nomenclature is not only a change of terms but has a wider meaning indicating a change in the ideology of the Judaeans toward their religion.

A story about the Pharisees is given in the Talmud. It is stated that one Sadducee said to John Hyrcanus I (in the Talmud he is called Jannaeus) that the Pharisees were not loyal to him. He inquired how he could find it out and was told that he should give them an oath, an oath of allegiance. One man by the name of Judah said to John Hyrcanus, "Too much for you the crown of kingdom, [60] leave the crown

[56] 49.6,   [57] Ibid. ναὸν.
[58] 50.1.
[59] I. Mac. 4. 41, 48:
[60] Kid. 66. רב לך כתר מלכות Cf. Num. 16.7. רב לכם בני לוי Cf. also *Ant.* 13. 16, 5(291),

of priesthood to the descendants of Aaron," *i.e.* the true children of Aaron, the descendants of Zadok. [61]

John Hyrcanus I, who had been a follower of the Pharisees, now became angry with them and left them, joining the Sadducees. This passage recording the rift between him and the Pharisees is significant. The story begins with the statement that one man, a Sadducee, told Hyrcanus that the "Pharisees" were not loyal to him. The Sadducees called their opponents Pharisees. [62] However, at the end of the story, where the Talmud itself relates the consequence of the rift, the name Pharisees is not mentioned but sages is given. [63] This again shows that the term Pharisees was never applied by the sages to themselves but only by the Sadducees. At the end of his life John Hyrcanus contemplated declaring himself king. This was opposed by the Pharisees who maintained that the crown of the kingdom belonged to a scion of David. Some of their extremists even thought that Hyrcanus was not a true heir of the high priesthood, not being a scion of Zadok. Josephus also wrote about the rift between the Pharisees and John Hyrcanus I. Josephus named the Sadduceean spokesman Jonathan while the Talmud has Eleazar. The critic of Hyrcanus was named Eleazar by Josephus while the Talmud named him Judah. According to Josephus Eleazar told Hyrcanus, "If you wish to be righteous give up the high priesthood and be content with governing the people." [64] This does not contradict the talmudic statement that his critics were against his contemplation of becoming king. Josephus plainly said that he should be content with having the title of leader of the people, the title which was given his father by the Great Synagogue.

The word *Perushim* in the Talmud had the connotation of separatists, those who made a point of separating themselves

---

[61] Cf. I Mac. 7. 14.
[62] ‎לבם של פרושים עליך‎.
[63] ‎ויבדלו חכמי ישראל בזעם‎.
[64] Ant. Ibid. καὶ μόνον ἀρκείτω σοι τὸ ἄρχειν τοῦ λαοῦ.

from particular objects for some reason. The Talmud states that after the destruction of the Second Temple there were many *Perushim* who separated themselves by not eating meat nor drinking wine as a sign of mourning for the Temple. [65] The Talmud also refers to a man named Judah and his son who separated themselves from the academy and settled in the south. [66] The Mishne in Hag., which gives different degrees of impurity has "The garments of the *Am Haretz* are unclean to the *Perushim*" *i.e.* those who separate themselves from uncleanliness. "The garments of the *Perushim* are unclean to those who eat *terumah*, teruma is more sacred than maaser. The garments of those who eat teruma are unclean to Hallow things. [67] This Mishne, as indicated by the previous Mishne, deals with the degrees of purity and impurity and not with groups. [68]

The Talmud also makes reference to seven types of *Perushim*, those who separated themselves to show their exclusiveness and piety. The Mishne calls them the plague of the *Perushim*. [69] The seven types enumerated in the Talmud, who separated themselves from the rest of the people, were consciously dishonest. [70] One of them—a man who walked with closed eyes, stumbled and hurt himself, saying that he did this so as not to look at women. [71] This as well as the other six types of *Perushim* were those who separated themselves from the rest of society to show that they were superior in piety and more devoted to the precepts of God. These

---

[65] Talmud B.B. 60 כשחרב הבית בשניה רבו פרושין בישראל שלא לאכול בשר ושלא לשתות יין.

[66] Pes. 70 תניא יהודה בן דורתאי פירש הוא ודורתאי בנו והלך וישב לו בדרום.... אמר רב אשי ואנן טעמא דפרושים ניקו ונפרש.

[67] M. Hag. 2.4. בגדי עם הארץ מדרס לפרושין בגדי פרושין מדרס לאוכלי תרומה בגדי אוכלי תרומה מדרס לקודש בגדי קודש מדרס לחטאת.

[68] Ibid. 5. הטובל לחולין והוחזק לחולין אסור למעשר טבל למעשר והוחזק למעשר אסור לתרומה טבל לתרומה והוחזק לתרומה אסור לקודש טבל לקודש והוחזק לקודש אסור לחטאת.

[69] M. Sotah חסיד שוטה ורשע ערום ואשה פרושה ומכות פרושין.

[70] Yer. ibid. זו מכת פרושין נגעו בו.

[71] Bab. ibid. 22. פרוש נקפי זה המנקוף את רגליו.

types of men were stamped as the plague of the *Perushim*, separatists from society.

In the Talmud it is related that when Jannaeus Alexander was on his death bed he told his wife not to fear the *Perushim*, Pharisees, nor the non-*Perushim* but to beware of those persons like *Zimri* who are wicked and present themselves as righteous like Phinehas, grandson of Aaron who killed Zimri.[72] It was perfectly proper for Jannaeus Alexander, who was a Sadducee, to call his opponents *Perushim*, Pharisees.

The name, *Perushim*, originally coined as a term of reproach and contempt, became at a later time one of respect. An analagous use of contemptuous terms in names may be found throughout history. In the eighteenth century there came into existence a sect named Hassidim. The Jews who opposed their theories were nicknamed by them *Mitnagdim*, a term of contempt. The opponents of the Hassidim did not called themselves *Mitnagdim*, but did so at a later date and it ceased to be a term of contempt. In the sixteenth century reformers arose against the pope. The catholics termed them protestants, a name of contempt. Later the term Protestants was adopted by all Christians who opposed catholicism. The Friends were nicknamed Quakers by other Christians. In later days, however, many Friends so called themselves. History is replete with examples of this nicknaming propensity. Similarly the word *Perushim* became one of respect and its original meaning was lost. Josephus who used the term probably did not know how it arose.

Jannaeus Alexander before his death advised his wife to beware of the "tainted", *i.e.*, hypocrites. Unscrupulous people often join a popular movement merely to further their own interests. Assocation with a distinguished group casts its aura of respectibility upon questionable characters. Certainly evil and designing persons joined the Pharisees for

[72] Sotah 22, אמר ינאי מלכא לדביתיה אל תיראי מן הפרושין ולא ממי שאינן פרושין אלא מן הצבועין שדומין לפרושין שמעשיהן כמעשה זמרי ומבקשין שכר כפנחס.

their own purposes. Undoubtedly there were many hypocrites among the Jews of that period as there were among other peoples.

Pious and humble men who abandoned worldly affairs attired themselves in black garments and walked slowly with downcast faces.[73] The wearing of black signified humility and piety. (The wearing of black garments is still considered a symbol of piety.) Dishonest men, in order to make people believe that they were righteous and trustworthy, wore black clothes. Species of hypocrisy prevailed in those days. *Tephilin* contained Pentateuchal passages and hence could be worn by those who observed the physical laws of cleanliness and were spiritually pure.[74] The wearing of them by a person indicated that he was pious and observed the laws. However, in many cases, the wearing of *tephilin* gave rise to hypocrisy. In the Palestinian Talmud it is related that a man who wore *tephilin* refused to return a sum of money that had been placed with him and he denied ever having received it. The man who had intrusted the money to him said, "I had confidence in the *tephilin* which you wore."[75] He made this statement because *tephilin* were worn only by pious people. Not all the Judaeans during the Second Commonwealth wore *tephilin*. It seems that even during the Middle Ages not all the Jews wore *tephilin*.[76]

The Pentateuchal injunction that "It shall be for a sign unto thee upon thy hand, and for a memorial between thine eyes[77] may have had its origin as phylacteries but lost its original significance during the Second Commonwealth. To render *tephilin* by the term phylacteries is erroneous.[78] The

---

[73] Cf. Ben Sirach 19.23, ἔστι πονηρευόμενος συγκεκυφὼς μελανία.
[74] Cf. Shab. 49; Yer. Ber. 2.3.
[75] Ber. Ibid. עובדא הוה בחד בר בש דאפקיד גביה חבריה וכפר ביה .אמר ליה לא לך הימנית אלא לאלין דברישך הימנית
[76] ואין תימא על מה שמצוה זאת רפויה בידנו שגם בימי חכמים היתה רפויה Tosafot Shab. 49.
[77] Ex. 13. 9; Deut. 6.8.
[78] See below p. 122.

Greek word φυλακτήρια phylacteria has the meaning of talisman, protective charm. The wearing of *tephilin* is not for the purpose of a protective charm but to remind the wearer of the power of God.

The Pharisees as leaders of the people sought to solve their religious problems. They offered to explain why the virtuous suffered and the wicked prospered. The Pharisees formulated the concept of the future world, teaching that the soul was incorruptible, that it held an immortal element and that reward and punishment were in store for those lived virtuously and wickedly respectively. They held that the body was a prison for the soul and that after death the soul would be released from it. [79] Some of these views were held by other peoples but the Pharisees either adopted them and shaped them according with their views or developed them independently.

The Pharisees held that men were the children of God and were under His Providence. Although they thought that every deed depends on fate and God, they believed in the freedom of man to act as he thinks, that he can exercise his will and act virtuously or evilly. But they also maintained that there was some cooperation of fate with men's deeds. The Sadducees denied both resurrection and providence, [80] neither of which is mentioned in the Pentateuch. They believed, however, that God takes care of the Jewish people as a whole but not as individuals.

The differences between the Sadducees and the Pharisees about the idea of God went much deeper. The Sadducees, who followed the Pentateuch literally, maintained that Yahweh is the God of the Judaeans only, that he is the creater of heaven and earth, superior to all other gods, that He is an ethnic God, that He is the God only of the descendants of Abraham, Isaac and Jacob who cannot worship other gods. They held that other peoples could not join the Judaeans and

---

[79] *Ant.* 18. 1, 3(12-15).
[80] Ibid. 13.5,9(171-173).

worship Yahweh. They did not recognize proselytism. The Pharisees, on the other hand, believed that Yahweh is the God of the universe, of all peoples and that anyone could join Jews and worship him. Thus the Pharisees favored proselytism.[81] This view had already been propagated by some of the prophets. The very pronunciation of Yahweh was changed, it was no longer pronounced as it is written. The Talmud states that while it is written *yod he* it is pronounced *alef dalet*,[82] in other words it is written Yahweh but pronounced *Adonai* to indicate that the God of the Jews is not an ethnic God but the God of the universe. Some of the biblical books have the word *Adonai* preceding Yahweh. The traditional pronunciation is *Aaonai Elohim*, the Lord God. We are, however, confronted with the problem: If the original pronunciation of these four letters *yod he waw he* was to be pronounced *Elohim* why was it not so written? The word *Elohim* occurs frequently in the Bible. As a matter of fact the Septuagint renders these two words κύριος κύριος Lord Lord.[83] Those who rendered the biblical books into Greek read it *Adonai Adonai*.

The expression ארני יהוה is found only four times in the Pentateuch. In Deuteronomy 3. 23, where Moses began to beseech God to let him enter the land beyond the Jordan in the words אדני יהוה tradition rendered the words Lord God. Again in 9. 26 where Moses prayed to God not to destroy the children of Israel in the words אדני יהוה here again tradition renders the words Lord God. It is a probability that in these two places where the word אדני יהוה preceded Yahweh it should be read אֲדֹנָי[84] and should be rendered my Lord Yahweh. In Exodus 23.17 the text has פני האדן יהוה which tradition renders the Lord God. The Septuagint renders it the "lord

---

[81] חביבים גרים.
[82] Yer. Sanh. 10.1. נכתב ביוד הא ונקרא באלף דלת.
[83] Cf. Is. 22. 12, 16; 30. 15; 40.10; 65.13; Jer. 7.20. Those who rendered the biblical books into Greek read it *Adonai Adonai*. Some Greek manuscripts of Ezekiel have *Adonai*.
[84] Cf. Numb. 11. 28; 12. 11. Cf. also Gen. 15. 2; 8.

thy God." [85] The authors of the Septuagint had the reading in the Pentateuch פני יהוה אלהיך. This reading is partially substantiated in the Sifre.[86]

The expression of *Adonai* Yahweh occurs frequently in the Bible, sometimes only Yahweh without the addition of *Adonai*, and in a few instances only *Adonai*. In the book of Ezekiel *Adonai* Yahweh predominates, while in the book of Joel *Adonai* Yahweh does not occur, only Yahweh.

It seems that the word *Adonai* was added in the Bible when the Judaeans no longer considered Yahweh an ethnic God but the God of the universe. They no longer pronounced Yahweh as spelled but *Adonai*, Lord of the universe. Only the high priest in the Temple pronounced the name of God as it was written. How he pronounced the four letters we do not know. All the theories advanced as to how the four letters were pronounced are only guess work. Neither can it be explained why in some books of the Bible we find *Adonai* Yahweh, in some Yahweh, and in some passages only *Adonai*. We may, however, say with certainty that in the Pentateuch, the oldest, most sacred and revered book, the expression *Adonai* Yahweh does not occur.

With the successful revolt of the Hasmoneans the Pharisees gained great power. Their domination in the matters of religion can be said to have begun. Now they endeavored to put their views into practice. First they sought to democratize the institutions of the Judaeans, beginning with the Temple.

According to the Pentateuchal law sacrifices were brought to the Temple every day, morning and afternoon. The Sadducees, who consisted of the wealthy class and who sought to monopolize the Temple, maintained that the daily sacrifices should be considered private matters so that any individual could provide the lamb slaughtered in his own name. Only the rich could afford the luxury of such a sacrifice. They

---

[85] Κυρίου τοῦ θεοῦ σου.
[86] והלא כבר נאמר את פני האדון יי אלהיך ומה תלמוד לומר אלהי ישראל.

could either bring a lamb for the daily sacrifice or offer to the Temple treasury the necessary money for purchasing it.

The Pharisees, on the other hand, from the time of the establishment of the Judaean community maintained that religion should not be a matter of interest to a few people but that it should be so to all persons, which meant that all should participate in the religious ceremonies, Israelites as well as the priests. Hence the Pharisees now established the rule that the daily sacrifices should be provided by the entire Judaean community. The money for their purpose now came from the funds of the Temple treasury to which every Judaean had contributed his equitable portion. [87]

But the Pharisees were not entirely satisfied and sought to further democratize the institution of the daily sacrifice. They wanted the entire people to participate in the slaughtering of the daily sacrifice in the morning and the afternoon. To this end they instituted the following arrangement: The Israelite inhabitants of each city, town and village were divided into twenty-four divisions called *Maamadot* (communal divisions). The members of each *Maamad* were to go to the Temple to take part in the ceremony of the slaughtering of the daily sacrifices. The members of these communal divisions represented the entire inhabitants of Judaea. But not all Israelites of the division could go or wished to go to Jerusalem. Therefore it was arranged by the Pharisees that those who remained at home should gather in their respective cities and towns on the days on which they were supposed to be in the Temple and read portions of the Pentateuch relating to the sacrifices. [88] The synagogue, which became a vitally important institution in the religious life of the people, is a later development of the *Maamadot*. [89]

The Pharisees were not satisfied only to democratize the services in the Temple and to make it an institution for the

---

[87] Cf. Men. 65; S. Zeitlin, הצדוקים והפרושים.
[88] M. Tan. 4.2; S. Zeitlin, ibid.
[89] Cf. S. Zeitlin, ibid. p. 13.

entire people but they endeavored to adjust religion to life. They therefore modified many laws, the written and the oral. They strove to bring these into consonance with life. The Sadducees opposed all modifications. Tannaitic literature records many instances where they complained against the Pharisees because of their innovations. The Pharisees utilized many occasions to demonstate the validity of their views. [90]

The Pharisees gained full control over the religious life of the Judaeans in the later days of the Second Commonwealth. Josephus wrote that when a Sadducee was appointed judge he had to follow the Pharisees' views, otherwise the people would object to him. [91] The teachings of the Pharisees became normative Judaism. The Sadducees now became the heretical group. History reverses itself. Originally the Sadducees were the orthodox, strict in observance of the Pentateuchal law and opposed to the oral law. The Pharisees, *Perushim*, had been the separatists, dissenters, had been regarded as heretics, innovators. Later the Pharisees became the orthodox, whose views the people followed. The Sadducees, *Zadukim*, were now regarded as heretics because they did not adhere to the views of the Pharisees. The term *Zaduki* now became a nickname for heresy, a term of reproach and contempt.

The Synoptic Gospels tell of controversies and conflicts between Jesus and his disciples with the Pharisees. These disciples called the Pharisees hypocrites. It is to be deplored that this unjustifiable nomenclature for the Pharisees should be attached to them and be so given in the dictionaries. A historical injustice has thus been perpetrated upon them.

In the charges and counter changes between the Pharisees and Jesus and his disciples are reflected their diverse philosophies concerning the nature of society. The Pharisees as leaders of the Judaeans were responsible for their welfare and they had to take note of their deeds. A person could be punished only if he committed a transgression of the law.

---

[90] Ibid. p. 18.
[91] *Ant.* 18. 1,4(17); Ibid. 13.10, 6(298).

A court had to have evidence in order to condemn a person. It could not punish one for wishing to commit a crime. Jesus and his disciples, being idealists, dreamed of establishing a utopian society. They believed that a person should never even in his mind transgress the law. They did not take into consideration the weaknesses of humanity. In the Sermon on the Mount it is said, "Ye have heard that it hath been said an eye for an eye a tooth for a tooth, but I say unto you that ye resist not evil but whosoever shall strike thee on the right cheek turn to him the other also. And if any man will sue ye at the law and take away thy coat let him have thy cloak also." [92]

The law of talio stated in the Pentateuch was not to be enforced by the state since injuring a person was not considered a crime against society, it was a private delict. This was a matter to be settled between the litigants. The injured person could demand whatever satisfaction he desired even to the extent of removing the eye of the person who caused the loss of his eye. Talio was the ultimate and extreme satisfaction which the plaintiff could exact. However he might take compensation with money. [93] The Pharisees felt the need of the abolishing of the law of *talio* and did abolish it. According to the newly enacted law the injured man had the right only to demand monetary satisfaction for the loss of his eye, [94] for the pain and suffering, for medical care, for disability and for humiliation. This form of retribution has been followed in the courts of all civilized peoples. Jesus, as a moralist, appealed to the people that they should not only not demand satisfaction by *talio* but that they should not resist evil at all. They should be meek to their oppressors; if one smites a person

---

[92] Mat. 5. 38-42.
[93] Cf. *Ant* 4. 8, 35(280). "He that maimeth a man shall undergo the like, being deprived of that limb whereof he deprived the other, unless indeed the maimed man be willing to accept money; for the law empowers the victim himself to assess the damage that has befallen him and makes this concession, unless he would show himself too severe."
[94] Cf. Talmud M.K. 83.

on the cheek the injured man should turn the other cheek to be punished twice. This may be great moral teaching but could a society really function on such principles? Have the followers of Jesus ever practiced this way of life? Not only have the Christians made war against non-Christians but they have made war against each other. The literal words an eye for an eye (modified and abolished by the sages during the Second Commonwealth) was followed more among the Christians than the teachings of the Sermon on the Mount.

We have the right to maintain that some controversies between the Pharisees and Jesus and his disciples could not have occurred during their lifetime. The Gospel according to Mark relates, "Then came to gather unto him the Pharisees and certain of the scribes, which came from Jerusalem. And when they saw some of his disciples eat bread with defiled, that is to say with unwashed hands, they found fault for the Pharisees and all the Judaeans, except they washed their hands oft, eat not, holding the tradition of the elders." [95] The institution of washing the hands before a meal was instituted at the earliest a few years before the destruction of the Temple, [96] long after the time of the crucifixion of Jesus. Thus, historically, such a controversey could not have occurred during the time of Jesus. The statement, according to the Gospel of Mark, "For the Pharisees and all the Judaeans, except they wash their hands oft, eat not," is an anachronism to say the least. At the time of Jesus for a Judaean who was in the status of uncleanliness the washing of the hands was not sufficient to become clean, he had to be submerged in water. [97] A person who was not defiled could eat without washing the hands.

Matthew states that Jesus accused the Pharisees of being hypocrites, "They make broad their phylacteries," [98] he said,

[95] Mark 7.3.
[96] S. Zeitlin, "The Halaka in the Gospels" *HUCA*, 1.
[97] Cf. ibid.
[98] Mat. 23.5

and added, that they wanted to be called rabbis.[99] The *tephilin* are not phylacteries. To repeat, they were not used as a talisman, a charm for protection against evil spirits.[100] The author of this passage did not know the meaning of *tephilin*, thinking that they were phylacteries. Furthermore the term *rabbi* came into vogue after the destruction of the Second Temple.[101] The title rabbi was not used by the Judaeans at the time of Jesus. This is anotner anachronism. which may shed light on this passage.

It cannot be denied that the disciples of Jesus were strongly opposed to the Pharisees and considered them adversaries, and in the heat of arguments they accused their former teachers, the Pharisees, of being hypocrites for not accepting Jesus as the Messiah. The Pharisees, on the other hand, considered the disciples of Jesus transgressors and deceivers who wanted to destroy Judaism as it was propagated by them throughout the centuries. No historian writing on the Pharisees can rely solely upon the denunciations of them in the Gospels. In order to write about the Pharisees one must be well versed in the literature of their own creation, the tannaitic.

It has been maintained that the Pharisees were narrow nationalists, in contrast to the prophets who were universalists. Such a view betrays lack of knowledge of the tannaitic literature and the essence of Phariseeism. The canonization of the prophetic books, Isaiah, Jeremiah, Amos and Micah, making their views fundamental for Judaism, was accomplished by the Pharisees. They were responsible for abolishing the term "House of Yahweh" and substituting the term "Sanctuary." They thereby emphasized that the God of Israel is universal, that no house could contain him, that he is everywhere. The Pharisees were far from being narrow nationalists. They were the first to maintain that anyone, regardless of race, can be converted to Judaism since Judaism is a universal religion.

[99] Ibid. 7.   [100] See above p. 114.
[101] See S. Zeitlin, Who Crucified Jesus? Pp. 139-140.

On the other hand a theory has been advanced that the Pharisees were truly Hellenized. This view likewise betrays total lack of knowledge of the Pharisaic literature. It cannot be denied that many views held by the Pharisees, such as the resurrection of the soul, believing in reward and punishment after death, were held by other peoples. This does not prove that the Pharisees were Hellenized. Ideas permeate the world due to the progress of civilization. One people does not necessarily copy from another. If it should be granted that the idea of resurrection was adopted by the Pharisees from other people this does not indicate that they were thoroughly Hellenized. The idea of the resurrection of the spirit was not the only foundation of Phariseeism. The Pharisees, as we have endeavored to show, were the heirs of the prophets who stressed the idea of the universality of God. The Pharisees encouraged proselytism and opposed theocracy. They held that a scion of the family of David should be the secular ruler of the people. This view later developed into the idea of a Messiah, the anointed of God. They emphasized particularly that the oral law is binding and on a par with Written Law, i.e., making the oral law statutory law.

In order to establish a legal system by which the Pentateuchal laws could be interpreted, to make them in consonance with life, and in order to make the oral law statutory, the Pharisees employed hermeneutic devices like *kal wa-homer* inference *a minori ad maius*, from the less important law to the more important; and *gezerah shawah*, inference by analogy of words. It has been contended that these hermeneutic devices are good illustrations of the thoroughly Hellenistic framework of Pharisaic thought. This again shows a lack understanding of tannaitic literature. It should be noted that Hillel was not the originator of the principle of *a minori ad maius*. It is already found in the Pentateuch. [102] Hillel only

---

[102] E.g., Gen. 44.8, הן כסף אשר מצאנו בפי אמתחותינו השיבנו אליך מארץ הן בני ישדאל. Cf. also Ex. 6.12. כנען ואיך נגנב מבית אדניך כסף או זהב לא שמעו אלי ואיך ישמעני פרעה.

perfected the three hermeneutic devices, (The Tosefta made reference to seven hermeneutic devices [103] but they are a later development of the three.) and employed them to make the unwritten law statutory. Not only the Sadducees opposed this method but also the school of Shamai did not adopt it. As a matter of fact even in a later time the school of Shamai did not employ the hermeneutic device of *gezerah shawah*. [104]

To utilize the rabbinic literature for the study of the Pharisees one must analyze it critically. Not all rabbinic literature can be used for the history of the Pharisees. There is a vast difference between the tannaitic and the amoraic literature and between the Palestinian and Babylonian. The later rabbinic literature is not a source for the history of the Pharisees. Many writers who have dealt with the Pharisees employed the later Babylonian literature and thus they distorted the history of the Pharisees.

To cite an example: The *Megillat Taanit*, which was composed circa 65 C.E., records that on the 28th of the month of Tebet the Synagogue sat in judgment and that a semiholiday was declared. Besides the aramaic text of the *Megillat* there exist also commentaries or scholia in Hebrew, explaining the events mentioned in the Megillah. The scholium on this event interpreted it that on that day the Pharisees were victorious over the Sadducees, that the Sadducaean Sanhedrin was abolished and therefore a holiday was declared on that day. The scholia on the *Megillat Taanit* were composed during the Middle Ages and hence have no value whatsoever on the history of the Pharisees. To use the scholia as a source for the history of the Pharisees is tantamount to the usage of Rashi's commentary on the Talmud as a source for the history of the Second Jewish Commonwealth and of

---

[103] Tos. Sanh. 7.11.
[104] See M. Bezah 1.8, אמרו בית שמאי גזירה שוה חלה ומתנות Cf. however Tos. ibid. אמרו בית הלל גזירה שוה חלה ומתנות From internal evidence we may say with certainty that the reading of the text, as recorded in the Tosefta is the original text.

the Tannaim. Such a method is not historical, to say the least, and is confusing and misleading.

In order to write on the Pharisees one must also deal with the history of the Judaeans during the Second Commonwealth. Parties are not created in a vacuum. They do not arise as the result of a whim of a leader or leaders. They are the result of political, social, economic and religious forces. Parties are indeed the creation of the people and in turn mold its history. Both are interwoven. To fully comprehend the Pharisees and their theological development one must follow step by step the history of the Judaeans. The history of a people may have a zig zag deviate course but the main characteristics always remain. This is also true of parties. Parties adapt themselves to ever changing historical forces but their main characteristics remain.

The Sadducees, it will be recalled, were those who after the Restoration opposed Zerubbabel and the effort to establish the Judaean community on a secular basis. They sought the establishment of a theocracy and favored Joshua, of the family of Zadok. When the Judaean state was established they supported Jannaeus Alexander, who was not of the Zadokite family, for the kingship and high priesthood. On the surface this would seem anomalous. In reality the ideology of the Sadducees had not changed. They had followed Joshua because they believed that he would serve their interests. They had been in favor of theocracy because it would give the high priest full authority over the Judaean community. They now supported Jannaeus Alexander although he was not of the Zadokite family, because of their ideology. They saw in him their ideal who, by his military genius, had placed the Judaean state on a firm foundation. They approved his policy of conquest to add more territory to Judaea for they were strongly nationalistic. They always believed that the Judaeans were the chosen people of God. However, when proselytism did became the norm of Judaism proselytes were not condidered in the eyes of the Sadducees on a par with the native Judaeans—they were considered half Judaeans.

The Sadducees, who regarded the unwritten law as not binding, however, followed them when they became statutory. But they always opposed the unwritten law which was based on tradition and any new laws which were based on inferences from the Pentateuch. The essential characteristics of the Sadducees with regard to religion, people and law remained the same throughout history.

The Pharisees, who opposed theocracy, believed that the kingship of the people should be vested in a scion of the family of David, and hence were opposed to Jannaeus Alexander. They did not hold that the Judaeans are the chosen people of God.

After the civil war which raged between the sons of Jannaeus Alexander, which was really one between the Sadducees and the Pharisees, the latter dedicated themselves solely to the advancement of religion. They were quietists.

The reign of Herod and the oppression of the Romans brought about two offshoots from the Pharisees. Josephus named one (followers of) the Fourth Philosophy. [105] The other whom Josephus called deceivers, wicked, [106] were really the Apocalyptic Pharisees. The former were militant, nationalistic and followed the principle that terror must oppose terror. Later they were called Sicarii because they concealed a *sica*, dagger, under their garments. [107] The Apocalyptic Pharisees, like the Sicarii, preached the gospel of no lordship of man over man and equality of men; they held that the only ruler

---

[105] *Ant.* 18. 1, 6(23-25). Josephus named the "Fourth Philosophy," because this group came fourth after the Sadduccees, the Pharisees and the Essenes.

[106] *Jewish War*, 2.13, 4(258-259). "Besides these there arose another body of villains, with purer hands but more impious intentions, who no less than the assassins ruined the peace of the city. Deceivers and impostors, under the pretence of divine inspiration fostering revolutionary changes, they persuaded the multitude to act like madmen, and led them out into the desert under the belief that God would there give them tokens of delieverance."

[107] *Jewish War*, ibid. (254-257).

over men is God. They differed from the Sicarii in opposing terror and violence. They preached love, "If anyone seeketh to do evil unto you do well unto him and pray for him." [108] This was their watchword and guide. They believed that God, either through himself or a Messiah, who would be a scion of the family of David, by a miraculous act would annihilate their oppressors. Since the salvation of the people would not come through arms but by act of God the Apocalyptists declared themselves messengers of God, claiming that they had supernatural power by which to smite the Romans and save the Judaeans. They held that the suffering of the people was the chastisement of God, that they are his beloved children and that He would never forsake them. They believed He would restore Jerusalem to its glory and proclaim His kingdom. The Pharisaic Apocalyptists were the forerunners of Christianity. The Pharisees saw dangers in the views and deeds of the adherants of the Fourth Philosophy and the Apocalyptists.

The view that the Judaeans, the Israelites, are the chosen people of God was emphasized in the Pentateuch and in other books of the Bible and, as noted before, was held by the Sadducees. When the Christians became entrenched they maintained that they were the true Israelites and are the chosen people of God. [109] Hence the Judaeans abandoned the name of Judaean and called themselves Israelites and maintained that they are the chosen people. [110] They now called their land, originally called Judaea, *Eretz Israel*, the Land of Israel. This was done to combat the contention of the Judaean Christians.

The view that the Jews are the chosen people was both the result of the Sadduceean influence and a reaction against

[108] See The Testament of the Twelve Pariarchs (The Testament of Joseph) 18. 2.
[109] Cf. Origen, *Against Celsus*, 5. 42, 50; Tertullian, *Adversus Iudaeos*, 3.
[110] Cf. ibid., S. Zeitlin, "Judaism as a Religion," *JQR*, 1944, pp. 88-91.

Christianity. After the destruction of the Second Temple the Sadducees, as a group, ceased to exist but some of their views were not entirely eradicated. One strong exponent of the view that the Jews are a chosen people was Jehudah ha-Levi (1085-1142). He held that although the Torah was given to the Jews, its acceptance was free to every one. Nevertheless he maintained that those who were not of the Jewish race, even though they embraced Judaism, could never acquire the gift of prophecy. He said that since Judaism is the historic, ethnic religion of the Jewish people anyone who embraced the Jewish religion becomes a member of the Jewish people and would be rewarded for his deeds but he would never be equal with those who are racially Jews. [111] Judah ha-Levi stated that when God revealed himself on Mount Sinai and gave the Torah to the Children of Israel; He did not say "I am the God who created the Universe but I am the God who brought you out of the land of Egypt." [112] He adhered to the view of the Sadducees who followed the Pentateuch literally and maintained that Yahweh is the God of the children of Israel because he took them out of the land of Egypt. The view of "peoplehood" held by many contemporary Jews is in accordance with that held by the Sadducees. The Pharisees strongly opposed the view that the Jews are a chosen people. They held that Judaism is the chosen religion.

In the liturgy of the festivals are recited the words, "Thou didst choose us from among all peoples; Thou didst love and favor us." [113] Here the view of chosen people is stressed. This again is due both to the influence of the Sadducees and the reaction against Christianity. However, when a person who has become a convert to Judaism, regardless of his race, yellow or negro, when he is called to the Torah he

[111] *Kusari*, 27, וכל הנלוה אלינו מן האומות בפרט יגיעהו מן הטובה אשר ייטיב הבורא אלינו אך לא יהיה שוה עמנו מפני שאנחנו נקראים הסגולה מבני אדם.

[112] וכן פתח אלהים דבריו אל המון ישראל אנכי ד אלהיך אשר הוצאתיך מארץ מצרים ולא אמר אני בורא העולם ובוראכם.

[113] אתה בחרתנו מכל העמים אהבת אותנו ורצית בנו.

makes the following blessing, "Blessed art Thou, Adonai, our God, King of the universe, Who has chosen us from all peoples. [114] Hence a person not of the Jewish race, who might be of the yellow or negro race, when called to the Torah proclaims himself as being one chosen above all other peoples. This is the Pharisaic view that the God of Israel is the God of the universe and that the whole human race are his children. Judaism is the chosen religion. Anyone who accepts Judaism is the spiritual descendant of Abraham, Isaac and Jacob. The Pharisees opposed the idea of a chosen race and the view of "peoplehood."

The Pharisees molded Judaism. Judaism of today is based on their teachings. Their view that the Pentateuchal and the subsequent oral law should be interpreted and amended in consonance with life made the Jewish religion a living one. Their maxim that law was for man, not man for the law, [115] gave substance to the life of the people, and made it possible for them to withstand the calamities which almost annihilated them. Their view of the universality of God not only had an impact on western civilization but made possible the survival of the Jewish people.

The nations of antiquity that were conquered by different empires have disappeared from the historical arena because they had ethnic gods. Their gods were conquered and they as ethnic peoples disappeared. The Jews were conquered by the Romans; their national life was destroyed, their land was taken away from them for a while but the Jews have not disappeared from the historical arena. This is primarily due to the teachings of the Pharisees—the universality of God, that God is everywhere and is not bound to one particular country. In the hearts of the Jews Judaea, Eretz Israel, was always considered the Holy Land, the Land of Israel, the land that always belonged to them. They never abandoned the hope that a new state would be reestablished in the land of Israel.

[114] ברוך אתה אדני אלהינו מלך העולם אשר בחר בנו מכל העמים ונתן לנו את תורתו·

[115] Yoma 86. היא מסורה בידכם ולא אתם מסורים בידה·

THE SADDUCEES AND THE PHARISEES—
A CHAPTER IN THE DEVELOPMENT
OF THE HALAKHAH

FOREWORD

Two methods may be employed in the study of the *Halakhah*. It can be studied either dogmatically or historically. As a dogmatic study, *halakhah* is just a series of laws, little or no attention is focused on the author or development. A judge is required to render a decision based solely on these accepted laws. As an historical study, however, one examines the evolution of the law and the basis for each statute. In this essay we will employ the historical method.

While the term *Zedoki* is found often throughout the Talmud, it has no connection whatsoever with the *Zedokim,* Sadducees, who flourished during the Second Commonwealth period. This sect totally disappeared with the destruction of the Temple and the term *Zedoki* became synonymous for apostate and heretic.

Although we attempt to prove in this essay that a group named *Perushim,* Pharisees, never existed, rather the term *Perushim* was a title of reproach employed by the Sadducees in referring to their adversaries, nevertheless, we bow to the weight of tradition and employ the term in its generally accepted sense.

Translated from the Hebrew by Mordekai Shapiro. Originally published in *Horeb*, Number 62, 1936.

INTRODUCTION

In relating the history of the Hasmoneans, Josephus tells us that already at the time of Jonathan, brother of Judah the Makkabee, there existed three sects among the Jews—the Sadducees, the Pharisees, and the Essenes.[1] We have no reason to doubt Josephus' assertion that even before John Hyrcanus these sects existed in Judaea.

Numerous hypotheses have been advanced with regard to the origin of the word Sadducees. The consensus of opinion is that the word Sadducees is derived from the name of the High Priest Zadok, a contemporary of King Solomon.[2] Proof for this theory can be found in tannaitic literature.[3]

These *Zedokim*, led by the High Priest of the Zadok family, were a rich, influential, aristocracy. It was their contention that only a member of their family can serve as a High Priest in the Temple.[4] They acknowledged as binding only the written law. Tradition, or interpretation of the written law, was rejected. The emergence of this party can be traced to the time of Ezra the Scribe. At that time, he and his associates on their return from Babylon attempted to interpret the Torah in accordance with the tradition of the elders. By doing this, they aroused the opposition of the Zadok family who monopolized the Temple, and the leadership over the Jews. The Zadokites—or Sadducees—strongly contested the ideas of Ezra and his associates. The followers of Ezra were dubbed Perushim, Separatists, who, from their point of view, separated themselves from the Jews.

Many suggestions likewise have been offered as to the origin of the name Pharisees. Some scholars are of the opinion that the word Perushim has its origin in the word for interpreter פרש [5], others maintain that the word stems from פרש to separate that is, the members of this sect separated themselves to avoid Levitical defilement. They further maintain that these *Perushim* were scrupulous about the laws of uncleanliness, avoiding not only the uncleanliness of the pagan, but also that of the *Ame Ha'aretz*.[6]

After a careful examination of all the tannaitic literature, however, we conclude that there was no sect among the Jews called "Pharisees." The word was coined and used by the Sadducees who resented the reforms and the new laws which were adopted by Ezra and his associates. These Jews, the followers of Ezra, they nicknamed *Perushim,* Pharisees—they had separated themselves from the Jews.[7] Thus, the name *Perushim* was a nickname of reproach and contempt. An analogous use of a contemptuous name may be found in Jewish history of the Eighteenth Century, when the sect of the Hasidim came into existence under the leadership of Rabbi Israel Baal Shem Tov. The Jews who did not accept his new theories were nicknamed by his associates as *Mitnagdim,* those who opposed not only the new sect of Hasidim but even, from their viewpoint, Judaism itself. Another example may be found in the rise of the Reform movement in the Sixteenth Century against the Pope. The Catholics at that time contemptuously called opponents of the Church—Protestants—implying not only opposition to the Pope and the Church but to the essence of Christianity. History is replete with examples of this nicknaming propensity.[8]

Although the term *Perushim* appears often in tannaitic literature it is never in the sense of party, group, or sect. It has, rather, the general meaning of separatists, of people who separated themselves from one thing or another. For example, after the destruction of the Temple, many refrained from eating meat or drinking wine because the daily sacrifice could no longer be offered, and the libation of wine was discontinued; these folk are referred to as *Perushim,* separatists.[9]

The term Perushim, when it does appear referring to a sect, adversaries of the Sadducees, it is only in some form of dialogue. The Sadducees say, "We protest against you, Pharisees." The Pharisees retort, "We protest against you, Sadducees."[10] One cannot prove from these sort of dialogues that there existed a specific sect called *Perushim.* The words *Zedokim* and *Perushim* are here merely used as a conversational convenience. A modern historian might record a controversy in the form of a dialogue between the Hasidim and the *Mitnagdim*. The Hasidim would say, "We are against you, *Mitnagdim;*" and the *Mitnagdim* would answer, "We are against you, Hasidim." The words used in such a dialogue would not prove that there was a sect by the name of *Mitnagdim*. There was a sect called Hasidim who called the opponents to their theories *Mitnagdim*. In a similar manner those among the Jews who opposed the theories of the Sadducees were called by the Sadducees, *Perushim*, Pharisees.

While Josephus may refer to Pharisees, Sadducees, and Essenes as three sects of Jews, the use of the term Pharisee does not, in any way, establish their existence as a sect, per se. Josephus uses the word Pharisee to identify the opponents of the Sadducees. As a modern historian, writing a Jewish history of the Eighteenth Century, would recount the conflicts between the Hasidim and the *Mitnagdim,* knowing full-well no such sect actually existed, so Josephus writing his history uses the nomenclature created by the Sadducees to identify their opponents.

That there was no Pharisaic sect can be further proved from tannaitic literature. We frequently find the phrase "the Sages said," but we never find the expression "the Pharisees said." There is not found one *halakhah* given in the name of the *Perushim*. Furthermore in the famous story recorded in the Talmud *Kiddushin* concerning the break between John Hyrcanus (Alexander Jannai) and the *Perushim,* the very same *baraita* which quotes Eleazar ben Po'irah as saying "O King Jannai, the hearts of the *Perushim* are against thee," concludes the narrative with "and the Sages of Israel departed in anger." [11] The use of the term "Sages of Israel" rather than *Perushim* clearly indicates that the sages did not employ the term Perushim when referring to themselves but was used by their opponents, the Sadducees.[12]

The Sadducees who comprised chiefly the high priestly families and the upper classes were the first to adopt the customs of the Hellenes. As a rule, the upper classes of subjugated peoples adopt the customs of their conquerors and are willing to become assimilated. An absolutely wealthy group, the Sadducees lusted for all material pleasures. Their gold and silver vessels were often displayed.[13] Yet, their economic situation was such that they were compelled to deal with the Greeks. It is for this reason that they acquainted themselves with the Greek way of life.

With the success of the Hasmonean revolt, Judaea emerged as a free state, rid of her Syrian oppressors. Simon, Mattathias' son, was appointed High Priest as a temporary measure, "until a true prophet shall arise." [14] John Hyrcanus, his son and successor encouraged by his great military victories and territorial conquests, sought, prior to his death, to be crowned King. Though, the Sadducees had always been anxious to maintain the High Priestly office exclusively for the family of Zadok (indeed for the 800 years from the reign of Solomon to Johnathan the Hasmonean the high priesthood had remained in the Zadok family), they united, at this time behind John Hyrcanus. This again illustrates the tendency of the wealthy, upper class to be associated with the ruling family. The Sadducees were for a strong nationalistic state and even in some ways imperialistic. That is, it was their intention to conquer cities and countries, to add to Judaea. John Hyrcanus' military exploits demonstrated to them just such a policy, that is why they supported him.

The appointment of Simon, son of Mattathias as High Priest was a major event in the lives of the Jews. The Sadducees who had always maintained that the High Priesthood belonged to the family of Zadok, now saw this high office transferred to a family of common-priests. They had to compromise with these new conditions. Though they retained their name and their power as a political party, they took on somewhat different characteristics. They were now strictly the wealthy class—landlords and high state officials.

During the reign of Herod many Sadducees were either killed or forced to leave the country. But their influence did not cease. Indeed, they were no longer as influential as they had been under the Hasmoneans. Nevertheless, those Sadducees who did compromise with Herod and adapted to the new conditions were able to continue Saducean policies. A new aristocracy was then emerging to replace the Hasmoneans. They were the Boethusians, so named for they were the family of Boethus the High Priest, Herod's father-in-law.[15] Once again the High Priestly family had been changed. The new group developed the characteristics of an upper class and Boethusian and Sadducee became synonymous.

We have endeavored to show that the Pharisees were not a party in the generally accepted sense of the word. They were the people at large. They stood aloof from the forces of assimilation. The Hellenistic culture did not penetrate into their ranks. When Antiochus sought to destroy Judaism, they supplied the martyrs, they sacrificed their lives for their beliefs. When the Hasmoneans arose against the Syrians they provided the rank and file of the Hasmonean forces. Through their valiant efforts, Judah and his brothers were able to overwhelm the Syrians and free Judaea from persecution. Towards the end of the reign of John Hyrcanus, however, a clash erupted between him and the Pharisees. The story behind this schism is related in a *baraita*.[16] "It once happened concerning the King Jannai . . . and there was a man there, frivolous, evilhearted, and worthless, named Eleazar ben Poirah, who said to King Jannai, 'O King Jannai, the hearts of the Pharisees are against thee.' 'Then what shall I do?' (asked the King) 'Test them by the plate between thine eyes.' (He advised him to have them take an oath of allegiance by the Holy Name on the plate.) [17] So he tested them by the plate between his eyes." (He wanted the Pharisees to take the oath, but the Pharisees refused to do so.) [18]

Prior to the Hasmonean uprising, Jerusalem was controlled by the Sadducees, while after the victory we find the Pharisees rising to power. The Sadducees enjoyed a brief interlude of power at the time of Jannaeus Alexander, only to lose that power completely with the rise of Herod. Thus Josephus writes, "the Sadducees having the confidence of the wealthy class alone but no following among the populace, while the Pharisees have the support of the masses." [19] As such, from the time of Herod until the destruction of the Temple, that is, from the time of Hillel the Elder until Rabban Johanan ben Zakkai, Judaism was guided and lived in the Pharisaic tradition. Josephus writes that, "all prayers and sacred rites of divine worship are performed according to their exposition." [20] The reason for this is that from the time of John Hyrcanus until Herod, both religious and civil leadership were wielded by one individual. When John Hyrcanus became a Sadducee, and through the reign of his son Jannaeus Alexander, the people were absolutely forbidden to live according to Pharisaic teachings. In fact, all Pharisaic innovations were abolished. During the reign of the Hasmoneans there was no separate religious and civil authorities, both positions were held by one family. Beginning with Herod, however, the situation changed and the authority was partitioned. The priesthood was controlled by the Boethusians and the State was controlled by the family of Herod. Herod appointed and dismissed High Priests at will, to prevent any one priest from gaining too great an influence over the people.

The Hasmoneans freed the Jews from Syrian persecution through military strategy and statesmanship. The Pharisees enabled the Jews to overcome the Hellenistic influence and to survive many other catastrophes. The institutions which emerged during that period and continued until our day were established by the Pharisees. Indeed, Judaism was formed by the Pharisees.

THE HALAKHAH

The main point of conflict between the Sadducees and the Pharisees centered in the Halakhah.

These halakhic controversies may be divided into three groups. A) Religious B) Social C) Dogma and Beliefs.

Religious

The Daily Offering

In the tractate *Menahot* we learn of the controversy between the Sadducees and Pharisees regarding the daily sacrifice (*Tamid*). The Sadducees maintained that any individual who wished to provide lambs for the daily sacrifice could do so directly or could donate to the Temple treasury the money required to purchase them. The Pharisees felt that the daily offering should be funded out of the communal treasury.[21] The reason behind this argument may be explained as follows. In the early days of the Second Commonwealth, the daily sacrifice was considered a private sacrifice, and hence was brought only by the wealthy. The poor, unable to afford to donate lambs or the money required to purchase them were virtually excluded from participating in the daily offerings. Since the upper class was made up mostly of Sadducees, they had a virtual monopoly on the daily-offering. By maintaining that an individual donates the sacrifice they simply excluded anyone too poor to afford the expense. The Pharisees were in favor of democratization of the Temple and the institutions connected with it. They opposed the monopoly the Priests had over the Temple and sought to bring the people closer to the service. They maintained that the daily sacrifice should be a communal offering purchased with public funds from the whole Jewish people. This is the main point of this controversy.[22]

As they were interested in having these daily sacrifices become a national institution, the Pharisees were not satisfied with the mere purchase of the cattle with communal funds. They wished the entire nation to participate in the ceremony of the slaughtering of the *tamid,* morning and afternoon. To accomplish this, the Israelites, the inhabitants of the cities, towns and villages, were divided into twenty-four divisions called *ma'amadot.*[23] The members of each *ma'amad* were supposed to go to Jerusalem, to the Temple, to take part in the ceremony of the slaughtering of the daily sacrifice. The members of the divisions represented the entire Jewish people. As not all the members of the *ma'amad* could go or wished to go to Jerusalem, the part that actually went represented the *ma'amad* and the entire Jewish people. The members that remained at home gathered in their respective cities and towns on the days on which they were supposed to be in Jerusalem and read the Pentateuchal account of the creation."²⁴ Thus they had to assemble twice daily throughout the year, morning and afternoon; on Sabbaths three times, morning, *musaf,* and afternoon; on the Day of Atonement four times, morning, *musaf,* afternoon, and *ne'ilah.* We may even postulate that the Israelites of each *ma'amad,* when they assembled in their respective places, not only read the biblical account of the creation but also read the portions of the Torah relating to the daily sacrifice and recited the liturgy of the Temple service. As a result, it became necessary for each group to establish a permanent place for assemblies. This place was called the *bet ha'knesset,* house of assembly. Those who gathered there came to be called *bnei-ha'knesset;* the supervisor was called *hazan-ha'knesset,* and the group leader was known as *rosh-ha'knesset.* Herein lies the the basis of the institution called *bet ha'knesset,* synagogue.²⁵

Feast of Weeks

According to the Sadducees the Feast of Weeks—*Azeret*—had to fall on a Sunday. "The Boethusians (Sadducees) said that *Azeret* must follow the Sabbath." The Pharisees maintained that it should fall on the fiftieth day after the Omer was brought, that is fifty days after the sixteenth of Nisan irrespective of the day of the week.²⁶ This controversy about the date of the Festival of Weeks is due to the fact that in the Bible this holiday has no fixed date. The two other holidays—Passover and the Feast of Tabernacles—have fixed dates. The former falls on the fifteenth of Nisan, and the latter on the fifteenth of Tishri. The Torah is rather vague as to the date of the Feast of Weeks. "Seven weeks shalt thou number unto thee; from the time the sickle is first put to the standing corn shalt thou begin to number seven weeks. And thou shalt keep the feast of weeks. . . ."²⁷ The book of Leviticus adds, "And you shall count unto you from the morrow after the Sabbath from the day that you brought the sheaf of the wave offering; seven weeks shall there be complete; even unto the morrow after the Sabbath of the seven weeks shall you number fifty days."²⁸ The Feast of Weeks is to be celebrated on the fiftieth day of the Omer and depends solely on the Omer. But the Omer sacrifice also has no specific date. "When you come into the land which I give unto you, and you shall reap the harvest, then ye shall bring the sheaf of the first fruits of your harvest unto the priest, and he shall have the Omer . . . on the morrow after the Sabbath the priest shall wave it . . .

And you shall count unto you from the morrow after the Sabbath . . . fifty days." [29]

Originally the Jews employed a solar calendar. Both, Passover—on the fifteenth of Nisan, and the Festival of Tabernacles on the fifteenth of Tishri, fell only on Sunday. In the early days of the Second Commonwealth the calendar was changed from solar to lunarsolar. The months were reckoned by the moon but the years were reckoned by the sun. In order to harmonize these lunar months with the solar years, a nineteen year cycle was set up during which seven of those years were leap years of thirteen months each.[30] Since the years in the new calendar had either 354 days (plain year) or 384 days (leap year) they were not divisible by seven, and it was no longer possible for the fifteenth of Nisan and the fifteenth of Tishri to fall on Sunday every year. It was therefore decided that these festivals are to be celebrated according to the date of the month, without regard for the day of the week it happens to fall on. The Feast of Weeks, as we said, was dependent on the day of the Omer, which was "on the morrow after the Sabbath." The Sadducees interpreted the verse literally and insisted that the Feast of Weeks be celebrated on Sunday, regardless of the date of the month. The Pharisees, on the other hand, insisted on reckoning the Feast of Weeks as the fiftieth day after the Omer, no matter what day of the week it was. They thus interpret the "morrow after the Sabbath" to mean the day after the first day of Passover—the sixteenth of Nisan, whatever day of the week it happens to be.[31]

Cutting the Omer on the Sabbath

According to the tannaitic source, the Sadducees prohibited the offering of the Omer on the Sabbath.[32] The reason was this: If we should assume that the Omer could fall on any day of the week, including the Sabbath, work could have to be done in the fields on that day to reap the Omer, resulting in a desecration of the Sabbath. The fact that sacrifices were brought to the Temple on the Sabbath could not be used to refute this stand because this was done by the priests in the Temple and was allowed under Biblical law. The Sadducees refused to permit a non-priest to reap the Omer on the Sabbath even though it was for the Temple service, thus emphasizing their policy of segregation of priest from Israelite even in service to God. The Pharisees, on the other hand, believed that, if in the Temple, a priest was permitted to labor on the Sabbath in the natural process of the ritual, an Israelite may be permitted to reap the Omer on the Sabbath as part of the Temple service. Thus, the Tosefta records that if the day of the offering up of the Omer falls on Saturday, the Sabbath may be violated to reap the Omer.[33]

We can now understand a Mishneh in Menahot. When the sixteenth of Nisan fell on a Sabbath, the farmers who were to reap the Omer would ask, "Is today Sabbath?" the reply was given, "Yes." ("Is today Sabbath?" again the reply was, "Yes.") Then the farmers would inquire "May we reap today"? the answer returned was, "Yes." ("May I reap? . . ."). Each separate matter was questioned three times and each time the reply was, "Yes! Yes! Yes!" The reason this procedure was carried out was because of the Boethusians (Sadducees) who maintained that the Omer must not be reaped at the conclusion of the first day of Passover but at the conclusion of the Sabbath day.[34] The Sabbath was repeatedly mentioned by the farmers to demonstrate publicly that even an Israelite may cut the Omer on the Sabbath for presentation in the Temple, thus overriding the Sabbath laws with the same allowance given priests in the Temple.

It is therefore evident, that the controversy between the Sadducees and the Pharisees did not center on differing interpretations of biblical verses, but from different points of view regarding the essence of the Judaean state. The Pharisees endeavored to make the Judaean religion the concern of every individual, by encouraging them to participate in the religious rituals. While in the pre-Hasmonean period, religious life centered entirely around the priests, and the Israelites had nothing to do with the Temple service, it was soon after that the influence of the Pharisees strengthened and the sages sought to gain Israelite participation in the ritual alongside the priests. It was at that time that the daily sacrifice became a public offering, funded from the communal treasury and the participation of the Israelites in the actual ritual became reality with the institution of the *Ma'amadot*. In an even greater assumption of authority, they extended the allowance given the priests to labor on the Sabbath while participating in the ritual and included those Israelites who might have to profane the Sabbath for the same ritualistic purposes. They, therefore permitted Israelites to reap the Omer, even on the Sabbath.

The Pharisees strove to eradicate the disparity between the aristocracy —the priest, and the masses—the Israelites.

Beating the Willow on the Sabbath

It is from a Tosefta that we learn of the Saducean opposition to performing the willow-beating ceremony on the Sabbath.[35] They maintained that if the seventh day of the Feast of Tabernacles falls on Saturday, the willow-beating ceremony is to be cancelled rather than desecrate the Sabbath by performing prohibited work. The Pharisees felt that the Israelites should be permitted to participate in the willow-beating ceremony, since it was part of the Temple ritual, and as such, none of the Sabbath restrictions apply to those rituals performed in the Temple regardless of who performs them, priest or Israelite.

A very interesting story is told in a *baraita*. Once, the seventh day of the Festival of Tabernacles fell on the Sabbath, bundles of willows were brought to the Temple on Friday in preparation. The Boethusians found the willow branches and hid them under heavy stones so that they should not be used. The next day, the *Ame ha'Aretz* discovered the hiding place, removed the willow branches from beneath the stones, and brought them to the altar to perform the ceremony, even though it was the Sabbath.[36] This clearly indicates that the Saducean (Boethusian) opposition to performing this ceremony on Sabbath was to stress their ideology of segregating the Israelites from priests. It was the privilege of the priests alone to perform in the Temple on the Sabbath, while the Israelites were restricted.

The question now arises, why the keen interest displayed by the *Ame ha'Aretz* in insuring that the ceremony be performed; that they especially went to recover the willows from their hiding place. It has been my contention that the term *"Ame ha'Aretz"* during the Second Commonwealth period, referred to the farmer-folk.[37] In this case, the account in the *baraita* is illuminating. According to an old tradition, the world is judged on the Feast of Tabernacles as to whether the coming year will have the proper rainfall or be a year of drought.[38] The four species carried during this festival are used in order to obtain the favor of God that He may give rain. Now we can understand why the *ame ha'aretz,* the farmers, were so interested in the cermony of the willow-branches. They believed that the performance of this ritual was essential, to insure proper rainfall.

Burning of the Red Heifer

According to the Mishneh, the burning of the red heifer is to be performed only by a *t'bul yom,* i.e., one who had become unclean, immersed himself during the day but did not wait until sunset. This was in opposition to the Sadducees who felt that "it must be performed only by those who had become clean with sundown."[39] I think the basis for this controversy may be explained as follows. According to the Pentateuchal laws one who has been defiled by a minor defilement is required to perform ritual immersion and then wait until sundown to be considered ritually pure. Bathing alone was not sufficient to restore ritual cleanliness, he had to wait until sunset for the process to be complete.[40] From the time of his immersion, as he waited for the sun to set, he was considered a *t'bul yom*. The Pharisees, maintained that this status only applied to a priest if he wants to eat *Terumah*. That is, if a priest is defiled by minor defilement, the immersion is not sufficient to render him ritually clean to partake of the *Terumah*, he must wait until sundown. With regard to other aspects of ritual purity, however, the ritual ablution is deemed sufficient to render a person ritually clean without the requirement of waiting for sundown.[41]

This helps to explain the controversy regarding the preparation of the red heifer. According to the Bible, this service must be performed by a ritually clean priest. Since the burning of the red heifer was performed publicly with much pomp and ceremony, the Pharisees utilized this opportunity to demonstrate to the people that the law was in accordance with their interpretation. Before burning the red heifer, the priest who was to do so was purposely defiled. A place for ritual immersion was prepared and he was told to go bathe and arise to burn the heifer.[42] This was strictly enforced, in opposition to the Saducean view, to emphasize that a priest who was defiled by a minor defilement need not wait until sunset, but became ritually clean following the ritual bath. This is the basis for this controversy.

The Nizzok

From the Mishneh in *Yadaim* we learn of a controversy regarding *Nizzok*. "The Sadducees say, 'We complain against you, Pharisees, because you declare clean the *Nizzok*.' The Pharisees say, 'We complain against you, Sadducees, that you declare clean the stream of water that comes from a cemetery.'"[43] All the commentators who have discussed the Mishneh and the scholars who have dealt with the matters of dispute between the Pharisees and Sadducees, have taken for granted that the word *Nizzok* implies pouring from one vessel into another. They thus interpret the Sadducees as saying, "We find fault with you, O Pharisees, because in case a man pours a liquid from a clean vessel into a vessel that is unclean you maintain that what is left in the upper vessel remains clean," and that the Pharisees rejoin thereto, "We find fault with you too, O Sadducees, that ye declare clean the stream of water that issues from a cemetery."[44] This interpretation of the Mishneh is unacceptable. Firstly, there is no talmudic evidence that the Sadducees ever declared unclean the water that remained in the upper vessel when part thereof had been poured into an unclean vessel. Secondly, the retort attributed to the Pharisees has nothing to do with the question propounded by the Sadducees. The Sadducees are represented as asking the Pharisees why the water in the upper vessel is declared clean when part had been poured into an unclean vessel. The Pharisees are represented as answering with a query of their own. Why do the Sadducees declare the water which flows from a cemetery—an unclean source—as clean. The response of the Pharisees is totally irrelevant and bears no relation, at all, to the original problem.

It is frequently the case that equivocal expressions lead to misinterpretations. One such expression is *Nizzok*. Since it generally has the connotation of pouring out from one vessel into another,[45] the commentators were misled into applying that definition to this particular passage. It seems to me, however, that the word *Nizzok* in this Mishneh is the *nif'al* form of the word יצק, and refers to the status of that which has received the water.

The dispute may then be explained as follows. According to the Pentatenchal law, if water was put upon seed, the seed becomes susceptible to Levitical uncleanliness.[46] No distinction is made between seed which is attached to the soil and that which is detached. The Pharisees, interpreted the word 'seed' to mean that only seed detached from the soil becomes susceptible to Levitical uncleanliness when water has been put upon it, but not while the seed is still attached to the ground.[47] The dispute resolves itself thus: The Sadducees objected to the Pharisaic distinction between detached and attached seed for the purpose of pollution susceptibility if water was poured upon seed.[48] It is to this that the Pharisees respond that the Sadducees themselves, as strict interpreters of the Bible, distinguish between that which is attached and detached. There is no greater source of defilement than the cemetery, yet, the stream which flows from it is rendered clean according to the Pentatench, because the stream remains attached to the soil.[49] According to this idea we can readily see the relationship between the answer of the Pharisees and the question posed by the Sadducees. This not only explains the Mishneh, but also the basis of the controversy.[50]

"The Scriptures Defile the Hands"

The Sadducees and Pharisees also argued regarding the holy scriptures. According to the Mishneh, the Sadducees opposed the Pharisaic edict that the holy scriptures defile the hands. "Said the Sadducees, 'We protest against you, O Pharisees, that you say the Holy Scriptures defile the hands and the book of '*Homirom*' does not defile the hands'."[51] The question arises. Why did the Pharisees declare that the Holy Scriptures should defile the hands? Indeed the entire subject of "Defilement of the Hands" requires scrutiny. Why should the hands alone be defiled and not the entire body? From what we know about the laws of purity in the Bible, if any part of the body, say a leg or hand touched any unclean object, the entire body is considered in a state of Levitical uncleanliness, not just that particular member.[52]

The decree that the Holy Scriptures defiled the hands was aimed against the priests, just as were most of the other eighteen decrees which the schools of Shammai and Hillel adopted at the conclave in the year 65 C.E. One of these decrees was *sefer*, the book, i.e., if the *sefer* came in contact with *Teruma*, the *Teruma* became defiled and could not be eaten by the priests. This decree was directed against the priests who were mostly Sadducees. With this decree the Pharisees made it impossible for the priests to read the Pentateuch and to eat the *Teruma*. According to the Talmud, the *sefer*, the Pentateuch, does not defile *Teruma* but renders it unfit. Thus the *sefer* was put in the "second degree" of defilement, which only makes *Teruma* unfit but not ordinary food.[53] With the decree that the *sefer* makes *Teruma* unfit, the Pharisees did not gain their entire end, as the priests could avoid contact of the *sefer* with *Teruma*. So they decreed that the *sefer*, which is only of "second degree" of defilement, makes the hands which touch the *sefer* not impure in the "third degree" but in the "second degree", as the *sefer*. Therefore, the hands which touch the book, the *sefer*, make the *Teruma* unfit for eating.[54] With this they accomplished their end, i.e., that the priests could not read the *sefer* because it would defile the hands and hence, they could not touch *Teruma* until evening, as washing the body was not sufficient to render them pure in connection with *Teruma*. When the Scriptures were canonized, the same law was applied, namely, as the *sefer* defiled the hands, thus the Scriptures defiled the hands.

Only the Sefer Torah which was in the *Azarah* did not defile the hands.[55] The reason this particular scroll was excluded from the decree, is so that it should not defile the High Priest when he read from it on the Day of Atonement. But, if this *Azarah* Scroll is removed from the Temple it defiles the hands just like all other holy scrolls. The laws of Levitical uncleanliness did not apply to anything which was kept in the *Azarah* for ritualistic purposes. While all liquids can defile, the blood and the water of the ritual slaughter-house were not susceptible to defilement as long as they were kept within the Temple confines. Similarly, the musical instruments used by the Levites in the Temple, were also excluded from the laws of levitical purity.[56]

We can now understand the opposition of the Sadducees to this Pharisaic rule regarding the Holy Books. Indeed the whole idea of the ruling was aimed against the Sadducees. The retort of R. Johanan ben Zakkai now takes on added significance. He is reported to have told the Sadducees that they too agree that the bones of a mule are ritually clean while the bones of Johanan the High Priest were ritually unclean, adding that their uncleanliness is proportionate to the love for them. A mule's bones are insignificant, to be considered mere dust, but the bones of Johanan the High Priest are esteemed, that is why they can defile. Similarly regarding the Holy Books. Those which have been canonized are important, they defile the hands; those which have been excluded, are deemed insignificant, like the bones of a mule and do not defile. The canonized works are analogous to the bones of Johanan the High Priest, in that they are for serious study and interpretation, not for ordinary use.[57]

The basic supposition regarding the Holy Books, that something which should not be handled indiscriminately will defile the hands, will enable us to understand a difficult Mishneh in *Pesahim*. The Mishneh tells us that the Paschal lamb after midnight, *Nothar,* and *Pigul,* all defile the hands.[58] The Talmud adds that the reason *pigul* defiles the hands is because of certain suspect priests who may have maliciously rendered the sacrifice as *pigul*. *Nothar* was considered to defile the hands because of those lazy priests who were too indolent to consume the sacrifice within the allotted time.[59]

It is not without hesitation that I beg to add my own reasoning to this decree, besides those reasons given in the Talmud. The Paschal sacrifice, though past the legal eating time (midnight), is still considered an object of holiness—that is why it defiles the hands. Similarly, *Nothar* and *pigul,* while they are forbidden to be eaten still maintain their holiness as sacrifices and also defile the hands. The hands which now become defiled are considered defiled in the 'second degree' and just as if the hands had touched the Holy Books they now can render *Terumah* unfit for use.[60]

It is well known that the Sadducees accepted the 'written law' while rejecting the 'oral law'. What was their attitude towards the Prophets and the Hagiographa? Did the Sadducees reject these too, or did they accept them and reject only the ancestral law? Many scholars have already dealt with this problem. It is my opinion that the Sadducees accepted all of the canonized books of the Prophets. The books of the

Hagiographa, however, while part of Jewish literature, were not canonized until 65 C.E. The Sadducees were strongly opposed to their inclusion in the Holy Scriptures. The notions of resurrection expressed in the book of Daniel and the concept of reward and punishment discussed in other books were doctrines that the Sadducees totally rejected. They could not accept such books into the canon.

The Mishneh in *Yoma* tells us that in order to keep the High Priest awake on the eve of the Day of Atonement he was required to expound the law. If he was not a scholar, unable to expound, "the sages would expound before him. If he were versed in reading, he read, and if not they read before him. And from what did they read before him? From Job, and from Ezra, and from the Chronicles . . . and the book of Daniel."[61] The Palestinian Talmud adds that they also read from the books of Proverbs and Psalms.[62] Some believe the reason that these readings were selected from the Hagiographa was to test the High Priest, to determine if he was a Sadducee. Since these books contain concepts of resurrection, and reward and punishment, ideas alien to Sadducean philosophy, the reaction of the High Priest to their recital would clue us as to his identity. Similarly, Psalms and Proverbs were also read. These books attributed to Kings David and Solomon, fathers of the Davidic dynasty and major opponents of the Sadducees, would certainly be opposed by a Sadducean High Priest.[63]

Some scholars maintain that the Sadducees rejected the books of the Prophets as well as the Hagiographa.[64] These notions are incorrect. If the Sadducees rejected the Prophets, too, then the book of Samuel, which glorifies King David would have been a more appropriate reading than Chronicles. If the purpose of these readings was to test the High Priest's reaction to the concepts of resurrection and reward and punishment, then why read from Chronicles, of all books? Certainly, we are correct, then, in assuming that the Sadducees accepted the Prophetic books as strongly as they accepted the Pentateuch. The purpose of reading to the High Priest from the Hagiographa was not to determine if he were a Sadducee, nor to test his belief in resurrection, or his acceptance of the Davidic dynasty. The Mishneh is telling us that if the High Priest was a scholar he interpreted the biblical works—the Pentateuch and the Prophets. The word דרש , to interpret, is not limited to *halakhah*—oral law—but applies also to the written word, e.g., *Mikra Ani Doresh*.[65] But, if the High Priest was not a scholar, unable to interpret on his own, then scholars interpreted these books for him. If he could read but was not capable of understanding the interpretations of the other scholars, he would read certain scriptures. If he could not read at all, they read for him from the Hagiographa. The term קרא —read—is used in relation to the Hagiographa, and not the word דרש —interpret—because the Hagiographa was not yet part of the canon and could only be read and not studied and interpreted.

By the same token, the fact that the Hagiographa was not canonized until 65 C.E. explains why there are no *haftorot* from that section of the Bible. The holy books, at that time, were the Pentateuch and the Prophets. A portion of the Pentateuch was read and a selection of the Prophets was read as a *haftorah*. By the time the Hagiographa was canonized, the *haftorot* for the Sabbaths and the Festivals had already been established.

The Water Libation

The Tosefta and the Mishneh provide the sources for the controversy regarding the water libation. According to the account of the Mishneh, it was requested that the priest who offered the libation should raise his hand with the pitcher so they could see where the water was being poured. An incident is recorded where a priest poured the water at his feet, the enraged throng pelted him with their citrons. The *tosefta* adds that the priest was a Sadducee.[65a] From this we see that the Sadducees opposed pouring the water onto the altar. While the Talmud does not offer a reason for this controversy, the essence of the argument may be explained as follows. The Pharisees sought to limit the libation ritual to the Temple by maintaining that the water must be poured onto the altar. It is well known that water libations were an integral part of ancient sacrificial rites.[66] The water was poured on the ground as an offering in return for proper rainfall. This method of worship is found among the ancient Hebrews also. This is attested to in the book of Samuel. "And Samuel said, gather all Israel at Mizpeh, and I will pray for you to Adonai. And they gathered together at Mizpeh and drew water and poured it out before Adonai." [67]

According to an old Jewish tradition the world is judged on the Feast of Tabernacles as to whether it should have rain in the coming year.[68] The book of Zechariah records the prophet as saying that those who did not go to Jerusalem on the Festival of Tabernacles would have no rain.[69]

Most likely, the Sadducees wanted to continue the ancient practice of pouring the libation on the ground—whenever one desired to do so. The Pharisees did not believe that pouring water on the ground is the way to insure proper rainfall. Rain is a divine gift [70] and only through prayer to

God can one plea for rain, not by pouring water on the ground. The Pharisees, realizing that the ancient magical practice had become well entrenched among the people and virtually impossible to eradicate, compromised and limited the libation only to the altar in the Temple. A similar change had taken place with the entire sacrificial cult. In ancient days, people offered sacrifices wherever and to whatever they desired. The form of worship by sacrifice had become so ingrained it was impossible to abolish it. A compromise was made and sacrifices were permitted, limited to a Temple altar and only to the God of Israel.[71] The Sadducees, as the wealthy land owners and much desirous of a proper rainfall,[72] sought to maintain the observance of the ancient practice of pouring the water on the ground lest there be no rain, at all. (A Sadducean priest would prefer not to pour the water at all, rather than conform to the Pharisaic mode of pouring it on the altar.) It was fear of the Pharisees and the general public who followed Pharisaic teachings that forced the Sadducean priest to pour the water altogether. Since he had to pour the water, he decided it would be preferable to pour it on the ground rather than the altar. In order to insure that the ritual was performed in the Pharisaic manner, the priest was warned to raise his hand so the people could see where the water was being poured.[73]

Incense

A *baraita* in Yoma records of a controversy between the Sadducees and Pharisees regarding the burning of the incense on the Day of Atonement. The *baraita* relates that once, on the Day of Atonement, a Sadducean high priest offered the incense in accordance with the views of the Sadducees, i.e., outside the curtain prior to entering the Holy of Holies. When he came out he was elated. Whereupon his father said to him, "Although we are Sadducees, we are fearful of the Sages," we have to follow their point of view.[74] The Pharisees maintained that the high priest must prepare inside the curtain, from within the Holy of Holies, not outside.

Tradition has explained this controversy as a variance of opinion in the interpretation of the relevant biblical verses. The verse, "For I appear in the cloud upon the ark cover," was interpreted by the Sadducees to mean that the smoke should rise from the incense before the High Priest enters the inner sanctum. The Pharisees, cited the verse, "And he shall put the incense upon the fire before Yahweh," and interpreted it to mean that the high priest should enter the inner sanctum and then prepare the incense.[75] An interesting explanation of this controversy has been offered by Dr. Lauterbach.[76] The Saducean priests believed that God was present in the Holy of Holies. They hesitated entering that inner sanctum without a smoke screen because they feared coming face to face with God and die. "For man shall not see me and live." To them the instructions in the Bible are very clear. "And he shall put the incense upon the fire before Yahweh, that the cloud of the incense may cover the arkcover that is upon the tesimony, that he die not . . . For I appear in the cloud upon the arkcover." Because of this fear of death they decreed that the high priest should put the incense upon the coals while he was still outside the curtain. The smoke rising from the burning incense would then obstruct his vision as he passed the curtain and entered the Holy of Holies. The Pharisees, however, maintained that God's presence is universal and not confined to the Holy of Holies. They maintained that the high priest should enter the Holy of Holies with open eyes and have no fears that his life would be endangered, since God was invisible and could not be seen with human eyes. In opposition to the Saducean view they decreed that the high priest should carry the incense and the coals separately into the Holy of Holies, and only when inside was he to put the incense on the fiery coals and let the smoke rise as an offering.[77]

Social

False Witnesses

As we know from the tannaitic sources, there was a controversy between the Sadducees and Pharisees regarding the laws of false witnesses. The Sadducees held that false witnesses are to be executed only after the defendant had already been put to death The Pharisees maintained that these false witnesses are to be executed once the verdict has been rendered.[77a] The general notion is that the Pharisees held that once the defendant had already been executed the witnesses can no longer be punished. This is not true. The Pharisees never expressed the view advocating the release of false witnesses once the defendant had been executed. The controversy pertained only to the time after the announcement of the verdict. The Sadducees held that the false witnesses were to be executed only, if through their false testimony an innocent person was actually executed. The Pharisees maintained that they be executed once the verdict had been rendered and it was determined that they had, in fact, borne false testimony.[78]

It would appear on the surface that the Pharisees had a more stringent attitude on this matter than did the Sadducees. This contradicts what we know about these sects, namely, that the Sadducees were rigid in judging offenders but that the Pharisees were more lenient in matters of punishment.

When analyzing the Pharisees' point of view, however, one can readily see that, in this case as in others, not only were they lenient but they applied logic. According to the Pentateuch, one who gave false testimony was to suffer the same penalty as the accused would have suffered through the false testimony, the Sadducees maintained such a witness could be executed only after the accused man was put to death. The Pharisees introduced a new principle into the laws of false testimony, by classifying "false witnesses" into two categories: The first included those whose testimony was merely contradictory. If it was found that witnesses testified falsely, their statement not being in accord with the facts, or disagreeing with other witnesses' testimony, the Pharisees held that the case should be dismissed and the witnesses not punished. The second included those who plotted against an innocent person, and who were not present at the murder. They deserved capital punishment even if the verdict of death had only been pronounced against the accused, though not yet carried out. If the accused had already been executed, the Pharisees held with the Sadducees that such false witnesses should be put to death. The Sadducees did not differentiate between the two categories. While on the surface one could assume that the Pharisees were rigid, and it was so assumed, they actually were lenient, since they made an important distinction between the two types of false witnesses.

The law of "once he has died, they are not to be killed," is not Pharisaic, nor is it found in any tannaitic source attributed to the Pharisees. It is mentioned in a *baraita* in the name of *"Berebi."* [79] It is possible that this law was enacted after the Sanhedrin had been abolished and capital cases were no longer tried.

An interesting story involving Judah ben Tabbai is found in a Tosefta. "May I be consoled that I acted properly in killing that false witness (before the defendant was executed), in opposition to the Boethusians (Sadducees) who claim that the witness is executed only after the defendant's sentence had been carried out? Said Simon ben Shetah, 'May I have consolation for you have shed innocent blood. For just as the Torah has instructed to confirm an act only based on the testimony of two or three witnesses, so the laws of 'false witnesses' applies only to two! At that time Judah ben Tabbai took upon himself never to render a halakhic decision without the accordance of (Simon) ben Shetah."[80] Judah ben Tabbai, who served as *Nasi,* declared that he had once ordered the execution of a person who had testified falsely, although his testimony could not lead to actual condemnation of the accused, since, according to the Pentateuch, the testimony of two people is required to convict and to sentence the accused to death. He, nevertheless, ordered the execution of this witness to emphasize his opposition to the Sadducean view that false witnesses are not killed until the defendant has been executed. Simon ben Shetah, serving as *ab-bet-din,* disapproved of the action and reproached him for having shed innocent blood. To emphasize opposition to the Sadducean interpretation was no excuse to execute the witness, for just as biblical law requires the testimony of two witnesses for conviction, so, in the case of alibi witnesses there must be two of them to render punishment for false testimony.

The biblical use of the word *'Ed,'* in the singular, seems to indicate that we are speaking of one witness. This is evident in both the Septuagint and in Josephus. Onkelos, too, renders it in the singular. "If a false witness rise up against a man to testify evilly . . . if the witness be a false witness, he hath testified a falsehood against his brother; then shall ye do unto him as he proposed to do unto his brother."[81] Simon ben Shetah told Judah ben Tabbai that the use of *'ed'*—witness—in the singular does not imply 'one witness'; rather it refers to 'witness' in a collective sense. Thus by inferring the laws of 'alibi witnesses' from the laws regarding honest testimony we learn that just as two are needed to convict and sentence a defendant so must two witnesses testify falsely for the court to have the power to punish them.[82]

Slavery

A Mishneh records a controversy between the Pharisees and the Sadducees regarding slaves. "The Sadducees say, 'We protest against you, O Pharisees, for ye say, "My ox or my ass that has caused an injury is culpable, but my bondman or bondwoman that has caused an injury is exempt;" if, in the case of my ox or my ass concerning which I be liable for any injury caused by them, then all the more in the case of my bondman or bondwoman regarding whom injunctions are laid upon me must I be liable for any injury they cause!' The Pharisees replied to them, 'Nay! As ye contend respecting my ox or my ass that have no understanding, would ye also contend of my bondman or my bondwoman that do have understanding? For if I provoke them to anger, they might go and set on fire another's shock of grain, and it would be I that would have to pay compensation?' "[83] The Sadducees, as we have pointed out, were the wealthy estate owners. They held that a slave is a mere object, the property of the owner, like the ox and the ass. Just as the owner is responsible for the damages caused by his animals so is he culpable if his slave caused damages. The Pharisees endeavoring to raise the status of the slaves, sought to rectify, as much as possible, the inequality which existed in Judaean society. The Pharisees maintained that a gentile slave could not be compared to irrational animals. A slave was a human being, with understanding, to learn to be responsible for his own acts. By ruling that the owner is responsible for the deeds of his slave is to lower the human being, created in God's image, to a despicable level.

The Mishneh states that the Sadducees held that gentile slaves were obliged to perform *mitzvoth*.[83a] It is strange that they, the Sadducees, should have entertained this view. From what we know of them, we may rightly assume that they held that the gentile slave is an object, without any rights or obligations. The *halakhah* that a gentile slave had to undergo circumcision was enacted much later. During the Second Commonwealth, a gentile slave could not perform *mitzvoth*. He was in the category of an animal. Upon his death, his master could not accept condolensces, as would be the case in the death of his cattle. Rabban Gamaliel had to excuse himself when he accepted condolence on the death of his gentile slave, by saying that his slave was different, a righteous person.[83b] The Sadduceean statement that a slave had to perform *mitzvoth* actually referred to a Noachite *mitzvoth, Jus gentium*.

Female Inheritance

A Tosefta records a controversy in regard to female inheritance. The Sadducees upheld the rule of female inheritance. A man who had died while his father was still alive is survived by a daughter and a sister. Upon the death of the father, his estate is equally divided, according to the Sadducees, between his daughter and the daughter of the previously deceased son (his granddaughter). The Pharisees maintained that the entire estate belongs to the daughter of the deceased son, while the daughter of the present deceased has no share at all, in her father's estate.[84] Many explanations have been offered regarding this controversy.[85]

On the surface it appears that the Saducean point of view is based on simple logic. In reality they were following the Pentateuchal law while the Pharisees were arguing from the unwritten law. According to the Pentateuch, a daughter could inherit only where there were no sons. Therefore, the Sadducees maintained that the two women, the daughter and the granddaughter, should share the inheritance, since there were no sons living. The Pharisees contended, that the granddaughter should inherit the entire estate of the grandfather. Their contention was based on the law which the sages introduced regarding testamentory succession. The new law of inheritance was that a person could make a will, *daithka,* whereby part of his property could go to whomever he designated, even to a total stranger. The Pharisees' contention was based on the assumption that if the father had desired that his daughter should inherit part of his property, he would have written a will *daithka,* bequeathing a share to her. He did not do so; which meant, according to the Pharisees, that he did not want his daughter to inherit any part of his wealth. Therefore, they maintained that the daughter could not share any part of the inheritance of her father and that the inheritance should go entirely to the granddaughter. The Pharisaic ruling both asserted the significance of their legal innovation of testamentory succession and registered their objection to the strict interpretation of the Pentateuchal law.[86]

NOTES

1. Josephus, *Antiquities* XIII 5.9.
2. Abraham Geiger, *Urschrift und Uebersetzungen der Bibel* (1854), pp. 101-158.
3. The members of this sect were called *Zedokim*. *Zedoki* is derived from Zadok the High Priest, father of the dynasty. See J. Wellhausen, *Die Pharisäer und die Sadduzäer* (Hannover, 1924). J. Derenbourg. *Essai sur l'histoire et la géographie de la Palestine* (Paris, 1867). H. Graetz, *Geschichte der Juden* III (Leipzig, 1874). E. Schürer, *Geschichte des Jüdischen Volkes im Zeitalter Jesu Christi* (Leipzig 1886-90) II, ch. 26. A. Geiger, *K'vutzat Ma'amarim* (Berlin, 1877).
4. cf. Klausner, *ibid.*
5. Wellhausen, *op. cit.* Schürer, *op. cit.* Graetz, *op. cit* Rudolf Leszynsky, *Die Sadduzäer* (Berlin, 1912). I. Halevi, *Dorot Ha'rishonim* (Frankfurt, 1897). Aptowitzer, *Parteipolitik der Hasmonaerzeit im Rabbinischen und im Pseudoepigraphischen Schrifttum* (Vienna, 1927). J. Z. Lauterbach, *The Pharisees and Their Teachings HUCA* VI (1929). B. Revel, "Leszynsky's Sadduzäer," *JQR*, n.s. VII, pp. 429-438. S. Zeitlin. *The History of the Second Jewish Commonwealth, Introduction.*
6. Geiger, *K'vutzat Ma'amarim*. G. F. Moore, *Judaism in the First Centuries of the Christian Era.*
7. The notion that *Perushim* was a name invented by their adversaries was expressed by Aptowitzer in *Parteipolitik* (1927), xxvii and Tchernowitz, *Toldot Ha'halakhah* II, p. 259. I have first presented this idea in my review of *The Pharisees*, by R. T. Herford, *JQR* XVI (April, 1926). Cf. Lauterbach, "The Saducees and Pharisees: A Study of their Respective Attitudes towards the Law," *Studies in Jewish Literature issued in honor of Dr. K. Kohler* (Berlin, 1913), pp. 176-198.
8. See S. Zeitlin, *The History of the Second Jewish Commonwealth* (Dropsie: Phila., 1933, pp. 42-43.
9. B.T. *Baba Batra* 60b. ת״ר כשחרב הבית בשניה רבו פרושין בישראל שלא לאכול בשר ושלא תניא יהודה בן דורתאי פירש הוא ודורתאי בנו והלך וישב לו *Pesahim* 70b. לשתות יין אמר ר׳ יוחנן See also P.T. *Yoma* 42a בדרום... אמר רב אשי ואנן טעמא דפרושים ניקו ונפרש קדשים נדחין בשעת מסעות טמאים פרושים כשאחד ואחד במחיצתו.
10. M. *Yadaim* 4.6-7 אומרים צדוקים קובלין אנו עליכם פרושים... אומרים פרושים קובלין אנו עליכם צדוקים.
11. *Kiddushin* 66a. See also Lauterbach, "The Saducees and Pharisees."
12. See P.T. *Yoma* 3a שהרי הצדוקין אומרין... אמרו להן חכמים The general notion is that M. *Hagigah* 2.7 "בגדי עם הארץ מדרס לפרושין" refers to the Pharisees. But, from the very Mishneh it is clear that perushim does not refer to a sect at all, rather to those who separated themselves from the *Ame ha'Aretz* and maintained levitical purity even while eating ordinary food. The Mishneh is clearly speaking about levels of purity. "בגדי עם הארץ מדרס לפרושין בגדי פרושין מדרס לאוכלי תרומה בגדי אוכלי תרומה מדרס לקודש בגדי קודש מדרס לחטאת. יוסי בן יועזר היה חסיד שבכהונה והיתה מטפחתו מדרס לקודש". The explanation is quite obvious. Since the *Ame ha'aretz* are not at all careful about levitical purity, their garments are considered pollutants to those who maintain levitical purity while partaking of ordinary food. The garments of these scrupulous folk are considered pollutant to those who eat *Terumah*, i.e. priests. The garments of these priests, levitically pure enough to eat *Terumah* will render "hallowed food' unclean. The garments of those

who partake of the "hallowed food" are not considered pure enough not to despoil the sin-offering. Each represents a higher level of sanctity and requires a higher degree of purity. The reason that the tablecloth used by Jose b. Joezer will despoil hallowed objects may be explained thusly. The Sages held that the sword used to kill a person has the same degree of impurity as the corpse itself, i.e. it is an *Abi Abot ha'Tumah* (B.T. Pesahim 14b) and one who comes in contact with the sword is deemed an *Ab ha'Tumah*. According to Jose b. Joezer, however, only one who comes in contact with the corpse is an *Ab ha'Tumah*. Contact with the sword will only render one a *Rishon le'Tumah* (B.T. *Abodah Zarah* 37b). It follows, therefore, that that which according to Jose b. Joezer is a "fourth degree impurity" (*revii*-fourth degree) and a non-pollutant to a hallowed object, is only of the "third degree" (*shelishi*-third degree) according to the Sages and will render a hallowed object impure. See my article, "The Semikah Controversy between the Zugoth," *JQR* VIII, April, 1917.

That this Mishneh is dealing with levels of purity and not with sects is quite evident from the Mishneh just preceding it. טבל למעשר אסור לחולין הוחזק לחולין אסור למעשר. טבל למעשר הוחזק למעשר אסור לתרומה. טבל לתרומה הוחזק לתרומה אסור לקודש. טבל לקודש הוחזק לקודש אסור לחטאת. חגיגה ב. ו.

Klausner maintained that that which is recorded in B.T. *Sotah* 22b refers to the Pharisees, "ת״ר שבעה פרושין הן פרושי שיכמי, פרושי נקפי, פרוש מאהבה, פרוש מיראה". However the term *perushim* in this baraita refers to those who separated themselves from the mundane to show that they were pious and God-fearing people. Actually, though, they did it for their personal pleasure, often to deceive everyone else. (See P.T. *Sot.* 20a).

The Mishneh *Sotah* 3.4 records פרושים ומכות פרושה ואשה ערום ורשע שוטה חסיד" "הרי אילו מבלי עולם. This too does not refer to the Pharisees, but rather to a group who have separated themselves from mundane, worldly pleasure. The author of this saying is R. Joshua, the same who voiced his displeasure at those who had refrained from eating meat and drinking wine (B.T. *Baba Batra* 60b).

13 *Ab' d'Rabbi Nathan* 5.
14 I Maccabees 14.41.
15 Cf. *Ant.* XV 9.3. Boethus was the grandfather of Herod's wife Mariamne 2.
16 B.T. *Kid.* 66a.
17 Cf. Gen. 26.3 "והקמתי את השבעה". Onkelos renders this verse, "ואקם ית קימא". אבי השביעני—אבא קיים עלי Ibid. 50.5 וישבעו איש לאחיו—וקיימו גבר לאחוהי Ibid. 31 אשר נשבענו שנינו—דקימנא תרוינא Ibid. 20–42 וישבע עוד דוד—וקים עוד דוד I Samuel 20.3 Ibid. 24.22–23 השבעה לי—קיים לי וישבע דוד—וקים דוד Rashi interprets "test them with the plate" to mean "that Jannai should place the plate on his forehead, forcing them to rise out of respect for the Holy Name imprinted on the plate. thus they will be revealed for what they are. Although he was not partaking in actual service, Jannai was permitted to do what he did, for one is permitted to derive pleasure from the priestly vestments." See also *Tosafot, Kidd.* 66a. The fact that the *Targum* renders שבועה as קיימא lends plausibility to explaining הקם להם בציץ as referring to an oath of allegiance.
18 The name Jannai here refers to John Hyrcanus. Often the Talmud refers to Kings—especially Hasmonean Kings—as Jannai. This story has its parallel in

Ant. XIII 10.5, and *Wars* I 3.8. Friedlander thinks that this story refers to Alexander Jannai, while John Hyrcanus remained a Pharisee until his death. It is difficult to agree with this opinion. The Talmud *Berakhot* 29a states explicitly that John Hyrcanus became a Sadducee before he died. Klausner, *Historia* p. 117, writes that towards the end of his life, John Hyrcanus split with the Pharisees. See also B.T. *Kidd.* 66a כרוכה ומונחת בקרן ... ״רומסים ותורה זוית ... ויהרגו כל חכמי ישראל Cf. *Ant.* XIII 10.6 that Hyrcanus split with the Pharisees, abolished their laws and innovations, and punished their followers.

19 *Ant.* XIII 10.6.
20 *Ibid.* XVIII 1.3.
21 B.T. *Menahot* 65a, שהיו צדוקים אומרים יחיד מתנדב ומביא תמיד מאי דרוש את הכבש האחד תעשה בבקר ואת הכבש השני תעשה בין הערבים, מאי אהדרו את קרבני לחמי לאשי תשמרו שיהיו כולן באין מתרומת הלשכה.
22 The Sadducees based their view on the fact the word תעשה was in the singular. The Pharisees emphasized the word תשמרו which is plural.
23 See B.T. *Taanit* 4b, ״אלו הן מעמדות לפי שנ׳ צו את בני ישראל וכי האיך קרבנו של אדם קרב והוא אינו עומד על גביו, התקינו נביאים הראשונים כ״ד משמרות על כל משמר ומשמר היה מעמד״.
See also Tosefta and P.T. on this source. These "watches" were made up of priests and Levites, while the *ma'amadot* were Israelites. Cf. Henry Malter, *The Treatise Ta'anit of the Babylonian Talmud* (New York: 1930). The Talmud credits the prophets with this innovation. (״אין אלו אלא דברי נביאות״) Cf. B.T. *Erubin* 60b and *Tosafot* commentary thereon.)
24 B.T. *Taanit* 4b, ״וישראל שבאותו המשמר (המעמד) מתכנסין בעריהן וקורין במעשה בראשית״ *Ibid.* 27a, ״אלו הן ת״ר... ואנשי מעמד מתכנסין לבית הכנסת״. P.T. *Taanit* 67a, מעמדות... מתכנסין בעריהן וקורין במעשה בראשית״.
25 See S. Zeitlin, "The Origin of the Synagogue," *PAAJR* II (1931), pp. 69–81. Jews gathered in their synagogues at least once a week, to read a portion of the Law and hear the words of the Sages. See *Contra Apionem* II 17. In *Antiquities* XVI 2.3, Josephus writes that the Jews gathered on the Sabbath to study the Law. Augustus Caesar called the synagogue *'sabbatien'* because the Jews gathered there for study on the Sabbath.
Incidentally, the term בית הכנסת does not mean 'house of prayer.' It is rather an assembly hall used for various purposes, e.g. the Assembly halls of the *Ame ha'Aretz*, and the Assembly halls of the Gentiles. It also refers to those places where items were stored, e.g. wood. See P.T. *Baba Bathra* 18a.
26 B.T. *Menahot* 65a ״תספרו חמישים יום, כל ספירות שאתה סופר לא יהיו אלא חמישים״. Tos. *Rosh Ha'shanah* 1 ״פעם אחת שכרו בייתוסין (צדוקים) שני עדים לבא ולהטעות את״ P.T: *Rosh Ha'shanah* 57a החכמים, לפי שאין בייתוסין מודים שתהא עצרת אלא אחר השבת ״שהיו אומרים עצרת לאחר השבת״.
27 Deut. 16.9.
28 Lev. 23.15–16.
29 *Ibid.* 9–15.
30 See S. Zeitlin, "Notes Relatives au calendrier Juif," *REJ* LXXXIX (1930), pp. 349–359.

31 ממחרת השבת ממחרת היום טוב B.T. *Menahot* 65b
32 B.T. *Menahot* 65a; Tos. *Men.* 10.23, מפני בייתוסין, (צדוקים) שהיו אומרים אין קצירת העומר במוצאי יו״ט אלא במוצאי שבת.
33 *Ibid.*
34 *Ibid.*
35 Tos. *Sukkah* 3.1.
36 *Ibid;* B.T. Suk. 43b.
37 See S. Zeitlin, "The Ame ha'Aretz," *JQR* XXIII (July, 1932), pp. 45–61.
38 "ובחג נידונין על המים". M. *Rosh Ha'shanah* 1.3 and Tosefta.
39 M. *Parah* 3.7 ומטמאין היו את הכהן השורף את הפרה מפני הצדוקים שלא יהו אומרים. Tos. *Parah* 3.8 ומטמאין היו הכהן השורף את הפרה מפני הצדוקין במעורבי שמש היתה נעשית שלא יהו אומרים במעורבי שמש נעשית.
40 Cf. Deut 23.12 וטמא עד הערב וטהר וכבא השמש יבא אל המחנה Lev. 11.32.
41 *Sifra, Shmini.* וטמא עד הערב... טהור לחולין מבעוד יום ולתרומה משתחשך *Sifra, Emor.* מה ישראל שאינם אוכלים בתרומה במעורבי שמש הרי הן אוכלין במעשר טבולי יום Tos. *Parah* 3.6. מעשר נאכל בטבול יום ותרומה נאכלת במעורבי שמש
The first Mishneh in *Berakhot* probably belongs to the period after the 18 *decrees*. Immersion was no longer sufficient for eating Terumah and the priest had to wait until evening. The Mishneh set the time for the reading of *Sh'ma* with the time the priests entered to eat *terumah*. This was the signal that the sun had set and it was already evening. See B.T. *Ber.* 2a מכדי הכהנים אימתי קא אכלי בתרומה משעת צאת הכוכבים Cf. Tos. *Ber* 1.1 משעה שהכהנים זכאין לאכול בתרומתן Cf. B.T. *Baba Kama* 114b מעשה באדם אחד שהיה מסיח לפי תומו ואומר זכורני כשאני תינוק ומורכבני על כתפו של אבא והוציאוני מבית הספר והפשיטוני את כתנתי והטבילוני לאכול בתרומה לערב.
42 M. *Parah* 3.7 ובית טבילה היה שם.
43 M. *Yadaim* 4.7.
44 See *Rashi* and other commentaries on the Mishneh.
45 M. *Makhshirin* 5.9.
46 Lev. 11.38 וכי יתן מים על זרע.
47 Tos. *Makhshirin* 1.1 בית הלל אומרים על התלושין בכי יותן ועל המחוברין אינן בכי יותן. Cf. *Sifra Shmini, ibid.*
48 According to our notion, the word ויצוק refers to the water which fell on the seed, i.e. in the passive voice—the seed upon which water has fallen. Such seed which is still connected to the ground has not been made susceptible. If this is the case, then the most important identifying factor of the law was not even mentioned—the SEED upon which water was poured. This is the style of the early tannaitic halakha. Another example is Hillel's innovation of פרוזבול. The word is Greek, πβος βουλή —before the court. Hillel decreed that a creditor may draw up a contract stating his right to collect the debts whenever he pleases. This contract is then deposited before the court. The main point of this innovation is the contract which is submitted to the court, yet, it is not mentioned at all in the title of the innovation. To cite a further example. Tosefta *Makhshirin* 3.4, R. Joshua b. Perahiah states that grains shipped from Alexandria are ritually unclean because of their אנטליא 'Antilia' is a Greek word, ἀντλίον, meaning 'pail'. R. Joshua b. Perahiah. mantained that the grain which has come from Alexandria

has been made susceptible to pollution by the water which was poured on it from the pail. (In Egypt there was little rain. Fields were nourished by hand). Again this illustrates that mode of concise halakhic writing, leaving out the most important elements.

The *Baraita* (*Sotah* 48a; Tos. *Sot.* 13.10; P.T. *Sot.* 9a) states that John Hyrcanus made a decree concerning the דמאי. '*Demai*', too is Greek, δῆμοι, the *Ame ha'Aretz*, the farmers. Hyrcanus' decree was that those who purchase produce from the *Ame ha'Aretz* are required to separate the required tithes from that produce. The reason being that the *Ame ha'Aretz* are suspected of not having separated those tithes. (See S. Zeitlin, "The Ame ha'Aretz", reference in note 37). The name of the decree is one word, '*Demai*'—the *Ame ha'Aretz*. The main element, produce, is not mentioned. Such was the Tannaitic style, to offer the *halakha* in a concise manner.

49 Lev. 11.36 "אך מעין ובור מקוה מים יהיה טהור".
50 Tchernowitz offers a different explanation for the controversy of the '*Nizzok*'. The Pharisees protested the Sadducees' view of '*nizzok*,' that they permit the pouring of 'water which was collected' over one who is ritually unclean, instead of requiring him to make the proper immersion in a ritual bath. (Tchernowitz feels that '*nizzok*' is the pouring of 'collected waters' over a ritually unclean body. The reflexive form denoted the one over which such water is being poured). To this the Pharisees answered that the Sadducees proclaim as clean the stream which flows from the cemetery. This answer has nothing to do with the question. According to Tchernowitz the Mishneh should be reversed, "אומרים פרושים קובלים אנו עליכם צדוקים שאתם מטהרים את אמת המים הבאה מבית הקברות". Thus, the Pharisees are the ones who open the dialogue by protesting against the Sadducees. But, there is not one place in the Talmud where we find the Pharisees as the initiators of a dialogue with the Sadducees. The Sadducees always open the debate. Besides, the Pharisees have nothing to protest or complain about. Jewish life was conducted in accordance with their teachings. The Sadducees complained against the Pharisees because they were opposed to their innovations. The Sadducees were against the idea of creating laws which the Bible never mentioned. The Sadducees were always the protestors. The Pharisees always offered the rejoinder.

51 M. *Yadaim* 4.6.
52 Logically speaking, if a hand is defiled, the whole body becomes defiled. Cf. M. *Hag.* 2.5 "נטמאו ידיו נטמא גופו".
53 P.T. *Hag.* 79b "השלישי פוסל בתרומה והרביעי בהקדש".
54 M. *Yadaim* 3.2 "כל הפוסל את התרומה מטמא את הידים להיות שניות ... כתבי קדש שניים מטמאין את הידים".
55 M. *Kelim* 15.6 "כל הספרים מטמאין את הידים חוץ מספר העזרה".
56 Tosefta *ibid.* "ספר עזרא (העזרה) שיצא לחוץ מטמא את הידים. נבלי בית לוי טהורים כל". Cf. M. *Kelim* 15.6. "המשקין טמאין ומשקה ביה מטבחיא טהורין"
57 M. *Yadaim* 4.6. See also the Tosefta. Perhaps Rabban Johanan b. Zakkai used

the bones of John Hyrcanus as an example, because John is reported to have become a Sadducee before he died.

58 M. *Pesahim* 10.9 "הפסח אחר חצות מטמא את הידים הפגול והנותר מטמא את הידים".

59 *Ibid.* ch. 5.

60 In a similar vein we can understand why it was decreed that "flesh of desire defiles the hands," ("שבשר תאוה מטמא את הידים"). If the *ma'aser behemah* was redeemed for money and that money was used to purchase animal or fowl, that meat can defile the hands. "תני בן בג בג אומר ונתת הכסף בכל אשר תאוה נפשך... בראשונה היו אומרים לוקחין בהמה לבשר תאוה והיו מבריחין אותו מעל גבי המזבח חזרו לומר לא יקחו אפילו חיה אפילו עופות" P.T. *Ma'aser Sheni* 1; Tosefta. "משגזרו שיהא בשר תאוה מטמא את הידים אמרו אין לוקחין חיה לבשר תאוה... אבל לא העוף לבשר תאוה". See Tos. *Niddah* 9, "בראשונה היו אומרים בשר תאוה טהור חזרו וגזרו עליו שיהא מטמא את הידים". The reason being that the sanctity of the *ma'aser sheni* has been extended to this meat. "הלוקח בהמה לזבחי שלמיו או חיה לבשר תאוה יצא העור לחולין". This Mishneh antedates the decree of בשר תאוה מטמא את הידים).

61 M. *Yoma* 1.6.

62 *Yoma* 39a.

63 Aptowitzer, *Parteipolitik*, XXV.

64 Tchernowitz, op. cit., p. 320.

65 B.T. *Taanit* 5b. *Sukkah* 51b, דרשיה ר' מנחם בר' יוסי *Sotah* 21a, קרא אשכחו ודרוש להאי קרא. *Sukkah* 3. Yer. *Ibid.* 14.

65a M. *Suk.* 4.9; Tosefta ibid. 3.

66 William Robertson Smith, Lectures on *The Religion of the Semites.*

67 I Samuel 7.6.

68 B.T. *Rosh ha'Shanah* 16a, P.T. *Rosh ha'Shanah* 57a "בחג נידונין על המים".

69 Zechariah 14.19.

70 M. *Taanit* 2.1.

71 *Lev. Rabbah* 22, "לפי שהיו ישראל להוטים אחרי ע"ז במצרים והיו מביאים קרבניהם לשעירים דכתיב ולא יזבחו עוד את זבחיהם לשעירים... והיו מקריבין קרבניהם באיסור במה ופורעניות באות עליהן אמר הקב"ה יהיו מקריבין לפני בכל קרבנותיהן באהל מועד ויהיו נפרשים מע"ז". Cf. Maimonides, *Guide for the Perplexed*, part 3, ch 32 "והוא שא"א לצאת מן ההפך אל ההפך פתאם, ולזה א"א לפי טבע האדם שיניח כל מה שהרגיל בו פתאם... מפני השאיר השם· מיני העבודות ההם והעתיקם מהיותם לנבראים... וצונו לעשותו לו ית'. ... ושיהיה הקרבן לו".

72 Tosefta *Rosh Ha'shanah* 1 "ניסוך המים בחג שהוא פרק גשמים שיתברכו עליך גשמים". Cf. P.T. *Rosh Ha'shanah* 57 "אמור מעתה ניסוך המים בחג שיתברכו לפניך המים".

73 Louis Finkelstein (*Harvard Theological Review*, 1920, p. 194), maintains that the controversy arose regarding the water libation because the Sadducees were the rural, land owners while the Pharisees were urbanized, lived in the cities. He points out that the cities are in great need of rain. Hence, the Pharisees were very careful in the performance of the water libation. The Sadducees, on the other hand, did not want rain at that particular time, as it would dampen their

holiday spirits. Since the water libation is not mentioned in the Bible, they saw no reason to perform the ritual.

Finkelstein's theory defies both logic and historical fact. Land owners need more rain than city people. One who lives in the city can easily quench his thirst on wine, milk, or any liquid he desires. Farmers need rain water. Besides, the people in the city could collect the rain water in barrels or reservoirs for future use. Farmers of that period were not familiar with irrigation. They needed rain. Josephus, in describing the hardships endured by the Judaeans of besieged Jerusalem, does not mention that they lacked water. In his description of the siege of Jotapata, however, a serious shortage of water is mentioned. Even Dio, the Roman historian, who writes that the Roman legions who laid the siege of Jerusalem suffered from a lack of water, does not mention that a similar condition existed inside the city. From Antiochus to Titus, Jerusalem was often besieged by foreign forces. Josephus, as well as the authors of the books of Maccabees, in describing the famine and suffering in besieged Jerusalem, never once mention a water shortage. Clearly, during the Second Commonwealth period, there was no lack of water in Jerusalem.

Finkelstein's basic theory that the controversies between the Sadducees and Pharisees are all economically oriented is incorrect. The controversies themselves disprove this notion. It is obvious, from the nature of the arguments that the basis for all the debates was varied ideas about the very essence of Judaism.

A general notion is held connecting the Bet ha-Shoebah celebration with the water libation ritual. An examination of the tannaitic sources will show that the Bet ha-Shoebah is not at all connected with water but with fire. M. *Suk* 5.2, "וארבעה סולמות על כל מנרה ומנרה... ובידיהן כדי שמן... לא היתה חצר בירושלים שלא היתה מאירה מאור בית השואבה. החסידים ואנשי מעשה היו מרקדין לפניהם באבוקות". Tosefta, P.T. *Suk.*, "מעשה ברבן שמעון בן גמליאל שהיה מרקד בשמונה אבוקות של אור... ואמרו אבותינו שהיו במקום הזה אחוריהם אל היכל... והמה משתחוים קדמה לשמש". A forthcoming article will be devoted to the nature of the Bet ha-Shoebah celebration. Cf. volume I "The Beth Ha-Shoebah" pp. 176.

[74] "מעשה בביתוסי (צדוקי) אחד שהקטיר... שהיו הבייתוסין (צדוקים) אומרים הקטר על שבחוץ שנאמר וכסה ענן הקטורת את הכפרת אשר על הארן ולא ימות, אמרו להם חכמים והלא כבר נאמר ונתן הקטרת על האש לפני ה' כל שמקטיר אין מקטיר אלא לפניהם... כשיצא אמר לאביו כל ימיכם הייתם דורשים ואין אתם עושין עד שעמדתי אני ועשיתי אמר לו אבא אף על פי שאנו דורשים אין אנו עושין שומעין אנו לדברי חכמים". Tos. *Yoma* 1. Cf. B.T. *Yoma* 19a; P.T. 39a.

Tos. *Yoma* 1. Cf. B.T. *Yoma* 19a; P.T. 39a.

[75] See P.T. *ibid.* "שהרי צדוקים אומרים יתקן מבחוץ ויכנס... כי בענן אראה על הכפרת אמרו להן חכמים ונתן הקטרת על האש לפני ה'".

[76] See J. Z. Lauterbach, "The Pharisees and their Teachings," *HUCA* VI (1929) pp. 69–139.

[77] Cf. M. *Yoma* 5.1 "ומתפלל תפלה קצרה... שלא להבעית את ישראל". Tosefta, *ibid.* "מעשה בכהן אחד שהאריך אמרו לו מה ראית להאריך אמר להם מתפלל אני עליכם... אמרו

"לו אף על פי כן אי אתה רשאי לשנות".
See P.T. *Yoma* 42c; B.T. 53a.

77a M. *Makkot* 1.6 "אין העדים זוממים נהרגין עד שיגמר הדין שהרי הצדוקין אומרים עד שיהרג, שנאמר נפש תחת נפש אמרו להם חכמים והלא כבר נאמר ועשיתם לו כאשר זמם לעשות לאחיו והרי אחיו קיים, ואם כן למה נאמר נפש תחת נפש יכול משעה שקבלו עדותן יהרגו ת"ל נפש תחת נפש הא אינן נהרגין עד שיגמר הדין".

78 They are not executed until after the verdict has been announced.

79 B.T. *Makkot* 5b "תנא בריבי אומר לא הרגו נהרגו הרגו אין נהרגין".

80 Tosefta *Sanhedrin* 6. According to the Mekhilta, Simon had the witnesses executed to show opposition to the Sadducees. Geiger and Finklelstein maintained that the *Mekhilta* text is the original text. This has no foundation. Aside from the fact that there are four texts which read different from the *Mekhilta* (Tosefta *San.*; P.T. *San.*; B.T. *Mak.*, *Hag.*), we can show from Talmud *Hagigah* that Judah b. Tabbal was responsible for the killing of the witnesses, not Simon b. Shetah. "ת"ר שלשה מזוגות הראשונים, שאמרו שלא לסמוך, ושנים מזוגות אחרונים, שאמרו לסמוך, היו נשיאים ושניים להם אב"ד דברי ר' מאיר, וחכמים אומרים יהודה בן טבאי אב"ד ושמעון בן שטח נשיא... בשלמא ר' מאיר דאמר שמעון בן שטח אב"ד ר"י בן טבאי נשיא היינו דקא מורה הלכה בפני שמעון בן שטח".
The Talmud sought to prove R. Meir's view that Judah b. Tabbai was the 'nasi' at the time. The Tosefta was brought as proof that he was the '*nasi*', killed the witness and then resigned to not render a decision without consulting Simon b. Shetah. It is clear that the Tosefta is the original text.
Cf. P.T. *Hag.* 77b "אנן תנינן יהודה בן טבאי נשיא ושמעון בן שטח אב"ד, אית תני תני ש"ומחליף, מאן דאמר יהודה בן טבאי נשיא עובדא דאלכסנדריא מסייע לו".
Regarding the argument between R. Meir and the Sages on Judah b. Tabbai as *nasi*, both are correct. Until he had ordered the execution of the witness he was, in fact, the *nasi*. After the incident and the protests of Simon b. Shetah, "he took upon himself not to render a decision without Simon b. Shetah." In orther words, Simon b. Shetah had been appointed the *nasi*.
Cf. Tosefta Pesahim 4 "בו ביום מינו את הלל נשיא והיה מורה להם הלכות פסח".

81 Cf. however *Targum Jonathan b. Uzziel* "ארום יקומון סהדין שיקרין בבר נש לאסהדא ביה סטיא... והא סהדי דשקר בפום סהדין שיקרא אסהידו באחוהין ותעבדון להן היכמא דחשיבו למעבד לאחוהון".

82 See S. Zeitlin, "The Semikhah Controversy between the Zugoth," *JQR* VIII (April 1917) pp. 499–517.

83 M. *Yadaim* 4.7.

83a ibid.

83b Cf. M. *Ber* 2.8.

84 Tosefta *Yadaim* 2 "אומרים ביתוסין (צדוקים) קובלני עליכם פרושים מה את בת הבאה מכח בני שבא מכחי הרי יורשתני, בתי הבאה מכחי אינו דין שתתרשני, אומרים פרושין לא אם אמרתם בבת הבן שכן חולקין עם האחין תאמרו בבת שאין חולקין עם האחין".
See B.T. *Baba Batra* 115b "שהיו צדוקין אומרים תירש הבת עם בת הבן".

85 See Geiger, *K'vutzat Ma'amarim*. Finkelstein feels that this controversy is based on the question of immortality of the soul. The Pharisees who believed in this

doctrine considered the son as if he were still alive. Therefore, although he is dead, he can pass his inheritance on to his daughter, to the total exclusion of his sister. The Sadducees, who did not believe that the soul remains after the body had died, held that when the son died his father's estate is transferred to his sister. That is why his daughter also shares in the inheritance. (See his article in *HUCA* VI). If this is the correct reason for the Sadducean view, the son's daughter should not get anything at all.

[86] See S. Zeitlin. "Testamentary Succession: A Study in Tannaitic Jurisprudence," *JQR* 1967.

THE PHARISEES AND THE GOSPELS

Foreword

THE literature on the Pharisees would make a complete library. Students of Judaism as well as of Christianity have written on all the sects which existed among the Jews during the Second Commonwealth, particularly on the Pharisees. Pharisaism became popular with the students of the New Testament, since to understand primitive Christianity a thorough study of the Pharisees is indispensible. However, some of the literature which was written on the Pharisees was one sided, because the writers gave their preference to one set of sources—Josephus, the New Testament, Apocryphal literature. They ignored the tannaitic literature—the product of the Pharisees. Some of them who made use of the tannaitic literature did not fully understand the sources in the original language.

The Pharisaic Halakah, or rather the disputes of the Sadducees with the Pharisees, are found only in the tannaitic literature. Tradition, however, adds more controversies on the Halakah between the Pharisees and the Sadducees. They are recorded in the *scholion* to *Megillat Taanit*. This *scholion* was written at the end of the amoraic period. Jewish students who wrote on the Pharisees did not differentiate between the tannaitic sources and the *scholion*. Hence,

Reprinted from *Essays and Studies in Memory of Linda R. Miller*, 1938.

we find explanations by these scholars of Halakic controversies between the sects, which historically never occurred, e. g. the *lex talionis*. According to them the Pharisees were against the law of *talio* while the Sadducees were for it. That there was a controversy between the Pharisees and the Sadducees on *lex talionis* is found only in the *scholion*. The tannaitic literature does not know anything about such a controversy. In fact, there was no such controversy.

Again, some Jewish students went a little further and ascribed to the Pharisees many Halakot which came from the School of Hillel, or even some of the halakot of Rabbi Akiba and Rabbi Eliezer. This too is not scientifically accurate. We must deal only with the halakot which are recorded in the tannaitic literature as controversies between the Pharisees and the Sadducees. The halakot of the Schools of Hillel and Shammai, of Akiba and Eliezer, etc., belong to the history and the development of the halakah, but have nothing to do with the Pharisees. With the destruction of the Second Temple, the Sadducees ceased to exist as a party and, thus, the Pharisees likewise disappeared as opponents. It is true, however, that the so-called Pharisees had great influence on the Halakot of the Schools of Hillel and Shammai. Thus, the teachings of the so-called Pharisees had great influence not only on the Tannaim and the Amoraim, but also upon the rabbis of the later periods.

In another study on the Pharisees I collected all

the Halakic controversies between them and the Sadducees,[a] ignoring, however, the halakic controversies between the two sects according to the *scholion*. In this essay I give all the Halakic differences between Jesus and the Pharisees as recorded in the Synoptic Gospels.

Numerous hypotheses have been advanced with regard to the name of Pharisees. Some scholars are of the opinion that the word *Perushim* has its origin in the word פרוש that stands for *"interpreter."* Others maintain that the word Pharisees has the connotation of *separation*. That is the members of this sect separated themselves from uncleanliness, hence *Perushim*. However, I advanced the theory in my early studies on the Pharisees,[b] that there was no such sect among the Jews at the time of the Second Commonwealth called Pharisees. The word was coined and used by the Sadducees who resented the new laws and reforms which were developed by the followers of Ezra. These Jews were nicknamed *Perushim* (Pharisees), i. e. they have separated themselves from Jewish Law. Thus the name Perushim was a nickname and a term of contempt. The scholars during the Second Commonwealth never called themselves *Perushim*. We do do not find in the entire tannaitic literature Halakot stated in the name of the *Perushim* (Pharisees). When we do have the word *Perushim* in the tannaitic literature as applied to a particular party opposed to the

[a] Comp. הצדוקים והפרושים N. Y. 1937.
[b] *The history of the Second Jewish Commonwealth, Prolegomena,* Ch. viii.

Sadducees, it is found only in the form of a dialogue. The Sadducees say, "We protest against you Pharisees." The Pharisees retort, "We protest against you Sadducees." Likewise the authors of the Gospels tell us that Jesus opposed the Halakot which were based on the "tradition of the Elders." By refuting these Halakot Jesus opposed the Pharisees since the so-called Pharisees stood for tradition. Hence the name Pharisees was used. Josephus, in his works mentioned the name Pharisees and Sadducees. However, this does not prove that there was a Pharisaic sect recognized as such. Josephus used the word Pharisees as the opponents of the Sadducees. As a modern historian writing the history of the eighteenth century would recount the conflicts between the *Hasidim* and the *Mitnagdim* although no such sect as *Mitnagdim* actually existed. Thus, Josephus writing his history, used the word Pharisees coined by the Sadducees to mark contemptuously their opponents. History is replete with such examples.[c] The Pharisees were the people who accepted the Oral Law and lived according to the tradition of the Elders and the scribes. The Sadducees opposed tradition. They accepted only the Torah and the Prophets.

Though I endeavored to establish that there was no such sect as the "Pharisees," nevertheless I use the word "Pharisees" for the sake of convenience, and in order to avoid confusion.

[c] See more *ibid.*; *idem*, *The Jews, Race, Nation or Religion*, pp. 32–35.

The word Pharisees has become a synonym for hypocrites. Undoubtedly the influence of the Gospels is responsible for this identification of Pharisaism with hypocrisy. In the Gospel according to Matthew, 23.13, we find, in the name of Jesus, the expression "Pharisees, hypocrites." The problem is for us to determine: Were the Pharisees really hypocrites? and, further, did this expression, "Pharisees, hypocrites," come from Jesus, or is it a later interpolation? Were they added by the early Christians at a time when great animosity existed between the Jews and the early Christians? And, therefore, the expression "Pharisees, hypocrites" was never used by Jesus.

I. The Sermon on the Mount

Before answering these questions we believe that a short analysis of the Sermon on the Mount is in place. In the Sermon on the Mount, we find that Jesus apparently was opposed to the teachings of the Bible, as when he said, "Ye have heard that it hath been said, An eye for an eye, and a tooth for a tooth: But I say unto you, That ye resist not evil: but whosoever shall smite thee on the right cheek, turn to him the other also. And if any man will sue thee at the law, and take away thy coat, let him have thy cloak, also. And whosoever shall compel thee to go a mile, go with him twain. Give to him that asketh thee, and from him that would borrow of thee turn not thou away."[1]

However, we cannot assume that Jesus was against the Bible, since he, himself, said "Think not that I am come to destroy the law, or the prophets: I am not come to destroy but to fulfil. For verily I say unto you, till heaven and earth pass, one jot or one tittle shall in no wise pass from the law till all be fulfilled."[2] Moreover, how could Jesus be against the Bible, since his entire mission as the son of David, as the Messiah, and even as the Son of God was based on words of the Bible? How could he oppose one portion of the Bible and maintain the other portion? He had to uphold, to fulfil the Bible in its entirety. The question, therefore, remains to be explained what was the meaning of Jesus' statement, "Ye have heard that it hath been said, An eye for an eye, and a tooth for a tooth: But I say unto you . . . ." It seems that Jesus in fact never opposed the Bible but he differed with the Pharisees in the interpretation of the biblical precepts.

It has already been pointed out that the *lex talionis* was never practiced during the Second Jewish Commonwealth. Lately much has been said on the *lex talionis*. Some try to prove the superiority of the ethical teachings of the Gospels over those of the Bible, while, on the other hand, many scholars, Jewish as well as

---

[1] Mat. 5, 38–42.   [2] Ibid. 17, 18.

Christian, have tried to prove that, in reality, the *lex talionis* was never practiced among the Jews during the time of Jesus. Although the Bible indeed says, "An eye for an eye . . .,"[3] actually this Halakah has never been applied and hence the ethical teachings of Jesus cannot be considered as superior to the Jewish teachings of that period.

To comprehend the biblical law, "An eye for an eye," we must first analyse the biblical laws relating to Wrong, private and public. The Bible, as well as the ancient Roman law, considered *Furtum*, (Theft), Injuries, as *Private Delict*, that is, the State had no right to interfere.[4] The *actio furti* can be brought by the person who was injured, not by the State, as it is practiced in our modern law. Only in cases like blasphemy against God, cursing God, could the Jewish State bring charges against the offender and punish him. This is quite evident from the story recorded in *Leviticus* where the entire Jewish community stoned the man who cursed the name of God.[5] That the offense of cursing God was to be punished by the State, is well brought out in the story of King Ahab, when he wanted to take away Naboth's vineyard. To accomplish this, Queen Jezebel wrote to the Elders in the King's name to have two men testify that Naboth

---

[3] Ex. 21, 24; Lev. 24, 20; Deut. 19, 21.
[4] Comp. Shon, Institutes of Roman Law. Oxford, 1901.
[5] Lev. 24, 14–16. ורגמו אותו כל העדה...ונקב שם ד' מות יומת רגום ירגמו בו כל העדה.

cursed God and for this he was put to death, and thus Ahab could legally take away his vineyard.[6] In the same manner, the State could execute the man who desecrated the Sabbath openly.[7] Likewise, in the case of any man who worshipped foreign gods, the State had to take charge and execute him.[8] Adultery was considered a sin against the State and was to be punished by the State.[9] According to the Bible, any man who acted against the decision of the High Priests, or the Judge, was liable to execution by the State.[10]

Homicide, however, was not considered a crime against the State. In primitive society, the kin of the family was supposed to avenge the death of any of the members of the tribe by killing the murderer.[11] Since murder may occur even by accident, without any intention to kill, Moses legislated that the slayer may flee to a city of refuge, to prevent the suspected murderer from being killed by the "Avenger of the Blood." If the slayer could prove that the man was killed by accident, and that he was not his enemy at all, he had to remain in the "City of refuge" until the death of the High Priest. The authorities of the city had no right to deliver him to the "Avenger of the Blood."

---

[6] 1 Kings 21, 7–16. ויבאו שני האנשים בני בליעל וישבו נגדו ויעדהו... לאמר ברך נבות את אלהים ומלך ויציאהו מחוץ לעיר ויסקלהו באבנים וימת.

[7] Num. 15, 35 מות יומת האיש רגם אתו באבנים כל העדה.

[8] Deut. 17, 5–7 וסקלתם באבנים ומתו ... יד העדים תהיה בו בראשונה להמיתו ויד כל העם באחרונה.

[9] Comp. Lev. 20, 10 ff.

[10] Comp. Deut. 17, 12.

[11] Comp. The Code of Hammurabi.

He was to be protected by the authorities of the city. However, if it was proven that the accused had not killed the man by accident but deliberately, the authorities had to deliver him to the "Avenger of the Blood," who was supposed to slay him.[12] From the description given in the Bible in relation to homicide, we may safely say that homicide was not a crime against the State but against the family of the victim, and hence the kin of the family had to avenge the murder. The authorities had only to decide if this murder was committed by accident or deliberately.[13] The execution, however, was carried out by the "Avenger of the Blood."[14] Apparently Moses could not entirely exclude cases of homicide from the jurisdiction of the tribes, but had to compromise. He limited the power of the tribes by instituting the Cities of Refuge. That the institution of "Avenger of the Blood" was in force during the First Temple we have no definite statement. But from the story recorded in 2 Samuel, we may infer that the system of "Avenger of the Blood" was still practiced during the period of the First Temple. It is recorded there that

---

[12] Numb. 35, 15–19 ... לנוס שמה כל מכה נפש בשגגה ... רצח הוא מות יומת הרצח
Comp. also Deut. 19; Joshua, 20. גאל הדם הוא ימית את הרצח

[13] Numb. 35, 24 גאל הדם ובין המכה בין העדה ושפטו. Joshua, 20, 9 ימות ולא
ביד גאל הדם עד עמדו לפני העדה. Comp. also Gen. 38, 24, the story about Tamar. When Judah was informed that Tamar was "with child by whoredom" Judah fixed her penalty to put her to death הוציאוה ותשרף.

[14] Deut. 19, 12: ומת הדם גאל ביד אותו ונתנו. Comp. Num. 35, 19–21. The Avenger of the Blood had no right to take ransom but he had to put the murderer to death.

Joab killed Abner for the blood of Asahel, his brother, which may mean that Joab was the "Avenger of the Blood."[15] However, after the Jews returned from Babylon, the institution of the "Avenger of the Blood" was abolished. There were no Cities of Refuge, since the Jews were not divided into tribes any more. The Sanhedrin, a court, was established to take care of all the cases of homicide. During the period of the Second Jewish Commonwealth, homicide was therefore considered a crime against the State and not against the individual or the family. The State and not the individual had to punish the offender.

According to the Bible, *furtum* (theft) was considered *private delict*.[16] If a man had stolen property from his fellow man, he had to pay a fine to the owner of the property. If it was an ox, he had to pay double; but if he had slaughtered or sold the ox, he had to pay a fine of five times its value. If it was a sheep, fourfold.[17] From the Bible, as well as from the Tannaitic literature, we may say that only the man who was injured could demand a fine from the thief; the State had no power to interfere.[18] It was a case entirely between the man who suffered through the loss, and

---

[15] 2 Sam. 3, 27.

[16] *A private delict* gives rise to an obligation; the law intends that delinquents shall be punished by becoming liable to a personal action at the suit of the injured party, the object of such action being either to recover damages or a penalty קנס, or to recover both damages and penalty. Comp. Shon's *Institutes of Roman Law*.

[17] Ex. 21, 37.

[18] The *actio furti* can be brought by the person who was injured by theft.

the thief. Injury, and bodily mutilation, likewise were considered private wrongs. The person had the right to fix the punishment and if he suffered the loss of an eye or the loss of a tooth, he was provided with the right to take out an eye or a tooth from the offender. The Twelve Tables similarly provided that bodily mutilation was punishable with *talio*.[19] The law of *talio*, as it is described in the Bible, "An eye for an eye," was not for the State to enforce since it was not a crime against Society, and the State had no right to interfere. It was not for the State to punish the offender. It was a case between the person who inflicted the injury and the man who was injured. The man who suffered the loss of an eye or any other member of his body could absolve entirely the man who caused the injury or could demand any satisfaction even to taking out the eye of the man who caused the loss of his eye. *Talio* was the extreme satisfaction which the plaintiff might demand. However, he might get his satisfaction with money as he was the sole judge.[20]

Our interpretation is also borne out by Josephus when he says, "He that maimeth any one, let him undergo the like himself, and be deprived of the same member of which he hath deprived the other, unless he that is maimed will accept of money instead of it;

---

[19] *Membrum ruptum*.

[20] The right of action is confined to the outraged person himself and does not pass to his heirs. A fine (קנס) according to Tannaitic law as well as according to Roman law cannot be collected by the heirs till after *litis contestatio* has taken place.

for the law makes the sufferer the judge of the value of what he hath suffered, and permits him to estimate it, unless he will be more severe."[21] From this it is quite obvious that Josephus considered injury as a *private delict*, i. e., a case between the injured and the offender.

In the early days of the Second Jewish Commonwealth, the Pharisees abolished *talio*. This was done by a legal fiction, since the man who suffered the loss of an eye had the right only to take out an eye exactly like his, in size and color; and since it is impossible for two men to have precisely the same organs in every respect, the injured could not make use of the law of *talio*.[22] Thus, by this legal fiction, the law of *talio* was abolished. The injured had only the right to demand satisfaction with money for the loss of his eye, for the pain, for medical care, for disability and for humiliation.[23]

When Jesus said, "It has been said, An eye for an eye, but I say unto you, Resist no evil," he did not refer to the Jewish State, as the State had no right to inflict the punishment "An eye for an eye," but he referred to individuals. Jesus, being the moralist, appealed to the people that they should not demand satisfaction by *talio*, but on the contrary they should not resist evil at all, "but whosoever shall smite thee

---

[21] Ant. 4, 8, 35.
[22] B. K. 83b. הרי שהיתה עינו של זה גדולה ועינו של זה קטנה האיך אני קורא ביה עין תחת עין.
[23] נזק צער רפוי שבת ובושת.

on thy right cheek, turn to him the other also." So Jesus in his statement was not preaching against the Bible. The difference between Jesus and the Pharisees consisted in the following. The Pharisees abolished *talio* by legal fiction, making it impossible for the plaintiff to demand an eye for his eye, while Jesus appealed to the plaintiff not to demand an eye for an eye and not to resist any evil by repaying evil.

The difference between Jesus and the Pharisees was not only the interpretation of the law but also its administration. The Pharisees, who were the leaders of the State, had to interpret the biblical laws by which Society was to be governed. Jesus, on the other hand, was not interested in applying the laws by which Society was to be governed, but as an ethical teacher he appealed to the people to abstain from any evil so that there would be no necessity for courts and judges. When in the Bible we find punishment for evil-doing, it is due, according to Jesus, to the fact that man's nature is bad. By changing his nature there would be no need for punishment. With this point of view, we can understand the other sayings of Jesus in the Sermon on the Mount, and his other differences with the Pharisees. This is well illustrated by his saying, "It hath been said, whosoever shall put away his wife, let him give her a writing of divorcement: But I say unto you, that whosoever shall put away his wife, saving for the cause of fornication, causeth her to commit adultery: and whosoever shall marry her that is divorced committeth adultery."[24]

Here again, Jesus was not against the biblical law that a man may give a bill of divorce, but his opinion was that Mosaic permission to divorce was due to sin and not to the original plan of man's creation, where it is indicated that man and wife should be as one flesh. Therefore Jesus was against divorce except in case of adultery. The person who married a divorcee was committing an act of adultery.

This is clear from the following statement of Jesus, "They say unto him, why did Moses then command to give a writing of divorcement, and to put her away? He saith unto them, Moses, because of the hardness of your hearts suffered you to put away your wives: but from the beginning it was not so. And I say unto you, Whosoever shall put away his wife, except it be for fornication, and shall marry another, committeth adultery: and whoso marrieth her which is put away doth commit adultery."[25]

On the question of divorce, the difference between Jesus and the Pharisees may be found in the following: According to Jesus, Moses permitted divorce because of the hardness of the hearts of man, which was due to sin and not to the original plan of man's creation, where it is written they should be one flesh.[26] The

---

[24] Mat. 5, 31–32; comp. Mat. 19, 3–9; Mark 10, 2–12; Luke, 16, 18.
[25] Mat. 19, 7–9. Comp. Mark, *ibid.* Luke, 16, 18.
[26] Gen. 2, 24. והיו לבשר אחד.

Pharisees, on the other hand, (the school of Hillel), granted that the idea was they should be one flesh, but maintained that in case the husband cares no longer for his wife (or, as Akiba puts it, has found a woman he likes better)[27] the original plan of man's creation, symbolized as "one flesh," is not carried out, and hence it is better that they separate — thus permitting the husband to divorce his wife. It is interesting to note that the school of Shammai, the conservative school, had the same idea as Jesus, that no man may divorce his wife save on account of adultery,[28] which would make it evident that they are no longer "one flesh." *The moralists and the conservatives sometimes meet.* Similarly in the law, "an eye for an eye," R. Eliezer, the Shammaite, held that the man who lost his eye may demand the satisfaction of taking out the eye of the offender.[28a] Jesus, from a different point of view, held the same opinion as R. Eliezer, but he appealed to the people not to exercise this privilege.

Similar differences regarding law as taught by the Pharisees, and the ethical teachings of Jesus, may be demonstrated in the other sayings of Jesus. "Ye have heard that it was said by them of old time, Thou shalt

---

[27] Gitin, IX, 10: ‎וב"ה אומרים אפילו הקדיחה תבשילו, ר"ע אוטר אפילו מצא אחרת ‎נאה הימנה. Comp. also Ant. 4, 8, 23. See W. Allen, Commentary to St. Mat. However, to protect the woman economically and to make divorce more difficult for the husband, the rabbis instituted the Ketubah. See more about the Ketubah S. Zeitlin, The Origin of the Ketubah, JQR. 1933, pp. 1–7.

[28] Gittin IX, 10: ‎ב"ש אוטרים לא יגרש אדם את אשתו אלא א"כ מצא בה דבר ערוה.
[28a] See B. K. 84a.

not commit adultery: But I say unto you, That whosoever looketh on a woman to lust after her hath committed adultery with her already in his heart. And if thy right eye offend thee, pluck it out, and cast it from thee: for it is profitable for thee that one of thy members should perish, and not that thy whole body should be cast into Gehenna."[29] The Pharisees, as the leaders of the State, would punish a person only when he committed an actual act of adultery, but they could not punish a man for his intention. Although the Pharisees considered the coveting of a woman as a sin, this sin, however, could not be punished by a Court. Jesus, on the other hand, who was a moralist, maintained that to covet a woman is as much a sin as to commit the act of adultery itself, and, therefore, according to him, "if thy right eye offend thee, pluck it out and cast it from thee."

Jesus said: "Again ye have heard that it was said to them of old time, Thou shalt not forswear thyself, but shalt perform unto the Lord thine oaths: But I say unto you, Swear not at all."[30] According to the Bible, if a man swore he must pay his oath to God.[31] Jesus, however, maintained that a man has no right to swear at all.[32] The same difference between law and

---

[29] Mat. 5, 27–30.

[30] Ibid. 33–34.

[31] Deut. 23, 24 מוצא שפתיך תשמור. See Allen, Com. to St. Mat. Comp. Strack-Billerbeck, *Kommentare z. N. T.* Mat. 5.

[32] See Ben Sirah, 23, 9: "Accustom not thy mouth to an oath and be not accustomed to the naming of the holy one." Comp. also Ecc. V, 3–5; IX, 2.

ethics is again indicated by Jesus when he says: "Ye have heard it was said to the ancients, Thou shalt not commit murder, and whosoever shall do so, shall be in danger of the judgment. But I say unto you, That every one who is angry with his brother shall be liable to the judgment, and whosoever shall say to his brother, Raca, shall be liable to Sanhedrin, but whosoever shall say, thou fool, shall be liable to the Gehenna of fire."[33] According to biblical law, only an act is liable to judicial prosecution. If a man committed murder, he is liable to the judgment. According to Jesus, even for inner feeling a man is liable to the judgment of God. The words τῇ κρίσει in the first passage, have the meaning of court. The words τῇ κρίσει in the second sentence, however, must be understood in a different sense from the first. The clauses can be explained in the following manner, "Thou shalt not commit murder," which follows by Jesus' antithesis, "Whosoever is angry is liable to the judgment of God."[34] "You shall not call your brother Raca" followed by Jesus with this antithesis, "But whosoever shall call his brother fool is liable to the judgment of God." The higher moral teachings of Jesus as antithetic to law and the nature of mankind are defined in his saying: "Ye have heard that it hath been said, "Thou shalt love thy neighbour and hate thine enemy. But I say unto you, Love your enemies, bless them

[33] Mat. 5, 21–22.
[34] Comp. Zahn, Mat. also Allen, ibid.

that curse you, do good to them that hate you and pray for them which despitefully use you and persecute you."[35]

According to Jesus, a man is supposed not only to love his neighbour but also to love his enemy. This is not in accordance with the biblical teaching,"Love thy neighbour."[36] (Jesus' statement "hate thine enemy" does not occur either in the Bible or in the Tannaitic literature). Here we must say that Jesus, the ethical teacher, did not fully comprehend the nature of human beings. It is possible for a man to love his friend, even not to despise his enemy, but it is totally impossible for him to love his enemy. Therefore, the ethical teachings of the rabbis are more applicable than those of Jesus. Hillel said, "What thou hatest for thyself, do not do to thy fellow."[37] Similarly, the author of the Book of Tobit said, "What thou thyself hatest, do to no man."[38] These teachings of the rabbis may not be superior to those of Jesus, but they are more in accordance with human nature.

From the perspective of history, we must say that Jesus failed. Nineteen centuries after Jesus' advent, his ideas of love and equality between man and man are not yet fulfilled. Men are not only not ready for the Messianic age, but hatred still exists in the hearts

[35] Mat. 5, 43–44.
[36] Lev. 19, 18 ואהבת לרעך כמוך.
[37] Shab. 31a, דעלך סני לחברך לא תעביד זו היא כל התורה כולה.
[38] Tobit 4, 15. Comp. also *The Twelve Patriarchs*, The Testimony of Joseph: "If any man seek to do evil unto you do him a good turn and pray for him."

of his followers. People hate their fellow men, not because they committed wrong against them, but because they have different ideas about state, politics, religion or economics. The Kingdom of Heaven upon earth is still as far away now as in the days of Jesus, when he preached equality between man and man, and love for all, even for his enemies.

In analyzing the sayings of Jesus in his Sermon on the Mount, we have seen the difference between the teachings of Jesus and the teachings of the Pharisees. The Pharisees, leaders of the Jewish people, although maintaining that ethical teachings are important for the development of human nature, insisted on the fulfillment of the law, always taking care of equity in the law. A State cannot exist unless it is maintained by law and order. On the other hand, Jesus, not being interested in the State, appealed to his fellow men to refrain from doing evil, saying, "That ye resist not evil: but whosoever shall smite thee on thy right cheek, turn to him the other also." Having pointed out the difference between Jesus' teachings and the Pharisees', we shall be able to understand their different attitude to the Halakah.

II. THE HALAKAH

From Matthew we learn that a controversy existed between Jesus and the Pharisees on the Halakah in relation to the Sabbath. "At that time Jesus went on the sabbath day through the corn; and his disciples were an hungred, and began to pluck the ears of corn, and to eat. But when the Pharisees saw it, they said unto him, Behold, thy disciples do that which is not lawful to do upon the sabbath day. But he said unto them, Have ye not read what David did, when he was an hungred, and they that were with him; how he entered into the house of God, and did eat the shewbread, which was not lawful for him to eat, neither for them which were with him, but only for the priests? Or have ye not read in the Torah how that on the sabbath days the priests in the Temple profane the sabbath and are blameless? But I say unto you, That in this place is one greater than the Temple. But if ye had known what this meaneth, I will have mercy, and not sacrifice, ye would not have condemned the guiltless. For the Son of man is Lord even of the sabbath day."[39] According to the Bible, no work can be done on the Sabbath day. However, sacrifices were brought to the Temple on the Sabbath and the priests performed their duties on this day. This was not considered profaning the Sabbath. The Pharisees maintained that if in a Temple a priest may work on the Sabbath, Israelites may likewise be permitted to work on the Sabbath if it is work for the Temple, and therefore they permitted them to bring the Omer on the Sabbath. They also permitted them to profane the Sabbath in order to save a man's life. Jesus and his disciples went on the Sabbath day to the cornfields,

[39] Mat. 12, 1–8, Mark, 2, 23–28; Luke, 6, 1–5.

where his disciples plucked the ears of corn to eat, and performed an act which the Pharisees considered a profanation of the Sabbath, since it had nothing to do with the Temple and was not purposed to save a man's life. Jesus contested the Pharisees' point of view by saying, "Have you not read in the Torah how that on the sabbath days the priests in the Temple profane the sabbath and are blameless?"[40] However, the Pharisees did not consider them as priests, or that it had to do with the services of the Temple. Jesus again contested their statement by saying, "Have ye not read what David did, when he was an hungred and they that were with him; how he entered into the house of God and did eat the shewbread, which was not lawful for him to eat?" The Pharisees, on the other hand, believed that David ate of the bread in the Temple to save his life, but the disciples did not eat the ears of the corn to save their lives. Again, the Pharisees did not believe that Jesus, the Son of Man, is the Lord of the Sabbath Day. The Pharisees were always ready to amend the laws of the Sabbath and to make it possible for the people to observe the Sabbath.[41] That the Sabbath was made for man and not man for the Sabbath, was the contention of the Pharisees.[42] They also

---

[40] This is omitted in Mark and in Luke.

[41] Comp. Yoma 86b: היא מסורה בידכם ולא אתם מסורים בידה. See also S. Zeitlin, *The History of the Second Jewish Commonwealth*, Prolegomena. p. 50, n. 158b.

[42] Comp. Yoma 85b: כדי שישמור שבתות הרבה שבת אחת עליו חלל. Mechilta לכם שבת מסורה ואי אתם מסורים לשבת, כי תשא. Comp. also the statement of Hillel אפילו בשבת. Shab. 19a, Tosefta Erub. 3, 7. עד רדתה אפילו בשבת.

objected to Jesus healing on the Sabbath because they did not believe that Jesus had the art of healing. It is true that the Pharisees allowed any medical treatment to be performed in the case of life being at stake, but the Pharisees did not believe in Jesus' power to heal. And when Jesus, indeed, according to the Gospels, restored one man's hand to its strength, the Pharisees — according to the same authority — accused Jesus of doing this with the power of the "chief of the devils," that he cast out the devils by Beelzebub, chief of the devils.[43]

From the Synoptic Gospels we learn that the Pharisees accused Jesus that his disciples did not fast, "And John's disciples and the Pharisees were fasting: and they come and say unto him, Why do John's disciples and the disciples of the Pharisees fast, but thy disciples fast not? And Jesus said unto them, Can the sons of the bride-chamber fast, while the bridegroom is with them? As long as they have the bridegroom with them they cannot fast. But the days will come when the bridegroom shall be taken away from them, and then will they fast in that day."[44] Fasting among the Jews was quite common.[45] We are told David fasted when his child was sick[46] and we are told R. Zadok fasted for forty years to ward off the destruction of the Temple.[47] Fasting was always considered as one of the

---

[43] Mat. 12, 14, 22–24; Mark, 3, 1–6; Luke, 6, 6–11.
[44] Mat. 9, 14–15; Mark, 2, 18–20; Luke, 5, 33–35.
[45] Comp. Mishnah and Tosefta Taanit.
[46] 2 Sam. 12, 21–23.
[47] Gittin 56a.

principle means of alleviation of calamities. Likewise in time of public suffering, like drought, public fasts were decreed.[48] According to the general opinion, that is the contention between the Pharisees and Jesus.

It seems to me, however, that these fasts which the Pharisees charged that Jesus' disciples did not observe, were the so-called National fasts, namely the fasts of the Ninth of Ab, Tenth of Tebet, Ninth of Tammuz[48a] and the fast in the Seventh Month, all of which were connected with the destruction of the First Temple. From Zechariah we learn that after the return of the Jews from Babylon and after the Second Temple had been built, the Jews asked the prophet Zechariah if they should continue to fast on the days that were instituted in commemoration of the destruction of the Temple. The prophet answered the Jews in these words: "The fast of the Fourth month and the fast of the Fifth, and the fast of the Seventh and the fast of the Tenth, shall be to the House of Judah joy and gladness and cheerful feasts."[49] This, however, does not indicate that the Jews did not continue to fast during the Second Commonwealth. The Prophecy of Zechariah was not fullfilled and the Jews had no occasion to declare these fasts as cheerful feasts. Not all the Jews returned to Palestine. The Kingdom of David

---

[48] See Mishna and Tosefta Taanit, Jerus. ibid. 65b. שלשה דברים מבטלין את הגזרה תפילה תשובה וצדקה.

[48a] Jer. 39, 2.

[49] Zech. 7, 3; 8, 19, צום הרביעי וצום החמישי וצום השביעי וצום העשירי יהיה לבית יהודה לששון ולשמחה ולמעדים טובים

was not restored. On the contrary, they suffered first under the Greeks and then under the Romans. Neither King Alexander Janai nor Herod were ideal kings and, therefore, they had no reason to abandon the fasts. They continued to fast on the days in memory of the destruction of the Temple and destruction of their kingdom. We may even prove from Josephus that these fasts were actually observed during the Second Commonwealth. According to Josephus, Pompey captured Jerusalem on a fast day,[50] i. e., on the Ninth of Tammuz. Likewise we learn from Josephus that the capture of Jerusalem by Herod and Sosius was on a fast day, namely on Wednesday, the Tenth of Tebet.[51] It is, therefore, quite evident that the fast days were observed during the Second Commonwealth.[52] With this interpretation we can grasp the full meaning of the controversy between the Pharisees and Jesus. The Pharisees accused Jesus that his disciples did not fast on the National fast days. To this Jesus replied, "Can the sons of the bride-chamber fast, while the bridegroom is with them? As long as they have the bridegroom with them they cannot fast. But the days will come when the bridegroom shall be taken from them, and then will they fast in that day." With this parable Jesus meant to say that his disciples need not fast, as He, the Messiah, was among them

[50] Ant. 14. 16, 4.
[51] Ibid. 16. 16, 2.
[52] See S. Zeitlin, *Megillat Taanit*, Ch. 3.

and, therefore, the fast days in memory of the destruction of the Temple need not be observed. "But the days will come when the bridegroom shall be taken from them, and then they will fast in that day." That is to say, when Jesus shall be taken away, his followers will fast.[53]

According to the Synoptic Gospels the Pharisees objected to Jesus for his association with Publicans and sinners, "And when the Pharisees saw it, they said unto his disciples, Why eateth Your Master with publicans and sinners?"[54] The reason why the Pharisees did not want to break bread with the publicans and sinners was not due to pride or to exclusiveness. For the Pharisees, the table was not merely a place for eating and drinking and satisfying their human needs but it was as well a place for learned discussion and prayers. Again, it was very hard for the Pharisees, who observed the laws of purity and impurity, to eat with publicans and sinners who were neither versed in the laws of purity and impurity nor did they observe them. Jesus, on the other hand, denied the "tradition of the Elders," and hence did not observe the laws of purity and impurity according to the Pharisees' conception. He could, therefore, associate with the publicans and sinners by eating with them. Jesus, seeking a new ethical social order, looked for help from the lower classes, and from them he drew his followers.

---

[53] Jesus was considered the bridegroom of the ecclesia.
[54] Mat. 9, 11; Mark, 2, 16; Luke, 5, 30.

The Synoptic Gospels tell us that there was a contention between the Pharisees and Jesus about the institution of "Washing the hands" and "Corban." "Then came together unto him the Pharisees and certain of the scribes, which came from Jerusalem. And when they saw some of his disciples eat bread with defiled, that is to say, with unwashen hands, they found fault. For the Pharisees and all the Jews, except they wash their hands oft, eat not, holding the tradition of the Elders. And when they come from the market, except they wash, they eat not. And many other things there be, which they have received to hold, as the washing of cups, and pots, brazen vessels, and of tables. Then the Pharisees and scribes asked him, Why walk not thy disciples according to the tradition of the Elders, but eat bread with unwashen hands? He answered and said unto them, Well hath Esaias prophesied of you hypocrites, as is written, This people honoureth me with their lips, but their heart is far from me. Howbeit in vain do they worship me, teaching for doctrines the commandments of men. For laying aside the commandment of God, ye hold the tradition of men, as the washing of pots and cups; and many other such like things ye do. And he said unto them, Full well ye reject the commandment of God, that ye may keep your own tradition. For Moses said, Honour thy father and thy mother, and Whoso curseth father or mother, let him die the death. But ye say, If a man shall say to his father or mother, It is

Corban, that is to say, a gift by whatsoever thou mightest be profited by me, he shall be free. And ye suffer him no more to do aught for his father or his mother; Making the word of God of none effect through your tradition, which ye have delivered: and many such like things do ye."[55]

The Pharisees complained of Jesus that his disciples trespassed the tradition of the Elders, for they ate without washing the hands. To understand this complaint it is necessary to give a short analysis of the institution of washing the hands. According to the Bible, any one disqualified on account of minor impurity had to leave town and undergo *Tebilah* and after that wait until the evening.[56] This law, which worked great hardship, was modified by the Pharisees. By the method of exegesis, the Pharisees explained the biblical expression מחנה (Camp) to mean מחנה שכינה.[57] Similarly in the matter of sunset. For, according to the Bible, mere bathing of the body in water would not have been sufficient to render the person pure, unless the sun had set on him thereafter,[58] and he was called in the Talmud טבול יום. The Pharisees, however, ordained that if the person had taken the prescribed bath he was *ipso facto* pure and it was not necessary for him to wait until sunset.[59] A few years before the destruc-

---

[55] Mark, 7, 1–13; Mat. 15, 1–6.
[56] Lev. 15, 16; Deut. 23, 11. ויצא מחוץ למחנה. Comp. Ant. 3, 2, 3.
[57] Pes. 68a.
[58] Lev. 22, 7 ובא השמש וטהר.
[59] Sifra Shemini 8 וטמא עד הערב טהור לחולין מבעוד יום ולתרומה משתחשך.

tion of the Temple, the schools both of Shammai and Hillel adopted the eighteen measures which put every Jew in a state of ritual uncleanliness[60] and, therefore, according to the law, every Jew would have to undergo Tebilah, which would be very impracticable. Therefore the rabbis declared that it was not necessary to undergo *Tebilah*, but that it was sufficient to wash the hands. This was the underlying reason for the institution of washing the hands.

The disciples of Jesus ate without washing their hands, that is, they denied the tradition of the Pharisees and their decrees in which they declared that every Jew was in a state of impurity and hence before eating had to wash his hands. For this the Pharisees reproached Jesus. Jesus answered them with a counter charge that the Pharisees were rejecting the laws of God in keeping up their own tradition. "And he said unto them, Full well ye reject the commandment of God, that ye may keep your own tradition. For Moses said, Honour thy father and thy mother; and whoso curseth father or mother, let him die the death. But ye say, If a man shall say to his father or mother, it is Corban, that is to say, a gift, by whatsoever thou mightest be profited by me; he shall be free."[62] All the commentators of the Gospels maintained that the word Corban means a gift to God, and so Gould trans-

---

[60] Comp. S. Zeitlin, Lex Dix-Huit Mesures, *REJ*. LXVIII, 29 et seq.
[61] Idem. The Halaka in the Gospels and in relation to the Jewish Law at the time of Jesus, *Journal of Jewish Lore And Philosophy*. 1919, 357–373.
[62] Mark. 7, 9–11.

lated this passage, "But . . . say, 'if a man say to his father and his mother anything in which you may be profited by me is Corban (That is, an offering), you no longer permit him to do anything for his father or his mother.' The meaning of this passage would be that "by which you might have received advantage from me is thereby dedicated as an offering."[63] From this we can see that the Commentators thought the word "Corban" meant an offering to God. The word "Corban" in the Bible is always translated by LXX, δῶρον gift, an offering. Apparently a scribe thought that the word *Corban* had the meaning of gift, and so he added in Mark the word ὅ ἐστιν δῶρον, that is a gift. In Matthew he left out the word *Corban* entirely, and he gave the interpretation of it as δῶρον, a gift. However, in some versions of the Gospel, according to Mark, the phrase ὅ ἐστιν δῶρον is not found, and in some versions of the Gospel, according to Matthew, we have the readings κορβάν ὅ ἐστιν δῶρον. From this we can readily see that the word *Corban* was in Matthew as well.[64] In the Syriac version of the Gospels we have the word "Corban" only, and the words, "that is a gift," are omitted.

[63] See Gould, Comm. l. c. See Rawlinson, "If a man shall say to his father or his mother, that wherewith thou mightest have been profited by me is Corban that is to say given to God ye no longer suffer him to do aught for his father or his mother". Comp. also McNeile, "That by which you might have received advantage from me is hereby dedicated as an offering".

[64] Comp. Tischendorf, N. T. Lipsiae, 1896. See also H. B. Swetee, *The Gospel according to St. Mark*, a. l.

On the basis of the readings which we have now in the Gospels all the commentators took the word *Corban* to mean a gift, and they constructed this passage accordingly. "That by which you might have received advantage from me is hereby dedicated as an offering." The word *Corban*, however, mentioned in the Gospels, does not have the meaning of a gift but a vow.[65] In this sense a vow is found quite often in Tannaitic literature,[66] and hence this passage in Matthew should be translated accordingly, "But you say whosoever shall say to the Father or to the Mother a Corban (a vow), anything wherewith thou mightest be profited by me, shall not honor his father."

With this interpretation we can further understand the contention between the Pharisees and Jesus. The Pharisees reproached Jesus (or his disciples) for transgressing the tradition of the Elders. To this Jesus replied, "The Pharisees with their tradition transgress

[65] Josephus mentioned the word *Corban* twice, once in B. J. 2. 9.4 where he said "that sacred treasure which is called Corban" the word Corban here is an allusion to the Chamber where was kept the money of the gifts to the Temple. In *Contra Apionem* 1, 22 Josephus says "this is declared by Theophrastus, in his writings concerning laws for he says that 'the laws of the Tyrians forbid men to swear foreign oaths', Among which he enumerates some others and particularly that called *Corban*, which oath can only be found among the Jews, and declares what a man may call a thing devoted to God" διαλέκτου δῶρον θεοῦ.

Josephus, who wanted to prove that the ancient Greek world was acquainted with the Jews said that already Theophrastus, who lived *circa* 372 B.C., said that the Tyrians used the word *Corban* for an oath which according to Josephus is derived from the biblical word *corban* meaning a "gift to God." However, the word "Corban" was also applied to a vow. See also Ant. 4, 4.4.

[66] Mishna Ned. 1, 1. Tosefta ibid.

the commandments of God by saying that if a man took a vow not to honor his father he must keep the vow, by which they nullify the biblical law of God where it is written, Honor thy father and thy mother."

According to the Pharisees, a vow must be kept since it is written in the Bible that a man should not break his word.[67] But if a man took a vow against biblical precept he must keep his vow and not observe the precept[68] for which undoubtedly, according to them, he will be punished for not observing the precept. However, to avoid a clash between two commandments in the Bible, namely, "Honor thy father and thy mother" and "he shall not break his word" if a man took a vow not to honor his father and mother, the Pharisees introduced a legal fiction by which he could absolve his vow. This is called in the Talmud הפרת נדרים. Thus, according to the Pharisees, if a man takes a vow against a biblical precept, his vow can be absolved.[69] According to Jesus, no vow can be taken against a biblical precept. This is a bone of contention between the Pharisees and Jesus. The law that a vow can be absolved was in existence among the Jews much before the time of Jesus. This is quite evident from a story found in the Palestinian Talmud

---

[67] Deut. 23, 24: מוצא שפתיך תשמר; Nu. 30, 8: לא יחל דברו.
[68] Tosefta Ned. 1, 6 קונם סוכה שאני עושה ולולב שאני נוטל ותפילין שאני נותן אסור. Ibid. 4 הנודר מן הכתוב בתורה הרי זה אסור בנדרים.
[69] M. Ned. 11, הרי זה ... קונם שאיני נהנה לאבא. Comp. also דברים שבינו ובין יפר אביו ואמו שפותחין לו בכבוד אביו ואמו.

that Simon ben Shetah dissolved the vows of one hundred and fifty Nazirites.[70]

All the students who interpreted this passage of Matthew found difficulty in explaining the charge of Jesus against the Pharisees.[71] All of them were of the opinion that the Pharisaic view found in the Mishnah is a direct contradiction of the view attributed to them by Jesus. Some are of the opinion that in the time of Jesus the Pharisees may have had a different point of view, others hold that Jesus brought an unjust charge against the Pharisees.[72] However, the difficulties which confronted the students are due to an interpolation in the Gospels where we have ὅ ἐστιν δῶρον. Hence, their interpretation is baseless.

III. "Pharisees Hypocrites"

As it was pointed out before, the expression, "Pharisees hypocrites," in Chapter 23 of the Gospel according to Matthew, is quoted often in the name of Jesus. In this chapter Jesus' attack against the Pharisees

---

[70] Jer. Naz. 54b: שלש מאות נזירים עלו בימי שמעון בן שטח מאה וחמישים מצא להם פתח. The idea that the law dissolving vows is a new Halakah is unfounded. In the Mishna, Hag. 1, 8 where we read the rules concerning dissolving of vows fly about the air and they have no authority upon which to depend, היתר נדרים פורחים באויר ואין להם על מה שיסמכו does not mean to say that these laws came in a later period. See Tosefta ibid. I, 9: היתר נדרים פורחים באויר ואין להם על מה שיסמכו אבל חכם מתיר לפי חכמתו הלכות שבת חגיגות ומעילות מקרא מועט והלכות מרובות כהררים התלויות בסערה [בשערה] ואין להם [ויש להם] על מה שיסמכו.

[71] See Hart, *JQR*. 1907, pp. 615–650. Mann, Amer. J. of Th., 1917. Belkin, Journal B. L., 1936.

[72] See Chwolson, *Das letzte Passamahl*; Klausner, *Jesus of Nazareth*, p. 306.

showed his great anger and animosity against the Pharisees. "Woe unto you, scribes and Pharisees, hypocrites!" He accused them of different hypocrisies. Jesus reproached the Pharisees that their interpretations of the laws were a burden upon the people. "For they bind heavy burdens, and grievous to be borne, and lay them on men's shoulders; but they themselves will not move them with one of their fingers." This accusation against the Pharisees as well as the other accusations are not justifiable. The Pharisees always strove to bring the Halakah into consonance with life and they amended the Pentateuchal law if such were life's demands. The Pharisees were always ready to harmonize religion and life, and indeed brought about many reforms in religious life, such as the laws of Erub which made the Sabbath less burdensome. Likewise, they amended the laws of purity and impurity, which would have been extremely burdensome to the people if they had been enforced according to the Torah.[73] The Halakah for the Pharisees was not stringent but elastic, and the Pharisees always strove to make the Halakah easy for the people. They were the people.

It is true that some of the people who called themselves Pharisees acted otherwise; and they were hypocrites.[74] Already Alexander Janai in the Testament to

---

[73] See S. Zeitlin, The Takkanot Ezra, *JQR*. 1917, pp. 61–79. Idem. Prolegomena, p. 50.

[74] Sota, 22b. Comp. Jerusalmi, ibid. 20a.

his wife said, "Don't fear the Pharisees or the non-Pharisees, but the people who are wicked and try to persuade the people they are pious."[75] It is possible that Jesus had in mind this kind of Pharisee. The Pharisees themselves condemned such individuals and always advised the people to be on guard. It is probable that the author of the Assumption of Moses refers to this kind of a Pharisee, when he says, "And in the time of these, destructive and impious men shall rule, saying that they are just . . . . Devourers of the goods of the (poor) saying that they do so on the ground of their justice, but in reality to destroy them, complainers, deceitful, concealing themselves lest they should be recognized, impious, filled with lawlessness and iniquity from sunrise to sunset: saying: 'We shall have feastings and luxury, eating and drinking, and we shall esteem ourselves as princes.' And though their hands and their minds touch unclean things, yet their mouths shall speak great things, and they shall say furthermore: 'Do not touch me lest thou shouldst pollute me in the place (where I stand) . . . "[75a]

It cannot be denied that the disciples of Jesus were particularly opposed to the Pharisees and had many arguments with them. It is quite likely that in the heat of the arguments they accused the Pharisees, their former teachers, as being hypocrites for not accepting Jesus as the Messiah. It is a matter of course

[75] Ibid.
[75a] Assumption of Moses chap. 7, v. 2-10.

THE PHARISEES AND THE GOSPELS

that people who have a common belief in religion, or common ideas in politics or in economics, accuse each other more severely than people who have nothing in common. The Pharisees with their teachings were in a great measure responsible for the ideas which brought about Christianity. The Pharisees with their ideas about the Future World and reward and punishment and Providence made possible the teachings of Jesus and his disciples. There was no great resentment shown against the Sadducees, since they had nothing in common with the disciples of Jesus, nor with their people.

It seems to me, however, that the entire chapter 23 of Matthew does not belong to the original Matthew (certainly not to the Logia) and was interpolated later, and hence the words, "Pharisees hypocrites" never came from the mouth of Jesus.

The expression Rabbi as a technical name occurs several times in this chapter. "And greetings in the markets, and to be called of men, Rabbi, Rabbi. But be not ye called Rabbi, for one is your Master, even Christ; and all ye are brethren." The word "Rabbi" as a technical expression was not known to the Jews until the destruction of the Second Temple. The scholars used their own names but never affixed to them the title of Rabbi, for example, Hillel, Simon ben Shetah, etc. Only with the advent of Gamaliel the title "Rabban" was affixed, which meant, our Master.

The reason thereof was that up to the time of Gamaliel two men stood at the head of the Sanhedrin, one a Nasi and the other an Ab bet din; while in the time of Gamaliel the position of Ab bet din was abolished and entire authority was invested in Gamaliel alone. Hence the title was given him "Rabban" "Master."[75b] The word "Rabban" is derived from "Rab" meaning "Elder," "Master." At the time of the destruction of the Second Temple the title "Rabbi" was given to all the scholars who received authorisation to decide the law. The scholars who did not receive any authorisation to decide the law were not called Rabbis but scholars.[76] Hence it is surprising to read that Jesus was given the title of Rabbi when there was not yet such a title in his time. At the time of Jesus people used to address each other by the word אדון, מר.

The word Rabbi which is found in this chapter may therefore throw light on the authenticity of the entire chapter. Jesus is usually addressed as "Teacher" διδάσκαλε.[77] Even when the Pharisees and the "Scholars of the Law" approached him, they always called him "Teacher" and not "Rabbi."[78] We would expect from the Pharisees and the "Scholars of the Law" when they asked Jesus questions on the law, that they should

---

[75b] In the Acts 5, 34 Gamaliel was called νομοδιδάσκαλος, a teacher of the law.

[76] See S. Zeitlin, Beginnings of Christianity and Judaism, *JQR*. 1937 pp. 392–393.

[77] Mark, 9, 17; Passim.

[78] Comp. Mark, 12, 14, 32; Luke, 20, 21, 39; Matt. 22, 35–36.

address him as "Rabbi" if such a title had already been in vogue.⁷⁹

In the story of the betrayal of Judas of Iscariot, the expression "Rabbi" occurs. The Gospel according to Matthew tells us, "Now he that betrayed him gave them a sign, saying, Whomsoever I shall kiss, that same is he: hold him fast. And forthwith he came to Jesus and said, Hail, Rabbi, and kissed him."⁸⁰ The same account is given in the Gospel according to Mark, "And as soon as he was come, he goeth straightway to him, and saith, Rabbi, Rabbi; and kissed him."⁸¹ In the account given in the Gospel according to Luke, the word "Rabbi" is omitted; "And while he yet spake, behold a multitude and he that was called Judas, one of the twelve, went before them, and drew near unto Jesus to kiss him."⁸² The Gospel according to John gives an entirely different version of Judas' betrayal. He does not follow the account that is given in the Synoptic Gospels about Judas' betrayal of Jesus by a kiss, but according to him, Judas knew the place where Jesus met his disciples and led the officers to arrest

---

⁷⁹ Dalman (The Words of Jesus, p. 331) "It is unnecessary to give proofs that רבי was the usual form of address with which the learned were greeted for the time of Jesus. Its use is expressly attested in Matt." However, the word Rabbi as a technical expression was not used among the Jews at the time of Jesus; this is quite borne out by the Tannaitic literature. The usual form of address with which the scholars were greeted at the time of Jesus was the word אדוני or in the Aramaic form ריבוני or מר.

⁸⁰ Matt. 26, 49.
⁸¹ Mark, 14, 45.
⁸² Luke, 22, 47.

Jesus. "And Judas also, which betrayed him, knew the place: for Jesus ofttimes resorted thither with his disciples. Judas then, having received a band of men and officers from the chief priests and Pharisees, cometh thither with lanterns and torches and weapons."[83] Thus, we see that the word "Rabbi" in connection with the tale of Judas is found only in Matthew and Mark, while omitted in Luke. John gives altogether a different version. We may therefore assume that the word "Rabbi" found in the first two Gospels was later interpolated.

In Mark 9,5, the word Rabbi occurs: "And Peter answered and said to Jesus, Rabbi ῥαββί it is good for us to be here; and let us make three tabernacles, one for thee, and one for Moses, and one for Elias." However, in Matthew 17,4, where the same passage occurs, the word κύριε is found instead of Rabbi while Luke 9,33 has Ἐπιστάτα. Again, in Mark 10,51, the word ῥαββει-ῥαββουνι is given, but some Mss. have instead κύριε.[84] The expression Rabbi is found again in Mark 11,21. However, some Mss. omit the word Rabbi,[85] and so in Matthew 21,20 the word Rabbi does not occur.

To summarize, we believe that this essay demonstrates that the Pharisees were not hypocrites. It was only in the heat of the arguments between the disciples of Jesus and the Pharisees that the disciples accused

---

[83] John, 18, 3.
[84] Comp. *Die Schriften des Neu Testamentes*, Herman Freiherr Von Soden, Goettingen, 1913.
[85] See *ibid.* ad loc.

the Pharisees of not accepting the doctrines of Jesus and called them hypocrites for not stretching the law to suit the interests of the early Christians. Again, if Jesus ever had any controversy with the Pharisees he did not call them hypocrites. The expression "Pharisees hypocrites" in Chapter 23 of Matthew, must have been interpolated after the time of Jesus. This is borne out by the fact that the expression "Rabbi" which appears often as a technical term for "teacher" was not yet in use in the time of Jesus.

IV. The Gospel according to John

The name Pharisees is mentioned many times in the Gospel according to John. Unlike the Synoptic Gospels we do not find in John any animosity towards the Pharisees. Neither do we find the phrase "Pharisees, hypocrites." One man named Nicodemus,—a Pharisee — even joined Jesus.[86] Nor do we find there any halakic controversies between Jesus or his disciples with the Pharisees.

In John V, we are told that Jesus healed a person who had been sick for thirty eight years. On a certain Sabbath Day the man arose, "and took up his bed and walked." To this the Jews objected since it is not permitted to carry anything on the Sabbath. The Gospel continues to say that when the Jews became aware that Jesus cured this man on the Sabbath they

---

[86] John 3, 1–22.

began to persecute Jesus and "sought to slay him because he had done these things on the Sabbath day." Jesus answered them, "My Father worketh hitherto and I work. Therefore, the Jews sought the more to kill him, because he not only had broken the Sabbath but said also that God was his Father making himself equal with God."[87] Here John does not refer to the Pharisees at all, but to the Jews who were eager to persecute him for profaning the Sabbath and for "making himself equal with God," while the Synoptics tell us that the Pharisees reproached Jesus for profaning the Sabbath.[88]

In John IX, it is told that Jesus cured a blind man, "and it was the Sabbath day when Jesus made the clay and opened his eyes." When this man was brought before the Pharisees they asked him how he had received his sight. He told them "He put clay upon mine eyes, and I washed, and do see. Therefore said some of the Pharisees 'This man is not of God because he keepeth not the Sabbath day'." Others said, "How can a man that is a sinner do such miracles? There was a division among them."[89] In this story likewise we do not see any animosity between the Pharisees and Jesus as is recorded in Synoptic Gospels. According to John some of the Pharisees even admitted that Jesus was performing miracles, hence he could not be a sinner.[90]

---

[87] Ibid. 5, 8–18.
[88] Comp. Mat., 12, 10; Mark 3, 2; Luke, 6, 6–7.
[89] 9, 16.
[90] Ibid. Comp. also 11, 47.

From the same Gospel we learn that some of the rulers of the Synagogue believed in Jesus; but they did not have the courage to confess openly their belief.[91] In John VII, we are told that the leaders and the Pharisees sent officers to bring Jesus to them. The officers, however, returned without Jesus. The Pharisees reproached them for returning without Jesus. The officers answered, "Never man spake like this man. Then answered them the Pharisees, 'Are ye also deceived? Have any of the rulers or the Pharisees believed on him? But these people who knoweth not the law are cursed. Nicodemus saith unto them 'Doth our law judge any man before it hear him, and know what he doeth?' "[92] Even in this story we do not find the great animosity between the Pharisees and Jesus as is found throughout the Synoptic Gospels.

What is the reason for this difference? How can we explain the difference in attitude towards the Pharisees in the Synoptic Gospels and in the Gospel according to John? It seems to me that this difference in attitude is due to the different audiences for whom the Gospels were written. The Synoptic Gospels were written for the Jewish-Christians, while the Gospel according to John was written for the Gentile-Christians. With this idea we can fully understand why John does not mention any Halakic disputes between the Pharisees

---

[91] "Nevertheless, among the chief rulers also many believed on him but because of the Pharisees they did not confess him lest they should be put out of the synagogue"; 12, 42.

[92] 50–52.

and Jesus, since they did not interest the Gentile-Christians some of whom were perhaps unaware of the existence of the Pharisees and, therefore, he records merely the controversies between the Jews and Jesus. Since the Synoptic Gospels were written for the Jewish-Christians the disputes between the most important group in the Jewish people and Jesus are recorded.

It is of interest to note that the disputes between the Pharisees and Jesus, as recorded in the Synoptic Gospels, are on halakic matters. The Pharisees reproached Jesus for eating without washing his hands and because he or his disciples plucked the ears of corn on the Sabbath day. In John, on the other hand, the disputes between the Jews and Jesus were not about the halakah but rather on the miracles of Jesus, not because he profaned the Sabbath but because he said that "God is his Father and he is equal with God." The Jews objected to Jesus because he said, "I am the bread which came from heaven."[93] The Pharisees, according to John reproached Jesus not because he did not follow the traditional law but because of his claim to divinity.[94]

It is well known that the Gospel according to John does not portray Jesus as the Messiah, the Son of David, but rather stressed that Jesus is "The Lamb of God—The Son of God." Since it was written for the

---

[93] 6, 41.
[94] "This man is not of God because he keepeth not the Sabbath day." The Jews also objected to Jesus saying, "I am the light of the world."

Gentile-Christians the idea of Messiah, the Son of David, would not have any appeal for them. That the Gospel according to John was written not for the Jewish-Christians but for the Gentile-Christians may be proved by his usage of the word Ἰουδαῖοι Judaeans, Jews. The name Judaeans, Jews, is used in John over sixty times, while in the Synoptic Gospels the expression Judaeans, Jews, is mentioned only in connection with the trial of Jesus,[95] or when it was used by Gentiles.

In the Gospel according to Matthew the expression Judaeans is mentioned in connection with the wise men who came "from the east to Jerusalem, saying 'Where is he that was born King of the Jews?'."[96] Here the word Jews is given because it came from Gentiles. In the same manner is to be explained the word Jews mentioned in the Gospel according to Luke. "And a certain centurion's servant, who was dear unto him, was sick and ready to die. And when he heard of Jesus he sent unto him the eldest of the Jews, beseeching him that he would come and heal his servant."[97] The name Jews is quite appropriate here since it came from a Gentile,[98] while in the Gospel

---

[95] "The King of the Jews."
[96] 2, 1-2.
[97] 7, 3.
[98] Comp. also Mat., 28, 15 "This saying is commonly reported among Jews until this day." The reason for using the name Jews is due to the fact that the saying is reported "until this day." See Luke 23, 50 "He was of Arimathaea, a city of the Jews." However, in Mat., 27, 57; Mark 15, 42; John 19, 38, where the same story is recorded the phrase "a city of the Jews" is not mentioned. In Mark 7, 3 it is told "For the Pharisees and

according to John the expression Judaeans is recorded throughout the entire Gospel. In John, when the feast of Passover or the Feast of Tabernacles is mentioned, the author always adds the "Jews' Passover"[99] and "the Jews' Feast of Tabernacles,"[100] while the Synoptic Gospels never says *Jews' Passover*, but Passover, without mentioning the Jews.

As we said above the name Jews occurs throughout the Gospel according to John. However when a dialogue is recorded between a particular Jew and Jesus, the word *"Israel"* is used. When Jesus saw Nathanael coming to him, he said "Behold! An Israelite indeed ... Nathanael said unto him, 'Rabbi, thou art the son of God ... Thou art the King of Israel."[101] Likewise the name of *Israel* was used in the dialogue between Nicodemus and Jesus.[102] I have already pointed out in my essay *The Jews: Race Nation or Religion?* that the Christians did not use the word *Israelite*, but Judaeans, when speaking or writing of the Jews. The name Judaeans was a nickname and a term of contempt for the people who rejected Jesus,

---

the Jews except they wash their hands oft eat not holding the tradition of the elders." This is an explanatory remark of the previous account, "And when they saw some of his disciples eat bread with defiled hands they found fault."

This explanatory remark is most likely a later interpolation. In fact, in Mat., where the same story is given, we do not find this explanatory remark.

[99] 2, 13 "And the Jews' Passover was at hand." Comp. also, 6, 4; 11, 55.
[100] "Now the Jews' feast of Tabernacles was at hand."
[101] 1, 47–49.
[102] 3, 10.

while those who believed in Jesus were the true Israelites.[103] Therefore, in the Gospel according to John, which was written for Gentile-Christians, the name Judaeans is recorded, but in the dialogue between Jesus and a Jew who was his adherent, the name Israelite was given. That the Gospel according to John was written not for the Jewish-Christians but for the Gentile-Christians can be confirmed from another expression which is used only in this Gospel. I refer to the phrase "Your law"—"Their law,"[104] a phrase which never occurs in the Synoptic Gospels. In the Gospels according to Matthew and Luke we find the word law mentioned quite often but never "Your law" or "Their law." Pilate, the Gentile, when telling the Jews that they should judge Jesus, used the expression "Your law" . . . "Judge him according to your law." In answering Pilate the Jews used the phrase "Our law."[105]

It is worth noting that in the Synoptic Gospels we find the expression "Your tradition" in the disputes between the Pharisees and Jesus.[106] The reason for this is that the Synoptic Gospels were written for the Jewish-Christians who accepted the Bible but rejected tradition. Hence the phrase "Your tradition" is quite proper.

---

[103] Comp. p. 34; see also John 12, 13 The Jews who believed in Jesus called him the "King of Israel." However Pilate called Jesus the "King of the Jews." Ibid. 18, 33; 19, 3.
[104] 8, 17; 10, 34; 15, 26.
[105] John, 18, 31; 19, 7.
[106] Mark, 7, 15; Mat., 15, 3.

Another problem that confronts us is the expression "Rabbi" as a technical name which is used in John quite frequently. As we have demonstrated before, the word Rabbi was not known to the Jews at the time of Jesus. It came into use at the time of the destruction of the Second Temple. Is there a possibility that the expression Rabbi in the Fourth Gospel was not exactly reproduced? The prevailing opinion among the New Testament scholars is that the Gospel according to John was written not earlier than the last quarter of the first century C.E. We may assume that the word Rabbi used in the Johannine text reflects the time when the Gospel was compiled; namely, the end of the first century when the word Rabbi as a technical name was in use among the Jews. This is not exceptional in the Fourth Gospel. There are other elements which lead us to surmise that they were incorporated in the Johannine text at the time when the Gospel was written. In the account given of the trial of Jesus, according to the Johannine text, the Jews said to Pilate, "It is not lawful for us to put any man to death." However, as has been proved already by Jüster, the Jews at the time of Jesus exercised the right of capital punishment.[107] The Sanhedrin had the power to inflict capital punishment. The expression, "It is not lawful for us to put any man to death" portrays

---

[107] See Juster, *Les Juifs dans l'Empire Romain*, V, 2, 127–149. See also S. Zeitlin JQR. 1937, p. 388.

the conditions of the time when this Gospel was written. After the destruction of the Second Temple, namely, when the Jews, in fact, did not possess the right to inflict capital punishment.

In the previous passages we endeavored to show that the reason why the Gospel according to John does not record halakic disputes between the Pharisees and Jesus is due to the fact that this Gospel was written for the Gentile-Christians, some of whom may not have known of the existence of the Pharisees, and certainly had no interest in the Halakah. On the other hand the Synoptic Gospels were written for the Jews and therefore we find recorded halakic controversies between the Pharisees and Jesus. There is no doubt that the Gospel according to Matthew was written for the Jewish-Christians. Likewise there can be no doubt that the Gospel according to Luke was written for the Jewish-Christians. From the contents we are sure that they were written for the Jews. Both of these Gospels insist on the observance of the Old Testament Law, as Luke said "And it is easier for heaven and earth to pass than one word of the law to fail."[108] Both Gospels also trace the geneology of Jesus to King David. This shows that these Gospels were written for the Jews since they expected a Messiah from the family of David. However, we are not altogether sure whether the Gospel according to Mark was written for the Jews.

[108] 16, 17.

Many New Testament students maintained that this Gospel was written for the Gentiles.[109] Their contention is based on the fact that the Gospel according to Mark contains explanatory remarks of Hebrew terms, customs and geographical places in Palestine. It seems to me, however, that this is not strong enough proof for the assumption that the Gospel according to Mark was written for Gentiles. We must not forget that tradition places the writing of this Gospel in Rome[110] where the Jews were not well acquainted with the new Halakah which was introduced in Palestine, and they were not very familiar with the geographical and topographical places in Palestine. It would be only logical for the author to give explanatory remarks. In Chapter VII (3-4) the author explains the Jewish custom of washing the hands: "For the Pharisees, and all the Jews except they wash their hands oft, eat not, holding the tradition of the elders. And when they come from the market except they wash, they eat not and many other things, thereby, which they have received to hold as the washing of cups and pots, brazen vessels and of tables." This was a later interpolation.[111] Besides, we have grounds to assume that

[109] See E. P. Gould, *The Gospel According to St. Mark*, p. xviii.
[110] Thus according to Clement of Alexandria, see Eusebius' *Church History*, 2, 15. Comp. also H. B. Sweete, *The Gospel According to St. Mark*, introd. Chap. III.
[111] See S. Zeitlin, The Halakah in the Gospels and in relation to the Jewish Law at the time of Jesus, *Journal of Jewish Lore and Philosophy*, 1919, 357-373.

the custom of washing cups and pots was not yet in existence in the time of Jesus. It is also of great interest to note that the Greek word used for pots ξεστῶν is abbreviated from the Latin word *sextarius*, and hence this explanatory remark can not prove that this Gospel was written for Gentiles.[112]

That the Gospel according to Mark was written for the Jews can be clearly surmised from the passage XIV, 62 "And ye shall see the Son of man sitting on the right hand of power, and coming in the clouds of heaven." By the expression, "the right hand of power," the author referred to the right hand of God. In tannaitic literature we find a word "Power" גבורה as one of the names of God. This shows that the Gospel according to Mark had in mind the Jews who were acquainted with the different attributes of God.

Likewise, it is of some significance that Mark,[113] like Matthew and Luke,[114] tells us that Peter wished to erect three tabernacles — one for Jesus, one for Moses and one for Elias. In this narrative the author of the Gospel wanted to give a permanent position to the Jewish law in Christianity. This would show that the Gospel according to Mark, as well as the Gospels of

---

[112] There are other Latinisms used in Mark which are not found in the other Gospels like κράβαττοα (2, 4) which is the Latin word *"grabatus."* As to the language in which the Gospel According to Mark was originally written see Blass, "Philology of the Bible," Chap. II. Comp. also C. Torrey, *The Four Gospels: A New Translation*, New York, 1933. See also R. Markus, *Harvard Theological Review*, v. 27, pp. 211.

[113] 9, 5.

[114] Mat. 17, 4; Luke 9, 33.

Matthew and Luke, were written for the Jewish-Christians. There is a possibility, perhaps, that Mark, who wrote his Gospel in the city of Rome, had in mind not only the Jews of the Diaspora but Gentiles as well.

It is well known that Judaism was the mother of Christianity. The Pharisees, with their ideas of the Future World and Reward and Punishment, were responsible for the ideas which brought about Christianity. Paul himself said that he was a Pharisee, the son of a Pharisee. Christianity is not only indebted to Judaism, but to the Jews as well, particularly to the Jews of the Diaspora who paved the way for the Apostles to preach the Gospel of an invisible God. The Jews who lived in the Greco-Roman World refused to worship the gods of the cities in which they dwelt. They worshipped only one God — the God of the Universe.

The Gentiles, on this ground, maintained that the Jews were not loyal to the state since they did not worship the gods of the state. This fact was the source of the hatred of the pagan world for the Jews. The Gentiles could not understand why the Jews, who dwelt in Alexandria, or in Antioch, and enjoyed all privileges, should not worship the god of the city, as did the other inhabitants. The Jews, however, were firm in their refusal to worship the god of the city. They did not allow other gods to be placed in their synagogues. The Jews, with their uncompromising attitude to the pagan world, incurred the constant hostility of their neighbors. In many cities they were almost annihilated. Thousands upon thousands of Jews were killed in many cities of the Hellenistic world, but the Jews, with their belief that there is only one God, and He is the God of the Universe, made it possible for Paul, the Apostle to the Gentiles, to preach his gospel. The ground was paved for Christianity to gain recruits among the pagan world. Thus the Jews of the Diaspora, who shed their blood upholding the idea of a Universal God, were in great measure responsible for the spread of Christianity through the Greco-Roman world. Therefore we may truly say that the blood of the Jews was the seed of the Church.

*
* *

ADDITIONAL NOTE

In the preceding discussion I advanced the theory, that the author of the Gospel according to John used the idioms and expressions which were current among the Jews at the time of the composition of that Gospel, which did not take place before the last quarter of the first century C.E., i. e. after the destruction of the Second Temple. This theory can be further substantiated by the fact, that in this Gospel the Festival of Unleavened Bread is called Passover. In the Bible, as is well known, the name Passover is applied only to the Paschal Lamb, while the Festival itself is called the Festival of Unleavened Bread, חג המצות. It is only after the destruction of the Temple that the name Unleavened Bread was abandoned and the name Passover was given both to the Festival and to the Paschal Lamb, and it is this name that is used throughout the tannaitic literature. In the Gospel according to John the name Unleavened Bread does not occur, but the name Passover is used instead. Comp. John 2, 13, *the Jews' Passover*; 23, *Passover*; 6, 4, *Passover a Feast of the Jews*; 11, 55, *the Jews' Passover*; 12, 1, *before the Passover*; 13, 1, *before the Feast of Passover*; 18, 39, *at the Passover*; 19, 14, *preparation of the Passover*.

In the Synoptic Gospels, however, the Festival of Passover is still called the Festival of Unleavened Bread, whereas the name Passover is applied to the Paschal Lamb. Comp. Mat. 26, 17: "Now the first day of Unleavened Bread . . . to eat the Passover." Mark, 14, 1: "After two days was the Passover and the Unleavened Bread." In this verse all translations render πάσχα by the Feast of Passover. The Greek text, however, does not have the word ἑορτή the word πάσχα by itself refers to the Paschal Lamb, and the word ἄζυμα refers to the Festival. Comp. also Mark, 14, 12: "And the first day of Unleavened Bread when they killed the Passover"; Luke, 22, 1: "Now the Feast of Unleavened Bread drew nigh which is called Passover." (Comp. Josephus, Ant. 18, 2, 2: "the Feast of Unleavened Bread, which we call the Passover"); Luke, 22, 7: "Then came the day of Unleavened Bread, when the Passover must be killed."

THE ORIGIN OF THE PHARISEES REAFFIRMED

THE GENERAL VIEW IS THAT THE Pharisees originated at the time of Jonathan the Hasmonean. This contention was maintained by Christian and Jewish theologians. This theory was supported by the fact that Josephus, in *Antiquities*, first made reference to the Pharisees in connection with his account of Jonathan.[1] According to these theologians the Pharisees came into being during the second part of the second century BCE.[2] Dr. Louis Finkelstein strongly adhered to this theory. In his book, *The Pharisees*, published in 1938 and republished in 1962, he argued that the Pharisees came into being during the Hasmonean period.[3]

I propounded the idea that the origin of the *Perushim*, Pharisees, dated shortly after the Restoration, i.e. during the latter part of the fifth century BCE. The nomenclature *Perushim*, Pharisees, was a nickname of reproach applied by the Sadducees to a certain group of Judaeans. It was at the time of the canonization of the Pentateuch that there arose a difference of views in regard to the unwritten laws. One group maintained that only the laws recorded in the Pentateuch were binding, while the customs and laws which had come into vogue among the people, i.e., the unwritten laws were not binding. This group consisted of the high priests who were of the Zadokite family, known by the name of *Zadukim*, Sadducees, the sons of Zadok. The other group who maintained that the unwritten laws were as binding as the laws in the Pentateuch were considered heretics in the eyes of the high priestly family, the *Zadukim*, Sadducees. Those

[1] *Ant.* 13.5.9 (171-173).
[2] Cf. E. Schürer, *Geschichte des Jüd. Volkes* 2.
[3] Cf. p. 76.

Reprinted from the *Jewish Quarterly Review*, New Series, Vol. 59, 1969.

who held these heretical views were nicknamed *Perushim*, Pharisees, separatists, who had separated themselves from the God of the Judaeans and from the people. This radical view was certainly considered heretical in the eyes of the *Zadukim*, Sadducees.

In my writings, particularly in the article "The Pharisees", *JQR* October 1961, and in the Appendix to the second edition of *The Rise and Fall of the Judaean State*, Vol. I,[4] I endeavored to show that the Pharisees could not have come into being in the early Hasmonean period. The Hasmonean were not of the Zadokite family. At that time the influence and the power of the Sadducees were in decline while the Pharisees were in the ascendancy in influence. Furthermore how could the *Zadukim*, Sadducees, nickname those who opposed them *Perushim*, Pharisees, separatists? From whom did they separate?

The argument of the scholars is that Josephus, in *Antiquities*, mentioned for the first time Sadducees and the Pharisees during the period of Jonathan, hence they maintained that these groups came into being during the period of Jonathan.

In refuting this view I wrote, "Josephus in his account of the sects which existed during the time of Jonathan did not say that they arose at that time. He wrote: 'Now at this time there were three schools of thought among the Judaeans which held different opinions concerning human affairs.'[5] The expression 'there were' indicates that these sects were in existence before that time. Josephus had no occasion to refer to the Sadducees and the Pharisees previously. The reason that he refers to these sects at the time of Jonathan is that the Essenes came into being at that time. Similarly in his first work, *Jewish War*,[6] Josephus referred to the Pharisees, Sadducees and Essenes for the first time during his account of the time when Augustus Caesar declared Judaea a province of Rome.... The reason that Josephus referred to these

---

[4] pp. 444a-444k.
[5] Κατὰ δὲ τὸν χρόνον τοῦτον τρεῖς αἱρέσεις τῶν Ἰουδαίων ἦσαν.
[6] 2. 8.1-2 (117-166).

sects at the time of Archelaus is that Judah the Galilean organized a group to oppose the Romans, a group that Josephus named the Fourth Philosophy." [7]

Dr. Louis Finkelstein, in a recent article, "The Origin of the Pharisees Reconsidered", in *Conservative Judaism*, Winter 1969, wrote, "If the Pharisees were an organized group early in the fourth century B.C.E., it would be natural for their opponents adhering to the teachings of the high priesthood, to be called Sadducees, after the House of Zadok, whose prerogatives they defended." [8] In another passage he wrote, "The Pharisees existed as a distinct group as early as the beginning of the fourth century B.C.E." [9] Thus Dr. Finkelstein abandoned his early theory and accepted my view without referring to my writings. He even used some of my arguments in refuting the view that the Pharisees came into being during the time of Jonathan. In Note 2 he wrote, "Josephus specifically states that 'At that time [i.e., at the time of Jonathan] there were among the Jews three sects" (*Antiquities* XIII 5.9). However, he does not suggest that the different groups originated at that time." [10] In the person of Dr. Finkelstein I gained a convert who now accepts my view that the Pharisees came into being at an earlier period. The difference between us is that I maintain that the Pharisees came into being in the latter part of the fifth century while he argues that they came into being in the early part of the fourth century. There is no wide difference of time. While I am glad to obtain converts to my views I did not feel lonesome. According to my thinking I marshalled impregnable arguments for the early date of origin of the Pharisees.

Dr. Finkelstein is to be commended for his courage in retracting his previously strongly defended opinion as to the date of the origin of the Pharisees. It seems to me that by

[7] P. 444i.
[8] P. 32.
[9] P. 25.
[10] P. 32 note 2.

his recent view he militates against his previous writings about the Pharisees, particularly against the two volumes, *The Pharisees: The Sociological Background of their Fate*.

Dr. Finkelstein bases his new thory on a flimsy evidence. He supports himself on a passage in Tosefta Yadaim, chap. 2. The passage reads: "The Morning-Bathers say to the Pharisees, 'We complain of you, O Pharisees, because you speak the Name in the morning, before bathing,' the Pharisees replied, 'We complain of you, O Morning-Bathers, because you speak the Name, with a body containing defilement.' " [11] Dr. Finkelstein maintains that, "The Name to which the Pharisees and the Morning-Bathers refer in this argument was certainly the Tetragrammaton. The various ciphers employed for the Divine Name are never described as "the Name" in Mishna or Tosefta." [12] I question this assertion. Dr. Finkelstein quotes a Tosefta Berakot 5.12 where it is stated, "If a gentile recites a blessing pronouncing the Name, one is required to answer 'Amen'. If a Samaritan recites a blessing pronouncing the Name, one does not answer 'Amen' unless one hears the whole blessing." He further states, "As prof. Saul Lieberman explains in *Tosefta Kifeshutah, ad loc.*, the point made in Tosefta is that a gentile is not forbidden to pronounce the Name needlessly. Therefore if he pronounced the Name in any blessing, one may say, 'Amen'. A Samaritan is forbidden to do so, therefore, we cannot answer 'Amen' if he mentions the Name, unless one hears the entire blessing, and knows that it is an appropriate one." [13]

The text in Tosefta reads as follows גוי המברך בשם [את השם] [14] עונים אחריו אמן כותי המברך בשם אין עונים אחריו אמן עד שישמע כל הברכה. There is a strong doubt that the word כותי *cuti* is the correct reading. This passage of the Tosefta

[11] אומרין טובלי שחרין קובלנו עליכם פרושין שאתם מזכירין את השם בשחרית בלא טבילה אומרין פרושין קובלנו עליכם טובלי שחרין שאתם מזכירין את השם מן הגוף שיש בו טומאה.
[12] Pp. 25-26.
[13] Note 5.
[14] Cf. ed. Zuckermandel.

is recorded twice in the Palestinian Talmud but varies. The text in the Palestinian Talmud reads as follows גוי שברך את השם עונים אחריו אמן בשם אין עונים אחריו אמן[15]. In this text we note a difference השם and בשם. The meaning of this passage is: If a gentile blesses God one may answer 'Amen'; however if a gentile in his blessing uses the Name of God, Tetragrammaton or Adonai, one may not answer 'Amen' because he may have in mind another god. Undoubtedly this Tosefta is not only corrupt but is based on the Palestinian Talmud.

If we should assume that the word כותי *cuti* is a correct reading in the Tosefta it would be in accordance of the opinion of Rabbi, who held that a *cuti* is considered a goy.[16] A *goy* who uses the name of God in his blessing one should not answer Amen.

The word השם has the connotation God as the words גבורה and מקום. These terms are not to be translated. The word גבורה is not to be translated Power, מקום is not to be translated Place, they are ciphers. The term הקדוש ברוך הוא is not to be rendered the Holy One be blessed, it is a cipher for God. So the word *haShem* is not to be rendered as the name God but is a cipher for God. קידוש השם is to be rendered sanctification of God, not the sanctification of the name of God. אם ירצה השם has the connotation *Deo volente*. One may ask how the word *haShem* became a cipher for God. The answer is in Mishne Yoma.

According to the Mishne Yoma the high priest on the Day of Atonement rendered confessions and prayers to God. In his prayers he used the Tetragrammaton. In recording the prayers the composer of the Mishne could not use Yahweh, Tetragrammaton, that the high priest used. This would be against the third commandment of the Decalogue wherein is stated, "Thou shall not take the name of Yahweh thy God

---

[15] Meg. 1.9; Suk. 3.10. Cf. also Yer. Ber. 8.8 גוי שברך את השם עונה אחריו אמן.

[16] Yer. Ber. 7.1 ‎··· כותי כגוי דברי רבי

in vain." Thus the composer of the Mishne substituted *haShem* for Yahweh. "O *haShem*, I have committed iniquity... forgive, I pray..."[17] Thus the word *haShem* became a cipher for God.

We have made clear that there is a difference between השם and בשם. The former is a cipher for God, while the latter has the connotation in the name of God.[18]

It is stated in Mishne Sanhedrin that a blasphemer, one who blasphemes God, is not guilty of capital offence unless he pronounces *haShem*, the Name,[19] which may mean Tetragrammaton. In the same tractate it is stated that a man who curses his father or mother is not culpable unless he curses them בשם [20], with the Name. It is indeed doubtful whether during the Second Commonwealth and later the Jews knew how to pronounce the Tetragrammaton. It was pronounced only by the priests in the Temple in such a manner that the bystanders could not follow them.[21] The Mishne Sotah records that the priests in their blessings—in the Temple used *haShem* as it is written, outside the Temple they used בכינוי [22] a cipher. The sages of the Middle Ages differed as to the meaning of כינוי. One held that the priests used the terms *Eel*, E-l-o-h-i-m. Another held that the priests used the term Adonai.[23] It is questionable if the word Adonai is a כינוי cipher. The Talmud states that while it is written *yod he* it is pronounced *alef dalet*,[24] in other words it is written Yahweh but pronounced Adonai. Adonai is a pronunciation of Yahweh, not a different

---

[17] 3.7 אנא השם כפר נא • • • אנא השם עויתי פשעתי•
[18] בראשונה הוא אומר אנא השם ובשניה הוא אומר אנא בשם. Cf. however B. Yoma 36.
[19] 7.8 המגדף אינו חייב עד שיפרש השם•
[20] המקלל אביו ואמו אינו חייב עד שיקללם בשם•
[21] Kid. 71 שהבליע את השם בנעימת אחיו הכהנים. Cf. also Yer. Yoma 3.7.
[22] 7.6 במקדש אומר את השם ככתבו ובמדינה בכינויו•
[23] Cf. Tosafot ibid. 38 דבינו הלל פירש בספרי בכינוי כגון אל אלקים צבאות ולא מסתבר דהכי תיסק אדעתא דשבושי קרא למימר יברכך אלקים במקום שם בן ארבע אותיות אלא בכינוי יש לומר בקריאת אלף דלת.
[24] Yer. Sanh. 10.1 נכתב ביוד הא ונקרא באלף דלת•

name of God, as כיני. I doubt that the word Adonai can be considered a כיניו cipher.

In the Biblical period Yahweh was a proper name, the God of Israel, an ethnic God. After the Restoration those who adhered to the view of the university of God maintained that Yahweh is not an ethnic God but is God of the universe, the God of all peoples. To propagate this view they declared that the word Yahweh in the Pentateuch should be pronounced Adonai to signify that He is the Lord, Master of the Universe.[25]

The expression Adonai Yahweh occurs in the Bible. The word Yahweh following the word Adonai is pronounced E-l-o-h-i-m. We are confronted with the problem: If the original pronunciation of the four letters was to be pronounced E-l-o-h-i-m why was it not so written? As a matter of fact in Isaiah, Ch. 22.12, 15 the Septuagint renders these two words Κύριος Κύριος.[26] Dr. Finkelstein correctly remarked that in Ch. 9 of Daniel, which is of a late composition, only the word Adonai occurs. It is singular that in the book of Ezekiel the word Yahweh frequently occurs. However when the Prophet used the words "thus said" or "said" he has Adonai Yahweh, "thus said Adonai Yahweh."[27] The Septuagint renders these two words Κύριος Θεός.[28] To sum up: The injunction that the name Yahweh should not be pronounced but it should be pronounced Adonai was introduced shortly after the Restoration.

The Mishne (Berakoth 9.5) states, "It was instituted that a man [a Jew] should salute his fellow men by pronouncing the Name; for it is written, and behold, Boaz came from Bethlehem, and said unto the reapers, 'Yahweh be with you' ... It is time to work for Yahweh; they have rendered void thy law. R. Nathan says: They have rendered void thy law

---

[25] Cf. S. Zeitlin, "The Pharisees" *JQR* Oct. 1961, pp. 115-117.
[26] Cf. also ibid. 30.15; 65.13.
[27] נאם אדני; כה אמר אדני
[28] See S. Zeitlin, *op. cit.* p. 116.

because it was time to work for Yahweh." והתקינו שיהא אדם שואל את שלום חברו בשם שנאמר והנה בעז בא מבית לחם ויאמר לקוצרים יי״י עמכם ויאמרו לו יברכך יי״י.... ואמר עת לעשת ליי״י הפרו תורתך רבי נתן אומר הפרו תורתך עת לעשת ליי״י.

This *takkana* was introduced to counteract the Judaean Christians. When a Judaean Christian met a fellow Judaean Christian he greeted him with, "Peace in the name of God and the Lord Jesus Christ." Paul in his Epistles always addressed his fellow men with the greeting, "Peace from God and our Lord Jesus Christ." The Apostolic Fathers did likewise when they addressed their fellow men. The sages therefore introduced the *takkana* that when a Jew greets another Jew he should greet him, Peace in the Name, the Tetragrammaton, which was pronounced Adonai, our God, thus emphasizing that there is only one God and that Jesus is not Christ the Messiah and cannot be called Lord.[29] The word בשם meant that a Jew should pronounce the Four Letters in saluting his fellow man. As was noted before hardly any Jew knew how to pronounce the Tetragrammaton. Here what is meant is that in saluting he should use Adonai our God.

We understand why the sages held that in emergency we may disregard the law. According to the Decalogue one is forbidden to take the name of God in vain. Greeting each other with the name Adonai our God was taking the name of Adonai in vain. However, due to the danger from the Judaean Christians who were still a part of the Judaean people and who greeted each other with the phrase, "Peace in the name of Jesus Christ our Lord" [30] the sages disregarded the prohibition against mentioning the name of God in vain.

In this essay I constantly use the word Yahweh. I must emphasize that the word Yahweh is not a transliteration of the Tetragrammaton. We do not know how the Four Letters were pronounced. There can be no objection, therefore, to the writing of the word Yahweh in secular writings.

[29] Cf. S. Idem., *The Zadokite Fragments*, pp. 25-26, note 59a.
[30] Cf. Ibid.

Furthermore, according to the Mishne Yadaim 4.5, no transcription was considered sacred unless it was written in the Assyrian script; i.e., the square script, on parchment with ink.

לעולם אינו מטמא עד שיכתבנו אשורית על העור ובדיו.

Some writers, being scrupulous, wrote Yahweh in the old Hebrew script, since, according to the Mishne, what was written in the old Hebrew script was not sacred. In some of the Scrolls, claimed to have been discovered in Qumran, the word Yahweh is written in the old Hebrew script. The scholars who claim great antiquity of the Scrolls maintain that the writing of Yahweh in the old Hebrew script sustains their view. However it appears that they are not well versed in the rabbinic literature. The writing of Yahweh in the old Hebrew script is based on the Mishne Yadaim.

As was stated before, Dr. Finkelstein based his theory of the origin of the Pharisees on a Tosefta Yadaim. He writes, "A passage in Tosefta Yadaim shows conclusively that the Pharisees existed as a distinct group as early as the beginning of the fourth century B.C.E. For according to it the Tetragrammaton was still pronounced by the contemporary Pharisees in their prayers." [31] The Tosefta reads אומרין טובלי שחרין קובלנו עליכם פרושין שאתם מזכירין את השם בשחרית בלא טבילה אומרין פרושין קובלנו עליכם טובלי שחרין שאתם מזכירין את השם מן הגוף שיש בו טומאה. "The morning-bathers say to the Pharisees, 'We complain against you, O Pharisees, because you mention the Name in the morning before bathing.' The Pharisees reply, 'We complain against you, O morning-bathers, because you mention the Name, from a body containing defilement' ".

I wonder how Dr. Finkelstein came to the conclusion that the Pharisees originated early in the fourth century BCE on the basis of this Tosefta. As noted before the word השם in the Talmud has the connotation God, the Tetragrammaton and Adonai. The usage of Adonai is already found in the book of Ezekiel. When the Prophet Ezekiel used the expressions

[31] P. 25.

"thus said" or "said" he always employed Adonai. During the Second Commonwealth the Jews did not know how to pronounce the Tetragrammaton but employed Adonai. The complaint of the Morning-Bathers against the Pharisees that they mention השם has the meaning of mentioning God or Adonai in the morning before bathing. The term טובלי שחרית Morning-Bathers does not occur in the tannaitic literature, it does occur twice in the Talmud—once in the Palestinian [32] and once in the Babylonian.[33]

To fully comprehend the complaint of the Morning-Bathers against the Pharisees we shall present the development of the laws of impurity and purity. According to the Pentateuch any one who had nocturnal pollution or a minor impurity had to leave town and undergo *tebilah*, immersion, and after that wait until sunset.[34] This law was modified by the Pharisees. By method exegesis the sages explained the Pentateuchal expression מחנה (Camp) to mean מחנה שכינה. Similarly in the matter of sunset. For, according to the Pentateuch, mere bathing of the body in water would not have been sufficient to render a person pure unless the sun had set on him thereafter, and such a person was called טבול יום. The Pharisees, however, ordained that if the person had taken the prescribed bath he was *ipse facto* pure and it was not necessary for him to wait until sunset.[35] A few years before the destruction of the Temple the Pharisees declared that it was not necessary to undergo *tebilah*, immersion, but that it was sufficient to wash the hands.[36] This was the underlying reason for the institution of washing the hands before meals. A Jew upon arising in the morning before rendering a blessing to God, mentioning Adonai, had to wash his hands in appre-

---

[32] Ber. 3.4.
[33] Ibid., 22.
[34] Deut. 23.11; Lev. 15.16.
[35] Cf. Sifra Shemini 8 וטמא עד הערב טהור לחולין מבעוד יום ולתרומה משתחשך.
[36] Hulin 106 וידיו לא שטף במים אמר רבי אלעזר בן ערך מכאן סמכו חכמים לנטילת ידים מן התורה. Cf. S. Zeitlin, *HUCA* I, pp. 369-371.

hension of nocturnal pollution. Many Jews, scrupulous in the laws of impurity and purity, maintained that the washing of hands is insufficient but that a person must undergo *tebilah*, immersion, in the morning before mentioning the name of God. This was the core of the complaint of the Morning-Bathers against the Pharisees. The Pharisees replied, "We complain against you, O Morning-Bathers, because you mention השם from a body containing defilement." The reply of the Pharisees is not found in the standard text of the Tosefta. However, Samson of Sens, in his Commentary on the Mishne Yadaim, had a text of the Tosefta which had the reply of the Pharisees.

The Church historian Eusebius, in describing the sects among the Jews, quotes Hegesippus, "Now there were various opinions among the circumcision, of the children of Israel, against the tribe of Judah and (Christ) Messiah as follows: Essenes, Galileans, Hemerobaptists (Daily-Bathers), Masbothei, Samaritans, Sadducees and Pharisees."[37] Eusebius, in recording the sects of Jews, mentioned Daily-Bathers.

The Hemerobaptists were not identical with טובלי שחרין. The former were probably the followers of John the Baptist who preached baptism for repentance and forgiveness of sins.[38] They may have been the followers of Bannus whom Josephus joined for a while. In describing Bannus Josephus wrote,[39] "who dwelt in the wilderness, wearing only such clothing as trees provided, feeding on such things as grew of themselves, and using frequent ablutions of cold water, by day and night for purity's sake, I became his zealous

[37] *Ecclesiastical History* 4.22 ἦσαν δὲ γνῶμαι διάφοροι ἐν τῇ περιτομῇ ἐν υἱοῖς Ἰσραηλιτῶν κατὰ τῆς φυλῆς Ἰούδα καὶ τοῦ Χριστοῦ αὐταὶ Ἐσσαῖοι Γαλιλαῖοι Ἡμεροβαπτισταὶ Μασβώθεοι Σαμαρεῖται Σαδδουκαῖοι Φαρισαῖοι. This is a difficult passage. The author placed the Samaritans, Galileans and Pharisees as being against the tribe of Judah and the Messiah (Christ). The placing of the Pharisees and Samaritans together is incongruous. Essenes is written Ἐσσαῖοι as Philo has it. Josephus always has Ἐσσηνοί.

[38] Mark 1.4-6; Matt. 3.1-6.

[39] *Vita*, 1.11-12.

follower. With him I lived for three years." There is a striking similarity between the way of life of Bannus and that of John the Baptist. Both lived in the desert and preached baptism for repentance and spiritual purity. Before the destruction of the Temple many Jews practised baptism for repentance and spiritual purity.

On the other hand the טובלי שחרית Morning-Bathers were Jews who were scrupulous in the laws of impurity and purity. They opposed the Pharisaic innovation that the washing of hands in the morning is sufficient in rendering prayers and mentioning the name of God. The Morning-Bathers came into being shortly before the destruction of the Temple, at the time that the Pharisees in interpreting the laws of impurity and purity instituted that the washing of hands was sufficient to render a person pure in the case of minor impurity as nocturnal pollution. The Tosefta Yadaim, which states that the Morning-Bathers complained against the Pharisees because they mention the Name in the morning before bathing, is of the first century CE.

Dr. Finkelstein, who has retracted from his former position and advances the theory that the Pharisees came into being in the early part of the fourth century BCE, does not explain the forces which brought about their origin. A group of men, the Pharisees, which guided the life of the Jews during most of the period of the Second Commonwealth and influenced Judaism throughout the ages. Assuredly there must have been ideological forces which brought about their origin. Movements which last for centuries do not spring from a vacuum. Parties and sects which mold the life of a people are not the result of a whim of a person. There must be historical forces which bring them into the arena of history.

To repeat, I wrote at the beginning of this essay that I advanced the theory that the Pharisees came into being shortly after the Restoration. The name Pharisees is a nickname of contempt applied by their opponents the Zadokites. This group, nicknamed Pharisees, maintained that Yahweh, the God of Israel, is not an ethnic God but the God of all peoples. They also maintained that the Temple which was built should not be called the House of Yahweh as it is designated in the Bible—God has no particular house, He is everywhere. After the Pentateuch was canonized in the year 444 BCE this group maintained that the unwritten laws were as binding as the laws in the Pentateuch. The Zadokites and their followers were opposed to all these ideas.[40]

It is understandable that those who argued that the oral laws were on a par with the Pentateuchal laws and that Yahweh is a universal God, to be pronounced Adonai, were considered heretics in the eyes of the Zadokites and their followers. Those who held these heretical views were nicknamed *Perushim*, Pharisees, separatists, men who separated themselves from the Judaean people and from the God of Israel. These historical forces brought about the rise of the so called Pharisees. What was considered heresy in the early part of the Second Jewish Commonwealth later became normative Judaism.

[40] Cf. S. Zeitlin, *The Rise and Fall of the Judaean State*, 1, pp. 9-32; Appendix to the Second Edition, 1968; "The Pharisees" *JQR* October 1961.

THE ESSENES AND MESSIANIC EXPECTATIONS

A Historical Study of the Sects and Ideas During the Second Jewish Commonwealth

JOSEPHUS in his book *Jewish Antiquities*[1] in dealing with the history of Jonathan, the Hasmonean, gives an account of the different sects then in existence, the Pharisees, the Sadducees, and the Ἐσσηνοί,[2] Essenes. The first two sects are mentioned in tannaitic literature and the gospels, but not the Essenes. Philo also refers to the Essenes calling them Ἐσσαίων,[3] Essaions. Pliny the Elder cites them as Essenes.[4] Since all three sects were Jewish, they all undoubtedly bore Jewish names. In the tannaitic literature we have the Hebrew names for the Pharisees and Sadducees, namely פרושים, *Perushim* and צדוקים, *Zedukim*; but we do not have the Hebrew name there for the Essenes.

Before we can have a full understanding of the Essenes we should know something about the Pharisees and the Sadducees. These two sects arose shortly after the Restoration. When the Jews were permitted to return from Babylon by the proclamation of Cyrus, two parties grew up, one under the leadership of the High Priest Joshua, a descendant of Zadok, the first high priest under Solomon, and the other under Zerubbabel, a descendant of the Davidic dynasty. Their views as to the reorganization of the new

---
[1] 8.171–3, comp. also *ibid*. 18.18–22; *Jewish War*, 2.119–166.
[2] Comp. also *Ant*. 15.370; 17.346, where the reading is Ἐσσαῖοι.
[3] *Quod omnis probus liber sit* (*Every Good Man is Free*).
[4] *Natural History*, 5.15.

Reprinted from the *Jewish Quarterly Review*, New Series, Vol. 45, 1954.

Jewish community in Judaea differed. Joshua wanted to establish the new community as a theocracy wherein the religious and secular affairs would be under the high priest, as was prescribed in the Pentateuch.[5] Zerubbabel opposed to the new community as being a theocracy, recommended that the head of the community be a civil leader, one who was of the family of David, as the prophets had maintained. He held that the affairs of the Temple should be managed by the high priest only. The Pharisees went even farther contending that religion should be brought in consonance with life and that the law should be made elastic. Being opposed to theocracy they were called *Perushim*, separatists, persons who separated themselves from the Jewish people and broke with the Pentateuch.[6] Since they maintained that Jewish leadership should be vested in a scion of the Davidic family they were charged with being opposed to the Torah and hence were considered heretics.

The *Zedukim*, the Sadducees, were the orthodox group. They opposed any innovation in the law. They abided only by the Torah and such laws as they had received from their forefathers.[7] It was they who coined the nickname *Perushim*, Pharisees.

After the Hasmonean victory over the Syrians, a Commonwealth was established in Judaea. Simon became the head of the new free Jewish state. Although he was a priest, but not a descendant of Zadok, the High Priesthood was given to him. The office did not come to him by

---

[5] Comp. the writer's essays on the Sadducees and Pharisees. *The History of the Second Jewish Commonwealth, Prolegomena*; *Religious and Secular Leadership*; *Who Crucified Jesus?*; פרק הצדוקים והפרושים, בהתפתחות ההלכה.

[6] Idem, *Prolegomena*.

[7] *Ant.* 18.16. φυλακῇ δὲ οὐδαμῶς τινων μεταποίησις αὐτοῖς ἢ τῶν νόμων. Comp. Josippon, הצדוקים ולא היו מאמינים לכל מסרת ... ולכל פירוש כי אם לתורת משה לבדה.

inheritance.⁸ Religious matters were vested in a new institution created to handle them — the *Beth Din*, the *Sanhedrin*.⁸ᵃ The high priest exercised his rights over the Temple only, and not over the Jewish people.⁹ The Sanhedrin became the tribunal which controlled the religious life of entire Jewry.

The *Perushim*, the Pharisees, who before the Hasmonean period were a minority group, became a majority group with the establishment of the Commonwealth, while the Sadducees now became a minority group. These two groups differed not only in their views about the management of the State, but also on essential matters in the Jewish religion. The Sadducees maintained that the Jewish religion was ethnic, a heritage of those born Jews. The Pharisees denied that the Jewish religion was ethnic, but held that any one who embraced Judaism was on an equal status with those born of Jews.¹⁰ Further, the Pharisees believed in the immortality of the soul, and reward and punishment in the future world, which the Sadducees did not. The Pharisees now denounced those who rejected these views as heretics. The Sadducees became the heretic group though they had once been the orthodox. The term Sadducees now became one of opprobrium — the equivalent of heresy. This process has frequently occurred. What has been considered orthodoxy has later become heresy, and vice versa.

The study of history involves not only the presentation of past events, but should bring lessons for understanding the present and even serve as a guide in shaping the future.

---

⁸ Comp. I Macc. 14.28–41.

⁸ᵃ Comp. S. Zeitlin, *JQR*, April, 1952; S. Hoenig, *The Great Sanhedrin*, Philadelphia, 1953.

⁹ Comp. S. Zeitlin, *JQR*, *ibid.*, 1952.

¹⁰ *Idem*, "Judaism as a Religion," *JQR*, 1944, pp. 193–9.

Cicero well said that history is a teacher of life.[11] By this he meant that knowledge of the past would enable man to shape his destiny. One might almost say that the true historians are supplanting the prophets of old. By setting forth the true state of affairs and the forces behind them, historians furnish leaders serviceable means to mold the life of a nation. Hence the leaders of the Third Jewish Commonwealth, i. e., the leaders of Israel, must take into consideration the historical shaping of events during the Second Commonwealth. Events in the Second Commonwealth can prove fruitful in guiding life in the Third Jewish Commonwealth. I have dealt elsewhere with the forces that resulted in the destruction of the Second Commonwealth;[12] yet then, as today, there were different religions and political parties in the country, and we have at present a group like the Sadducees who would permit no innovation to be introduced in Jewish law. Yes, we have a Sadducee group now in Israel. They maintain that all the laws which were handed down from our forefathers must be strictly observed. They will allow no departure therefrom to be tolerated. They are not interested in bringing religion into consonance with life. They, or at least their religious leaders, have the same type of mentality as the Jews in Eastern Europe from whence they themselves came.[13] They do not grasp the fact that a State of Israel has come into being. A Pharisaic movement unfortunately is not yet noticeable in Israel. There have not appeared on the horizon religious leaders who possess not only the full knowledge of rabbinic lore, but who have the courage to make the law applicable to modern life in Israel.

The lack of a progressive religious leadership in Israel,

[11] *Historia Magistra Vitae.*
[12] גלינות, Tel Aviv, 1954.
[13] S. Zeitlin, "Is a Revival of a Sanhedrin in Israel Necessary for Modification of the Halaka?" *JQR*, 1952.

comparable to that of the Pharisaic movement of the Second Jewish Commonwealth, is due largely to the fact that the present leaders are interested only in making Israel an industrial state. Humane studies have not been encouraged, and have even been neglected. The Hebrew University which many Jews hoped would be a beacon to the entire Jewry stresses only the sciences at the expense of Jewish studies. An ordinary Levantine state will have *no spiritual effect* upon the Jews of the Diaspora.

The Essenes

The name Essenes by which Josephus designates the sect is not Hebrew. Being, however, a Jewish sect they must have borne a Hebrew name. What was it? When did the sect originate? What causes led to its emergence? It did not come into existence by chance or whim. It had existed for a long time. The organization we must assume was brought about by important factors.

The general opinion is that the term Essenes is derived from the Aramaic form חסין[14] and that their Hebrew name was *Hassidim*. Let us trace the origins and reason for the Hebrew name. In the First Book of Maccabees we are told that when the Jews were persecuted for their religion the *Hassidim* joined Mattathias.[15] The Greek word for them is Ἀσιδαίων which is a rendering of the Hebrew חסידים. The *Septuaginta* translates the Hebrew word חסידים, *Hassidim* by ὅσιοι, saints, pious.[16] On the other hand in the First Book of Maccabees the Greek translator has Ἀσιδαίων. This shows that the author had in mind a particular group

---

[14] E. Schürer, *Geschichte*, 2; Klausner, כרך, היסטוריה של הבית השני, שלישי, 116, שהאיסיים הגדישו את הסאה הפרושית קצת יותר מדאי... שהפרושיות והאיסיות נבעו שתיהן כאחת ממקור אחד.
[15] 2.41.
[16] Ps. 149.1, ἐκκλησία ὁσίων, 5, 32.6, 37.28.

called *Hassidim*. This is substantiated by the fact that in Chapter 7.13 of the same book, the author says that when Demetrius appointed Alcimus high priest Ασιδαίων, the *Hassidim* joined the latter. The author says in verses 16–17, that Alcimus betrayed the Jews and slew 60 in one day, "According to the one who wrote, 'the flesh of thy ὁσίων, saints and their blood.' "[17] The Hebrew undoubtedly had the word *Hassidim*, saints. Here the translator rendered it ὅσιοι, saints because the passage was taken from another book and refers only to pious people and not to a particular group. Hence the translator rendered the word חסידים ὅσιοι, pious. The author of the Second Book of Maccabees relates in 14.6 that when Alcimus came to Demetrius complaining about Judah Maccabee, he said, "These Jews who are called Ασιδαῖοι *Hassidim* whom Judah Maccabee leads." The author did not use the word ὅσιοι saints, pious, but the word Ασιδαῖοι, *Hassidim*, which indicates clearly that he had in mind a particular group who bore the name *Hassidim*.

Josippon who made use of the Second Book of Maccabees as the source for his history of the time of Antiochus Epiphanes,[18] calls those who were tortured and who died for their strict adherence to Judaism, *Hassidim*. In that part of his history where his source was Josephus, he uses the word *Hassidim* where Josephus uses the term *Essenes*. Where Josephus says there were three sects, Pharisees, Sadducees and Essenes, Josippon has Pharisees, Sadducees and *Hassidim*.[19] In his account of the assassination of Antigonus, the brother of King Aristobulus, Josephus refers to a man named Judah — an *Essene* who had foretold

---

[17] Comp. *ibid.* 79.2–3 שפכו דמם כמים ... בשר חסידיך, τὰς σάρκας τῶν ὁσίων.

[18] Comp. our Introduction to II Macc. ed. Dropsie College.

[19] הפרושים ... הצדוקים ... והחסידים חלק אחר.

the tragic death of Antigonus.[20] Josippon says — this man Judah was a member of the *Hassidim*.[21] Josephus in another place relates that a man named Menachem, an *Essene*, had once prophesied to Herod that he would some day be king of Judaea.[22] Josippon says that this man, Menachem, was a member of the *Hassidim*.[23] In short, the author of Josippon identifies the Essenes with the *Hassidim*. This book of Josippon was composed at a very early period, either at the end of the second century or the beginning of the third century CE.[23a] When the sect of the *Essenes* was still in the memory of the people, the author of Josippon was well aware that the term *Essenes* in Josephus' writings was the Hebrew name for the *Hassidim*.

There is a probability, however, that the name Essenes given by Josephus has the connotation of oracle, prophecy. As we know, the Essenes were credited by Josephus with having the power of prophecy.[24] In speaking about the vestments of the high priests in the third book of the *Antiquities*, he calls the *hoshen, essen*, and adds that these words signify *logion* (oracle) in Greek.[25] He says that the group he calls Essenes wore a linen cloth on their loins. Each member received a small hatchet and a loin cloth which was a sign of purity. It is true that the high priests wore a *hoshen* or the *essen* on their breasts, while this group whom Josephus calls Essenes wore a loin cloth. As it was believed that the *hoshen* or *essen* was the means of giving the power of

---

[20] *Ant.* 13.311, Ἰούδαν τινά Ἐσσηνὸν (Ἐσσαῖον).
[21] יהודה מן החשובים אשר לחסידים.
[22] *Ant.* 15.373. Ἐσσηνῶν Μανάημος ὄνομα.
[23] בעבור מנחם ... אשר לחסידים.
[23a] See A. A. Neuman, *Landmarks and Goals*, pp. 35-7.
[24] The Essenes were also known as interpreters of dreams. Josephus (*Ant.* 17.346) relates that Simon, the Essene, once interpreted a dream of King Archelaus and that this interpretation proved correct.
[25] ἐσσην μὲν καλεῖται, σημαίνει δὲ τοῦτο κατὰ τὴν Ἑλλήνων γλῶτταν λόγιον, (3.163).

prophecy to the person who wore it, the men of this particular group who wore the loin cloth were also credited by Josephus with the power of prophesying. It is therefore possible that Josephus called this group Essenes because of this. The fact that he called these men who wore a loin cloth Essenes, i. e., because they foretold the future, is not surprising. He called another group whom he regarded as terrorists, *Sicarii*, because they wore under their garments a dagger called *sica*;[26] he coined the word *Sicarii* because the men wore a *sica*.

We may surely assume that this group whom Josephus called *Sicarii*, robbers, had a Hebrew name by which they called themselves. Unfortunately the sources are silent.

Philo called the Essene sect Ἐσσαῖοι *Essaioi*. He thought this name was "a variation, though the form of the Greek is inexact, of ὁσιότης (piety), is given them, because they have shown themselves especially devout in the service of God."[27] It seems he knew they were called *Hasside* which has the connotation the pious, the holy. In explaining to his Greek readers the term *Essaioi*, he said, "It is a derivation although not exact of the Greek word ὁσιότης holiness, piety." From his account it is again evident that the members of this group were called in the Hebrew חסידים *Hassidim*.

Having shown that the Hebrew name of the sect whom Josephus called Essenes was *Hassidim*, we may ascertain when the group was organized and present the causes which led to its origin. We learn from the books of the Maccabees and from Josephus that Antiochus Epiphanes, for political as well as other reasons with which I dealt elsewhere,[28] persecuted the Jews for adherence to their religion. A

---

[26] *Jewish War*, 2.254–57.
[27] *Every Good Man is Free*, 75.
[28] Comp. our Introduction to II Macc. ed. Dropsie College.

segment of the Jews followed his policy in the Hellenization of the Jews, among whom were the high priest Jason, the brother of the high priest Onias, Simon, the captain of the Temple, Onias-Menelaus, and others. Zeus was brought into the Temple. Those who circumcised their children were tortured and crucified. Those who kept the Sabbath were put to death. The youth of the priesthood took part in athletics, and in order not to be recognized as Jews they covered their circumcision by drawing forward the prepuce.

Another group now arose in Judaea who were meticulous in the observance of the Torah and all the precepts they had received from their forefathers. They were ready to face torture and death for observance of the law. Once the members of this group gathered in a cave on the Sabbath to observe this holy day. When Antiochus' men came upon them and gave them the alternative to leave the cave and profane the Sabbath or to be burned alive, they chose the latter. A thousand men, women and children were burned at the stake.[29] One extreme always begets another. The first group which was extreme was the Hellenists who were ready to give up Judaism for Hellenism. They were headed by Jason and Menelaus. The extreme members of this group who were called lawless, renegades, and traitors by the authors of the books of the Maccabees and by Josephus, were responsible for the emergence of the other group of extremists. The חסידים, *Hassidim*, not only defied the decrees of Antiochus Epiphanes but opposed all form of compromise in the way of Jewish life. They were called *Hassidim* in the First and Second Book of Maccabees,[30] but Josephus called them *Essenes*.

The tragedy at the cave where a thousand men, women

---
[29] I Macc. 2.32–7.
[30] I Macc. 2.41, 7.13; II Macc. 14.6.

and children were burned alive without having resisted their enemies gave a strong stimulus to others to be loyal to Judaism and oppose Hellenism and the decrees of Antiochus with arms. Many of these people who previously met the edicts of Antiochus with the silent scorn of non-resistance now joined Mattathias and his son Judah in their revolt against the Syrians. Not only the Pharisees and many of the Sadducees, but also the Hassidim joined in this revolt.

When Demetrius ascended the throne, the Hellenization policy of Antiochus Epiphanes was abandoned and Alcimus was appointed high priest. When Demetrius offered them religious freedom, the *Hassidim* who previously fought in the army of Judah deserted him and supported Alcimus. Alcimus was of the high priestly family of Zadok,[31] the son of Joseph who was the son of Tobiah. Alcimus, however, did not trust the *Hassidim*, and in his distrust he killed sixty of them. This treacherous act caused the *Hassidim* again to fight in Judah's army. When Jonathan, brother of Judah Maccabee, won religious freedom for the Jews and was appointed the high priest by Alexander Balas and later by Demetrius, the *Hassidim* deserted him. They opposed him because the Hasmoneans strove to make Judaea a free state, which they did not approve of, and because he was not of the high priestly family. Later they also opposed the election of his brother Simon as he was not a descendant of the family of Zadok. According to the Pentateuch, God had promised the high priesthood to Pinchas, the progenitor of Zadok.[32] Since the building of the First Temple, all the high priests were descendants of the family of Zadok. They were the only lawful high priests. The appointment of Jonathan and also the subsequent

---

[31] See our Introduction to II Macc.
[32] Num. 25.11–13.

election of Simon to the high priesthood were not according to Jewish law and tradition.

It is true that when Simon was elected high priest by the Great Synagogue of priests, Levites and Israelites, a condition was made that he should be priest "until a true prophet should arise."[33] This, however, could not placate the *Hassidim*, the Essenes, particularly when his son John Hyrcanus became high priest and even contended for the kingdom. With the election of Simon as high priest, the *Hassidim*, the Essenes, considered the Temple profaned since Simon had no right to enter the Holy of Holies.

We now realize what Josephus meant when he tells us that the Essenes did not send any animal sacrifices to the Temple;[33a] it was that they did not recognize the high priesthood of the Temple. Also, they did not use oil because it was a part of the Temple sacrifice. Jerome relates that the Essenes abstained from eating meat and drinking wine.[34] This was due to the fact that they did not recognize the sacrifices which were brought into the Temple, and wine as well as oil was a part of the sacrifice; hence they abstained from using all three, wine, meat and oil. Schürer thinks Jerome's statement is based upon gross carelessness in rendering the words of Josephus.[35] It is true that Jerome quotes this from a passage in Josephus' book, *Contra Apionem*, where there is no mention of the Essenes; however, Schürer's statement that the Essenes ate meat and drank wine is based on the words of Josephus, τροφὴν καὶ ποτόν. This is a careless rendering. The word τροφὴν should be ren-

[33] I Macc. 14.41.
[33a] *Ant.* 18.19; comp. also Philo *op. cit.*
[34] *Josephus in secunda Judaicae captivitatis historia et in octavo decimo antiquitatum libro et contra Apionem duobus voluminibus tria describit dogmata Judaeorum: Pharisaeos, Sadducaeos, Essaeonos. Quorum novissimos miris effert laudibus, quod et ab uxoribus et vino et carnibus semper abstinuerint.* Hieronymus adv. Jovinian. 2.14.
[35] *Geschichte*, 2.

dered "a meal," and the word ποτός is "a drink." It would be absurd to assume that the Essenes drank wine every morning with each meal. Josephus meant they drank water. As a matter of fact, after the destruction of the Second Temple when sacrifices were no longer brought into the Temple, many Jews abstained from eating meat and drinking wine, since sacrifices had ceased and wine had formed part of animal sacrifices.[36]

From the fact that the Essenes were the *Hassidim*[37] and

---

[36] Comp. Tosefta Sota 15, משחרב בית המקדש רבו פרושים בישראל ולא היו אוכלין בשר ולא היו שותין יין ניטפל להן ר' יהושע אמר להן בניי מפני מה אין. אתם אוכלין בשר אמרו לו נאכל בשר שבכל יום היה תמיד קרב על גבי המזבח ועכשיו בטל. . . . נשתה יין. . . ועכשיו בטל. Comp. also Talmud b. B. B. 60.

[37] Professor Baer in his article, היסודות ההיסטוריים של ההלכה published in *Zion*, 1952, maintained that the term Essenes has the connotation of a people who separated themselves by their character of piety and purity from the rest of the people. נניע לידי מסקנה, כי שורש המלה מציין איש שהוא נבדל משאר אנשים ע"י תכונות של אצילות ופרישות. He found a connection between the Essenes in the city of Ephesus and the Essenes of Judaea. קשה להכחיש שקיים לכה"פ איזו קשר מילולי בין ה ἐσσῆves של העיר אפסוס וה עשְמ של קאלימכוס ולבין ה ἐσσηνοί היהודים. He points out that the priests in Ephesus, who were called Essenes, refused to associate with other persons for a certain period.

This etymology of the term Essenes is ingenious but it cannot hold ground. First, a pious Jewish sect such as the Essenes would not have a Greek nomenclature, they must have borne a Hebrew name. Furthermore, Professor Baer did not explain how the Essenes came into existence. What were the causes which brought about the rise of the sect? Undoubtedly he knows as a historian that no sects or parties can arise as the result of a mere whim of some person or persons. There is no connection between the Essenes and the priests of the city of Ephesus.

Professor Baer is right in having the Hebrew term אסנים instead of איסיים which all the Hebrew writers have hitherto employed. Professor Klausner (*op. cit.* v. 3, p. 110, n. 4) says that the word occurs in Josippon. בבירור אין למצוא את השם "איסיים" קודם ליוסיפון, שממנו שאב שם זה ר' עזריה מן האדומים. This statement is *incorrect*. The word איסיים *does not* occur in Josippon.

The comparison which Professor Baer makes between the halakot and the Greek laws is not borne out.

He often has not grasped the meaning of the halaka, neither the historical significance nor the literal meaning. For example in speaking about the pacificism of the Hassidim-Essenes, he says that the prohi-

that they came into existence as a reaction against the Hellenization forced upon the Jews by Antiochus and the high priests Jason and Menelaus, we can readily understand their reasons for their conduct. In the days of the persecution they were the first to scorn the edicts of Antiochus. They were ready to forfeit their lives for the meticulous observance of the law and to face torture. This characteristic of readiness to sacrifice themselves for the law remained with them throughout their history. Josephus says that the Romans "tried their (Essenes) souls through and through by every variety of test. Wrecked and twisted, burned and broken ... they refused to yield to either demand, nor ever once did they cringe to their persecutor or shed a tear."[38]

Our main sources about the Essenes are the works of Josephus, his book *Jewish War* written a few years after the destruction of the Temple, and his *Antiquities* which contains additional material written more than 20 years later. Philo refers to the Essenes in his *Every Good Man is*

bition to manufacture armament is reflected in the Mishne Shabbat. כדוגמא לשמירת מסורת עתיקה אצל חכמי המשנה המאוחרים נזכיר גם סימן לנטיות הפאציפיסטיות של החסידים, האסנים עוסקים גם באמנויות, אבל — לפי דברי פילון — רק באלה שעוזרים לעניני שלום, אם כי — כפי שנאמר במקום אחר — מותר להם לשאת נשק, כשהולכים בדרך. לאיסור של עשיית כלי מלחמה נמצא הד במשנה שבת יד: לא יצא איש לא בסייף ולא בקשת . . . ואם יצא חייב חטאת. ר' אליעזר אומר תכשיטין הן לו. וחכמים אומרים אלא לגנאי . . . . כאן הם שוב דוגמא מעניינת לצורת הבאתם של הלכה עתיקה עד מאד, ומאידך יש ללמוד מכאן על שיטתם של החסידים הראשונים להסיק מסקנה מעשית מתורת הנביאים השמורה בלבם (p. 45). This Mishne, however, makes no reference to manufacturing of armaments. It says that a man should not carry a sword or any other arms on the Sabbath day. Rabbi Eleazar held that a person doing so is not guilty of any offence against the law, since armaments are considered ornaments, while the sages had a different opinion on armaments. This Mishne does not allude to any pacificism of the *Hassidim*, Essenes. From internal evidence we may postulate that the halaka mentioned in the Mishne does not go back to great antiquity.

[38] *Jewish War*, 2.152.

Free and in his *Hypothetica*.[39] There is also a short paragraph about the Essenes in the work *Natural History*[40] by Pliny the Elder. The main source, however, is Josephus. Philo never met any Essenes and he described them from hearsay, or he made use of documents, whereas Josephus lived in the same country with them. Furthermore, he came into contact with them. As he said, for a while he was a member of this sect.[41] Hippolytus in his book *The Refutation of all Heresies*[42] gives a full account of the Essenes largely taken from Josephus' work *Jewish War*. There are some discrepancies between his account and that of Josephus. Hippolytus added passages that are Christological, not found in Josephus' account, nor did the ideas recorded by him constitute a part of the philosophy of the Essenes. For the other passages the author may have used another work unknown to us.

The Organization of the Essenes

Both Josephus and Philo give us accounts of the Essenaic organization. Philo says that there were four thousand members, a number also given in *Antiquities* by Josephus. He does not give this number in his book *Jewish War*; so we do not have to accept it. He says that they lived in large numbers in every town,[43] whereas Philo says "they (the Essenes) lived only in villages."[44] Josephus is more

---

[39] Comp. also Eusebius, *Praeparatio evangelica*, 8.11; idem, *Ecclesiastical History*, 4.22.
[40] 5.15, 73.
[41] Comp. *Vita*, 10.
[42] *Elenchos*, 9.18–30. Hippolytus' authorship of this work has been questioned. There can be no doubt, however that the work belongs to the latter part of the second century or the early part of the third century. For our purpose the authorship has no great significance.
[43] Μία δ' οὐκ ἔστιν αὐτῶν πόλις, ἀλλ' ἐν ἑκάστῃ μετοικοῦσιν πολλοί.
[44] κωμηδὸν οἰκοῦσι τὰς πόλεις ἐκτρεπόμενοι.

authoritative, as he lived among them in Judaea. He
divided them into different classes. He states that any
one who wanted to join them had to go through a period of
probation, first for a year, during which he remained outside of the sect; then having given proof of good character
he was accepted, but was not yet allowed to enter their
assemblies; and before doing so he was placed on probation
for two more years. Josephus also set forth their daily
routine. He says that they began the day by offering hymns
to God, adding, "as though entreating him (the sun) to
rise."[45] After being dismissed by their superiors, they
worked in the fields or at manual crafts until the fifth hour,
11 o'clock, when they performed ablutions which were
followed by a common meal. Before this a priest said
"grace," and after the meal he proferred thanks to God.[46]
Apparently the table meal was a substitute for the altar.
In like manner the Jews after the destruction of the Temple
considered the table at which they partook of their meal
a substitute for the altar, and if a priest was present he
pronounced the "grace." The Essenes had their own priests
who traced their lineage to the family of Zadok. The
Essenes gave their tithe of corn, which was required to be
given by all Jews, to their own priests.[47] After the meal
they resumed work, at which they continued until time
for the evening meal.

The Essenes were very particular about their food. They
ate only that which was prepared by one of their own group,
the reason being they did not recognize the priesthood of
the Temple; therefore, the giving of the tithe which the

---

[45] It is assumed that this hymn referred to the proclamation of *Shema*.
Shema is not a prayer nor a hymn, nor can we accept the view that the
Essenes recited the benediction of יוצר אור "that formest the light."
This benediction originated among the Jews of Babylonia.

[46] προκατεύχεται δ' ὁ ἱερεὺς τῆς τροφῆς . . .

[47] *Ant.* 18.22. ἱερεῖς δὲ ἐπὶ ποιήσει σίτου τε καὶ βρωμάτων.

Israelites were required to give to their own priests from their produce was not consummated, as the priesthood of the Temple was not recognized as priests by the Essenes.

Josephus relates that when an Essene was convicted of a crime he was expelled from the sect. This meant he was destined to die of starvation, unless some members took pity on him and gave him food, as he was forbidden to partake of the food of other men.[47a]

The Essenes were particular about the laws of purity. They were constantly performing ablutions. Their garments were white and were regarded sacred.[48] Josephus relates that if a senior member was touched by a junior member, he had to take a bath "as after contact with a pagan."[49] Pagans, according to the old halaka, were not susceptible to impurity.[50] They were not considered unclean even if they touched a corpse. They did not cause uncleanliness to a Jew when he came in contact with them.[51] According to the old halaka only Jews could transfer uncleanliness by contact. However, in the year 65 CE all pagans were declared in a state of uncleanliness and any Jew who came into contact with them had to resort to ablutions;[52] hence Josephus' statement "as after contact with a pagan" must refer to the period after 65 CE when he wrote his book. Apparently he wanted to point out the rigidity of the Essenes in the laws of purity.

The Essenes were very strict in observing the laws of the Sabbath. They prepared their food on the eve of the

---

[47a] Apparently the Essenes followed the Pentateuchal injunction ונכרת האיש ההוא מקרב עמו "that man shall be cut off from among his people."

[48] ἱερὰς ... ἐσθῆτας ...

[49] καθάπερ ἀλλοφύλῳ συμφυρέντας.

[50] Comp. S. Zeitlin, תרצ״ח "חורב", הוצאת הבית השני, טומאת נכרים בזמן.

[51] Idem, ibid.

[52] Ibid.

Sabbath, on the day of *Parasque*.[53] They did not kindle a fire on that day. Josephus says further, on this day "they do not venture to remove any vessels or even to go to stool."[54] He was right when he said they were stricter in observing the laws of the Sabbath than the rest of the Jews, since the Pharisees liberalized these laws and made the Sabbath a day of pleasure. They always strove to bring the laws into consonance with life. On the other hand, the Essenes were an ethical group living for themselves, apart from the rest of the Jews.

In their strict observance of the Sabbath the Essenes in the time of Antiochus assembled in a cave, and when their enemies approached and demanded the profanation of the holy day, they did not defend themselves even by throwing stones at them. This type of religiosity continued with them throughout their history.

The Essenes were opposed to slavery. There were two groups of Essenes one of which was opposed to marriage. Josephus says they did not condemn marriage in principle, but "they wished to protect themselves against a woman's wantonness, being persuaded that none of the sex kept her plighted troth to one man."[55] Philo goes a little farther in his explanation of why the Essenes did not marry. He writes, "For no Essene takes a wife, because a wife is a selfish creature, excessively jealous and an adept at beguiling the morals of her husband and seducing him by her continued impostures. For by the fawning talk which she practises and the other ways in which she plays her part like an actress on the stage she first ensnares the sight and hearing, and when these subjects as it were have been duped she cajoles the sovereign mind. And if children

---

[53] Josephus, *op. cit.*
[54] *Ibid.*
[55] *Ibid.*, 121.

come, filled with the spirit of arrogance and bold speaking she gives utterance with more audacious hardihood to things which before she hinted covertly and under disguise, and casting off all shame she compels him to commit actions which are all hostile to the life of fellowship."[56] This view possibly was entertained by Philo himself and not by the Essenes. It is true that in ancient times women were not considered dependable or reliable. In his *Antiquities* Josephus says the reason why women can not be witnesses in court is, "because of the levity and temerity of their sex."[57] In order to perpetuate their group, the Essenes adopted children whom they reared in their way of life.

The other group of the Essenes, Josephus says, were in full agreement with their fellow members in every respect except on the question of marriage. They held that the propagation of the people was a command, and maintained that if every one followed the principles of his fellow members, the race would die out quickly. This dissenting group married, but only after putting their prospective wives on three-years probation and after reassuring themselves that their prospective wives were capable of bearing children. The reasons given by Josephus and Philo why the Essenes were opposed to marriage are largely correct. Women in the ancient world, particularly certain groups among which we may include the *Hassidim*, were looked upon as untrustworthy. We believe there was another reason why the Essenes were opposed to marriage. It is that wedlock was closely connected with the laws of impurity. It not only was difficult for a man, but especially for a woman, to carry out the laws fully, and the Essenes were meticulous about purity; they underwent ablutions every morning and wore white clothes as a sign of purity; furthermore, after a

[56] *Hypathetica*.
[57] 4.219.

woman was freed from her impurity after giving birth, she had to bring a sacrifice to the priests at the Temple,[58] the priests of which the Essenes disapproved.

The Essenes were a well organized group and had overseers. Their clothing was communal and they had a communal treasury. Since they lived in many cities, the house of fellow-Essenes was open to any one who had migrated. If one of them was accused of misbehavior, he was brought before a court of one hundred whose decisions were final. They avoided taking an oath because it was in accordance with the Pentateuchal laws not to take the name of the Lord in vain.[59] They were considered pious and ethical, and their word was accepted even by the rulers of the country. When Herod demanded that every Jew take an oath of allegiance to him, he absolved the Essenes from this obligation.[60]

Josephus says that after God, the Essenes "held most in awe the name of their law-giver, any blasphemer of whom is punished with death."[61] The word lawgiver was taken to mean Moses. This passage in Josephus is ambiguous, to say the least. Why should an Essene be punished with death for blaspheming the name of Moses? Although we have a law in the Pentateuch that he who curses the name of God shall be put to death,[62] it is questionable if the Essenes ever resorted to capital punishment.[63] Their severest punishment was excommunication from the group,

---

[58] Lev. 12.2–8.
[59] Ex. 20.7. Comp. Targum Onkelos, לשוא.
[60] *Ant.* 15.371.
[61] μετὰ τὸν θεὸν τοὔνομα τοῦ νομοθέτου κἂν βλασφημήσῃ τις εἰς τοῦτον κολάζεται θανάτῳ.
[62] Lev. 24.13–16.
[63] Capital punishment was imposed only by the Sanhedrin, *Bet Din* which was not recognized by the Essenes, since it came into existence after the establishment of the state of Judaea. The Sanhedrin of course is not mentioned in the Pentateuch.

which was tantamount to death by starvation. Hippolytus who undoubtedly copied Josephus' text says, "They honored the lawgiver next to God. If anyone was guilty of blasphemy against the lawgiver he is punished."[64] He does not have the word "death." Hippolytus evidently did not have the word "death" in Josephus' text, otherwise he would have used it.

Beliefs and "Messianic Expectations"

The Essenes believed in fate, that all things were preordained by God. They held that anyone who was appointed ruler should be respected, and that no ruler attained his office except by the will of God.[65] This applied not only to their own rulers but also to the rulers of the Judaeans. A king like Herod, they believed, should be respected because it was God's will that he attained this high office.[66]

They believed in immortality of the soul, that it is imperishable and never dies. As Josephus says, they believed the soul emanates from the finest ether, that it is a prisoner of the body but is freed from it after death.[67] They believed the righteous would be rewarded after death, while the souls of the wicked would undergo everlasting punishment. The Essenes, according to Philo, used to assemble in the synagogue on the Sabbath,[68] to read the

---

[64] τιμῶσι δὲ τὸν νομοθέτην μετὰ τὸν θεόν καὶ εἴ τίς εἰς ταῦτον βλασφημήσει κολάζεται. (9.25.)

[65] *Jewish War*, 2.140.

[66] Comp. *Ant.* 15.37–4. Menahem the Essene said to Herod: "You will reign for God has deemed you worthy."

[67] *Jewish War*, 2.154–5. "The body is corruptible and its constituent matter impermanent, but that the soul is immortal and imperishable. Emanating from the finest ether αἰθέρος, these souls become entangled, as it were, in the prison-house of the body, to which they are dragged down by a sort of natural spell; but when once they are released from the bonds of the flesh, then, as though liberated from a long servitude, they rejoice and are borne aloft."

[68] οἳ καλοῦνται συναγωγαί.

Torah. One would read aloud and another would expound difficult passages. Josephus does not use the word synagogue. He says they used to come together in a particular place.[69] The practice of assembling on the Sabbath to read the Torah was not singularly an Essenaic custom. Josephus tells us in his book *Contra Apionem* that the Jews used to assemble on the Sabbath to listen to the reading of the Torah.[70] The term synagogue in Philo may have the connotation of assembly for any purpose as well as for the reading of the Torah, but not for the saying of prayers. They had another term for the house of prayers, *proseuche*.[71]

Hippolytus says that all the Jewish sects expected a Messiah. Undoubtedly this was true in the end of the second century CE.[72] Most of the Jews expected a Redeemer to free them from the Romans, and to reestablish their state and rebuild the Holy Temple. During the Second Commonwealth, however, the Jews did not expect a Messiah in the sense that we understand the term today. They believed that God would help them to vanquish their enemies as he had done in the time of David and Judah Maccabee. Only one group, the Apocalyptists, a Pharisaic sect, believed that a Redeemer would eventually free the Jews from their oppressors, and that he would be the Messiah endowed with supernatural powers.

The word משיח Messiah has the meaning of anointed one. The priests and kings during the period of the First Temple all were anointed with oil.[72a] This anointment was considered divine and they were called the Lord's anointed משיח ה'. Even a pagan king who was anointed was surnamed Mes-

---

[69] *Op. cit.*
[70] 2.175.
[71] Comp. S. Zeitlin, "The Origin of the Synagogue," *AAJR*, 1931.
[72] Comp. note 42.
[72a] Comp. also *The Testament of Levi*, 8.4, "anointed me with holy oil"; Ps. 23.5; 45.18; 133.2.

siah, like King Cyrus.[73] In the time of the Second Commonwealth neither the priests nor the kings of Judaea were anointed.[73a] They were no longer called the Lord's anointed. The term Messiah came to have a new meaning, — those who were anointed by the holy spirit. Jesus who was called Messiah, Christ, by his followers was never anointed with oil. The gospels do not record that Jesus was ever anointed with oil by John the Baptist or any one else.[74]

There were two offshoots from the Pharisees. One was the sect organized by Judah, the Galilean which sponsored the Fourth Philosophy, whose aim was to fight the Romans and force the leaders of the Jews to make war against them.[75] Its methods were terroristic. It was a minority group, and as it could not expect victory in open battle it resorted to other tactics. All the members of this sect kept a sica (dagger) hidden under their garments and assassinated anyone whom they suspected of being pro-Roman. They spread terror among the leaders of the Jews. Because of their practice of carrying a *sica* concealed in their garments Josephus called them *Sicarii*.[76]

The other offshoot of the Pharisees was called the "Apocalyptists" because they believed in the revelation of God. Their views agreed with followers of the Fourth Philosophy in their hatred of the Romans, and they regarded their own leaders wicked and traitorous because they sold themselves out to the Romans. They were opposed, however, to terroristic methods. Being against fighting the Romans with arms, they looked for divine intervention for the

---

[73] Isa. 45.1. כה אמר ה' למשיחו לכורש.

[73a] Comp. also Yoma, 52, משננו ... שמן המשחה.

[74] It is never stated in the apocalyptic literature where the name Messiah frequently occurs, and his functions described, that he will be anointed with oil.

[75] Comp. Josephus, *Jewish War*, 2.118.

[76] *Ibid.* 254–57; 7.252–55.

freedom of Israel. They preached that the day would come when the Messiah would be sent by God to free them and punish their oppressors and all evildoers. They believed that the Messiah existed before creation, and that he would eventually reveal himself and be glorified by all the people of the earth. He would sit on the throne of his father David.[77] The *Apocalyptists* were the forerunners of Christianity.

Only in apocalyptic literature like the Book of Enoch, Psalms of Solomon, The Testament of the Twelve Patriarchs, etc., is the idea of the Messiah well developed, while in the apocryphal literature such as the four books of the Maccabees, Judith, The Wisdom of Solomon, the Letter of Aristeas, Tobit, etc., regardless of where the books were written, in Judaea or the Diaspora, there *is no mention* of Messianic expectations.

The Jews of the Second Commonwealth did not look toward a Messiah. Most if not all histories of the Second Jewish Commonwealth *are vitiated* with the idea of Messianic expectations. Jewish as well as Christian theologians have interpreted certain biblical and apocryphal passages as referring to a Messiah, the Christian theologians to their Messiah and the Jewish to theirs. I have no quarrel with them. On the contrary, I admire their theological efforts. All honor to the theologians. A people must have a sacred theology. My objections are to the historians who are deluded by the idea that Messianic expectations occupied the Jews during the Second Commonwealth, and who write books on Messianic expectations.[78] They not only deceive

---

[77] Comp. Psalms of Solomon; Enoch; The Testaments of the Twelve Patriarchs.

[78] I refer to writers who speculate on the Messianic expectation and its origin during the Second Commonwealth. The Jews then except the Apocalyptists, did not expect a Messiah. I do not refer to authors who deal with Messianic expectations after the destruction of the

their readers, *but they distort the entire Jewish history of that period.* Messianic expectations came in only after the destruction of the Second Temple. During the Second Commonwealth, the *Apocalyptists* expected a Messiah, but the Jews in general did not have any notion about the coming of a Messiah. It originated with the *Apocalyptists* who, because they were opposed to terroristic methods, propagated the doctrine that God would send them a prophet, a man of supernatural power to vanquish their enemy.

In neither the works of Philo nor of Josephus is there any mention of a Messiah or any inkling of Messianic expectations. It has been generally assumed that Josephus did not mention the Messiah because he feared his benefactors, the Flavian family. This assumption has no validity. If he had been aware that the Jews expected a Messiah, he would have said so, but he probably would have used in this connection such appellatives as "charlatan" and "imposter," so that the Romans should not suspect him of any seditious views. In describing the *Apocalyptists* he says, "They were deceivers and imposters, under the pretense of divine inspiration fostering revolutionary changes. They persuaded the multitude to act like madmen and led them out into the desert under the belief that there God would give them tokens of deliverance."[79] If Josephus had known of the Messianic expectations among the Jews he would have given an account of the movement in such a way as to make sure that the Roman authorities would not suspect him of belief in such expectations.

Temple. The Jews at that time speculated on the coming of the Messiah. The book of Dr. A. H. Silver, *A History of Messianic Speculations in Israel*, is an important and valuable work.

[79] *Jewish War*, 2.258–9. Comp. also *ibid.* "Besides these (the Sicarii) there arose another body of villains, with purer hands but more impious intentions, who no less than the assassins ruined the peace of the city."

Hippolytus says that the Jews believed in a Messiah but denied that Christ was the Messiah, and that they held he would be a scion of David, "not from a virgin and the Holy Spirit, but from a woman and a man." ... "They [the Jews] allege," he writes, "that this Messiah will be king over them, a warlike and powerful individual, who after having gathered the entire nation of the Jews and having done battle with all the Nations, will restore for them Jerusalem the royal city. And into this city he will collect the entire nation, and restore the ancient customs, that it may fulfil the royal and priestly functions, and dwell in confidence for a period of time, and that a war would next be waged against them after being thus congregated, and in this war Messiah would fall by the edge of the sword. Shortly after this there will be the conflagration and termination of the universe."[80]

Hippolytus' account of the Jewish belief in the Messiah, which undoubtedly reflects in some way the ideas of the Jews of his time, is illuminating. It sheds light on rabbinic utterances in regard to the Messiah. According to a talmudic statement the Jews believed in two Messiahs, one of the tribe of Joseph, or rather who was an Ephraimite, and the other a scion of David. The Messiah ben Ephraim would be killed in battle[81] and then the ben David Messiah would arrive. Thus the Talmud corroborates Hippolytus

---

[80] γένεσιν μὲν γὰρ αὐτοῦ ἐσομένην λέγουσιν ἐκ γένους Δαβίδ ἀλλ' οὐκ ἐκ παρθένου καὶ ἁγίου πνεύματος, ἀλλ' ἐκ γυναικὸς καὶ ἀνδρός ... φάσκοντες τοῦτον ἐσόμενον βασιλέα ἐπ' αὐτούς, ἄνδρα πολεμιστὴν καὶ δυνατόν, ὃς ἐπισυνάξας τὸ πᾶν ἔθνος Ἰουδαίων πάντα τὰ ἔθνη πολεμήσας, ἀναστήσει αὐτοῖς τὴν Ἱερουσαλὴμ πόλιν βασιλίδα, εἰς ἣν ἐπισυνάξει ἅπαν τὸ ἔθνος καὶ πάλιν ἐπὶ τὰ ἀρχαῖα ἔθη ἀποκαταστήσει βασιλεῦον καὶ ἱερατεῦον καὶ κατοικοῦν ἐν πεποιθήσει ἐν χρόνοις ἱκανοῖς. ἔπειτα ἐπαναστῆναι κατ' αὐτῶν πόλεμον ἐπισυναχθέντων. ἐν ἐκείνῳ τῷ πολέμῳ πεσεῖν τὸν Χριστὸν ἐν μαχαίρῃ, ἔπειτα μετ' οὐ πολὺ τὴν συντέλειαν καὶ ἐκπύρωσιν τοῦ παντὸς ἐπιστῆναι.

[81] Tal. Suk. 52. שראה משיח בן יוסף שנהרג. Comp. also IV Ezra, 7.28.

that a Messiah would be killed in battle. Most scholars hold that the conception of a Messiah ben Ephraim is based on the 12th chapter of Zechariah.[82] A conception using this type of reasoning is not sound and historians should not accept it. It belongs in the realm of theology rather than in that of history. An idea which becomes deeply rooted in a people may be the outgrowth of religious, political, or social conditions. Leaders in order to propagate the idea then quote scripture to support it.

After the destruction of the Second Temple, the adherents of the Fourth Philosophy whom Josephus called the *Sicarii*, continued to agitate for a new revolt against Rome. They caused disturbances in Egypt,[83] in Cyrenaica[84] and in Judaea proper. This agitation gained many recruits. When Trajan died in 117 during the war with the Parthians, the Jew of Judaea began to prepare for war against the Romans. This preparation which began in 122 culminated in an open struggle in 132. The man who headed this revolt was named Simon, and many proclaimed him King Messiah. One of his great followers was Rabbi Akiba. Simon was named bar Kokba, i. e., King Messiah,[85] and he apparently maintained that he was of the family of David.[86] The revolt ended with the greatest catastrophe for the Jews.

After this debacle the Jews were in a state of deep gloom and depression. Their national and spiritual life suffered a great setback. The explanation which was advanced that Simon was not the Messiah but was a deceiver, *Bar Koseba*,

---

[82] Comp. *ibid.* וספדה הארץ ... חד אמר על משיח בן יוסף שנהרג.
[83] *Jewish War*, 2.410–19.
[84] *Ibid.* 7.437–44.
[85] Comp. Yer. Tan. 4. אמר [בר כוכבה] ר' עקיבה כד הוה חמי בר כוזבה דין הוא מלכא משיחא. Comp. also Targum Numb. 24.17 דרך כוכב ... כד יקום מלכא מיעקב ויתרבא משיחא. Comp., also *The Testament of Judah*, 24.1, "shall arise the star," כוכב, i.e. Messiah.
[86] Yer. *ibid.* עקיבה יעלו עשבים בלחייך ועדיין בן דוד לא בא.

gave them no solace. They looked to their leaders for a better explanation than that they had been deceived. A theory was set up that this collapse was only temporary, that although Simon was the Messiah, he was not of the Davidic family, but of the Ephraim family, and that as a matter of fact the killing of the Ephraimite Messiah had already been foretold by the Prophet Zechariah. Subsequently the other Messiah who would be of the Davidic family would appear and wreak vengeance upon the gentiles. This had been foretold by Zechariah.[87] Some were of the opinion that there would be no Messiah, but that God would reveal himself and destroy all the enemies of the Jews, and that He would gather all the Jews from the four corners of the earth into the Holy Land. These enemies were designated under a collective name, *Gog* and *Magog*. These names were derived from Ezekiel.[88]

The reason the Jews expected a Messiah of the Davidic family is well known; however, the source of the expectation that another Messiah would come and that he would be an Ephraimite still needs clarification.

There had been rivalry between the Judaean and the Ephraimite tribes. The first king over the ten tribes was Jeroboam, an Ephraimite, who revolted against Solomon. We learn from the Pentateuch that when Moses sent men on the mission to investigate the land of Canaan, they came with discouraging reports, except Caleb of the tribe of Judah, and Joshua the son of Nun, of the tribe of Ephraim.[89] Since the two latter brought in good reports about the land of Canaan, God rewarded both tribes. David was of the tribe of Judah, while Joshua, the first ruler after Moses, came

---

[87] On the Messiah ben Ephraim, see C. Torrey, *JBL*, 1947; H. H. Rowley, *The Servant of the Lord*, pp. 64–75.
[88] 38–39. Comp. Eduy. 2.10.
[89] Num. 13–14.

from the tribe of Ephraim. These two tribes would later be associated in that the first Messiah would be an Ephraimite,[90] and the second would be of the Davidic family.

There is a legend in rabbinic literature that the Ephraimites left Egypt before the day God set for the exodus, and consequently they were slain.[91] This is analogous to a second redemption. In the first redemption the Ephraimites were killed, because they forced the time of the redemption in leaving Egypt ahead of the time set. Later the Messiah of Ephraim was also killed because the Jews forced the time of redemption before the predestined time.

On the other hand, some Jews even after the time of Bar Kokba did not believe in any Messiah. They expected God himself to save and redeem them from their enemies. The author of the book The Assumption of Moses, which was composed in the year 140 CE,[92] calls those who led the Bar Kokba revolt pestilent men and deceivers. Normative Judaism or Pharisaic Judaism still continued to oppose any idea of a Messiah. Rabbi (Judah the prince) who was the leader in normative Judaism composed the Mishne[92a] which was to be second in authority to the Bible. He does not

---

[90] Comp. Targum of Jonathan, Ex. 40.11, מטול יהושע ... דעל ידוי עתידא ארעא דישראל לאיתפלגא ומשיחא בר אפרים דנפיק מינה.

[91] See Tal. Sanh. 92, בני אפרים שמנו לקץ וטעו; Targum of Jonathan Ps. 78.9, כד הוו יתבין במצרים אתרברבו בני אפרים מנו קצא וטעו ונפקו תלחין שנים קדם קצא ... ואתקטלו ביום סדרי קרבא. Comp. Midrash R. Song of Songs, 2, שדחקו את הקץ ונכשלו ... ואחד בימי כוזבא ואחד בימי שותלח בן אפרים.

[92] Comp. S. Zeitlin, "The Assumption of Moses and the Revolt of Bar Kokba," *JQR*, 1947.

[92a] The word משנה has the connotation "study" and "second." The halakot which Rabbi Judah collected and codified was called משנה i.e., second to the Pentateuch. The transliteration of the word משנה Mishna hitherto used is incorrect. In the edict issued by the Roman government fobidding the study of the משנה the term δευτερωσις (second) was employed. (Comp. Justinian *Novellae*, 146.1-2) Thus it is evident that in Palestine the word משנה was pronounced *Mishne*. In this essay I therefore transliterate the word משנה Mishne. I hope to present a full study of the Mishne and Tosefta in the near future.

mention Messiah — an omission which would be impossible if normative Judaism believed in one. It is true that the words "the days of Messiah" occur in the first chapter of *Berakot*[93] and in the last chapter of *Sota*;[94] however, these passages are later additions after the death of Rabbi. As the name of Rabbi is mentioned in the passage of Sota,[95] we may assume that these words were introduced after his death. In the passage of Mishne *Berakot* of the Babylonian Talmud, the text reads כל להביא לימות המשיח, whereas in the Mishne of the Palestinian Talmud the text has as follows: כל ימי חייך עולם הבא להביא את ימות המשיח. In my opinion the words ימות המשיח "the days of Messiah" point to a later interpretation; however, it is *a fact that Messiah is not mentioned in the entire Mishne*. It is stated there that all the Israelites would have a share in the future world. Those who did not believe that the Torah was revealed by God would not have such a share. Resurrection, the Future World, and Revelation are stressed in the Mishne.[95a] Since Messiah is not mentioned, we have conclusive proof that even after the destruction of the Temple, normative Judaism for a century and a half did not entertain the idea of a Messiah.

Pharisaic or normative Judaism dominated Jewish life after the Bar Kokba catastrophe. The books of the Apocalyptists were banned and the people were forbidden to read them under the risk of losing their portion in the future world.[96] Nevertheless the ideas of the Apocalyptists, particularly in reference to the idea of a Messiah, were not eradicated. In times of persecution and under suffering and

---

[93] וחכמים אומרים ימי חייך העולם הזה כל להביא ימות המשיח.
[94] בעקבות משיחא חוצפא יסגא.
[95] משמת רבי בטל ענוה ויראת חטא.
[95a] (Comp. also Yer. Pea 1) האומר אין תחיית המתים ואין תורה מן השמים.
[96] ואלו שאין להם חלק לעולם הבא... ר' עקיבא אומר אף הקורא בספרים החצונים. See Joshua Bloch, *On the Apocalyptic in Judaism*, Philadelphia, 1952.

distress, the Jews did turn to the idea of a Messiah, believing he would save them and take revenge on their enemies. The Jewish sages, the Tannaim and Amoraim, were occupied with the idea of the advent of a Messiah. Some of them foretold the day of his coming, and also described the turmoil and anguish which would precede it.[97] Christianity undoubtedly gave an impetus in shaping the conception of the supernatural Messiah among the Jews.

The idea of a Messiah undoubtedly afforded great spiritual comfort to the Jews, especially during their persecutions, but it also brought many catastrophies to them. Many false Messiahs appeared, and the Jews suffered spiritually as well as politically. After the great massacre of the Jews in 1648, a false Messiah named Sabbatai Zevi appeared, and he held great sway over the Jewish people regardless of class distinction. The ignorant as well as the learned accepted him as the true Messiah. The Jews had to have an outlet for their great misfortunes in which almost a third of the people, was destroyed.

We may say with some assurance that the recent establishment of the State of Israel has saved the Jewish people from the rise of a false Messiah, as an aftermath of one of the greatest catastrophies which has befallen the Jews, when about six million, more than a third of their number, the flower of the people, were exterminated. Such a catastrophe could not but have raised great mental disquietude, particularly among the orthodox Jews. The questions would have been raised, where was Providence, where was the God of Israel, the protector of His people? The answer might have been the rise of false Messiahs as an outlet. But the establishment of the State of Israel gave a partial answer to various perplexities. The State of Israel is,

[97] Comp. Tal. Sanh. 97–9. Many rabbis vehemently opposed those who set dates for the coming of the Messiah.

according to the belief of some orthodox Jews אתחלתא דגאולה "the beginning of the redemption."

Although the Jews have not succumbed to false Messiahs, they did not escape the intellectual decline characteristic of pseudo-Messianism. We refer to the literature of symbolism and mysticism which has become prevalent among the Jews, — a literature which is a synchronized Judaism and Christianity, but is neither Judaism nor Christianity. The literature is the production of so-called neo-orthodox. Neither the orthodox nor the liberals indulge in such a literature.[98] Unfortunately it is published by creditable publishers and national organizations. although it surely is a passing fad; nevertheless it does great harm to the youth who are not well versed in Judaism. In Israel, however, the people do not indulge in this pseudo-theological literature.

Conclusion

The Essenes mentioned by Philo and Josephus are the *Hassidim* referred to in the first two Books of Maccabees and in Josippon. They arose in the year 169–168 BCE, at the time of the persecutions of Antiochus Epiphanes. The Sadducees and the Pharisees had come into existence shortly after the Restoration, a few centuries before the rising of the Essenes. The Essenes joined the army of Judah Maccabee for a brief period, but later when religious freedom was obtained by the Hasmoneans, one of whom was appointed high priest, they formed themselves into a separate group. While they recognized the State of Judah they did not recognize the high priesthood. In due time fanatics and malcontents joined their ranks. They cherished belief

---

[98] We may safely assume that Maimonides even in his time, the thirteenth century, would have branded such literature as belonging to the type of obscurantism.

in immortality of the soul, and reward and punishment. They accepted the Pentateuch and perhaps the prophets, but rejected belief in a Messiah. This group is not mentioned in tannaitic literature nor in the Gospels, because they did not participate in the affairs of the Jewish people, religiously or politically.

Mention is made in the Gospels of false prophets and false Messiahs;[99] undoubtedly these refer to the Apocalyptists. Even the "Fourth Philosophy," the followers of which Josephus called the *Sicarii*, is referred to in Acts,[100] but there is no mention of the Essenes. This shows that the early Christians neither were influenced by them nor had to combat them.

Some are of the opinion that Essenism is actually a phase of Pharisaism; in other words, that the Essenes were the extreme wing of the Pharisees.[101] Such an opinion is a travesty of Jewish history of the Second Commonwealth and a reflection upon Pharisaism. The Pharisees strove to amend the law, to put religion into consonance with life. They modified the strict laws of impurity. They made the vigorous laws in connection with the Sabbath more liberal. They favored proselytism.[102] Their views were in direct opposition to the doctrines of the Essenes. Some hold that the Essenes were Apocalyptists. This is untrue. The Apocalyptists were an off-shoot of the Pharisees and adopted their teachings. They propagated also the idea of a supernatural Messiah, which the Essenes did not entertain.

---

[99] Comp. Matt. 24.5–11; Mark 13.32; Acts 5.36.

[100] Acts 21.38 .... ἄνδρας τῶν σικαρίων.

[101] See note 14.

[102] Comp. S. Zeitlin, "Judaism as a Religion," *JQR*, 1944, p. 195, "The rabbis [Pharisees] regarded the proselytes very highly and extolled those who gave up their idols and accepted the God of Israel, commending them even more than those who were born Jews."

The Apocalyptists in order to persuade the multitude to join them indulged in prophecies, foretelling that God himself or through a Messiah would deliver them from the yoke of the Romans, and that their enemies would be avenged. The Essenes as a whole did not resort to prophesying. Some of them were seers and confined themselves to foretelling the fortunes or misfortunes of an individual, as one of them had foretold the assassination of Antigonus, and another one the ascendency of Herod to the throne of Judaea. We have here the crux of the difference between the Apocalyptists and the Essenes. The former were interested in the Jewish people as whole, while the latter were interested only in individuals. Again, the Apocalyptists were not opposed to marriage while the Essenes were. Some believe that the Essenes were communists since they had no private possessions and had a communal treasury. This again is untrue. They opposed slavery and the accumulation of wealth because they believed slavery, money and women led to corruption. They were individualists, interested in saving their own souls, and not in helping the people as a whole. Further, they recognized the State of Judaea. The Apocalyptists or communists would not recognize it, particularly a king like Herod. The Essenes, on the other hand, thought that since God gave the kingdom to Herod, he should be honored and respected as a king.[103] Incidentally, opposition to marriage was not a communist trait.

Some hold that John the Baptist was one of the followers of Essenism. In the Gospels he is pictured as one who went to the people and besought them to repent of their sins. His baptism was an immersion to be freed from sin, while the immersions of the Essenes were for levitical purity. John the Baptist strove to proselyte people. The Essenes

[103] Comp. *Ant.* 15.374.

never set out to proselyte. It was made difficult for anyone to join them. They required years of probation before accepting a person, while the Pharisees, Apocalyptists and John, the Baptist, went to the people and sought to convert them. With them it was not necessary for a proselyte to go through a period of probation. John, the Baptist, may have been of the type of ascetic like the hermit Bannus, whom Josephus described in his book *Vita*, who dwelt in the wilderness, and wore such clothing as the trees provided, and ate such articles of food as grew of themselves.

Some connected the Essenes with the Therapeutae whom Philo described in his book *The Contemplative Life*. Their name Therapeutae, Philo says, is derived either from the word ϑεραπευταί "cure," because they profess ϑεραπεύειν the art of healing, or associated it with worship, for they were the servants of God. Sometime ago this treatise of Philo was quite rightly recognized as spurious.[104] Philo's account of the Therapeutae is not in accordance with his account of the Essenes. There was no common ground between these two sects. The Therapeutae, according to Philo, lived in Egypt. The Essenes never emigrated from Judaea which was for them the Holy Land, while they held that the land of the gentiles was defiled. No Essene-*Hassid* would live in a defiled country. The Therapeutae undoubtedly were the early Christian monks; there is no connection whatsoever between them and the Essenes.[104a]

The Essenes were considered heroes in the time of Antiochus Epiphanes when they defied him in his edicts against the laws of the Torah; however, they could not adapt themselves to the revolutionary ideas which pre-

---

[104] The present writer is of the opinion that the *Questions and Answers to the Pentateuchal Passages* is also not the work of Philo.

[104a] Neither is there any connection between the *Hassidim*-Essenes and the Pythagoreans.

vailed after the establishment of Judaea as a free state. When *Theocracy* was substituted for *Nomocracy*, and the high priest was no longer of the Zadokite family, the Essenes considered these changes a transgression and even a nullification of the religion which they had received from their forefathers, and for which they sacrificed their lives in the time of Antiochus Epiphanes.

The revolutionary changes which the Pharisees were instrumental in bringing about, were accepted by the Jewish people. The Essenes then isolated themselves and lived a rigid life apart, strictly observing the old laws, but ignoring the Temple. Their fanaticism remained with them throughout their history. Their ranks were filled by the adoption of children whose parents probably had perished in the civil or foreign wars. There was another type of recruit which joined them, a determined and discontented people who hoped to find salvation for forsaking the mundane affairs of life. These joined the pious group, the *Hassidim*, Essenes, because thereby they could indulge in prayers and resort to ablutions.

Josephus says that any one who had joined the Essenes and had tasted their philosophy did not desert them.[105] It is quite understandable and natural that malcontents and refugees who had lost their place in society found happiness in the midst of the Essenes, where they were taught that they would be rewarded for their sufferings and their rigid life in the future world, when their souls would be freed from their mortal body in which they were now imprisoned.

The fanaticism and at the same time heroism, which the Essenes, *Hassidim*, displayed in the time of Antiochus Epiphanes were also shown by them at the time of the war

---

[105] ταῦτα μὲν οὖν Ἐσσηνοὶ περὶ ψυχῆς θεολογοῦσιν, ἄφυκτον. δέλεαρ τοῖς ἅπαξ γευσαμένοις τῆς σοφίας αὐτῶν καθιέντες.

with the Romans. Josephus says that during this war they were tortured "in order to induce them to blaspheme their lawgiver or to eat some forbidden thing. They refused to yield to either demand, nor ever once did they cringe to their persecutors or shed a tear."[106] Probably generals or officers of the Roman army demanded, after their capture, that they swear by the genius of Caesar and say, "Away with the atheists."

Since the Essenes did not reject the State of Judaea, some of them participated in the war against the Romans. One Essene named John was a general in the Judaean army.[107]

After the destruction of the Temple, the Essenes settled on the west side of the Dead Sea where they dwindled and finally disappeared without leaving a trace, having never had any influence either on Judaism or Christianity. Pliny, the Elder, who described the Essenes after the destruction of the Temple, wrote that on the west side of the Dead Sea "is the solitary tribe of the Essenes, which is remarkable beyond all the other tribes in the whole world, as it has no women, and has renounced all sexual desires, has no money and has only palm-trees for company. Day by day the throng of refugees is recruited to an equal number by numerous accessions of persons tired of life, and driven thither by the waves of fortune to adopt their manners. Thus through thousands of ages (incredible to relate) is a race in which no one is born who lives on for ever, so prolific for their advantage is other men's weariness of life."[108]

---

[106] *Jewish War*, 2.152. Ἰωάννης ὁ Ἐσσαῖος, comp. also 3.11.
[107] *Ibid.*, 2.567.
[108] *Ab occidente litora Esseni fugiunt usque qua nocent, gens sola et in toto orbe praeter ceteras mira, sine ulla femina, omni venere abdicata, sine pecunia, socia palmarum, in diem ex aequo convenarum turba renas-*

The Essenes probably wrote books. If they did so, they discoursed on angelology, immortality of the soul, laws of impurity and most likely levelled diatribes against women. Both they and their literature disappeared, without leaving a vestige, since neither the Jews nor the Christians had any interest in them.

Had it not been for Philo and Josephus who strove to present to the Hellenistic world the high moral excellence of a group of Jews, who opposed slavery, who shunned wealth, who lived in communal groups, and were especially devout in the service of God, we would not know of the existence of the Essenes. Josephus probably knew nothing of the origin of the sect any more than he did of the origin of the Pharisees and the Sadducees. He was as ignorant of the reason for their nomenclature as many modern historians are of the origin of the names given to the different political and religious sects which flourished during the Middle Ages.

The Essenes thus, who came into being as heroes and martyrs for Judaism, disappeared through isolation and self-suicidal measures. They could not reconcile themselves to the progressive ideas advanced by Pharisaism, nor the ideals upon which the new state of Judaea had to develop. Do not the *Hassidim*, the *Essenes*, furnish us with a valuable religious and political lesson to-day?

---

citur large frequentantibus quos vita fessos ad mores eorum fortuna fluctibus agitat, ita per seculorum milia (incredibile dicta) gens aeterna est in qua nemo nascitur: tam fecunda illis aliorum vitae paenitentia est.

The Origin of the Idea of the Messiah

THERE IS A saying in the Talmud "either the sword or the book."[1] This could be interpreted that one who seeks to combat injustice and is a fighter for ideas and ideals cannot produce great scholarly works. On the other hand a true scholar cannot engage in public affairs, for his place is in an ivory tower. Dr. Abba Hillel Silver has shown that this saying refers only to the average person, not to a person of superior intellect and gifted with original ideas. Such a person combines valor in fighting for his ideas and ideals and those faculties required to produce scholarly works of permanent value.

Doctor Abba Hillel Silver, who is approaching his seventieth birthday, has devoted his life to the service of the Jews. He was the main champion in defending the Jewish rights in *Eretz Israel* (Palestine) before the United Nations. History will record the great indebtedness which the State of Israel owes to him.

While Dr. Silver was engaged in the struggle for the rights of the Jews he, at the same time, produced scholarly works in which he displayed sound learning and showed keen historical insight. He has a masterful style and exhibits great courage in expounding his views.

The first of Dr. Silver's scholarly works was *A History of Messianic Speculation in Israel,* in which he traces the messianic speculations among the Jews from the end of the first century to that of the seventeenth century. This book shows a vast knowledge of the sources and literature of this period as well as the author's acute mind in dealing with this complicated subject. Some of his other books are *Religion in a Changing World, Where Judaism Differed,* and the latest, *Moses and the Original Torah,* in which Moses is presented as a living reality, a challenge which very few scholars have been able to accomplish. All of Dr. Silver's works are of lasting value.

In the volume dedicated in honor of Doctor Abba Hillel Silver's seventieth birthday, it is fitting to have an article on the origin of the

[1] Abodah Zarah 17.

Reprinted from *In The Time of Harvest,* New York, 1963.

idea of a messiah, since the first fruit of Dr. Silver's thought was on the messianic expectation.

I

The messianic expectation among the Jews was both a blessing and a curse. The hope for a messiah gave them strength and courage during the centuries of the Middle Ages, dark ages, in their privations and degradations. They underwent great sufferings but they hoped that this would not be prolonged. They believed that the Promised Messiah would come soon, redeem them from their misery, and bring them back to their homeland, the Land of Israel, where the kingdom of Israel would be reestablished under the scepter of a scion of the family of David. Their motto was "to hope and to suffer." The expectation of a Messiah, indeed, made their survival possible. It kept alive the hope that at a not too distant time the Messiah would come. They besought God in their prayers to hasten the coming of the promised Messiah.

On the other hand, the longing and expectation of the Messiah brought misfortune and suffering to the Jews. Many opportunists and adventurers, observing the persecution and degradation of the Jews and being aware of their hopes for a Messiah, took advantage of the situation by proclaiming themselves either messiahs or prophets of messiahs. These messianic movements were catastrophic to the Jews. One of the latest was Sabbatai Zevi's messianic movement in the seventeenth century. Almost all the Jews of that period succumbed to it, rich and poor. Even the intelligent classes—bankers, doctors, and rabbis, believed Sabbatai Zevi to be the true messiah. The propaganda for this movement was led by one Nathan, who proclaimed himself to be a prophet. He was a demagogue, adventurer, and forger. He showed great ability, we may say genius, in the organization of the movement. Sabbatai Zevi's messianic movement was calamitous to the Jews as were all the others. In fact, the Jews have not yet fully recovered from the aftereffects of the collapse of the Sabbataian movement.

True, there were men who honestly believed themselves to be messiahs. They arrived at this belief because of their ascetic way of living and through their engrossment in the studies of mysticism and Kabbala. They fasted and prayed and thus their minds became deranged—they saw visions that God destined them to be messiahs to redeem His people and lead them to the Promised Land. This type of false messiah also brought great suffering to the Jews. The messianic expectation, as stated previously, was both a blessing and a curse. It

II

The word *Mashiaḥ*, messiah, *christos* in Greek, has the connotation of being anointed. We learn from the Bible that Aaron, the first priest; the Tabernacle and the vessels in it were anointed with oil.[2] The anointment signified that they were divine and belonged to Yahweh. The Prophet Samuel anointed Saul, the first king, and in doing so said, "Is it not that Yahweh hath anointed thee to be a *nagid* over His inheritance."[3] Saul thus became divine and thus became *Mashiaḥ* of Yahweh.[4] Later when the Prophet Samuel anointed David to become king, the same nomenclature, *Mashiaḥ* of Yahweh, was given to him.[5] God promised David that the kingship would be an inheritance of his family and would last forever.[6]

The term *Mashiaḥ* was not only applied to the Jewish kings and high priest but also to foreign kings. Cyrus, the king of Persia, was called the *Mashiaḥ* of Yahweh.[7] The word *Mashiaḥ* was used in the Bible as an adjective, not as a noun. The term "messiah" as a noun appears only in the late apocalyptic literature and in the New Testament. On the other hand, during the Second Commonwealth neither the kings nor the priests were anointed with oil. Therefore an explanation is necessary as to how the term *Mashiaḥ*, "messiah," appears later in the Hebrew literature as a person and aroused the idea in the minds of the people that God would send a *Mashiaḥ*.

The early Church Fathers, to prove that Jesus was the true messiah, *Christos*, maintained that there were references to Jesus as the messiah in the Pentateuch and in the other books of the Bible. To combat the views of the Church Fathers the rabbis interpreted the same verses as containing prophecies of the Jewish *Mashiaḥ*. To cite a few examples: The verse in Genesis 49:10 reads, "The scepter shall not depart from Judah, Nor the ruler's staff from between his feet, As long as men come to Shiloh; And unto him shall the opinions of the people be." Origen interpreted this passage as referring to the "Christ of God," Jesus.[8] The Targum, according to Jonathan, interprets it as referring to the Jewish *Mashiaḥ*. The verse in Isaiah 11:1 reads, "And there shall come forth a shoot of the stock of Jesse and

---

2 Exodus 40:9–15.
3 I. Samuel 10:1.
4 *Ibid.*, 26:11.
5 *Ibid.*, 16:13; II Samuel 19:22.
6 *Ibid.*, 7:8–16.

7 Cf. Isaiah 45:1. "Thus said Yahweh to his *mashiah* to Cyrus."
8 *Against Celsus*, B. 1, 53. "For He came for whom these things were reserved, the Christ of God."

a twig shall grow forth out of his roots." Justin Martyr interpreted this verse as a prophecy for the coming of Jesus.[9] The rabbis interpreted it as referring to the coming of the Jewish *Mashiaḥ*. In Chapter 53 of Isaiah the suffering of the servant of Yahweh is described. The Church Fathers interpreted it as referring to the Passion of Jesus. Barnabas, one of the Apostolic Fathers, interpreted this chapter as referring partly to Israel and partly to Jesus.[10] Origen, in his treatise Against Celsus, said that the Jews believed that the prophecies in this chapter referred to the whole people of Israel regarded as one individual. He denied this contention and held that the prophecies and suffering related in this chapter referred to the sufferings and the death of Jesus Christ.[11] The Targum, according to Jonathan, interpreted this chapter as referring to *Mashiah*, the Jewish Messiah.

The Church Fathers as well as the rabbis injected their ideas of the messiah into the Biblical passages. However, as we have previously stated, there is no indication anywhere in the Bible of the coming of a personal messiah, natural or supernatural. The word *Mashiab* appears in the Bible several times. It has the connotation of anointed and refers to the high priest [12] or to the king, of the family of David. In the Book of Psalms the word *Mashiaḥ* is found several times. It appears in Chapter 84:10, "Look upon the face of Thine *Mashiaḥ*." This seems to refer to the anointed high priest. In Chapter 89:39, "But Thou hast cast off and rejected, Thou hast been wroth with Thine *Mashiah*." This seems to refer to the family of David. Similarly in verse 52 the word *Mashiab* refers to the family of David. Again in Chapter 105:15, "Touch not My *Mashiab* and do My prophets no harm." This refers to the anointed priest. The psalmist beseeches the people not to harm the priest and the prophet. It seems that this verse is dislocated and should come at the end of the chapter. In the book of Lamentations 4:20, we read, "The breath of our nostrils, the anointed of the *Mashiaḥ* of Yahweh, was taken in their pits; of whom we said: 'Under his shadow we shall live among the nations.'" The words "*Mashiah* of Yahweh" refer to King Josiah. In the book of Daniel the word *mashiab* occurs twice. In one place the author designates *mashiab* as *nagid*, ruler.[13] This undoubtedly is a reference to the high priest who, during the Second Commonwealth, was the spiritual as well as the secular ruler of the people.[14] In the other place the

---

9 Cf. *The First Apology*, 32. "A flower has sprung from the root of Jesse this Christ."

10 *The Epistle of Barnabas*, 5. "For the scripture concerning him relates partly to Israel, partly to us, and it speaks thus: 'He was wounded for our iniquities. . ..'"

11 B. 1.55. ". . . My Jewish opponent replied that these predictions bore reference to the whole people. . . . And who is this person save Jesus

author wrote, "And after three score and two weeks shall the *mashiaḥ* be cut off." [15] Here the author refers to the elimination of the priesthood of the Zadokite family. The book of Daniel, as we have it today, was composed after Judah Makkabee purified the Temple.[16] These passages were cited to show that in the Bible the word *mashiaḥ* has the connotation of anointed and refers to the high priests or to the kings of the family of David. Modern theologians, Christian and Jewish, have injected the idea of the expectation of a personal, supernatural messiah into the Biblical passages. All histories of the Second Commonwealth are vitiated with the idea of messianic expectations.

True, the prophets do speak of a millennium—a period of happiness and prosperity when there will be no more wars between nations, and people will live in peace with one another. But this is not an expectation of a personal messiah. We must differentiate between a millennium and a messiah. The Prophet Isaiah, who according to tradition was of the family of David,[17] voiced a longing for a period when a descendant of Jesse, that is, of the family of David, imbued with the spirit of Yahweh, would rule. That day would be the time of the millennium, when "The wolf shall dwell with the lamb, and the leopard shall lie down with the kid; and the calf and the young lion and the fatling together; and a little child shall lead them" (11:6–10). There are messianic expectations in this passage. Isaiah hoped that a time would come when the Jews would prosper and live in peace as before at the time of King Solomon, a descendant of Jesse. Isaiah was a great patriot and nationalist. As a parallel we may cite the hope of a devotee of the Bourbon dynasty that the grandeur of France will be restored as in the time of Louis XIV.

That the Jews during the first part of the Second Commonwealth did not have the expectation of a personal messiah is evident from the literature produced during that period. The word *mashiaḥ* does not occur in the book of Ben Sirah nor does it occur in the other apocryphal literature—Tobit, Judith, The Wisdom of Solomon, I Maccabees. In the latter it is stated that when the high priesthood was given to Simon the Hasmonean, a clause was inserted, "Until a true prophet will arrive in Israel." [18] From this we may deduce that Jews believed prophecy would be restored but there is no indication that they expected a messiah. Even in II Maccabees, wherein physical resurrection [19] and the hope that all Jews would be gathered in Judaea

Christ, by whose stripes they who believe on Him are healed."
12 Cf. Leviticus 4:3.
13 9:25.
14 Cf. also I Chronicles 9:11.
15 9:26.
16 Cf. *I Maccabees*, ed. Dropsie, p. 32.
17 Talmud Megillah 10.
18 Chap. 14:41.
19 See Chap. 7.

are given prominence, the word *mashiaḥ* does not occur—the author believed this would be accomplished through the intervention of God.

The term "messiah" occurs only in the apocalyptic literature; once in the Testament of the Twelve Patriarchs,[20] twice in the Book of Enoch,[21] and twice in the last two chapters of the Psalms of Solomon.[22] The first two books mentioned as well as the last two chapters of the Psalms of Solomon (17th–18th) were written after the time of Herod. We may even assume that "Lord Messiah" in Chapter 17 is a later Christian interpolation.[23] The word "messiah" also occurs in IV Ezra [24] and the Apocalypsis of Baruch.[25] the messiah is portrayed in this literature as being a scion of David who will rule over Israel and free the Jews from their foreign yoke. The Jews believed that the messiah would be a supernatural being and yet a son of David. In the Book of Enoch the son of David is named "the anointed of God," [26] "the Elect One," [27] "the Son of Man," [28] "the Son of God." [29]

This, then, is our paradox. The idea of a supernatural messiah is mentioned only in the apocalyptic books which were considered "outside books," profane—there had been an edict against reading them [30] —nevertheless the idea of a messiah possessing supernatural power became deeply rooted among the Jews, almost an article of faith. What were the forces which gave rise to the idea of a supernatural messiah? We have pointed out that the term *mashiaḥ* had the connotation of high priest, or King David and his son Solomon, who had been anointed with oil. What were the causes which brought about this persistent idea of a supernatural messiah? Ideas which have a profound influence and are lasting are not created in a vacuum or by the whim of a person, however important he may be.

To comprehend the origin of the idea of a supernatural messiah we must briefly review the political and spiritual conditions which prevailed at the time of the Restoration. At the head of the exiles who returned from Babylonia were two men, who represented influential political factions with diametrical ideological views. One was Joshua, the grandson of Seraiah, the high priest who had been killed by the Babylonians, representing the high priesthood. The other leader was Zerubbabel, the grandson of King Jehoiachin, representing the Davidic royal family. A clash developed between these two factions

---

20 *The Testament of Reuben*, 6:8.
21 48:10; 52:4.
22 17:6; 18:8.
23 Cf. H. E. Ryle and M. R. James, *Psalms of the Pharisees commonly called the Psalms of Solomon*, ad loc.
24 Cf. 5:29; 12:32.
25 29:3; 39:7; 40:1; 70:9. Cf. also S. Zeitlin, "The Apocrypha," *Jewish Quarterly Review*, 1947, pp. 239–248.
26 48:10.
27 49:2; 51:1.

as to how the Judaean community should be organized. The adherents of Joshua maintained that the community should be ruled by the high priest, the vicar of God. In other words that it be established as a theocracy. The followers of Zerubbabel held that the new community should be ruled by a scion of the family of David. The ideology of Joshua triumphed. Zerubbabel disappeared from the political and religious arena. The Judaean community was established as a theocracy.[31]

Although the Judaean community took the form of a theocracy, the idea that a scion of the family of David should rule over Israel was not obliterated from the minds of the people. Many Judaeans still hoped that ultimately the Judaean State would be ruled by a descendant of the family of David. This hope was cherished especially among the lower classes. It was so deeply held among the Judaeans that the author of I Maccabees, in giving the Testament of Mattathias the Hasmonean, said that David "inherited the throne of an everlasting kingdom."[32] Similarly Ben Sirah, writing in his book about Phineas, the grandson of Aaron to whom God gave the high priesthood forever, said that God made a covenant with David, the son of Jesse, to whom he gave an everlasting kingdom.[33]

The followers of Joshua were of the high priestly family of the Zadokites, the Sadducees. They were strict adherents to the written law. Although they recognized the unwritten law then in vogue, they did not hold it binding. To them only the laws of the Torah were binding. Since they strictly followed the Torah they held that Yahweh is an ethnic God, the God of the descendants of Abraham, Isaac, and Jacob, with whom He made a covenant and whose children He brought out of Egypt. Hence they still called the Temple built after the Restoration the House of Yahweh, using the same nomenclature applied to the Temple built by King Solomon. The followers of Zerubbabel maintained that the unwritten laws are on a par with the written laws, the Torah. They held that anyone who transgressed the unwritten laws would be liable to punishment as if he had transgressed the written laws.[34]

The group that held that the oral law is on a par with the Pentateuchal laws; that the new community should be established under the leadership of a scion of the Davidic family and not under the

---

28 62:14; 69:26.
29 69:4; 105:2.
30 M. Sanhedrin 11:1.
31 Cf. S. Zeitlin, *The Rise and Fall of the Judaean State*, 1962, pp. 6–12.
32 I Maccabees 2:57.
33 47:11.
34 Cf. S. Zeitlin, "The Pharisees," *Jewish Quarterly Review*, October, 1961, pp. 97–129; idem., op. cit.

leadership of a high priest; and that Yahweh is the God of all peoples and not an ethnic god was considered heretical by the Zadokites, the high priestly family. This group was called *Perushim*, Pharisees, separatists, by the Zadokites who maintained that they separated themselves from the Judaeans, the people of Yahweh. Down to the successful revolt under the leadership of the Hasmoneans the Pharisees had no influence over the affairs of the Judaean community but they had the confidence of the rank and file of the people.[35]

The Pharisees endeavored to solve the vexing problems of individuals—why did the righteous suffer and the wicked prosper? They taught the people that there was a future world where there would be reward and punishment—the reward for good deeds in this world and punishment for the wicked. They also impressed upon the minds of the people that the soul is immortal. The physical body dies but the soul lives forever. These theological views gave meaning and essence to the lives of the people, for they now felt that their good deeds in life were not in vain and were certain that they would be rewarded for them. That life in this world is passing while the future world is eternal became an article of faith. During the entire period of the Second Commonwealth the Pharisees stressed the views that one day leadership over the Jews would be vested in a scion of the family of David, and that there would be reward for the righteous and punishment for the wicked in the future world.

When the Hasmoneans succeeded in throwing off the yoke of the Syrians and eliminated the high priesthood of the Zadokite family, the influence of the Pharisees ascended. Daniel's words that the *mashiah* will be cut off, that is,[36] eliminated, refers to the abolishment of the high priesthood of the Zadokite family.

When the Judaean Commonwealth was established in 141 B.C.E. the Great Synagogue confirmed the high priesthood of Simon, the Hasmonean, and proclaimed him the ruler of the State. In this declaration there was a clause "until a true prophet will arise in Israel." The kingship was not given to him. With this act theocracy was abolished. But the view that Judaea should be a theocratic state was not entirely obliterated from the minds of all the people. Some of them longed for its re-creation. When the Roman general, Pompey, was in Syria, a deputation of Judaeans came to him asking that the kingship of Judaea be abolished and that the affairs of the community be placed in the hands of the high priest as in the olden days when the high priest was ecclesiastic as well as civil ruler over the people.[37]

35 Ibid.
36 9:26.
37 *Antiquities* 14. 3.2 (41).
38 *Ibid.*, 17. 11:2. (313–314).

In other words, they wanted Judaea to be a theocratic state. Similarly, after the death of Herod a deputation of Judaeans went to Augustus Caesar with the same petition.[38]

When Jannaeus Alexander assumed the kingship over Judaea the Pharisees bitterly opposed him. This brought about a civil war which ended tragically for the state. The Pharisees recognized that their struggle first with Jannaeus Alexander and later their participation in the civil war between John Hyrcanus and Aristobolus was catastrophic, so they abandoned political activity, devoting themselves to religion. They became quietists and legalists. However, there were groups among the Pharisees who continued to fight for the freedom of Judaea. Josephus tells that when Judaea was made a province of Rome in the year 6 C.E., Quirinus was sent by Rome to take a census of Judaea with a view to levying taxes upon the people. This aroused great opposition among the Judaeans. A man named Judas of Galilee organized a new group whose doctrines Josephus called the Fourth Philosophy.[39] This group was so named because Josephus deals with the Essenes, Sadducees, and Pharisees as philosophies, and names this group as the Fourth Philosophy. Josephus wrote about this group, "These men agree in all other things with the Pharasaic notions; but they have an inviolable attachment to liberty and say that God is to be their only ruler and Lord." He further said that Judas "incited his countrymen to revolt, upbraiding them as cowards for consenting to pay tribute to the Romans and tolerating mortal masters after having God for their Lord." [40] The followers of Judas from time to time resorted to seditious acts against the Romans. They also acted vigorously against their countrymen who submitted to the Romans. They considered as traitors such Judaeans who betrayed the freedom of their people. They held that terror must oppose terror.

Not being able to engage in open battle against the Romans and their followers, the Judaeans, the members of the Fourth Philosophy, resorted to the use of the *sica* (a short dagger) to assassinate those who favored peace with the enemy. From their use of the *sica* they received the name Sicarii [41] (not to be confused with the Zealots). Josephus referred to the Sicarii as robbers, brigands. He maintained that they were responsible for the destruction of the Judaean state and the burning of the Temple.

Of course the verdict of Josephus is a gross distortion of realities, for he himself said that hunger for freedom and liberty had motivated their actions. A speech which Josephus put in the mouth of Eleazar, son of Jairus, the last leader of the Fourth Philosophy before the fall

39 *Ibid.*, 18. 1.1(1–5); (23–25); *Jewish War* 2: 8.1 (107–108).
40 *Antiquities* 18. 1.6 (23–24).
41 *Ibid.*, 20. 8.10 (185–186).

of Masada, could not have come from the mouth of an ordinary robber: "Long since, my brave men, we determined neither to serve the Romans nor any other save God, for He alone is man's true and righteous Lord." He concluded his speech with the following, "For it is death which gives liberty to the soul and permits it to depart to its own pure abode, there to be free from all calamity; but so long as it is imprisoned in a mortal body tainted with all its miseries, it is in sober truth dead, for association with what is mortal ill befits that which is divine." [42] An ordinary brigand could not have uttered such noble sentiments, as Josephus would have us believe.

Josephus mentioned another group which he called wicked as were the members of the Fourth Philosophy. He gave no name to this group. In writing about these two groups he said that although their hands were purer than those of the Sicarii their intentions were more impious. "Deceivers and imposters under pretense of divine inspiration, fostering revolutionary changes," he said of them. "They persuaded the people to act like madmen, and led them out into the desert under the belief that God would there give them tokens of deliverance." [43]

This group was the Apocalyptists. Its members believed in the revelation of God and, therefore, the appelation of Apocalyptists is appropriate. The Apocalyptists as well as the members of the Fourth Philosophy, the Sicarii, were offshoots of the Pharisees. These two groups had the same objectives: to free the Judaeans from the yoke of the Romans as well as from the Herodean dynasty. They both maintained that God is the only ruler over man, but they differed in their methods of advocating this view. The members of the Fourth Philosophy held that terror must oppose terror. To free the Judaeans and destroy their adversaries, force and violence, even murder, were justified. The Apocalyptists were opposed to acts of terror and the use of violence. They preached love, their watchword was, "If one seeketh to do evil unto you, do well unto him and pray for him." [44] The Apocalyptists were God-fearing people who believed that God had not forsaken the Judaeans but only chastised them. They believed that He would reestablish Israel under His anointed *Mashiah*, that a scion of the family of David would rule in Zion and destroy the persecutors of His people as well as all the sinners. They considered *Mashiah* the anointed of Yahweh, not an ordinary human being, but

---

[42] *Jewish War* 7. 8.6–7 (321–380).
[43] *Ibid.*, 2. 13. 4 (259).
[44] See *The Testament of the Twelve Patriarchs;* The Testament of

Joseph 18.2.
[45] Cf. *Enoch* 51:2. "For in those days, the elect one shall arise and shall choose the righteous and the holy

THE ORIGIN OF THE IDEA OF THE MESSIAH

one possessed of supernatural powers.[45] The Apocalyptists, aware of the might of Rome, knew that the Judaeans could not free themselves from the Romans by force. They believed that God would perform miracles to free His people. They introduced the idea of a supernatural *mashiah*, who would reveal himself in due time, vanquish the Romans, free Israel, and sit on the throne of his father David. Then the millennium would come, looked forward to by the prophets of old.

The Apocalyptists were a mystic religious group. Mysticism is belief in truths which are beyond comprehension and understanding. People whose minds are deranged by physical or mental suffering are led to join such groups, and in doing so they become fanatics. On the other hand, opportunists and adventurers join such groups out of selfish motives. Josephus refers to one, Theodas, who "persuaded a great part of the people to take their effects with them and follow him to the river Jordan, for he told them he was a prophet, and that he would by his command divide the river, and afford them an easy passage over it. Many were deluded by his words." [46] He also wrote about a man from Egypt who claimed to be a prophet. He "advised the people to come along with him to the Mount of Olives where he will perform miracles."[47] The Apocalyptists, however, in general were sincere, pious people. They believed that their revelations were given by angels and through supernatural powers, that the kingdom of God was approaching, and that the *Mashiah* of Yahweh would reveal himself in all his glory.

The normative Pharisees opposed both the Sicarii and the Apocalyptists. They may not have shared the view of Josephus that the Apocalyptists were imposters, charlatans, but they maintained that the Apocalyptists were deceiving themselves; that their views were in opposition to the true views of the Pharisees; and hence that the Judaeans would be led astray. The Pharisees believed that God would some day free His people from the Roman yoke, that the kingship would again be in the hands of *Mashiah* of Yahweh, a scion of David, but that the king would not possess supernatural power and would not perform miracles. In this view they greatly differed from the Apocalyptists.

The terms "*Mashiah* of Yahweh" and "son of David" are synonymous and interchangeable. The term *mashiah* in the Bible refers to David and his descendants. The author of Lamentations, deploring

---

from among them . . . and the elect one shall in those days sit on My Throne." See *Psalms of Solomon* 17:23, "Raise up unto them their king, the son of David."
46 See *Antiquities* 20. 5. 1 (97–99).
47 *Jewish War* 2. 13. 5 (261–262); Cf. also *Acts* 21:38.

the untimely death of King Josiah, calls him the *Mashiah* of Yahweh.[48] The Talmud says that Rabbi Akiba called Bar Kokba "King *Mashiah*." One of Rabbi Akiba's colleagues said to him, "Grass will grow through thy jaws, and the time of the son of David has not come."[49] The term "son of David" and "king *mashiah*" are synonymous.

The gospels according to both Matthew[50] and Luke[51] trace the genealogy of Jesus to David, while Mark, who does not give the genealogy, states that Jesus is the son of David.[52] John, who stresses the view that Jesus was the son of God, nevertheless wrote, "But some said, Shall Christ come out of Galilee? Hath not the scripture said, that Christ cometh out of the seed of David and out of the town of Bethlehem where David was?"[53] According to the gospels Jesus was greeted with the words, "Blessed be the kingdom of our father David," "Hosanna to the son of David."[54] On the cross on which Jesus was crucified the words "Jesus of Nazareth, king of the Judaeans" were inscribed in Hebrew, Greek, and Latin.[55] *Mashiah*, messiah, Christ were synonymous in their minds with "son of David" and "king of the Judaeans."

After the burning of the Temple, and particularly after the tragic collapse of the Bar Kokba revolt, the belief in a supernatural messiah who would rebuild the Temple and restore the Jewish state gained sway over the minds of the people. This was their only hope. Physical revolts ended in catastrophe and they looked for their salvation, redemption, to a supernatural *mashiah*. Not all the sages,[56] however, shared this view and it never became an article of faith. Rabbi Judah the Prince, in codifying the Mishnah, does not refer to the belief in a *mashiah*. Reference is once made to the days of *mashiah*.[57] In the Mishnah it is stated that those who do not believe in Revelation and resurrection will not have a share in the world to come.[58] Denial of the coming of *mashiah* is not included in this category. Many Tannaim and Amoraim, however, believed in the coming of the *Mashiah*

---

48 4:20.
49 *Yerushalmi. Taanit* 4; *Midrash R. Lamentations* 2.
50 1:1–16:
51 3:24–31.
52 12:35.
53 7:41–42.
54 *Mark* 11:10; *Matt.* 21:9.
55 *Iesus Nazarenus, Rex Iudaeorum*.
56 Cf. also Maimonides *Mishne Torah*, Hilkot Melachim. Maimonides held that Messiah would be a mortal, a king, a descendant of the house of David, a man wiser than Solomon, and a prophet next in greatness to Moses.
57 *Mishnah Berachot* 1.6. The phrase, "the footsteps of the *mashiah*" occurs in the *Mishnah Sotah* 9. 15. This part, however, is a later addition; the name of Rabbi Phineas ben Jair is mentioned in this Mishnah which indicates that it was interpolated after the time of Rabbi Judah.
58 *Mishnah Sanhedrin* 10. 1.

THE ORIGIN OF THE IDEA OF THE MESSIAH

and even indulged in predictions as to the time when he will reveal himself.

Belief in a supernatural *mashiah,* a scion of the family of David, was first brought forth by the Apocalyptic Pharisaic group. It did not greatly influence the Judaeans during the Second Commonwealth, but after the destruction of the Second Temple, and particularly after the revolt of Bar Kokba, it gained stimulus and shaped the life of the Jewish people throughout the centuries. The idea of a supernatural *mashiah* became the cornerstone of Jewish survival, as is admirably portrayed by Doctor Abba Hillel Silver in his book *A History of Messianic Speculation in Israel.*

PROSELYTES AND PROSELYTISM DURING THE SECOND COMMONWEALTH AND THE EARLY TANNAITIC PERIOD

IN THE RABBINIC LITERATURE the term for a convert to Judaism, a proselyte is *ger*. It has another connotation in the Pentateuch, sojourner, one who came to live in the country for a while. The Pentateuch refers to the children of Israel as *gerim* who came from the land of Canaan to live in Egypt.[1] The Pentateuch as well as the early prophets did not recognize conversion. Yahweh was held to be an ethnic God, the God of the children of Abraham, Isaac and Jacob with whom He made a covenant. Yahweh was the God of the descendants of those whom He had brought out of Egypt, the land of slavery. Hence those who were not descendants of Abraham, Isaac and Jacob and whose ancestors were not slaves in Egypt could not worship Yahweh.

During the time of the Second Commonwealth the Judaean religion went through a revolutionary transformation due to the influence of the prophets and the teaching of the Pharisees. Yahweh was no longer believed to be an ethnic god, the God of the Judaeans alone; now He was held to be the God of the entire universe. The four letters, the Tetragrammaton, were now pronounced *Adonai*, the Lord of the universe. Anyone could accept Him. Hence conversion not only became possible but desirable.[2]

The author of the book of Ruth relates that Ruth, the Moabite, who after her husband's death returned to Judaea said to her mother-in-law, Naomi, "Thy people shall be my people, and thy

---

[1] Ex. 23: 8. כי גרים הייתם בארץ מצרים.

[2] Cf. S. Zeitlin, *The Rise and Fall of the Judaean State*, I. Idem. "The Pharisees," *JQR* (Oct. 1961), 29–33; 269–281.

Reprinted from the *Harry Austryn Wolfson Jubilee Volume*, New York, 1965.

God my God."³ These words could not have been uttered when conversion was unheard of. The author wanted to stress the desirability of conversion. According to the Pentateuch "an Ammonite or a Moabite shall not enter into the assembly of Yahweh; even to the tenth generation shall none of them enter into the assembly of Yahweh forever."⁴ The author of the book of Ruth made Ruth say, "Thy people shall be my people, and thy God my God" and she later married Boaz, a leading man of Judah. King David, the anointed of God, was a descendant of this union. It is true that later the Sages, in order to reconcile the contradictory and opposing view between the book of Ruth and the book of Deuteronomy, said that the Pentateuchal prohibition regarding the Moabites referred only to the male but not to the female.⁵ At a still later period the Sages advanced the view that the Pentateuchal prohibition regarding the Moabites did not refer to the period after the time of Sennacherib, the king of Assyria.⁶

The author of the book of Judith relates that one of the generals of Holofernes named Achior, an Ammonite, after the victory of the Israelites over the hosts of Holofernes, "joined unto the house of Israel."⁷ The book of Judith is not based on historical facts. It is fictitious. It may be that some current event prompted the author to write the book. It is primarily a religious book, emphasizing that righteousness will ultimately triumph, and that the Jews will be victorious over their enemies as long as they observe the laws of God. He also brought out the idea of proselytism, purposely making the general of the Holofernes army an Ammonite who spoke in favor of the Jews. He said to Holofernes

---

³ 1:16. עמך עמי ואלהיך אלהי.

⁴ 23:4. לא יבא עמוני ומואבי בקהל ה' גם דור עשירי לא יבא להם בקהל.

⁵ *M. Yeb.* 8, 3. עמוני ומואבי אסורים ואיסורן איסור עולם אבל נקבותיהם מותרות מיד.

⁶ *Yad.* 4. בו ביום בא יהודה גר עמוני לפניהם בבהמ"ד אמר להם מה אני לבא בקהל א"ל ר' גמליאל אסור אתה א"ל ר' יהושע מותר אתה... כבר עלה סנחריב מלך אשור ובלבל את כל האומות... והתירוהו לבא בקהל. *Tosefta ibid.*, 2, 17.

⁷ 14:10.

that as long as the Jews will observe the laws of God none can vanquish them. Ultimately this Ammonite general became a convert to the Jewish religion. The author emphasizes that Ammonites, like any other foreigners, are welcome to become converts to Judaism and a member of the Judaeans.

In the books of Ruth and Judith conversion to Judaism is clearly stated. The former, a canonical book, states that Ruth, a Moabite, became converted to Judaism. The latter, an apocryphal book, states that an Ammonite was converted to Judaism. These two conversions are in direct contradiction to the laws given in Deuteronomy against the Moabites and the Ammonites. The book of Ruth was written in Judaea and the book of Judith was written in the Diaspora. Both books were written in the period when the Judaeans were influenced by the Pharisees who held that Yahweh is the God of the universe, the father and the ruler of all mankind.

In the book of Esther it is related that after Haman was hanged the Jews "had gladness and joy. And many from among the peoples of the land מתיהדים; for the fear of the Judaeans was fallen upon them."[8] The word מתיהדים is rendered by the JPS translation "became Jews." The same rendering is given in the authorized version. Rashi, in his commentary on the word, has מתגיירים "became converts." The translation of the word, מתיהדים to mean that the people of the land became Jews, is faulty. At the time of the composition of the book of Esther there could not have been conversions to Judaism. That Yahweh was the God of the Universe was not yet the prevailing belief of the Judaeans. The word מתיהדים is to be rendered "they pretended to be Judaeans," i.e., the fear of the Judaeans which fell upon the people of the land made them pretend to be Judaeans. A similar word is given in the story that when King Jeroboam sent his wife to the prophet Ahijah to inquire about the illness of his son she disguised herself in order that the prophet should not recognize her.[9] The expression

---

[8] ורבים מעמי הארץ מתיהדים כי נפל פחד היהודים עליהם.
[9] I Kings 14:5–6. והיא מתנכרה... למה זה את מתנכרה.

given is מתנכרה "she will feign herself to be another woman." Similarly in the book of Samuel it is related that when Ammon fell in love with Tamar, his sister, and wanted her to come to him, his friend Jonadab advised him to התחל "to pretend to be sick."[10] Thus it is clear that the words מתנכרה, מתיהדים have the connotation "to pretend to be what one is not."

When conversion to Judaism was made possible, the term for it was מומר changer, i.e., one who changed his god for the God of Israel.[11] Conversion became prevalent at the time when theocracy was abolished and nomocracy, i.e. the rule of the law was established. Thus a convert to Judaism was called a changer to the law. One who left the Judaeans and adopted another religion was termed a changer of the law, i.e. he changed his religion.[12] Josephus wrote that when Epiphanes, the son of King Antiochus, refused to marry Drusilla, the sister of King Agrippa, the reason was that he did not want to change to the Judaean law,[13] he did not want to be a changer. On the other hand one who left Judaism was also called a changer. The author of III Maccabees said that Dositheus was born a Jew but became a Hellene, using the phrase "he changed his laws."[14] Similarly the author of II Maccabees used the expression "change" in the case when a Jew changed his laws for the customs of the pagans.[15] In the Tannaitic literature a person who abandoned Judaism for another religion was termed מומר, a changer.

In the later Tannaitic literature a convert to Judaism was called a *ger*. The word *ger* occurs frequently in the Pentateuch where it has the connotation of a stranger, a newcomer to the land of Israel. The same term was applied to one who became a convert to Judaism, a newcomer to the Jewish people. In the Septuagint the word *ger* is translated *proselytos* with the same connotation, a newcomer to a foreign land. When the word *ger* was applied

---

[10] II Sam. 13:5–6. שכב על משכבך והתחל... וישכב אמנון ויתחל.
[11] Jer. 2:11. ההימיר גוי אלהים... ועמי המיר.
[12] *Pes.* 96. המרת הדת. *Suk.* 56. שהמירה דתה.
[13] *Ant.* 20.7.1 (139). ...'Ιουδαίων ἔθη μεταλαβεῖν [μεταβαλεῖν].
[14] 1:3. μεταβαλὼν τὰ νόμιμα. [15] 6:24.

to a convert to Judaism the same Greek word *proselytos* also came to mean a convert to Judaism. However one who left Judaism was still named מומר, changer.

Neither the term *ger*, in the sense of a convert to Judaism, nor the term *proselytos*, with the same connotation, occurs in the early literature of the Second Commonwealth. It is true that in a story related in the Talmud about a foreigner who came to Hillel to be converted to Judaism the word *ger* is used.[16] We have to bear in mind, however, that the story does not come from Hillel but was related at a later period. The word *proselytos*, in the sense of a convert to Judaism, does not occur in the apocryphal literature nor in the writings of Josephus. Philo employs *proselytos* three times in his writings. In two instances he copies the term from the Septuagint which renders the word *ger* by *proselytos*, a sojourner.[17] In the third instance he may have used *proselytos* in the meaning of convert to Judaism.[18]

Originally a *proselyte* did not have to undergo particular rites. That he had rejected idols and accepted the God of Israel as the God of the universe was sufficient. In the above mentioned story about the foreigner who came to Hillel to be converted, Hillel said to him, "What is hurtful to you do not do to your fellow man, the rest is commentary; go and study." Hillel implied that when the foreigner accepted the God of Israel as the God of the universe he had already embraced the main principle of Judaism. The next principle was the relationship between man and man, and this he should study. To use a later rabbinic expression, — one who denies idol worship recognizes the entire Torah.[19] In the story related in *Antiquities* about the conversion of Izates, the son of Queen Helena, a Jew named Ananias persuaded him to

---

[16] *Shab.* 31. מעשה בנכרי [גוי] שבא לפני שמאי אמר ליה גיירני ע״מ שתלמדני כל התורה כולה כשאני עומד על רגל אחת דחפו באמת הבנין שבידו בא לפני הלל גייריה אמר ליה דעלך סני לחברך לא תעביד זו היא כל התורה כולה ואידך פירושה היא זיל גמיר.

[17] *On Dreams,* 2.272; *Special Laws,* 1.308.   [18] *Ibid.* 51.

[19] *Sifre* (I, sect. 111, ed. Horovitz, p. 116, bot.) כל הכופר בע״ז מודה בכל התורה. Cf. *Meg,* 13 כל הכופר בע״ז נקרא יהודי.

embrace Judaism and did not exact any rites, even that of circumcision. He told Izates that "worship of God was of a superior nature to circumcision."[20] However, when another Jew, Eleazar whom Josephus portrayed as very learned in the law, entered the palace and found Izates reading the Laws of Moses, he reproached him for not being circumcised saying, "You do not consider, O king! that you unjustly break the principle of those laws, and are injurious to God Himself; for you ought not only to read them but chiefly to practice what they enjoin you. How long will you continue to be uncircumcised?"[21]

Circumcision actually became a *sine qua non* for any man who wanted to embrace Judaism. To again quote Josephus who stated that Agrippa gave his sister Drusilla in marriage to Azizus, King of Emesa, only upon the condition that he be circumcised. Circumcision became imperative for Jews as Tacitus said: the Jews adopted circumcision, "to distinguish themselves from other peoples by this difference."[22] It was indeed a mark of distinction. By remaining uncircumcised a person transgressed the Pentateuchal law all the time. Again, when Antiochus Epiphanes forced Hellenization upon the Judaeans he prohibited circumcision and ordered anyone discovered to be circumcised to be put to death. Thus the Jews throughout the ages emphasized the importance of circumcision. However, halakicly, legal, a Jew who was uncircumcised was considered a Jew but regarded as מומר לדבר אחד.[23] According to the Halakah, if it happened in a family that children died resulting from circumcision a new born child was exempted from circumcision.[24]

According to Rabbi Joshua if a pagan became a convert to Judaism and underwent ritual immersion but was not circumcised he was considered a proselyte, a Jew.[25] According to the school of Hillel circumcision *ex opere operato* is valid.[26] If a pagan was

---

[20] 20. 2. 4 (45–46). [21] Ibid. (47–48).
[22] *Hist.* 5.5. *Circumcidere genitalia instituerunt ut diversitate noscantur.*
[23] Cf. *Hulin* 4. [24] *Ibid.*
[25] *Yeb.* 46. טבל ולא מל ר' יהושע אומר הרי זה גר.
[26] *Tos. Shab* 15, 9. גר שנתגייר כשהוא מהול... אין צריך (להטיף ממנו דם).

circumcised before he was converted to Judaism he did not have to undergo another ritual. According to Rabbi Eliezer if a pagan who wanted to embrace Judaism was circumcised but had not undergone the ritual of immersion he was considered a proselyte, a Jew.[27] Immersion for proselytes was not instituted as a ritual *per se* for converts to Judaism. It became a requirement for proselytes for another reason. At the Conclave in the year 65 C.E. it was decreed that all gentiles are *ipso facto* unclean, in the category of a *zab*.[28] In consequence of this decree any gentile who wished to enter the Jewish community had to undergo the ritual of immersion. This was the underlying reason for the institution of baptism for proselytes and was introduced after the year 65 C.E. Rabbi Joshua laid stress on baptism while Rabbi Eliezer laid stress on circumcision.[29]

Prior to the year 65 C.E. pagans were not deemed susceptible to the laws of impurity and were never subject to the laws of impurity and purity. Many statements to this effect are found in the Tannaitic literature that pagans are not susceptible to the laws of impurity ...הגוי והבהמה,[30] and also that pagans affected by leprosy do not impart impurity.[31] Therefore a pagan, not being considered unclean, was not obliged to be baptised upon becoming a proselyte. Hence baptism with regard to proselytes is not mentioned in the aprocryphal literature nor in the writings of Josephus when reference is made to converts to Judaism. According to the Tannaitic literature a proselyte, besides undergoing the rituals of circumcision and baptism, had to offer a

---

[27] *Yeb.* 46. גר שמל ולא טבל רבי אליעזר אומר הרי זה גר תני גר שמל ולא טבל
טבל ולא מל הכל הולך אחר המילה דברי רבי אליעזר רבי יהושע אומר (אף) הטבי־
לה מעכבת. *Yer. Kid.* 3, 12.

[28] *Tos. Zabim* 2, 1. כובין לכל דבריהם. Cf. also, S. Zeitlin, "L'origine de L'institution du Baptême pour les Prosélytes," *REJ* (1934).

[29] Cf. S. Zeitlin, "The Halaka in the Gospels and its Relation to the Jewish Law at the Time of Jesus," *HUCA*, 1.

[30] *Tos. Neg.* 7. 10. Cf. also *Tos. Oh.* 1. 4. שמת [גוי] נכרי ...הגוי והבהמה;
טהור מלטמא במשא שאין טומאתו אלא מדברי סופרים. *Ibid. Nida* 9, 14. Cf. also ואין הגוים מיטמים בזיבה, ed. Weiss, 74d), ריש פ׳ זבים) *Sifra*.

[31] *Tosefta, Neg.* 2, 13. ...בהרת בגוי.

sacrifice.³² This sacrifice consisted of two doves. Such a sacrifice was brought by a *zab*.³³ Hence the sacrifice which had to be brought by a proselyte was not because he embraced Judaism but because he was no longer in the status of a *zab*. The rituals of baptism and sacrifice were introduced for proselytes because they were no longer considered *zabim* and had the right to enter the Jewish community. The rituals of baptism and sacrifice for proselytes were introduced after the year 65 C.E.

Jews were zealous to make proselytes and regarded them as superior to natives. Horace also refers to the eagerness of the Jews to proselytize.³⁴ The Gospel of Matthew relates that Jesus accused the Pharisees of proselytizing, "Woe unto you scribes and Pharisees, hypocrites, for you compass sea and land to make one proselyte."³⁵ Justin Martyr also accused the Jews of sending men to preach against Christianity, "You select and send out of Jerusalem chosen men throughout the land to tell that the godless heresy of the Christians had sprung up."³⁶ The historian Dio, in writing about the Jews, stated, "The country (Palestine) has been named Judaea, and the people themselves Judaeans. I do not know how this title came to be given them, but it applies also to all the rest of mankind, although of alien nationalities, who affect their laws. This class exists even among the Romans, and though often repressed has increased to a very great extent and has won its way to the right of freedom in its observances."³⁷ From this account it is clearly indicated that there were many proselytes even among the Romans.

Many in the pagan world followed the Jewish customs and practices. Was this due to the zeal of the Jews to spread their religion or to the decline of Hellenism and the yearning of the pagans for mysteries? The spread of the observance of Jewish customs, particularly of the Sabbath and the kindling of the lights, was probably the result of all of these causes. Josephus, in *Contra*

---

³² *Ker.* 9.   ³³ Lev. 15:14; cf. also *ibid.* 12:6–8.
³⁴ *Sat.* 1.4.143. *ac veluti te Iudaei cogemus in hanc concedere turbam.*
³⁵ 23:15.
³⁶ *Dialogue With Tryhpo*, 108.   ³⁷ *Roman History*, 37.

[9] PROSELYTES AND PROSELYTISM 879

Apionem, wrote "The masses have long since shown a zeal to adopt our religious observances, and there is not one city, Hellene or barbarian, nor a single nation to which our custom of abstaining from work on the seventh day has not spread, and where the fasts and the lighting of the lamps and many of our prohibitions in the matter of food are not observed."[38]

The Roman writers also showed their acquaintance with the Sabbath and other Jewish customs. Horace makes reference to the Sabbath, "Today is the thirtieth Sabbath," he said, "Would you affront the circumcised Jews?"[39] Ovid also refers to the Sabbath, "On that day," he writes, "less fit for business, whereon returns the seventh day feast that the Syrians of Palestine observe."[40] In another place he wrote, "Nor let Adonis bewailed of Venus escape you, nor the seventh day that the Syrian Jew holds sacred."[41] Juvenal in his satires makes reference to Sabbath observance and other Jewish customs, "Some who have had a father who reveres the Sabbath, worship nothing but the clouds, and the divinity of the heavens, and see no difference between eating swine's flesh from which their father abstained and that of man; and in time they take to circumcision. Having been wont to flout the laws of Rome, they learn and practice and revere the Jewish law, and all that Moses committed to his secret tome, forbidding to point out the way to any not worshipping the same rites and conducting none but the circumcised to the desired fountain. For all which the father was to blame, who gave up every seventh day to idleness, keeping it apart from all the concerns of life."[42] Some Roman writers misunderstood the significance

---

[38] 2. 282.

[39] *Sat.* 9. 69. *hodie tricesima sabbata; vin tu curtis Iudaeis oppedere?*

[40] *Artis Amatoriae,* 1.415. *Quaque die redeunt rebus minus apta gerendis, Culta Palestino septima festa Syro.*

[41] *Ibid.,* 75. *Nec te praetereat Veneri ploratus Adonis, Cultaque Iudaeo septima sacra Syro.*

[42] *Quidam sortiti metuentem sabbata patrem nil praeter nubes et caeli numen adorant, nec distare putant humana carne suillam, qua pater abstinuit mox et praeputia ponunt; Romanas autem soliti contemnere leges Iudaicum ediscunt*

415

of the Sabbath and attributed the ceasing of work on that day to laziness of the Jews.[43]

The observance of Jewish customs became widespread among the pagans. Many of them, although not converted to Judaism, were God fearing יראי ה׳, יראי שמים, and worshipped the God of Israel, without becoming *gerim*. Poppea, the mistress wife of Nero Caesar, was attracted to Jewish customs. Josephus called her a religious woman.[44] From the writings of Josephus we learn that many in the pagan world were attracted to Judaism and revered the God of Israel. In his book, *Antiquities*, describing the wealth of the Temple, he stated, "For all the Judaeans throughout the habitable world, and those who revered God, even those from Asia and Europe, had been contributing to it for a very long time."[45] During the time of the revolt against the Romans in Syria the pagan population arose against the Judaeans who lived there and massacred them. Josephus wrote that although the Judaeans were annihilated, the Syrians were still in a state of fear, "For although believing that they had rid themselves of the Judaeans, still each city had its Judaizers who aroused suspicion; and, while they shrunk from killing off hand this equivocal element in their midst, they feared these neutrals as much as those who were of foreign religion."[46] In describing the massacre of the Judaeans in Damascus Josephus wrote that the pagans feared their own wives, "who with few exceptions adhered to the Judaean customs, and so their efforts were mainly directed to keeping the secret from them."[47] In describing the status of the Jews in Antioch and the wealth of the synagogue Josephus wrote, "They were constantly attracting to their religious ceremonies multitudes of the

---

et servant ac metuunt ius, tradidit arcano quodcumque volumine Moyses non monstrare vias eadem nisi sacra colenti, quaesitum ad fontem solos seducere verpos sed pater in causa, cui septima quaeque fuit lux ignava et partem vitae non attigit ullam. Sat. 14, 96–106.

[43] Cf. also Tacitus, *Hist*. 5.4. *dein blandiente inertia septimum quoque annum ignaviae datum.*

[44] θεοσεβής. *Ant*. 20. 8. 11 (195).

[45] σεβομένων τὸν θεόν. *Ibid*. 14. 7. 1 (110).

[46] *Wars* 2. 18. 2 (463).   [47] *Ibid*. (559–560).

Hellenes, and these they had in some measure incorporated with themselves."[48] Not all of those who revered the God of Israel and accepted Jewish customs became proselytes. Josephus, in his book *Contra Apionem*, made the following statement, "Many of them have agreed to adopt our laws; of whom some have remained faithful, while others, lacking the necessary endurance, have again seceded."[49]

A *ger* was one who accepted Judaism without qualification. If a pagan wanted to become a proselyte but stipulated that he would not adhere to one of the precepts he was not accepted as a *ger*. There were *no* semi-proselytes. A *ger torshab* was a foreigner who lived in the land of Judaea. He had to observe the Noachite laws, i.e., *jus gentium*.[50] The fearers of *Adonai* were pagans who, although they worshipped their own gods, yet feared and revered the God of Israel. The psalmists already made reference to the fearers of *Adonai*.[51] From the book of Kings we learn that the Kutim, who were transported from their land by the Assyrians to the land of Israel, worshipped their gods yet feared *Adonai*.[52] The term "fearers of Heaven", which was originally applied to the pagans who feared and revered the God of Israel, was later applied to pious Jews.

A proselyte was considered on a par with a native Jew.[53] However those who adhered to the view, as did the Sadducees, that Yahweh is an ethnic God, the God of the descendants of Abraham, Isaac and Jacob with whom He had made a covenant and whom He brought out of the land of Egypt, regarded the proselyte as not the equal of a native Jew. Although this view was contrary to the philosophy of the Sages of the Second Commonwealth and the Tannaitic period and rejected by them it did influence later Judaism.

---

[48] *Ibid.* 7. 3. 3 (45). [49] 2. 10 (123).
[50] Cf. *Ab. Zarah* 64. איזהו גר תושב כל שקיבל בפני ג׳ חברים שלא לעבוד עבודה זרה דברי רבי מאיר וחכמים אומרים כל שקיבל עליו שבע מצות שקבלו עליהם בני נח
[51] Ps. 115:13. Cf. also S. Zeitlin, "The Hallel," *JQR* (July, 1962), 24–25.
[52] II Kings 17:33.
[53] Cf. *Mekilta, Mishp.* 18. כמה חביבים הגרים... ונקראו הגרים אוהבים.

THE OFFSPRING OF INTERMARRIAGE

A Mishne in Kiddushin states that the offspring of a union between a Jew and a non Jewess is like the mother, not a Jew.[1] However in the case of a union betwen a non Jew and a Jewess the offspring is a Jew, like the mother. Many reasons are given in the Talmud for this. The Amoraim endeavored to point out the reasons for this distinction by citations from verses in the Pentateuch[2] and from the book of Ezra, but not altogether successfully.

Law must be based on logic, otherwise it is not law. True, decrees are made seemingly without logic but there must be underlying reasons for their enactment. What is the logic and the underlying reason for this particular law?

This law in the Talmud was deduced from Deuteronomy where it is stated, "Neither shalt thou make marriage with them: Thy daughter thou shalt not give unto his son, nor his daughter shalt thou take unto thy son. For he will turn away thy son from following Me." This Pentateuchal injunction applied equally to intermarriage of daughters as well as sons. The clause, "For he will turn away thy son from following Me,"[3] is only a homiletical interpretation that "thy son" referred only to the son whose mother was a Jewess; but if the mother was not a Jewess he was not called "thy son." Furthermore this injunction referred only to the seven peoples who originally inhabited the land of Canaan.

It has been maintained that in order to define who is a Jew the mother is the only criterion because we do know

[1] Kid. 3.12. הולד כמותה ואיזה זה ... ונכרית.
[2] אמר רבי יוחנן משום רבי שמעון בן יוחי כי יסור את בנך מאחרו בנך הבא מישראלית קרוי בנך ואין בנך הבא מן הנכרית קרוי בנך אלא בנה.
[3] כי יסור את בנך.

Reprinted from the *Jewish Quarterly Review*, New Series, Vol. 51, 1960.

who is the mother but we cannot be assured as to who is the father. Also it is maintained that with regard to "genealogical privileges" the offspring follows the father. Thus if a priest married the daughter of an Israelite the offspring if a male would be a priest. However this argument does not carry weight and may be disposed of. It is stated that if a pregnant woman was asked whose child she was carrying and she answered that of "A", a priest, both Rabban Gamaliel and Rabbi Eleizer said "She is believed."[4] This in spite of the fact that the unborn child was the offspring of illicit relations. The child if a male, would be a Kohen, a priest, and could eat *terumah*, holy food that was prohibited to Israelites. Furthermore he would be allowed to enter the inner part of the Temple and offer sacrifices to God, prohibited to Israelites under penalty of death.

It is true that according to the Talmud the words "She is believed" referred to the woman, that she could marry a priest[5]. According to some authorities they meant that if the child were a female she could marry a Kohen.[6] However the talmudic statement referring to her or to the daughter is a later deduction and is based on a halakah that is also late.[7]

The words in the Mishne "She is believed" do not mean that she could marry a Kohen, or that her daughter could marry a Kohen if she gave birth to a girl. The words pertain to the offspring that her child would be of the priestly family, thus if the child is a male he would be a Kohen. Otherwise it was not necessary for the woman to say that the father of the unborn child was a Kohen. She could have said that the father was an Israelite of good birth. If she is believed she would not be disqualified from marrying a Kohen; nor would be the offspring if it was female be disqualified from marrying

[4] היתה מעוברת ואמרו לה מה טיבו של עובר זה מאיש פלוני וכהן הוא רבן גמליאל ורבי אליעזר אומרים נאמנת.
[5] להכשיר בה.
[6] להכשיר בבתה.
[7] מאי בדוקי אלימא שבודקין את אמו ואומרת לכשר נבעלתי נאמנת.

a Kohen. The word Kohen in this Mishne cannot be taken to mean an Israelite of good birth,—it means a priest.[8] Rashi in his commentary on this Mishne in Kid. 74 saw the difficulty of this talmudic interpretation when he wrote: וכהן הוא כלומר מיוחס. When the word כלומר is used by Rashi it means that he saw a difficulty in the talmudic text.

May I venture to suggest the underlying reason for the enactment of the law,—namely that the offspring whose mother is not a Jewess and whose father is a Jew is not a Jew. This law was enacted during the time of Nehemiah and was motivated by political and religious reasons.

It is well known that after the Restoration there was great dissension between the Samaritans and the Judaeans which led to secession. The Samaritans maintained that the Temple should be built on Mount Gerizim, to which there is reference in the Pentateuch.[9] On the other hand the Judaeans maintained that the Temple should be rebuilt on the site where it had stood on Mount Zion, in Jerusalem. The Judaeans had only historical support because this was where the Temple stood at the time of King Solomon, while the Samaritans had Pentateuchal support. It was in order to combat the contentions of the Samaritans that the historical books of the Bible were canonized.[10] The book of Kings states that God had chosen Jerusalem as the place where His House should be built.[11] The Samaritans tried to halt the building of the

---

[8] The first part of the Mishne, wherein it is stated ראוה מדברת עם אחד ואמרו לה מה טיבו של איש זה איש פלוני וכהן הוא רבן גמליאל ורבי אליעזר אומרים נאמנת The words "she is believed" refers to her, that she is not disqualified from marrying a Kohen. The second part of the Mishne where it is said: היתה מעוברת ואמרו לה מה טיבו של עובר זה מאיש פלוני וכהן הוא רבן גמליאל ורבי אליעזר אומרים נאמנת The words נאמנת "she is believed" refers to her offspring. If she gave birth to a girl her daughter is not disqualified from marrying a Kohen, if the child is a male he would be a Kohen.

[9] Deut. 27, 12.

[10] Cf. S. Zeitlin, "The Book of Jubilees and the Pentateuch" *JQR* 1957, pp. 231-2.

[11] II Kings 21, 7.

Temple by denouncing the Judaeans to the Persian government, accusing them of building a fortress and planning a revolt.[12]

During the life of Nehemiah Sanballat the Horonite was governor of Samaria. He wanted to halt the construction of the walls around Jerusalem which Nehemiah had commenced. He hired prophets to prophesy that the Judaeans would meet with disaster by the building of the walls and to charge that Nehemiah was planning to become king of Judaea.[13] But Nehemiah was not deterred and went on with the building of the walls until they were completed.

Sanballat did not cease his scheming to build a temple on their sacred mount, Mount Gerizim, and to make it supreme over the Temple in Jerusalem. Priests are essential to the temple according to the Pentateuchal law. The Pentateuch gave the high priesthood to Phineas and his descendants as an eternal covenant.[14] The Zaddokites were the descendants of Phineas. Sanballat, in order to comply with the law—that priest of the Zaddokite family should serve in the temple which he contemplated building gave his daughter in marriage to Menasah the grandson of the High Priest Eliashib.[15] Thus his son-in-law would become the high priest in the temple on Mount Gerizim. The descendants of this union would be high priests and priests of the Zaddokite family and also his descendants. The designs of Sanballat were a serious threat to the Temple in Jerusalem. The Samaritans had the support of the Pentateuch that Mount Gerizim was a place for blessing and not Jerusalem.[16] Now Sanballat could have priests of the high priestly family of Zaddok to serve in his temple. To remove this danger a law was enacted that the offspring of a mixed marriage where the mother is not a

---

[12] Ezra 4, 12-16.
[13] Neh. 6, 5-13.
[14] Num. 25, 13.
[15] Neh. 13, 28; cf. Josephus, *Antiquities* ll. 302 303
[16] Deut. 27, 12.

Jewess should not be considered Jews. Sanballat's daughter was not Jewish, she was a Horonite. Hence according to the enacted law, the children of this union could not be Jews. Although the father in such a union be of the high priestly family his children could not be priests nor even Jews. [17] This law brought to naught all the schemes of Sanballat. It prevented the priests of his temple from being considered Jews. The schism between the Samaritans and the Judaeans came to open conflict. The final break between them occured in the year 332 BCE when Sanballat's grandson, bearing the same name, received permission from Alexander of Macedon to build a temple on Mount Gerizim. [18] Eventually in 128 BCE the temple on Mount Gerizim was entirely destroyed by John Hyrcanus I.[19]

There is another instance in Judaean history when the leaders enacted a law to destroy any rivalry with the Temple in Jerusalem. During the persecutions by Antiochus Epiphanes when the High Priest Onias III fled to Egypt Ptolemy VI gave him permission to build in Heliopolis,[20] The leaders in Judaea, feared that the temple might attract many Judaeans and would be a rivalry with the Temple in Jerusalem, enacted a law that the land outside of Judaea be regarded as in a state of defilement.[21] Hence no shrine coud be considered sacred if built on ground which is defiled.

[17] In the time of Nehemiah the Judaeans held that Yahweh is their God because He made a covenant with their forefathers and took them out of bondage, from the land of Egypt. Hence one who was not a descendant of Abraham, Isaac and Jacob was not a Judaean. Those who believed in an ethnic god did not recognize proselytism, and hold that one who was not of the race of the Judaeans could become a convert to the Judaean religion. Only when the view of the Pharisees became the norm of Judaism that the God of Israel is a universal God was proselytism encouraged. See further my forthcoming book *The History of the Second Commonwealth.*

[18] Ant. ll. 323-24.
[19] Ibid. 13, 254-56.
[20] See Maccabees II, ed. Dropsie College, pp. 78-80.
[21] See S. Zeitlin, *The History of the Second Jewish Commonwealth Prolegomena*, 1933, pp. 26-29.

In my review of Justice Silberg's book, *Personal status in Israel*, I wrote that there are different methods of studying law, the dogmatic and the historical. The dogmatic method implies the study of laws as they are, without any investigation of the underlying reasons for their origin. The historical method is the study of the origin of the laws and the factors which brought about their enactment. In this essay my purpose was to set forth the causes which brought about the enactment of the law of offspring of intermarriage. I avoided any dogmatic conclusions.

THE JEWS: RACE, NATION, OR RELIGION?

A Study Based on the Literature of the Second
Jewish Commonwealth

Reprinted from a Monograph published by The Dropsie College of Hebrew and Cognate Learning, 1936.

FOREWORD

In this essay I use the term Jews, although the Judaeans— the Jews, after they lost their independence and Judaea was conquered by the Romans, ceased to call themselvee Jews. Instead they began to use the name Israelites exclusively. Similarly, the Judaeans never called the land of Israel— *Erez Yisrael*, Palestine. This name was given to the land of Israel by their enemies. However, I have adopted the terms "Jews" and "Palestine," which are in common use, for the purpose of clarity and convenience, and in order to avoid confusion.

The greater part of this essay was originally published in the *Jewish Quarterly Review*. Wherever forms of the Greek words, ὁμόφυλος and ἀλλόφυλος, are found, they are quotations from Greek sources.

INTRODUCTION

The problem whether the Jews constitute a nation or a religious group was for the first time brought up during the French Revolution. In the General Assembly which met in Paris in the year 1789 the royalists (the anti-Semites), like l'Abbe Maury, maintained that the Jews constitute a definite nation and therefore cannot be considered as citizens of France, while the liberals, the friends of the Jews, like Mirabeau and Robespierre, maintained that the Jews were entitled to equal rights, since they did not constitute a nation but a religious community. This question was debated in other countries at the time of the Jewish emancipation. Later this problem was taken up by the Jews themselves. Some of them argued that the Jews were a nation, while others were of the opinion that they formed only a religious group (see I. Kaufmann, גולה ונכר, תל אביב).

It is not my intention to define whether the Jews of our own days should be considered as a nation or a religious group. It is, however, my aim to present the opinion of the sages of the Second Commonwealth.

It is well known that in the entire Jewish history, only during the period of the Second Commonwealth did the Jews have their own state, their own country, their own government, and at the same time were scattered over the entire globe. In that period Judaism was molded and cemented. We may say that the Jewish Constitution was framed at that period. The Pentateuch as well as the teachings of the Prophets were canonized; the Halakah was formulated. The ideas and the ideals which made it possible

1

for the Jews to endure the different persecutions, privations and degradations in the centuries of the Dispersion, were promulgated in that period. Our moral standards and religious institutions are directly traceable to the Second Commonwealth.

The entire Western world was at that time revolutionized by the destruction of paganism and the rise of Christianity. That change in Western civilization was largely due to the influence of Judaism as perpetuated by the Pharisees.

Although the term "race" is comparatively a new term, it has not yet been established etymologically whether its origin may be Slavonic or even Semitic, from the word ראש—head. (See *We Europeans* by Julian S. Huxley and A. C. Haddon, London 1935, p. 18). However, the conception of *race* was known in the period of the Second Commonwealth and was used in the sense of descendants of a particular person or of a clan. In the Bible the word בני, זרע had the connotation of *race* which the Greeks defined by the term *Genos*. In the Septuagint the biblical word בן נכר is translated ἀλλογενής. In the talmudic literature, race is sometimes defined by the word גזע.

In the same manner the term nation, although a modern term, can be very well applied to the time of the Second Commonwealth. A unity of a certain group, occupying a definite territory and closely associated with each other by common history, governed by the same laws, was considered a *polis*, a state—or in a wider sense, an *Ethnos*, a nation.

The term *Ethnos* is used by the Greek writers Aristotle, Strabo, Dio and others, at times as a political state, at other times as a people.

The meaning of *Ethnos* and *Genos* may be best demonstrated by the manner in which they were used by the Greek writers; thus Aristotle, in *Politics*, VII, 6, says: "The nations

INTRODUCTION 3

ἔθνη inhabiting the cold places and those of Europe are full of spirit but somewhat deficient in intelligence and skill ... The peoples of Asia on the other hand are intelligent and skilful in temperament ... the Greek race Ἑλλήνων γένος participates in both characters, just as it occupies the middle position geographically ... The same diversity also exists among the Greek nations Ἑλλήνων ἔθνη compared with one another." When Aristotle speaks of the Greeks in general he uses the term *Genos*; when he discusses the different states of the Greeks he uses the term *Ethnos*. (Comp. also ibid. III, 1).

In the biblical literature the word גוי (*goy*) is used to designate *Ethnos*—nation.[1] Later, under the influence of the Church, the word *goy* was used in the Talmud when referring to Gentiles, for in the New Testament and in the writings of the early Church Fathers, the term *Ethnos* was always applied to non-Jews.

In this essay I confine myself only to the Halakot of the early Tannaim, since the later Tannaim, after the period of Bar Kokba, cannot represent the ideas of the Jews during

---

[1] See II Sam. 7.23; I Chron. 17.21; ומי כעמך כישראל גוי (ἔθνος) אחד בארץ. And who is like thy peoples, like Israel, a nation one in the earth. This dictum is attributed to King David: hence before the ten tribes separated from Judah. In the time of David the entire Jewish people constituted one *goy* (*ethnos*) one nation, one kingdom. Comp. Ezek. 37. ועשיתי אותם לגוי (ἔθνος) אחד בארץ .... ומלך אחד יהיה .... ולא יהיה עוד לשני גוים (ἔθνη) "and I will make them one nation in the land ... and one king ... and there shall be no more two nations." According to Justin Martyr, *Apology* I, 53, the word גוים, ἔθνη in the Prophets applies to the Gentiles, while the *Judeans* (the Jews) are referred to as *Israelites*. After the coming of Christ, the Christians were designated by the term *Israelites*, (*Dialogue with Trypho*, 135). The Jews, however, maintained that the Christians were of another religion, ἀλλόφυλοι (*Epistle of Diognetus*, V). Thus the word ἀλλόφυλοι has the connotations, "of another religion" rather than "of another race," since during the first century of Christianity the Jews constituted a large percentage of its converts, numbering among them most of its leaders. Comp. note 56.

431

the Second Commonwealth. Undoubtedly there was a reason for some of the Halakot which are not in accordance with the early Halakah.

I have not limited myself to the Halakot only, but I took into consideration the entire literature of that period: the Apocrypha, Josephus, Philo, the New Testament, pagan writers, as well as the writings of the early Church Fathers.

The study of Judaism has occupied many scholars, Jews and Christians alike. Many books have been written on this subject. These studies, however, are not limited to one particular period. The authors, desiring to prove their point of view on Judaism, quote statements from the vast talmudic and rabbinic literature in support of their thesis. They failed to see, however, the development in Jewish history. The Halakah in the talmudic or in any other later period cannot give us a true conception of the Judaism of the Second Commonwealth, nor can Maimonides' Judaism represent the Judaism of any other period.

Far be it from me to say that the ideas formed by the sages of the Second Commonwealth must be followed now and that the Constitution[2] which was framed by them must be observed in its entirety. Their own point of view was that the Halakah may be amended so that it could meet the needs of the people and the time. Their motto was that *the Halakah was instituted for the people, and not the people for the Halakah.* The Jewish Constitution, however, cannot be abrogated on the whim of a part of the people, even though they may think that that would benefit the entire Jewry.

The conclusions presented in this essay are based only on the impartial studies of the original sources. Though

---

[2] The idea of constitution has been well defined. "L'ensemble des institution et des lois fondamentales, destinées à régler l'action de tous les citoyens." Holland, *Jurisprudence*, p. 361.

there may be some who would be reluctant to accept the views expressed here, but *we have to abide by the documents*.

In this essay are reflected the opinions of the Jews up to the Bar Kokba period. I intend to analyze this problem from Bar Kokba up to the close of the Talmud. It would be both of interest and importance to make a study of the same problem from the talmudic period up to the French Revolution. This would necessitate a study of the entire rabbinic literature, particularly the Responsa, as well as the writings of the Church Fathers and the different decrees of the states where the Jews dwelt during the Middle Ages. This, however, is not a work for one man. So vast and comprehensive is the literature that it would require the service of a group or a *collegium* of scholars working cooperatively. If a Maecenas were to make such a *collegium* possible, he would certainly contribute towards a better understanding of Judaism and the history of the Jewish people. Such a *collegium* might also be utilized by those organizations that safeguard the Jewish rights in this tempestuous age. This *collegium* could furnish authoritative information on internal and external Jewish problems.

I know that the material needs of the Jewish people today are great and urgent. The cultural side, however, must not be overlooked, for on it depends the survival of the Jewish people.

THE JEWS: RACE, NATION OR RELIGION—WHICH?*

It is my purpose to discuss the attitude of the Palestinian Jews of the Second Commonwealth toward the Jews of the Diaspora. Did they regard the Jews of Babylon, Egypt and the great centers of Asia Minor as a part of their own nation? Did they look upon them as members of one race—the Hebrew race? Did they consider them co-religionists only, adherents of the same religion? Further, how did the Palestinian Jews regard the Gentiles, who in large masses accepted Judaism, either of their own volition as did the Adiabenes[1] or under compulsion as did the Idumaeans and the Ituraeans?[2] Were these new groups considered as part of the Jewish people or were they regarded merely as co-religionists?

Race: a group of persons, or animals, or plants, connected by common descent, posterity of (person), house, family, tribe, or nation (*Oxford Dictionary*). The descendants of the same ancestor; a family, tribe, people, or nation taken as the same stock (*Webster's New International Dictionary*).

Nation: 1) a people connected by ties of blood, generally manifested in community of language, religion, customs. 2) A body of inhabitants of a country united under a single government (*Webster's New International Dictionary*). An extensive aggregate of persons, so closely associated with each other by common descent, language, or history, as to form a distinct race or people, usually organized as a separate political state and occupying a definite territory. (*Oxford Dictionary*).

People: A body of persons united by a common character, culture, or sentiment. (*Webster's New International Dictionary*). A nation may comprise two or more peoples; also, it may be comprised of a portion of a people.

[1] Comp. *Ant.*, XX, 2.
[2] Ibid. XIII, 9.

To shed light on this problem is of great importance, as it will not only clarify the history of the Second Jewish Commonwealth, but will also reveal the development of the philosophy of Jewish history after the destruction of the Second Temple; for, during this period, Judaism was moulded and reached its culmination. The Bible was then canonized. The teachings of the Prophets became the guiding principles for the Jews. In the period of the First Temple the Prophets were looked upon as dreamers. Their words were considered a menace to the state. Many of the Prophets were persecuted by the Kings of Israel. In the period of the Second Temple, the ideals of the Prophets became the ideals of the people. Judaism, under the influence of the Prophets and the Pharisees, was cemented. Judaism of today is an outgrowth of the teachings of the Pharisees of that period. The institutions which are in existence among the Jews in our own days either emerged or were established in the period of the Second Commonwealth.

I

JUDAEANS

Before the Assyrian period there was no Jewish Diaspora; the Jews were settled in Palestine. The idea that the God of Israel is the only God of the whole universe, had not yet been accepted by the entire Jewish people. Even at the time of King Saul, those Jews, who for some reason or other left Palestine, were no longer considered part of the Jewish people. When David was compelled to flee the country in fear of Saul, he complained to the King that he would no longer be able to worship the God of Israel, but would have to worship other gods. "For they have driven me out this day from abiding in the inheritance of the Lord, saying, 'Go serve other gods,' " he said.[3]

In the days of David and Solomon, the Hebrew State was formally established. However, a division came about after the death of Solomon. Ten tribes separated themselves from Rehoboam, the son of Solomon, and established their own kingdom in the North. The tribes of Judah and Benjamin remained with the family of David, and kept Jerusalem as their capital. Samaria finally became the capital of the Northern Kingdom. These states made war upon each other, and occasionally they concluded alliances. The best informed minds undoubtedly deplored the division of Israel. One Prophet named Edad reproached Pekah, the son of Remaliah, for taking captives from the country of Judah and Jerusalem, for he considered them brothers.[4] However, another Prophet, named Jehu, reproached King Jehoshaphat for making an alliance with Ahaziah, King of Israel.[5]

The kings of the North were called Kings of Israel, while the kings of the South were called Kings of Judah. By what name did the people of both these countries refer to themselves? Did the people who lived in the North call themselves Israelites, and did the people who lived in the South call themselves Judaeans? We cannot be certain. The author of the book of Jonah tells us that Jonah said he was a Hebrew when his fellow-passengers on the boat asked him from what country and people he came.[6] He

---

[3] I Sam. 26.19. כי גרשני היום מהסתפח בנחלת ד' לאמר לך עבד אלהים אחרים. The exile is compelled to serve the gods of the land in which he is a resident. See H. P. Smith, *Intern. Comment. a. l.*

[4] II Chron. 28.11. והשיבו השביה אשר שביתם מאחיכם.

[5] Ibid. 20.37. בהתחברך עם אחזיה פרץ ד' את מעשיך וישברו אניות ולא עצרו ללכת תרשיש.

[6] Jonah 1.9. Comp. *Ant.*, IX, 10, γένος ἔλεγεν Ἑβραῖος.

437

did not call himself an Israelite.⁷ On the other hand, the author of the Book of II Kings called the people of the South Judaeans in his account of the victory of Rezin, the King of Syria, over Ahaz, King of Judah. The author says that Rezin drove the "Judaeans" out of the city of Elath.⁸ When Rabshakeh, the general of Sennacherib, appealed to the inhabitants of Jerusalem to submit to the Assyrians, the author says that he spoke to them in the language of the Judaeans.⁹ The prophets of Judaea always delivered their messages to the kings of Judah and the inhabitants of Jerusalem in the name of God, the Lord of Israel.¹⁰ They never used the expression, God the Lord of Judah.

About the year 722 B. C. E., the Assyrians conquered the Northern State and exiled most of the people to other countries; since then the Northern Kingdom ceased to exist. Many people of the Northern Kingdom joined the kingdom of Judah. In the year 586 B. C. E., the kingdom of Judah also ceased to exist. The city of Jerusalem was taken by Nebuchadnezzar and most of its inhabitants led to Babylon.

Although the Prophets recognized the fact that the Northern Kingdom and the Southern Kingdom constituted two different states and two different nations, they looked forward to the time when these two nations would again be united as one state, as a single nation in one country ruled by one king. This is clear from the beautiful vision of Ezekiel when he compared these two kingdoms to two different pieces of wood, "Behold, I will take the stick of

---

⁷ Comp. II Chron. 13.18 where the word בני ישראל occurs, also II Sam. 17.25, ועמשא בן איש ושמו יתרא הישראלי. Comp., however, I Chron. 2.17 ואבי עמשא יתר הישמעאלי.

⁸ II Kings 16.6 וינשל את היהודים. See also Jer. 32.12; ibid. 34.9; comp. Deut. 15.12.

⁹ II Kings 18.28, ויקרא בקול גדול יהודית.

¹⁰ Ibid. 19.20, passim. See also II Chron. 15.13.

Joseph, which is in the hand of Ephraim, and the tribes of Israel his fellows, and will put them with him, even with the stick of Judah, and make them one stick, and they shall be one in mine hand ... Behold, I will take the children of Israel from among the heathen, whither they be gone, and will gather them on every side, and bring them into their own land: And I will make them one nation in the land upon the mountains of Israel; and one king shall be king to them all; and they shall be no more two nations, neither shall they be divided into two kingdoms any more at all."[11]

About fifty years after the destruction of the Temple, the Persian government permitted the Jews to return to Judaea. In spite of many obstacles, the Temple in Jerusalem was rebuilt. Since that time, the inhabitants of Judaea were always called Judaeans. In the books of the Prophets of the Post-Exilic Period, like Ezra and Nehemiah, the name of Israel is still used, but the name of Judaeans is most prevalent. Later, the name "Israel" disappears and the name "Judaeans" takes its place entirely. In the Book of Esther, the name of Israel is not mentioned at all. The word יהודים Judaeans appears throughout the book. When the author of the book relates that many people of the land accepted Judaism, he used the word מתיהדים, "Judaized." According to the same author, Mordecai was called a Judaean, although the author gives his genealogy as a descendant of the tribe of Benjamin, and not of the tribe of Judah.[12]

---

[11] Ezek. 37.15–25, הנה אני לקח את בני ישראל מבין הגוים ... ועשיתי אותם לגוי אחד בארץ בהרי ישראל ומלך אחד יהיה לכלם למלך ולא יהיה עוד לשני גוים ולא יחצו עוד לשתי ממלכות עוד.

[12] Esth. 2.5 איש ימיני ... ושמו מרדכי ... איש יהודי היה. The Talmud already noticed the difficulty by asking why Mordecai is called a Judaean when it is stated that he is from the tribe of Benjamin. Comp. Meg. 12b קרי ליה יהודי ... וקרי ליה ימיני.

Josephus in the first ten books of the *Antiquities*, where he relates the history of the Jews up to the Restoration, uses the term Hebrews. After that period, he calls them Judaeans. The word Judaeans is applied to the inhabitants of Judaea, in the entire Hellenistic literature. Josephus says that the Jewish people are called Judaeans because they are descended from Judah.[13] In another place he gives another reason, namely that they were inhabitants of the country of Judaea.[14] It is possible that originally the people who lived in Judaea were called Judaeans because they were descended from the tribe of Judah, since the tribe of Judah really predominated. Later the name Judaeans was applied to all inhabitants of Palestine, regardless of the tribe from which they came. The name was now connected with the country. Still later all the Jews, regardless of where they lived, were designated as Judaeans by the Gentiles, since the land of the people was called Judaea.

In the Elephantine Papyri the name *Yahud*, Judaean, is used. However, some Jews were here called Aramaeans.[15] It is possible that the Jews who came from Samaria and

---

In the Book of Daniel the name Judaeans occurs a few times, since it refers to Daniel, Hananiah, Mishael and Azariah, who were the children of the captivity of Judah, מן בני גלותא די יהוד. Comp. Dan. 3.8, 12; 5.13; 6.14.

[13] Comp. *Ant.* XI, 7. That is the name they are called by from the day that they came up from Babylon, which is taken from the tribe of Judah, which came first to these places, and hence both they and the country gained that appellation.

[14] Comp. *Contra Apion* I, 22, "and took their name from the country they inhabit which is called Judaea." See Dio, *Roman History*, XXXVII, 16, "They have also another name that they have acquired; the country has been named Judaea, and the people themselves Ἰουδαῖοι Judaeans. I do not know how this title came to be given to them."

[15] Comp. A. Cowley, *Aramaic Papyri of the Fifth Century*, p. xv. There was a Jewish military settlement in Elephantine and Syene; they among others were put in charge of the fortresses of Elephantine and Syene as a defense of the southern frontier of Egypt against Ethiopia. Comp. also Ezek. 16.3, אביך האמרי ואמך חתית.

THE JEWS: RACE, NATION OR RELIGION 13

were mixed with Aram were called Aramaeans while the Jews who came originally from the Southern Kingdom were called Judaeans.[16]

In the first chapters of I Maccabees, the name of Israel is often used, but later on where the victory of Judas Maccabeus over the Syrians and the establishment of a Jewish State are described, the name Judaeans is used quite frequently. In the official documents sent by the Jews to the Spartans and to the Romans, only the name Judaean is used.[17] Likewise, in the official communications from the Romans to the Jews the term *Ethnos Joudaion*, the Jewish Nation, is given.[18] The word Israel never occurs in these official documents. In the letters from the Syrian kings, Alexander Balas and Demetrius II, to the Jews, the term *Ethnos Joudaion* is used.[19] In II Maccabees, the name Judaeans appears throughout, and the word Israel as designating the Jewish people does not occur. Again in the official documents which passed between the Syrian kings and the Jews, and the Romans and the Jews, the name Judaeans is recorded.[20]

In the tannaitic literature of the Second Commonwealth, the expression יהודים, Judaeans, is given. The author of *Megillat Taanit* tells us that a holiday was declared on the twenty-eighth of Adar, since on that day good tidings reached the Judaeans.[21] A story is related in the Talmud that those Alexandrian Jews who lived in Jerusalem and

---

[16] See Cowley, ibid., p. 16. Comp. also Strabo, *Geog.*, I, 2, 34.
[17] I Macc. 12.6. Ἰωνάθαν ἀρχιερεὺς καὶ ἡ γερουσία τοῦ ἔθνους καὶ οἱ ἱερεῖς καὶ ὁ λοιπὸς δῆμος τῶν Ἰουδαίων Σπαρτιάταις τοῖς ἀδελφοῖς χαίρειν; Ἰωνάθαν ὁ ἀρχιερεὺς καὶ τὸ ἔθνος τῶν Ἰουδαίων.
[18] ἔθνει Ἰουδαίων.
[19] ἔθνει τῶν Ἰουδαίων.
[20] I Macc. 11–12.
[21] אחת בשירתא טבתא ליהודאי. Some readings in the *Megillat Taanit* have והוה פרקו לבית ישראל. This, however, is not found in Yer., nor in the Parma. Ms. See S. Zeitlin, *Megillat Taanit*, p. 68.

who became betrothed were deprived of their prospective wives by other Jews who married them. The sages of that period wanted to declare the children of these marriages illegitimate. Hillel, however, was of the opinion that the offspring of these marriages were legitimate, since in the *Ketubah*, the marriage contract, there was a clause which read: "When you come to my house, you shall be my wife according to the laws of Moses and the Judaeans."[22] From this story we readily see that in the official documents used among the Jews in Palestine during the Second Commonwealth the expression *Jehudim*, Judaeans, was used and not the word Israel. One of the Jews who was killed in a caravan on the way to Antioch is referred to as a יהודי, *Jehudi*, according to a story recorded in the name of Rabban Simon the son of Gamaliel.[23] From this we may safely surmise that the Jews of Palestine were named Judaeans, not Israelites. In the entire rabbinic literature of the time of the Second Jewish Commonwealth, we never find the name "Israel" used for the Jewish people. The term Israel was used only in contrast to Priest and Levite; it was used only to distinguish the different castes which were in existence in Jerusalem at the time of the Second Jewish Commonwealth, "a community of Priests, Levites, of Israelites, and of proselytes."[24]

---

[22] Yer. Ket. 29a. כשהיו בני אלכסנדריא מקדשין נשים ... כשתיכנסו לביתי כדת משה וישראל. According to the Tosefta תהויין לי לאנתו כדת משה ויהודאי. This undoubtedly is a corrupt reading, as after the destruction of the Temple the Jews called themselves Israelites, and the term Judaeans was no longer in use, so the form of the *Ketubah* was changed accordingly to read כדת משה וישראל. As that is the case it can be proven by the Mishna which still has the reading ואלו יוצאות שלא בכתובה העוברת על דת משה ויהודית ... ואיזוהי דת יהודית because the *Ketubah* had originally the clause כדת משה ויהודאי. Comp. also Ned. 11.12 בראשונה היו אומרים ג' נשים יוצאות ונוטלות כתובה ... נטולה אני מן היהודים.

[23] Tos. Yeb. 14.7 אמר רבן שמעון בן גמליאל מעשה בקולאר של בני אדם שהלכו לאנטוכיא ובחזירתן אמרו לא נהרג ממנו אלא פלוני יהודי.

[24] Yer. Kid. 65c קהל כהנים, קהל לוים, קהל ישראלים, קהל גרים.

Likewise, the Jews who lived in the neighboring countries of Palestine, where the Hellenistic culture was dominant, were named Judaeans. This was due to the fact that during the period of the Second Commonwealth, the Jews were known to the Hellenistic world not only as members of a particular state or country, but also as followers of a different culture from their own. In the decrees of Julius and Augustus Caesar granting different privileges to the Jews of Asia Minor, the name Judaeans is given.[25]

The Jews of Egypt as well as the Jews of Syria were called Judaeans. The Jews of Egypt who were under the Ptolemies and the Jews of Syria who were under the sovereignty of the Seleucides constituted two different groups politically and economically; and undoubtedly under these two dynasties the Jews took part in the long wars, fighting each other, one group being called Alexandrians and the other Antiochans. At the time of the wars between Antiochus III and Ptolemy V, the Jews of Palestine sided with the Syrians, as the High Priest thought they would thus benefit more, since most of the Jews lived in the upper lands. In the later wars between the Syrians and the Egyptians, the Judaean policy was changed in favor of the Alexandrian court. The Jews believed that if Palestine were united with Egypt, Judaea would benefit more because the number of Jews living in Egypt had greatly increased.[26] Even at that early time the Jewish people who lived in Palestine and in the Diaspora did not constitute one nation.

It is well known that the majority of the Jews did not return to Palestine when the Persian government issued

---

[25] *Ant.* XIV, 2–24; XVI, 2–7. See Dio, *Roman History*, XXXVII, 17: "But it applies also to all the rest of mankind, although of ἀλλοεθνεῖς who affect their customs."

[26] See S. Zeitlin, *History of the Second Jewish Commonwealth*, pp. 3–4.

an edict permitting them to return to their homeland and rebuild the Temple. They remained in Babylon, their adopted country.[27] Were these Jews of Babylon also universally known as Judaeans, as were the Jews of Palestine, or were they called Israelites? From tannaitic sources we have reason to believe that they were not called "Judaeans," but "Israelites." Rabban Gamaliel, in his epistle to the Jews of Babylon and to the other Jews of the Diaspora, addressed them all as the "Exiled of Israel."[28] He did not apply the word Judaeans to them.

It seems that the Jews in some localities in the Diaspora called themselves "Hebrews." This is substantiated by the fact that in some inscriptions which came down to us from Corinth the words "Synagogues of Hebrews" are found.[29] Paul, in his epistle to the Corinthians, calls himself "a Hebrew."[30] In his epistle to the Philippians he refers to himself as "a Hebrew from Hebrews," Ἑβραῖος ἐξ Ἑβραίων.[31] When he was arrested in Jerusalem he appealed to the people in the Hebrew language telling them that he was a Judaean, on the ground that he was brought up in the city of Jerusalem and received his education at the feet of Gamaliel and that he served the High Priest and

---

[27] *Ant.* XI, 5.2. "But then the entire body of the people of Israel λαὸς τῶν Ἰσραηλιτῶν remained in that country; wherefore there are but two tribes in Asia and Europe subject to the Romans, while the ten tribes are beyond the Euphrates till now δέκα φυλαὶ πέραν εἰσὶν Εὐφράτου ἑωσδεῦρο and are an immense multitude." This was apparently the opinion of the Jews of that time that the ten tribes, the Israelites, בני ישראל are in Babylon.

[28] See Tos. Sanh. 2.6. מעשה ברבן גמליאל וזקנים שהיו יושבין על גב מעלות בהר הבית ... לאחנא בני גלותא דבבל ובני גלותא דימדי ושאר כל גלותא דישראל. Comp. also Yer. ibid. 18d; Yer. Ma'as. Sh. 56c; Sanh. 11b.

[29] [συνα] γωγή Ἑβρ [αίων]. See B. Powell, "Greek Inscriptions from Corinth," *Amer. Journal of Archaeology*, VII, 60–61, 1903; A. Deismann, *Light from the Ancient East*, p. 13, n. f.

[30] II Cor. 11.22.

[31] Phil. 3.5.

the Senate zealously.[32] Thus, Paul in his epistles addressed to the dwellers of the cities of the Diaspora called himself a "Hebrew," while in Palestine he classified himself a "Judaean," like the people of Judaea. That the Jews of the Diaspora were called Hebrews can be proven by an early Mishna where it is stated that on a writ of divorce one witness was a Hebrew, the other a Hellene.[33]

In the Book of Judith, which is a story almost identical with the narrative given in the Book of Esther, the term "Judaeans" is not mentioned, but the words "Children of Israel" and "Hebrews" are recorded throughout. According to the story, the great King Nebuchadnezzar invaded the valley of Esdraelon, situated in the north where the Jews lived. It is singular that the entire invasion was concentrated in the north, around the city of Bethulia,[34] outside of Judaea. When Judith came to the camp of Holofernes and was asked who she was, she replied that she was a daughter of the Hebrews.[35] Likewise, when after the victory of the Jews over Holofernes' army, Achior, the Ammonite, circumcised himself and became a Jew, he was said to have "joined the people of Israel."[36] The author does not use the expression "judaized" like the author of the Book of Esther.[36a] We are confronted with the problem why the author of the Book of Judith used throughout the name Israel and not Judaeans, like the author of the Book of Esther. It is probable that the change of the term was due to the character of the story. For the plot was laid at the time of Nebuchadnezzar before the Restoration, and in

---

[32] Acts 22.3. Ἐγὼ μὲν εἰμι ἀνὴρ Ἰουδαῖος.
[33] Mishna Giṭ. 9, אחד עברי ואחד יוני. Comp. Yer. B. B. 17.
[34] About the city of Bethulia, see Charles, *Introduction to Judith.*
[35] Judith 10.12. θυγάτηρ εἰμί των Ἐβραίων.
[36] Ibid. 14.10. καὶ προσετέθη πρὸς τον οἶκον Ἰσραὴλ.
[36a] Comp. also B. J., II, 18.2. Ἰουδαΐζοντας.

445

the northern part of Palestine where the Israelites lived. We may even say that the Book of Judith was really written in the Diaspora in Babylon and not in Palestine, as some scholars suggested.[37] Hence the term "children of Israel" and not "Judaeans" was used, as the term Judaeans was not employed in Babylon.[37a] It is worth noting that the name of the heroine of this book is Judith. The name Judith is found in the Bible in Chronicles; it is the name of a woman who was descended from the tribe of Judah.[38]

Josephus, in his narrative of the history of the Jewish people from the time of the Restoration, used three different terms for them: *Genos*, γένος; *Ethnos*, ἔθνος; and *Phule*, φυλή—φῦλον. In describing the history of the Jews in Palestine he usually used the term ἔθνος Ἰουδαίων or Ἰουδαίων

---

[37] See the interesting article by P. Churgin in *Horeb*, I, pp. 48–71. It is likely that Judith was not included in the Canon because it was written in the Diaspora. Comp. further S. Zeitlin, *An Historical Study of the Canonization of the Hebrew Scriptures*, 1933.

In the Book of Susanna the term Judaeans occurs a few times. On the surface it would seem that it would be a contradiction to the statement we made that the Jews in Babylon called themselves Hebrews or Children of Israel, but not Judaeans, as the plot of the story of Susanna was laid in Babylon. This objection, however, can be easily removed, as Charles already pointed out, "The earlier form of the story seems to have no connexion with Daniel or Babylon." (*The Apocrypha*, Vol. I, p. 642). As a matter of fact, some of the manuscripts do not contain the first six verses where the name Babylon occurs. That this story was not written in Babylon may be substantiated by internal evidence. When Daniel said to one of the men who accused Susanna, "O, thou, seed of Canaan (some manuscripts read "Sidon") and not of Judah." It is quite evident that this book was not written in Babylon, but in Palestine, since he contrasts Canaan (Phoenicia) with Judah. Were this book written in Babylon he would not make a comparison with Phoenicia, but he would use a city in the neighborhood of Babylon.

[37a] When Alexander the Great asked the Shechemites whether they were Jews, they answered they were Hebrews who lived in Shechem. *Ant.* XI, 8.

[38] I Chron. 4.18. See also Gen. 26.34.

ἔθνος, the Jewish nation.[39] He never used the expression "Hebrews." Likewise he never referred to them as children of Israel.[40] As to the Jews of the Diaspora, those who dwelt in Babylon he called Hebrews or Judaeans;[41] occasionally when he spoke about the internal conditions of the Jews in Egypt he added the term *Ethnos*.[42] The Jews in the time of Josephus were self-governing bodies in Egypt as well as in Babylon, and he readily could have applied to them the expression *Ethnos* as a group who had common political interests. Before the time of Augustus Caesar the Jews had their own Ethnarch. When the Ethnarch died Augustus did not appoint another one in Egypt. He instituted instead a *Gerusia*, a Senate;[43] the Jews of Egypt lost many specific rights on account of the change in the form of government. Likewise, when Augustus Caesar banished Archelaus, the son of Herod, from the kingdom, he did not select another king for Judaea, but appointed a procurator instead.[44]

The Jews of Babylon were not controlled politically by those of Palestine. The kings of Judaea did not have authority over the Jews who dwelt in Babylon. Even when the High Priests were appointed by the Romans as Ethnarchs over the Jews in Palestine, they could not exer-

---

[39] The word γένος has different meanings: race, descendant, birth. ἔθνος may mean "nation" or any number of persons having the same social, economic and cultural interests. φυλή has the meaning of tribe, race, clan, kind.

The Septuagint translates the word גוי by *Ethnos* and עם by λαός. In the New Testament the word *Ethnos* refers to people, not to the Jewish race. Similarly, in the writings of the Church Fathers the words *Ethnos* and *Genos* refer to non-Jews. See, e. g., Eusebius, *C. H.*, IV, 6.

[40] The term "Hebrew" is used by Josephus when he refers to the language, customs, laws, or to the history of the Jewish people.

[41] Comp. *Ant.*, XVIII.

[42] Comp. *B. J.*, VII, 423; also *Cont. Ap.* passim. When Josephus speaks of the Jews of Babylon, he does add the term *Genos*. See *Ant.*, ed. Niese, XVIII, 378, according to the Mss.

[43] Philo, *In Flaccum*, 10, γενάρχης. Comp. *Ant.* XIX, 5, ἐθνάρχας; also 14.   [44] *B. J.*, 2.7.

cise their authority over the Jews beyond the Euphrates. These Jews were citizens of Parthia, with their economic and social interests which were adverse to those of the Romans; the welfare of Parthia was the first consideration of its Jewish inhabitants. Hence they could not be ruled by the political leaders of Palestine. Their affinity to the Jews of Palestine was in religion alone. They sent their sacrifices and gifts to the Temple;[45] they made pilgrimages to Jerusalem, the religious city, the metropolis of all Jewry. The spiritual life of the Jews, especially in regard to the regulation of the holidays, was controlled by the Sanhedrin in Jerusalem.

In social-economic life they were entirely independent of the Sanhedrin in Jerusalem. In the deeds of sale as well as in the writs of divorce they did not use the era which was applied in Judaea, i. e., they did not date the years according to the dynasty of the Hasmoneans or the Roman Caesars, but they used the era which was common in Babylon. They dated the documents according to the Seleucidan era.[46]

That Josephus was very careful in differentiating the term Hebrews from that of Judaeans is apparent from many passages. As we saw, he used the term Hebrews as applicable to the Jews only up till the Restoration, and the term Judaeans for the Jews after the Restoration. In *B. J.*, IV, e. g., he calls Joshua the captain of the Hebrews, since he had lived before the Restoration.[46a]

---

[45] Comp. *Ant.* XVI, 6; XVIII, 9.

[46] דתניא בגולה אין מונין אלא למלכי יוונים. See 'Ab. Zarah 10a. The Babylonian Jews counted the era to מלכי יוון, i. e., to the Seleucidan dynasty.

[46a] See, however, *Ant.* VI, where the name Jews occurs. This is an anachronism or a slip. A like anachronism is found in Book VIII where Josephus relates that Solomon began the building of the Temple in the month Iyar (instead of Ziv which is in the biblical text). In fact the name Iyar was unknown to the Jews till the Babylonian period and is used only in the post-Exilic literature.

THE JEWS: RACE, NATION OR RELIGION   21

Likewise, Josephus in his speech to the Jews, appealing to them to submit to the Romans, pointed out that in the time of Hezekiah God helped the Jews without resorting to war, (*B. J.*, V). He used the term Hebrews, not Judaeans, since Hezekiah lived before the Restoration.

Philo similarly distinguishes between the term Hebrews and the term Judaeans. When he speaks about the Jews before the time of Ezra he uses the term Hebrew, but when he writes about the Jews after the return from Babylon he uses the term Judaean. In recording the story of Balak and Balaam (Num. 23–24) he uses the term Hebrews, although in the Bible the name "Hebrew" is not mentioned, but Jacob and Israel. The Bible has "How goodly are thy tents, O Jacob." In Philo we read:[47] "How goodly are thy dwellings, thou host of the Hebrews!"[48] When speaking of the Jews in general or when referring to the Jews of his own time, Philo always uses the term Judaeans.

II

CO-RELIGIONISTS

As we said before, during the Second Jewish Commonwealth there was another group of Jews who were Jews in religion only: the Idumaeans and the Adiabenes. Josephus could not apply the term Jewish *Ethnos* to them, since they did not assimilate with the Jews so as to become one *ethnic group* and they continued to live as separate states. The

---

[47] מה טבו אהליך יעקב משכנתך ישראל. The Septuagint reads: ὡς καλοί σου Ἰακώβ, αἱ σκηναί σου, Ἰσραήλ. Philo, ὡσ καλοί σου οἱ οἶκοι, στρατια Ἑβραίων.

[48] Similarly the Bible reads מן ארם ינחני בלק מלך מואב מהררי קדם לכה ארה לי יעקב ולכה זעמה ישראל. The Septuagint, ἄρασαί μοι τὸν Ἰακώβ, καὶ δεῦρο ἐπικατάρασαί μοι τὸν Ἰσραήλ. Philo, ἐκ Μεσοποταμίας μετεπέμψατό με Βαλάκης μακρὰν τὴν ἀπ' ἀνατολῶν στειλάμενον ἀποδημίαν, ἵνα τίσηται τοὺς Ἑβραίους ἀραῖς.

Adiabenes had their own *Ethnos*,[49] as the Idumaeans had theirs.[50] The Idumaeans called themselves a kindred nation,[51] perhaps because of the tradition that they were the children of Edom, Esau, the son of Isaac.[52] They were so near to Judaea, geographically, that they intermarried with the Judaeans. Josephus could not apply to them the word *Genos* Ἰουδαίων or Ἑβραίων, neither ἔθνος Ἰουδαίων nor Ἑβραίων, since they were not of the Jewish race, nor did they have a common history.

Josephus, speaking about the Idumaeans and the Adiabenes calls them *homophulon* "ὁμόφυλον",[53] co-religionists. That the term ὁμόφυλον means co-religionist can be readily proved from his context. He tells us that during the war carried on against the Romans, the Idumaeans upon the request of the zealots dispatched an army to Jerusalem to re-inforce them. Upon approaching Jerusalem, the Idumaeans found that the gates were closed against them by the command of the High Priest. The leaders of the Idumaeans reproached the High Priest by saying, "This city is sup-

[49] *B. J.*, IV, 9.11. Ἀδιαβηνῶν βασιλέως.
[50] Comp. Strabo, *Geog.*, XVI, 2.34.
[51] *B. J.*, IV, 4.4 συγγενέσι.
[52] According to Strabo, *Geog.*, XVI, 2.34, the Idumaeans were originally Nabataeans—an Arabian people.
[53] *B. J.*, I,2. Ἀδιαβηνῆς ὁμοφύλους. Ibid. II, 16.4. Thackeray, in his translation of *B. J.*, p. 475, said: "Proselytes would have been a more correct term than kinsmen." Thackeray failed to see that the term ὁμοφύλους has the connotation of relationship, affinity rather than *kinsmen*. The term ὁμόφυλος did not always render the meaning, the same tribe or countryman. This is substantiated by Strabo, *Geog.*, I, 2, "For the nation of the Armenians and that of the Syrians and Arabians betray close relationship, not only in their language, but in their mode of life, and in their bodily build." τὸ γὰρ τῶν Ἀρμενίων ἔθνος καὶ τὸ τῶν Σύρων καὶ Ἀράβων πολλὴν ὁμοφυλίαν ἐμφαίνει κατά τε τὴν διάλεκτον καὶ τοὺς βίους. καὶ τοὺς τῶν σωμάτων χαρακτῆρας, καὶ μάλιστα καθὸ πλησιόχωροι εἰσι. The relationship between the Judaeans, Idumaeans and the Adiabenes was indeed very close, since these nations followed one religion which had a common effect on their mode of life.

THE JEWS: RACE, NATION OR RELIGION 23

posed to welcome ἀλλοφύλοις people of other religions for worship, and yet you closed the gates against your co-religionists, ὁμοφύλων."[54] That the word ὁμοφύλων has the meaning of co-religionist may be seen from other passages of Josephus. In recounting the destruction of the Temple he said that one million one hundred thousand perished and that most of them were ὁμόφυλον, but not natives of Jerusalem.[55] The word *homophulon* here must mean co-religionist, since on the same page he said that it was not to be wondered that there were so many people assembled in Jerusalem. He explained this by saying that the Jews who came to celebrate the festival of Passover were caught in the war and remained during the siege. He said that the Jews used to slaughter about two hundred fifty-five thousand and six hundred paschal lambs on the eve of Passover; an average of one lamb for ten men, not counting men and women who could not partake in this celebration on account of uncleanliness or on account of being ἀλλοφύλοις who came to worship. The word ἀλλοφύλοις must here mean the exclusion of those not of the Jewish religion. Hence *homophulon* must refer to co-religionists.

Josephus in describing the Temple says that there were tablets in the second wall written in Latin and Greek in which "ἀλλόφυλον" were warned not to penetrate further within;[56] "ἀλλόφυλον" must mean people not of the Jewish

---

[54] B. J., IV, 4.4.

[55] Ibid. VI, 9.3. τούτων τὸ πλέον ὁμόφυλον μὲν ἀλλ' οὐκ ἐπιχώριον.

[56] Ibid. V, 5.2. The word ἀλλόφυλον must have the connotation of people of other religions rather than of other races. Proselytes although coming from other nations or races are allowed to go into עזרת ישראל. Clermont-Ganneau had discovered some slabs which had inscriptions μηθένα αλλογενῆ εἰσπορεύεσθαι ἐντὸς τοῦ περὶ τὸ ἱερὸν τρυφάκτου καὶ περιβόλου. See also Mommsen, *The Province of the Roman Emp.*, N. Y., Vol. II, p. 205. It is possible that the word ἀλλογενῆ

religion. Josephus in appealing to the Jews to submit to the Romans used the *homophulon* term; he said, "μέμνησο δ' ὡς ὁμόφυλος ὢν παραινῶ καὶ 'Ιουδαῖς ὢν ἐπαγγέλλομαι,"[57] "and I will never injure my *race*."

The term ἀλλόφῦλος Josephus applied to people of other religions and not to people of other races. This is quite evident from Josephus' remark that the Jews were not allowed to marry women of ἀλλόφῦλος.[58] This term can be interpreted only to refer to women of another religion. There was no law either in the Bible or in the early Halakah

was translated from Latin *alienigenae* or from the Hebrew word בן נכר. The Septuagint renders the word בן נכר, ἀλλογενής. See Ex. 12.43; Ezek. 40.9.

Josephus in *Ant.*, XV, 11.5, used the term τον ἀλλοεθνῆ. Here Josephus apparently used a corrupted source. The entire passage of Josephus which describes the gates of the Temple does not agree with the Mishna Mid. 3. See also note 80. Josephus tells, ibid. V, 5.2, that one court was open to the women. ἀνεῖτό γε μὴν ταῖς τ' ἐπιχωρίοις καὶ ταῖς ἔξωθεν ὁμοφύλοις ἐν ἴσῳ πρὸς θρησκείαν ὁ χῶρος. Thackeray's translation of this passage reads as follows: "This court was, however, thrown open for worship to all Jewish women alike whether natives of the country or visitors from abroad." The word "Jewish" is not mentioned at all in the passage. ὁμοφύλοις has undoubtedly the meaning here of co-religionist, which is to say the court was open for worship to women, whether natives (Judaeans) or from foreign countries, of the same religion as the Judaeans. That the word ἀλλόφυλον has the meaning of foreign religion rather than foreign *race* can be proved further from another passage in Josephus, *Ant.*, XVIII, 9. Josephus tells us that a certain Jewish general in Babylon, by the name of Anileus, after defeating his opponent took his wife and married her. This woman brought along with her the gods of her country and worshiped them. The Jewish friends of Anileus reproached him, saying that he did not act in a manner according to the Hebrews, by marrying ἀλλόφυλον. They reproached him not because he married her, but because she brought her idols with her and worshiped them in his house. This proves sufficiently that ἀλλόφυλον is rendered here as foreign religion. Comp. also *Ant.* VIII, 7; XII, 4.

[57] *B. J.*, VI, 2.1.

[58] *Ant.*, XVIII, 9.5. Josephus in *Ant.*, XI, 5.4, tells us that Ezra and Nehemiah reproached the Jews for marrying foreign wives. He used the term ἀλλοεθνεῖς. See note 80.

THE JEWS: RACE, NATION OR RELIGION   25

prohibiting the Jews from marrying foreign women if they accepted the Jewish religion.[59]

It is certain that Gentiles who accepted Judaism, i. e., became proselytes, were permitted to marry Jewish women. They were not only ὁμόφυλος co-religionists, but the children of Israel.[60]

Although Herod was not of the Jewish race, since his father, Antipater, was an Idumaean, yet he was a Judaean. Herod's opponent, King Antigonus, called him half a Jew,[61] because neither his father nor his mother, Kupris, was of the Jewish race.[62] In the eyes of Antigonus he was a Jew by religion only and not by race. However, his descendants were Judaeans in the full sense of the word.[63] We are told in the Mishna that when King Agrippa, the grandson of Herod, read the Torah on the holiday of Tabernacles, he shed tears when he reached the verse, "from among thy brethren shalt thou set king over thee," apparently because he felt that he could not be considered a "brother" since

---

[59] See Kid. 4.1.

[60] According to R. Jose, a priest may marry a daughter of a proselyte בת גרים. Rabbi Simon was of the opinion that a priest may even marry a girl who embraced Judaism when she was not yet three years and a day old, which is against the biblical law where it specifies that a priest may marry only a virgin of the children of Israel, Ezek. 44.22, מזרע בית ישראל.
According to the Talmud, the Halakah is according to R. Jose, Yer. Ḳid. 66a, הלכה כר יוסי. Josephus in *Contra Apion* states that priests were allowed to marry *homoethnos*, which corresponds to the point of view of R. Jose that a priest may not marry a proselyte but she must be of the same religion and of the same people.

[61] *Ant.*, XIV, 15.2.

[62] Herod's mother Kupris was an Arabian. *B. J.*, 8.9; comp. *Ant.*, XIV, 7.3.

[63] Eusebius, *Church History*, I, 6, said that Herod was γένος ἀλλοφύλου. The reason is that according to the version of Africanus, Herod was not Idumaean; Antipater was taken a prisoner from Ascalon, where his father was a slave at the Temple of Apollo. Comp. also Justin Martyr, *Dialogue with Trypho*, 52. However, according to Josephus, Herod was of the Jewish *Ethnos*. Comp. *Ant.*, XIV, 12.1.

his ancestors were Idumaeans. The sages consoled him by saying, "You are our brother."[64] This meant that they considered Agrippa, although racially not of Jewish stock, a full Jew. He was ὁμοεθνος of the same people and ὁμόφυλος of the same religion.[65] A story is told in Josephus that a man named Simon, a fanatic, very zealous concerning the Jewish tradition and learned in the Jewish Law, maintained that Agrippa who was not of Jewish descent had no right to go into some of the inner chambers of the Temple.[66] Agrippa, who was by nature very human, called Simon and asked him why he was thus disqualified. Simon could offer no objection[67] because, according to the Jewish Law, Agrippa was a Judaean, a full Jew, regardless of his ancestry. As a matter of fact, in the time of the Second Jewish

[64] Sota 7.8. ‎אנריפס‎ .... ‎וכשהגיע ללא תוכל לתת עליך איש נכרי זלנו עיניו דמעות‎
‎אחינו אתה‎.

[65] According to Yer. Sota 22a ‎חנינה בן גמליאל‎ took issue with the sages who called Agrippa ‎אחינו אתה‎ and he said, ‎הרבה חללים נפלו באותו היום שהחניפו‎ ‎לו‎. This is due to the fact that some of the Tannaim looked upon the Herodian dynasty with contempt.

Dr. Baron, in his article "Historical Outlook of Maimonides" in the *Proceedings of the American Academy for Jewish Research*, Vol. VI (1935), p. 68, n. 133, says: "It is questionable, nevertheless, whether Maimuni knew that Agrippa's mother was Glaphyra, a non-Jewess. His partial Jewish descent through his grandmother, the Hasmonean Mariamne"... Such, however, is not the case. Agrippa was the son of Aristobulus and Bernice, the daughter of Salome. Both of his parents were Jews. See *B. J.*, I, 28.1: "For Alexander had by Glaphyra two sons, Tigranes and Alexander; and by his marriage with Bernice, Salome's daughter, Aristobulus had three, Herod, Agrippa and Aristobulus." See also *Ant.*, XVII, 1. On the basis of this error, Dr. Baron attempts to change a correct reading in Maimonides' ‎ולא היה לו אב מישראל‎ to read ‎ולא היתה‎ ‎לו אם מישראל‎ which is wrong. Were Agrippa's mother a non-Jewess, Agrippa would be considered, according to Maimonides, a non-Jew. See Rashi, Sota 41a ‎שאמו מישראל‎ which corresponds to Maimonides' reading, ‎ולא היה לו אב מישראל‎. The Rabbis erroneously believed that Agrippa was the son of Herod who was ‎עבדא דחשמונאי‎.

[66] δικαίως δ' ἂν εἴργοιτο τοῦ ναοῦ τῆς εἰσόδου προσηκούσης ταῖς ἐγγενέσιν.

[67] *Ant.* XIX, 7.4.

Commonwealth there was no pure Jewish race, since many Gentiles, converts to Judaism, lived in Palestine and the Diaspora, and they constituted a part of the *Jewish people* but not of the *Jewish race*.

Although the Jews were a mixed race at the time of the Second Commonwealth, they were a purer race than any other of that time. This was due to a singular cause. In order to join the Jewish people, it was necessary not only to accept the Jewish religion first, but to be circumcised, a rite not so easy for other people to submit to. Therefore the mixture was not so great as among other races. The idea that a pure race was no longer in existence at that time was recognized by the Jewish leaders of the first generation after the destruction of the Temple. They allowed an Ammonite proselyte named Judah to become a member of the community of Israel, i. e., to have the privilege of marrying a daughter of the Israelites.[68] This was against the biblical law which forever prohibits any Ammonite from joining the community of Israel.[69] The Tannaim allowed the Ammonite to join the community of Israel on the theory that there was no Ammonite race and that there were no more pure races in existence, since Sennacherib, the Assyrian King, mingled the nations by his wars.[70]

Philo, like Josephus, used the term $\delta\mu\delta\phi\bar{\upsilon}\lambda o s$ to designate co-religionist, not countryman, as it is usually translated. This may be demonstrated by the following passages from Philo: King Agrippa on appealing to Gaius Caesar not to put his image in the Temple of Jerusalem told him that not only would the Jews of Judaea permanently remain friendly to him, but also the Jews who inhabited

---

[68] Yad. 4.4, בא יהודה גר עמוני . . . והתירוהו לבא בקהל.
[69] Deut. 23.4. Nehem. 13.1.
[70] Yad. 4 בא סנחריב . . . ובלבל את כל האומות.

Asia Minor, as well as those who lived beyond the Euphrates.[71] Gaius granted the request of Agrippa, but accused him of being more desirous of serving his ὁμοφύλους than him, Caesar.[72] ὁμοφύλους does not mean countrymen, i. e., the Jews of Egypt, since Agrippa appealed to him in the name of the entire Jewry, even that beyond the Euphrates who were not under the rule of the Romans.[73]

In another passage Philo tells us that Isidorus, noting the contempt of Gaius for the Jewish embassy of Alexandria, said to him that he would hate them and their ὁμόφυλοι more if he became aware that they were the only people who refused to offer any sacrifice to him.[74] Here again the word ὁμόφυλοι must mean co-religionist, as Isidorus wanted to emphasize to Gaius the point that not only the Alexandrian Jews, but the entire Jewish people, refused to bring sacrifices to Gaius, and therefore the word ὁμόφυλοι cannot mean countrymen.

Again Philo in explaining the biblical laws says that God told the Jews to select a king "from among thy brethren" and not from strangers, using the words τον ὁμόφυλον και συγγενῆ[75] which mean that the Jewish king must be of the Jewish religion and related by blood, that is of the same people and of the same religion.[76]

Philo, like Josephus, when he speaks of members of other religions uses the term ἀλλόφυλοι. This may be satisfactorily proven from a passage in which he tells us that in the city of Jamnia, one of the most populated cities of Judaea, there lived besides the Judaeans ἀλλόφυλοι mem-

---

[71] *Legatio ad Gaium*, 36–41.
[72] Ibid. 42.
[73] καί τοῖς πανταχοῦ τῆς οἰκουμένης Ἰουδαίοις. The word οἰκουμένης should be rendered the Roman world.
[74] Ibid. 45.   [75] *De Special. Leg.*, IV, 3.
[76] It is interesting to note that Philo, in quoting the biblical words מקרב אחיך .... לא תוכל לתת עליך איש נכרי renders οὐκ ἀλλότριον ἀλλ' ἐκ τῶν σων ἀδελφῶν but gives the explanation τόν ὁμόφυλον καί συγγενῆ.

bers of other religions who brought considerable trouble to the Judaeans by violating their national laws. The heathens discovered that Gaius Caesar felt bitter towards the Jews because they refused to allow his image in their Temple. They thought that the proper moment had arrived to take revenge upon their fellow-citizens, the Jews, by erecting a great altar in honor of Gaius Caesar.[77] The term ἀλλόφυλοι therefore must mean not foreign people, but chiefly those of other religions, as we know that anyone, regardless of nationality or race, may become a Judaean by accepting the Jewish religion.[78]

Philo quite often uses the words *Joudaion Ethnos*. These words, mistakenly, have been translated as *The Jewish Nation*. It is quite certain that Philo in many instances did not mean the Jewish nation in the modern sense of the word. This is apparent from his statement that Abraham was the founder of the *Joudaion Ethnos*.[79] He could not have implied that Abraham was the founder of the Jewish nation, as a political state. It would have been more suitable to apply the term to David. Indeed, it would have been more applicable to Jacob than to Abraham, since the latter had more than one son—Isaac and Ishmael—and thus should be considered as the founder of two nations.[80]

[77] *Legatio ad Gaium*, 30.
[78] Philo stressed the religious point that these ἀλλόφυλοι gave trouble to the Judaeans by violating the Jewish customs.
[79] *De Vita Mosis*, I, 2, Ἰουδαίων ἔθνος.
[80] Eusebius, *Church History*, II, 5, says that Philo was sent to Rome in behalf of Ἀλεξάνδρειαν ὁμοεθνῶν. The term ὁμοεθνῶν should be translated "his people."

It is probable that Josephus in saying that priests were allowed to marry only *homoethnos*, meant that priests may marry only daughters of the same people and of the same religion. Likewise, Josephus' statement that no ἀλλοεθνῆ may enter the Temple is again to be understood that members of other religions as well as of peoples may not enter the sanctuary. Comp. also *Ant*. XV.

Undoubtedly, Philo meant to say that Abraham was the founder of the Jewish people as a religious community. It is well known that Abraham was the first to recognize God, as the God of the universe. And thus he is regarded as the founder of the Jewish religion, and so of the Jewish people. The same idea was expressed by the Tannaim when they said that a proselyte may invoke the name of God by the prayer which reads, "God, our God, and the God of our fathers," since Abraham is the father of all those who worship the God of Israel.[81] Thus Philo, the Jewish philosopher of the Diaspora, was of the opinion that the unity of the Jewish people was based not on state, but on religion. In the opinion of Philo as well as of the Tannaim the Jews do not constitute a nation; their unity is rooted in common cultural and religious interests.

III

ISRAELITES

Up to the destruction of the Temple, as we already pointed out, the Jews of Palestine were called יהודים, Judaeans. Their language was called עברית in the rabbinic

---

[81] See Yer. Bik. 64a. גר עצמו מביא וקורא . . . והטעם כי אב המון גוים נתתיך.
In speaking of fortunes and misfortunes which may befall humanity, Philo states (*On Joseph*, XXIII): "That these are dreams is attested not only by single men, but by cities, peoples, countries, by Greeks, by the world of the barbarians, by dwellers on the mainland, by dwellers on islands, by Europe, by Asia, by West, by East." μάρτυρες τῶν ἐνυπνίων οὐκ ἄνδρες μόνον, ἀλλὰ καὶ πόλεις, ἔθνη, χῶραι, ἡ Ἑλλας, ἡ βάρβαρος, ἠπειρῶται, νησιῶται, ἡ Εὐρώπη, ἡ Ἀσία, δύσις, ἀνατολή. He uses his terms decidedly in an ascending order, thus: single man, cities, *Ethnos*, countries, etc. The word *Ethnos*, therefore, must be regarded as referring to something between cities and countries. It cannot be translated as nations, for that would be the same as χῶραι. Philo, in using the term *Ethnos*, undoubtedly meant people, for a country may contain two or more peoples. Thus, in his own country—Egypt—there were at least three peoples: the natives (Egyptians), Hellenes and the Jews.

THE JEWS: RACE, NATION OR RELIGION   31

literature,[82] and by Josephus Hebrew. Josephus often tells us that he spoke in the Hebrew tongue.[83] Palestine was called ארץ, the land,[84] not *Erez Yisrael*. The Diaspora was called חוץ לארץ, "beyond the land."

After the destruction of the Temple the word Judaeans disappears entirely from the Talmud. The name Israel now became the only term for the Jews. Up to the time of the Hadrianic period we sometimes do find the word Judaeans, but after that it disappears entirely, and the name Israel supplants it.[85] After Judaea was conquered

---

[82] See Mishna Yad. 4 תרגום שכתוב עברית et passim.

[83] B. J., VI, 97. Comp. also *Ant.*, XVIII, 6.10. B. J., VI, 2.1. ἐβραΐ-ζων. Sometimes it may refer to Aramaic, see Acts 21.40, 26.16.

[84] Comp. Yer. Shebu. 36d, 37a, תני איזו היא הארץ ואיזו היא חוץ לארץ, et passim. See also Mak. 7a. After the destruction of the Temple, when Palestine came to be called *Erez Yisrael* by the Jews, many early passages in tannaitic literature were amended to read accordingly. During the Second Commonwealth, the Jews of the Diaspora referred to Palestine as the Holy Land. See Philo, *Leg. ad Gaium*, 30. Jerusalem was called the Holy City, ibid. 36. B. J. II, 16.4 et passim. Comp. also Sanh. 107 ירושלים עיר הקדשה. See, however, Yer. Hag. 77d. ירושלים עיר הגדולה.

[85] The word Judaeans occurs in the Talmud only when used by Gentiles or when a Jew is represented as speaking to a Gentile. Otherwise the word Israel is used throughout. Comp. e. g., Midr. Lam., כהלוקא די יהודאי, יהודאי, ההוא גברא יהודאי יתי, חד יהודאה בעי למשאל מרדו. See also Git. 57, בשלמך, לא נצרוך לחרובא כי יהודאי, פריקחן דיהודא או יהודאי יהודא או ארמאי ארמאי, בהדין סבא דיהודאי. Yer. Shebu. 4, בך יהודא. Comp. also Tos. 'Ab. Zarah, ומזמנין כל היהודים. See Midr. Lam. עד בתרתין נשין Comp. ibid. דאת מכבש ברברין (barbarians) כבש אילו יהודאי זניין באשקלון מתכשין... דחויין אפיך כיהודאתא... כולא שרי ושביק ליך אלא על. Comp. also Yeb. 62b; דאמרת לי חזיין אפיך כי יהודאתא לא שרי ולא שביק ליך Pes. 113b, יהודי הדר בלא אשה. The manuscripts, however, read אדם, which, undoubtedly, is the correct reading. The change is due to the Christian censor, because the statement אדם would naturally be against celibacy which was practiced by the Christian bishops. Therefore they changed from אדם הדר to יהודי הדר. The term Judaeans also occurs in the Talmud with reference to the *Ketubah*, since the *Ketubah* contains the clause כדת משה ויהודאי. See above p. 320. Comp. Ket. 7.6. העוברת על דת משה ויהודאי. See also Ned. 11.12. In some of the *Responsa* we again find the term Judaeans. This is due entirely to the influence of the Christians. The word Judaeans also occurs in the Talmud in relation to the Book of Esther. Comp. Meg. 13a; Yeb. 62b; 'Ab. Zarah 26a.

459

by the Romans, particularly after the last struggle of Bar Kokba, the Jews ceased to exist as a nation. They were not even allowed to enter Jerusalem, their metropolis. They segregated themselves as a religious group without a country of their own. They spoke different languages, those of the countries in which they dwelt. Their tongue which before the destruction of the Temple was called Hebrew עברית, was now called the "Sacred Tongue,"[86] not the language of the people, but the language of prayers and of the Bible. Judaea which in the time of the Second Jewish Commonwealth was called the Land, now was called the Land of Israel.

The word Israel does not have racial or national implications, but a religious significance. This is confirmed by at least one passage of the Tosefta which states that if one vowed to derive no benefit from Israel, he was forbidden to derive benefit not only from Israelites, but also from proselytes.[87] Since the word Israel had no racial connotation, but a religious one, a proselyte, although he was not of the Jewish race, was an Israelite.

The Greeks, the Romans and the Christians continued to call the Jews by the name of Judaeans, not Israelites. Since the term Judaeans was applied to the Jews when they had their own state, the term was still employed by the Hellenistic world,[88] although the Jews after the destruc-

---

[86] Comp. M. Sota 9, בלשון הקודש; Yer. Meg. 71b et passim; also Targum Jonathan Gen. 45.12. בלישן בית קודשא.

[87] Tos. Ned. 11.4. הנודר מישראל אסור אף בגרים.

[88] It is of interest to note that some pagan historian of the latter part of the second century used the term Ἑβραῖοι and not Ἰουδαῖοι. See Th. Reinach, *Texts*, p. 158. It is due probably to the fact that some pagan writers who were friendly to the Jews did not want to use the expression Ἰουδαῖοι, because it was regarded as a term of reproach. Thus, in the literature of the Ebionites the term "Hebrew" is found instead of "Judaean." Eusebius who was a great admirer of Philo and

tion of the Temple called themselves Israelites. Furthermore, Judaeans in the eyes of the Greeks and Romans were not only members of another state, but were considered by the Hellenes and by the barbarians, Judaeans, not only in religion but in their whole mode of life. The Jews had introduced a new philosophy and a culture greatly at variance with that of the rest of the world. Judaism and Hellenism were two distinctly different cultures. Any Jew, regardless of his racial ancestry and of the place where he lived, whether in Palestine, Egypt, or Asia Minor, was, in the eyes of the Hellenes, a Judaean,[89] as any Hellene who lived in Athens, Sparta, Egypt or in a city of Asia Minor was classified as a Hellene, distinct from barbarians and Jews.

The Christians continued to apply the term Judaeans to the Jews. For the Christians, Israel was the Chosen People. But after the Jews had rejected Jesus, who according to the early Church Fathers is alluded to in the Bible by the name of Israel,[90] the Jews ceased to be Israelites in the eyes of the Christians. Paul said, "For they are not all Israel which are of Israel,"[91] but only those who believed in Jesus. Paul further says that the Gentiles before they accepted Jesus as the Christ were alien to the commonwealth of Israel; however, with their acceptance, "Those who were far were made nigh by the blood of Christ."[92]

Josephus calls them Hebrews (*C. H.* II, 4; I, 5), although both lived in the period of the Christian era. Likewise Eusebius says that Peter and the first fifteen bishops were of Hebrew descent (ibid. II, 16; IV,5).
  [89] See Dio, *Roman History*, XXXVII.
  [90] Comp. Justin Martyr, *Dialogue with Trypho*, 100, also the *Epistle of Barnabas*, 12.
  [91] Romans, 9.6.
  [92] Ephesians, 2.13.

Therefore, the Jews were called Judaeans by the Christians and ceased to be considered Israelites.[93]

It is probable that the Jews began to use the name Israel exclusively in order to refute the Christian point of view that they were not of the heritage of the religion of the Patriarchs, Moses and the Prophets. The Jews by adopting the name of Israel wanted to demonstrate that only they continue the old religion of Israel which God revealed to Moses and the Prophets.

The name Judaeans, which was applied by early Christians as a nickname and a term of contempt to the people who rejected Jesus,[94] was later accepted by the people. The word Jews is derived from Judaeans.[95] An analogous use of a contemptuous name may be found in a few instances. The name Pharisees was coined and used by the Sadducees against the followers of Ezra. They nicknamed them *Perushim*, Pharisees—they had separated themselves from the Jews. This name was later adopted by the followers of Ezra. Another instance may be given: In the 18th century the sects of Hassidim nicknamed all the Jews who did not accept their theories as *Misnagdim*, as opposed not only to the new sect of Hassidim, but even,

---

[93] According to the early church, the Christians were the true heirs to the Covenant. See *Ep. of Bar.*, 13. From the Julian Apostate we may infer that the Christians considered themselves Israelites "Now since the Galilaeans (Christians) say that, though they are different from the Jews, they are still, precisely speaking, Israelites." *The Works of the Emperor Julian* (*The Loeb Classical Library*), Vol. III, p. 393.

[94] See Juster, *Les Juifs dans l'Empire Romain*, I, 173, n. 4.

[95] Likewise the words *Juif, Jude, Zhid* are derived from the term *Judaean*.

It is interesting to note that after Bar Kokba the Romans, as well as the Christians, no longer referred to the country as Judaea, but called it Palestine. They did not want to associate this country with Jews and referred to it as Palestine. The modern Jews, however, not knowing the reason why the Christians called it Palestine, adopted this name.

THE JEWS: RACE, NATION OR RELIGION

from their viewpoint, to Judaism. This name, however, was used by all the Jews who opposed the Hassidim. Another example may be found in the rise of the reform movement against the Pope. The Catholics called the people who protested against the church Protestants. History is replete with such examples.

We may be safe in saying that the Jews after the last attempt to win national independence in the time of Bar Kokba, which ended with a catastrophe, identified themselves as a religious community, just as the Christians did. After the destruction of the Temple, the term חבר היהודים, Commonwealth of the Judaeans, was no longer used, and Synagogue of Israel, כנסת ישראל, a theological term, was applied to the entire Jewish community, as ἐκκλησία τοῦ θεοῦ, the Church of God, was used by the Christians. The leader of the Jews was no longer called Ethnarch, but ἀρχισυναγωγος, the ruler of the Jewish community or Patriarch. Julian the Apostate, in his edict to the Jews, does not address them as *Ethnos Joudaion*,[96] as did Julius and Augustus Caesar, because in his time the Jews did not constitute an *Ethnos* but a religious community, a synagogue, כנסת ישראל.

Even before the destruction of the Temple, the religion united the Jews of Palestine and the Diaspora and made them as one people. Therefore, anyone who accepts the Jewish religion automatically joins the Jewish people. A proselyte must circumcise himself. Circumcision was a symbol of the covenant which God made with Israel.[97]

---

[96] Th. Reinach, *Texts*, p. 209. Ἰολιανὸς Ἰουδαίων τῷ κοινῷ.
See Mommsen, *H. Z.*, 89. Comp. however, Juster, *Les Juifs dans l'Empire Romain*, Vol. II, p. 19. There is no question that after Bar Kokba the Jews did not constitute a nation, and so the Romans considered them a people, but not a state.
[97] Gen. 18.2.

From the point of view of the Halakah a proselyte who did not go through the ritual of circumcision was still a good proselyte.[98] According to the school of Hillel, circumcision *ex opere operato* is valid. If a man was circumcised before he was converted to Judaism he did not have to go through another ritual.[99] The Jews, however, demanded circumcision from the proselytes, since it was a sign of distinction of the Jewish people from the rest of the world.[99a] They were very particular about this. When the Hasmoneans conquered other nations they forced circumcision upon them.[100] Even the Herodian family demanded circumcision from Gentiles who wanted to marry their daughters.[101] It became for the Jewish people a *sine qua non*.

On the other hand, a Jew who accepts another religion is no longer a member of the Jewish people, according to the early Halakah. He may be considered a Jew by birth

---

[98] Yeb. 46a. טבל ולא מל ר' יהושע אומר הרי זה גר.

[99] Tos. Shab. 15 גר שנתגייר כשהוא מהול . . . אין צריך (להטיף ממנו דם). This is in accordance with the principle of the school of Hillel which stressed the spirit rather than the letter of the Law. Since circumcision is to indicate the Covenant which God made with Israel and also to differentiate between a Jew and a non-Jew (see Tacitus, *Hist.*, 5), a convert to Judaism who had already been circumcised need not undergo another ritual. Comp. Solomon Zeitlin, "Les Principes des Controverses Halachiques entre les écoles de Schammai et de Hillel," *REJ*, XCIII (1932), 73–83.

[99a] Circumcision became a symbol of the unity of the Jewish people and a mark of differentiation from the rest of the world. Comp. Tacitus, *Hist.*, V, 5. "Circumcidere genitalia instituerunt ut diversitate noscantur." Comp. also the story of Shechem (Gen. 34) of whom the sons of Jacob demanded circumcision for marrying Dinah. Hence Paul looked upon circumcision as a symbol peculiarly Jewish. "Behold, I, Paul, say unto you, that if ye be circumcised, Christ shall profit you nothing. For I testify again to every man that is circumcised that he is a debtor to the whole law." (Galatians 5.2–3). Since by circumcision one joins the Jewish people, Paul, the Apostle to the Gentiles, fought bitterly against circumcision, more than other precepts and ceremonies of the Jews.

[100] See *Ant.*, XIII, 9. Comp. also I Macc. 2.46.

[101] See *Ant.*, XX, 7.

only; he belongs to another religion and has excluded himself from the Jewish people. According to the early Tannaim he is in the same status as a גר תושב, a heathen who resides in Palestine, and he is considered a בן נכר, a foreigner.[102] However, if one is born of Jewish parents and is not circumcised, he is considered a Jew and he is entitled to all Jewish privileges. He is only named in the Talmud a heretic, ומשומד מומר לדבר אחד.[103]

If a Jew disregards all the precepts he is still considered a Jew. When a Jew openly profanes the Sabbath, however, the Talmud says that he is מומר לכל התורה כולה.[104] The severity of this provision was due to the fact that the Christians substituted Sunday as the Day of the Lord, instead of Saturday. The Tannaim of that period, therefore, laid great stress on the observance of the Sabbath. Likewise, this severity may have been due to the fact that by profaning the Sabbath one also denies the creation of the world by God and the covenant which God made with Israel.[105]

In this essay it was demonstrated that the Jews during the Second Commonwealth did not constitute one nation. The Jews of the Diaspora in Egypt and in Babylonia were not under the political leadership of the Palestinian Jews.

---

[102] Comp. Yer. 'Er. 24b. גר תושב ועבד תושב משומד בגלוי פנים הרי הוא כנוי לכל דבר. Also Yer. Shek. 46b. מכם להוציא את המשומדים. According to the Sifra, p. 3 (ed. Venice) a convert is not even a בן ברית—מכם להוציא את המשומדים . . . מה ישראל מקבלי ברית אף הגרים מקבלי ברית, יצאו המשומדים שאינן בני ברית. Comp. also Targum Onkelos to Ex. 12.43, where the translation of זאת חקת הפסח כל בן נכר לא יאכל בו is given as כל בר ישראל דישתמד לא יכול בו. According to the Targum a convert is called a בן נכר and like a heathen cannot partake of the paschal lamb. See also Targum, according to Jonathan, ad locum, כל בר עמטין או בר ישראל דאסתלק ולא הדר לא יכול בו.

[103] Ḥul. 46b.

[104] 'Er. 69b. ישראל המחלל שבת. See Tos. ibid. 7. מחלל שבת בפרהסיא. Comp. also 'Ab. Zarah 64b. בפרהסיא אין צריך לבטל רשות.

[105] Comp. Ex. 20.13; 31.13.

They were citizens of their own respective countries. What really united the entire Jewry was their religion, their culture. The Jews of the Diaspora looked upon Judaea as the Holy Land. Only a minority of the entire Jewry lived in Judaea. In Egypt alone there were a million Jews[106] and in Asia Minor and along the Mediterranean coast to the Black Sea there were almost as many as in Egypt.[107] Babylon possessed a still greater number of Jews than did Egypt. Josephus and Philo both claimed that there was not a single place in the world where the Jews did not live.[108]

The spiritual needs, however, of all the Jews in the Diaspora and their laws were directed in Judaea by the Sanhedrin. The religion, indeed, became the rock upon which Judaism was built. Only the literature of the Palestinians survived and made an impress on Jewish life, while the literature of the Jews of the Diaspora did not influence Jewish life and disappeared.[108a] Even the writings of Philo still extant owe their preservation to the interest of the Church Fathers in them.[109]

Although the Jews like the Christians segregated themselves as a religious community, nevertheless there was a vast difference between the two religions. In Christianity, though it came from the hills of Judaea, Jerusalem was not the metropolis of their religion, and hence Paul said,

---

[106] Philo, *In Flaccum*.
[107] Comp. ibid. 7; *Leg. ad Gaium*, 36.
[108] Philo, *In Flaccum*, 7; Josephus, *Contra Apion*; *B. J.*
[108a] However, when the center of Judaism shifted from Palestine to Babylon, and later to other countries, Jewish life was greatly influenced by the cultural accomplishments of these centers.
[109] Even the writings of Josephus owe their preservation to the Fathers of the Church. Neither Josephus nor Philo are even mentioned in the entire talmudic literature. Jewish history is greatly indebted to the Church for preserving these works, without which the history of the Second Jewish Commonwealth could not have been written.

"But Jerusalem which is above is free, which is the mother of us all."[110] Similarly, Jesus said, "Upon this rock I will build my Church."[111] The Jewish religion, on the other hand, was not only followed by the Judaeans who lived in Palestine, but by all the Jews in the world. The Jews who lived in the Diaspora not only sent their sacrifices[112] and gifts to the Temple, but they themselves from time to time used to go to the Holy City of Jerusalem to worship the God of Israel. Ever since the days of the Prophets and the time of the Second Jewish Commonwealth, Jews have hoped for the time when all the adherents of the Jewish religion, the Israelites, would be together in Palestine. This hope did not cease after the Temple was destroyed. Still more did they look forward to the day when Jews the world over would return to Jerusalem, the Messianic Age. For thousands of years the Jews have prayed to God in their synagogues for the rebuilding of the city of Jerusalem and for gathering together all the Jewish people.[113]

The Pharisees had the foresight to realize that the Judaeans would not maintain their independent state against the Roman aggressor for a long time. They knew that the Judaeans were surrounded by hostile pagans to whom Jewish culture and religion were foreign. The Phari-

---

[110] Galatians, 4.26.
[111] Matt. 16.18.
[112] *Ant.*, XVIII.
[113] Palestine was always regarded by the Jews as their ancient home to which they strove to return. According to the Tosefta 'Ab. Zarah 4, שישיבת ארץ ישראל שקולה כנגד כל מצות שבתורה the hope of the Jews for the coming of the Messianic age, so that they could return to Palestine, was one of the main reasons for the emergence of the different Messiahs in Jewish history. This historic craving for Palestine throughout the centuries undoubtedly helped to develop the movement of Zionism. Also the numerous persecutions of the Jews helped to bring about the rise of the various Messiahs and the final growth of Zionism.

sees strove to strengthen the Jewish culture so that even on losing their independence they would be able to continue their lives as Jews without a country. They made their religion and not the land or even the language the center of the Jewish people. With this they made it possible for the Jews to keep alive in the face of massacres, inquisitions and persecutions; to surmount the debilitating influence of the Exile; to remain loyal even at the time of emancipation and assimilation.

The Sadduceans, who were interested only in the political upbuilding of Judaea and ignored the development of the Jewish religion and its culture, disappeared entirely after the collapse of the Jewish state. After the city of Jerusalem was razed there was no *raison d'être* for their existence.

The idea of the Pharisees was to give unity and strength to the Jews in the centuries of wandering, privation and degradation. For the Pharisees, Judaism was a living religion. The Halakah was not rigid but elastic. They took full cognizance of the demands of the time by amending the Halakah. The Pharisees always strove to bring religion into consonance with life. They introduced different *takkanot* so as to amend and to modify the Halakah through legal fiction or interpretation,[114] for the purpose of harmonizing religion and life.

To summarize: We believe that this essay demonstrates that in the early days of our history there was distinctly a Hebrew race. By the time of the Second Commonwealth

---

[114] A *Takkana* תקנה is a modification of biblical laws or earlier Halakah. It is by its very nature permanent and universal, applicable to all Jewry, irrespective of the land they inhabit, and is valid for all time. It can never be annulled, but merely modified, or even suspended as a "temporary measure," הוראת שעה. "Temporarily," however, may mean a very long period.

there was no longer a pure Hebrew race. Only the Jews who lived in Palestine constituted the Jewish nation and called themselves Judaeans. The Jews of Babylon were not members of the Jewish nation. They were only united to the Jews of Palestine by religion and culture. They called themselves Hebrews or Israelites. After the destruction of the Temple, the Jews segregated themselves as a religious group, כנסת ישראל, and no longer called themselves Judaeans but Israelites.

ADDENDA to note 85

Comp. Targum to Ex. 1.19; 2.7; 5.3; 7.16; 9.1 10.3; Jonah, 1.9. See, Targum to Deut. 15.12; Jer. 34.9. See Yer. Ma'as. Sh. 55b. Git. 43b. See also Targum to Gen 40.15; 41.12; 43.32.

WHO IS A JEW?

A Halachic-Historic Study

IN A TIME when peoples who never enjoyed statehood have become independent states and are now members of the United Nations and on *a par* with the great nations of the world; in a period when men are no longer satisfied with subduing their own world but are striving to conquer outer space, accepted definitions are disputed and are subjected to new revisions.

The Jews, who lost their statehood almost nineteen centuries ago, have recently established an independent state, the State of Israel, in the very land where their forefathers had lived and where their kingdom had flourished. Throughout the centuries the Jews considered this land their land — religiously, historically and legally. Through the ages the Jews have expected a redeemer, the Messiah, who would reestablish them in the land of their forefathers. When the State of Israel was proclaimed only a small minority of the Jews lived there. It is understandable that with the establishment of the State of Israel, when the majority of the Jews were living in the Diaspora, the question who is a Jew should arise, since under the Law of Return any Jew enjoys the right to immigrate to Israel and to become an Israeli citizen without any obstacles

The question — who is a Jew — first arose after the French Revolution when the Jews were politically emancipated, the Jews themselves did not ask this question. It arose at the National Assembly of France, after the Revolution, when it was debated whether or not the Jews

Reprinted from the *Jewish Quarterly Review*, New Series, Vol. 49, 1959.

should enjoy equal rights with the rest of the French people. The liberals like Abbé Grégoire and particularly Clermont-Tonnere and Robespierre, maintained that the Jews were only a religious community like Catholics and Protestants, that the term Jew had the connotation of religion, and hence were entitled to the rights which were enjoyed by the other religious groups. On the other hand the nationalists, the reactionaries Abbé Maury and Rewbell maintained that the Jews were a nation, that the term Jew had the connotation of nationality, and therefore they could not enjoy rights as other Frenchmen but should be protected by French law as aliens.[1] The same question, whether the Jews were a religious group or a nation, came up again in the Constitutional Assembly in the State of Batavia (now Holland), after she gained her freedom.[2]

When Christianity became the dominating religion of Rome the policy of the Church was shaped according to the teachings of the Church Fathers. The Church regarded the Jews as an ethnic group — a nation. It prohibited anyone not only a Christian but even a pagan from embracing the Jewish religion. Those of Jewish parentage were allowed to remain Jews. The Church forbade marriage between Christians and Jews and severely punished those who transgressed.[3] Throughout the Middle Ages the Christians, whether hostile or favorable to the Jews, looked upon them as a ethnic group. The Church maintained that the Jewish religion was an ethnic religion, not a universal.[4] The Church did not exterminate the Jews as it did the pagans who did not embrace Christianity because the

---

[1] "Le mot juif n'est pas le nom d'une secte, mais d'une nation." Comp. Leon Kahn, *Les Juifs de Paris*, Paris, 1898; S. Zeitlin, *JQR*, 1944, pp. 98–102.

[2] *Ibid.*, pp. 103–108.

[3] Comp. *ibid.*, pp. 85–98.

[4] *Ibid.*

Jews were the guardians of the Bible in which the Christians found evidence that Jesus was the messiah. The Church who permitted the Jews to exist in order to demonstrate the truth of Christianity. The Jews who rejected Jesus were subjugated and suffered.

The Jews did not surrender their idea of Judaism. They believed that Judaism was a universal religion and that the Jews were the people of God. The Jews never asked themselves who they were. Anyone born of Jewish parents was a Jew; they considered anyone who embraced Judaism a Jew.

The Jews themselves are now raising the question — who is a Jew and what is Judaism. Some maintain that Judaism is a religion and that the connotation of Jew is religious. Others are of the opinion that the Jews are a nation. Still others believe that Judaism is a "civilization." Lately the term "peoplehood" for the Jews has been employed.

The Jews are not a *new* people, they are one of the oldest peoples in the world. Judaism is one of the oldest religions in the world, and the oldest in the Western world. Both Christianity and Islam are the daughters of Judaism. The Jews have a history of thousands of years and therefore, in order to have a clear definition of who is a Jew we must review their history from their early days down to the present without prejudice or favor. No definition of who is a Jew can be made *de novo*; it must be based on historical evidence.

Originally the word Jew had a genealogical as well as geographical connotation. The people were called יהודים, Judaeans, Jews, because they were descendants of Judah, the son of Jacob. During the time of the First Temple there were two different states. There was a Judaean state in the South and the people living there were called

בני יהודה the men of Judaea. The country was called Judaea. The king of the land was called מלך יהודה, the King of Judaea the language was called Judaean, the people living in the North were called the children of Israel; the land was called ארץ ישראל, the Land of Israel; and the king was called מלך ישראל, the King of Israel. The two kingdoms, the Southern and the Northern, constituted two different nations. They worshipped different gods. The Southern people believed in the God of Israel who dwelt in the Temple of Jerusalem, who had brought them out of the land of Egypt, while the Northern people whose first king Jeroboam, built "two calves of gold" and told the people that these were the gods who broughtout their ancestors out of Egypt.[5] The prophets of both the Southern and Northern States were opposed to the division of the tribes of Israel, and looked toward a time when the two states would be united into one kingdom, the Kingdom of Israel worshipping one God of Israel.

The God worshipped in the Southern Kingdom was an ethnic God who had made a covenant with their forefathers, Abraham, Isaac and Jacob. They worshipped him because he led their forefathers out of Egypt and brought them to the land of Canaan as he had promised them.[6] In the Northern Kingdom Jeroboam who built two "calves of gold" and told the people, "Here is your god Israel which brought you out of the land of Egypt,"[7] laid emphasis on the fact that they should worship the god who brought them out of the land of Egypt. The people of the Northern Kingdom worshipped different gods at different times according to the advantages they could derive from them. One who was not a descendant of Abraham, Isaac and

---

[5] I Kings 12.27–8.   [6] Comp. Jer. 11.3–5.

[7] I Kings 12.26, ויעש שני עגלי זהב ... הנה אלהיך ישראל אשר העלוך מארץ מצרים.

Jacob, and who was not of the racial stock of those who had been enslaved in Egypt and had entered the Promised Land, could not join. In other words there were no proselytes.

The prophets protested against the conception of an ethnic God. In the Book of Isaiah we have the following words: "Thus saith the Lord: The heaven is My throne, and the earth is my footstool; Where is the house that ye may build unto me? And where is the place that may be My resting-place?"[8]

About the year 722 BCE the Assyrians conquered the Northern State and exiled most of the people to other countries; since then the Northern Kingdom ceased to exist. Many people of the Northern Kingdom joined the Kingdom of Judah. In the year 586 BCE the Kingdom of Judah also ceased to exist.

In the year 538 BCE King Cyrus of Persia issued a proclamation permitting the Judaeans to return to their homeland Judaea. Only a small minority of them left Babylonia for Judaea. A revolution ensued among the Judaeans at that time which had a far reaching influence in shaping Jewish history and the history of the civilized world. The Judaeans who were polytheists and henotheists became monotheists — recognizing but one God, the God of the people of Israel, regardless of whether they lived in the land of Judaea or elsewhere. The Judaeans belonged to one community, the followers of the God of Israel. In Judaea, where a new Jewish community was organized, a theocracy was established, i. e. the rule of God. The Judaeans were governed by a priest under the authority of God.

The inhabitants of Judaea were always called Judaeans. In the biblical books of the Post-Exilic period, Ezra and

---

[8] Isa. 66.11; Ezek. 37.15–25.

Jeremiah, the name Israel is still used, but the name Judaeans is most prevalent. Later the name Israel disappears and that of Judaeans takes its place. In the book of Esther the name of Israel is not mentioned. The word יהודים, Judaeans, appears throughout the book. The author relates that after the downfall of Haman many people of the land מתיהדים, Judaized. The author's meaning of מתיהדים, Judaized, is ambiguous. Does he infer that the people of the land accepted the God of the Judaeans and they became a part of the people?[9]

Mordecai was called a Judaean in the Book of Esther although in the genealogy given he is a descendant of the tribe of Benjamin. Josephus, in the first ten books of the *Antiquities*, where he relates the history of the people down to the Restoration, uses the term Hebrews. After that period he calls them Judaeans. The name Judaeans is applied to the inhabitants of Judaea in the Hellenistic literature as well as in the tannaitic. Josephus said that the people were called Judaeans because they were the descendants of Judah.[10] In another place he gives another reason, namely that they were the inhabitants of the country of Judaea.[11] Thus the term Judaeans, Jews, had a tribal connotation, a particular group of men who lived in a country called Judaea.

The people of Judaea were united with their brethren under one flag from the time of the Restoration until the time of Alexander of Macedon. All of them lived in the Persian Empire. When Alexander conquered this empire they continued to be united. They so continued some time after his death when his empire became divided. Later Judaea was conquered by the Ptolemies and the Judaeans were united with their brethren who lived in Egypt but

---

[9] See below p. 257. [10] *Ant.* XI. 7.
[11] *Contra Apionem* I, 22.

no longer united with those in Babylonia. When Judaea became a part of the Seleucid Kingdom the Judaeans again were united with their brethren in Babylonia. When Judaea became an independent state, the State of Judaea, they became separated from their brethren in Babylonia and Egypt.

Ecclesiastical and secular authority was vested in the hands of the high priest from the time of the Restoration on, first by the Persian kings and later by the Ptolemies and the Seleucids. The high priest during this entire period was the vicar of God and he had the sole authority over the people in civil matters.

The high priest was shorn of both authorities, religious and secular with the establishment of the state of Judaea. Theocracy was abolished and nomocracy was established. In nomocracy there can be no representative of God. The High priest authority was limited to the temple, while the secular authority was held by the ethnarch and later by the kings. A new institution was established for religious matters, the *Bet Din*, the Sanhedrin which dominated the religious life not only in Judaea but also in Babylonia and Egypt. When the Diaspora extended to other parts of the world, the religious life was dominated by the laws promulgated by the *Bet Din*.

It is axiomatic that the people who lived in Judaea were called Judaeans, Jews. Many Judaeans left Judaea after the destruction of the first Temple, and went to Egypt where they settled and continued to consider themselves Judaeans. Again when Ptolemy I conquered Judaea many Judaeans were captured and were settled in Egypt. Thus the Egyptian Diaspora was originally made up of Judaeans and they were known as Judaean Jews.[12] It is not certain whether their coreligionists in Babylonia, who had not

---

[12] Comp. S. Zeitlin, *The Jews: Race, Nation or Religion*, 1936.

migrated to Judaea at the time of the Restoration, were called Judaeans, Hebrews or Israelites. However it appears that the Diaspora in Asia Minor living under Seleucid domination were called Hebrews and in some parts Israelites.

The conception of God was further revolutionized with the establishment of the Second Commonwealth. The Judaeans were monotheists since the time of the Restoration — they believed in their God, the God of their people. He was an ethnic God. Through the increased influence of the Pharisees, who maintained that God is universal — the God of the entire human race, the Judaeans were not only monotheists but became strong believers in a universal God. This was one of the contentions between the Sadducees and the Pharisees. The Sadducees believed in a national God, an ethnic God of the Judaeans while the Pharisees believed that their God is the God over the entire universe. The Judaeans accepted him but held that anyone, regardless of nation or race, can accept the God of the Judaeans, the God of the Universe.

So long as the people adhered to the idea of a racial God, an ethnic God, there could not be any convert to the religion of the Judaeans. The word *ger*, which frequently occurs in the Bible, has the connotation of stranger, a newcomer in the land.[13] Converts were welcome after the acceptance of the idea that the God of the Judaeans is a universal God. The word *ger* in the Bible, which we previously mentioned, had the connotation newcomer and now came to be applied to any person who became a convert, a newcomer to the religion of the Judaeans, one who became a part of the Jewish people. The term *proselytos*, by which the Septuagint translated the word *ger* in the

[13] כי גרים הייתם בארץ מצרים.

Bible, came to mean a convert to Judaism in the late Hellenistic Jewish literature.

Josephus did not yet use the term proselyte for those who joined the Judaeans. When he related the story of Sylleus, the son of Bodas, king of Arabia, who wanted to marry Salome, the sister of king Herod, the king agreed to this marriage on the condition that Sylleus would accept the Judaean customs, laws.[14] When Helena, Queen of Adiabene, and her son Izates joined the Judaean religion Josephus wrote that they changed their way of life, accepting the Judaean customs, laws.[15]

Was a ceremony required from a proselyte to the Judaean religion? We deduce from the early literature of the Second Jewish Commonwealth that no ceremony was necessary. The rejection of idols and the acceptance of the God of Israel as the God of the universe was all that was required. It is related in the book of Ruth that the heroine, Ruth, in accepting the Judaean religion, simply said to her mother-in-law, "Thy people shall be my people, and thy God is my God." A story is recorded in the Talmud of a non-Jew who came to Hillel asking to be converted to the Judaean religion on the condition that he be instructed in the entire Torah while standing on one foot. Hillel welcomed him and said, "What is hateful to you do not do to your fellow-men, the rest is commentary; go and study."[16] Hillel, in accepting the non-Jew as a proselyte to the Judaean religion, acted on the assumption that the non-Jew who came to him to be converted had already renounced his idols and accepted the God of Israel as the God of the universe. Hence he had to follow the precepts

---

[14] *Ant.* 16.17 (225) Ἰουδαίων ἔθεσι.

[15] *Ibid.*, 20.2 (38) ... Ἰουδαίων ἔθεσιν ...

[16] Shab. 31: בא ..... מעשה בנכרי [נוי] אחד שבא לפני שמאי אמר ליה גיירני לפני הלל גיירה אמר ליה דעלך סני לחברך לא תעביד זו היא כל התורה כולה ואידך פירושה היא זיל גמור.

of God like any Jew. Since circumcision is a precept of God
and had to be performed on the eighth day after the child's
birth it had to be done for a convert immediately as otherwise he would be continually transgressing God's law.
However circumcision was not a *sine qua non* for those
who wanted to accept the Judaean religion, although later
it became imperative for proselytes. Hillel said to the non-
Jew that he should not do to a fellow-man what was hateful
to himself. According to Hillel the Judaean religion was
based on two principles — the recognition and love of
the God of Israel as the God of the universe, and love of
one's fellow-men. Josephus, in his account of the conversion
of Izates to the Judaean customs, the Judaean way of life,
said that Izates wondered whether he could be a true
Judaean without being circumcised, since circumcision was
fraught with danger to him because of the reaction of his
subjects, the Abidenes. His teacher, Ananias relieved his
anxiety by telling him that he could worship God without
being circumcised, that the worship of God is superior to
circumcision.[17] Josephus further relates that once when
Izates was reading the Laws of Moses a man, named
Eleazar, who was grounded in the laws of his country,
reproached Izates and said that he was breaking these laws
while reading the Laws of Moses, since he was not circumcised. This does not mean that circumcision was a *sine
qua non* for proselytes. Eleazar simply advised Izates that
when one transgressed the laws of Moses he ought not
read the laws of Moses.[18]

It is related in the book of Judith that, after Holofernes
was slain, Achior, the Ammonite, believing in God, was
circumcised, "and joined unto the house of Israel."[19]

[17] *Ant.* 20.2 (41) . . . θεῖον σέβειν . . . εἶναι κυριώτερον τοῦ περιτέμνεσθαι . . .
[18] *Ibid.* (44).   [19] 14.10: και περιετέμετο τὴν σαρκα . . .

Achior, who believed in God and joined the house of Israel, followed the laws of God, and performed the first precept of God, that of circumcision.

Circumcision became a *sine qua non* for proselytes after the destruction of the Second Temple. The demand for the circumcision of proselytes is understandable: First, the proselyte indicated by this act his acceptance of the Judaean religion, and furthermore the Jews underwent persecutions for observing this commandment. Antiochus Epiphanes prohibited circumcision and the Jews suffered death for its observance. Secondly, Paul maintained that God made a covenant with Abraham not by circumcision.[20] To combat the Paulinian doctrine the sages maintained that God made a covenant with Abraham by circumcision, and since that time circumcision became known by the phrase ברית של אברהם, "covenant of Abraham."[21] Therefore the Jews stressed the importance of circumcision and demanded it from proselytes.

What is the underlying reason for the ritual of baptism for proselytes? A conclave was held in the year 65 CE where certain measures were adopted, one of them being the pronouncement that all non-Jews were declared to be *ipso facto* unclean in the degree of זב, *zab*.[22] Any Jew who was unclean in the degree of a *zab* was obliged to be baptized after purification and to bring a sacrifice. A non-Jew, who was declared to be unclean in the degree of a *zab*, who wished to join the Jewish community, had to be baptized since by entering the Jewish community he became purified. Besides being baptized the poselyte had to offer a sacrifice, just as a Jew who had been purified from his uncleanliness had to bring a sacrifice besides being baptized. The sac-

---

[20] Romans 4.1–13.
[21] והמפר בריתו של אברהם אבינו... אין לו חלק לעולם הבא.
[22] Tos. Zab. 2.1: הגוים... טמאין כזבין לכל דבריהם. Comp. also S. Zeitlin, *HUCA*, Vol. 1.

rifice brought by the Jew was two pigeons, a similar sacrifice was brought by the proselyte.[23] It is evident from this that the baptism for the proselyte was invoked not because he accepted the God of the Judaeans but because he became pure of his uncleanliness, which was in the degree of a *zab*.

The Talmud records a controversy over the question of what was the imperative requirement of one who wanted to become a Judaean. According to Rabbi Eliezar if the candidate was circumcised but not baptized he was a *bona fide* proselyte. According to Rabbi Joshua if he was baptized and not circumcized he was a *bona fide* proselyte.[24] Rabbi Joshua, a Hillelite, held that if a non-Jew wanted to become a Jew he would have to follow all the precepts of God and therefore would have to be circumcised, but maintained that circumcision was not a *sine qua non* for proselytism. Baptism was a *sine qua non* for proselytism according to Rabbi Joshua since as a non-Jew he was in the state of uncleanliness. Therefore when he wanted to become a Jew he had to take the levitical immiersion. It was the opinion of the sages that both circumcision and baptism were imperative for those who wanted to become proselytes.

This law recorded in the Talmud in the name of the sages is really the opinion of Rabbi Jose[25] who lived after the Hadrianic period. The reason that his name was not mentioned is that the law would have had to be decided against him as the opinion of one individual and Rabbi Joshua held an opposing view. Therefore the view was given in the name of the sages. There is a talmudic prin-

---

[23] Tos. Shek. 3; Ker. 8–9.
[24] Yeb. 46: גר שמל ולא טבל ר' אליעזר אומר הרי זה גר ... טבל ולא מל ר' יהושע אומר הרי זה גר. Comp. also Yer. Kid. 3.12.
[25] וחכמים אומרים ... אין גר עד שימול ויטבול ... מאן חכמים ר' יוסי.

ciple that where there is the opinion of an individual rabbi and the majority are against him the law was decided according to the opinion of the majority. According to a later halachah, if a non-Jew wanted to embrace the Jewish religion and was willing to follow all the precepts of God with the exception of one or two he was not considered a proselyte.

The sages regarded the proselytes very highly and extolled those who gave up their idols and accepted the God of Israel, commending them even more than those who were born Jews.[26] They compared the proselytes to Abraham, who had been brought up in idol worship and later abandoned it. It is true that there is an opinion in the Talmud hostile to proselytism,[27] but this was the opinion of an individual and had no influence. The general attitude toward proselytism was highly favorable, this is evident from the halachah, according to which a priest may marry the daughter of a proselyte[28] since in the eyes of the sages a proselyte was a full fledged Israelite. Rabbi Simon held that a priest may even marry a girl who embraced the Jewish religion before she was three years and a day old.[29] These opinions are at variance with a biblical command which stated that a priest should marry only a daughter of an Israelite.[30] The Talmud records that some of the outstanding sages were descendants of proselytes.

The Pharisees canonized the book of Ruth in order to show that a proselyte was a true Israelite, The genealogy of King David is traced there to Ruth, who was a Moabite,

---

[26] Comp. *JQR*, 1944, pp. 194–98. חביב הגר לפני הקב"ה מן אותן אוכלסין שעמדו על הר סיני.

[27] Yeb. 47: דאמר ר' חלבו קשים גרים לישראל כספחת.

[28] Comp. Yer. Kid. 4.6: עד שיוולדו בקדושת ישראל.

[29] גיורת שנתגיירה פחותה מבת שלש שנים ויום אחד כשירה לכהונה.

[30] Comp. Ezek. 44.22: מזרע בית ישראל; comp. also Yer. Bik. 1.4: גר עצמו מביא וקורא.

and who embraced the Jewish religion. According to the Pentateuch a Moabite cannot enter the community of God and it does not differentiate between male and female. The Pharisees in canonizing the book of Ruth wanted to show that a Moabite proselyte was favored in the eyes of God by showing that King David, the pride and glory of all the kings, the author of the book of Psalms, was a descendant of a proselyte, a Moabite. There was no prohibition against intermarriage if the partner became a proselyte. The Talmud prohibited intermarriage only if one of the contracting parties remained a pagan. In *Antiquities* Josephus related a story about a Jewish warrior in Babylonia, who married a pagan woman; there was strong opposition by his coreligionists because the woman continued to worship idols.[31] Josephus further related that this marriage brought great misfortune to the entire Jewish community.

Marriage between Jew and non-Jew is not recognized. If the mother is Jewish so is the child,[32] but if the mother is not Jewish the child is not considered a Jew although his father is a Jew.[33]

In the *Maarib*, October 31, 1958, it was stated that Premier David Ben-Gurion reported before a committee that a girl, from the Kibbutz גבעת השלושה, whose mother was not Jewish, went to the rabbi of Petach Tikva to be converted. When the rabbi asked from where she came she answered from the Kibbutz גבעת השלושה. The rabbi refused to convert her because in that kibbutz the candles were not lighted on the eve of Sabbath. At first Premier Ben-Gurion expressed astonishment over the action of the rabbi. Then he said that the rabbi was right as he acted according to the halachah, according to which

---

[31] *Ant.* 18.9 (345)

[32] Comp. Yeb. 45: והלכתא נכרי [נוי] ועבד הבא על בת ישראל הולד כשר בין בפנויה בין באשת איש... כיון דאמו מישראל אחיך קרינן ביה.

[33] Comp. Kid. M. 3,12: אין בנך הבא מן הנכרית קרוי בנך אלא בנה; הולד כמותה.

if a proselyte accepts the entire Torah with the exception of one point, even a special point of the Soferim, he is not acceptable.[34]

In my humble opinion the rabbi of Petach Tikvah erred. According to the Tosefta, if a proselyte said that he wants to accept the entire Torah with the exception of a special point of the *Soferim* he cannot be considered a proselyte.[35] The meaning of the Tosefta is clear that if the person who came to be converted openly said that he is opposed to a a particular precept, — it may even be rabbinical, — he cannot be converted. But if a person comes to be converted without stating any limitations then he is acceptable for conversion. We must assume from the fact that since the person came to be converted he is willing to accept the entire Torah. The fact that this girl came from a kibbutz where the Sabbath candles were not lighted is not sufficient grounds for her rejection. Her case is not worse than if she had come from a pagan community. A rabbi in accepting a woman convert has only to instruct her in the precepts for women.[36] If she does not follow these precepts she is on the par with other Jewish women who do not follow them. Unless the rabbi of Petach Tikvah had other grounds for rejecting this girl or she had openly expressed unwillingness to follow the precept of lighting the candles on the eve of Sabbath he committed a halachic error. One should follow the principle of Hillel to welcome converts.[37]

[34] ‎. . . הלכה לרב בפתח־תקוה להתגייר. הרב שאל אותה: מאיין את? ענתה: מגבעת השלושה, אמר הרב לא אוכל לנייר אותך, את צריכה להדליק נרות בערב שבת ובגבעת השלושה אין מדליקים נרות, בשעת המעשה זועזעתי. אבל לאחר שעיינתי בהלכה—ראיתי. שהרב צדק. הרב של פתח־תקוה נהג לפי הלכה . . . ר' יוסי ב"ר יהודה אמר: אם הוא מקבל התורה כולה, אבל דקדוק סופרים אחד לא—אין מקבלים אותו, וזהי הלכה . . . ‎הוא עשה לפי ההלכה.

[35] Tos. Demai 2.4; T. Bek. 30.

[36] Yeb. 47. ‎ומודיעין אותה מקצת מצות קלות ומקצת מצות חמורות . . . ואין מרבים. Comp. also ‎מסכת גרים: ע"מ שתהא זהירה בנדה. ‎עליו ואין מדקדקים עליו ובהדלקת הנר.

[37] Comp. *ibid.*: ‎. . . אשרך ‎אומרים לו דברים טובים ונכונים.

The word used for religion in the early tannaitic literature and in Josephus was דת יהודית, "Law of the Judaeans." As previously noted, with the establishment of the Second Jewish Commonwealth Theocracy was abolished and Nomocracy was insituted. Therefore in the tannaitic literature we have the word for religion דת, law. The words used in tannaitic literature are "The Law of the Judaeans."[38] Similarly in Josephus we have "Judaean Laws, Judaean Customs." Josephus, in referring to Antiochus who became a renegade, converted to another religion, said "He changed the Judaean customs, laws."[39] The author of III Maccabees, said that Dositheus, a Jew by birth — who accepted the pagan religion, changed his ancestral laws.[40] Likewise in the tannaitic literature there is applied to a Jew who rejected his religion the expression המיר את דתו "he changed his law."[41] Josephus sometimes used the term $\vartheta\rho\eta\sigma\kappa\epsilon$ία for religion. In describing the massacre of the Jews in Damascus he stated that the women, with few exceptions, were converted to the Jewish religion.[42] In describing the massacres of the Jews in Syria he wrote that the Syrians, although believing that they had rid themselves of all the Jews, suspected their own people because each city had Judaizers.[43] This is the only instance in which Josephus used the term "Judaizers." We cannot assume Josephus meant that each city had many converts, otherwise he would not have said that the Syrians suspected their own people as they would have known which of them had joined the Judaeans. What Josephus meant by the term "Judaizers" was that there were many Syrians who were in

---

[38] דת יהודית.
[39] *Jewish War* 7.50: ... μεταβολῆς ... τῶν Ἰουδαίων ἔθη.
[40] μεταβαλὼν τὰ νόμινα.
[41] Suk. 56: שהמירה דתה; Pes. 96: הטרת הדת.
[42] ... Ἰουδαϊκῇ θρησκεία. (*Jewish War* 2.561).
[43] ἰουδαΐζοντας.

sympathy with the Judaeans and followed some of their customs. The translation of the phrase ורבים מעמי הארץ מתיהדים (Esther 8.17), "many of the people of the land became Jews" is wrong. The true meaning of the sentence is, "Many of the people feigned to be Jews for fear of the Jews fell upon them."[44] The Septuagint renders this passage, "Many of the Gentiles were circumcised and sided with the Jews."[45] The Vulgate has "Many of the other nations joined themselves to their (the Jews) worship and ceremonies."[46]

Josephus, relating the story of a Babylonian Jew who married a pagan who continued to worship idols, said that he did not act according to the laws of the Hebrews.[47] In dealing with the people of Judaea he employs the phrase "Laws of the Judaeans." In recording the events of their coreligionists in Babylonia he uses the phrase "Hebrew Laws." Again we may deduce from this that the people who lived in Judaea were called Judaeans while their coreligionists who lived in the Diaspora were called Hebrews. Paul, in his epistle to the II Corinthians (11.22), says that he is a Hebrew; and again, in his epistle to Philippians (3.5), he refers to himself as "an Hebrew of the Hebrews." However when he was arrested in Jerusalem he said that he was a Judaean.[48] This apparent contradiction can be explained. When Paul was in Judaea he claimed to be a Judaean and when he was in the Diaspora he considered

---

[44] Comp. I Kings 14.5, והיא מתנכרה, she will feign herself to be another woman. The word מתיהדים could not have had the meaning that the people became Jews, since at the time the book of Esther was written, there could not have been proselytes to Judaism.

[45] καὶ πολλοὶ τῶν ἐθνῶν περιετέμοντο καὶ Ἰουδάϊζον. (Sided with the Jews, or imitated the Jews).

[46] *in tantum ut plures alterius gentis et sectae eorum religioni et ceremoniis iungerentur.*

[47] ... Ἑβραϊκὰ οὐδὲ ὁπόσα νόμοις ...

[48] Acts 22.3. Comp. also I Cor. 9.20: "Unto the Jews I became as a Jew."

himself a Hebrew — among the Judaeans he was a Judaean, among the Hebrews he was a Hebrew.

The word Judaism, having the connotation of religion, first occurs in the Second[49] and the Fourth Books of Maccabees.[50] These books were composed in Antioch.[51] It seems that the Judaean way of life, which dominated their co-religionists in the Diaspora, became synonymous with their religion, hence the term *Judaismos* was employed. Ignatius, the third bishop of Antioch who lived in the first century of our era, used the term *Judaismos* a few times, but he also coined a similar term for the Christian religion, *Christianismos*, an antonym for *Judaismos*. In his epistles to the Philadelphians, 6, he said, "But if any one interprets *Judaismos* (Judaism) to you, do not listen to him; for it is better to hear *Christianismos* (Christianity) from the circumcised than *Judaismos* from the uncircumcised."

The author of the Second Book of Maccabees who coined the term *Judaismos*, Judaism, for religion used as its antonym *allofulismos*, heathenism.[52] In the Fourth Book of Maccabees where the term Judaism is employed for religion the author does not use the word Judaeans, Jews, but Hebrews. The reason for not using the term Judaean and using the word Hebrews is readily explained. Since this book was written in the Diaspora the people who professed Judaism called themselves Hebrews.

After the destruction of the Second Temple and particularly with the rise of Christianity, when the Christians maintained that they were the true Israelites, the term Judaean was abandoned. The Jews called themselves Israelites in order to combat the contentions of the Christians. The term כנסת ישראל, "the Assembly of Israel" was

---

[49] 2.21.   [50] 4.26.
[51] See *The Second Book of Maccabees*, ed. Dropsie College.
[52] μεταβεβηκέναι εἰς ἀλλοφυλισμόν.

coined. The word Judaean no longer appeared in the Talmud and the word Israel was used. The term Jew, Judaism, became the term for religion.[53]

In the early days after the destruction of the Temple the Romans regarded the Jews as a religious community. When the Romans captured Jerusalem they levied against the Jews a special tax of two drachmas to be paid annually to Jupiter Capitolinus just as formerly it has been contributed by the Jews to the Temple in Jerusalem. This tax was called *fiscus Judaicus*.[54] It was not levied on the Jews as an ethnic group, it was rather a religious tax levied upon those who professed the Jewish faith, regardless of where they lived whether in Judaea or in the Diaspora and whether they were born as Jews or as proselytes.

The Romans, in levying this tax *Fiscus Judaicus*, to be paid to *Jupiter Capitolinus*, sought to emphasize the victory of Jupiter, the Roman god over the God of the Jews. The Roman historian, Dio, tells us that when the Romans subjugated Judaea Vespasian and Titus received the title *Imperator* but not of *Judaicus*.[55] It was the custom of the Roman Caesars when they received the title of Imperator for their victories over a particular nation to append the name of the nation to the title of Imperator. However, in the case of their victory over Judaea they did not append the title *Judaicus*. The reason for this was that Judaism at the time of the destruction of the Temple was already held by the Roman people to be a religion. Thus Vespasian and Titus could not accept the title *Judaicus*. If they

---

[53] We have ישראל, בן ישראל, עם ישראל. We do not have the expression עם יהודי.

[54] Suetonius, Domitian 12: *Praeter ceteros Iudaicus fiscus acerbissime actus est; ad quem deferebantur, qui vel improfessi Iudaicum viverent vitam vel dissimulate origine imposita genti tributa non pependissent.* Comp. also Dio, 65.

[55] *Ibid.*: Καὶ ἐπ' αὐτοῖς τὸ μὲν τοῦ αὐτοκράτορος ὄνομα ἀμφότεροι ἔλαβον το δὲ δὴ τοῦ Ἰουδαϊκοῦ αὐδέτερος ...

accepted this title it would have meant that they were accepting the religion of the Judaeans. They considered those who lived in Judaea as only a part of their coreligionists who lived in the Diaspora.

The fact that the Roman authorities considered the Jews as a religious group, not a nation, was in a way reponsible for the survival of the Jews in the Roman Empire. The Jewish religion in the Roman Empire was a *religio licita* and received many privileges in the period of the early Caesars. The Jews had the right to worship their God without any disturbance, the right to build synagogues. The historian Lampridius tells us that Alexander Severus respected the privileges of the Jews and also allowed the Christians to exist unmolested.[56] Thus he grouped together the Jews and the Christians as religious sects. Although Judaea as a state was captured by the Romans, the Judaeans had the same privileges as their coreligionists in the Diaspora had always enjoyed since they were regarded by the Romans as a religious group.

What really saved the Jews from extinction after the destruction of their state *was* their religion. During the Second Commonwealth the Pharisees laid great stress on religion. In opposition to the Sadducees who maintained that the Jewish God is an ethnic God, the God of the Jews or those who are the descendants of Abraham, Isaac and Jacob, the Pharisees maintained that God is universal, that anyone is welcome to join the Jews who accepted Him, maintaining that He can be worshipped anywhere and that He is not bound to any particular land. This idea of a universal God saved the Jews from oblivion.

In the ancient times there were many nations, many empires. The Jews were a small people. Most of the old nations, even the empires, are extinct. We learn of them

[56] *Iudaeis privilegia reservavit Christianos esse passus est.*

only from the museums and from archaeologists who have discovered some remnants of their culture. The Jews still live in spite of all the persecutions which they had undergone throughout the ages. *The survival of the Jews lies only in their religion.* The nations who have disappeared had national gods. When they were conquered their gods were also conquered and ceased to be their gods. Their gods were placed in captivity in a pantheon. The Jews worshipped the God of the Universe regardless of their country. When the Jewish state was conquered their God was not conquered. They continued to worship Him no matter where they lived and this is the reason for their continuation.

With this in mind we can fully understand why the Northern State, the Ten Tribes, disappeared since they worshipped a local god, the god of the land, the god of their people. When they were conquered by the Assyrians their god was conquered. They disappeared as other nations disappeared when they were conquered, as the Sumerians and Hittites had disappeared. On the other hand the Southern Kingdom, the Judaeans, conquered later by the Babylonians, were in exile only fifty years. Fortunately when they returned they had the guidance of leaders who understood that the belief in a local god is not true religion. As previously mentioned the Judaeans abandoned polytheism and became monotheists. Later under the influence of the prophets and the guidance of the Pharisees they came to recognize the universality of God. This is the reason for the disappearance of the Ten Tribes of Israel and the continuation of Judaeans as the people of Israel.

When Christianity became the dominating religion of the Roman Empire the policy held by the Church was that Judaism was a superstition and must be confined only to the people who were stubborn and would not see the light of the truth. Proselytism to Judaism was prohibited under penalty of death. For the Church Judaism was not a universal religion but an ethnic religion, a religion confined to one people called Jews. Hitherto Judaism was considered a *religio licita*. However when Christianity became the religion of the Empire the Jewish religion was no more a *religio licita*, it was called odious and abominable.[57] Any one who came in contact with Judaism was said to be contaminated. The Christians looked upon the Jews as a people confined to their superstition which must not be allowed to spread to other people.

The Jews, however, did not surrender their idea that Judaism is a universal religion. They would have welcomed other people but being subject to Christian authorities who prohibited proselytism even to pagans to Judaism, they could not make proselytes. As previously indicated, in retort to the Christians they called themselves Israelites and their religion, Judaism. Their language and culture was called Hebrew and so it was throughout the ages. Thus the term Jews has no other connotation *but* religion. The Jews are a religious community, united with their brethren throughout the world by religion. Thus there are American Jews, French Jews, English Jews and Israeli Jews. Since Judaism represents the genius of one people, the people of Children of Israel, they are united not only by religion but also by historical bonds. Christianity, unlike Judaism, is not the genius of one people. It arose in the hills of Judaea and later embraced many cultures, many nations and races either by persuasion and more by conquest. Thus it has the elements of many different cultures and is not confined to one people.

In our historical definition the Jews are a religious community. Some may question how can the Jews be defined

[57] See S. Zeitlin, *Judaism as a Religion*.

as a religious community when many of its members are not religious and some of them are atheists, not believing in God. The answer is simple — Judaism as a universal religion considers even the atheists a part of the community.[58] The halachah is that even if a Jew accepted another religion he is still a Jew.[58a] If a Jew has married and has accepted another religion his wife is still bound to him. If she wishes to be free, in order to marry some one else, she was to receive a *get* from him (a religious writ of divorce).[59] Some analogy can be drawn here. A person who was born in the United States, or has become a citizen, must follow the laws of his country and if he does not he is punished but he is still a citizen. He cannot renounce his citizenship unless he relinquishes it in another country. States have boundaries. Judaism, as a universal religion, *has no boundaries*, Therefore one born a Jew, or one who has accepted Judaism, can not renounce Judaism. He may be a sinner in the eyes of God but he is still a Jew. If a non-Jew has accepted Judaism he can never renounce it. The halachah is clear — If a non-Jew has accepted Judaism and returned to his old religion or changed to another religion he is still a Jew.[60] His marriage according to the Jewish law is valid, his religious divorce is valid. In a word, this proselyte even if he returns to his old religion, is still a Jew. The same theology is held by the Catholics, who maintain that Catholicism is a universal religion — once a Catholic always a Catholic.

---

[58] Comp. Kid. 36: ואומר בנים לא אמן בם וכי תמא כי לית ביה הימנותא הוא משומד לע"ז ... ובכלל בנים הוא ... :194 שו"ת הרשב"א see also דמוקרי בנים ... כי פלחי לע"ז לא מקרו בנים ואומר בנים משחיתים.

[58a] Yeb. 47: ישראל מומר קרינא ביה. Comp. also תשובת הגאונים ... וישראל משומד ... אלא אפיקורס הוא ואם חזר משמדותו תשובתו תשובה וא"צ טבילה.

[59] ישראל מומר קרינא ביה וקידושיו קדושין.

[60] אור זרוע See also דאי הדר ביה ומקדש בת ישראל, ישראל משומד קרינא ביה גר טבל ... דאי הדר ביה ומקדש בת ישראל מומר הוא וקדושיו קדושין וצריכה 604: גט דישראל רשע הוא. Comp. also S. Zeitlin, *Judaism as a Religion*.

The non-Jewish world did not differentiate between the observant and non-observant Jew. The Nazis sent the observant and non-observant and even the atheists to the gas chambers. To them all of these were Jews, even those who had accepted Christianity.

As was noted before, the question who is a Jew arose in Israel in connection with the "Law of Return," which entitles all Jews to immigrate to Israel without any obstacles. Many of the immigrants were married to non-Jewish women and had children. According to international law they are legally married. Since they were married under the laws of the countries where they had resided, the civil courts of Israel had to recognize such marriages. Under the "Law of Return" these immigrants were allowed to enter the State of Israel without any obstacles. A dispute arose between the civil authorities and the religious leaders over the identity cards. The civil authorities wanted to have the word "Jew" on their identity cards but the religious leaders objected to this. According to religious law, the halachah, marriage between a Jew and a non-Jewish woman is not recognized and the children of such a union are not Jews.

The view of the religious leaders carries great weight. For two thousand years the word *Jew* has had the connotation of religion. Again according to the halachah, which goes back to great antiquity, the marriage between a Jew and a non-Jewish woman is not recognized and the children of such a union are not Jews unless the mother had accepted Judaism prior to her marriage. True the halachah is not static, it is plastic, it cannot be abrogated but it can be interpreted. *Only religious leaders may interpret and amend the halachot.* Furthermore it is easy for the women who accompanied their husbands to Israel to accept Judaism as the ceremony is a simple one.[61] The fact that they did not

[61] Comp. Tosefta to Yeb. 47a: הא דבעי ג' היינו דוקא לכתחלה אבל מדיעבד

accept Judaism is an indication that they wished to adhere to their old religion. To this they have full right. No one in the State of Israel may coerce them to accept Judaism. In our democratic way of life we must respect all religions, and all religions should be welcome in Israel. We must strive to have complete separation of religion from state.

In the *Maarib*, previously referred to, it was stated that Mr. Ben-Gurion is anxious to have the name "Jew" on the identity cards and passports in order to emphasize that the Israelis are Jews.[62] This is a good thought. We have observed that unfortunately many students from Israel, coming to America, insist that they are Israelis but *not* Jews. Simply writing the word Jew on the identity cards will not make "certain" Israelis conscious of their Jewishness. A thorough *Jewish education* is needed to make them conscious that they are Jews and a part of the Jews of the Diaspora.

Again the apellation of the word Jew on the identity card can only be applied to those who were born Jews or who had accepted Judaism regardless of whether they are observant or not observant, whether they are believers or atheists. The word Jew cannot be applied to those who have non-Jewish mothers. It would be interesting to know whether the civil authorities in Israel would apply the term Christian on the identity cards of Christians. If this were the case then the civil authorities would be intervening in religious matters which are not in their province. Similarly, the United States has the right to define who is an American but not — who is a Jew or who is a Christian. To have the

אטבלה להיא נכרית לשם אנתתא אמר רב 45: Yeb. also .Comp .חד נמי כשר
להיות גירות גמורה: .Comp. also Rashi *ad loc*. יוסף יכילנא לאכשורי בה ובבתה
ואע"פ שלא טבלה לשם גירות... דטבילת סלקא לה לשם גירות דנכרית לא טבלה לגדרותה.

[62] אבל נולד כאן דור חדש, שברובו הגדול אינו דתי, אם יהיה רק ישראלי ולא יהודי — ישנה סכנה, צריך שידע שהוא יהודי.

word *Jew* on the identity cards and passports alongside that of Israeli may lead to unpleasant and even to grave consequences for the Jews of the Diaspora.

In the same paper it was reported that the Secretary of Justice, Mr. P. Rosen, suggested a compromise: Those who are born Jews should have "Jew" on their identity cards; those who are of mixed marriage to have "Jew by adoption" on their cards. For example — a person born in France is a Frenchman and it is so noted on his identity card, but if he became a French citizen — on his identity card would appear "Frenchman by adoption."[63] It appears that Mr. Rosen has erred. If the person became a French citizen his children, born in France, will be citizens by birth. However, neither the children of intermarriage whose mothers are non-Jewish, nor their children, would be Jewish according to the halachah, unless they accepted Judaism. If they do accept Judaism they are equal to those Jews who can trace their genealogy to great antiquity.

To reiterate — the acceptance of Judaism is now a simple ceremony for male or female.

In the same paper there is also reported that the prime minister said that he is opposed to any religious war.[64] He expressed this view with full consciousness of the history of the Jews. The religious war which broke out between Alexander Jannaeus and the Pharisees was the *beginning of the end* of the Second Jewish Commonwealth.

The civil authorities must avoid clashes with the religious leaders, always bearing in mind that through the fanaticism of religious men and their zeal for religion, Judaism, the victory over Hellenism and over the High Priests Jason and Menelaus was made possible. The religious men

---

[63] רוזן הציע פשרה: אם ההורים הם נשואי תערובת — יכתבו בתעודת הזהות. לאומית יהודית מאומצת׳ כמו שיש כדבר הזה במדינות אחרית.

[64] חששתי מאוד ממלחמת־דת ואני חושש ממנה גם עכשיו.

were responsible for the establishment of the Second Commonwealth and for the Festival of Hanukkah which is celebrated to day by the religious and secular men alike. If not for their religion the Jews would not have survived nor would there be the State of Israel, nor would there be Christianity.

Unfortunately the religious leaders in Israel have the psychology and mentality which developed among them in the ghettoes of Poland, Lithuania and Roumania. They seek to preserve the Judaism and the religious practices which were in vogue in Europe without recognizing the fact that these religious laws were once enacted as a safeguard for Judaism to survive in the ghettoes, and some were used as a prevention from assimilation with other people. These laws have outlived their purpose in the free State of Israel.[65] Religious life in Israel is indeed in a chaotic state. There is not only a wide gulf but a feeling of hostility prevails between the secularists and the religionists. The religionists, who are a minority of the population, want to enforce the religious rites of Eastern Europe on the young generation of the land. The religious leaders of today should seek to bring religion into consonance with life emulating the wisdom of the sages of the Second Jewish Commonwealth who did so. Although the Pentateuch was the basis of the Jewish law and was the constitution of the people the sages did not hesitate to interpret and amend the pentateuchal laws.

Following are two examples of many pentateuchal laws which were interpreted and amended by the sages. According to the Pentateuch a Jew was not allowed to walk out of his house on the Sabbath day. To make the Sabbath

---

[65] See S. Zeitlin, "The Halaka: Introduction to Tannaitic Jurisprudence," *JQR*, 1948; *idem*, "Is a Revival of a Sanhedrin in Israel necessary for Modification of the Halaka?" *JQR*, 1952.

enjoyable the word מקום was interpreted to mean city. Later the law was amended so that a Jew had the right to walk two thousand cubits outside of the city. In order to make the Sabbath still more enjoyable and to make it possible for a Jew to observe it comfortably the sages amended the law further by introducing the *Erub*.[66] According to the Pentateuch the blood of the paschal lamb had to be sprinkled on the side posts and on the lintel of the house. This was against the spirit of the Jews who abhorred blood. The sages interpreted this pentateuchal injunction as referring to the paschal lamb which was sacrificed in Egypt but not to the "Passover of generations," i. e. to the paschal lamb which was offered during the Second Jewish Commonwealth.[67] The sages interpreted this pentateuchal law in spite of the fact that the words of the Pentateuch explicitly read: "And ye shall observe this thing as an ordinance to thee and thy sons forever. And it shall come to pass when you come to the land which the Lord will give you according as He had promised that ye shall keep this service."[68] The sages of the Second Jewish Commonwealth made religion a moral force.

If the religious leaders of Israel would have the foresight, wisdom and courage to make Judaism a living religion it would have great influence on the entire Jewry. They should follow the principles of the sages of the Second Jewish Commonwealth who interpreted and modified the laws in order to make religion a vital force. The religious leaders should strive to adjust the halachot by interpretation to the religious and social needs of the Jewish people. To be a

[66] *Idem*, "The Takkanot of Erubin," *JQR*, 1951.
[67] See Tos. Pes. 8: פסח מצרים נאמר בו והגעתם אל המשקוף ואל שתי המזוזות מה שאין כן בפסח דורות פסח מצרים מקום אכילה שם לינה ופסח מצרים אוכלין במקום אחד ולנין במקום אחר.
[68] Exod. 12.7, 23–24.

497

מחמיר, to be strict in the application of the laws does not require great learning — any one can be strict.[69]

Some may be apprehensive that the modification of the laws through new interpretations will arouse great opposition from the ultra orthodox. Undoubtedly it will do so; this is to be expected. The sages during the Second Commonwealth were also confronted with great opposition from the Sadducees who were the ultra orthodox of that time.

To sum up: The answer to the question "Who is a Jew?" is that anyone who is born of a Jewish mother or one who has embraced Judaism, regardless of whether he observes or does not observe the precepts is a Jew. Judaism is a universal religion and no one can exclude himself. The religious authorities have not the right to exclude any Jew. This definition is the verdict of Jewish history. No one can ignore history. It is futile to pass over history. The term Jews, like Christians, has a religious connotation. Unlike Christianity, Judaism is the creation of one people, the bond is deep. The Jews are also united by their history and to a great degree by Hebrew culture. Since Judaism represents the genius of one people there is also the ethnic element which unites them. The bond between the Jews of the Dispora and the Jews of Israel is even greater. The land of Israel is not only the cradle of Judaism but Judaism as we know it today was molded there. Throughout the ages the Jews of the Diaspora longed for the establishment of a messianic kingdom in the land of Israel. The Jewish kingdom had flourished there and the prophets uttered their prophecies. After they were exiled from their land they *never* abandoned their love for the land of Israel nor did

---

[69] Comp. Rashi Bezah 2: דההירא עדיף . . . אבל כח האוסרין אינה ראיה שהכל יכולין להחמיר.

they relinquish their religious or legal rights over the Holy Land. During the Second Jewish Commonwealth the Jews of the Diaspora looked upon Jerusalem as their spiritual metropolis and they regarded the Temple as the religious center of the entire Jewry. The bond between the Jews of the Diaspora and the Jews of Israel is strong. The Jews of the Diaspora need Israel. Israel needs the Jews of the Diaspora. The Jews of the Diaspora have great vitality.

If Israel should become an ordinary, democratic industrial state it would be a great tragedy for Jewry and humanity as a whole. An ordinary Levantine state even a highly democratic one will have no effect upon Judaism and upon humanity.

We have deep faith in the secular and religious leadership of Israel, believing that Israel will again be a beacon of light which will shed its beams not only over the mountains of Judaea and Galilee but over the entire Jewry by emulating the spiritual forces of the prophets and the Pharisees whose ideals and ideas gave substance to the Jews and also revolutionized the civilized world.

THE NAMES HEBREW, JEW AND ISRAEL

A Historical Study

"WHAT's in a name?" asked Juliet in Shakespeare's play. By this was meant that a name has no particular significance. This may apply to the name of an individual, but not to that of a nation. The name of a people has significance, particularly when during various periods of their history they have changed their name. Such changes cannot be ascribed merely to chance or caprice. A nation must have a historical reason for changing its name.

The Book of Exodus begins, "These are the names of the children of Israel who came into Egypt with Jacob," and then the names of the eleven sons who came with him follow. The words, "children of Israel" here give the name of a particular person, Jacob, who was surnamed Israel. The term *Bne Israel*, children of Israel, applied to the entire people who came out from Egypt. Sometimes only the word Israel is mentioned without the word *bne*, the children.

In the Book of Deuteronomy the nomenclature for the people, with some exceptions is Israel and not the children of Israel, which means that "Israel" had become a definite name for the people.[1] In the early prophetic books, like Joshua and the Judges, we sometimes find the name "Bne Israel," but here it does not have the connotation of the children of a particular person but the name of a particular people. A division arose among the people in the time of David. The majority followed the son of the martyred

---

[1] Comp. Deut. 27.9, הסכת ושמע ישראל היום הזה נהיית לעם.

Reprinted from the *Jewish Quarterly Review*, New Series, Vol. 43, 1953.

King Saul, while the tribe of Judah accepted David as the king. Later all the people were united under the sceptre of David, and his son Solomon became king of all Israel. After Solomon's death the people of Israel were divided into two kingdoms, the northern and the southern. In the former, the kings were called the Kings of Israel,[2] while in the latter the kings were called the Kings of Judah, and the inhabitants were designated Judaeans.[3] When the prophet Jeremiah advised the king, Zedekiah, to submit to the Babylonians, he replied, "I am afraid of the Judaeans that are fallen away to the Chaldeans, lest they deliver me into their hand and they mock me."[4] Thus, we see that the inhabitants of Judaea were called Judaeans. We are also told that the Babylonians carried into captivity three thousand twenty-three persons, Judaeans.[5] We also learn from Jeremiah that the people who fled from Judaea to Egypt after the assassination of Gedaliah, the son of Ahikam, were called Judaeans,[6] and that their language was *Yehudith*[7] — Judaic. The country was The Land of Judah,[8] and the cities were known as the cities of Judah.

The northern kingdom was named *Eretz Israel*,[9] The Land of Israel, or simply Israel. The people were called Israel,[10] but we cannot say for certain what the language was known as, because the sources are silent. The God of the people was always called the God of Israel. The prophets of Judaea in delivering their messages to the kings of Judah and the inhabitants of Jerusalem in the

[2] מלכי ישראל.
[3] II Kings 16.6, וינשל את היהודים.
[4] Jer. 38.19, comp. also *ibid.* 36.23, ויהי כקרוא יהודי.
[5] *Ibid.* 52.28.
[6] *Ibid.* 41–44.
[7] יהודית.
[8] ארץ יהודה.
[9] ארץ ישראל, comp. II Kings 5.5
[10] הישראלי, II Sam. 17.25.

name of God, always used the expression "The God of Israel," never "The God of Judah."

The term Hebrew, in reference to the people of Israel, does not occur either in the Pentateuch or the Prophetic books. It is used in connection with slaves or with foreigners (non-Jews). When the wife of Potiphar complained to her husband about Joseph she referred to him as "a Hebrew,"[11] and the butler of the king of Egypt also spoke of Joseph as "a Hebrew." It is related in Exodus that when the king of Egypt determined to exterminate all the newly born males of the children of Israel, he referred to both the midwives and the women as Hebrews.[12] When the daughter of Pharaoh found a male child in the bulrushes, she said, "This is one of the Hebrew children."[13] It is further related that Moses, when grown up, saw an Egyptian smite a "Hebrew," and later that he saw two "Hebrews" smite one another.[14]

The term Hebrew is employed in the laws regarding slavery set forth in the Book of Exodus.[15] When Jeremiah reproached the Jews for not setting their slaves free, he also used the term Hebrew;[16] in other instances the term Judaeans is employed in the Bible. The term Hebrew is often used in the Book of Samuel,[17] wherein the stories of the wars between the Philistines and the Jews are related. When Jonah was asked to which people he belonged, he answered that he was a Hebrew.[18]

[11] איש עברי, Gen. 39.14; see also 40.15, 41.12.
[12] Ex. 1.15, 16, 19.
[13] 2.6.
[14] *Ibid*. 2.11, 13. Comp. also *ibid*. 3.18, ובאת אתה וזקני ישראל אל מלך מצרים . . . אלהי העברים בא אל פרעה ודברת אליו . . . כה אמר . . . אלהי העברים עד מתי מאנת.
[15] 21.2, עבד עברי.
[16] 34.9.
[17] 4.13.
[18] 1.9, עברי אנכי.

After some of the exiled people returned to the land of Judaea they always were referred to as Judaeans. The name Israel is still used in the books of the prophets of the post-exilic period, like Ezra and Nehemiah, but the name Judaeans is most prevalent. Later the name Israel disappears, and that of Jews takes its place entirely. The term יהודים Judaeans appears throughout the Book of Esther. When the author of the book relates that many people of the land became Jews, he uses the word מתיהדים. Mordecai is called a Judaean, although the author gives his genealogy as a descendant of the tribe of Benjamin.[19]

The word Judaeans is applied to the inhabitants of Judaea in the entire Hellenistic literature as well as in the tannaitic literature of the Second Commonwealth.[20] Josephus says that the people of Judaea were called Judaeans because the inhabitants were descendants from the tribe of Judah.[21]

During the long period, however, from the Restoration to the destruction of the Temple, many people from other tribes settled in Judaea, as well as many Gentiles who then lived according to the laws of that country. Therefore, Josephus in his book *Against Apion*, which was written after the destruction of the Second Temple, says that the new residents were called Judaeans because they lived in Judaea, regardless of their original tribes and ancestry. Many proselytes who lived in Judaea in the time of the Second Commonwealth accepted the way of life there. They were called Judaeans — Jews.

The word יהודים *Judaeans* is used in the tannaitic literature. We are told in *Megillat Taanit* that a holiday was

---

[19] איש ימיני ... ושמו מרדכי ... איש יהודי היה.
[20] In I Mac. the name Israel is used, see my Introduction to I Mac. ed. Dropsie.
[21] *Ant.* XI.7.

declared on the 28th of Adar because on that day good tidings reached the Judaeans.[22] It is related in the tannaitic literature that the Alexandrian Jews living in Jerusalem, who became betrothed, were deprived of their respective wives by fellow-Jews who subsequently married them. The sages of that period wanted to declare the children of these marriages illegitimate. Hillel, however, was of the opinion that the offspring of these marriages were legitimate since there was a clause in the Ketubah, the marriage contract, which reads "When you come to my house, you shall be my wife according to the laws of Moses and the Judaeans."[23] It is evident from this that the expression Judaeans was used in the official documents current among the people in Judaea during the Second Commonwealth, and not the words Israel or Hebrew. We never find the term Israel denoting the people of Judaea, in the entire tannaitic literature of the time of the Second Commonwealth. The term Israel was used only in contrast to the priests and Levites. The country was called Judaea, or sometimes the land of Judaea. The tannaitic literature of that period used the term הארץ the "land."[24] The language of the people was called Hebrew.[25]

Thus it is evident that the people of Judaea were called Judaean — Jews. But what of the people who lived in the Diasporas? Were they called Judaeans—Jews, Israeli or Hebrews? The term Jews was applied in Egypt to the inhabitants who settled there and followed the same religion

---

[22] אתת בשורתא טבתא ליהודאי. See S. Zeitlin, *Megilat Taanit*, p. 68.

[23] Yer. Ket. 29a, כשהיו בני אלכסנדריא מקדשין נשים... כשהיכנסו לביתי ואילו יוצאת שלא בכתובה העוברת. Comp. also תהויין לי לאנתו כדת משה ויהודאי. See also Ned. 11.12, ונוטלות על דת משה ויהודית... ואיזוהי דת יהודית כתובה... נטולה אני מן היהודים, see S. Zeitlin, *The Jews, Race Nation, or Religion*, 1936.

[24] See Yer. Sheb. תני איזו היא הארץ ואיזו היא חוץ לארץ.

[25] תרגום שכתוב עברית.

as the inhabitants of Judaea. The reason they were called Judaeans — Jews, was that many Judaeans — Jews, fled to Egypt after the destruction of the First Temple and established a colony there. When other co-religionists later came to Egypt and were absorbed by the Jewish colony there, they adopted the same nomenclature, Judaeans — Jews. Furthermore, the two Jewries of Egypt and Judaea were united under one flag, the Ptolemaic. The two Jewries were a part of the Ptolemaic Empire from the year 320 BCE, almost to the time of the Hasmonean revolt, except for a short period. Many Jews who migrated to Alexandria either came voluntarily or had been brought there from Judaea by the Ptolemaic kings. Thus it is quite logical that they should be called Judaeans — Jews, throughout the entire period of the Second Commonwealth; the Jews in other countries, Babylonia, Syria, and Antioch, however, did not call themselves Jews. They were called Israelis and Hebrews. When the king of Persia allowed the Jews to return to their own land, Judaea, only a few did so. The great majority many of whom were descendants from the ten tribes of Israel remained in Babylonia. They continued to call themselves Israelis. The Jews of Antioch called themselves Hebrews; during the Greek and Roman period they were politically separated from the Jews of Judaea. In the Hellenistic period, however, they were a part of the Seleucid Empire, while the Judaeans except for a short interval were a part of the Ptolemaic Empire. The Jews of Antioch, after the establishment of the Judaean state, remained under the Seleucid Empire which was hostile to the Judaeans, and many wars were fought between them. That the Jews of Antioch called themselves Hebrews, is evident from the Fourth Book of Maccabees which was composed in Antioch.[26] The term Hebrews is used here

[26] See M. Hadas, Introduction to IV Mac., ed. Dropsie.

throughout. The Epitomist of the Second Book of Maccabees who was an Antiochen[27] likewise used the term Hebrews, and not Jews in his account of the martyrdom. The expression "the synagogue of the Hebrews" occurs in inscriptions which have come down to us from Corinth,[28] which indicates that the people in Corinth were called Hebrews and not Jews. That the people who lived in Judaea were called Judaeans — Jews, and that those who lived in the Diaspora were called Hebrews or Israeli are well illustrated by the different nomenclature used by Paul. When he was arrested in Judaea he said, "I am a Jew,"[29] since he was brought up in the city of Jerusalem and received his education from Gamaliel. In the letter to the Philippians, however, Paul said he was of the stock of Israel, the tribe of Benjamin, a Hebrew of the Hebrews.[30] In II Corinthians he remarked, "Are they Hebrews? So am I. Are they Israelites? So am I."[31] In the letter to the Romans he said that he was an Israelite of the seed of Abraham, of the tribe of Benjamin.[32] Thus, when Paul was in Judaea he called himself a Judaean like the rest of the inhabitants of Judaea, the Jews, while when he was in the Diaspora he called himself a Hebrew, or Israeli, as the people (Jews) of the Diaspora did.

Not only the term religion but its conception was unknown in the ancient period. The Bible speaks of a righteous man as one who followed the precepts of God, and of a wicked man as one who transgressed them and worshipped foreign gods. The righteous man in the later period was

[27] S. Zeitlin, Introduction to II Mac., ed. Dropsie.
[28] See B. Powell, "Greek Inscriptions from Corinth," *American Journal of Archaeology*, VII, 60–61.
[29] Acts 21.39; 22.3. ἐγώ εἰμι ἀνὴρ Ἰουδαῖος.
[30] 3.5. φυλῆς Βενιαμὶν Ἑβραῖος ἐξ Ἑβραίων.
[31] 11.22. Ἑβραῖοί εἰσιν κἀγώ Ἰσραηλῖταί εἰσιν κἀγώ.
[32] 11.1. ἐγώ Ἰσραηλίτης εἰμί, ... φυλῆς Βενιαμίν.

designated a pious man, one who worshipped God, who followed the precepts and was humble among his fellowmen. There was no word to describe the way of life of the Jews as a people.

When the Jewish state was established in the year 141 BCE theocracy automatically disappeared, and a new system, nomocracy, was inaugurated, i. e., the Jewish religion underwent a change; heretofore it had been based on faith, now it was controlled by law, and the term דת *dath* became the nomenclature for what we now know as religion.[33] Thus a pious Jew was characterized as one who observed the laws of his forefathers, the laws of God. The earliest appearances of the term Judaism are in the Fourth Book of Maccabees and in the Epitome of the Second Book,[34] both of which were composed in the Diaspora, in the city of Antioch. Judaism became a term for the religion followed by those who accepted the Jewish way of life regardless of race or nationality. It is understandable that the term Judaism was coined in Antioch, since the people there adhered to the same religion as the Judaeans, although politically and economically they were divided. They had been under the flag of the Seleucids and later had come under the Roman flag. Judaea was a politically independent state; however, the Antiochian Hebrews had one religion which was moulded by the Judaeans through the religious Sanhedrin and through the Temple. Hence they coined the term Judaism, although in name they were Hebrews and politically separated from Judaeans. In contrast to Judaism they coined the word *Hellenism*[35] which means the culture and way of life of the Hellenes, and also the word *Allofulismos*[36] which means the religion and way of life of

---

[33] Comp. S. Zeitlin, "Judaism as a Religion," *JQR* 1944, pp. 179–225.
[34] Ἰουδαϊσμος, 2.21.
[35] Ἑλληνισμός, 4.13.   [36] ἀλλοφυλισμός, *ibid*.

the heathen who were not Hellenes. This definition of Judaism, as expressing the religion of the Jews could not have been coined in Judaea.

The term Judaism in the sense of religion was coined by Jews of the Diaspora. Josephus in his account of Izates Adiabene's embracement of Judaism, used the term "the Jewish custom."[37] He usually used the term θρησκεία *Threskeia*,[38] worship. Neither he nor the authors of the Apocrypha which was composed in Judaea ever used the term *Judaism*. He sometimes used the term *ioudaikos*[39] in the sense of the characteristic of the people but not in the sense of religion.

The people in the Diaspora who adhered to the Jewish religion lived in the midst of different cultures and various religions. While they were a part of the general population politically they were different religiously, and thus they coined the term Judaism to express their religious differences from the Hellenes. The term Judaism became in the Hellenistic world and later in the Roman, one that denoted a particular religion which differed from others. This term is used in the Epistle of Galatians[40] and later became a common term in the Christian world.[41] The Jews adopted this term, Judaism יהדות[42] to define their religion, disregarding other terms. Even the term Jew was used in the Hellenistic and Roman world, and later in the Christian Church, not as signifying a racial characteristic of the

---

[37] *Ant.* 20.34. ὡς Ἰουδαίοις πάτριον or "'Ιουδαίων ἔθη." (*ibid.* 139).
[38] Comp. *ibid.* 13.198. καὶ τῆς θρησκείας τοὺς, and *passim*.
[39] Ἰουδαϊκῶς, *Jewish War*, 6.17. Comp. also Galatians 2.14. εἰ σὺ Ἰουδαῖος ὑπάρχων ἐθνικῶς καὶ οὐκ Ἰουδαϊκῶς ζῇς.
[40] 1.13. Ἰουδαϊσμῷ.
[41] Comp. The Epistles of Ignatius, "For Christanismos (χριστιανισμὸς) did not base its faith on Judismos."
[42] Comp. M. R. to Esth. 7. כך הם לא שינו אלהיהם ודתוהם והחזיקו ביהדותן; ובגדולת יהודתי (יוסיפון); על שם היהדות לבדה.

people, but as a distinctive term for a particular religion, although this religion was embraced not only by Judaeans, i. e., of the stock of Jacob but by others. The Roman historian, Dio Cassius, who lived toward the end of the second century CE said, "I do not know how this title (Jew) came to be given them but it also applies to all the rest of mankind although of foreign nationalities who affected their customs. This group exists even among the Romans."[43] We can deduce from these words of Dio, as well as from those of others which have come down to us that the word Jew became a term not of a particular race or nationality but of the devotees of a particular religion. The Church to some extent followed the same principle; however, when it became the dominating religion in the Roman Empire it prohibited anyone from embracing Judaism under penalty of death.[44] If a Jew embraced Christianity he ceased, in the eyes of the Church, being a Jew and became a Christian, since the term Jew implies a follower of Judaism. A Jew by birth or adoption, however, in the eyes of the synagogue can never renounce his religion.[45] He will always be regarded as a Jew, just as a born Catholic will always be regarded as such by the Church.

After the destruction of the Second Temple, particularly after the catastrophe of Bar Kokba, the people who called themselves Judaean-Jews, changed their name to that of Israel. The reason was due to the fact that the "Judaean Christians" maintained that they were the true Israelites,

---

[43] ἥ τὲ γὰρ χώρα Ἰουδαία καὶ οὗτοί Ἰουδαῖοι ὠνομάδαται. The country has been named Judaea, and the people themselves Judaeans-Jews. ἡ δὲ ἐπίκλησις αὕτη ἐκείνοις μὲν οὐκ οἶδ' ὅθεν ἤρξατο γενέσθαι φέρει δὲ καὶ ἐπὶ τοὺς ἄλλους ἀνθρώπους ὅσοι τὰ νόμιμα αὐτῶν καίπερ ἀλλοεθνεῖς ὄντες ζηλοῦσι καὶ ἔστι καὶ παρὰ τοῖς Ῥωμαίοις τὸ γένος τοῦτο. XXXVII.

[44] See S. Zeitlin, "Judaism as a Religion," *JQR* 1943, pp. 234–41.
[45] *Idem, ibid.*, pp. 28–40.

the chosen people. They held that the Judaeans-Jews who rejected Jesus were not the true Israelis with whom God made a covenant; any Gentile who accepted Jesus as the Christ was a true Israeli. According to the early Church Fathers, Jesus is alluded to in the Bible by the name Israel; hence they maintained that the Judaeans who rejected Jesus as the Messiah were rejected by God and were no longer the chosen people, and that they were not spiritually descendants from the Israelis with whom God made a covenant. To counteract the contention of the Christians, the Judaeans-Jews now assumed the name Israel.[46] Therefore, the term Jew with few exceptions does not occur in the entire tannaitic or amoraic literature,[47] only that of Israel. The term Jew occurs only in relation to a non-Jew. The documents which previously had the term Judaeans, were now changed and the term Israel substituted. The phrase, "according to the laws of Moses and the Judaeans," in the marriage contract, was now changed to "the laws of Moses and the Israel."[48] The country which during the Second Commonwealth was called Judaea, or simply the *Land* was now called ארץ ישראל *Eretz Israel*. The Romans and Christians surnamed the land of Judaea Palestine after Bar Kokba's defeat to emphasize the fact that the land did not belong to the Jews. On the other hand, the Jews stressed the name *Eretz Israel* to point out that the country was theirs.

In summing up, the name Israel originally had a racial connotation. Jacob was surnamed Israel. His descendants were called *Bne Israel*, the children of Israel, and sometimes simply Israel. When after the death of Solomon the descendants of Israel broke up into two kingdoms, the

---

[46] Idem, *The Jews: Race, Nation or Religion*, pp. 30–40.
[47] Idem, *ibid*.
[48] כדת משה וישראל.

northern and the southern, the kings of the former were called the kings of Israel, and the land was known as the land of Israel, and in all probability the people were called Israeli. The kings in the latter kingdom were called the kings of Judah; the country was the land of Judah and the people were Judaeans. The language was called *Yehudit*.

After the Restoration, particularly when the independent state was proclaimed, the name of the new state was The Commonwealth of the Jews. The country became known as Judaea. Their language was no longer called *Yehudit* but Hebrew.[48a] Although there were two kingdoms, the inhabitants of both were descendants of one progenitor; they were the children of Israel; they were of one racial group. Proselytes to their religion were not admitted. In the time of the Second Commonwealth, however, there were many proselytes from other nations and races to the Jewish fold. Proselytes from other peoples were not only welcomed but were encouraged.[49] The Judaeans-Jews were no longer one ethnic group. All the descendants of Israel did not live in Judaea. They lived in different countries and were politically separate from Judaea. They even bore different nomenclatures. Those who lived in Judaea were called Judaeans-Jews, those who lived in Antioch were called Hebrews, and those who lived in other countries of the Diaspora were called Israelis. All of them were the spiritual descendants of Israel regardless of locality or race. One spiritual force united all of them, and that is the religion which was highly developed in Judaea and Jerusalem and had a moulding power over all the Diaspora. The name of the religion was given as Judaism and the name Israel or Hebrew never became associated with the religion; the

[48a] Comp. *Jewish War*, VI.97; IV Mac. 12.7; M. Yad. 4. תרגום שכתוב עברית. In Nehemiah the term יהודית is still used.

[49] See *JQR* 1944, pp. 193–200.

term Judaism as the nomenclature for the religion was not coined in Judaea but by the Diaspora Jews which is very significant. The term Judaism, therefore, is to be associated only with religion and not with a civilization.

When the British relinquished their authority over Palestine on May 14, 1948, a new State by the name of Israel was proclaimed. This name, given to the State, was rightfully chosen. The State could not have been named Judaea as the people would have been called Judaeans-Jews. It is true that the name Israel had been adopted by the Jews themselves since the time of Bar Kokba, but this was because the Christians had held that they themselves were the true Israelis. The term *Keneset Israel*, the Synagogue of Israel, was coined to indicate that Israel after Bar Kokba became a religious community in contrast to the *ecclesia* of the Christians, but the term Israel was not used in the sense of religion. Judaism was employed in the sense of religion in contrast to Christianity.

The term Israel for the new State is suitable in many ways. The first government established by the Jews in the time of Saul was called Israel. He was the first king of Israel. Since the term Israel has no connotation of religion, a Moslem or Arab or a Christian Arab can be a citizen of the State of Israel; however, if the State were called Judaea, the inhabitants would be called Judaeans-Jews. The name Judaea would be exclusive; a Moslem or a Christian could not be called Jewish. I pointed out elsewhere[50] that when the Romans subjugated Judaea, Vespasian and Titus received the title Imperator but not Judaicus. It was the custom of the Roman Caesars when they received the title Imperator for their victories over a particular nation to attach the name of that nation to the

[50] *Ibid.* 1943, p. 227.

title of Imperator; however, in the case of the victory over Judaea they did not append the title Judaicus.[51] The reason for not appending this title was that it had the connotation of religion; Titus would not attach the title of a foreign religion to the title of Imperator.

Some may argue that the term Israel is not suitable for the new State since it has been constantly referred to as Israel for the last eighteen hundred years in the Talmud as well as in rabbinic literature. We had such statements, for example, as "All Israelis have a portion in the future world"; "Israel, although he has sinned is still Israel"; and the expression, "the Laws of Israel" These critics believe that the name Israel will lead to confusion. To whom did these references apply — to the people of the State of Israel only or to all the Jews? The objections to the use of the term Israel for the state have no validity. Jews were not disturbed by such fears in the Second Commonwealth, when the country was called Judaea and the people Judaeans-Jews. We have in the Pentateuch the well-known creeds, "Hear, O, Israel, the Lord our God is one;" and "Now, Israel, what doth the Lord thy God require of thee but to fear the Lord thy God and to walk in all His ways and to love Him with all thy heart and with all thy soul?"[52]

The Jews of the Second Commonwealth were not worried that these decrees might *not* apply to them. They knew quite well that although they called themselves Jews, the Pentateuchal statements referred to the entire stock of Israel. It is clear also that phrases in the Talmud referring to "Israel," take in all the Jews of the stock of Israel, not only the inhabitants of Israel. The Jewish people are of the

---

[51] Dio. LXV.
[52] Comp. also Deut. 5.1, ולמדתם ... שמע ישראל את החקים ואת המשפטים אותם; ועתה ישראל מה ד' אלהיך שאל מעמך כי אם ליראה את ד' ללכת בכל דרכיו, *ibid.* 10.12; Num. 24.5, מה טבו אהליך יעקב משכנתיך ישראל.

oldest peoples which exist. Many changes have taken place during their long history owing to their ascendency or decline, the periods of their triumphs or the periods of their defeats, respectively. The terms, Hebrew, Jew, Israel are in themselves distinctive marks of changes in the development of the people.

There can be no doubt that the establishment of the State of Israel is a definite change and even a revolutionary one in the life of the Jews, and for that matter in world history, as was the case in the Second Commonwealth. Those who are witnessing this revolutionary event cannot fully grasp its significance. Only the future generations will be able to evaluate it.

Again, there can be no quibbling about changes that must be made in the ritual as well as in the halakot, particularly those which originated in the Diaspora.

I pointed out above that in the marriage contract during the Second Commonwealth there was the phrase, "according to the laws of Moses and the Judaeans." After Bar Kokba this was changed to read, "according to the laws of Moses and Israel." Now another change is called for.

The choice of the name Israel had prophetic significance and indicates a political demarcation between the Jews of the Diaspora and those of the State of Israel. Both groups are united by religion, history and to a great degree by common ancestry, but they are divided politically. The Israeli of the State of Israel are Jews by religion, and this unites them with all the Jews of the Diaspora. The Jews of the Diaspora are not bound to Israel politically. They are citizens of their respective countries to which they owe their allegiance.

JEWISH RIGHTS IN PALESTINE

THE critical position that Palestine occupies in the peace of the Near East — possibly in the peace of the world — has turned the eyes of mankind towards that strife-ridden, harassed, little land. The United Nations, through its appointment of an investigating commission, has manifested this universal concern over the fate and destiny of Palestine.

In this essay our aim is to clarify on the basis of authentic original sources what rights inhere in the Palestine situation for the Jews and other peoples from the standpoint of religion, history, and law. Partisan literature on Palestine has tended to confuse fundamental basic issues. Extravagant claims and counter-claims are but poor counterfeit substitutes for the realities of history. At this crucial historic moment, when the fate of Palestine is about to be weighed in the councils of the United Nations, we propose to review the sources to be found in Jewish, Christian, and Mohammedan literature which throw light upon the religious, historic, and legal claims to Palestine.

1. RELIGIOUS CLAIMS

Palestine, as the land of Israel, has been religiously connected with the Jews from their beginnings down to modern days. In the Pentateuch God promised the patriarchs in a covenant that their children would inherit this land provided they in return would accept Him as their God. The God of Israel was regarded as the God of the land.

According to the prophets the Israelites were exiled

from their land because they did not worship the God of the land. Ezekiel in his vivid and memorable vision compared the Israelites who had given up hope of ever returning to the homeland to "dry bones." "Our bones are dried up," they cried, "and our hope is lost; we are clean cut off." But the prophet, to encourage them and to inject new life in their "dried bones," in the name of God replied: "I will put My spirit in you and ye shall live and I will place you in your own land."[1]

After the return to the homeland, the people no longer considered God to be connected with the land of Israel only; He is the God of the universe.[2] However, the land of Israel remained the holy land for all the Jews of the world. Jerusalem was the mother city, the Holy City, for all the Jews; and it was so named by Philo.[3] Josephus likewise called Jerusalem the Holy City,[4] for it is the mother city of all the Jews of the inhabitable globe.

During the time of the Second Commonwealth the Jews of the entire Diaspora made pilgrimages to the Holy Land, and sent sacrifices to the Temple. These pilgrimages never ceased throughout the history of the Jewish people. The ancient rabbis spoke of the Jews living there as assured of a portion in the future world.[5] According to them, the precept to settle in Palestine was equal to the sum total of all the other precepts of the Torah.[6] Even a breach in the observance of the strict laws of the Sabbath was sometimes overlooked, when it was done in the interest of acquiring property in Palestine.[7] Throughout the Middle Ages the Jews and the land continued an integrated entity.

[1] Ez. 37.
[2] See my study, "Judaism as a Religion," *JQR*, 1943, pp. 327–43.
[3] *Legatio ad Gaium*, 36.
[4] *Jewish War*, II, 16, 4, (397); VII, 8, 7 (379).
[5] Yer. Shek. 3, 3. מי שקבוע בארץ ישראל ... שבן עולם הבא הוא.
[6] Ket. 110b. אמרו ישיבת ארץ ישראל שקולה כנגד כל המצות שבתורה.
[7] B. K. 80b. והלוקח בית בארץ ישראל כותבין עליו אונו אפילו בשבת.

Judah ha-Levi, the celebrated poet and philosopher of the 12th century, voiced the belief that God had selected Israel as the Chosen People. He also selected Palestine of all the countries of the earth as His favorite abode. True, God was the Creator and Master of the entire universe but the land of Israel was especially dedicated to Him. While other countries were ruled by angels, God Himself ruled the land of Israel, which He gave as an inheritance to His people. The divine election of Israel was interwoven with the selection of the land. Only through the land of Israel, it was believed, could the Jews advance to perfection.[8]

Judah ha-Levi's passionate love for Palestine, so glowingly revealed in his elegaic poems, immortalized his peoples' love and longing for the Holy Land. His heart was in the East even though his body was in the West. He left his home for his beloved Palestine, braving the dangers and hazards of the journey. A legend relates that when he entered Jerusalem an Arab came galloping along and trod him down. He died kissing the soil of Jerusalem, and the last word he uttered was his *Song of Zion.*

Nachmanides, who was born shortly after the Latin kingdom was destroyed by Saladin and who witnessed the conquest of Palestine by the Mamelukes, said that since the Jews left Palestine, no nation could or would hold Palestine. The land belongs to the children of Israel. It was the particular domain of God.[9]

This conception became a part of Jewish theology. According to the rabbis, only in Palestine could a prophet arise, for only there could the Holy Spirit be found.

Of the three universal religions, Judaism, Christianity and Islam, only Judaism is continuously interwoven with

[8] Comp. Kuzari, II, 11–24.
[9] Comp. Naḥmanides, Lev. 18.25.

Palestine. The Christians did not consider Judaea, now known as Palestine, of any great importance in connection with their religion. When Jerusalem was besieged by the Romans the Christians did not defend the city, as did their Jewish brethren, but left for Pella.[10] For them Judaea was not a Holy Land. Only the places of Jesus's birth and burial were considered *loca sancta*.[11] For the Jews, however, the entire country of Palestine was considered a Holy Land. Other cities and places were regarded as holy in the eyes of the Christians. Indeed, St. Jerome wrote in one of his letters: "The court of heaven is equally open from Jerusalem and Britain."[12]

[10] Eusebius, *The Church History*, IV, 5.

[11] The earth where Jesus was buried was considered holy and was used as a means of exorcism of evil spirits. *Acceperat autem ab amico suo terram sanctam de Hierosolymis adlatam, ubi sepultus Christus die tertio resurrexit.* "Now he (Hesperius) had received from a friend of his own some holy earth brought from Jerusalem, where Christ, having been buried, rose again the third day." *De Civitate Dei*, XXII, 8. In the early centuries of Christianity devout Christians used to go to Jerusalem to visit the holy places. We are told that Arculfus, a bishop of Gaul, went to Jerusalem for the sake of the holy places.

The first to call Palestine the Holy Land, *Terra Sancta*, was Pope Urban II, who, in addressing the Council of Clermont (in the year 1095), said: "*Quam terram merito Sanctam diximus, in qua non est etiam passus pedis quem non illustraverit et sanctificaverit vel corpus vel umbra Salvatoris, vel gloriosa praesentia Sanctae Dei genitricis, vel amplectendus Apostolorum commeatus, vel martyrum ebibendus sanguis effusus.* The name, Holy Land, applied to Palestine, thus was for the first time emphasized by Pope Urban II and has been frequently used down to our own time. However, neither in the New Testament nor in the writings of the Church Fathers, was the term Holy Land ever applied to Palestine.

[12] *et de Hierosolymis et de Britannia aequaliter patet aula caelestis; ... Antonius et cuncta Aegypti et Mesopotamiae, Ponti, Cappadociae et Armeniae examina monachorum non uidere Hierosolyman, et patet illis absque hac urbe paradisi ianua. beatus Hilarion, cum Palaestinus esset, in Palaestina uiueret, uno tantum die uidit Hierosolymam, ut nec contemneret sancta loca propter uiciniam nec rursus deum loco cludere uideretur.*

"Anthony, and all the swarms of monks of Egypt and Mesopotamia, of Pontus, Cappadocia, and Armenia, saw not Jerusalem; and the gate of Paradise is open to them without (a knowledge of) this city. The

Christianity, in truth, arose in Jerusalem; but the early Christians gave up the earthly Jerusalem and spoke only of the Heavenly Jerusalem. "But Jerusalem which is above is free, which is the mother of us all,"[13] wrote Paul to the Galatians. St. Augustine also spoke of a heavenly Jerusalem but not of the Jerusalem on earth. For him the true Jerusalem, the eternal one, was in heaven, "Whose children are all those who live according to God on the earth."[14] Judaism, on the other hand, while also speaking of a heavenly Jerusalem always emphasized the earthly Jerusalem. The heavenly Jerusalem, moreover, could only be realized after the earthly Jerusalem has been re-established. This is well expressed in the Talmud. God said: "I will not enter the heavenly Jerusalem until I reenter the earthly Jerusalem."[15]

Rome, the city where Peter and Paul were executed, became the center of Christianity and its symbol. For the Christians Rome became the Eternal City. James Bryce well characterized this fact when he said: "To be a Roman was to be a Christian, and this idea soon passed into the converse. To be a Christian was to be a Roman."[16]

Judaism, on the other hand, recognized no holy places outside Palestine. The Jews who lived in the Diaspora were always connected spiritually with the Holy Land. They never ceased to pray for the coming of the Messiah, when Palestine would be the center of the religion of the entire world, when the prophecy of Isaiah about the uni-

blessed Hilarion, though he was a native of Palestine, and lived in Palestine, only saw Jerusalem on a single day; that he might not appear to despise the holy places on account of their nearness, nor, on the other hand, to confine God to place." *Epistula*, LVIII, 3. Comp. also CVIII.

[13] 4.26.

[14] *Id est ueram Hierusalem aeternam in caelis, cuius filii homines secundum Deum uiuentes peregrinantur in terris. De civitate Dei*, XVII, 3.

[15] Tan. 5a. אמר ר' יוחנן אמר הקב"ה לא אבא בירושלים של מעלה עד שאבוא לירושלים של מטה.

[16] *The Holy Roman Empire*, chs. 5-9.

versal fellowship of man would be fulfilled. In a word, in Christianity only those places connected with Jesus's birth, his sojournings and the holy sepulcher were particularly sacred, not Palestine as a whole. For Judaism Palestine is central to the most important aspects of Jewish theology.

As to Islam, Palestine can hardly be said to have played an important part in Islamic thought. While the roots of Christianity stem from Palestine, Islam flowered in the desert of Arabia. The Koran does not make mention of Palestine; its religion is focused on Mecca.[16a] It is true that the Koran (Sura 17) relates that Mohammed was transported at night from the sacred Temple of Mecca to the Temple of Jerusalem, and, according to tradition, was carried through the seven heavens to the presence of God and was brought back to Mecca the same night. But, apart from this, Palestine never became an integral part of the religion of Islam.

Mohammed, in order to break with Judaism and Christianity, particularly the former, substituted Friday for the Sabbath; Ramadan was established as a month of

[16a] In Koran, Sura 21, Mohammed is reported as saying: "We delivered him (Abraham) and Lot by bringing them into the land wherein we have blest all creatures." According to some commentators, this land is Palestine. Baiḍāwī, however, takes the meaning to be that God brought Abraham and Lot from Iraq to Syria, اى من العراق الى الشام.

Again, in Koran, Sura 5, Moses implores the Jews to "enter the Holy Land (ارض المقدسة) which God hath decreed you." Here, too, most commentators refer the expression to Palestine. Baiḍāwī, however, records an opinion that it denotes the Mountain (of Sinai) and its environs. "There is an opinion that it means the Mountain (Sinai) and its surroundings." (Baiḍāwī 5.24) In any event, Palestine did not figure to any appreciable extent as a Holy Land in Islamic thought and was not so considered by the True Believers, whereas to the Jews it always possessed a sacred character. The author of II Maccabees, which dates as early as c. 125 B. C. E., (Chapter 1, 7) designates Palestine as ἀγία γῆ (Holy Land).

fasting; and *qiblah* — the direction to be observed during prayers — even was changed from Jerusalem to Mecca. Pilgrimage likewise was directed to Mecca, which was made a holy city instead of Jerusalem.

From time to time the Moslems do go on pilgrimages to such places as the Temple area, Hebron and the Nebī Mūsā, but these are only places of local pilgrimages. The Koran commanded all believers to make pilgrimages to Mecca (Sura 3). There is a tradition that if a Moslem has not made at least one pilgrimage to Mecca he might just as well have died a Jew or a Christian. On the other hand, according to Jewish tradition, any Jew who lives in Palestine is assured of a part in the future world.

To summarize: there are places in Palestine which became holy to Christianity and to Islam, but the land as a whole was not considered holy by these two religions. Palestine as a Holy Land is connected with Judaism only.

2. Historical Claims

One may argue that while it is true that Palestine is considered the Holy Land for the Jews, historica it is not their land since they lived there but a short time and legally they lost title to it, when Palestine was conquere by the Romans. What are the historical facts? The following is a brief resumé.

The land of Canaan, later known as Judaea and Palestine, was conquered by the Hebrews under the leadership of Joshua approximately two thousand years before the present era. In the early days, there was no union among the Hebrews: they were divided into tribes. They were subjugated for a time by different neighboring nations. Subsequently, some of the tribes united. The first real union among the Jews came about when Saul was elected king. This was some time at the end of the second millennium before the Common Era. After him David ruled over all Israel, and was succeeded by his son, Solomon. On Solomon's death the United Kingdom was divided.

The Northern Kingdom was conquered by the Assyrians and later, in 587–6 B. C. E., Judaea was captured by the Babylonians. Not all the Jews, however, were exiled from the land. According to the II Book of Kings the poorest people were left in Judaea. In 538 B. C. E., Cyrus, the king of Persia, gave the Jews permission to return to their homeland. The Temple was rebuilt later, and the Jews were settled in a free, autonomous land under the leadership of their High Priests. Thus the Jews were in exile less than fifty years, and even during that time some Jews, the poorest among them, remained in Palestine to farm the land.

In the year 333 B. C. E. Alexander defeated Darius and became ruler of the Persian Empire, including Palestine which was then called lower Syria (Coelo-Syria). With the conquest of Judaea by Alexander, the status of the land was not changed. The Jews, ruled by their High Priests, remained there. After the death of Alexander the land became a part of the Ptolemian empire and later a part of the Seleucidean empire but the Jews continued to live in Palestine uninterruptedly. Before Judaea became an independent state, Judas Maccabeus made a political alliance with the Romans.[17]

Pompey, the Roman general, captured Jerusalem in the year 63 B. C. E. With the conquest of Judaea by Pompey, changes occurred in the political life of the Jews but no change took place in their religious life. Even later when Judaea became a province of Rome, the Jews enjoyed a measure of autonomy in their land. It was still considered the land of the Jews.

[17] See I Mac. 8.

In 70 C. E. Vespasian conquered Judaea and put an end to its political independence. But the Jews were not exiled from the land. The Romans punished only those who participated in the revolt against them. The Jews continued to live in the land under the autonomy of their religious Sanhedrin.

After the revolt against Hadrian (132–135 C. E.), the Jews were forbidden to enter Jerusalem but they were allowed to live in Galilee. The center of Jewish life was shifted from the South to the North, Tiberius becoming the main seat of Jewish learning and the residence of the Sanhedrin.

In the Fourth Century, when the Roman Empire was divided, Palestine became a part of the Eastern Roman Empire, Byzantium. Although the Jews were greatly humiliated and persecuted and their religion only tolerated, they continued to live in the land. In the year 615 Khusraw, King of Persia, aided by the Jews, conquered Jerusalem. In 628 the Byzantine king Heraclius reconquered Palestine. A few years later (636 C. E.), the Arabs, sweeping in from the desert with great fanaticism, holding the sword in one hand and the Book in the other, put an end to the dominance of the Byzantian Empire over Syria and Palestine. The Eastern Roman Empire was eliminated from the Middle East. It is told that when the city of Jerusalem surrendered to the followers of Mohammed a condition was laid down that no Jew should be allowed to remain in Jerusalem. However, this agreement was not honored by Omar. We know that the Jews not only were not disturbed in Palestine, but a community was organized and flourished in Jerusalem.

Omar, the conqueror of Palestine, was succeeded by Abu-Bakr. Later Ali became caliph. After the assassination of Ali, Mu' Āwiyah was proclaimed caliph in Iliyā' (Jerusalem) in the year 661, and Damascus became the capital. With Mu' Āwiyah the dynasty of the Omayyad caliphate began and lasted to the year 750. This dynasty was opposed by the 'Abbāsids, descendants of an uncle of Mohammed. In 750 Abu-al-'Abbās declared himself caliph and established his capital in Bagdad. The families of these two dynasties, the Omayyads and the 'Abbāsids were not Palestinian Arabs, but came from South Arabia. In 969 the Fatimids (Shiites from Northern Africa) conquered Egypt and soon afterwards Palestine, but about a century thereafter, the Saljūq Turks captured Jerusalem and restored it to the 'Abbāsid caliphs. In 1098 the Fatamids again reconquered Palestine.[18]

In the year 1096 the First Crusade was organized to march on Palestine to retake the holy places from the Moslems. In 1099 Jerusalem fell before the Crusaders. The capture of Jerusalem by the Christians was celebrated by savage butchery of Jews and Moslems alike. For a while Jerusalem became the center of the Latin Kingdom.

Saladin, in the year 1187, defeated the Crusaders near Hittin (Lower Galilee) and recaptured Jerusalem, thus ending the Latin Kingdom. The last hold of Christianity in the extreme North of Palestine was destroyed by the Egyptian Mamelukes in the year 1291.

The Mamelukes were a dynasty of slaves of different races and nationalities who absorbed the power in Egypt. The word "Mameluke" bears the meaning of slave. For more than two centuries the Mamelukes ruled Palestine. Their hold over Palestine came to an end with the advance of the Osman Turks. In 1517 Selim I captured Jerusalem and brought Palestine under the empire of the Turks. The Turks ruled Palestine until October 1917 when General Allenby captured Jerusalem and brought their domination to an end.

[18] See P. Hitti, *History of the Arabs*, London, 1937.

The point of this brief survey of the changing rulers of Palestine is to indicate that the Jews never left Palestine. For almost a thousand years they had their own rule—they ruled Palestine. Even after the Jewish state was destroyed the Jews remained in Palestine, even if at times their numbers were not great. There was no period when there were no Jews in Palestine, and however humble Palestine Jewry may have been at times, the Jews of the world looked forward to the day when Elijah would blow the trumpet to herald the coming of the Messiah and the return of the Jews to Palestine.

The Palestinian Arabs or the Arabs of Trans-Jordania never ruled Palestine. Palestine had been conquered by the Arabs who came from the South. As stated above, the dynasties of the Omayyads and the 'Abbāsids were not natives of Palestine. Certainly the Mamelukes and later the Turks not only were not Palestinian Arabs, but were of an entirely different race; they were not even Semitic.

Thus the historical claim of the Jews to Palestine is not a fallacy, as Ibn Saud maintained in his recent letter to the late President Roosevelt; they are based on unchallengable historical facts.

Equally unfounded are Ibn Saud's claims to Palestine as an Arabic country in the same letter: "The Arabs were the first inhabitants and they dwelt there for a period of 3,500 years before Christ and have remained there since Christ until the present day. They ruled it alone or with the Turks for a period of about 1,300 years, whereas the disjointed reign of the Jews did not exceed 380 confused and sporadic years." That this is a fantastic claim has been clearly indicated.

Palestine up to 734 C. E. was never an Arabic country and was never so considered by geographers and historians. Josephus as well as the Roman geographer Strabo placed

Arabia beyond the boundaries of Palestine, or as it was then called, Judaea. On the other hand, the Jews held sovereignty in the country not for "380 confused and sporadic years," but from about 1028 B. C. E. until the year 70 C. E. when Jerusalem fell before the Romans. And even after the fall of Jerusalem the Jews in Palestine as we indicated were ruled by their own patriarchs and the Sanhedrin. Furthermore, as we shall soon point out, when Palestine became a province of the Roman Empire, the Jews were considered an associate people.

3. Legal Rights

One may say, of course, that Judaism is the only religion rooted in Palestine and that the Jews have a historical claim on Palestine. But can one say they have a legal claim since the country was captured by the Romans? Did not the title to the country pass from the Romans to the later conquerors?

When Titus captured Jerusalem in the year 70 C. E. neither he nor his father Vespasian appended the title *Judaicus* to their title of Emperor as was the custom of Roman victors when they conquered a country.[19] The reason why Vespasian did not append the title *Judaicus* was two-fold. First, Judaism at that time was considered a religion, and he could hardly adopt the title *Judaicus*.[20]

Secondly, Vespasian did not append the title *Judaicus* because he did not annex Judaea to the Roman Empire. Josephus said that the Emperor took Judaea for himself as a private possession.[21] The special tax (*fiscus Judaicus*)

[19] Dio Cassius, 65 καὶ ἐπ' αὐτοῖς τὸ μὲν τοῦ αὐτοκράτορος ὄνομα αμφότεροι ἔλαβον τὸ δὲ δὴ του Ἰουδαϊκου οὐδέτερος ἔσχε.

[20] See S. Zeitlin, *JQR* XXXIV, 2 (1943).

[21] *Jewish War*, 7. 6,6 (217), "receiving the country as his private property οὐ γὰρ κατῴκισεν ἐκεῖ πόλιν ἰδίαν αὐτῷ τὴν χώραν φυλάττων ὀκτακοσίοις δὲ μόνοις ἀπὸ τῆς στρατιᾶς διαφειμένοις χωρίον ἔδωκεν εἰς κατοίκησιν ὃ καλεῖται μὲν Ἀμμαοῦς ἀπέχει δὲ τῶν Ἱεροσολύμων σταδίους τριάκοντα.

that Vespasian levied on the Jews after the War, was levied not only on the Jews of Judaea, but on all the Jews of the Empire, even on the proselytes.[21a] This religious tax demonstrated the victory of Jupiter over the God of Israel. Vespasian as the representative of Jupiter on earth, appropriated the land for himself.

From the Roman historian Tacitus we learn that Titus insisted that the Temple should be burned as a prime necessity "in order to wipe out more completely the religion of the Jews and the Christians." He held, that "these religions, although hostile to each other, nevertheless sprung from the same source. The Christians had grown out of the Jews. If the root were destroyed the stock would easily perish."[22] Thus by the destruction of the Temple, the Romans hoped to destroy the Jewish and Christian religions.

The Jews continuing to live in Judaea were not considered as *peregrini dediticii*, that is, aliens whose country had been destroyed and who now had no country. Thus, when Emperor Caracalla conferred the Roman *civitas* (citizenship)[23] on all aliens, excepting only the *peregrini dediticii* who had no country which they could claim as their home, the Jews were among those who received Roman citizenship. They were even called Romans[24] and enjoyed all the privileges and rights in their land, Palestine. The Jews lived under their own administration, under an ethnarch, the head of the Jewish community in Judaea. The Church Father Origen, who lived in the third century and who

---

[21a] Dio, *Epitome* LXV; Suetonius, *Domitian* XII.

[22] *At contra alii et Titus ipse evertendum in primis templum censebant quo plenius iudaeorum et Christianorum religio tolleretur: quippe has religiones, licet contrarias sibi, isdem tamen ab auctoribus profectas; Christianos ex Iudaeis extilisse: radice sublata stirpen facile perituram.* (Fragments of the Histories).

[23] *Lex Antoniona de civitate.*

[24] *Iudaei Romano. Cod. Theod.* II, 1, 8 (398).

spent some time in Judaea, observed that the Jews had their own ethnarch and their own courts.

That the Jews were not considered a conquered people but rather *socii populi Romani*, an associate people of the Romans, can be inferred also from the fact that they had the privilege of accepting public offices in the Roman government or declining them. This privilege which the Jews enjoyed, was even incorporated in the Roman law as late as 321 C. E.,[25] a privilege which could not have been enjoyed by a people who had no country.

That the Jews were an associate people of the Romans can be also learned from their participation with the Romans in the war against Persia. When Sapor was victorious over the Romans and conquered many cities in Judaea, among them Caesarea, thousands of Jews were killed in this war; they were killed as Romans. On the arrival of this news to the Jews of Babylonia, Samuel, (the spiritual head of Babylonian Jewry), did not tear his garments as a sign of mourning.[26] Since he was a Persian patriot, he considered the killing of these Jews not as a specific Jewish catastrophe; they were killed as participants with the Romans in the war against Persia. The Talmud relates that King Sapor prided himself on the fact that he never killed a Jew.[27] Apparently, he did not consider the thousands of Jews killed in Caesarea as Jews; for him they were Romans.

That the Jews did not lose title to Palestine can furthermore be attested by historical and legal facts. The Jews continued to exercise the right of owning slaves as well

[25] *Cunctis ordinibus general lege concedimus Iudaeos vocari ad curiam. Verum ut aliquid ipsis ad solacium pristinae observationis relinquatur, binos vel ternos privilegio perpeti patimur nullis nominationibus occupari.* Ibid. 16, 8, 3.

[26] M. K. 26a והא אמרו לי' לשמואל קטל שבור מלכא תריסר אלפי יהודאי במזינת קסרי ולא קרע.

[27] *Ibid.* א'ל שבור מלכא לשמואל תיתי לי דלא קטלי יהודי מעולם.

as the right of manumission,[28] which *peregrini dediticii* did not have.[29] As late as the year 429 the Palestinian Sanhedrin was still recognized in the Eastern Roman Empire.[30] The authority of the Jewish patriarchs was likewise acknowledged.[31] Clearly the Jews enjoyed citizenship, and were not aliens in their own land.

According to international law, if a power conquers a country, the title of the country passes from the vanquished government to the conqueror, either by treaty or even without treaty. If a country, however, was previously conquered and its conqueror was afterwards defeated by another power, the later conqueror acquires title to all the rights and privileges held by the previous government.

Though the Romans conquered Palestine, they did not annex it to the Empire. When the Persians and later the Arabs conquered Palestine from the Romans, they occupied

---

[28] According to the Roman law only citizens had the right to own slaves and the right to manumit them.

According to Eusebius the Emperor Constantine passed a law to the effect that no Christian should be a slave to a Jewish master on the ground that it would not be right that those whom Christ had ransomed should be subjected in slavery to a Jew. (*The Life of Constantine*, IV, 27). Constantine, in passing this law that a Jew could not have slaves who were Christians, specified the religious reason, but not the legal. If the Jews were not citizens, the Emperor would have emphasized the fact that aliens had no right to own slaves.

[29] *Manumissio vindicata*, is a form of manumission by means of *in jure cessio*. Peregrinus cannot acquire property by *mancipatio*. Peregrinus, however, enjoyed rights under *jus gentium*.

[30] Comp. *Cod. Thed.* 16, 8, 29. *Iudaeorum primates, qui in utriusque Palaestinae synedriis nominantur vel in aliis provinciis degunt, quaecumque post excessum patriarcharum pensionis nomine suscepere, cogantur exsolvere.*

[31] *Iudaei Romano ... Sane si qui per conpromissum ad similitudinem arbitrorum apud Iudaeos vel patriarchas ex concensu partium in civili dumtaxat negotio putaverint litigandum sortiri eorum iudicium iure publico non vetentur: eorum etiam sententias provinciarum iudices exequantur, tamquam ex sententia cognitoris arbitri fuerint ad tributi. Ibid.* II, 1, 10. Thus, in the year 398 C. E., in the time of the Emperors Arcadius and Honorius, the Jewish patriarchs and the courts were recognized.

the country but could not annex the title which the Romans themselves did not possess. When the Turks conquered Palestine from the Mamelukes, they, too, held the country as an occupying power only. Thus the rights of the Arabs and the Turks to Palestine were based on *possession* but not on *title*. They never conquered Palestine from the Jews, and the Jews never gave up title to the land.

In conclusion, we may say that Judaism is the only religion and the Jews are the only people in the world who, from earliest times to modern days, are identified religiously, historically and legally with Palestine.

JEWISH RIGHTS IN PALESTINE

BY

Prof. ARNOLD J. TOYNBEE

❧

JEWISH RIGHTS IN ERETZ ISRAEL (PALESTINE)

BY

Prof. SOLOMON ZEITLIN

CORRESPONDENCE

Reprinted from the *Jewish Quarterly Review,* New Series, Vol. 52, 1962.

JEWISH RIGHTS IN PALESTINE

By Arnold J. Toynbee, England

Rights may perhaps be defined as claims which are recognised as being valid not merely by the claimants themselves but by a general consensus of disinterested parties. In the current dispute over Palestine, the immediate claimants are the Palestinian Arabs on the one side and the Jews now in Palestine on the other, while many other Arabs and other Jews sympathise in varying degrees with those Arabs and those Jews who are immediately concerned. All the Arabs and all the Jews in the World, added together, amount to no more than a small minority of the human race. The majority, to which I happen to belong, is also concerned in the Palestine dispute, though it is disinterested in the sense that it has no local claims. Nevertheless, its concern is a most legitimate and most respectable one. We are concerned that, in Palestine as everywhere else, human rights shall be vindicated, whatever these rights may be deemed to be by a consensus of the disinterested majority. We are concerned that wrongs shall be righted and that sufferings shall be relieved. We are also concerned that a local quarrel in Palestine shall not give rise to a world war that might destroy the human race.

In this world forum, claims based on alleged divine revelation to the Jewish, Christian, and Muslim communities must be left out of account, because the adherents of these three religions together, and, a fortiori, the adherents of any single one of them, are only a minority of the human race. The majority does not recognise the doctrines of any of the three as being true. The Jewish, Christian, and Muslim communities each claim to be 'the chosen people' of one and the same god. The rest of the human race does not agree that any of these three mutually incompatible claims entitles the claimants to special privileges. The Jews claim that, in the second millennium B.C., this same god made a gift of Palestine to their Israelite forefathers and authorised, or even commanded, them to conquer the country by force of arms and to exterminate its existing inhabitants. The Christians claim that the Jewish founder of their religion, Jesus, was the son of the same god, and that he was born in Bethlehem, was brought up in Nazareth, and was crucified, was buried, and came to life again on the outskirts of Jerusalem. The Muslims claim that the prophet Muhammad ascended to Heaven from the Temple area at Jerusalem on the Night of Power. These claims have no validity for agnostics, Hindus, Buddhists, Confucians, Shintoists. Therefore, in the world forum that has the last word to say about rights, there is no place for any claims on Palestine that are made, in the name of alleged divine revelation, by Jews or by Muslim and Christian Arabs. The case must be argued in terms of human rights that are more or less universally recognised as being valid.

I submit that the human rights of the native inhabitants of a country have an absolute priority over all other claims upon that country, and that these overriding rights are not forfeited if the native inhabitants are dispossessed of their homes and property. This is a violation of their rights, not a cancellation of these. The native inhabitants' rights may not be the only valid rights in connexion with a country. But other peoples' rights in connexion with it, if there are any, are valid only in so far as these can be exercised without damaging the rights and the legitimate interests of the native inhabitants.

What are the rights, if any, that can be claimed by outsiders? Outsiders may have rights that are religious. Palestine is a 'holy land' for the adherents of each of the three Judaic religions; so I should say that, subject to the overriding rights of the native inhabitants, the Jewish, Christian, and Muslim communities throughout the World have a right of access to Palestine for their pilgrims, a right of residence in Palestine for seminarists and religious devotees, and a right to maintain in Palestine places of worship and also hostels, hospitals, colleges, monasteries, and other religious or philanthropic institutions. Happily it is possible to arrange for the exercise of these religious rights in Palestine for all the three claimant religions side by side and simultaneously, and also to arrange for their exercise without encroaching on the overriding rights of the country's inhabitants.

This right of access to Palestine for religious purposes has, I believe, always been granted to Jews and Christians by Muslims during the long periods during which the Muslims have been in a majority among the inhabitants of Palestine and during which the government has been in Muslim hands. This Muslim policy is a consequence of the Prophet Muhammad's instructions in the Qur'an. He has ruled that Jews and Christians, as well as Muslims, are 'people of the Book', and that it is therefore the duty of a Muslim Government to tolerate and protect its Jewish and Christian subjects so long as these submit to its authority and pay a surtax. The right of access was not so well assured to Jews and Muslims, I believe, during the interlude of Crusader Christian rule in Palestine; and, in so far as Jews and Muslims were hindered, under this regime, from entering Palestine and residing there for religious purposes, they were, I should say, being wrongfully deprived of their religious rights.

Jews had previously been excluded from Palestine, except for Galilee, by the Roman Government after the Romano-Jewish wars, until the liquidation of Roman rule in Palestine by the Arab conquest. This, too, was a violation of the Jews' religious rights, but in this case the blame is shared with the Roman Government by the fraction of the Palestinian Jewish community that was predominant at the time of the Romano-Jewish wars, namely the Zealots. If the Pharisees, instead of the Zealots, had had the upper hand, it seems probable that these wars would not have been fought and that the Jews would not have been subsequently excluded from the greater part of Palestine by the Roman Government. The difference in attitude and policy between the Pharisees and the Zealots was that the Pharisees gave religion precedence over politics whereas the Zealots gave politics precedence over religion. Considering the Jewish Zealots' attitude and temper, the exclusion of the Jews from Palestine by the Roman Government was a safeguard for its military and political security that was perhaps inevitable.

The Jews also claim rights in Palestine on the ground that, during the greater part of the time between the conquest of Palestine by the Israelites in and after the second millennium B.C. and the extermination of the Jewish community in Palestine (with the exception of Galilee) by the Romans in the first and second centuries of the Christian Era, the greater part of Palestine was inhabited by their ancestors. The Israelite and Jewish occupation was never complete (it never extended to the Philistine country, for example). Moreover, the Israelites were only one of many peoples, ending with the Arabs, who established themselves in Palestine successively, and the Israelites were also far from being the first comers. They made their first entry into Palestine not more than about 3400 years ago, and the pre-Israelite civilizations in Palestine date back to about 8000 or more years ago on the evidence of the excavations at Jericho. At the same time, out of all the pre-Arab inhabitants of Palestine, the Israelites are the only community that has living representatives at the present day in the shape of the Jews; and, as living representatives of the former kingdom of Judah, which was one fraction of the historical Israel, the Jews do, in my opinion, have a right to a special position in Palestine which no other present-day non-Palestinians possess. At the same time, the Jews' historical rights in Palestine, like the Jews', Christians', and Muslims' religious rights in Palestine, are valid only in so far as they can be exercised without injury to the rights and the legitimate interests of the native inhabitants ot the country.

The Jews' historical rights in Palestine and the native

inhabitants of the country's overriding human rights were both recognised by Britain in the Balfour Declaration. In this instrument, the British Government recognised, and undertook to uphold, the Jews' right to a 'national home' in Palestine, subject to the stipulation that this undertaking was to be implemented without injury to the rights and interests of the existing inhabitants of the country. Thus, in the Balfour Declaration, Britain recognised the rights of two parties and entered into an obligation to uphold both sets of rights. This two-fold obligation was afterwards written into the mandate for the temporary administration of Palestine that was conferred on Britain by the League of Nations. This was a mandate of the so-called 'A' class, in which it was stipulated that the mandatory power was to prepare the country under mandate for eventual self-government and independence. At the dates when the Balfour Declaration was made and the mandatory regime was inaugurated, more than 90 per cent. of the living population of Cisjordanian Palestine consisted of Muslim and Christian Arabs. In Transjordania, the population was and is wholly Arab except for a small minority of Circassian refugees who came from the Caucasus at the time of the Russian conquest of the Caucasus, and who were settled in Transjordania by the Ottoman Imperial Government.

Both the Balfour Declaration and the British mandate for Palestine were imposed on the Arab majority of the native population against their will by British force of arms. If the local Arabs had been allowed to exercise the human right of choosing a political regime for themselves, they would have voted for immediate independence. The native Arab majority of the population of Palestine has never agreed that the imposition upon it of the Balfour Declaration and the British mandate was either legally or morally valid. Let us, however, provisionally assume these to have been valid for the sake of the argument. This would entitle Jews, as well as the native Arab majority, to be at home in Palestine, and would also entitle the Jewish community in Palestine to increase its previous numbers by immigration; but this Jewish right of immigration would still be limited by the overriding stipulation that the rights and interests of the existing inhabitants must not be injured. This would mean that Jewish immigration must not be admitted in so great a volume that it would overwhelm the native population of Palestine and would reduce them to the unfavourable position of becoming a minority in their own country. Thus the obligation undertaken by Britain, under the Balfour Declaration and under the mandate, to the existing inhabitants of Palestine required Britain, while fostering Jewish immigration into Palestine, to keep it within limits within which it would not prejudice the position of the Palestinian Arabs. It would also have been reasonable that these native inhabitants of Palestine should have had some say in the decision of the question of what the maximum amount of Jewish immigration should be.

In the event, the rights of the native Arab majority in Palestine that were recognised and guaranteed in the Balfour Declaration and the mandate have been violated (i) by the establishment of the Jewish state of Israel in Palestine, (ii) by the expropriation of the great majority of the Arab inhabitants of the Palestinian territory on the Israeli side of the present armistice line, (iii) by the removal of all restrictions on Jewish immigration into the territory now held by Israel, while most of the native Arab inhabitants of this territory have become dispossessed refugees. The resulting situation is an unhappy one for all parties. The wrongs done to the Palestinian Arab refugees remain unrighted; Israel remains insecure.

The blame for this unhappy outcome of the Balfour Declaration and the mandate rests primarily on the former mandatory power, Britain. She has failed to carry out the obligations, undertaken by her, towards the native Arab inhabitants of Palestine. Their rights and interests have not been safeguarded; a large proportion of them have been deprived of their homes and their property. On the other hand, the Jews have got much more in Palestine than they were promised and than is warranted by their historical rights. They have got not merely a national home but a state, and this at the cost of grave injustice to the Palestinian Arabs.

In the second degree the blame rests on Germany. If the Nazis had not committed unprecedented atrocities against the European Jews, first in Germany and then in the other European countries that the Germans invaded and temporarily occupied in the Second World War, there would not have been the pressure that there was to turn Palestine into an asylum for the Jews fleeing from the threat of death at German hands. But German crimes against European Jews do not excuse Britain for having failed to fulfil her undertakings to the Palestinian Arabs. The genocide of six million European Jews was not committed by Arabs; it was committed by Germans. Yet it is the Palestinian Arabs, not the Germans, who have been made by Germany's fellow-Westerners, the Western victors in the Second World War, to pay for Germany's crimes. The Palestinian Arabs have, in fact, been treated as if they did not have human rights.

Britain ought not to have allowed Palestine to be swamped by European Jewish refugees—as it has been to the Palestinian Arabs' grave detriment. Britain ought to have abolished all restrictions on the immigration of European Jews into her own territory, and on their earning their living there. So ought the United States, and therefore a share of the blame for what has happened rests on her too. The United States alone could have absorbed all the Jewish refugees from Europe, and she would have gained greatly if she had performed this act of humanity.

An exponent of Jewish historical claims in Palestine may perhaps plead at this point that the establishment of a state of Israel in Palestine in 1948 was a legitimate implementation of an historical Jewish right. It was, it may be argued, the re-establishment of a past situation. In the past, there has been a series of Israelite and Jewish states in Palestine: the pre-Exilic kingdoms of Israel and Judah, and the post-Exile Jerusalemic Temple state, Hasmonaean kingdom, and Herodian kingdom. The previous existence of this series of states legitimises the establishment of the present state of Israel, according to this argument. The post-Jewish inhabitants of Palestine have no valid rights in Palestine as against the descendants of the previous Jewish inhabitants.

When the Jewish historical claim to a special position for Jews in Palestine is carried to the point at which its implementation inflicts wrongs and sufferings on the present-day Arab inhabitants, the Jewish claim runs up against the statute of limitations. This is an almost universally accepted principle of law. Its general acceptance is due to its being commended by both humanity and expediency. The principle is that ancient rights, even if valid originally, lose their validity in course of time if they have fallen into desuetude and have consequently been superseded by other rights that have been validated by a long period of usage. It is rightly held that the hardship and injustice that would be caused by the annulment of long-since-established subsequent rights is bound to outweigh the satisfaction that would be produced by a re-validation of the ancient rights for the benefit of remote descendants of the people, dead many generations ago, by whom those ancient rights were once possessed. This legal doctrine is humane, because it declares in favour of the lesser amount of suffering and injustice in cases in which a living and an extinct right conflict. The doctrine is also expedient because, without it, no right, however long exercised, would ever provide any legal security of tenure. Every current right could then be annulled at any moment by some more ancient one, and this one in turn by some more ancient one still, and so on in an infinite regress.

In the Palestinian case in point, it was reasonable that the survivors of the deportees of 586 B.C., together with their children and grandchildren, should be repatriated in 538

B.C. Their living link with Palestine was still unbroken. We may guess that their re-installation in Palestine did cause some disturbance, and perhaps even hardship, to the Judaean peasantry whom Nebuchadnezzar had left undisturbed and whom the restored exiles labelled, somewhat contemptuously, 'the People of the Land'. On this analogy, it would likewise be reasonable if the Palestinian Arabs who were deprived of their homes and property in A.D. 1948 were to recover these in A.D. 1996. On the other hand, the interval between the date of the dispossession of the Palestinian Jews by the Romans and the date of the establishment of the present state of Israel is so long that the principle of the statute of limitations tells, in this case, decisively in favour of 'the People of the Land' who have become established in Palestine within the last eighteen hundred years. More than this length of time has elapsed since the Romans evicted the Jews from Palestine, except for Galilee, in the Second Romano-Jewish War, which ended in A.D. 135.

As to any legal title to the ownership of Palestine, as distinct from the human title derived from long-standing possession of the country, none of the successive occupying peoples has any title unless we accept the barbarous claim that a valid legal claim can be derived from an act of military conquest. Military conquest was the means by which Palestine came to be possessed in turn by the Middle Kingdom of Egypt, by the Amorites, by the New Kingdom of Egypt, by the Hebrew peoples and the Philistines, by the Assyrians, Babylonians, Persians, Macedonians, Romans, Arabs, Saljuq Turks and Crusader Franks, by Saladin and his Mamluk successors, by the Ottoman Turks and their British successors, and, latest but not necessarily last, by the Israelis. Successful military revolt against the Seleucid Macedonian power was the means by which the Hasmonaean Jewish kingdom in Palestine won its independence for the period of about two-thirds of a century running from the death of the Seleucid Emperor Antiochus VII Sidetes to the Roman occupation of

Palestine in 63 B.C. The pre-Hasmonaean Jerusalemic Temple-state and the post-Hasmonaean Herodian kingdom were brought into existence by the fiat of a conquering power—the Temple-state by the Persian Empire and the Herodian state by Rome.

In 1947 the United Nations assumed to itself the right to partition Cisjordanian Palestine into two areas which were to be respectively under Arab and under Jewish rule, and it is this decision of the United Nations that gives the present state of Israel any legal title that it may have, as distinct from the so-called 'right of conquest'. This title deriving from the United Nations is, however, of doubtful validity for two reasons.

In the first place, the United Nations, as so far constituted, has no jurisdiction over the internal affairs of any country, and to decree that a country shall be partitioned is certainly an interference with its internal affairs. If, for instance, the Government of Continental China were one day to expel the Kuomintang Chinese from Taiwan, and if the United Nations were then to decree that the state of Delaware should be detached from the United States and should be placed at the disposal of the Kuomintang Chinese refugees, it is certain that the United States would deny that the United Nations possessed jurisdiction, and that it would resist by force of arms any attempt, made in pursuance of this imaginary decree of the United Nations, to instal the Chinese refugees in Delaware in place of the present American population of the state.

The second reason why the 1947 decision of the United Nations is of doubtful validity is because it has been rejected by both the Arabs and the Israelis. The Arabs rejected it in toto at the time. The Israelis claim that the United Nations' decision to assign a part of Palestine to a Jewish state has given the state of Israel a legal title. At the same time, they reject, as being null and void, the frontiers, laid down in 1947 by the United Nations, between the parts of Palestine that the United Nations was assigning to a Jewish state and to an Arab state respectively. But the two provisions of the 1947 resolution of the United Nations necessarily stand or fall together. The United Nations could not, and did not, take it upon itself to partition Palestine without deciding, at the same time, where the dividing line was to run. Israel cannot have it both ways. In rejecting the United Nations frontier, she is at the same time rejecting any legal title that the United Nations resolution might be deemed to have given her. If she wishes to secure this title, then she must accept the frontierline that is part and parcel of it.

To my mind, claims made on legal grounds, as well as claims made on historical grounds, are of little consequence compared to present human rights. As I see it, Jews, and, equally, Christians and Muslims, have a human right of free access for religious purposes to a country that is their common holy land. As I see it again, the Jews, being the only surviving representatives of any of the pre-Arab inhabitants of Palestine, have a further claim to a national home in Palestine, but this only in so far as it can be implemented without injury to the rights and to the legitimate interests of the native Arab population of Palestine. In my opinion this population's human rights to their homes and property override all other rights in cases where claims conflict. This principle is, in my belief, valid in Palestine to-day because it is valid at all times and places. It has surely been violated by the establishment of the state of Israel and by the dispossession of those Palestinian Arabs who are now refugees.

JEWISH RIGHTS IN *ERETZ ISRAEL* (PALESTINE)

By SOLOMON ZEITLIN, Dropsie College

FROM TIME to time sweeping statements by Dr. Arnold J. Toynbee concerning Palestine, Israel or Judaism appeared in the public press. As a rule, they were highly charged personal opinions couched as generalized statements without historical proof or validity. One of Dr. Toynbee's more recent utterances while on a lecture tour in Canada was an annihilating denial that the Jews had any rights in Palestine. This appeared to us an astounding declaration contrary to the logic and facts of history. We therefore invited Dr. Toynbee to present his views on this subject in the *Jewish Quarterly Review* in a scholarly manner as befitting a journal of this character, stating at the same time that I would also present my own opposing point of view in the same issue.

Dr. Toynbee kindly accepted our invitation with this understanding. In all candor, it must be stated at the outset that the article here presented by Dr. Toynbee proved disappointing in not conforming to scholarly standards either in form or substance. It bears no documentation. None of the allegations is based on primary sources and it is marred by numerous historical inaccuracies of an elementary character. In brief, as we will show, the views stated herein are not what one would expect of a trained historian. They cannot be described otherwise than the personal views of Professor Toynbee without the support of literary sources and historical facts. They are *ex cathedra* statements, punctuated with half truths and inspired with the eloquence of bias and prejudice. We propose to analyze his assertions and submit them to the test of original sources in the course of which the rights of the Jews in Palestine will be clearly vindicated.

Professor Toynbee's argument reduces itself to three major

propositions: A. The religious claims of the Jews in Palestine confer upon them no special status, because Christians and Muslims likewise have religious claims to Palestine. B. The claim based on legal title to the land is not valid because Palestine was occupied by Jews for relatively short historical periods and on the other hand it was overrun by conquering armies and was occupied by various sovereignties for many more centuries. Consequently the tenuous legal title was torn to shreds. C. Finally, even if credence be granted to historical and legal claims, Dr. Toynbee appeals to the statute of limitations.

We shall examine these arguments seriatim, and in the process we shall quote copiously Dr. Toynbee's own words so as to retain as far as possible the flavor of Dr. Toynbee's style of arguments.

Regarding the Jewish religious identification with the land of Israel, Dr. Toynbee cites the alleged parallel claims of Christianity and Mohammedanism. He writes, "The Christians claim that the Jewish founder of their religion, Jesus, was the son of the same god and that he was born in Bethlehem, was brought up in Nazareth, and was crucified, was buried, and came to life again on the outskirts of Jerusalem. The Muslims claim that the Prophet Mohammed ascended to heaven from the Temple area at Jerusalem on the Night of Power."

He states further, "Palestine is a 'holy land' for the adherents of each of the three Judaic religions." Consequently, "The Jewish, Christian and Muslim communities throughout the World have a right of access to Palestine for their pilgrims, a right of residence in Palestine for Seminarists and religious devotees, and a right to maintain in Palestine places of worship and also hostels, hospitals, colleges, monasteries and other religious or philanthropic institutions."

Superficially, these statements may sound plausible and persuasive to the unguarded reader. What Dr. Toynbee fails to account for is the vital difference in the historic ties, in the spiritual quality and the degree of the indispensability of

Palestine for the wholeness of the religion in Judaism in contrast to the two daughter religions.

The Christians did not consider Palestine, now Israel, of any great importance in connection with their religion. Only the places of Jesus' birth and burial were considered *loca sancta*,[1] holy places. St. Augustine wrote in his book, *De Civitate Dei*, that in the early centuries of Christianity devout Christians used to go to Jerusalem *to visit the holy places.*[2] Palestine as a whole was not the Holy Land to the early Christians. Christianity arose in Jerusalem but Paul gave up the earthly Jerusalem and spoke only of a heavenly Jerusalem. "But Jerusalem which is above is free, which is the mother of us all," wrote Paul to the Galatians.[3] St .Jerome wrote in one of his letters, "The Court of heaven is equally open from Jerusalem and Britain."[4] St. Augustine also spoke of a heavenly Jerusalem but not of the Jerusalem on earth. For him the true Jerusalem, the eternal one, was in heaven, "Whose children are all those who live according to God on the earth."[5] Judaism also speaks of a heavenly Jerusalem but emphasizes the earthly Jerusalem; the heavenly Jerusalem, however, can only be realized when the earthly Jerusalem has been established. It is well expressed in Talmud, God said,

---

[1] Cf. Jerome, Epist. 58. 3. ... *Antonius et cuncta Aegypti et Mesopotamiae, Ponti, Cappadociae et Armeniae examina monachorum non viderunt Hierosolymam et patet illis absque hac urbe paradisi jianua beatus Hilarion, quum Palaestinus esset, in Palaestina viveret, uno tantum die vidit Hierosolymam ut nec contemnere sancta loca propter viciniam nec rursus deum loco claudere videretur.* ... Antony; and all the swarms of monks of Egypt and Mesopotamia, of Pontus, Cappadocia and Armenia, saw not Jerusalem; and the gate of paradise is open to them without (seeing) this city. The blessed Hilarion, though he was a native of Palestine, and lived in Palestine, only saw Jerusalem on a single day . . . . .

[2] *De Civitate Dei*, 22. 8.

[3] 4.26.

[4] *et de Hierosolymis et de Britannia aequaliter patet aula caelestis.*

[5] *De Civitate Dei*, 17. 3.

"I will not enter the heavenly Jerusalem until I re-enter the earthly Jerusalem." [6]

Rome, the city where Peter and Paul were executed, became the center of Christianity and its symbol. For Western Christianity Rome became the Eternal City. Pope Urban II, in addressing the Council of Clermont in the year 1095, was the first to call Palestine, *Terra Sancta*, the Holy Land. [7] His purpose was to inspire the Christians to join the crusade and organize armies to the land already known to them as Palestine to seize it from the rule of the Seljukes. (The Seljukes were not of Arabic stock). Neither in the New Testament nor in the writings of the Church Fathers was the term Holy Land applied to Palestine.

As to Mohammedanism, it can hardly be said that Palestine played an important part in Islamic thought. While the roots of Christianity stemmed from Judaea Islam came into being in the desert of Arabia. The Koran hardly makes mention of Judaea or Palestine; its religion is focused on Mecca. In the Koran, Sura 21, it is stated that Mohammed said, "We delivered him [Abraham] and Lot by bringing them into the land wherein we have blessed all creatures." Some commentators interpret the word "land" as referring to Palestine. Other commentators, however, take its meaning to be that God brought Abraham and Lot from Iraq to Syria. In Sura 5 it is stated that Moses implored the Jews to, "enter the Holy Land which God had decreed you." Here too many of the commentators maintain that the Holy Land refers to Palestine. Baidawi, however, records the opinion that the phrase "Holy Land" in this passage refers to the Mountain [of Sinai]. In

[6] אמה רבי יוחנן אמר הקבייה לא אבא בירושלים של מעלה עד שאבוא
לירושלים של מטה. (Tan. 5a)

[7] *Quam terram merito Sanctam diximus, in qua non est etiam passus pedis quem non illustraverit et sanctificaverit vel corpus vel umbra Salvatoris, vel gloriosa praesentia Sanctae Dei genitricis, vel amplectendus Apostolorum commeatus, vel martyrum ebibendus sanguis effusus.* The name Holy Land, applied to Palestine, thus was for the first time emphasized by Pope Urban II.

Sura 17 it is related that Mohammed was transported at night from the sacred temple of Mecca to the Temple of Jerusalem and, according to tradition, he was carried through the seven heavens to the presence of God and was brought back to Mecca the same night. Apart from the above vague allusions, Judaea, or Palestine, never became an integral part of the Muslim religion. In order to break with Judaism, Mohammed ordered that *qiblah*—the direction to be observed during prayers—should be towards Mecca instead of Jerusalem. Pilgrimages were ordered to Mecca which became the holy city instead of Jerusalem. There is a tradition that if a Muslim had not made at least one pilgrimage to Mecca he might just as well have died a Jew or a Christian. The Muslims from time to time do go on pilgrimages to such places as the temple area, where the Jewish Temple stood during the second Commonwealth, also Hebron and the Nebi Musa, but these are only places of local pilgrimages. The center of the Muslim religion is the city of Mecca, not Jerusalem. [8]

Judaea, or Palestine as a whole, did not figure to a great extent as the holy land in Christian or Islamic thought, whereas to the Jews Judaea was always a Holy Land integrated into the precepts and ceremonies of Judaism. The author of II Maccabees, which was composed before the destruction of the Second Temple called Judaea the Holy Land. [9] It was holy to the Jews before the destruction of the State and throughout the ages. For Judaism, Palestine, called *Eretz Israel*, the land of Israel, is the center of Jewish religion. To this day the synagogues are built facing the East in order that the prayers should be directed toward Jerusalem. In their prayers, Jews implored God to rebuild the Holy Land and the Holy City of Jerusalem. [10] The Jews of the

---

[8] The rabbis spoke of the Jews living in *Eretz israel*, Palestine as assured of a portion in the future world. Yer. Shek. 3.5.

[9] II Mac. 1.7. ἁγίας γῆς.

[10] "Return in mercy to thy city Jerusalem ... Rebuild it soon, in our days". "Jerusalem Thy holy city". "Make us walk upright to our land".

Diaspora were always connected spiritually with *Eretz Israel*. They prayed for the coming of the Messiah when *Eretz Israel* would be the center of religion for the entire world, when the prophecies of Isaiah would be fulfilled, and the teachings of the sages of old about the universality of God and the fellowship of man would be realized.

In a word, to the Christians, only the places connected with Jesus' birth, his sojournings and the holy sepulchre are sacred. For the Muslims only those places which tradition connects with Mohammed and Moses and other figures of their religion are sacred. For the Jews *Eretz Israel* as a whole is a Holy Land. All of its cities are considered holy, even those which were built after the destruction of the Second Temple. For them Tel Aviv, Haifa, the Negev are sacred. [11]

Strange indeed is the statement of Toynbee: "These religious claims have no validity for agnostics, Hindus, Buddhists, Confucians, Shintoists. Therefore, in the world forum that has the last word to say about rights, there is no place for any claims on Palestine that are made, in the name of alleged divine revelation, by Jews or by Muslim and Christian Arabs." It is true that other religions, Hindu and Buddhist, etc., do not accept Judaism, Islam, or Christianity but they do respect the conscience of other religious groups. They respect holy places of other religions. The Jews, Christians and Muslims also respect the holy shrines of Hindus, Buddhists etc. Even agnostics, although denying divinity, would not act contrary to the religious feelings of a people. Only the militant atheists and the Nazi Germans would destroy the shrines of religious people and would not take into consideration the feelings of religious groups. Even in ancient times the Hellenes and Romans showed reverence to shrines of other gods. The Jews who believed in one God did not revile the gods of other people. [12]

---

[11] Cf. Kelim, 1 ארץ ישראל מקודשת מכל הארצות

[12] Let none blasphem the gods which other cities revere, nor rob foreign temples, nor take treasure that has been dedicated in the name of any god. *Ant.* 4.8.10 (207).

As was noted before, Toynbee said, "The Christians claim that the Jewish founder of their religion, Jesus, was the son of the same god." The term the "same god" would imply the existence of other gods. Is Prof. Toynbee not aware that the Jews of that period believed in the universality of God, that God was the Lord of the entire universe and that there was no other God, and that the same view was held by the early Christians?

From the religious aspects, we now turn to the Jewish historical claims on Palestine. Are they valid? For this purpose we shall present a brief historical survey since the ancestors of modern Jews occupied the land of Canaan, which later became known as the Land of Israel, or Palestine.

Approximately 13 hundred years before the present era, the Children of Israel, under the leadership of Jushua, conquered the Land of Canaan. In the early days there was no union among the tribes of Israel. The first real union came about when Saul was elected king some time at the end of the second millenium before our era. After him David ruled over the united nation, and was succeeded by his son Solomon. After Solomon's death the Kingdom became divided into two parts; one—the Kingdom of Israel—in the North, and the other—the Kingdom of Judah—in the South. From the latter state, the name of Judeans, or Jews is derived.

The Kingdom of Israel was conquered by the Assyrians. Later, in 587 BCE, the Kingdom of Judah was conquered by the Babylonians. Not all the Judaeans were exiled from the land. The Babylonians carried the elite classes into captivity but allowed many Judaeans to remain. Gedalia, a Judaean, was appointed governor of the country. During the period of turmoil many neighboring nations took advantage of Judaea's helpless condition and annexed part of her territory. The Edomites invaded from the south and reached beyond Hebron. The Ammonities and the Moabites from the east, pared off some of the Judaean country as did the Philistines from the west.

When Cyrus, king of Persia, conquered Babylonia he gave the Judaeans permission to return to their homeland. The Temple was rebuilt and the Judaeans were settled as a free autonomous community in the land under the leadership of their high priests, who had religious and secular authority over them. [13] The captive Judaeans had been in exile less than fifty years, and during that time the common folk of the nation, the poor, the farmers, and many of the military castes, who escaped captivity remained in Judaea.

In the year 333 BCE, Alexander of Macedonia defeated Darius and became the ruler of the Persian Empire, including Palestine, which was then called Coelo-Syria, Lower Syria. With the conquest of Judaea by Alexander, the status of the Judaeans was not changed. They still were ruled by their high priests. When Coelo-Syria became a part of the Ptolemean Empire and later a part of the Seleucidean Empire, the Judaeans continued to live in the country uninterruptedly as an autonomous community. [14] When Antiochus Epiphanes forced his policy of hellenization upon them many defied his decrees. Those who opposed him were persecuted and put to death. The Judaeans were ready to die for the truth of their religion. They were the first martyrs in history. The persecutions by Antiochus Epiphanes against Judaism brought about a great religious revolt, which developed into a national war under the leadership of the Hasmonean family. It proved successful. In the year 142 BCE Judaea became an independent state. Simon the Hasmonean was elected high priest and ruler of the new independent State of Judaea. [15] Simon

---

[13] Cf. Ezra 7.25-6. "And thou, Ezra, after the wisdom of thy God that is in thy hand, appoint officers and judges who may judge all the people that are beyound the River ... And whosoever will not do the law of thy God, and the law of the king, let judgement be executed upon him with all diligence, whether it be unto death, or to banishment, or to confiscation of goods, or to imprisonment".
[14] Cf. *Ant.* 12.3.3 (138-146).
[15] Cf. I Mac. 14.46-49.

during his rulership concluded a political alliance with the Romans.[16]

About a century later, a civil war between the two brothers, John Hyrcanus and Aristobulus served as a pretext for Rome to intervene in the internal affairs in Judaea. Pompey the conquerer of Mithridates and Tigranes was in Syria in 63 BCE. He received deputations from the warring factions including a party that was opposed to any form of monarchy and who were willing to live under a foreign government as had their ancestors under Persia, the Ptolemies and the Seleucides.[17] Pompey made war against Aristobulus, captured the Temple, abolished the independence of Judaea, and placed the country under the supervision of the governor of Syria.[18] Gabinius, who succeeded Pompey, partitioned Judaea into five confederacies, *sunodoi*,[19] *sunedria*,[20] each of which had its capital. A similar policy was applied by Paulus the Roman general when he conquered Macedonia divided it into four confederacies, *sunodoi, sunedria*.[21]

After Julius Caesar defeated Pompey and hence became the ruler of Rome, he appointed Hyrcanus as the high priest and ethnarch, thus making him the ruler of Judaea.[22] Thus, he not only nullified Gabinius' division of Judaea but he restored her independence. He prohibited the stationing of troops in Judaea for their winter quarters and the exacting of money and provisions for their Roman army.[22] He placed Judaea among the states known as *Civitates sine foedere immunes et liberae*. These communities had self government, and no auxiliary troops could be stationed among them. They also had the right to impose custom duties. Caesar recognized the

---

[16] *Ibid.* 15.17. φιλίαν καὶ συμμαχίαν.
[17] Cf. *Ant.* 14.3.2 (41).
[18] *Ibid.* 14.4.4 (74).
[19] *Jewish War* 1.8.5 (170).
[20] *Ant.* 14.5.4 (91).
[21] Livy 45.32. *senatores, quos synhedros vocant, legendos esse, quorum consilio res publica administraretur.*
[22] *Ant.* 14.8.5 (151); 10.2 (194); *Ibid.* (204-205).

Judaeans a *socii et amici populi Romani*.[23] Judaea became again an autonomous state, but a satellite country, subservient to the interests of Rome. When the Parthians conquered Syria they made Antigonus king of Judaea; Rome appointed Herod king. In the time of Augustus Caesar, Herod was a *rex socius*, an allied king.

In 70 CE, Vespasian conquered Judaea and terminated its political independence.[24] The Jews however were not exiled from the land. The Romans punished only those who participated in the war against them. The Jews continued to live in Judaea under the rule of their religious Sanhedrin.

After the unsuccessful revolt against Hadrian (132-135 CE), the Jews were forbidden temporarily from entering Jerusalem, but they continued to live in their country. The center of Jewish life was shifted from the south to the north, Tiberias becoming the main seat of Jewish learning, and the seat of the religious Sanhedrin.[25] But there were other cities to the south where Jewish learning flourished, in the city of Caesarea,[26] and in Judaea proper, in the city of Lydda.[27] The Jews continued to live in Judaea, Gaza, Ascalon and Azotus (Ashdod).[28] Many Jews continued to live in Jerusalem. The Judaean Christians who still followed many of the Jewish customs and celebrated Pascha (Easter) on the 14th day of Nisan had their church in Jerusalem.

After Hadrian suppressed the revolt, the name of Jerusalem was changed to *Aelia Capitolina*. This name however was not

[23] *Ibid.* (185), φιλίαν καὶ συμμαχίαν.
[24] The Roman historian Dio (65) relates that when the Romans conquered Judaea, Vespasian and Titus received the title of *Imperator* but not of *Judaicus*. It was the custom of the Roman Caesars, when they received the title of *Imperator* for their victories over a particular nation, to append the name of the nation to the title of *Imperator*. However, in the case of their victory over Judaea, they did not append the title *Judaicus*.
[25] Cf. Talmud Sanh. 12a.
[26] רבנן דקסרין.
[27] חכמי הדרום.
[28] Cf. Yer, Sheb. 6.i.

perpetuated. The country was renamed Palestine. The Roman historian Dio Cassius who lived after the Hadrian period still called the country Judaea. The Church Father Jerome, in his letters, refers to the country as Judaea. The Jews never designated their country Palestine. They called it *Eretz Israel* the land of Israel. In other words the Jews never abandoned title to their country.

In the fourth century when the Roman Empire was divided, Judaea then known as Palestine became a part of the Eastern Roman Empire, Byzantium. Although the Jews were greatly humiliated and persecuted, and their religion was only tolerated by the Church, they still continued to live in *Eretz Israel*, their land.

For a short interlude (from 615 to 636), Palestine fell to the Persians and then again to the Byzantians under Heraclius. Finally in 636 an Arab invasion sweeping in from the desert put an end to the rule of the Byzantians over Syria and Palestine (Judaea). Under the Arabs, the Jews were allowed to live in Jerusalem, to practice their religion under the guidance and control of their religious leaders, who enjoyed high status under the rule of the Caliphate. This was equally true under the Omayyad Caliphate that ruled from its capital in Damascus till 750 and the Abbasid Caliphate that established itself in Baghdad since 750. The families of these two dynasties, the Omayyades and the Abbasids were not Palestinian Arabs but came from South Arabia. In 969 the Fatimids (Shiites) from Northern Africa, conquered Egypt and soon afterwards Palestine, but about a century thereafter, the Turks captured Jerusalem and restored it to the Abbasids Caliphs. In 1098 the Fatimids again reconquered Palestine.

In the year 1096 the first Crusade was organized to march on Palestine to retake the holy places from the Muslims. In 1099, Jerusalem fell before the Crusades. The capture of Jerusalem by the Christians was celebrated by savage butchery of Jews and Muslims alike. For a while Jerusalem became the center of the Latin Kingdom.

Saladin, in the year 1187, defeated the Crusaders near Hittin (Lower Galilee) and recaptured Jerusalem, thus ending the Latin Kingdom. The last hold of Christianity in the extreme north of Palestine was destroyed by the Egyptian Mamelukes in the year 1291.

The Mamelukes who were a dynasty of slaves composed of different races and nationalities took over power in Egypt. (The word Mameluke has the connotation of slave). They ruled Palestine for more than two centuries. Their domination over it came to an end with the advance of the Osman Turks. In 1517 Selim I captured Jerusalem and brought Palestine under the rule of the Turks. [29]

Turkey, in the First World War, joined forces with Germany. The Allies therefore declared war against her. In October 1917, the Allied forces under the command of General Allenby captured Jerusalem.

This brief outline of the changing rulers of Palestine shows that the Jews never left Palestine which they called the Land of Israel, and also that the Palestinian Arabs or the Arabs of Transjordania never ruled Palestine; it had been conquered by the Arabs who came from the desert. The Omayyades and the Abbasids were not natives of Palestine. Of course the Mamelukes and later the Turks were not Palestinian Arabs; they were not even Semites. On the other hand, the Jews never renounced the title to their homeland. There was never a period when there were no Jews in Palestine.

Now let us turn to Professor Toynbee: "As to any legal title to the ownership of Palestine, as distinct from the human title derived from long-standing possession of the country, none of the successive occupying peoples has any title unless we accept the barbarous claim that a valid legal claim can be derived from an act of military conquest." We here may agree with Professor Toynbee. Military conquest alone without a legal annexation is not valid. The Jews not only never gave

---

[29] See P. Hitti, *History of the Arabs*, London, 1937.

up their title to Palestine, adhering to the country as *Eretz Israel*, the land of Israel, but many remained to live in Palestine, even after the great catastrophe which befell them in the time of Hadrian; they were not considered *peregrini dediticii*, that is, aliens whose country had been conquered and who then had no homeland. When Emperor Caracalla conferred the Roman *civitas*, citizenship,[30] on all aliens, excepting only the *peregrini dediticii* who had no country which they could claim as their own, the Jews were among those who did receive citizenship. They enjoyed all the rights in their land *Eretz Israel*, Palestine. They lived under their own religious administration, under a Patriarch, the head of the Jewish community in *Eretz Israel*.[31] The Church Father Origen, who lived in the third century and spent some time in Palestine observed that the Jews had their own Patriarch and their courts.

The Jews during this period had the privilege of accepting or declining public office in the Roman Government,[32] a privilege which could not have been enjoyed by a people who had no country. The Jews continued to exercise the right of owning slaves as well as the right of manumission [33] which *peregrini dediticii* a people without a homeland, did not have.[34]

---

[30] *Lex Antoniona de civitate.*

[31] *Iudaeorum primates, qui in utrisque Palaestinae synedriis nominantur vel in aliis provinciis degunt, quaecumque post excessum patriarcharum pensionis nomine suscepere, cogantur exsolvere. Cod Thed.* 16.8.29. Cf. also Yer. Pea, רבי בר בא מקיים ארכנין Cf. also the Epistle of Emperor Julian the Apostate to Hillel II. τὸν ἀδεχφον Ἰουλον τόν αἰδεσιμώτατον πατριάρχην.

[32] *Cunctis ordinibus generale lege concedimus Iudaeos vocari ad curiam. Verum ut aliquid ipsis ad solacium pristinae observationis relinquatur, binos vel ternos privilegio perpeti patimur nullis nominationibus occupari. Ibid.* 16.8.3.

[33] See Yer. Git. 4.6. רבי טבלא זבין עבדיה ... אמתיה דרבי אדא ערקה לקלוסייא.

[34] According to Eusebius (*The Life of Constantine*, 4.27), Emperor Constantine passed a law to the effect that no Christian should be a slave to a Jewish master on the ground that it would not be right that those whom Christ had ransomed should be subjected in slavery to a Jew. Constantine, in passing this law that a Jew could not have

The Roman authorities acknowledged the rule of the Jewish Patriarch. The Caesars recognized the authority of the religious Sanhedrin. *Peregrini* could not acquire property by *mancipatio*; they however could do so under *jus gentium*. The Jews, however, enjoyed their rights, not as individual aliens, under *jus gentium*, but as an organized community in *Eretz Israel*, with their own Patriarch and their own religious codes. (The Jewish patriarchate was abolished through the influence of the Church). This proves that Romans, although they conquered the country, did not take away from the Jews the title to their land. Judaism was considered a *religio licita*, [35] a lawful religion in Rome while all Eastern religious rites were prohibited. This privilege would not have been granted if the Jews did not have a homeland.

Though when the Romans conquered Judaea they appointed governors with armies, they were really armies of occupation for the purpose of suppressing any revolt or disturbances which might arise. According to international law, if a power conquers a country, the title, to it passes from the vanquished people to the conqueror, either by treaty or even without treaty. In a country previously conquered whose conqueror was afterwards defeated by another power, the later conqueror acquires title to all the rights held by the previous government. When the Persians and later the Arabs conquered Palestine from the Romans they occupied the country, but could not annex the title which the Romans themselves did not have. When the Turks conquered Palestine from the Mamelukes they too held the country as a occupying power only. Thus the rights of the Arabs and the Turks to Palestine were based on possession but not on title. They never conquered Palestine from the Jews and the Jews never gave up title to the land Judaea.

slaves who were Christians, specified the religious reason, but not the the legal. If the Jews were *peregrini*, the Emperor would have emphasized this fact.

[35] The expression, *religio licita*, is not the technical name in Roman law, which rather speaks of *collegia licita*.

Professor Toynbee concedes tentatively that a case could possibly be made for the legitimacy of the historical support for Jewish rights in Palestine: "An exponent of Jewish historical claims in Palestine may perhaps plead at this point that the establishment of the state of Israel in Palestine in 1948 was a legitimate implementation of an historical Jewish right. It was, it may be argued, the re-establishment of a past situation. In the past, there has been a series of Israelite and Jewish states in Palestine. The pre-Exilic kingdom of Israel and Judah, and the post-Exile Jerusalemic Temple state, Hasmonean kingdom. The previous existence of this series of states legitimatizes the present state of Israel, according to this argument..." Forthwith, however, he seeks to demolish such claims by projecting the legal principle of the statute of limitation: "When the Jewish historical claim to a special position for the Jews in Palestine is carried to the point at which its implementation inflicts wrongs and sufferings on the present-day Arab inhabitants, the Jewish claim runs up against the statute of limitations. This is an almost universally accepted principle of law. The principle is that ancient rights, even if valid originally, lose their validity in course of time if they have fallen into desuetude and have consequently been superceded by other rights that have been validated by a long period of usage."

Thus Professor Toynbee dismisses the Jewish historical rights in Palestine, which the Jews throughout the ages called *Eretz Israel*, the land of Israel, on the principle of the statute of limitations. He says, "This is an almost universally accepted principle of law." Professor Toynbee is certainly aware that the principle of the statute of limitations does not apply to all crimes. It does not apply to homicide. Neither is the principle of statute of limitations applicable to peoples whose countries were taken away from them by force as long as they have not relinquished their legitimate rights. Poland was first divided in the latter part of the 18th century. Finally, in the second decade of the 19th Century, it was divided among

Russia, Prussia and Austria. Poland ceased to exist as a political state, but its national consciousness was not destroyed. After the First World War, when the Allies were victorious over Germany and Austria, Poland regained her political independence. The statute of limitations was not applied. Lithuania ceased to exist as an independent state at the end of the Middle Ages. At the time of the First World War much of her land was inhabited by Poles and Russians. After the victory of the Allies Lithuania became an independent state: the principle of statute of limitations was not applied. Many other examples can be cited. This principle is not applicable to peoples whose countries were taken by force and who never relinquished their rights to their country, regardless of whether their countries were conquered a hundred, five hundred or eighteen hundred years ago. Thus Toynbee's statement in dismissing the Jewish rights in Palestine on the basis of the statute of limitations is neither historically nor legally correct.

Professor Toynbee's opposition to the State of Israel leads him to attack the jurisdiction of the United Nations: "The United Nations, as so far constituted, has no jurisdiction over the internal affairs of any country, and to decree that a country shall be partitioned is certainly an interference with its internal affairs."

Again let us review the facts. Palestine was a part of the Turkish Empire. In the First World War, she joined with Germany. After the conclusion of the war, the League of Nations which was created by the Treaty of Versailles in the year 1919, empowered England to administrate Palestine.

On November 1917 Balfour issued a declaration in the name of the government which reads in part: "His Majesty's Government view with favour the establishment in Palestine of a national home for the Jewish people." In consequence of the Balfour Declaration, many Jews began to immigrate to Palestine. This greatly displeased some of the Arab leaders and led to violence on their part.³⁶ In 1929 they organized a bloody massacre of the Jews in Hebron. The Arab leaders resisted the Jewish immigration, because they believed that it would undermine the Arab economy. On the contrary, we know from the Greek and Roman historians during the Hellenistic and Roman period the Jews made Judaea (Palestine) a very wealthy country, one of the wealthiest in Asia Minor.³⁷ It had been a desert since it was overrun by the different califs and the Turks. When the Jewish immigrants started to come to Palestine they found the country, particularly Galilee infested with malaria. They had to fight the very elements to make the land again flourish. Their coming not only did not impoverish the Arabs but brought them wealth.

After the Second World War, the Jews appealed to the mandatory government to facilitate immigration, particularly of those who survived the gas chambers and were still interned in concentration camps. The Arabs opposed this and persuaded the mandatory government to keep the immigration to a minimum. This led to further acts of violence on the part of the Arabs and the Jews and also the mandatory government.

England tired of sitting as it were on a powder keg decided to submit the question of Palestine to the United Nations, which was the heir of the League of Nations. In the spring of 1947 the United Nations sent a committee of investigation to Palestine. A majority spoke in favor of partitioning Palestine into independent Arab and Jewish states. The Arabs strongly opposed the idea, and neither were the Jews very happy. On November 29,1947, the United Nations

[36] Leonard Stein, *The Balfour Declaration*, New York, 1961.
[37] Cf. *Justini Historiarum ex Trogo Pompeo*, 36.3. *Opus genti ex vectigalibus opobalsami crevere, quod in his tantium regionibus gignitur.* Pliny in describing balsam said: *uni terrarum Iudaea concessum.* (N.H. 12.54). Cf. also Diodorus, ... ἐξ ὁῦ πρόσοδον ἀδρὰν εἶναι συμβαίνει οὐδαμοῦ μὴν τῆς ἄλλης οἰκουμένης εὑρισκομένου τοῦ φυτοῦ τῆς δ' ἐξ αὐτοῦ χρείας εἰς φάρμακα τοῖς ἰατροῖς καθ' ὑπερβολὴν αὐθετούςης. (19.98).

General Assembly voted in favor of partition. The Arabs were bitter, while the Jews accepted this resolution. England refused to carry out the resolution of the United Nations unless it had the consent of both the Arabs and the Jews.

England announced that it would resign its Mandate over Palestine on May 15, 1948 when it would draw out all troops from the country. Chaos broke loose in Palestine. In February 1948 an army under Fauzi el Kaukji entered Palestine from the north. This army received supplies from the Arab League. In March and April serious fighting took place between the Arabs and the Jews. In spite of their lack of equipment the Jews emerged the victors, they too suffered heavy losses. The aim of the Arabs was to prove that the United Nations' decision caused chaos and was unworkable.

On May 1948, the State of Israel was proclaimed. The surrounding Arab states comprising Egypt, Transjordan, Syria, Lebanon and Iraq, now attacked her. Their army was completely routed by the newly organized army of Israel and they were forced to ask for a truce.

Where then is the logic of Professor Toynbee's contention that the United Nations has no jurisdiction to interfere in the internal affairs of Palestine? The League of Nations originally entrusted the mandate over Palestine to England. Since she relinquished her mandate, the United Nations, the heir of the League of Nations, had the jurisdiction to transfer Palestine to other agencies, which they did by partitioning it between the Arabs and the Jews.

Dr. Toynbee's animus toward Israel leads him from illogical positions to absurdity. Thus he says, "For instance, the Government of Continental China were one day to expel the Kuomintang Chinese from Taiwan, and if the United Nations were then to decree that the state of Delaware should be detached from the United States and should be placed at the disposal of the Kuomintang Chinese refugees, it is certain the United States would deny that United Nations possessed jurisdiction, and that it would resist by force of arms any attempt, made in pursuance of this imaginary decree of the United Nations, to install the Chinese refugees in Delaware in place of the present American population of the state." What a pitifully absurd parallelism! It would be interesting to know how many Kuomintang Chinese lived in the State of Delaware before the United States became a nation.

Professor Toynbee accuses the Jews of expelling the Arabs from Palestine. This is historically not true. In the Declaration of Independence of Israel one paragraph reads as follows: "WE APPEAL—in the very midst of the onslaught launched against us for months—to the Arab inhabitants of the State of Israel to preserve peace and participate in the upbuilding of the State on the basis of full and equal citizenship and due representation in all its provisional and permanent institutions." The leaders of Israel made every effort to pursuade the Arab population to stay and to pursue their normal life.

The blame for the exodus of the Arabs from Palestine must be put on their leaders who urged them to leave the country. The leaders of the Arab League labelled all who remained in the country traitors. They assured them that their stay in the neighboring, brotherly States would be temporary.[38] They promised them they would soon be able to return, and all the millions that the Jews had spent on land and on economic development would surely be easy booty for them, since it would be a simple matter to throw them to the bottom of the Mediterranean Sea.[39] Only about 20% of the Moham-

[38] Cf. R.E.M.P., (Research Group for European Migration Problems) The Hague. October 1959.
[39] Cf. ibid. p. 8. "The Greek Orthodox Archbishop of Galilea, Mgr. G. Hakim, stated in an interview: 'The refugees had been confident that their absence from Palestine would not last long, that they would return within a few days-within a week or two. Their leaders had promised them that the Arab armies would crush the "Zionist gangs" very quickly and that there was no need for panic or fear for a long exile". Cf. also *The Middle East and the Refugees*, Dec. 1958, p. 7. "Arab leaders, too, confirmed that the flight was not caused by Israel. On April 20, 1948, Jaml Husseini, (now an important advisor

medan Arabs and about 50% of the Christian Arabs remained in the country. The entire Drusian Community remained in the State of Israel.

The sufferings of the Arab refugees invoke the sympathy of all men of good will, Jew, Muslim and Christian. This however can be solved in a peaceful manner by both Israel and the neighboring Arab states. The Karelians have been absorbed by the Finns when Karelia was annexed by the Soviet Union, and West Germany absorbed the refugees of Silesia when it was annexed to Poland. With good will of both parties a solution can be found and must be found.

Professor Toynbee's bias against the Jews is revealed in all his writings concerning them. In his newly published book *Reconsideration*,[40] he writes: "In the Jewish Zionists I see disciples of the Nazis."[41] Pace Professor! How many Zionists put Christians into gas chambers? Such a comparison is a libel upon the Zionists and an insult to the intelligence of the readers of his book.

Professor Toynbee denies that he is an anti-Semite: "I have never felt any inclination to be anti-Semitic." Perhaps so. But he certainly has a distaste for Hebrew and he has no interest in Hebrew literature. "I have never learned even a smattering of Hebrew" he says, "Since childhood Hebrew has left me cold, whereas I have had a passionate desire to learn Arabic."[42] "I am ignorant of the Rabbinical Jewish literature and of the Jewish philosophy that flourished in an early Islamic and a medieval Western cultural environment. I know of the Pharisees, not through their own writings,

---

of King Saud of Saudi Arabia) Vice Chairman of the Arab Higher Committee, and one of its spokesmen in the fight against partition, told the U.N. Security Council that 'the Arabs would not submit to a truce, but prefer to leave their homes'."

[40] *A Study of History*, vol. XII, *Reconsiderations*, Oxford University Press, 1961.
[41] P. 628.
[42] P. 597.

but through the denunciations of them in the Gospels."[43]

Yet he presumes to write about the Pharisees and about the history of a people whose literature he admits he does not know. Popular writers and diletantes may depend on secondary literature but not a serious historian. He knows the Pharisees through the denunciations of them in the Gospels. Could an unprejudiced American historian write objectively about the Democratic Party relying upon the attacks of the Republicans during an election campaign? Or vise versa? A serious historian must make use of the literature of both parties, otherwise he writes propaganda and distorted history.

Professor Toynbee's lack of knowledge of Jewish life is evident throughout his writings. He says: "And Ituraeans were forcibly circumcised."[44] Josephus in his book *Ant.* 13.11.3 (318) wrote when Aristobulus conquered the Ituraens he gave them a choice,[45] either to leave the country or to follow the normal life of the Judaeans and be circumcised, if they wished to stay. He sought to do away with some of the cruelties of war. In ancient times when the Greeks and Romans conquered a city they either slaughtered all the people or sold them into slavery. Aristobulus acted in a more humane manner.

Prof. Toynbee asserted that "Idumaean contingent gave Jewry Herod; the Galilaean contingent gave Jesus."[46] Professor Toynbee does not go into the historical forces that brought about the rule of Herod and the coming of Jesus. Professor Toynbee further asserts, "Jesus was not a Christian; he was a Jew in belief and practice, though, being a Galilaean, he may have been a gentile by descent."[47] By implication he seeks to convey that Jesus was not a Jew by birth. He thus raises the racial question advanced by the well known

[43] P. 596.
[44] P. 502.
[45] εἰ βούλονται μένειν ἐν τῇ χώρᾳ περιτέμνεσθαι καὶ κατὰ τοὺς Ἰουδαίων νόμους ζῆν.
[46] P. 502.
[47] P. 516.

anti-Semite H. S. Chamberlain [48] and others. Here he rejects the accounts of Matthew and Luke who trace the genealogy of Jesus to King David, and even Mark who while he does not give the genealogy of Jesus states that Jesus was of the family of David. Paul also said that Jesus was of the seed of David, "Of this man's [David] seed hath God according to his promise raised unto Israel a Saviour, Jesus." [49] If Jesus was of the seed of David he could not have been "a gentile by descent". John, who does not trace the genealogy of Jesus to David, maintains that he is the Son of God. According to John's opinion neither could Jesus have been born of Galilean gentiles.

No one denies that Professor Toynbee has the privilege of rejecting the accounts of the birth of Jesus, as recorded in the Gospels, but he supports himself on the accounts about the controversies between Jesus and the Pharisees. He cannot reject one and accept another.

Prof. Toynbee follows this with another statement: "There is no evidence that he [Jesus] was not an orthodox Jew." [50] Apparently Prof. Toynbee does not know the definition of an orthodox Jew. "The claims to divinity", he says, "that are put in his [Jesus'] mouth in the Gospels are not evidence of this; they are evidence only of what his Christian adherents in the next generation believed about him. This belief is blasphemous in terms of Judaism; but the blashphemy is Christian: Jesus himself cannot be convicted of it. Jesus was not a pharisee; but a Jew could be an orthodox Jew without being a Pharisee in Jesus' time, as he can today." As a matter of fact an orthodox Jew is one who follows the laws enacted by the Pharisees and interpreted by the later rabbis. If he does not follow these laws he is a Jew, but not an orthodox Jew.

Professor Toynbee partially retracted his shocking des-

---

[48] *Die Grundlagen des neunzehnten Jahrhunderts*, 1898.
[49] Acts, 13.23.
[50] P. 516.

cription of Judaism as a fossil religion. He now states that "the contemporary Reform, Conservative, and Liberal movements in the Jewish diaspora have been 'defossilising' their practice of Judaism ... The unwritten Torah was dormant for 1,400 years, from the date of the closing of the Babylonian Talmud till the 'emancipation' of the Jews in the West in the Napoleonic Age." [51] He apparently never heard of Rashi and Maimonides and other great Rabbinic luminaries during the Middle Ages. The Torah was not dormant for 1,400 years; it is Professor Toynbee who has not been awake to realize the spirit and the development of Judaism. During the Middle Ages a school of commentators on the Bible developed; great poets were produced by the Jews. A system of theology was formulated, to mention only one that by Maimonides, whose book, *The Guide for the Perplexed*, exerted great influence on the Christian theologians. Thomas Aquinas who in his lifetime was accepted by the Dominicans as the greatest authority in theology, was influenced by Maimonides' works.

These are only a few instances of his many misstatements and distortions of the history of the Jewish people.

Some reviewers praised his writings saying that although he did not present microscopic details, he did present a true paronama. A panorama is true only when the details are authentic. When details are misrepresented and distorted the panorama cannot be true. Professor Toynbee's approach to history, his very method of writing history is fundamentally unsound. His writings are conditioned by personal bias, which may make them attractive as art. But they are dangerously misleading.

[51] *Ibid.*

CORRESPONDENCE

Dear Dr. Zeitlin,

I HAVE READ, WITH great interest, your article in the July 1961 number of the *Jewish Quarterly* on Jewish rights in Palestine, which is published in this issue together with an article of mine on the same subject. I should much appreciate it if, in a future issue, you would publish my present letter to you, commenting on your article, and would write your own comments for publication simultaneously.

The main thesis of my article is that the human rights of the inhabitants of a country override the historical claims of the descendents of people who were inhabitants of the same country a long time ago, but who have not constituted more than a small minority of the population for a long time past. In your article, I do not think you have taken direct issue with me over this thesis of mine. I should be interested to know whether you agree or disagree with it.

I hold that the Arab refugees from the territory now occupied by Israel have not forfeited their rights to their homes and property. What prevents them from recovering these is not what happened in 1948. It is the refusal of Israel, since then, to agree to their re-instatement. As you truly say, "the sufferings of the Arab refugees invoke the sympathy of all men of good will." Are you in favor of a solution that would recognize the Palestinian Arab refugees' rights and would re-instate the refugees? This lies in Israel's power, and is a request that has been made to the Israeli Government repeatedly by the Assembly of the United Nations.

You make the point that there never ceased to be some Jews in Palestine. At the time of the establishment of the British mandatory regime, however, the non-Arab inhabitants of Palestine, non-Jews and Jews together, amounted to less than 10 per cent of the population. Can you produce evidence that the percentage of Jews in the population of Palestine had ever been larger than that at any date since A.D. 135? This question is important, because a minority of less than 10 per cent cannot justly claim title to a country against a majority of more than 90 per cent.

You say that "the Jews never abandoned title to their country." You also note that the Children of Israel conquered the Land of Canaan about thirteen hundred years before the present era. Is the title that they claim founded on ,,right of conquest"? If so, it has been extinguished by the successive titles of a series of subsequent conquerors. If it is based on their having subsequently come to constitute a majority of the population (of the interior only, not the coast), I submit that the Jews were never more than a small minority of the population of Palestine from A.D. 135 until after the First World War, and that their previous rights as a former majority had, by then, expired long since under the statute of limitations.

A propos of the statute of limitations, you are mistaken in stating that this principle was not applied to Polish and Lithuanian claims after the First World War. The right of the Poles and the Lithuanians to have states of their own was recognized only in respect of territories in which these two nationalities were, and had been continuously, an overwhelming majority of the population. Each of these two nations put forward claims to large additional territories, inhabited by non-Polish and non-Lithuanian majorities, which the Poles and Lithuanians had conquered and ruled in the past. In contrast to Polish and Lithuanian claims to their own respective national habitats, in which they were in the majority, their claims to re-acquire their former dominions in territories inhabited by alien majorities were not recognized as valid by the rest of the World.

In the authorities that you cite apropos of the Romans' treatment of Palestine and the Jews, I cannot find any evidence that the Romans regarded or treated Palestine differently from any other of the many countries that they conquered and annexed. I here fellow Theodor Mommsen, *The History of Rome*, 'The Provinces, from Caesar to Diocletian', English translation, vol. ii, pp. 184-225. After the conversion of Judaea into a Roman province in A.D. 6, the Romans left the local Jewish community, as well as the Greek colonial city-states in Palestine, in possession of their local autonomy. This was the policy that the early Roman Government followed in all provinces. After A.D. 70 however, it abolished the Jewish Sanhedrin in Palestine; and, after A.D. 135, it turned Jerusalem into the Roman colony Aelia Capitolina, and placed this out of bounds for Jews. The Romans never recognized that the Jews had an unextinguished title to the possession of Palestine; and the differential treatment that they eventually gave to the Jews in Palestine was less, not more, favourable than their standard treatment of their subject populations.

I should be most interested to read your comments on the points that I have made in this letter.

Yours sincerely,
Arnold Toynbee

Dear Doctor Toynbee:

I welcome your letter in which you take issue with some of the views in my article, "Jewish Rights in Eretz Israel." It affords me the opportunity to elucidate some of the views which evidently you overlooked, judging by your present letter which, in the main, is a reiteration of your previous article without adding anything new or pertinent.

Your letter reiterates "the main thesis" of your article, that "the human rights of the inhabitants of a country override the historical claims of the descendents of people who were inhabitants of the same country a long time ago, but who have not constituted more than a small minority of the population for a long time past." You state bluntly that I have not taken direct issue with you over this "main thesis", and you ask me rhetorically whether I agree or disagree with your thesis. I am certain that any thoughtful, impartial person who read my article could entertain the slightest doubt whether or not I agree with your thesis. However, as you profess doubt, I shall make my reply crystal clear.

Surely you must know that the United Nations has struggled with the question of what constitutes human rights almost from its very inception. President Truman, in his address at the closing session of the Conference in San Francisco on June 26, 1945, stated hopefully, "Under this document [the Charter] there is good reason to expect an international bill of rights acceptable to all the nations involved. The bill of rights will be as much a part of international life as our own Bill of Rights is a part of our Constitution. The Charter is dedicated to the achievement and observance of human rights and fundamental freedoms." While the Charter is dedicated to the achievement of human rights, the Commission of the United Nations has not yet been able to draft or to define the principle of human rights acceptable to all members of this body. In dealing with human rights the Commission of the United Nations has always been confronted with the problem of how to avoid intervention into the affairs of a sovereign state.[1] It was recognized that in order to deal with the problems of human rights the consensus of all the states must be obtained. Thus far this has been impossible to accomplish. The reason for this lies in the very nature of the principle of human rights which involves a delicate balance between individual liberty and the rights of the state. At the 669th meeting held on March 15, 1961 it was still discussing this problem and to this day it has been unable to draft and to define the principle

[1] Cf. United Nations, Commission on Human Rights, Report of the Seventeenth Session (20 February-17 March 1961) Supplement No. 8; also United Nations Work for Human Rights, Dec. 1961.

of human rights in a manner acceptable to all members of the United Nations.

Your statement that human rights "are more or less universally recognized as being valid" appears strangely unanalytical. Even if as a humanist and historian you wish to disregard the legal and political aspects of the problem you must at least define what you mean by the principle of human rights. Does it refer to individuals, groups of people or nations?

You and I are in full agreement that every person should have the right to live in accordance with his conscience and without the interference of society or government and that no government should curtail such human rights of a peaceful individual citizen. No society should discriminate against individuals because of color, race, sex or religion. Every peaceful member of society is entitled to security, political and economic, liberty from arbitrary arrest and the pursuit of happiness. A group of persons constituting a minority is entitled to develop its way of life and culture. This type of human rights should be recognized universally that even these circumscribed human rights are still not universally recognized.

Without troubling to define how the concept of human rights affects the concept of sovereignty of states, you proceed forthwith to the "rights of the Arab refugees in Palestine," and you declare, "I hold that the Arab refugees from the territory now occupied by Israel have not forfeited their rights to their homes and property." I do not know whether these implications contained in your statement, "the territory now occupied by Israel", is due to loose phraseology or is deliberately intended to stress your attitude. In either case you are not stating the fact correctly. Israel is *not* occupying the territory not belonging to her. Israel is living in her own country which is her legal and historical home. The United Nations Committee, composed of various nations, United States, Russia, England, France and the smaller nations, Australia, Canada, Czecho-Slovakia, Guatamala, India, Iran, Netherlands, Peru, Sweden, Uruguay and Yugoslavia unanimously rejected the Arab claims to Palestine in 1947. The State of Israel has been recognized by most of the countries of the world and since 1949 Israel has been a member state of the United Nations. Israel is a sovereign state and the land she occupies is her own territory.

You continue, "What prevents them [the Arab refugees] from recovering these [lands] is not what happened in 1948. It is the refusal of Israel, since then, to agree to their reinstatement." Again you do not present the facts accurately. The Jews did not expel the Arabs from Palestine. The Arabs who fled Palestine abandoning their homes and property and consequently became refugees did so on the orders of their own leaders. The Arab League issued orders exhorting the people to seek temporary refuge in neighboring countries, with the promise that they would soon return to their own homes with the victorious Arab armies and obtain their share of the loot from the abandoned Jewish properties. [2] The Arab leaders victimized their brethren by drawing them away from their homes and using them as pawns in a political game, feeding them with the poison and hatred of vengeful passions against Israel. Azam Pasha, Secretary General of the Arab League, in May, 1948 assured them that it would be a war of Extermination (against Israel) and the momentous massacre will be spoken of like the Mongolian massacres and the Crusades. The Arab Higher Executives denounced all the Arabs who remained in Palestine as traitors. [3] Despite the pressure not all the Arabs left the country. The entire Drusian community, about 17,500, remained in the land. Many Arabs in Galilee and in other parts of the country remained. Today there are in Israel about 220,000 Arabs — over 155,000 of them Moslems and over 55,000 Christians. They have seven representatives in the Knesset.

The first act of Israel's emergence to statehood was the

[2] See *Research group for European Migration Problems*, 1957. Reprint of Vol. 5, n. 1, p. 8.
[3] *Ibid.*

Proclamation of its Declaration of Independence. In this document the government of Israel declared:

> We appeal—in the very midst of the onslaught launched against us for months—to the Arab inhabitants of the State of Israel to preserve peace and participate in the upbuilding of the State on the basis of full and equal citizenship and due representation in all its provisional and permanent institutions.

But unceasingly flagrant hatred has been fanned against Israel. Muhammed Hassanein Heykal wrote in Al-Ahran, Cairo, May 12, 1962, "The Israel-Arab problem can be solved only by war. And since Israel knows very well that we will not agree to anything less than her liquidation it is she who will start the war and will attack us in the near future." Al-Gomhouriya, May 14, 1961, stated, "We shall never agree to negotiation nor to bargaining nor to an armistice nor to declarations to the effect that if Israel will make concessions to the Arabs on her borders, or will allow them to return to Palestine, we will be prepared to enter negotiations with Israel and sign a peace settleement with her. No—a thousand times no..." With utter disregard of the facts and political realities you assert, "What prevents them [the refugees] from recovering these is not what happened in 1948. It is the refusal of Israel, since then, to agree to their re-instatement."

Could you in good conscience pose to me the question, "Are you in favor of a solution that would recognize the Palestinian Arab refugees' rights and would re-instate the refugees?" Would you suggest that I ask Israel to commit hara-kiri? The Arab refugees, numbering over a million in the Gaza Strip, Syria, Lebanon and Jordan, have been indoctrinated for over fourteen years with hatred against Israel, preparing them for the coming of the day of revenge when Israel will be destroyed and driven into the sea. Can Israel open her borders to those who are taught link their return with her destruction?

Would you suggest that Israel commit suicide by inviting self-destruction?

I shall reiterate what I wrote in my article "Jewish Rights in Eretz Israel" that the Arab refugee problem should be solved in a peaceful manner by Israel and the neighboring states. We understand that the Israeli government is willing to allow some of the refugees to return. Dr. Joseph E. Johnson, was in the Near East and discussed this matter with the Israel and Arab leaders. It is to be hoped that a solution will be found to ease this situation. As to the question of compensation Ambassador Michael Comay, Chairman of the Delegation to the United Nations, made the following statement, "My delegation is authorized to reaffirm the previous declarations of my Government that if a solution by integration in the Arab world were actually carried out, and if the international assistance offered in 1955 were available, Israel would be prepared to pay compensation, even before the achievement of a final peace settlement, or the solution of other outstanding problems." He further said, "In fixing the level of compensation, it would be necessary to take into account Jewish property in areas such as the Jewish Quarter of the Old City of Jerusalem, and the Jewish villages in the Jerusalem and Hebron districts." [4] He also called attention to the fact that the Jews who lived in Irak and Egypt who were forced to leave these countries their properties were confiscated by the governments. Before 1948 there were in Irak almost 180,000 Jews, now there are not quite 50,000. In Egypt there were approximately 90,000 Jews but today there are less than 14,000.

Having established, beyond any doubt, my judgment of your "main thesis", I may now reply to the historical questions you raised. You challenged me to "produce evidence that the percentage of the Jews in the population of Palestine had ever been larger (10 percent) than that at any date since

---

[4] Statement before the Special Political Committee of the Fifteenth General Assembly, on 28 November, 1960.

A.D. 135." This is my reply: Over two hundred years after 135 C.E., i.e. after the collapse of the Bar Kokba revolt, the Jews in Palestine were far in excess of the percentage you assigned to them. In the year 351 C.E. the Jews were strong enough and numerous enough to revolt against Rome in order to regain their political independence. Socrates, in *Ecclestiastical History*, [5] stated that the Jews were completely vanquished by the Roman army under Gallus. The Jewish revolt was powerful enough to require Emperor Constantine to send an army under Gallus to suppress the Jewish rebellion. Obviously the Jewish population in Palestine at that time could not be considered a small minority of less than ten percent. Furthermore as late as 614 C.E., in the struggle between the Persians and the Byzantians for the possession of Palestine, the Jews were courted as allies by both sides. They fought first on the side of the Persians [6] who promised the Jews to reestablish their kingdom in Jerusalem. [7] When the victorious Persians broke their promise the Jews cast their weight on the side of Heraclius because he solemnly vowed to restore the privileges of the Jews. With the aid of the Jews he counterattacked and defeated the Persians. But the Church leaders absolved Heraclius from his oath by declaring a special fast day, the Fast Day of Heraclius, as atonement for the Emperor's broken vow. [8] The Christians now had a free hand to massacre the Jews and many fled from the land to escape with their lives. The Jewish population subsequently was further decimated by the Crusaders. The resulting Jewish minority in Palestine was therefore an infliction forced upon them by brutal force. Subsequently their numbers were frequently restricted by

[5] Chap. XXXIII.
[6] Cf. Bar Hebraeus, *The Chronography*, ch. 9. Oxford University Press, London, 1932.
[7] Sebeos, *Histoire d'Heraculis*, tr. F. Macler; P. Marr, *Antioch Stratig, The Capture of Jerusalem by the Persians*, (in Russian); H. Hilkowitz, "The Participation of the Jews in Conquest of Jerusalem by the Persians" *Zion*, 1939, pp. 307-316, (in Hebrew).
[8] Sebeos, *ibid.* ch. 30.

special measures taken against their readmission to their homeland.

I stated in my recent article that the Jews never abandoned the title to their country and that in various degrees they lived in Palestine continually ever since the Children of Israel conquered the land about 1300 years before the present era. This statement you countered by asking, "Is the title that they claim founded on 'right of conquest'? If so, it has been extinguished by the successive titles of a series of subsequent conquerors." Your analogy surprises me, to say the least. Let us for the moment grant that Jews' claim for rights in Eretz Israel is based on the right of conquest. Is this in the same category as the conquest of Judaea by the Romans, Persians, the Arabs of the desert, the Mamelukes and the Turks? The Jews conquered the land from the Canaanites, Hittites, and the Amorites. How many of these people are here to claim title to this country today? Thousands of years have elapsed since the extinction of the Canaaites, Hittites and the Amorites. But the Jews are still alive to claim the right to their homeland, having never relinquished their title to the country or signed a peace treaty with any of the subsequent conquerors. When other powers took possession of Palestine the Jews did not relinquish their rights, regardless of their numbers, in their land—the Land of Israel.

You persist in misunderstanding the historic basis for the religious and legal claims of the Jews for their rights in Eretz Israel (Palestine). And then you fall back on "the statute of limitations" under which "their previous rights as a former majority had by then expired". Need I again point out that the statute of limitations is itself subject to limitations beyond which it is not applicable. For example, it does not apply to murderers. Nor is it applicable to peoples whose countries were wrested from them by force as long as they did not relinquish their legitimate rights and press their claims.

Instead of meeting this argument on its merits you cavil about the example of Poland and Lithuania, which I had cited as nations whose historic rights were restored after World War I. Granted that these nations, by and large, were still inhabiting by large majorities the countries to which they laid claim, how do you explain the situation vis a vis Vilna, which had no majority of either Poles or Lithuania (40 percent of the population of Vilna was Jews); [9] or the State of Grodno whose imhabitants had no majority of those nations. [10] Silesia is still another illustration. When the Germans conquered Silesia from the Poles the Polish population was reduced to a small minority. By the fortunes of war the Poles were able to expel the Germans—the majority population—and regain title to Silesia, though at that time they were perforce a small minority in the land.

Turning now to your concluding paragraph I find it incomprehensible that you, a historian of world prestige, should shun the evidence of original sources and thereby open yourself to error on the basis of a citation from an English translation of Theodor Mommsen's *The History of Rome*, "The Provinces from Caesar to Diocletian".

In categorical fashion—which, may I say, seems to be characteric—you state, "I cannot find any evidence that the Romans regarded or treated Palestine differently from any other of the many countries that they conquered and annexed." You base this sweeping statement on a chapter in Mommsen's book. Have you sought evidence elsewhere, as, for instance, in the Roman sources or, perchance, in the Hebrew documents of that period? Even Mommsen in his work, where he describes Emperor Severus Alexander's differentiation between the Christians whom he tolerated and the Jews whose ancient privileges he confirmed, [11] wrote, "Clearly the privileged position of the Jews as compared with the Christians comes here to light—a position, which certainly rests in its turn on the

---

[9] Cf. The Hebrew (Russian) Encyclopaedia, vol. 5, (St. Peterburg).
[10] *Ibid.* Vol. 6.
[11] *Iudaeis privilegia reservavit. Christianos esse passus est.* The *Scriptores Historiae Augustae, Severus Alexander*, XXII.

fact that the former represent a nation the latter do not." [12]

You equate the autonomy granted to the Jews from 6 C.E. to 70 C.E. with that granted by Rome to all other conquered provinces; after 70, according to your statement, Rome abolished the Jewish Sanhedrin in Palestine; and after 135 Jerusalem was barred to the Jews. You conclude, finally, that the differential treatment in Palestine which the Jews received from the Romans was less favorable than the standard treatment they accorded to other subject populations.

Each of these postulates is in contradiction to the clear evidence of the ancient sources. The Jewish patriarchat functioned in Palestine till 415 C.E. Origen (third century), who lived in Palestine for some time, in his Epistle to Africanus wrote, "How much, even now, where the Romans rule and the Jews pay to them two drachmas [13] has the ethnarch among them his power with the wish of the Caesar (Emperor) the privilege to rule his nation.... Even courts are secretly held according to the law, and even on various occasions

---

[12] P. 245, n. 1.

[13] When the Romans captured Jerusalem in the year 70, a tax of two drachmas, half a shekel, was levied to be paid annually to *Jupiter Capitolinus* as formerly was contributed by the Jews to the Temple in Jerusalem. (Josephus, *Jewish War*, 7.6.6). This tax was called *fiscus Iudaicus*. This tax was to emphasize the victory of Jupiter, the Roman god, over the God of the Judaeans. It had to be paid by all Jews, regardles of where they lived even if they or their forefathers had never lived in Judaea; it had also to be paid by converts to Judaism long after the Romans had conquered Judaea. (Dio, *Epitome of* b. LXV; Suetonius, *Domitian*, XII). Thus the *fiscus Iudaicus* was actually a religious and not a political tax. It is this tax that Origen refer in his epistle to Africanus when he speaks of the payment of two drachmas to the Romans. When the Church became the dominating religion in the Roman Empire, the Christians could not afford to receive a tax which signalized the victory of Jupiter, a pagan god. This tax was then abolished and different taxations were levied upon the Jews. The Jews had been paying a fixed sum of money to the patriarch, after Theodosius abolished the patriarchate he decreed that the sum of money previously paid to the patriarch should instead be paid to the empire which was called *Aurum Coronarium. Quam patriarchae quondam coronarri auri nomine postulabant.* Cod. Theod. XVI. 8. 29.

sentence of death is pronounced. This I, who have long lived in the land of this people, have myself experienced and ascertained." [14] This indication of the extensive power of the ethnarch [patriarch] is substantiated by the Theodosian Code. On October 20, 415 Theodosius removed Gamaliel (VI) from his post and thereby abolished the patriarchate. [15] Until then, the patriarchate had been in continuous existence for centuries and it was delegated by Rome to exercise ecclesiastical and civil authority over the Jews in Palestine.

The patriarch moreover had jurisdiction not only over the Jews but also over the other inhabitants, even over the Christians. This is clearly indicated in the sequel to the above quotation from the Theodosian Code, "He [Gamaliel] shall have no power to judge between Christians; and if a dispute shall arise between the Christians and the Jews it shall be decided by the governor of the province." [16] The curtailing of the

[14] Καὶ νῦν γοῦν 'Ρωμαίων βασιλευόντων, καὶ 'Ιουδαίων τὸ δίδραχμον αὐτοῖς τελούντων ὅσα συγχωροῦντος Καίσαρος ὁ ἐθνάρχης παρ' αὐτοῖς δύναται ὡς μηδὲν διαφέρειν βασιλεύοντες τοῦ ἔθνους ἰσμεν οἱ πεπειραμένοι, γίνεται δὲ καὶ κριτήρια λεληθόντως κατὰ τὸν νόμον καὶ καταδικάζονταί τινες τὴν ἐπὶ τῷ θανάτῳ οὔτε μετὰ τῆς πάντῃ εἰς τοῦτο παρρησίας, οὔτε μετὰ τοῦ λανθάνειν τὸν βασιλεύοντα. *Ep. ad Africanum* 14, PG. 11.

[15] *Quoniam Gamalielus existimavit se posse impune delinquere, quo magis est erectus fastigio dignitatum iulustris auctoritas tua sciat nostram serenitatem ad virum inl(ustrem) mag(istrum) officiorum direxisse praecepta ut ab eo codicilli demantur honorariae praefecturae, ita ut in eo sit honore, in quo ante praefecturam fuerat constitutus ac deinceps nullas condi faciat synagogas et si quae sint in solitudine, si sine seditione possint deponi, perficiat, et ut inter Christianos nullam habeot copiam iudicandi.* (16. 8. 22).

[16] ... *Si qua inter Christianos et Iudaeos sit contentio, non a senioribus Iudaeorum, sed ab ordinariis indicibus dirimatur.* That prior to this decree the Jewish courts tried cases between Jews and non-Jews is also shown in the tannaitic literature. It is stated in the Sifra Deut. that when there appeared before Rabbi Ishmael two litigants Jew and non-Jew and wanted the case be conducted in accordance with the Jewish law, he complied with their wish. If they asked that the case be tried according to the Roman law he did so.

The decree issued by the Emperors Arcadius and Honorius that all cases, even civil cases, had to be tried in Roman courts according to Roman law. The Jewish court could only be an arbitrary court in civil cases if the litigants agreed among themselves to accept its

power of the Jewish courts came after the abolition of the partriarchate and was due to the new policy dictated by the Church. Until 415 C.E. when the enactment of this decree took place the Jews in Palestine under the headship of the patriarch (ethnarch) were a self governing people within the Roman Empire.

Your statement, "After A.D. 70 however it abolished the Jewish Sanhedrin in Palestine" is historically incorrect. In 429 C.E., fifteen years after the patriarchate was abolished, Theodosius II issued a decree to "The primates of the Jews who are appointed in the Sanhedrin." [17]

Before the Roman government adopted Christianity as the state religion Judaism was recognized as a *religio licita* and the unique political status of the Jews in Palestine was fully recognized. The Jews in Palestine had their own patriarch, ethnarch, who had ecclesiastical as well as social and economic authority over the people. He had the right to appoint judges and archons, [18] civil leaders. The patriarch was responsible to the Roman government for the political tranquility of the Jews. From Constantine to Theodosius one of the world's greatest revolutions took effect—the merger of pagan imperial Rome with the Christian church. There emerged the shadow of the later Medieval Holy Roman Empire. Judaism was to be extirpated for the glory of the new faith.

For almost two thousand years the Jews have looked forward to the day of their return to Eretz Israel by the grace of God and by their own efforts. They revolted several times against the Romans to regain their country. When there was no longer any hope of return to their country by force they prayed to God and hoped for the reestablishment of a Jewish

---

decisions. This decree referred only to the Jews who lived outside of Palestine and who were considered Romans, *Iudaei Romano.* (II, 1. 10).

[17] *Iudaerum primates, qui in utrisque Palestnae synedriis nominantur vel in aliis provinciis degunt, quaecumque post excessum patriarcharum pensionis nomine suscepere, cogantur exsolvere.* (16. 8. 29).

[18] *Cf.* Talmud Yer. Ned. 42; Pea 21.

state in their homeland *Eretz Israel*. Throughout their long history since the destruction of the State of Judaea by the Romans the Jews underwent great physical and mental sufferings at the hands of Christians and Moslems, and at times were almost on the verge of annihilation. During the times of their persecutions many Jews committed suicide in order not to transgress their religion. The horrors of the gas chambers are still vivid in our minds. Now that history has granted them the privilege to which they were entitled, they deserve the acclaim and help of all men of good will throughout the world.

Sincerely yours,

SOLOMON ZEITLIN

THE ECUMENICAL COUNCIL VATICAN II AND THE JEWS

THE TEACHING OF THE CHURCH for over eighteen hundred years that the Jews were guilty of the crucifixion of Jesus, that they are deicides, was responsible for the spread and acceleration of anti-Semitism. We may say that the slaughter of the six million Jews was partly due to the evil effects of this accusation. The holocaust of the gas chambers led many Christians to examine the evil effects of this age old stigma that the Jews are deicides.

At the Second Session of the Ecumenical Council a summary of the draft on Jews was published in the *New York Times*, November 19, 1964, it read as follows:

> The Jewish people should never be presented as one rejected, cursed or guilty of deicide. What happened to Christ in His Passion cannot be attributed to the whole people then alive, much less to that of today. Besides, the church held and holds that Christ underwent his Passion and death freely, because of the sins of all men and out of infinite love.

The death of Jesus has historical and theological aspects. By the historical aspect we mean the need to investigate the reason why Jesus was put to death and who crucified him. By the theological aspect we mean the presentation by the Church of the death of Jesus Christ, the Son of God who ransomed with his blood the sins of men.

The sources dealing with the events which led to the death of Jesus are the Gospels. But the Gospels are swathed about with theological clothes. Furthermore, the Gospels contradict each other in many essential facts regarding the events which led to the crucifixion. The Gospels were written more than

Reprinted from the *Jewish Quarterly Review*, New Series, Vol. 56, 1965.

two generations after the death of Jesus. Even the Gospel according to Mark, which is the earliest, was written after the destruction of the Judaean State and this Gospel was based on logia. In his Epistles Paul makes scant reference to the crucifixion of Jesus.

The Apostolic Fathers mention only that Jesus was crucified under Pontius Pilate.[1]

With regard to outside sources, the passage about Jesus in Josephus that he was crucified by Pilate, was interpolated by the Church Father Eusebius.[2] The Roman historian Tacitus, speaking of the Christian sect, wrote, "Christus, the founder of the name, had undergone the death penalty in the reign of Tiberius, by sentence of the procurator Pontius Pilatus."[3] We would expect to find some reference to Jesus in the Palestinian Talmud but there is none. In the Babylonian Talmud there are some passages which make reference to the heresy of Jesus and to his crucifixion. These passages are of the period of the 3rd century CE and hence have no historical value.[4]

Thus sources, outside the Gospels do not give any historical material dealing with the events which led to the crucifixion of Jesus. The only remaining sources then are the Gospels. The historian dealing with the period of the crucifixion of Jesus must divorce the theological encasement from historical facts.

According to the Gospels, when Jesus was arrested by a

---

[1] Cf. Ignatius to the Smyrnaeans, 1, -2, "he is in truth of the family of David according to the flesh, God's son by the will and power of God, truly born of a virgin, baptised by John ... truly nailed in the flesh for our sake under Pontius Pilate and Herod the Tetrarch. ἀληθῶς ἐπὶ Ποντίου Πιλάτου καὶ Ἡρώδου τετράχου καθηλωμένον ὑπὲρ ἡμῶν ἐν σαρκί ... Cf. also Episttle to the Trallians 9.

[2] Cf. S. Zeitlin, "The Christ Passage in Josephus," *JQR*, 1928, pp. 231-255, idem., *Josephus on Jesus*, 1931.

[3] *Annals*, 15. 44. *Auctor nominis eius Christus Tiberio imperitante per procuratorem Pontium Pilatum supplicio adfectus erat.*

[4] Cf. S. Zeitlin, "Jesus in the Early Tannaitic Literature" *Abhandlungen Zur Erinnerung An Hirsch Perez Chajes*, Wien 1933, pp. 295-308.

cohort and brought to the house of the high priest where a *synedrion* was assembled, the high priest asked Jesus, "Are you the Messiah, Christ, the Son of the Blessed (Son of God) ?" Jesus replied, "I am and ye shall see the Son of Man sitting on the right hand of Power (God)." [5] When the high priest heard the words of Jesus he tore his clothes and said that there was no need for witnesses since he had heard with his own ears abusive language against God. Thereupon the entire synedrion, [assembly], thought such a man was liable to the death penalty. [6] Blasphemy, according to the Judaean law, was not punishable by death. Only when a person cursed God with the name of God was he guilty of a capital crime, and was put to death. [7] By Claiming to be the Son of God, Jesus was not liable to capital punishment. Jesus' declaration that he would sit on "the right hand of Power [God]" cannot be considered blasphemy nor false prophesy. Many pious Judaeans looked forward to the future world where they would sit in the company of God and enjoy the Divine Glory.

Again, according to the Gospels, Jesus was brought to the house of the high priest where the *synedrion*, [council], assembled. [8] The question arises—why was Jesus brought to the house of the high priest and why was a *synedrion* summoned when the ordinary procedure would have been to bring Jesus to the court house where the *Bet Din* tried religious cases?

According to Matthew and Mark, the scribes and the elders were assembled in the house of the high priest Caiaphas, and there Jesus was examined and indicted. According to Luke, Jesus was interrogated on the morning following his arrest when the elders, the high priests and the scribes assembled and brought him "into their *synedrion*." [9] Luke does not mention that the high priest accused Jesus of blasphemy;

[5] Mat. 26. 46-64; Mark 14. 43-62.
[6] Ibid. 64-67.
[7] Cf. M. San. 7.5.
[8] Mat. 26. 57, Mark. 14. 53-55.
[9] 22. 65.

Mark, on the other hand, does not record the crime of which the high priest accused Jesus before Pilate. Luke does state the accusation which the multitude brought against Jesus was that he perverted the nation and forbade the people to pay tribute to Caesar by saying that he himself was "a Christ, a King." When Pilate asked Jesus, "Art thou the king of Judaea?" Jesus answered, "Thou sayest it." [10] According to John, when Pilate asked the people, "Shall I crucify your King?" the chief priests answered, "We have no king but Caesar." [11] The fact that the high priest had to assert again and again that they have no other king but Caesar indicates that the crime of Jesus was political. The inscription which Pilate ordered to be inscribed on the cross in Hebrew, Greek and Latin was—*Iesus Nazarenus, Rex Iudaeorum*, "Jesus of Nazareth the King of the Judaeans." This inscription clearly indicates that Jesus was crucified as a political offender for claiming to be the King of the Judaeans. It was a Roman custom to write and explain the reason for the execution. [12]

In presenting a case an impartial historian as well as a jurist must pierce through all available documents without prejudice. Notice must be taken of contradictions and discrepancies in those documents. The motive which led to the commission of the act must be carefully scrutinized and investigated. With regard to the motive involved in the death of Jesus, the religious leaders of Judaea had no reason to put Jesus to death. Jesus in proclaiming himself the Messiah did not commit a religious offence. Many followers of the Pharisees—Apocalyptists looked forward to the day when the Messiah would reveal himself and redeem the Judaeans from the Roman yoke. [13] As was noted before, the sources for the trial and

---

[10] 23. 1-3.

[11] 19. 15.

[12] Cf. Suetonius, *Caligula* 32, *praecedente titulo qui causam poenae indicaret per coetus epulantium circumduceretur*.

[13] Cf. The psalms of Solomon 17.

crucifixion of Jesus are the Gospels. They contradict each other and there are irreconcilable discrepencies.

For an impartial historian there can be but one conclusion— the Jews had no part in the death of Jesus. The accusation was theologically motivated; historically it is a false and libelous accusation.

The Gospels, although they contradict each other, are in agreement that the high priests and their *synedrion* plotted the death of Jesus. Two points must be considered. First—The Gospels, as stated above, are not historical books; they have a theological slant. Further, they were written after the destruc- of the Judaean State. In the first centuries after the death of Jesus the Christians were a small group and they had to fight for their very existence. Many of them, if not the majority, were Jews who believed that Jesus was the true Messiah who arose from the dead. In their propaganda to prove that Christianity was the true religion, that they were the true Israelites, they claimed that the Jews, previously the chosen people, were no more. God had forsaken them. The Jews are the accursed people, responsible for the crucifixion of Jesus. For this God had punished them by the destruction of the State and the burning of the Temple. The early Christians asserted that God punished the Jews for their rejection of Jesus as their true Messiah and blamed them for the cruci- fixion. As long as the Jews do not recognize Jesus as the Christ, they are an accursed people. They can be redeemed of the guilt of the crucifixion only by accepting Jesus as the Messiah. The charge of the Church Fathers that the Jews are deicides, the killers of Christ, has been the Church's battle cry since the Second Century.

Eusebius, Hilary and Chrysostom, in their writings, charged the Jews with the crucifixion of Jesus, and declared that the blood of Jesus was perpetually on the hands of the Jews. Chrysostom considered the synagogues dens of idolatry and abodes of devils, even though there were no images in them. [14]

[14] See *C. Judaos* i, 4, 6.

The Jews, he said, used to murder their offspring with their own hands and were worse than wild beasts. "Even if they no longer murder their own children," he continued, "they murdered Christ, which is worse." [15] They do not worship God but worship devils. "God hates them," he added in a later section; and indeed He always hated them, but since the murder of Jesus he allows them no time for repentance. These homilies and writings poisoned the minds of Christians who came to look upon the Jews not as children of God but as children of devils, responsible for the crucifixion of Jesus, for whom there was no repentance and no redemption unless they accepted Jesus as the Christ.

In 1096 the first crusade was organized by the Christians against the Moslems to retake Jerusalem and the Holy Sepulchre. When the crusaders began to march towards Palestine the chronicle relates that they said, "While we are on the way to recover the Holy Sepulchre and take revenge on the Moslems, we find in our midst Jews who crucified Christ. Let us take revenge on them and destroy the Jews here unless they accept our religion." [16] This determination of the crusaders was a normal reaction resulting from the propaganda of centuries that the Jews were deicides, Christ killers. The crusaders saw the absurdity of the situation. They were going to retake the holy sepulchre and to die for it, while having in their midst the guilty ones who crucified their Lord.

It is true that many of the Christian hierarchy tried to protect the Jews from the crusaders. Bishop Johannes of Speyer sought to protect the Jews and to punish the crusaders but to no avail. [17] The masses could not understand why they were not permitted to kill the Jews since they had been taught that the Jews were deicides who killed their Lord.

---

[15] *Ibid.*
[16] הנה היהודים היושבים בינינו אשר אבותיהם הרגוהו וצלבוהו ... ננקמה מהם תחילה ונכחידם מגוי ולא יזכר שם ישראל או יהיו כמנו ויודו בבן ..
[17] Julius Aronius, *Regesten zur Geschichte der Juden*, p. 84.

They were going to fight and die for the recovery of the Holy Sepulchre; was there not more reason to kill the Christ killers at home?

With the period of the crusades the dark ages of the Jews began. Pope Innocent III, one of the most powerful popes, in his bulla to the archbishop of Sens and the bishop of Paris, set forth the policy of the Church towards the Jews in these words, "The Jews...by their own guilt are consigned to perpetual servitude because they crucified the Lord." [18] Thus the Jews became the servants of the Church because of their alleged crucifixion of Jesus. In another bulla he made the following statement, "Thus the Jews, against whom the blood of Jesus Christ calls out, although they ought not to be killed lest the Christian people forget the Divine Law, yet as wanderers they ought to remain upon the earth until their countenance be filled with shame and they seek the name of Jesus Christ, the Lord." [19] He compared the Jews to Cain who had killed his brother Abel and upon whom God had set a sign so that he should not be killed by any one who found him but should wander from place until the end of the world. Like Cain the Jews also were branded so as not to be slaughtered but to be doomed to wander from place to place. The policy that the Jews were perpetual slaves because of the crucifixion of Jesus was reaffirmed by Pope Gregory IX.

It is true that a number of popes protected the Jews from persecution. Pope Innocent IV said in his bulla that the charge against the Jews of using human blood for religious rites was false since the Jews, were prohibited from using even the blood of animals. [20] The good will of Innocent IV and other popes did not greatly improve the conditions of the Jews in Europe since for centuries the leaders of the Church held that the Jews were guilty of deicide, the killers of Christ, and there-

---

[18] Cf. Solomon Grayzel, *The Church and the Jews in the XIIIth Century*, pp. 114 f. *Etsi Judaos, quos propria culpa submisit perpetue servituti cum Dominum crucifixerint.*

[19] Grayzel, *op. cit.* pp. 126 f.

[20] Cf. *idem*, ibid. pp. 268-271.

fore must remain in degradation. When a community or state suffered some calamity the masses vented their wrath upon the Jews. It must be said also that the policy of the Church formulated by Innocent III and Gregory IX, that the Jews must not be entirely annihilated but remain as a living witness to the truth of Christianity, made possible the physical survival of the Jews during the Dark Ages. The popes, vicars of Christ, in pursuing their theology that the Jews, guilty of the death of Christ and therefore rejected by God, had to live in suffering and degradation as living witnesses to the truth of Christianity, thus they protected the Jews in many instances from total annihilation by various kings and demagogues

In modern times political freedom was granted to the Jews in Western Europe. The political freedom was granted to them on the principle that the Jews were a religious community. This emancipation was not successful. Although the Jews were given political rights as a religious group, the old accusation against the Jews,—that they were deicides—continued. The masses looked upon them as Christ killers. This is one of the reasons for the failure of the emancipation. The Jews were emancipated politically but not religiously.

In Eastern Europe the hatred against the Jews as the killers of Christ prevailed. When the Russian senate in 1742 enacted a statute to allow some Jews to transact business in Russia because it would greatly benefit the Russian people, the Empress Elizabeth commented in these words, "From the enemies of Christ I do not desire any benefit." With the ascent of Czar Alexander III to the throne there was an outbreak of pogroms against the Jews and harsh restrictions imposed upon them. On March 6th, 1890 Baron Horace Gunzburg personally submitted a memorandum to Alexander III, asking him to improve the economic conditions of the Jews and remove the political restrictions imposed upon them. In this memorandum Baron Gunzburg made clear to the Czar that these restrictions gave the impression to the masses that the government itself was interested in making the Jew a sufferer and a wanderer. The Czar did not reply to this memorandum but wrote on the margin that it was proper for the Jews to suffer because they killed Chirst, and their ancestors had said, "His blood be upon us and upon our children," and therefore the Jews were destined for suffering. [21]

The theology of the crucifixion, which the Church emphasized, that the Jews killed Chirst, that they are deicides and thus accursed, destined to suffer and live in degradation as eternal witnesses to the truth of Christianity brought immeasurable suffering and death to an innocent people. It was a cruel libelous accusation against the very people who gave Jesus to the world. It may be said without exaggeration that the seed of the propaganda that the Jews are deicides was also instrumental in helping the Nazis to slaughter six million Jews. The first physical outbreak against the Jews in Germany was the destruction and the burning of synagogues.

From its beginnings the Church stressed the Crucifixion as the cornerstone upon which Christianity was founded, that God in His infinite mercy gave his Son to be crucified as ransom for sinners. In the Epistle to Diognetus its anonymous author wrote, "Himself gave His own Son as ransom for us, the Holy for the wicked, the innocent for the guilty, the just for the unjust, the incorruptible for the corruptible, the immortal for the mortal." [22] Justin Martyr said that Christ was the paschal lamb, "For the pascha (paschal lamb) was Christ who was afterwards sacrificed as also Isaiah said 'He was led as a sheep to the slaughter'... and as the blood of the pascha saved those who were in Egypt, so also the blood of Christ will deliver from death those who have believed." [23]

[21] This memorandum was never presented by the czar to the government. During one of my trips to Russia I found it in the private archives of the Romanoff family and I made a photostat of this important document.

[22] 9. ... αὐτὸς τὸν ἴδιον υἱὸν ἀπέδοτο λύτρον ὑπὲρ ἡμῶν τον ἅγιον ὑπὲρ ἀνόμων τὸν ἄκακον ὑπὲρ τῶν κακῶν ...

[23] *Dialogue with Trypho* 111. Ἦν γὰρ τὸ πάσχα ὁ Χριστός ὁ τυθεὶς ὕστεροῦ ... ὡς δὲ τοὺς ἐν Αἰγύπτῳ ἔσωσε τὸ αἷμα τοῦ πάσχα οὕτως καὶ τοὺς πιστεύσαντος ῥύσεται ἐκ θανάτου τὸ αἷμα τοῦ Χριστοῦ.

Since Jesus was the paschal lamb he had to be sacrificed on a definite date, namely on the fourteenth day of Nisan when the paschal lamb was slaughtered or the fifteenth day of Nisan when the Hebrews were saved. The Church Father Irenaeus wrote:

> It is clear that the Lord suffered death in obedience to His Father, upon that day on which Adam died while he disobeyed God. Now he died on the same day in which he did eat. For God said, 'in that day on which ye shall eat of it, ye shall die by death.' The Lord therefore recapitulating in himself this day underwent His suffering upon the day preceding the Sabbath, that is the sixth day of the creation, on which day man was created; thus granting him a second creation by means of his passion, which is that (creation) out of death." [24]

Jesus was crucified to redeem mankind from the Original Sin. Thus he had to be crucified on a definite day—the day that Adam committed the Original Sin, Friday.

These two theologies based on the Crucifixion are in conflict. This conflicting theology was drafted at the Ecumenical Council Vatican II and was adopted by a great majority. It was said in the schema that the Jewish people as a whole during the time of Jesus was not responsible for the Crucifixion, "What happened to Christ in his Passion cannot be attributed to the whole people then alive, much less to that of today." Hence the Jewish people of today are not guilty of deicide. This means that *some Jews* at the time of Jesus were responsible for the Crucifixion. In the same schema it was further said, "The church held and holds that Christ

---

[24] *Contra Haereses* 5. 23. *Manifestum est itaque, quoniam in illa die mortem sustinuit Dominus abediens Patri, it qua mortuus est Adam inobediens Deo. In qua autem mortuus est in ipsa et manducavit. Dixit enim Deus: 'In qua die manducabitis ex eo, morte moriemini' Hunc itaque diem recapitulans in semetipsum Dominus venit ad passionem pridie ante sabbatum, quae est sexta coditionis dies in qua homo plasmatus est.*

underwent His Passion and Death freely, because of the sins of all men and out of infinite love." If Jesus went to his death freely and out of infinite love and to ransom the sin of men how can even some Jews be accused of the Crucifixion? Historically, the Jews were not guilty of the death of Jesus.

Modern Christians recognize that the guilt of deicide, is the root of hatred. They also recognize that anti-Semitism is a cancer gnawing at the vitals of civilization. Although the Jews are the real victims of this disease ultimately this pestilence will strike civilization as a whole. The slaughter of six million Jews by the Nazis, the burning of multitudes in the gas chambers, moved the conscience of modern Christians. To ameliorate the condition of the Jews many Christians and Jews endeavor to establish good will societies.

John XXIII, a great humanitarian and saintly pope, in the dark days of the holocaust interceded whenever he could and saved the lives of many Jews. With his deep love and compassion for all people he made changes in the liturgy to improve the relationship between the Church and the Jews. On Good Friday the Catholics, in praying for all peoples, have a prayer *pro perfidis Judaeis* and they ask God to have mercy on the *Iudaica perfidia*. Pope John XXIII ordered the words *perfidis* and *perfidia* be omitted. He contemplated calling an Ecumenical Council in which the theology of the Crucifixion in its relation to the Jews was to be discussed and possibly revised. His successor Paul VI summoned the Ecumenical Council. Some Jews, when they learned that the Ecumenical Council would reconsider the theology of the Crucifixion in relation to the Jews made pilgrimages to Rome and petitioned the Vatican. Among them was a professor, a theologian. It is to be assumed that those who ran to the Vatican did not go to instruct the Pope in the Church theology on the Crucifixion. They went to the Vatican to plead for "exoneration" and "forgiveness." Exoneration from what? Forgiveness for what? Historically, the Jews were not guilty of the crucifixion of Jesus. Jesus was crucified by the Romans as a rebel. It is not the Jews but the Christians who have to atone for the libelous accusation against the Jewish people.

Msgr. Newton, in his review of my book *'Who Crucified Jesus'*? in the *Catholic Biblical Quarterly*, April, 1943, wrote that my book is modern Israel's cry of not guilty. In my reply in the same journal, January, 1944, [25] I wrote, "If the book could be held to make a charge, that charge would refer to the cry of guilt to the Christian world for using the crucifixion of Jesus as a pretext for enslaving and persecuting the Jews throughout the ages. Modern Christians should recognize that the charge is a libel against a whole innocent people."

This running to the Vatican by some Jews, including the Jewish professor, was not only bad judgment and a type of *shtadlenot* below the dignity of modern Jewry, but was also harmful. Pleading for "exoneration" and "forgiveness" is to admit that the ancestors of modern Jewry were responsible for the crucifixion of Jesus. Some fundamentalists do want the Jews to assent to the fact that their ancestors were guilty of the crucifixion of Jesus. James Daane, Associate Editor of *Christianity Today*, in an article, "The Anatomy of Anti-Semitism," in the issue of March, 1964, wrote:

> The Jewish people could help eliminate anti-Semitism if they would admit, as honesty could do without violating the terms of the Jewish faith, that they did destroy a man. There is little, if anything, of such an admission in current Jewish concern about anti-Semitism. Let Jews, if they must, regard Christ as only a man; but let them admit that honesty and integrity demand—the destruction of a man by their ancient leaders's insistence that he be put to death.

Daane follows with advice to the Jews that as the Gentile was saved by accepting Jesus so the Jew can also be saved by accepting him. He propagates. "The reunion of Jew and

---

[25] Pp. 105-110.

Gentile in the oneness of the Church." [26] This is the logical conclusion of Daane and those who still maintain that the Jews at the time of Jesus were responsible for the Crucifixion, but wish to exonerate the Jews of today of this guilt. By this they hope to unite the Jew and the Gentile into the oneness of the Church.

The lobbying of some Jews for some amendation in the theology of the Church on the crucifixion is harmful historically. Judaism and Christianity are two different religions with different theologies. It is morally wrong to interfere with other theologies. The theology of the Church is a matter for Christians. The theology of the Synagogue is a matter for Jews.

The Jews can only expect that the forthcoming session of the Ecumenical Council will erase *the guilt of the Church* for the defamation of an innocent people, the people of the prophets.

The Apostolic Fathers who flourished during first century C. E, a generation or two after the crucifixion of Jesus, did not accuse the Jews of the Crucifixion. The Apostolic Father Ignatius, hostile to Judaism and the Jews, in his Epistle to the Magnesians, wrote, "It is monstrous to talk of Jesus Christ and practice Judaism." [27] In speaking of the death of Jesus he said that Jesus was persecuted under Pontius Pilate. [28] He did not accuse the Jews of the death of Jesus. Historically the Jews were not responsible for the crucifixion of Jesus.

The guilt of the Jews for the crucifixion of Jesus was brought forward by the early Christians when they were a small group that had to fight for their very existence. They strove to prove that Jesus was the true Messiah, Christianity the true religion, and the Jews no longer were the Chosen People of God. The Judaean State was destroyed and the

[26] Cf. S. Zeitlin, "The Crucifixion, A Libelous Accusation Against the Jews," *JQR* July, 1965, pp. 8-22.

[27] ἄτοπόν ἐστιν 'Ιησοῦν Χριστὸν λαλεῖν καὶ ἰουδαιζειν.

[28] Epistel to the Trallians 9, ἀληθῶς ἐδιώχθη ἐπὶ Ποντίου Πιλάτου. Cf. above note 1.

Temple in Jerusalem was burned. These were interpreted as punishments for their guilt of the death of the true Messiah, the Son of God. The theological teaching that the Jews were responsible for the crucifixion of Jesus aimed to prove that the Jews are living witnesses to the truth of Christianity and the falsehood of Judaism. But Christianity today no longer needs witnesses for its existence; it is well established. The Synagogue does not fight the Church. Jews are friendly towards Christians; Jews and Christians have much in common. Now Christianity has other enemies as does Judaism. Indeed, both Church and Synagogue have a common enemy.

Dialogues between Jews and Christians have become popular. This is contrary to the history of true Judaism. The Jews never indulged in dialogues with Christians. It is true that during the Middle Ages there were dialogues and disputations between Jews and Christians. They were enforced upon the Jews and the Jews were compelled to defend their religion. The dialogue between the Jew Trypho and Justin Martyr never took place. [29] Justin, in order to refute some of the arguments of the Jews and to prove the truth of Christianity, composed this dialogue. He placed in the mouth of Trypho arguments and charges against Christianity so that he might refute them. In the dialogue he proved that Jesus was the true Messiah whose coming was foretold by the ancient prophets, Christianity the true religion, the Jews were no longer the Chosen People of God, and Judaism was not the true religion.

The Jews do not wish to convert the Christians to Judaism nor be converted to Christianity. The Jews respect Christianity as it brought monotheism to the pagan world. Even in the Middle Ages when the Jews were persecuted by the Christians, Maimonides held that Jesus helped to prepare the way for the true King Messiah. [30]

The Jews are grateful to the Church for its preservation of

[29] Cf. S. Zeitlin, "Anti-Semitism" *Crozer Quarterly*, April, 1945.
[30] Cf. *Mishne Torah, Hilkot Melochim*, ch. 11.

great treasures of Jewish literature such as the Apocrypha—Apocalyptic literature, the writings of Josephus, and the writings of Philo. Were it not for the Church, the Hebrew Bible would have remained a book for the Jews alone, as is the Talmud. By its adoption by the Church the Hebrew Bible became a universal book which has had a tremendous influence on western civilization.

Jews and Christians are members of one human society. Having a common interest in the welfare of their country. they are members of one fellowship though they are separated by their religions. The Jews respect Christianity and against interfering with the theology of Christianity. The Jews follow the eternal words of the Prophet Micah.

> Let all the people walk each one in the name of his God, but we will walk in the name of Adonai, our God forever and ever. [31]

Dialogues between Jews and Christians are wrong historically. There may be dialogues between Jews and Jews but not between Jews and Christians. If there are zealots among Jews to make converts to Judaism they can find a field of activity in Asia and Africa where there still are tribes who worship idols.

There is a great need for the enlightenment of Christians about the true spirit of Judaism, particularly of the development of Judaism at the time when Christianity arose. There is also a great need to present the historical background of the *Parting of the Way*. Jews also need this enlightenment as many do not have a true conception and significance of the *Parting of the Way*. This can be accomplished by authoritative historical works that present the true spirit of Judaism.

[31] 4.5.

ADDENDUM

VERSION DEBATED IN THE COUNCIL SEPTEMBER 28-30, 1964 [32]
32. (On the inheritance common to Christians and Jews.) The Church of Christ gladly acknowledges that the beginnings of its faith and election, in accordance with God's mystery of salvation, are to be found already among the Patriarchs and Prophets. Indeed, all Christians believe that, as sons of Abraham by faith (cf. Gal. 3, 7), they are included in this Patriarch's vocation and that the salvation of the Church is mystically prefigured in the exodus of the chosen people from the land of bondage. Nor can the Church as a new creation in Christ (cf. Eph. 2, 15) and as the people of the New Covenant ever forget that it is a continuation of that people with whom God in his ineffable mercy once designed to enter into the Old Covenant and to whom he chose to entrust the revelation contained in the Books of the Old Testament.

Moreover, the Church does not forget that from this Jewish people were born Christ, according to the flesh, the mother of Christ, the Virgin Mary, as well as the Apostles, the foundation and the pillars of the Church.

Further, the Church was always mindful and will never overlook Apostle Paul's words relating to the Jews, "whose is the adoption, and the glory, and the covenants and the giving of the law, and the service, and the promises" (Rom. 9, 4).

Since such is the inheritance accepted by the Christians from the Jews, this Holy Council is resolved expressly to further and to recommend reciprocal understanding and appreciation, to be obtained by theological study and fraternal discussion and, beyond that, in as much as it severely disapproves of any wrong inflicted upon men wheresoever, it equally deplores and condemns hatred and maltreatment of Jews.

---

[32] *The Third Session*, Xavier Rynne, New York, Farrar, Straus & Giraux; *New York Herald Tribune*, September 30, 1964.

It is also worth remembering that the union of the Jewish people with the Church is a part of the Christian hope. Accordingly, and following the teaching of Apostle Paul (*cf.* Rom. 11, 25), the Church expects in unshakable faith and with ardent desire the entrance of that people into the fullness of the people of God established by Christ.

Everyone should be careful, therefore, not to expose the Jewish people as a rejected nation, be it in Catechetical tuition, in preaching God's Word or in worldly conversation, nor should anything else be said or done which may alienate the minds of men from the Jews. Equally, all should be on their guard not to impute to the Jews of our time that which was perpetrated in the Passion of Christ.

II. Revised Draft Declaration on the Church's Relationship toward Non-Christian Religions, approved in a first Vote on November 20, 1964 [33]

... As this sacred synod searches into the mystery of the Church, it remembers the bond that ties the people of the New Covenant to Abraham's stock.

With a grateful heart, the Church of Christ acknowledges that, according to God's saving desing, the beginnings of her faith and her election were already among the Patriarchs, Moses, and the prophets. She professes that all who believe in Christ—Abraham's sons according to faith—were included in the same patriarch's call, likewise that here salvation is typically foreshadowed by the chose people's exodus from the land of bondage.

The Church, therefore, cannot forget that she received the revelation of the Old Testament from the people with whom God in His ineffable mercy concluded the former Covenant. Nor can she forget that she feeds upon the root of that cultivated olive tree into which the wild shoots of the Gentiles

---

[33] *The Third Session* Xavier Rynne, New York; *New York Times*, November 19, 1964; *The Catholic Herald*, London, Dec. 4, 1964.

have been grafted (*cf.* Rom. 11, 17-24). Indeed the Church believes that by His Cross Christ our peace reconciled the Jews and Gentiles, making both one (*cf.* Eph. 2, 14, 16).

The Church, keeps ever in mind the words of the Apostle about his kinsmen: "Theirs is the sonship, the glory, the covenants, the giving of the law, the worship, and the promises. Theirs are the patriarchs, and of them is the Christ according to the flesh," the Son of Mary the Virgin (Rom. 9, 4-5).

No less does she recall that the Apostles, the Church's mainstay and pillars, as well as most of the early disciples who proclaimed Christ's Gospel to the world, sprang from the Jewish people.

Even though a large part of the Jews did not accept the Gospel, they remain most dear to God for the sake of the patriarchs. This is the witness of the Apostle as is the utterance that God's gifts and call are irrevocable (*cf.* Rom. 11, 28f). In company with the prophets and the same Apostle, the Church awaits that day, known to God alone, on which all peoples will address the Lord in a single voice and "serve Him shoulder to shoulder" (Soph. 3, 9; cf. Is. 66, 23; Ps. 65, 4; Rom. 11, 11-32).

Since the spiritual patrimony common to Christians and Jews is of such magnitude, this Sacred Synod wants to support and recommend their mutual knowledge and respect, a knowledge and respect that are the fruit, above all, of biblical and theological studies as well as of fraternal dialogues.

Moreover, this synod, in her rejection of injustice of whatever kind and wherever inflicted upon men, remains mindful of that common patrimony and so deplores, indeed, condemns hatred and persecutions of Jews, whether they arose in former or in our own days.

May all, then, see to it that in their catechetical work or in their preaching of the word of God they do not teach anything that could give rise to hatred or contempt of Jews in the hearts of Christians.

May they never present the Jewish people as one rejected cursed, or guilty of deicide. All that happened to Christ in His passion cannot be attributed to the whole people then alive, much less to that of today.

Besides, the Church has always held and holds now that Christ underwent His passion and death freely, because of the sins of all men and out of infinite love. It is, therefore, the burden of Christian preaching to proclaim the Cross of Christ as the sign of God's all-embracing love and as the fountain from which every grace flows.